Israel

AMS PRESS

NEW YORK

Israel
from its Beginnings to the Middle of the Eighth Century

By

ADOLPHE LODS
Professor at the Sorbonne, Paris

Translated by

S. H. HOOKE
Professor of Old Testament Studies, University of London

LONDON
ROUTLEDGE & KEGAN PAUL LTD.
BROADWAY HOUSE, 68-74 CARTER LANE, E.C.

Library of Congress Cataloging in Publication Data

Lods, Adolphe, 1867-1948.
    Israel, from its beginnings to the middle of the
eighth century.

    Translation of Israël, des origines au milieu du
viiie siecle.
    Reprint of the 1948 ed., 2d impression, published by
Routledge & K. Paul, London, which was issued in series:
The History of civilization, the early empires.
    Bibliography: p.
    Includes index.
    1. Judaism—History—To 70 A. D. 2. Bible. O. T.—
History of Biblical events. 3. Palestine—Religion.
I. Title.
BM165.L5713 1976   933   75-41180
ISBN 0-404-14569-8

Reprinted from an original copy in the collections
of the Ohio State University Libraries

From the edition of 1948, London
First AMS edition published in 1976
Manufactured in the United States of America

AMS PRESS INC.
NEW YORK, N.Y.

CONTENTS

v

CONTENTS

CONTENTS

BOOK II

THE RELIGION OF THE ISRAELITES IN PALESTINE

LIST OF PLATES

LIST OF MAPS

LIST OF ILLUSTRATIONS

FOREWORD

ISRAEL AND NOMADISM

THIS book is the first of the second section, in our scheme, and possesses a double interest, since it faces, so to speak, in two different directions.

It is connected with the volumes in the first section devoted to the East, and supplements them in several important respects, since it amplifies the references to the populations of Western Asia in vols. vi (From Clans to Empires), *viii* (Mesopotamia), *ix* (The Ægean Civilization). *But, with the exception of the Phenicians the contribution of these peoples, and above all of the little people of Israel, to universal history, has consisted mainly of those features which formerly caused their history to be known in a special sense as " sacred." It has been said, with reason, that here as in the history of the Greeks, we find " miracle," in that meaning of the word which we have given elsewhere.*

From a definite period, the Hebrew miracle lies at the springs of the religious and moral life of mankind, and dominates the beginnings of what has been called the Christian era. For this reason we have assigned this place, at the beginning of our second section, to a book on Israel which looks both backwards and forwards.

First of all let us set out the contribution of this volume to the general history of this part of Asia.

Lying at the cross-roads of the ancient world, the highway of wandering peoples and victorious hosts, traversed by trade and by the earliest movements of thought, Syria was the inevitable home of syncretism. In this region, constantly in contact and often in conflict with the grasping empires of Asia and Africa, and linked with the sea-going peoples, we find those groups of Semitic peoples, who, apparently from the beginning

*of the third millenium, had made their home on Syrian soil,
sharing in a civilization which may be called Mediterranean,
or belonging to the Mediterranean East, whose main elements
were derived from Egypt, Babylon, the Ægeans and the Hittites.*[1]
*For centuries these Semitic peoples continued to borrow or receive
from alien sources without producing any original contribution
of their own to civilization.*

*Nevertheless, a certain exclusiveness and a love of inde-
pendence were fostered, as in Greece, by the nature of the country
which, between the coastal plain and the desert was cut up by
mountain ranges, and allowed small groups, in separate districts, to live in a relative isolation, secluded from the main lines
of communication.*

*But the moment arrived, in the second half of the second
millennium, when the Semitic or Semitized inhabitants of this
historic region* [2] *were released from the pressure of " the superior
might of the great empires " (see p. 52) ; they were able to
escape from the entanglement of the political ambitions of their
neighbours, to resist the influences which had been brought to
bear upon them, and for four centuries to develop their own
potentialities.   This was the moment when Canaanite culture,
already long rooted in Palestine, was destined to meet and mingle
with a new element which various predisposing causes had
conspired to constitute an active ferment in Syrian history,
before it became a factor in world history, namely, the Hebrew
element.*

*One of the most valuable features of Professor Lods' book
consists in his close and accurate study of pre-Israelite Canaan,
making it possible to assess its contribution to the history of
Israel, when once the fusion was accomplished.   We believe
that this is the most remarkable success in this direction which
has yet been achieved.*

*The most characteristic feature of the elaborate civilization
of the Canaanites was its practical tendency.   If they did not
invent, they at least perfected and diffused the art of writing.
With little gift for the plastic arts, they possessed a remarkable
genius for commerce.   They had developed an urban life, and
for the defence of their cities had devoted themselves to the systematization of warfare.   Being, moreover, warlike by nature,*

[1] See pp. 74–82.
[2] On the question of race, see Pittard, *Race and History*, Part III.

and incessantly occupied in fighting, their petty kings weakened their power by constant rivalries. Their religion consisted of very various elements, and, to use a spatial metaphor, presents an appearance of stratification. Professor Lods' analysis of this early Canaanite religion, together with his subsequent study of the primitive religion of Israel, provides very useful material for the general history of religion, material of which we shall avail ourselves elsewhere.[1] The most typical feature of Canaanite religion consists in the cults of baals and astartes, local divinities who become political gods, overlords, arbitrary tyrants rather than righteous rulers, while they still retain some of their early connexions with physical phenomena. They were appeased by bloody and orgiastic rites whose ecstatic and tumultuous character are partly explained by their agrarian origin. The continued persistence of human sacrifice and other brutal rites, both here and among other Semitic peoples, springs from a natural cruelty which we have pointed out elsewhere.[2] The most striking characteristic of Canaanite culture is its low moral level : " A relatively high level of culture was accompanied by a distinctly lower stage of morality " (p. 149).

But the earliest tribes who bore the name of Israel, in their story as it is contained in the Book, *the Bible, appear before us with very different characteristics. In the account of their troubled history, " unique of its kind," we find the stamp of reality, " the note of primitive life," appearing through the legendary material.[3]*

Nevertheless, in spite of its value, this account is a source which can only be used scientifically with extreme caution.

Between the events of Genesis and the documents which contain them lie from twelve to fifteen hundred years of tradition, during which the processes of intermingling of sources, and of idealization, were at work : hence the necessity of avoiding overcredulity—even Renan was sometimes too ready to accept the material without question—and undue scepticism. Professor Lods has made use of the immense labour which has been

---

[1] On the nature of religion, and its place in history, the reader is referred to the Foreword to vol. xi which has been delayed, but will appear shortly.

[2] See Delaporte, *Mesopotamia*, Foreword, and J. de Morgan, *Les premières civilisations*, pp. 305–6.

[3] See J. de Morgan, *op. cit.*, p. 297 ; Renouvier, *Introduction à la philosophie analytique de l'histoire*, pp. 414, 462.

expended on the " sacred " text to disentangle the various redactional elements and their stages, to bring to light the presence of folklore and imaginative elements, instructive as these are, and to throw into relief in the light of archæology the historical contents of the documents. He combines wide learning with sound critical judgment : by searching analysis he eliminates doubtful hypotheses and forced interpretations ; his choice among plausible solutions is always guided by prudence. He treats the prehistory of the Israelites with cautious reserve. He shows how far the saga of the patriarchs is the product of the interweaving of stories of widely varying origin and character. In his treatment of the story of the sojourn in Egypt and the exodus, he disentangles " the prosaic reality " from its " supernatural halo."[1] He discerns the essential spirit of Israel under its garb of legend and in its sober dress of " prosaic reality " ; he follows its manifestations in the land of Canaan with ever increasing accuracy and detail. Here we find the secret of the profound fascination of this notable book.

The characteristics which the Israelites brought into Canaan from the desert were " strong passions," " a particularly lively and vivid imagination," " a fierce pride," and a love for " the free life of the nomad." The desert life was more than a memory, it left a permanent impress upon the national character.[2]

Professor Lods has movingly depicted " the life of these Bedouins, engaged in the rearing of sheep and goats."[3] Occasionally they might sow a grain-crop, when there was a possibility of a speedy harvest,—" it is the cultivation of fruit-trees that binds man to the soil "[4]—but the breeding of flocks which provide the nomad with food, clothing and tents rendered necessary a wide range of movement, limited, however, by agreement between the various groups in the matter of grazing areas and wateringpoints. Their resources, and no doubt their pleasures, were eked out by the practice of raiding. A nomad life carries with it a spice of adventure, and the nomad, after his fashion, is a corsair. " The desert and the sea possess common characteristics and offer similar allurements." [5]

Besides, this kind of " natural law " which, as Professor

---

[1] See pp. 162 *ff*, 171, 179, 188, 185. [2] See pp. 173, 190, 191, 207.

[3] *Cf.* L. Febvre, *Geographical Introduction to History*, Part III, Chapter IV (Characteristics of pastoral life) ; Pittard, *op. cit.*, Foreword, xvi–xviii ; Moret, vol. vi, pp. 196 *ff*.

[4] *Cf.* Febvre, *op. cit.*, p. 294 ; he adds " irrigation."

[5] See Pittard, *op. cit.*, p. xvii.

Lods points out, urges the nomads " to be for ever seeking to encroach upon the cultivated territory lying along the borders of their deserts," also drives them on, when the resistance weakens, to seek a settlement in those more fertile lands.[1] *The Israelites were no exception to this law ; they advanced from tent to house, from clan to fortified town, but at heart they remained unchangeable nomads.*

We shall agree with our author that it is impossible to emphasize this point too strongly. As we see them settling in Palestine, quickly becoming a sedentary people, learning from their predecessors their customs and acquiring their tastes (for there is no truth in the view that the conquest was savage and destructive) ; even when, as inevitably happens, they pass under the influence of a conquered people superior in culture, we shall find that they continue to evince, secretly or avowedly, a yearning for the nomad life.

From their primitive nomad mode of life they derived an invincible tendency to individualism, to segregate themselves in groups and to develop personality within the group. Lods points out that originally, in clan and tribe, neither the " elders " nor the war-chief were " autocrats " (p. 195): their authority depended on their personal prestige. It was above all the activity of Moses, that, after the exodus, brought Israel into existence as a nation. Moses is a legendary figure, but underlying the legend " there must have been a dominant personality," roused to action by the oppression of the Egyptians (p. 309). Without a central authority, and hindered by the dispersion of the tribes in the desert, he nevertheless succeeded in creating in the confederation of the Bene Israel " a national consciousness." " Jahweh would be Israel's God and ·Israel Jahweh's people. This often repeated formula seems to express the guiding idea of the activity of Moses " (p. 311).

Summing up in broad outline the political history of Israel, Lods brings out the increasing solidarity of the tribes, the state which grows out of the conditions of a settled mode of life and becomes a " monarchy." Gideon, Saul, David, Solomon— especially the two latter kings [2]*—added territory, power and*

---

[1] On the attraction which civilization has for nomads, see Febvre, *op. cit.*, pp. 282 *ff.* ; *cf.* Dussaud, *Les Arabes en Syrie avant l'Islam*, pp. 4 *ff.*

[2] Lods gives us a very delicately shaded portrait of David : " His was a character rich in contrasts, a chivalrous courage was set off

FOREWORD

magnificence to the kingship. But these developments owed nothing to the national character, which was neither monarchist nor imperialist: they arose out of external pressure causing resistance and conflict; they were the work of powerful personalities. But this very force of character, which fosters unification, is often also fatal to it by reason of the divisions which it gives rise to. In short, whatever may have been their personal significance, or the breadth of their political views, the chiefs, judges, and kings, never achieved any lasting results of a moral as opposed to a merely political nature.

The " ancient Bedouin individualism " was opposed to the idea of kingly power (p. 395). The ancient equality rebelled against the growth of social distinctions, against the development of latifundia: " Among nomads the poorest is actually the equal of the richest; all alike partake of the same simple food, wear the same coarse clothing, and inhabit the same primitively furnished dwelling, the tent " (p. 397). To the growing demands of luxury the old austerity of life presented an increasingly stubborn opposition based on a deep-rooted sense that the national spirit " was opposed to commercial activities on a large scale " (p. 371).

A crisis arose in which Canaanite culture and the whole of the new civilization springing out of it were rudely challenged, and a strong " conservative or reactionary " movement broke out (p. 419). It appeared chiefly among the champions of Jahweh. Such a one was Jonadab, the Kenite,[1] *who in the middle of the ninth century, founded a kind of brotherhood by imposing upon his clan " the religious duty of a perpetual observance of those nomad customs which they had hitherto followed as a matter of tradition " (p. 399; cf. pp. 209, 308).*

The surviving elements of nomadism, under the impulse of the wistful memories of an idealized desert life, gave birth to Jahwism. In spite of divisions and civil strife, that which

---

by a cunning that often bordered on duplicity. Cruel when reasons of state demanded it, he showed a tender affection for his sons to the point of weakness. Poet, musician, orator of persuasive eloquence, he cast the spell of his charm upon all who came in contact with him " (p. 365–6). For Solomon, a kind of Louis XIV, see pp. 366–72.

[1] The Kenites, a nomad Midianite tribe, ranging in the neighbourhood of Sinai, possibly a community of smiths, may have been the first worshippers of Jahweh. See pp. 317–18.

ensured Israel's fundamental unity and constituted its distinguishing characteristic was its religion.

Lods has most fittingly devoted special attention to tracing out and explaining the religious development of Israel.

First of all, there was the religion of the Hebrews in their nomad state, a religion whose practices must have persisted after the settlement in Palestine, although it became infused with a new spirit ; but in the history of this religion of nomad times, two periods are clearly discernible : the first, prior to Moses ; and the second, the period of Jahwism, which starts with Moses.

Lods deals in a very interesting manner with the early beliefs of the Hebrews, making use not only of Hebrew tradition, but drawing on his wide knowledge of classical and Semitic religions and of recent studies on primitive mentality.   We may refer once more to the remarks which we have made elsewhere concerning the origin of religion,[1] *and confine ourselves here to pointing out that among the Hebrews the relations of man with the universe do not, at first, appear to have been conceived of otherwise than as the majority of peoples have regarded them. For the Hebrews of the pre-Mosaic Age the world was peopled with powers and spirits : hence the cult of trees, springs and mountains, a fear-inspired veneration of the dead and of certain animals : " wherever he met with some unusual manifestation of energy, in the luxuriant oasis springing out of a parched desert, in the magic power of a chief or in the ecstasies of a seer, the early Hebrew recognized the presence of supernatural spirits " (pp. 241, 251, 265).   There is an efficacy which resides in things, even in words, indeed, there are individuals in whom this efficacy is concentrated : priests, ecstatics, chiefs.*

The plural elohim, which finally came to denote a god, originally designated divine powers or forces.   The guardian deities of the clan must gradually have acquired a more personal character.   In any case, there was one of these deities, the god of Sinai, belonging to the Kenite group, whose personality, through the influence of Moses, and for the same reason as the personality of Moses, acquired a unique significance.   " Jahweh was not the God of Israel until Moses " (p. 210) : we have seen that it was by means of the emphasis which he laid on the national God that he succeeded

[1] See *The Religious Thought of Greece.*

*in creating a national consciousness. But this god was still
only one among many. At the outset, possibly, he did not even
appear superior to any of the rest. The Israelites were " monolatrous " before they became monotheists, and " monolatry is a
form of polytheism." Monotheism does not begin until the
eighth century and does not become fully conscious until the
sixth (p. 257).*

*After the settlement in Canaan, the religion of Israel
assimilated foreign elements, but these elements were sufficiently
akin to Hebrew religion to render the process of assimilation
an easy one ; and, on the other hand, when the reaction set in,
the Israelites gradually succeeded in completely differentiating
their own religion from that of Canaan.*

*Not only did Canaanite practices creep in, giving rise to ritual
innovations which aroused numerous protests, but the foreign
gods who existed alongside of Jahweh, came to be worshipped
in Israel, to the great indignation of the genuine Jahwists ; the
point was even reached when, as in the case of Ahab, for instance,
political considerations caused a breach in the monolatry of Israel.*

*In any case, the Israelites transferred to their God, their
heavenly sheikh, to whom they ultimately assigned an abode in
heaven, that faith which they had in themselves, the pride and
passion which they had brought with them from the desert ;
they began to regard him as more powerful than other gods,
before they reached the point of conceiving of him as the true and
only God. Jahweh was their ally, a formidable and holy ally :
He had brought them out of Egypt ; He had led them into Canaan ;
He had given them their laws, guided them with His counsel and
loaded them with blessings. The trials of Israel were His
punishments. Jahweh was an austere and jealous God, but
ever increasingly to be regarded as a righteous God : more and
more did the demands which He required from the nation and
the individual present themselves as the demands of morality.
Jahweh loves Israel, but He loves righteousness more.*[1]

[1] Lods gives us an excellent description of the strange development of the doctrine of the after-life in Israel. The Hebrews long
held the belief in the real survival of the individual after death in
Sheol, without the idea of moral retribution. The dead possessed
magical powers ; they were *elohim*. Jahwism resisted the cult of
the dead as an insult to Jahweh ; and it presents the phenomenon
of a religion " in which the belief in the future life of the individual
was long an alien element, and was even regarded with more or less

*Inspired men played an important part in the creation of a
national conscience. Such were the prophets, the* nebi'im.
*These men embodied the old mistrust with which those " who
dwell in tents " regard city-dwellers and the devices of their
civilization. They it was who developed the potentialities of
the national character. They strove against foreign influences.
To the corruption of civilization, the lust for power and pleasure,
they opposed the ancient ideal of the simple life, an ideal which
they gradually transformed into one of moral perfection and
spiritual satisfaction.*

*The increasingly active and conscious rôle which the prophets
played in the history of Israel will be described in the succeeding
volume of this series. But even before the eighth century we
find them, in obscurity or with public acclamation, in communities or in solitude, displaying the characteristics of religious
ecstasy.* " Nabism," *in the form of collective ecstasy, accompanied by songs and dances after the manner of the dervishes,
is not peculiar to the Hebrews. But the distinctive note of the
Israelite prophets consisted in their moral energy in defending
the laws of Jahweh, an energy which placed righteousness before
the immediate interests of the nation (p. 423). And the time
was at hand when by " the deep-seated protest against the narrowness and poverty of a purely national religion " (p. 488) and
by the conception of one God, of absolute righteousness, by a new
interpretation of the expected day of Jahweh, and by the messianic
hope, prophetism would succeed in expressing the spirit of Israel
in a new form. " Gradually the idea of a religion made for a
people is replaced by that of a people chosen for the purpose of
preserving and spreading a belief."* [1].

*Thus we find the whole of Israel's national life deeply per-
meated with religion. To religion we turn for the explanation
and orientation of Israel's history. " Sacred " history is a
pragmatic philosophy of history. " The other religions of
antiquity have no historical element, in the strict sense, . . .
they are not based on history ; in their sacred writings, when
they possess any, we only find cosmogonies and myths. On the*

---

suspicion." Only towards the second century B.C. did there appear
" a new hope : the hope of a resurrection or immortality, bound up
with a judgment after death." (See pp. 218–30; 474-5.)

[1] Cournot, *Traité de l'enchaînement des idées fondamentales dans
les sciences et dans l'histoire*, p. 653.

*other hand, nothing could be simpler . . . or more concise than
the purely cosmogonic portion of the sacred books of the Jewish
people."* [1] *But this sober cosmogony displays a double tendency,
on the one hand a pessimistic trend (paradise lost) ; on the other
an optimistic note (the idea of a progressive creation and of the
beneficent nature of God's activities).* [2] *It is this latter, and
more specifically Hebrew tendency, which seems to be suited to
the idea of a directive purpose in history. Israel does not
possess the mythopœic faculty ; she seeks God in man and
history rather than in natural phenomena.* [3]

*But the history of Israel, wholly religious in character, even
when it has been stripped by the critic of its halo of sanctity, has
too often been " stylized," so to speak. We have heard much
about " a vocation " and " a providential rôle," about " the
monotheistic desert " and " the primitive intuition of the divine
unity." Even Renan, tracing out " the task which the breath
of God, that is, the soul of the world, has accomplished by means
of Israel,"* [4] *still betrays, in the ambiguity of his metaphors, the
power of the facts which is in itself a sufficient explanation of
the history.*

*Conceptions such as these, which are either too abstract or
too literary, are translated by Lods into actual history. His
knowledge, which is weighty without being heavy,* [5] *and his art,*

[1] Cournot, *op. cit.*, p. 655.

[2] See J. Delvaille, *Essai sur l'histoire de l'idée de progrès*, c. i.

[3] Israel's anthropomorphism is very different from that of the
Hellenes, being moral rather than imaginative or intellectual ; but
the development of the idea of personality, whence it arises, is quite
as active in the tribe as in the πόλις. The contrast between the
Semite and the Aryan is a favourite theme. Although the comparison which Renouvier has made between these peoples and their
languages, in his *Introduction à la Philosophie analytique de l'Histoire*,
is less known than Renan's, it possesses a lively interest, in spite
of its somewhat theoretic cast. It contrasts the " self-centredness "
of the Semite, his intensity of feeling, his power of concentration,
" utterly unlike abstract generalization," with the " Aryan feeling
for others and for nature " (see pp. 436, 441, 443, 445, 449). He
distinguishes among the Semites themselves those who possess " the
genius for foresight and commerce, industry and labour " (p. 442),
and those among whom there appeared " that absolute, ascetic,
narrow, strong and lofty attitude of spirit which produced . . .
those extraordinary religious phenomena which still exercise a potent
influence among us, after four thousand years " (p. 477).

[4] *Histoire du peuple d'Israël*, vol. i, p. xxix.

[5] A few discussions of a somewhat technical nature, dealing with
important points of history or belief, are printed in smaller type
and for the most part relegated to appendices.

which consists in a judicious blending of objectivity and sympathetic insight, carry the reader through all the phases of Israel's history and all the changing stages of its beliefs. In the converging of geographic and racial facts, individual experiences, and historical circumstances, he finds the explanation of Israel's unique destiny. By his emphasis on the fusion which took place in Canaan of two different Semitic elements, the sedentary and the nomad, he helps us to understand the ambivalent nature of this destiny. Sustained by hope and an unquenchable optimism, Israel, in the course of the ages, became the embodiment on the higher plane, of the Celestial City, and on the lower, of the earthly City.

HENRI BERR.

ADDENDA

p. 79, n. 3. ⸰ This inscription has been published by Dunand in the *Revue Biblique*, July, 1930, pp. 321-31.

p. 116, n. 3. *Add :* It is not certain whether this was the purpose of the channels found by R. Weill in the city of David, in Jerusalem (**REJ**, 1926, pp. 112-3): they are several metres from the nearest tomb.

p. 271, n. 6. *Add :* Perhaps the same rule was observed by the Jews of Elephantine when they mourned for the temple of their God which had been destroyed : " our wives have become as widows " (*Sachau Pap.* i., l. 20).

p. 397. *Add :* This far-reaching change in the structure of Israelite society involved corresponding changes in customary law. This body of law, as we find it in the civil enactments of the so-called Book of the Covenant, contains regulations dealing with cases arising out of agricultural disputes (Exodus xxii. 4, 5, 13-14). The immigrants must have taken these over from the Canaanites. This is the most natural way of explaining the resemblances and the differences observable between the " Book of the Covenant " and the Code of Hammurabi. The latter had, no doubt, passed into Palestine together with Babylonian language, script and culture. There does not seem to be any direct literary relation between these two collections of laws ; but there is an unquestionable connexion, as, for instance, in the definition of crimes and penalties. The Israelite legislators did not copy either the arrangement or the terms of the ancient Babylonian code, any more than those of the Hittite (*cf.* **XXXIII**), the Assyrian (*cf.* **CCXXXII**), or the Sumerian codes (*cf.* Clay, *Misc. Inscr. in the Yale Bab. Coll.*, 1915, pp. 18 *ff.*). But they assimilated the juristic conceptions common to the whole of the civilized East, while at the same time they freely adapted them to the needs of a society which was far less advanced, culturally, than that of the surrounding empires, and which, in spite of its environment, had remained in an almost " primitive " state. This explains the persistence of the bloodfeud in Hebrew law (Exodus xxi. 13), a custom which the Code of Hammurabi forbids by implication ; it also explains why the Hebrews retained the superstitious taboo—unknown to the Code of Hammurabi (art. 250-2)—which forbade the eating of the flesh of a slain ox (Exodus xxi. 28-32). *Cf.* V. Scheil, *La loi de Hammourabi*, 2nd ed., Paris, 1904 ; **CCLXXXII** ; P. Dugros, **RHP**, 1926, pp. 350-65.

p. 435, l. 9.　With regard to these hand-censers, see Stefan Przeworski, **SY**, 1930, pp. 133-45.

p. 483, n. 1.　*Add :* A. Audin and P. Bertie have put forth certain new and somewhat divergent hypotheses (A. Audin, *La légende des origines de l'humanité, précédée des onze premiers chapitres de la Genèse, introduction, traductions et notes critiques* by Paul Bertie, Paris, Rieder, 1930).

p. 484, n. 2.　*Add :* A. Audin believes that the narrative can be divided into two versions, each dealing with one only of the two trees ; but he is obliged to base these conclusions upon the assumption of the existence of two parallel recensions which have undergone radical modifications.

ISRAEL

FROM ITS BEGINNINGS TO THE END OF THE EIGHTH CENTURY

INTRODUCTION

I

Object and Plan of the Book

THE unique importance of the people of Israel, equal to that of Greece and Rome in the history of humanity, is due to its religion, the mother of Christianity, Judaism and Islam.

Hence the chief preoccupation of the historian who may be dealing with this small corner of the ancient world is naturally the study of the origin and development of the religion of Israel. But this study depends upon the success of a number of preliminary or subsidiary investigations. It depends upon the reconstitution of the history of Hebrew literature, so that the historian may start with definite conclusions concerning the age and value of the documents which he is using. It demands a knowledge of the country which formed the stage upon which the drama of Israel's destiny was played out. It presupposes a familiarity with the customs and institutions of Israel and a reconstruction, as far as that is possible, of the political history of the nation, its foreign relations, and the growth of its social institutions and organization. For it is a fact that .among no other people have the vicissitudes of the nation's life influenced more profoundly the history of its religion.

Space will not permit us to deal with these preliminary

inquiries as fully as their importance demands. Hence, instead of attempting a general picture of Hebrew life with its various features only barely sketched in, it will be better to confine our attention to the essential matter of Israel's religion, only giving such information concerning its political history and social changes as is necessary for the understanding of its religious development. Accordingly the main outlines of our account will be determined by the course of the evolution of the religion.

For many centuries after their settlement in Canaan the Israelites were faced with a very serious practical problem. Could they preserve their ancestral traditions, above all their religion—the worship of Jahweh—and at the same time adopt the civilization of the ancient inhabitants of Palestine, or were the two incompatible? It is becoming more and more clear that in the religious realm as in the rest, the conflict resulted in a compromise, and to a certain extent in fusion.

Hence it will be necessary to examine first each of the constituent elements—on the one hand the culture of Canaan, and on the other that of the ancient Hebrews—then the results of their clash. Out of this consideration arises the arrangement of this book. The first part of it will consist of an account of the state of Canaan before the Hebrew settlement; the second of the Hebrew people before their settlement in Canaan; and the third of the Israelites from their entry into Palestine until the middle of the eighth century.

Another volume of this series will deal with the subsequent history of the religion of Israel up to the time when it gave birth to still existing religions—Christianity and Rabbinic Judaism.

It is hardly necessary to justify the date adopted as the dividing line between the two parts of this history. It is in the middle of this century that we find the beginning of the Assyrian invasions, which, followed by the Babylonian, Persian, Greek and Roman conquests, resulted in the destruction of the Hebrew nation, and the transformation of the Jewish social order into a kind of church.

Moreover, it was above all at this point in their history that the first of those striking religious personalities whom we call the great prophets appeared. From them the ancient world received an entirely new conception of God and His relations with men. Outwardly the struggle between the authentic ancestral religion, and the religion and culture of Canaan during the eighth, seventh and sixth centuries, was as bitter as ever : resistance to Canaanite influence is the keynote of some of the great prophets and especially of their disciples (Hosea, Jeremiah, Ezekiel and the deuteronomic legislators). But in reality the aspect of the struggle has changed ; the burning question now is whether the Hebraic-Canaanite religion which was in fact the traditional religion of the nation, or the germ of a loftier conception of religion created by the prophets, would win the day. Here again the crisis ended in the compromise which is the Judaism of the post-exilic period.

It is to the prophets of the eighth and the following centuries that Judaism owes that unique and profoundly original element in the history of humanity, its ethical monotheism. Before they appeared the religion of Israel was an ancient religion, similar in all essential respects to the other national religions of the ancient world. The main interest of the subject of this volume, the periods which lie before the great prophets, is that here we can study the growth of that vast substratum of ancient ideas, beliefs and institutions which has persisted to a great extent even in Judaism, and on the other hand that we already find here the tendencies, the strivings which herald and explain the great religious upheaval which marks the birth-pangs of Israel's national existence at the beginning of the eighth century and its transformation at the time of the exile.

II

THE SOURCES

1. *Archæology and Epigraphy*

Our information concerning the conditions in Palestine and throughout western Asia during the period of Israel's birth as a nation is almost wholly derived from inscriptions and archæological remains.

Here we shall merely give a rapid summary, as we shall constantly be referring to our sources in detail in the course of our narrative.

At Jerusalem from 1864 researches had been carried on by C. Wilson, and after that date by the Palestine Exploration Fund (1867–70), by Guthe (**ZDPV**, t. V), and by others. But it was not until 1890 that the systematic exploration of the soil of Palestine began ; it has been followed up with ever-increasing success until the present time, save for the interruption of the war of 1914–18. In addition to Jerusalem,[1] the chief sites explored have been Tell el-Hesy—generally identified with Lachish,[2]—Tell es-Safi, Tell Zakariya, Tell Djudeideh, Tell Sandahanna—the ancient Mareshah [3]—Tell Taanach,[4] Tell Djezer—formerly Gezer [5] — Tell el-Mutesellim — Megiddo,[6] — Jericho,[7] Ain Shems,[8] Beisan,—formerly Beth Shan,[9]—Tabgha,[10] Balata—Shechem or Migdal-Shechem,[11]—en-Nasbeh—perhaps the ancient Mispah,[12]—Beit Mirsim—formerly Debir.[13]

An excellent summary of the results of these excavations, at least up to 1905, in P. Vincent's *Canaan d'après l'exploration récente*, Paris, Gabalda, 1907 (second thousand, 1914). The more recent undertakings can be conveniently followed in the well-documented accounts of Palestinian exploration in the *Revue Biblique* (Paris, Gabalda).

An interesting light is thrown by these excavations on the prehistoric period of Canaan, on the social conditions of the peoples who preceded the Hebrews, their art, their religion, their relations with the neighbouring kingdoms.

Hitherto they have yielded a very small number of *texts*

---

[1] **C** ; **CLXI** ; E. Baumann, **ZDPV**, 1913, pp. 1 *ff.* ; **CLXIII** ; **CLX** ; **REJ**, 1926, pp. 103–17.

[2] Flinders Petrie, **PEF**, 1890–92 ; **CXLVI** ; **CI**.

[3] **PEF, QS**, 1898 *ff.* ; **CII**.

[4] **MN**, 1902, pp. 13 *ff.* ; **CLIII** ; **CLII**.

[5] Macalister, **PEF, QS**, since 1902 ; **CXXXVIII**.

[6] Schumacher, **MN**, since 1904 ; **CLI**. An American mission is carrying on the total clearance of the mound.

[7] **CLIV** ; C. Watzinger, **ZDMG**, 1926, pp. 131 *ff.*

[8] **PEF**, 1911, pp. 41 *ff.* ; **PEF, QS**, 1911–12. Excavations continued by an American mission (Prof. Grant), **RB**, 1929, pp. 110–13.

[9] A. Rowe, **PEF, QS**, April, 1927 ; **RB**, 1926, pp. 124–6, 468–71 ; 1927, pp. 98–101 ; 1928, pp. 123–38, 318–19, 512–43 ; 1929, pp. 85–91, 555–66 ; **SY**, 1928, pp. 124–30.

[10] **RB**, 1925, pp. 583–5.

[11] E. Sellin, **ZDPV**, 1927, pp. 205–10 ; 265–73.

[12] **RB**, 1927, 414–18.

[13] **RB**, 1927, pp. 408 *ff.* ; 1929, pp. 103–7 ; W. F. Albright ; **ZATW**, 1929, pp. 1–17.

coming from the pre-Israelite periods. It is a characteristic fact that they are partly in Babylonian script and language (the tablets from Tell el-Hesy and Taanach), partly in Egyptian, (the steles from Beisan, the funerary inscription from Gezer).[1]

Excavations have been carried on in Syria, in the main since 1919, under the direction of the French Department of Antiquities, especially those at Djebel (Byblos), Saida (Sidon), Nerab, Tell el-Mishrifeh (Qatna), and Ras Shamra. These have a double claim on our attention, first because Syria and Palestine have always been closely linked both in their political vicissitudes and in their civilization, and secondly because one of the principal Syrian peoples, the so-called Phenicians, were a Canaanite people.[2] These excavations have thrown startling new light on the influence of Egypt in Phenicia from the beginning of the third millennium, and moreover on the origins of the alphabet, *i.e.* of the script which was ultimately adopted by the Israelites.[3]

Used with due precaution, epigraphic and other material from the later period of Phenician history will help us to discover features which the Phenicians [4] may have inherited from their Canaanite ancestors of the second or third millennium. The Carthaginian ritual shows certain affinities with the Levitical sacrificial order to which M. Dussaud has rightly called attention [5] and which call for explanation.[6]

The discoveries made at Serabit el-Hadim in the so-called Sinai Peninsula are particularly valuable for the history of the alphabet.[7]

The documents unearthed in Egypt and in Mesopotamia are an inexhaustible mine of information and facts of vital importance for the understanding of the history of Canaan both before and after the Israelite settlement. Such are the mention by Egyptian and Mesopotamian princes of expeditions into Syria from the third millennium and onwards,[8]

---

[1] **PEF**, 1906, pp. 121-2 ; *cf.* pp. 134-5, 148.
[2] P. 54.
[3] On the Syrian excavations, see the review **SY** ; summaries of it have been given in **CIX** and **CXI**, pp. 15-28.
[4] See **CXI**.
[5] **XVIII ; XIX**.
[6] See below, pp. 97-8 ; **RHP**, 1928, pp. 401-2 ; 410-11.
[7] See pp. 76-8.   [8] See pp. 43-6.

the list published by Prof. Kurt Sethe in 1926, of Asiatic states and princes cursed at the funeral of a pharaoh of the ninth dynasty ; [1] the Egyptian folk-stories of Sinuhe, belonging to the period of the twelfth dynasty, and of the predestined prince ; the narratives of the campaigns of Thothmes I and III ; the correspondence of the princes of Syria and Palestine with their overlords Amenophis III and IV, discovered at Tell el-Amarna, the inscriptions of Seti I, of Ramses II, of Merneptah, and of Ramses III ; the story of the journey of Wen Amon to Palestine and Phenicia in the time of Ramses XI (about 1100).

The direct influence of the Egyptian and Babylonian civilizations on Palestine is amply attested by archæology. Excavations in the Holy Land have yielded a great number of objects coming from Egypt or in the Egyptian style. On the other hand, Babylonian was the official language of Canaanite courts about 1400. The Babylonian and Assyrian myths of Creation, their codes (the Sumerian laws, the code of Hammurabi, the collection of Assyrian laws), their psalms, are plainly related to the similar narratives, laws and poetry found in Hebrew literature.[2] The Wisdom literature of Israel has drawn its inspiration from Egyptian sources.[3]

But Assyria, Babylon and Egypt, together with Syria and Phenicia, are not the only countries whose archæological material throws light on the early history of Palestine. Recent discoveries have recreated the history of a people whose political importance and advanced civilization could never have been suspected from the cursory biblical references nor even from the accounts of the campaigns of Ramses II, namely the Hittites. We are becoming increasingly acquainted with Hittite art in building, sculpture, and carving, with its history, and certain features of its religion ; we are beginning to understand its speech, even if its peculiar script has not yet been deciphered. Its legal code· has recently been translated, a code closely related to the most

[1] **AAW**, no. 5 ; see p. 44.
[2] The greater part of the Babylonian and Egyptian texts throwing light on the history of Palestine will be found together in **XXIII**, **XXXVI** ; the Assyro-Babylonian alone in **CXVIII** and in English in **LXXXIII**. See also **XCIII**, **XXXVII** and **XXXVIII**.
[3] *Cf.* Paul Humbert, *Recherches sur les sources égyptiennes de la littérature sapientiale d'Israel*, Neuchâtel, 1929.

ancient collection of Israelite laws.[1] Several indications allow us to suppose that this civilization, which for a brief space rose to such heights, influenced Canaan to no small degree, and that Ezekiel had good grounds for saying of Jerusalem " thy mother was a Hittite " (Ez. xvi. 3). The discovery in Palestine of pottery of the same type as the magnificent vases found in Crete has shown that Ægean culture also had its influence upon the Canaanite peoples. The Philistines moreover were in all probability Ægeans.

It is becoming more and more certain that several centuries before the Hebrew tribes became a nation the eastern Mediterranean region was the home of a civilization to which many peoples of various races had contributed. First the Canaanites, then the Israelites shared in this Mediterranean culture, just as the Jews later on were influenced by Hellenistic culture.

While archæology and epigraphy have thus an extremely important bearing on the environment in which the Israelite people developed, they have so far contributed very little direct evidence relative to the history of Israel.

In the lists of Palestinian towns and peoples conquered by the Pharaohs of the eighteenth and nineteenth dynasties, it has been claimed that the names Jacobel, Josephel, Simeon, Asher and Leviel occur. But the point is doubtful whether we have to do here with Israelite groups bearing these names or with Canaanite districts whose designations these groups adopted.[2]

An inscription, unfortunately rather vague and ambiguous, on the stele of Merneptah, the son of Ramses II, mentions an Israilu in the fifth year of this prince (1229).

The remains of pottery and of civil or military buildings unearthed by excavations in the Holy Land show that there has been no break of continuity between Canaanite and Israelite civilization.[3]

Among the Israelite remains recently brought to light, we find to the south-east of Jerusalem part of the walls and waterworks of the " City of David," that is, of the old citadel of Zion taken by David from the Canaanites and built over

---

[1] For the literature concerning the Hittites, see **CXII, XXXIII** ; Louis Delaporte, *Éléments de grammaire hittite*, Paris, Maisonneuve, 1921.
[2] See pp. 47, 49–50 etc.   [3] See p. 332.

by his successors, and also the tombs belonging apparently to the necropolis of the kings of Judah.[1]

Sheshonk I (about 945–924), on his return from an expedition into Palestine, caused himself to be depicted on the south wall of the great temple of Karnak receiving from the hands of the god Amon and the goddess of Thebes 165 prisoners, representing so many conquered cities.[2] This expedition is mentioned in the Hebrew book of Kings (1 Kings xiv. 25–6).

The site of Samaria, systematically explored by an American mission, has yielded antiquities whose Israelite origin is not doubtful, since the city was founded by Omri, King of Israel (about 887). A notable find in the palace of Ahab consisted of 75 ostraca, whose date has been established.[3] These texts, as well as other objects with inscriptions of early Israelite origin, 60 seals, 100 vase-handles with one or two words stamped in the clay, several weights,[4] are all, save two cuneiform tablets found at Gezer,[5] in Hebrew and in alphabetic characters, as against Prof. Naville's theory, according to which they should have been in Babylonian or in Aramaic.

As far as we know at present Israel is mentioned for the first time in the ninth century in a cuneiform text. The Assyrian king Shalmaneser III mentions Ahabbi Sir'lai, *i.e.* Ahab, King of Israel, among his enemies at the battle of Karkar (854).

We owe to the same monarch the first monument on which Israelites are depicted, from which we can gain some idea of their type, their dress and the produce of their country at that time : it is the famous obelisk representing the tribute sent to him by " Yaua of the land of Omri," that is to say, Jehu, King of Israel (842).

---

[1] **CLXIII** ; **REJ**, 1926, pp. 103–17.

[2] See **XXIII**[2], i, pp. 98–99, 105 ; ii, fig. 114.

[3] **LXXX** ; David G. Lyon, **HTR**, 1910, pp. 137–8 ; 1911, pp. 136–43 ; Vincent, **RB**, 1911, pp. 125–30 ; F. M. Abel, **RB**, 1911, pp. 290–3 ; H. Thiersch, **ZDPV**, 1913, pp. 49–57 ; Albright, **JPOS**, 1925, pp. 38–43 ; H. Gressmann, **ZATW**, 1925, pp. 147–50 ; J. W. Jack, **ET**, 1926–7, pp. 264–9 ; R. Dussaud, **SY**, 1925, pp. 314–38 ; 1926, pp. 9–29.

[4] See **III**, pp. 181–2, 196–7, 223–9 ; **SY**, 1925, pl. xliii.

[5] **III**, pp. 176–7 ; but they are of the seventh century (649 and 647) and therefore belong to the period of Assyrian domination.

About the same time, probably shortly after 842, Mesha, King of Moab, set up the stele whose speech and style strangely recall the vocabulary and modes of thought and expression of the biblical book of Kings. Upon it he recorded the victories which his god Chemosh had given him over Israel.

These archæological and epigraphic data have the inestimable value of establishing for us reliable chronological points of reference : the two Assyrian inscriptions of Shalmaneser, in particular, give us the first certain dates of Israelite history. But so far the monuments have yielded only the most fragmentary evidence directly relating to this history. Any attempt at reconstruction must always depend mainly upon sources of an entirely different character : namely, upon the literary sources which have survived owing to the fact that they found a place in the Hebrew Bible.

2. *The Literary Sources*

There are archæologists accustomed to dealing with inscriptions, that is to say with texts which have come down to us exactly as they left the hand of the stone-cutter contemporary with the events thereon recorded, who affect to despise literary records, accounts often written long after the periods which they describe, usually with apologetic or controversial aims, repeatedly copied and consequently changed, recast, full of scribal alterations.

The monuments of Hebrew literature do not seem to deserve either the complete distrust or the uncritical reliance of which they have so long been the objects. If they are read critically, taking into account the circumstances under which the books were composed and transmitted, it is permissible to draw from them many highly probable conclusions, and for certain periods, completely reliable information.

It is necessary of course, as for all documents of early date, to establish first of all, as far as possible, the sense of the primitive text, making use of all evidence still available. Not only must the traditional or *massoretic* (from the Hebrew *massoreth*, tradition) form of the Hebrew text be consulted, but also the ancient versions, especially the Greek, Syriac and Latin versions, made from manuscripts differing in various degrees from, and often better than those employed by the *massoretes* (the scholars whose labours produced the text which ultimately became the official Hebrew text).

With the text restored as far as possible, the next task of criticism consists in distinguishing between the various component elements of the books as we now possess them. All the historical writings of the Old Testament are, in fact, compilations from earlier works which the redactors have combined in an almost verbal reproduction, following the naïve method occasionally employed by the Assyrian annalists,[1] a method which was later employed by the Arab historiographers[2] and the mediæval chronicler. Devoid of all pride of authorship and intent only on making as complete a collection as possible of the traditions of the past, the Hebrew and Jewish scribes reverently copied and placed in juxtaposition the fragments of earlier histories which they had before them, regardless of the fact that these fragments were inconsistent with one another, or resulted in more or less complete doublets.

This explains why Genesis, as Vitringa (1683) and Witter (1711) had already recognized, and as Astruc (1753)[3] definitely proved, contains two narratives of the creation, one in Genesis i. 1–2, 4^a, culminating in the creation of man, while the other, beginning at Genesis ii. 4^b, makes the creation of man the first act of the divine activity. The episode which represents the wife of the patriarch as being taken into the harem of a foreign prince as the result of her husband's deception, and subsequently as being miraculously delivered, occurs three times in Genesis in variants on the original form (cc. xii, xx, xxvi). Twice David spares the life of Saul, in very similar circumstances, and carries on an almost identical conversation with his persecutor (1 Sam. xxiv. and xxvi.).

In the book of Joshua appear two totally different conceptions of the Hebrew settlement of Palestine. According to the predominant account Canaan was conquered in a single generation by the whole of the Hebrew tribes united under the command of Joshua. But scattered throughout the book there are episodes which presuppose, on the contrary, that

---

[1] **XXXV**, p. 238.
[2] *E.g.* Guidi, **RB**, 1906, pp. 509–19.
[3] **CXXXVI**, pp. 49–52 ; 54–5.

each of the tribes must have taken possession of its own
territory independently, and that the conquest was either
incomplete or very gradual.[1] It is natural to suppose that
the fragments which present such a different view of the
conquest come from another document. Now in this case
we are not limited to conjectures however plausible. We
have actual proof of their truth. The account of the settlement in Palestine from which the above-mentioned fragments in the book of Joshua have been taken still exists : it
has been preserved almost entire at the beginning of the
book of Judges, of which it forms the first chapter. Here
may be seen how the Jewish compilers used their sources :
the compiler of the book of Joshua cut up one of his documents and placed the fragments, almost without changing a
word, in the framework of another parallel narrative.

Finally it will suffice to compare the book of Chronicles
with the more ancient books of Samuel and Kings to reveal
a similar process of composition. The author of Chronicles
reproduces the text of Samuel and Kings almost verbatim,
only making here and there omissions or changes as it suited
his purpose, and adding such fresh information as he thought
fit.

Since such were the methods of redaction, it will be understood that by careful observation of doublets, abrupt changes,
differences of vocabulary and style, references to earlier
accounts, it is possible to distinguish the different hands
which have helped to produce the books as we read them
today. This has been the task of the generations of critics
since Astruc. Their accumulated labours have resulted in
certain conclusions which, in their broad outline, are almost
unanimously accepted today.[2]

The first six books of the Hebrew Bible, often united under
the title of the Hexateuch, are the result of the fusion of four
documents, each of which appears to be the work, not of a

[1] Jos. ix. 6ᵇ, 7, 14, 15ᵃᵝ, 16* ; xi. 13 ; xiii. 13 ; xiv. 12 ; xv. 13–19,
63 ; xvi. 10 ; xvii. 11–18 ; xix. 47.
[2] The simplest method of becoming acquainted with these conclusions and checking them, is to consult one of the translations of
the Biblical text where the various sources are indicated by letters
in the margin or by different colours : VI : XL ; Haupt, *The Sacred
Books of the Old Testament* ; Giovanni Luzzi, *la Bibbia tradotta dai
testi originali e annotata*, Florence, Sansoni, 1922.

single author but of a group of writers belonging to the same period or the same circle, a school :

1. The work known as the *Jahwist*, because its narrators assert in naïve fashion that earlier generations already called God Jahweh, comes from a school which flourished in Judah in the ninth and eighth centuries. It is designated by the letter J.

2. About the same time, but no doubt a little later, there was composed in the northern or Ephraimite kingdom the *Elohist* history (E), whose authors are careful always to employ the title *elohim* (the divinity), as the designation for God until the moment when He allows Moses to reveal Him by the distinctive name of Jahweh (Ex. iii.).

The authors of these two accounts, J and E, have a guiding idea, which is to show that it is Jahweh who has given the land of Canaan to Israel in fulfilment of a predetermined purpose. But, far from transforming the old traditions *ad majorem Dei gloriam*, they have reproduced them with such reverent accuracy that we can still discern under their accounts the original features of their various sources and reconstruct to some extent a history of oral tradition in ancient Israel.[1]

3. Very different is the character of the third school that contributed to the composition of the Hexateuch, the *Deuteronomist* school (D). Its principal contribution is the book of Deuteronomy, at least cc. i–xxxi of the actual book, a collection of laws and admonitions most certainly edited in the seventh and sixth centuries by the instigators and defenders of the great ritual and ethical reform arising from King Josiah's attempt in 622 to apply the principles of the prophets.

The Deuteronomist school of redactors have recast the earlier sources of J and E, already combined, in order to bring them into agreement with the ideas of the reformers.

4. Finally, after the abolition of the Temple ritual as a consequence of the destruction of Jerusalem (586), certain of the priests, among whom was the prophet Ezekiel, undertook the task of committing to writing the ritual laws before they were forgotten or changed, in view of the restoration to

[1] **XXVI**[3] ; **RHR, LXXXVIII**, pp. 57–63.

which they looked forward. From this *priestly* school (P), came several small collections of laws (Ez. xl.–xlviii; Lev. i.–vii. ; xi.–xv. ; xvii.–xxvi., etc.), and above all a great work cast in historical form describing how the various Jewish ritual institutions were successively established by Jahweh in the course of the ages : this is the Priestly Code (P). Many of the rites sanctioned by the priestly laws are extremely ancient, but they also introduce many new rules, for the priestly code undertook not only to codify the ancient customs, but also to purify them. These laws, edited during and after the exile (sixth and fifth centuries), appear to have been promulgated, at least in part, by Ezra towards the end of the fifth century.

The book of Judges contains ancient traditions edited in a parallel form by authors belonging no doubt to the schools of J and E. Among other things it has preserved the so-called song of Deborah (c. v.), which is certainly contemporaneous with the events which it celebrates. In the form in which they have reached us, these ancient fragments have been retouched by a deuteronomic redactor. Fortunately the editor has confined himself to inserting links between the fragments which he was reproducing. These links entirely alter the general meaning of the history ; but by removing them it is easy to recover the original form of the stories. The priestly school has only contributed to this book a version of its final episode (cc. xix.–xx.).

In the book of Samuel, the original documents, taken no doubt from two or three parallel accounts edited by the schools of J and E, are in the main merely combined ; the deuteronomic redactor has confined himself to minor additions. In this work we meet for the first time, side by side with primitive oral traditions, records which have certainly been edited shortly after the events which they describe : for example, certain official documents and especially a detailed account of the reign of David, which occupies almost the whole of the second book.

In the book of Kings the redactor, wholly imbued with the spirit of Deuteronomy, has given little more than summaries of his sources ; he has fortunately made an exception in favour of those sources relating to the development of the religion of Israel. Among these passages possessing primary documentary value for the period prior to the eighth century are 1 Kings i.–ii. ; xx. ; xxii. ; 2 Kings ix.–x.

The book of Chronicles is only of subsidiary value for the periods of Israel's history preceding the exile ; for this work depends almost entirely upon the books of Samuel and Kings. The greater part of the material peculiar to Chronicles bears the unmistakable stamp of the ritualist and dogmatic temper of post-exilic Judaism : it may be assigned in the main to the last editor of Chronicles, who lived in any case after Alexander the Great, and possibly at the beginning of the second century B.C.

In order to estimate the value of the evidence of the historical books of the Hebrew Bible, it is necessary to take into account both the length of time which separates the document in question from the events which it relates, and also the particular bias of the author ; for both these considerations may have more or less modified the facts.

It is hardly necessary to say that the remaining fields of Israelite and Jewish literature contain a large store of most valuable evidence for the history of the religion, ideas and customs of Israel.

The most ancient remains of Hebrew literature belong to what would be called today the *lyric poetry* of that people. Among the Hebrews, as among all peoples who have developed their own culture, verse preceded prose. Fragments of this early poetry have come down to us in the form of quotations made by the old annalists whose work has been embodied in the first nine books of the Hebrew Bible (the Pentateuch, Joshua, Judges, Samuel, Kings). Among them we find bridal odes,[1] funeral dirges,[2] war songs,[3] such as the song of Deborah; magic spells,[4] especially blessings and curses,[5] religious poems, prayers, hymns, oracles.[6] Already certain more literary forms began to appear, such as political

---

[1] Gen. xxiv. 60 ; Judg. xiv. 14, 18.

[2] 2 Sam. i. 17, 27 ; iii. 33–34.

[3] Call to arms : Ex. xvii. 16 ; 2 Sam. xx. 1 ; Songs of Victory : Gen. iv. 23–4 ; Judg. xv. 16 ; Ex. xv. 1–19, 20–1 ; 1 Sam. xviii. 6–7 ; perhaps Numb. xxi. 14–15 and 27–30.

[4] Jos. x. 12.

[5] Gen. iii. 14–19 ; Numb. vi. 24–6 ; Jos. vi. 26.

[6] Numb. xxi. 16–18 ; x. 35–6 ; 1 Kings viii. 12–13 (emend acc. to Sept. 1 Kings viii. 53) ; Judg. xvi. 24 ; Gen. xxv. 22–3 ; Numb. xii. 6–8 ; 2 Kings xiii. 17–19.

poetry, praises or satires directed towards a people or a tribe,[1] and gnomic poetry, proverbs or parables.[2]

The *prophetic books* give us information of first-rate importance concerning the religion of ancient Israel with which the prophets were contemporary. On many points they attacked it ; sometimes they mocked it ; they inveighed against it with passion ; but they had an intimate understanding of it, and a sharpened perception of its secret tendencies.

The prophetic literature also requires careful critical study before it can be used as historical evidence. Interwoven with the utterances of the prophets themselves or their immediate disciples it contains later material. A summary of the results of this critical examination will be given at the beginning of the volume dealing with the history of the prophetic movement.

3. *Comparative Folklore. Comparative History of Religion*

It follows from what has just been said that the strictly documented history of Israel only begins with the reign of David. Concerning the earlier periods, save for an inscription and some poetry, we only possess traditions which become more and more uncertain as they recede along the stream of time.

In order to discover whether these traditions have any historical foundation and to disentangle it, we must take into account the laws which govern the evolution of oral tradition, since it is possible that many of the features of these popular stories are themes borrowed from international folklore.

Moreover, especially for the insufficiently documented primitve stages, the general history of religions gives us many certain points of comparison, enabling us to check the scanty evidence of our texts.

We shall find examples of the help which the comparative method of study can give us in the chapters on the patriarchal traditions, the social organization and religion of the Hebrews in their nomad state, but it must be emphasized here that

---

[1] Gen. ix. 25–7 ; xvi. 12 ; xxv. 22–3 ; xxvii. 27–9 ; xlix ; Numb. xxiii and xxiv ; Deut. xxxiii.

[2] Judg. ix. 8–15 ; *cf.* 1 Kings v. 12–13 ; 2 Kings xiv. 9.

these methods must only be employed in a subsidiary fashion and with great caution. Our foundations must rest on the evidence of the monuments and the texts. Comparative methods can only prove fertile in results if they lead us along the lines of the documentary history, not if they undertake to correct it.[1]

III

THE COUNTRY

1. *Name. Boundaries. Relations with other Countries*

The country which formed the stage upon which the drama of Israel's destinies in the main unfolded itself has been called by many names, whose application has varied with changing ages and political vicissitudes. The name *Amurru*, used by the Babylonians, was also applied to the whole of Syria. The Egyptians used the names *Haru* and *Retenu* ; and the latter term, derived from the name Lotan, denoting a Horitè people, or from that of the town of Lod-Lydda,[2] was extended also to Syria. The name Canaan, employed by the indigenous inhabitants from the Tell el-Amarna period (about 1400), was sometimes confined to the country south of Carmel [3] or, on the other hand, it might embrace the whole of Phenicia.[4] As for the name *Palestine*, originally Syria Palestina, we owe it to the Greeks, who extended to the whole country the name of the coast-dwellers, the Philistines, with whom they were best acquainted.

However, in spite of these variations, the Palestinian region constitutes a sufficiently well-defined geographical unit.

The Mediterranean, at its eastern end, is bounded by a coast extending in an almost straight line from north to south for a distance of about 600 kilometres. This is the coast of Syria. The central part of.this coastline is bordered by a lofty mountain chain, the Lebanon range, whose crests slope precipitously to the sea. In the interior of the country, parallel to this chain runs the Antilebanon range, separated from the Lebanon by the deep and wide valley of Coele-Syria (hollow Syria), called today el-Beq'a, "the valley" *par*

---

[1] *Cf.* **RHR, LXXXVIII**, pp. 53–5, 63–4.
[2] Alt, **ZDPV**, 1924, pp. 169 *ff.*
[3] As by the Egyptians. [4] Gen. x. 16–18 ; *cf.* p. 54.

excellence. The southern end of Antilebanon is marked by the majestic dome of Hermon (2,759 metres), capped with snow during most of the year.

To the south of this immense natural boundary, where the two mountain chains end, the region of Palestine begins. It extends from north to south a distance of about 240 kilometres, or two-fifths of the entire Syrian coast.

When the Israelite writers wished to indicate the extreme boundaries of their country, they used the expression " from Dan to Beersheba," that is to say, they regarded as their northern frontier the above-named mountain ; Dan, the modern Tell el-Qadi, stood in fact at the foot of Hermon, near one of the sources of the Jordan As their southern boundary they took the Wady el-Ghazzeh which, when there is any water in it, flows a little to the south of Gaza, by Bir es-Seba'ah (Beersheba).

Other writers preferred the expression " from the entering in of Hamath to the river of Egypt."[1] This description corresponds fairly accurately, at least on the north side, with the above. For the expression which we translate " the entering in of Hamath " (*lebo' ḥamath*)[2] apparently denotes neither the neighbourhood of Hamath on the Orontes, a town situated more than 200 kilometres farther north, nor the region of Riblah in northern Coele-Syria, nor the locality of Ain-Lebueh,[3] 23 kilometres north of Baalbek, but the southern end of the Beq'a because this constituted the gateway into the territory of Hamath.[4] It is immaterial whether Hamath the great, on the Orontes, is in question, or, as some think,[5] a Hamath in Zobah, nearer, but the existence of which is far from certain.[6] As for the Wady Mizraim (the river of Egypt, or more probably, of Muzri, *i.e.*, of western Arabia), this denoted the Wady el-Arish, thirteen hours' march to the south-west of Gaza.

The Mediterranean forms the western boundary of the

[1] 1 Kings viii. 65 ; 2 Chron. vii. 8 ; *cf.* 2 Kings xiv. 25.
[2] Numb. xiii. 21 ; xxiv. 8 ; Jos. xiii. 5 ; Judg. iii. 3 ; Amos vi. 14 ; Ez. xlvii. 16, 20 ; xlviii. 1.
[3] As Dom Bonaventura Ubach has suggested (*La Biblia, III, El Nombres, El Deuteronomi,* Montserrat, 1928) ; *cf.* **RB,** 1928, p. 268.
[4] Ez. xlvii. 16, places the frontiers of Damascus and of Hamath here ; *cf.* **XX,** pp. 16–17.
[5] **III,** p. 11 ; *cf.* **XCII,** ii, p. 210 *n.* 1
[6] 2 Chron. viii. 3 ; *cf.* 1 Chron. xviii. 3 ; **XX,** p. 234.

I. C

land. On the east and south the Syrian and Arabian deserts constitute a frontier, ill-defined but even more efficacious than the waves of the sea against the invading hosts of the conqueror.

In virtue of its position, Palestine was an indispensable link in the chain which united the great civilized states of antiquity ; and on the other hand, the logic of circumstances forced upon it a relative isolation.

The two chief centres of ancient civilization from time immemorial were Babylon and Egypt. The space which separates these two countries is for the most part a series of deserts across which only occasional well-armed caravans can venture. But there was a way of avoiding the toilsome passage of these vast solitudes ; it consisted in going round them by way of the north. Leaving Babylon, the course of the Euphrates was followed to the point nearest to the Mediterranean. It was then only necessary to follow the belt of fertile country which runs from north to south between the sea and the desert and which constitutes Syria, in order to reach without difficulty, either Egypt, or the starting-point of the caravan routes leading to the equally civilized regions of southern Arabia.

It has been proposed to call these regions lying between Babylon and Egypt " the fertile crescent."[1] In one sense we might even speak of a complete ring ; for the countries occupied by the Semitic or Semitized peoples consist of a great central desert surrounded by an almost uninterrupted circle of lands more or less suited for cultivation and a settled form of life.

Syria was the inevitable highway of the conquerors who swept either from Egypt to the invasion of Asia, or from Babylonia, Assyria, Persia, Asia Minor, Europe, to seize the Nile valley. Trade and ideas followed the same route. It is easy to see that from a very early date these regions were thickly populated, and possessed great cities whose very situation lent itself to commerce. Here mingled the great streams of thought, art, industry and customs from Egypt, the plains of the Euphrates, and the Tigris, hither Asia, Arabia, Cyprus, the Cyclades, Greece.

On the other hand, the more these regions became popu-

[1] See **LXVIII**, p. 220, and the Map, p. 219.

lous, rich and civilized, the more they aroused the greed of conquerors. Syria was ever the prize of victory in the contest between the mistress of the Nile and the power that dominated the Euphrates, whether Babylon, the Hittite empire, or Asshur, Persia, the Greek empire of Alexander, or that of the Seleucids, whether it were the caliphs of Bagdad or the Sultan of Constantinople, in the time of Mehemet Ali, for example, or in 1914–18.

Palestine was on this highway of the civilization of the ancient East. No doubt exports from Phenician ports, Arvad, Byblos, Berytus, Sidon, Tyre, would travel by sea to Egypt in preference to the land route, and even for military expeditions the pharaohs often preferred to transport their troops by ship to one of the ports of the Asiatic coast, thus avoiding the unpleasant crossing of the desert to the south of Gaza. There was, however, a sufficiently heavy traffic across the land of Canaan.

Leaving aside the trade route .which led from Tyre to Damascus by way of Dan,[1] hardly touching Palestine, and likewise the desert routes which linked Hebron on the one side to Egypt by way of Beersheba, and on the other to Elath on the Red Sea by way of the land of Edom, we must make special mention of three great international highways crossing the country : [2]

1. The way of the sea coast. In order to show how much this was used from the earliest times, it will suffice to recall the inscriptions and bas-reliefs carved, along this route, on the rock of the promontory which juts out to the south of the estuary of the Nahr el-Kelb (Dog-river), 12 kilometres north of Beyrut. These are the actual traces of their passage left by the leaders of Egyptian, Assyrian, Greek and Roman armies, to say nothing of the French expedition of 1860, or of the allies in 1918.

2. The highway from Egypt to Damascus and the valley of the Orontes. After crossing the coastal plain of the Philistines, it passed over the chain of Carmel near Megiddo (the modern Tell el-Mutesellim), cut the plain of Jezreel, climbed the Galilean plateau, and there divided into two forks, one of which led to Coele-Syria, while the other crossed the Jordan to the south of lake Huleh, where the " bridge of

the daughters of Jacob " (fifteenth century) stands, and
from thence ascends to Damascus. This was no doubt the
way of the sea of which Isaiah speaks (viii. 23) ; in any case
it was the mediæval *via maris*. By this route Pharaoh Necho
reached the banks of the Euphrates in 609, when Josiah
attempted to stop his progress at Megiddo (2 Kings xxiii.
29–30).

By a slight change in the route it is possible to reach
Damascus by Shechem or by Dothan, then by Bethshan and
the fords below the lake of Tiberias. At Dothan Joseph,
according to the J tradition, was sold to a caravan of
Ishmaelites carrying a load of spices from Gilead to Egypt
on the backs of camels (Gen. xxxvii. 25–7, 28). According
to the version of E, he was carried off by Midianite merchants
passing near Shechem (xxxvii. 28[a]). Custom duties from
these convoys constituted for the local sheiks one of their
principal sources of revenue : when the revolting Shechemites
wished to strike Abimelech their king in a vulnerable
spot, they robbed the travellers on the highways (Ju. ix.
25).

3. A third main artery of communication was the route
which skirted the lands beyond Jordan along the edge of
the desert, and led from Damascus to Arabia and Elath at
the head of the Elanite gulf. This route, known as the
" pilgrim's way," *i.e.* to Mecca, is no doubt the " way of the
tent-dwellers," that is to say, the Bedouins, mentioned in
Judges viii. 11.

But although the land of Canaan, by reason of its geographical position, was drawn into the main stream of Oriental
civilization, none the less it secured to its inhabitants, or
to be precise a part of them, a relative isolation.

In fact, the great international highways of which we
have spoken, left outside their system large tracts of country
such as the hill country of Ephraim and Judah or the land
of Gilead. It was in these districts, on the margin of the great
stream of civilization, that the Israelites gathered themselves
into compact units, then into states. And it was in one of
these countries, namely in Judah, after the exile, that a
society could come into being whose ideal was to shut itself
off from all intercourse with the outside world.[1]

[1] Josephus, *c. Ap.*, i, 12 ; *cf.* Numb. xxiii. 9.

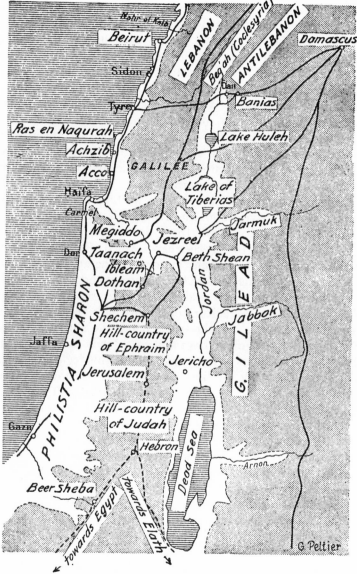

MAP I. ROUTES AND NATURAL DIVISIONS OF PALESTINE.

2. *Natural Divisions of the Country*

Another almost inevitable result of the configuration of the country was the separation of the population into a certain number of regional groups each having its peculiar interests and distinct mode of life.

The surface of Syria consists of a limestone plateau, which emerged after the upheaval which brought the Mediterranean basin into existence. At the close of the Tertiary period there occurred a deep subsidence in this plateau which is occupied today by Coele-Syria, the valley of the Jordan with the Dead Sea basin, and which is continued southwards by the Arabah, the Elanite Gulf, and the Red Sea. Palestine is thus divided into four parallel zones running from north to south : the coast, the plateau west of the Jordan, the valley of that river, and the Transjordanian plateau.

I. *The Coast* itself has three distinct aspects :

1. To the north of the cape called Ras en-Naqurah (probably the ancient Scala Tyriorum), the actual boundary between the French mandated territory and Palestine, the mountains being higher and closer to the sea give no room for plains where the culture of cereals may be carried on to any great extent. On the other hand, the shoreline, rocky for the most part, offers bays and roadsteads suitable for the building of harbours. The population of this region naturally acquired the mode of life of seafarers and traders. This became the site of· the great merchant city of Tyre.

2. From Ras en-Naqurah to Carmel is a transitional region. The mountains are further from the coast. A little coastal plain extends along the shores which are almost everywhere sandy. However there are ports, Achzib (Ecdippa, the modern ez-Zib), Accho (Ptolemais, St. Jean d'Acre) and the modern harbour of Haifa, near the ancient Sycaminum. Neither this part of the coast, nor the previous part, has ever been Israelite territory : it was possessed by the Phenicians.

3. To the south of the Carmel promontory the coast becomes almost a straight line. Lined by sandhills, it presents no natural anchorage. By great labour a few artificial landing-places, such as Jaffa and Gaza, have been created. While this region offers little encouragement to marine pursuits, the vast and fertile plains of Sharon to the

north, and Philistia to the south, due to an upheaval of the earth's surface to a height of 60 or 70 metres,[1] are admirably suited to agriculture. The highway from Egypt into Syria, passing through this region, caused strongly fortified trading cities to grow up along its route. During the Israelite period these were, for the most part, in the hands of the Philistines.

II. *The Cis-Jordan Plateau* is divided from west to east by a wide and deep plain, the valley of Megiddo or Jezreel, which constitutes a line of communication between the coast and the deep Jordan valley. The region of the Cis-Jordan heights is thus divided into three natural zones :

1. The mountainous region to the north of the plain of Jezreel varies considerably in elevation. There are fantastic summits, the highest of which is Djebel Djermak, 1,199 metres, and deep and extensive depressions. The fertility of the district is remarkable, owing to the abundance of springs. This smiling country which, under the name of Galilee, was destined to play a central part in the religious history of the world, had little or no part in the history of ancient Israel. Its Hebrew population was, in fact, very scanty. Furthermore, it was cut off from the main Israelite body by the formidable barrier of the plain of Jezreel.

2. This depression is the strategic key of Palestine. Here or in the neighbourhood were fought most of the great battles for the possession of the country : at Megiddo in the time of Thothmes III and later under Josiah, at the Kishon in the time of Deborah, on the mountains of Gilboa where Saul fell, at the Horns of Hattin (1187) at the time of the Crusades, at Mt. Tabor in the time of Bonaparte. In this valley trade and military routes crossed one another. It gave access by easy passes—the pass of Jezreel is only 123 metres high—to the Jordan valley and the Damascus region. Furthermore, this wide plain, which is becoming increasingly a grain-producing district, has been surrounded by a circle of cities inhabited from the stone age, and fortified from at least the sixteenth century B.C. : Megiddo, Taanach, Ibleam, Jezreel, with Dor on the coast and Bethshan to the east, formed a chain of strongholds which, remaining in the hands of the Canaanites, for centuries hampered communications

[1] **III**, p. 12.

between the Israelites of the hill-country to the south and
those of the Galilean heights.

3. To the south of the valley of Jezreel, the plateau presents an appearance very different from its northern aspect.
In the Israelite period the district was called the hill-country
of Ephraim, and further south the hill-country of Judah.
The variety of the Galilean landscape is here replaced by
uniformity : the rounded outline of the hills presents an
even range of heights (789 metres at Jerusalem, the highest
point Tell 'Azur, 1,011 metres). Streams are rare and
generally dry ; trees are almost entirely absent. The slope
which goes down to the Jordan, more precipitous than the
western slope, and hollowed into deep ravines by the rain, is
wild and sparsely inhabited ; it is of little use save for pastoral
activities. The important towns of the district stand on the
ridge of the plateau : Shechem, Bethel, Jerusalem, Bethlehem, Hebron. The reason is that the western slope being,
like the eastern, seamed by many deep gorges, the main road
of the district is obliged to follow the line of the watershed.
Owing to the nature of the soil and the isolated position of
these highlands, the greater part of the inhabitants depend
upon agriculture for a livelihood. Cereals, vines and olives
have always been the chief wealth of the country. Cattle-
rearing only prevails in the south, where wide stretches of
country are already " desert," which means not a sea of
sand, but stony plateaus, covered in winter and spring with
grass, thin but sufficing to feed the flocks of goats or sheep :
the word denoting desert in Hebrew has the etymological
meaning of " pasturage " (*midbar*).

III. *The valley of the Jordan*, as is well known, has the
uncommon peculiarity of lying below sea-level for most of
its length. While the three sources of the river spring from
heights of 330 metres (the Banias source, the ancient Cæsarea
Philippi), 520 (the Hasbani source), and 154 (that of Tell
el-Qadi), the lake of Huleh, formed by the union of the three
streams and often identified on insufficient grounds with
the " waters of Merom " (Jos. xi. 5),[1] is only two metres
above sea-level. The lake of Tiberias, formerly the Sea of
Chinnereth, which the Jordan passes through a little further
south, is already 208 metres below the shores of the Mediter-

[1] See the note in **VI.**

ranean. And the Dead Sea, in earlier times known as the Sea of the Plain, then the Salt Sea or Eastern Sea, and finally Lake Asphaltites, into which the river runs, is 393·8 metres below sea-level at the shore. As the lake is 399 metres deep, it follows that the depression is in all 793 metres below sea-level.

According to certain Israelite traditions (Gen. xiii. 10 ; xiv. 3), the present site of the lake was, in the time of Abraham, occupied by a fertile, smiling valley " like the garden of Jahweh." Apparently the formation of the Dead Sea, with the desolation of its shores, was attributed to a divine punishment, a rain of fire and brimstone or, according to another version, an upheaval of the earth, which destroyed the wicked cities of Sodom and Gomorrha. Geology gives a more prosaic explanation of the deathly appearance of the lake by the deposits of salt which the lake has left on its shores as it receded. It likewise explains the extreme saturation of its waters with chloride of magnesium (2,200 million tons), with chloride of sodium (2,000 million tons), and other solid matter (25 per cent. in all), by the intense evaporation caused by the tropical heat which prevails in that narrow gorge.[1] Only a few bacilli, such as that of tetanus, can live in that supersaturated solution of salts. The level of this inland sea must have varied considerably during the different glacial and inter-glacial periods ; the deposits left on the slopes of the neighbouring mountains show that it has been 426 metres above its present level.[2] In any case, the formation of the Dead Sea goes back far behind the beginnings of history, and its configuration does not seem to have changed much since, except for some subsidence of the soil on the south side.[3]

In the geographical unity of Palestine, the Jordan valley has its own independent existence. In the immediate neighbourhood of its sources, which are very abundant, as is usually the case with those which spring from limestone hill-country, the river passes through the alpine region of Hermon, then, above lake Huleh, through marshy country covered with

[1] *Cf.* **RB**, 1929, p. 239.
[2] *Cf.* **III**, pp. 16–17.
[3] On the Dead Sea, *cf.* **CXVI** ; P. Abel, **RB**, 1929, pp. 237–60 ; M. Blanckenhorn, **ZDPV**, 1896, p. 1 ; 1912, p. 113 ; **XCIX**.

reeds, where a few semi-nomad tribes pasture their herds of buffaloes. The slopes surrounding the lake of Tiberias, abounding in fish, are famous for a fertility which the historian Josephus is never tired of praising. In the time of Jesus, this region, now almost desert, used to support a large population of peasants and fishermen.

Below the lake of Tiberias, the aspect of the valley undergoes an abrupt change. The climate becomes tropical : at Jericho, " the city of palm-trees," date-palms yield their ripened clusters ; in the neighbourhood of the Dead Sea are found certain species of birds and plants which are only found besides in Egypt and the Indies. Nevertheless, the Jordan plain is a dreary desert ; the Hebrews called it the Arabah, " the steppe." This is due to the fact that it is impossible to use the river for purposes of irrigation. In earlier days when the river was much higher, it cut for itself

FIG. 1. SECTION OF THE JORDAN VALLEY.

a bed at least two kilometres wide with precipitous banks about fifteen metres high. At the present time, even at its highest, the river never reaches the foot of these natural quays. It has actually dug in its old river-bed a new course, three or four metres deep. Today the only vegetation in all the Jordan valley is found at the oases of Bethshan and Jericho, save for a kind of jungle (ez-zor) growing thickly in the immediate neighbourhood of the river. Although there may have been a few other grassy spots near Succoth, Penuel, Mahanaim, and Phasael, the general aspect of the Arabah must have remained the same from very early times. In the O.T. we hear of lions infesting the thickets by the Jordan (Jer. xlix. 19).

Another characteristic of the Jordan is that it is a dead river, unnavigable save near its source. Unlike most rivers, instead of being a link it is a barrier.

IV. *Transjordania.* Seen from the west from Jerusalem, for example, the blue line of the escarpment bounding the

Jordan valley on its eastern side wears the appearance of a mountain chain. In reality it is the edge of a vast plateau whose height ranges from 600 metres on the north to more than 1,000 on the south. This plateau, which is the complement and was once the continuation of that of Ephraim and Judah, is remarkable for the abundance of its streams. These in their rapid course to the Jordan and the Dead Sea cut deep ravines in the limestone plateau, dividing it into so many peninsulas. The three chief streams are the Yarmuk,[1] the modern Sheriath el-Munadireh, the Jabbok (Nahr ez-Zerqa) and the Arnon (wady el-Mojib). Geologically and geographically, the country east of the Jordan falls into clearly marked districts, of which the course of the Jarmuk forms the dividing line.

1. The nature of the country to the north of this river is essentially volcanic. An immense plain which today is known as the Golan (the Gaulanitis of the Greeks),[2] and the Hauran (the ancient land of Bashan or Batanea), stretches away to the east as far as Gebel Hauran, that is, to the group of extinct volcanoes also called the mountain of the Druses. This plain, whose soil is formed of disintegrated volcanic debris, is a splendid wheat-growing land. It is the granary of Syria. The Israelites never gained a permanent footing in this fertile country. It was occupied, probably shortly after their settlement in Palestine, by kinsfolk as keen as themselves to seize the choicest lands and as stubborn to defend them when taken, the Arameans.

2. In the Israelite period the region to the south of the Jarmuk bore the name of the mountain of Gilead. Here the soil is no longer volcanic, but the abundance of water produces a noticeably richer vegetation than is found on the plateau to the west of the Jordan. Moreover, real forests, never seen on the western side, now begin to appear. Arable country abounds, and the vines of the land were famous (Is. xvi. 8–10). But there were two occupations pre-eminently characteristic of the inhabitants of Transjordania, between the Jarmuk and the Arnon, these were

---

[1] *Mishnah Parah*, viii, 10.
[2] *Cf.* Golan in the Biblical epoch (Deut. iv. 43 ; Jos. xx. 8 ; xxi. 27 ; 1 Chron. vi. 56) and perhaps Giluni at the time of Tell el-Amarna (**TA(K)**, 185 ; **XX**, p. 506).

cattle-breeding, for which the country was admirably suited, and the struggle with the nomads. In comparison with the region north of the Jarmuk the width of the strip of country fit for settled occupation is three or four times less, and is closely hemmed in by the desert.

> " As for Gad, bands of plunderers hem him in ;
> but in his turn he shall press hard upon their heels."

The ancient oracle (Gen. xlix. 19) concerning the tribe of Gad, with its untranslatable play on words, aptly describes the mode of life of the inhabitant of these lands, ever on the alert to repel the predatory Bedouin. It is easy to understand that the people of this country, ever anxiously watching the desert, may often have been indifferent to the dangers of an entirely different kind which threatened their kinsmen on the western side of the river, as in the days of Deborah, and that indifference might easily change into hatred, as in the time of Jephthah.

It will be seen that the inhabitants of Palestine must have tended to fall apart into regional groups with divergent interests. Furthermore, while in Egypt or Mesopotamia the vital necessity of regulating the inundation compelled the inhabitants of those river-valleys to build up a central government, no similar necessity in Palestine forced the inhabitants of the same district into political unity. Historical circumstances might bring it about ; but geographical conditions tended rather to the isolation of each valley and each city. Even if nomads settled in these mountains, they could still maintain their immemorial detachment : the clan or the tribe being merely replaced by the town, the village or the district. Such, we shall see, was the state of the Canaanites, and for centuries continued to be the state of the Israelites.

3. Climate. Local Phenomena

Palestine belongs to that region of the earth's surface where there are only two seasons, one dry and scorching, the other rainy, " summer and winter " (Gen. viii. 22 ; Zec. xiv. 8 ; Ps. lxxiv. 17). The variation in temperature during these two seasons of the year is considerable on the plateaus. At Jerusalem, where precise observations have been recorded since 1860, the thermometer varies from 45 deg., Jan. mean temp., to 73 deg., Aug. mean temp. The extremes recorded are 39 deg. below zero and 112 deg. above. Hence the summer is very hot, and we can understand that in the religious belief of these countries the sun wears the guise of a terrible destroyer rather than of a benefactor. The Israelite who wishes to speak of his God as a protector, does not usually call him his " sun " (Ps. lxxxiv. 12), but his " shade " (Numb. xiv. 9 ; Ps. cxxi. 5, etc.).

With the exception of the burning plain of the Jordan, the climate renders conditions of life easy as far as food, clothing and shelter are concerned, and is neither relaxing nor depressing. The wide variation in temperature between the seasons, as between day and night (42 deg. mean variation at Jerusalem), tends to foster the adaptability of the physical organism. The shepherds who, like Jacob, were " consumed by heat by day and by frost by night " (Gen. xxxi. 40), became capable of great endurance. In winter the temperature drops enough to make a fire necessary (Jer. xxxvi. 22 ; Mark xiv. 54, 67) ; at Jerusalem the King had actually his " winter house " (Jer. xxxvi. 22), doubtless a chamber specially protected against the cold (*cf.* Amos iii. 15).

Palestine is in the region of the trade winds. There is also a regular alternation of land winds and sea breezes. Every day the west wind springs up on the shore about nine or ten in the morning ; it reaches Jerusalem about three, bringing with it, even in summer, some degree of freshness and moisture. It drops in the evening and springs up again at night. One of the writers of Genesis has naïvely transferred to Paradise the climatic conditions of Palestine, and depicts Jahweh as walking in the garden in " the cool of the day," *i.e.* in the evening when the refreshing sea-breeze blows (Gen. iii. 8). This peculiarity of the Palestinian climate explains why Boaz happened to be on his threshing-floor on the night of his romantic meeting with Ruth : the fact being that the Judean peasant avails himself of the sea-breezes to winnow his grain.[1]

Another wind much more frequently mentioned in Hebrew literature, is the terrible *qadim*, the east or more precisely the south-east wind, which we call the sirocco (from the Arabic *šarki*, eastern). Scorching in summer, freezing in winter, it brings from the Syrian and Arabian deserts clouds of fine

[1] Ruth iii. 2 ; *cf.* Hos. xiii. 3 ; Ps. i. 4 ; xxxv. 5 ; Job xxi. 18.

dust which make not only breathing but the smallest effort a misery. It dries up the springs and withers the vegetation. It raises whirlwinds of dust which tear up tents from their fastenings and overturn animals. In the story of Job it was one of these tornadoes which came from the desert, struck the four corners of the house and buried the ten children of the pious man under the ruins (Job i. 19). It is the east wind which is peculiarly "the wind of Jahweh" (Hos. xiii. 15; Isa. xl. 7), the breath of his nostrils.[1] The fact that the divine wind is not the kindly and regular sea-breeze, but the destructive and capricious sirocco, is characteristic of the religious mentality of the Semite, who finds the divine not in the normal course of nature but in its breach, in the unforeseen and incalculable, in the forces of nature which strike man with terror rather than in those which are beneficent.

In Palestine it is the rain which is the greatest of blessings. There are three periods in the rainy season which lasts from November to April:

1. The season of the *moreh* or *yoreh*, that of the early rains of autumn which make it possible for the plough to penetrate the soil baked by the drought of summer.

2. The season of the great winter rains or *gešem*.

3. The season of the *malqosh*, or spring rain without which the crops and fruits could not sustain the burning heat of the summer. If the spring rain failed or was insufficient, drought and famine resulted. After April there is no source of moisture for the vegetation save the dew which is fortunately always abundant.

For the Israelite it was one of the great advantages of his country that by a dispensation of Providence it was spared the toilsome necessity of irrigation characteristic of Egypt. There it was necessary to water the fields " by the foot," that is to say, by the great water-wheels which had to be turned by foot and hand (Deut. xi. 10–12). As a result the Canaanite peasant felt himself absolutely dependent upon the powers that sent down the kindly waters from above.

Storms in Palestine are less impressive and rarer than in Europe. However, by reason of the mentality referred to above in connexion with the east wind, this terrifying phenomenon vividly impressed the Semitic imagination and

[1] *Cf.* Job xxxviii. 1 ; Amos i. 2 ; **CXXIX**, p. 52.

entered largely into religious conceptions. Among the Canaanites Hadad was a storm god and Resheph a lightning god.[1] For the Israelite the thunder was the voice of Jahweh, who roared like a lion or uttered shouts of joy like one who treads the wine-press.[2] The lightning is his spear or his arrows.[3] The gleaming bow seen in the clouds after rain is no doubt laid there by Jahweh after he has used it to shoot out his arrows,[4] like the god Quzah among the Arabs,[5] or Indra among the Hindus.[6]

For the same reason the earthquake held a place in the religious conceptions of the Israelites quite out of proportion to its slight and relatively rare occurrence in Palestine. The only well-attested earthquake recorded in the O.T. is that which took place in the reign of Uzziah about 760.[7] However the trembling of the earth is a regular feature in the descriptions which historians, poets and prophets give of past, present or future epiphanies of Jahweh.

Extinct volcanoes are found in Palestine, especially in the Golan, but also in the heart of the country, such as Sheik Iskander (518 metres) to the south of Megiddo. The soil of Galilee and of the plain of Jezreel is partly volcanic.[8] It is possible that the Israelites may have seen one of the craters in activity. M. Schumacher claims to have found the traces of two lava-beds crossing the valley of Jezreel; in one of which he discovered a vase imbedded in the stone : according to him it dated from the third millennium, but according to other archæologists from the fifteenth century at the earliest.[9] However, the reminiscences of volcanic eruptions contained in certain Israelite theophanies [10] seem to have been derived

[1] See below, p. 127–9.
[2] Amos i. 2 ; Jer. xxv. 30 ; Zech. ix. 14 ; Ps. xxix. 3–9.
[3] Ps. vii. 13, 14 ; cxliv. 5 ; Hab. iii. 9–11.
[4] Gen. ix. 13–16 ; Ezek. i. 28.
[5] **XC**, p. 209 ; **LXXXIX**, p. 317.
[6] With the Babylonians, the bow of Marduk seems to become a star, perhaps Sirius (**XLII**, vi, 1, p. 33 ; **XCIII**, pp. 426, 431, 496 ; **XXXVII**, pp. 143–4).
[7] Amos i. 1 ; Zech. xiv. 5. Josephus makes mention of one, in 31 B.C., which had caused 10,000 (A. J., xv. 5, 2) or 30,000 (B. J., i. 19, 3) deaths.
[8] **III**, pp. 14–15.
[9] **CXXIX**, p. 75.
[10] Exod. xix. ; cf. Micah i. 3–4 ; Nah. i. 6 ; Deut. xxxii. 22 ; Ps. civ. 32 ; cxliv. 5.

rather from the traditions concerning Sinai, the distant mount of God.[1]

4. Flora and Fauna

Palestine has always been, perforce, a land of " tillage and pasturage." While the soil of the country provides excellent building-stone (for example, that taken from the great quarry at Jerusalem called " the cotton cave ") and potter's clay,[2] it is very poor in metals. The Deuteronomist indulges in a daring hyperbole when he says that " the stones of the land are iron and out of its hills thou mayest dig brass " (Deut. viii. 9). The nearest copper deposits are in Lebanon and Edom. There is an iron mine near Beirut,[3] and another at Gebel Mirad near Burmeh, to the north of the Jabbok.[4] The iron bedstead of Og, King of Bashan, was probably of basalt. It is significant that, according to Israelite tradition, the father of the smiths should be Tubal (Gen. iv. 22), the eponymous ancestor (Gen. x. 2), of the people called by the Assyrians Tabal, by the Greeks Tibarenians, and who dwelt in the region north of the Taurus, *ubi ferrum exoritur*.[5]

Cattle-breeding was the paramount activity in the south of Judah (the Negeb), in Transjordania and on the barren slopes running down to the Jordan, known as " the deserts " of Judah, of Engedi, of Tekoa, Gibeon, Ai, etc. Immense herds of small cattle pastured there, consisting no doubt then as now of fat-tailed sheep (Lev. iii. 9, etc.) and long-eared goats.

The breeding of kine was carried on in ancient times on a much larger scale than at present, and calves were freely slaughtered (Gen. xviii. 7–8 ; Amos vi. 4 ; Luke xv. 23, etc.).

The early Israelites used as beasts of burden the ass, the mule and the camel, but the latter seems to have been mainly used in the desert.[6] The horse, which seems to have been unknown in Babylon before the Kassite invasion, about 1760, and in Egypt before that of the Hyksos, expelled in

---

[1] See p. 176. [2] See p. 389.
[3] Mentioned by the geographer Idrisis (A.D. 1154), doubtless that of Murudj, which was worked by the Turks during the war of 1914–18.
[4] IV, p. 28.
[5] Inscription quoted in **CXLI**, p. 122 ; *cf.* Ezek. xxvii. 13.
[6] Ezra ii. 67, reckons 435 camels as against 6,720 asses.

1580,[1] was used by the Canaanites for their famous iron chariots,[2] but was not adopted by the Israelites until the time of Solomon for purposes of war and as a luxury. The prophets, with their rooted attachment to ancient customs, always regarded this animal with hostility as a symbol of heathen influence and godless militarism.[3]

Agriculture was the mainstay of the country. In early times barley, the food of the poor, was the principal sustenance of the Israelites settled in the mountainous parts of the country (Judges vii. 13–14). Later on they became great cheese-makers (Deut. viii. 8 ; 1 Kings v. 25). In the sixth century this formed one of the chief articles of commerce between Israel and Tyre (Ezek. xxvii. 17). They also culti-vated spelt, millet, flax and various kinds of vegetables ; the English name of one of these is a reminder that it was in Palestine that the Romans learnt to use it, the shallot, whose name comes from the Latin *ascalonia*. Together with corn the main objects of culture were the olive and the vine. The olive, still plentiful, in spite of the deforestation due to the short-sighted financial policy of the Turks, produced oil which was highly esteemed even at the court of the Pharaohs (Hos. xii. 2). The cultivation of the vine was much more intensively carried on in ancient times than at present ; we find the remains of winepresses and terraces in places which are now barren. The vine became a national product to such an extent that it was stamped upon Jewish coins as the national emblem. There were famous vintages, especially in Transjordania. The fig-tree with its fruits which ripened, so to speak, at all times of the year, furnished a most esteemed food (Hos. ix. 10 ; Mic. vii. 1). The Palestinian peasant's cherished dream was for each to dwell safely under his own vine and fig-tree. Nor must the date-palm be forgotten, formerly cultivated in the oasis of Jericho. The Roman government took over the monopoly of the date-industry, and exported its famous produce as far as the palace of the Cæsars.[4] The best-known products of the country were spices, honey, gum tragacanth, myrrh, pistachio nuts and almonds (Gen. xliii. 11).

---

[1] *Cf.* **XII**, pp. lxv–lxvi.   [2] *e.g.* Judges v. 22, 28. See p. 74.
[3] Hos. xiv. 3 ; Isa. ii. 7 ; xxxi. 1, 3 ; Mic. v. 9 ; Deut. xvii. 16.
[4] Josephus, A. J., xv, 4, 2, and B. J., iv, 8, 3 ; Pliny, H. N., xiii, 44.

The fact that the population of Palestine was, perforce, almost entirely engaged in agriculture, had a vital influence on the social and religious development of the peoples which settled in the country.[1]

A still much-disputed question is whether the soil of Palestine was much more fertile in the past than it is now, and whether it can have nourished a population five times or even ten times greater than today. It is a fact that the various branches of cultivation have been better managed at certain epochs, notably during the Roman occupation, than in our time. By means of irrigation, tracts of country which have now relapsed into the wild state, were then reclaimed from the desert, a fact which is attested by the frequent ruins of Greek and Roman cities found now surrounded by the steppe. But if the labour of man was then able to draw a more ample supply from the resources of the soil, it does not appear that the contention is well-founded that these resources were richer in ancient times, or that the climate of the country has changed.

The story of the huge bunches of grapes which the Israelite spies displayed on their return from their exploration of the country round Hebron, bunches which it took two men to carry, belongs to the same cycle of popular tradition as the story of the giants who were supposed to have been the original inhabitants of the land. The fantasy may be merely the expression of the bewildering impression of fabulous fertility which the land created in men accustomed to the desert, or it may represent the Israelite's feeling of pride when he compared the resources of his country with the sand and rocks of his kinsfolk the Edomites.

We may understand similarly the well-known phrase used by the Hebrew writers to describe the fertility of their country : " a land flowing with milk and honey." If the reference is to literal milk and honey, then we have not to do with a description of Palestine as a land of intensive cultivation, but rather as a region of cattle breeding and abounding in bees, that is, wild bees, for the Israelite does not seem to have practised apiculture.[2] The expression would have a

---

[1] See pp. 120–136 ; 400–3 ; 409–10.
[2] It was known, however, to the Hittites. *Cf.* Hittite Code, § 91–2 (**XXXIII**, pp. 71–2).

more direct reference to the fertility of the soil if we suppose that by honey is here intended a kind of syrup made of grapes, dates or figs [1] called by the indigenous inhabitants *dibs*, an Arabic word corresponding to the Hebrew *debash*, honey.[2] Or, again, if the formula be taken merely to imply that the produce of the country, its grain and fruits, were as sweet and pleasing to the taste as milk and honey.[3] A third possibility is that the words are an imaginative comparison of Palestine to Paradise, the fabulous garden where, according to some traditions, there flowed streams of milk and rivers of honey.[4] However we may take it, the phrase is the nomad's way of saying that Palestine is a land of plenty, a paradise, if you will, compared with the desert. Only Bedouins would have measured the fecundity of a country by the quantity of milk and honey which it could produce, since milk is the nomad's main source of food while honey is his favourite sweetmeat.[5] When Isaiah wishes to describe a time of return to the pastoral mode of life, he says : " butter and honey shall he eat " (Isa. vii. 21–5). Hence we cannot attach much importance to these poetic eulogies.

The fertility of the soil depends mainly on the water-supply, and this in its turn is affected by the extent to which the country is afforested. Now it would not appear that Palestine was, at least in the Israelite period, a well-wooded country.[6] When wood was needed for building on a large scale, it became necessary to import it from abroad, especially from the forests of Lebanon, at that time very extensive. There were certainly " forests " in Palestine ; a small town was called Kirjath-jearim, " the city of forests " (Joshua xv. 10). Ezekiel speaks of Judah under the metaphor of " the

[1] Called μέλι by Josephus, B. J., lv, 8, 3 (468) ; Pliny, H. N., xiii, 44.

[2] L. Bauer, **MN**, 1905, 2, pp. 65–71 ; S. Krauss, **ZDPV**, 1909, no. 3.

[3] Dalman, **MN**, 1905, 2, p. 28 ; *cf.* pp. 27–9.

[4] *Sib.*, iii, 741–9 ; v, 281–3 ; *cf. Slav. En.*, 8, 5 ; *Apoc. Paul*, ed. Tisch., p. 52 ; *Coran*, 47. *Cf.* **CLVIII** ; **CXXIX**, p. 81 ; **IV**, p. 20 ; **III**, p. 67, no. 1 ; **XXXVII**, pp. 594–5.

[5] Le Clerc had already pointed out that the Arabs have at least 80 words for this product (*Dissertatio de lingua hebraica*, § 5, in the preface to *Genesis*, Amsterdam, 1693).

[6] If one can believe the Egyptian story of the Predestined Prince (edited probably under the twentieth dynasty), Syria, as far as Naharina (in the Euphrates district), was only an immense hunting ground (**XXXVI**, ii, pp. 370–5).

forest of the south field " (Ezek. xx. 46). But the word was often used then, as now, to describe thickets of scrub-oak and thorns, rather than forests of tall timber. The jungle along the banks of the Jordan is called a forest. A further proof that tall trees were extremely rare in early times is that the words denoting " sacred tree " and those for the evergreen oak and the terebinth were constantly confused : hence trees of this kind must all, or nearly all, have been regarded as sacred.

There were also in early times, as now, immense stretches of desert in the interior of the country.

Hence the figures given in some of our texts must be discounted to a great extent : according to the priestly writer the Israelite warriors numbered 600,000 men at the time of the entry into Canaan, while in the time of David there were 1,300,000 of them according to 2 Samuel xxiv. 9. These figures require a population of two and a half millions in the first case, and of five millions in the second. The ancient song of Deborah, a most reliable document, gives the more modest estimate of the total number of spearmen in the whole battle-array of the tribes as 40,000 (Judges v. 8). Six hundred warriors constituted a large part of the fighting force of the tribe of Dan. Gideon pursued the Midianites with 300 followers. In his revolt against the Philistines Saul had at his disposal, according to one version, 3,000, according to another, 600 men (1 Sam. xiii. 2, 15). These facts throw suspicion on the high figures quoted above, even if we allow for the wholesale absorption of the Canaanites under David and Solomon. The Canaanites must have had an effective fighting force on a similar scale to that of the Hebrews, yet the invading Pharaohs, for their conquest, depended on armies which, according to Maspero, never numbered more than 30,000 men.[1]

Taking all the facts into account, we shall not be far wrong if we accept Benzinger's estimate of the population which ancient Palestine could support as about double that of the Holy Land today, that is, about 1,200,000, or 40 to 45 inhabitants per square kilometre.[2]

[1] **LXIII**, ii, p. 212.   [2] **III**, p. 24.

PART I

CANAAN BEFORE THE ISRAELITE SETTLEMENT

BOOK I

HISTORICAL DATA AND SOCIAL ORGANIZATION

CHAPTER I

THE HISTORY OF PALESTINE UP TO THE TWELFTH CENTURY

I

PREHISTORIC TIMES [1]

PALESTINE has been inhabited since the beginning of the Quaternary epoch. Deposits of worked flints have been found in the Belqa (the land of Moab and Ammon), which may possibly go back to the Eolithic period. [2]

The Palæolithic period, or age of stone implements, is represented in Palestine by objects, usually of flaked flint, belonging to the various types into which the European Stone Age has been divided: the same sequence of forms, apparently, occurs in the East as in the West:

1. *The Chellean.* The dwellers on the high plateaux of Jerusalem, Ammon, Moab, and Dera'at, had but a limited range of tools, such as axes, stone hammers and maces. They lived by means of hunting in the great forests with which the country was then covered.

[1] CLIX, pp. 373–426 ; IV, pp. 42–53 ; III, pp. 37–41 ; Buzy, RB, 1928, pp. 555–78.
[2] CLIX, pp. 397.

2. *The Mousterian-Solutrean.* As the climate became
milder, it became possible to settle in the valleys and the
coastal plains. Hunting still provided man with food as
well as skins for clothing. Pierced shells show that he had
begun to take an interest in personal adornment. The
earliest skeletal remains discovered in Palestine, consisting
of a human skull found in 1925 at Tagba, near the Lake of
Tiberias, display Neandertal characteristics.[1]

3. *The Solutrean-Magdalenian.* The return of the cold
forced the inhabitants to take refuge in caves. The piles
of bones found there indicate the species of animals which
furnished them with food : these were mainly stags, ante-
lopes, wild goats and gazelles. But there is evidence that
they also hunted the larger wild animals, aurochs, lions, cave

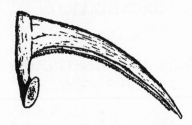

FIG. 2. NEOLITHIC SICKLE (GEZER)

bears. Some human bones found at Antelias near Beirut,
suggest by their appearance that they may have been the
remains of a cannibal feast.[2]

Various deposits, especially that found at Tahuneh, near
Bethlehem, belong to the period prior to the Neolithic, which
some prehistorians call the *Mesolithic.*[3]

The third, or Neolithic period, is the age of polished stone
implements and the earliest handmade pottery. The first
characteristic products of this stage are found in the upper
layers of the cave deposits of Phenicia and the Lebanon,
also in Mt. Nebo in Transjordania and at Khan Lubieh
in Galilee.[4]

It was at a later stage of the same epoch that some of
the future cities of Canaan began to be inhabited. Of these

[1] RB, 1925, pp. 583–5 ; ZATW, 1926, pp. 75–6.
[2] Blanckenhorn, ZDPV, 1912, p. 136.
[3] Buzy, RB, 1928, pp. 558–78.   [4] CLIX, p. 403.

the most notable was Gezer. The first inhabitants of Gezer settled in the natural caves with which the hill is honeycombed. Prof. Macalister has explored forty-four of these.[1] The cave-dwellers adapted them to their purposes, widening the walls with their stone picks, whose traces may still be seen, using the ledges as seats, cutting out niches as shelves for

FIG. 3. HAND-MILL (NEIGHBOURHOOD OF JERUSALEM).

small objects, making steps down into the subterranean passages, opening galleries between two caves, digging cisterns.

These " troglodytes " had already taken the first steps in agriculture, for they possessed sickles, ploughshares, primitive millstones for grinding corn (Figs. 2 and 3) ; like the modern Fellaheen and Bedouins,[2] they probably used

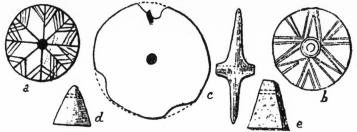

FIG. 4. NEOLITHIC CONES AND SPINDLES.

the pebbles of which piles are often found in their hearths, for baking their dough. They must have reared cattle, for many bones of cows, sheep, goats, pigs, camels and fowls have been found. Small perforated clay disks or cones also occur ; these seem to have been weights used for stretching

[1] IV, p. 44.
[2] CLIX, p. 406 n. 3. Other hypotheses, *ibid.*, pp. 406–7 and IV. p. 45.

the thread in weaving : hence they must have known the art of weaving cloth for purposes of clothing. The beginnings of art appear. Their pottery bears incised or redpainted linear ornamentation. On a kind of frieze in a cave at Gezer, there were found drawings of cows, buffaloes, stags, bearing some resemblance to the wonderful cave-

FIG. 5. TROGLODYTE PROFILE.

drawings of France and Spain.[1] Certain shapeless figurines, possibly cult objects, represent the first rude attempts at sculpture ; the marked prognathous character of some of these [2] suggests that the cave-dwellers of Gezer did not belong to the races which we call Semitic (Fig. 5).

The same conclusion follows from their manner of disposing of their dead, whom they cremated. In a cave at Gezer there was found a bed of ashes, about one foot deep, containing the remains of human bones, arranged in regular layers. An air-shaft still shows the signs of smoke. The discoverer calculates that this primitive crematorium was in use about 4000–2500 B.C.[3] Hence it must have been about the middle of the third millennium that the old inhabitants of Gezer were replaced by new-comers who were apparently Semites. This date would agree with the Tyrian tradition preserved by Herodotus that the temple of Melqart was founded about 2750.[4]

In any case the Gezer cave-dwellers seem to have believed in the survival of the dead, and even to have attributed to

[1] IV, p. 44.
[2] CLIX, pp. 155 (fig. 99), 156 (fig. 100).
[3] CLIX, p. 211.
[4] II, 44 ; cf. Dussaud, Scientia, 1913, p. 84 ; CXI, pp. 43–5.

PLATE I

1.   ROCK WITH CUP-MARKS, AT GEZER

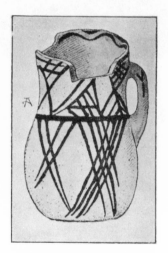

2.   EARLY CANAANITE POTTERY
(*See* p. 68)

PLATE II

TOMB OF AHIRAM
(See p. 78)

them certain powers ; for two metres from the entrance of
the cave in which the incineration was carried out, a " cup-
mark " was cut in the rock, and, judging from other instances,
was intended to receive libations.[1]

One of the sanctuaries of the Neolithic population of
Gezer has been discovered : it consists of a rock platform
with similar cup-marks and channels leading into a basin ;
close by is a cave, piles of bones, and symbols which leave
no doubt concerning the cultual use of the place.[2] The
cult there practised was apparently that of some chthonian
deity. Certain sanctuaries of this kind appear to have
been in use in the Israelite age ; the one at Ophrah, for
example, consisted of a " basin " (Judges vi. 11) and a rock
on which it was still the custom to lay the flesh of the victims

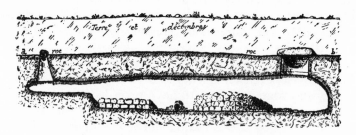

FIG. 6. INCINERATION GROTTO AT GEZER.

and to pour out the broth (Judges vi. 20).   The sacred rock
on which now stands the Kubbet es-Sakhra (the Dome of
the Rock), erroneously called the Mosque of Omar, was no
doubt held sacred by the pre-Canaanite inhabitants of Jerusalem, long before it was used as the site for David's altar,
and for that of Solomon's temple. It exhibits the usual
cup-marks and a funnel leading to a cave beneath, which has
been cut out of the rock.[3]

To the end of the Neolithic period, and in part to the
beginning of the Bronze Age,[4] must be assigned the megalithic
monuments found in great numbers, on the high plateaus of
Transjordania and less frequently on the mountains to the
west of Jerusalem. There are dolmens, that is, tables or
chambers made of huge slabs, menhirs or standing stones,

[1] **CLIX**, pp. 211, 407.   [2] **CLIX**, pp. 92–5, 407.
[3] **XLVI**, pp. 1–96, spec. 12–24.   [4] **III**, p. 41.

cromlechs or stone circles, cairns or piles of rocks, and cyclopean walls extending along certain roads. Excavations have established the fact that the dolmens were generally burial-places. Some of them possess cup-marks, suggesting that libations may have been offered there, but these may have been intended for the dead. The menhirs no doubt had various functions, funerary, votive and cultual, the same, as we shall see, as those of the standing stones erected by the Semites. The cromlechs, apparently, formed a sacred enclosure to protect a burial-place or sanctuary from the profane footstep. At the time of the Israelite settlement they still preserved their sacred character. The numerous spots called Gilgal, or more accurately, hag-gilgal, " *the circle*," were holy places of special sanctity, hallowed to Jahweh by the new settlers, and we know that one of them enclosed twelve sacred stones, erected, so it is related, by Joshua after the miraculous crossing of Jordan (Joshua iv. 8, 20–24).

Israelite popular tradition seems to have attributed some of these cyclopean monuments to a race of giants, the Rephaim, who were supposed to have preceded the Amorites : for example, the gigantic " iron bedstead " shown near Ammon, a region specially abounding in dolmens. It was said to have belonged to Og, King of the Amorites of Bashan, who was the last survivor of the Rephaim (Deut. iii. 11).

To what race did the builders of the megalithic monuments of Palestine belong ? Were they Semites, Indo-Europeans, or perhaps Hittites from Asia Minor ? We are not yet in a position to solve this problem. We are at least quite sure that they were not the kinsmen of the Gezer cave-dwellers, since instead of burning the dead, they buried them in the ground or in chambers of stone. They would seem to have reached a somewhat more advanced stage of civilization, as they no longer lived in caves but built themselves houses of stone, for the abodes which they built for the dead were, no doubt, more massive and enduring copies of those in which they housed the living.

II

THE HISTORICAL PERIOD

In the first half of the third millennium the prehistory of Palestine begins to give place to a history illuminated by monuments and inscriptions. The changing destinies of Palestine between 2900 and 1100 are linked up with those of the great Babylonian, Egyptian and Hittite empires ; the entire field of this history has been dealt with in detail in vol. vi. of this series. Hence we may confine ourselves here to a brief sketch.

It seems that the political history of the country between 3000 and 1100 may be divided provisionally into three great periods :

1. The period prior to 1926, which we may call the Babylonian period, because in it the over-lords of the lower end of the Euphrates valley repeatedly succeeded in bringing the region of Syria within the confines of their empire. At one time it was Sumerian or Accadian princes, such as Lugal-zaggisi about 2900, Sargon of Accad and Naram Sin about 2800, or Dungi, third dynasty of Ur, 2474–2358 ; at another it was Elamites, such as Kutur, or the so-called western Semites, such as Hammurabi, 2123–2081, and Ammizaduga, 1977–1957. The city of Qatna, the modern Tell el-Mishrifeh, to the north-east of Homs, possessed probably from the time of the third dynasty of Ur,[1] a temple dedicated to a goddess with the purely Mesopotamian name of Ninegal, and was under the authority of a Babylonian official (*shakkanaku*).[2]

The sway of these princes of lower Mesopotamia must have broken down from time to time, for they were not able to prevent the kings of Egypt, as Snefru (fourth dynasty, 2840–2680), Sahure (fifth, 2680–2540), and Pepi I (fourth, about 2500),[3] from invading the country.

From the beginning of the historical period Egypt was in specially close relation with Byblos, the port from which she received the cedars of Lebanon, whose wood and resin

[1] Dussaud, **SY,** 1927, p. 190.
[2] Virolleaud, **SY,** 1928, p. 95.
[3] ·See the autobiography of Uni (**CXLVII**) ; **XXIII,** i, pp. 80–1 ; **XXXVI,** ii, pp. 528–9.

were essential for the manufacture of coffins.[1] The foundation deposits of the great temple of Byblos contain many objects bearing the names of Pharaohs of the Old Kingdom, Mycerinus (fourth dynasty), Unas (fifth) Pepi.[2] There have been taken from the debris excavated in 1926 fragments bearing the cartouches of Pepi I, Pepi II and Cheops.[3]

On the other hand, a remarkable series of documents lately discovered show that towards the end of the eleventh dynasty (2000), the Asiatics (Ammu), among whom occur the Anakim, the Amorites (?), the inhabitants of Byblos, of continental Tyre (Usu), of two cities named Jarmuth, of Ascalon, Jerusalem (rushalim ?), of a Hamath, perhaps the one near Bethshan, or that in the land of Zobah,[4] could not have been subjects of the Pharaoh, but were enemies of the dynasty; for they are ritually cursed at the accession of a new king, by breaking the vases on which their names have been written.[5]

Whatever may have been the influence of Egypt at certain epochs on Syrian politics, one fact clearly proves that, before the twentieth century, Babylon had succeeded in establishing a strong and permanent suzerainty over these countries. It is a fact that the common use of cuneiform script and Accadian speech continued at least as late as the fourteenth century, not only in northern Syria,[6] but also in Palestine.[7] The bond between Babylon and Syria must have been particularly close under the first dynasty of Babylon and its illustrious ruler Hammurabi, if it is true that this dynasty was of Amorite, *i.e.* of Syrian origin.

2. In 1926 Babylon was taken in the course of a Hittite or a joint Amorite and Hittite invasion,[8] and the great House

[1] " Maxims of an Egyptian sage " (**LXIX,** p. 265).

[2] Montet, **SY,** 1927, p. 99.

[3] **SY,** 1927, pp. 97–8.

[4] See p. 17.

[5] **CLV**; Dussaud, **SY,** 1927, pp. 216–33; Lods, **RHP,** 1927, pp. 451–3; Albrecht Alt, *Aeg. Zeit.,* 1927, p. 39; **ZATW,** 1928, pp. 77–8.

[6] Accounts of the treasury of the goddess Ninegal found at Tell el-Mishrifeh (Qatna); *cf.* **SY,** 1928, pp. 90–6.

[7] Letters from Tell el-Amarna, Taanach and Lakish; see p. 72.

[8] From the fact that Marduk and Sarpanit were taken captive to the land of Hana on the Euphrates, M. Dussaud concludes that the true conquerors of Babylon were the Amorites, and that the Hittites were only called to their aid (**SY,** 1927, p. 222).

of Hammurabi fell. Shortly after, Lower Mesopotamia came under the sway of the Kassites, a barbarous race from the east, and the sovereignty which she had exercised over western Asia ceased for 1,300 years. The fall of Babylon ushered in a new era for Palestine, and one in which she seemed to have attained a certain amount of freedom from Egyptian intervention in her affairs. The Pharaohs of the twelfth dynasty, although Egypt was exceedingly prosperous under their rule, seem to have confined themselves to a purely defensive policy in regard to Asia.

Nevertheless, the spread of Egyptian civilization and even of her political influence in Syria at this period was remarkable ; a sphinx, of the twelfth dynasty, was found at Tell el-Mishrifeh (Qatna).[1] Byblos was governed by an envoy of the Pharaoh, an Egyptian official, the son of an Egyptian father and the husband of an Egyptian wife.[2] In the reigns of Amenemhet III and IV, Byblos had native princes with Semitic names (Abishemu, Ipshemuabi), but the objects found in their tombs show that they were vassals of the Egyptian king.[3] The same was probably true of Gezer, where the burials yielded many twelfth-dynasty objects,[4] and of Berytus (Beirut), where a sphinx has recently been found with the cartouche of Amenemhet IV.[5] The story of Sinuhe illustrated vividly the frequent intercourse between the local Asiatic chieftains and the great neighbouring kingdom in the time of Senusret (Sesostris) I. The same document says definitely that this king " did not desire the lands of the north "[6] and sent no expeditions there. We only know one war-like expedition into Asia made by a king of the twelfth dynasty, that recorded on the funerary stele of an officer of Senusret III :

His majesty marched northwards to strike down the Asiatics.
His majesty arrived at a province whose name was Sekmem.
His majesty made a good journey going (returning) to the palace
   of " life, prosperity, health,"
When Sekmem had fallen with Retenu the wretched,
While I acted as rearguard.[7]

---

[1] Dussaud, SY, 1927, p. 191.
[2] P. Montet, SY, 1927, pp. 90–2.
[3] Ibid., pp. 88, 92.   [4] IV, p. 58.
[5] SY, 1928, pp. 300–2.   [6] LXVIII, p. 267.
[7] Translation by Jean (XXXVI, ii, p. 129), according to VII.

It may have been Shechem which was thus taken by the Egyptian army ; but the rest of the story shows that they were attacked on the way home.

At the end of this period, Asia overflowed into Egypt, in the famous Hyksos invasion which still presents so many unsolved problems.

The victorious invaders were mainly Semites, if we may judge by the names of several of their chiefs (Jacobel, Anatel, Hiyan). Other names suggest that the flood contained elements belonging to various races, perhaps Kassites or Hittites, but particularly the Mitannites, who, after having overrun Babylonia and Syria, might have carried with them in their train a host of Semite Amorites. In any case, one of the Hyksos kings, Hiyan, founded a short-lived empire extending from the Tigris to Upper Egypt, of which Canaan constituted an important part. At Gezer a seal was found bearing his name with the title " lord of the lands."[1] His capital, Avaris, was on the Palestinian border of the Egyptian frontier.

3. Concerning the third period, which we call the Egyptian period, we are much better informed. After having driven out the Hyksos about 1600, the eighteenth-dynasty Pharaohs, especially Thothmes I and III, conquered the whole of Syria as far as the Euphrates : Thothmes III is reckoned to have made seventeen Asiatic campaigns.[2] The inhabitants were formidable opponents. They were particularly skilled in the art of fortification, which they had learnt from the Babylonians,[3] an art in which they were far superior to the Egyptians.[4] The already very numerous cities were " walled up to heaven," in the words of the Israelite spies (Deut. i. 28). But the country had no political unity : each city was an independent state, ruled by a king, or else a small republic governed by a council of elders, for instance, Tunip,[5] Irqata,[6] Gibeon.[7] In the hill-country these city-states probably ruled over a wider extent of territory than in the plain.[8]

---

[1] **IV**, p. 59.   [2] **L**, p. 18 ; **XII** ; **LVXII**.
[3] **CLIX**, pp. 81–9.
[4] Raymond Weill, **JA**, 1900, p. 82.
[5] Probably Dunipeh, 16 kilometres north-east of Mishrifeh, **XX**, p. 109.
[6] Arqa, north of Tripoli.
[7] According to Joshua ix, spec. v. 11.   [8] **III**, pp. 258–9.

However, the only kingdom of any serious importance in the whole region was that of the Mitanni, a race akin, no doubt, to the Hittites, with whom they had gods in common, Teshub and Hipa. The Mitannites were governed by an Aryan aristocracy. The seat of the kingdom was in the, Naharina, Aram-naharaim of the Hebrews, that is to say, on the two banks of the Euphrates, in the district of Aleppo,[1] Carchemish and Harran. It seems to have possessed a kind of hegemony in the coalitions formed among the petty Amorite states against Egypt. In the list of the peoples of upper Lotanu (central Syria) whom Thothmes III shut up and captured in " wicked Megiddo " (1479), we find the very interesting names of Y'-k-b-'-a-ra, *i.e.* Yacobel (Jacob) and Y-s-p-'a-ra, *i.e.* perhaps, Yosephel (Joseph).[2]

With remarkable political acumen the Pharaohs took advantage of the state of disintegration into which the country had fallen to secure a permanent authority at little cost to themselves. As a general rule they allowed each of the native kings to govern his own city, with the title of *hazanu*, reserving only the right to receive from them an annual tribute, on the condition that they should send their sons to be educated at the Egyptian court, in order to imbue them with its customs, and that an imperial commissioner should be sent from time to time to deal with matters of dispute of more serious importance. They depended on the skilful fostering of dissensions to prevent any of their vassals from acquiring a dangerous pre-eminence.

We can follow this regime of treating Palestine as a protectorate by means of the diplomatic archives of Amenophis III and IV (1415–1362), discovered in the ruins of the ephemeral capital of Amenophis IV, that strange religious reformer who sought to throw off the heavy yoke of Amon-Ra of Thebes and his priests, and to create an imperial religion which should unite in one worship both Egyptians and the inhabitants of his possessions abroad. These archives are contained in the famous Tell el-Amarna tablets in Middle Egypt. They comprise more than 320 letters addressed to

[1] Perhaps as far as Qatna and the neighbourhood of Ras Shamra (Virolleaud, *Antiquity*, 1929, p. 314 ; **SY,** 1929, pp. 304–5).

[2] This last identification is however disputed from the point of view of language : **L,** 36 ; Burchardt, **CV,** ii, p. 13, proposes to read *Yasuphel.*

kings of Egypt, nearly all written in Babylonian, about 1400 and onward, either by Asiatic rulers or by Syrian and Palestinian vassals of the empire.

The correspondence of the latter is mainly occupied with denunciation of one another, and with appeals, generally futile, for help from Egypt against one of their neighbours.

At the same time they call attention, with an occasionally desperate emphasis, to two dangers threatening the Empire, but apparently without succeeding in rousing the court from its habitual apathy. These were the advance of the Ḥatti in the north, and the inroads of the Ḥabiru, especially in the south, in the neighbourhood of Jerusalem, whose king ARAD-Ḥiba redoubles his cries of distress.

The Ḥatti of the letters are the Hittites, a group of peoples from Asia. Minor, differing in speech and perhaps in racial origin, but no doubt containing Indo-European elements. Their capital was at Ḥatti or Ḥattušaš (the modern Boghaz-Keuoi, near Angora), and were united under the forceful rule of King Ḥattusil, who was succeeded by his son Shubili-uliuma. The archives of these princes and their successors, found at Boghaz-Keuoi, are even richer than those of Tell el-Amarna, which they overlap to some extent. From the details contained in them we learn how the Hittites succeeded, even in the lifetime of Amenophis IV, in annexing the kingdom of Mitanni and in seizing northern Syria, owing to the treachery of an Amorite prince, Abdashirti, who while protesting his loyalty to the Egyptian crown was secretly a vassal of the Hittites.

We are still more directly concerned with the Ḥabiru. As soon as the Tell el-Amarna letters had been deciphered, their identification with the Hebrews was suggested (Hebrew *'ibri*). From the linguistic point of view the equation of the two names is unassailable. Nor is it necessary to regard the word Ḥabiru as a noun meaning "confederates" (*haberim*), here denoting the Hittites (so Sayce), or to find in it the name of Heber, a clan of the Israelite tribe of Asher (Jastrow). But later discoveries have brought to light perplexing facts.[1] The names of two individuals have been found with the qualifying word *habira*, that is to say, no doubt, "habirians"; and these names are not Semitic but Kassite. Several

[1] *Cf.* J. Lewy, **OLZ**, 1927, pp. 738–46, 825–33.

scholars have inferred from this that the Ḥabiru were Kassites, hence Indo-Europeans employed as mercenaries (so Halévy, Scheil, Hilprecht, Reisner, Lagrange).   On the other hand, a text deciphered by P. Scheil bears witness to the presence of Ḥabiru officers at Larsa, in Lower Babylonia, in the employ of King Rim Sin, six centuries before the Tell el-Amarna age.

The question arises whether we must not conclude from these facts that the word Ḥabiru was not originally a real proper name, but a general appellative meaning " those beyond," *i.e.* beyond the frontiers or beyond the desert, and connoting nomads of any race.   It may be observed that the Egyptians also used to denote the Bedouins by a word which was originally a common name for free-booters, *shasu*, and that the Sumerian SA.GAS, which is used in the Tell el-Amarna tablets, and still more·clearly in those of Boghaz-Keuoi as a synonym for abiru,[1] seems to have been pronounced in Semitic *ḥabbatum*, that is, free-booters.[2]   It would be natural for this general term to be applied to the Israelites when they were still wanderers, and Hebraized under the form *'ibri*.   It is significant that in the Hebrew texts this is always the name used by strangers to designate Israelites, it was never so used by themselves.   This lends considerable support to the view that the word was not a true proper name.

Moreover, it is *a priori* a plausible supposition that the Ḥabiru of the tablets of Tell el-Amarna and Boghaz-Keuoi, the nomad free-booters who were raiding Syria on the east and south, were Semites, or more accurately, Arameans. We shall deal later with the question whether they comprised any part of the future people of Israel.   Suffice it to remark here that in one of the Tell el-Amarna tablets [3] occurs the name of a town *Ša-am-ḫuna*, *i.e.* perhaps, Simeon (Hebrew, *shim'on*), although it cannot be said whether or not it is to be identified with the Galilean town called *Shimron* in the Masoretic Text of Joshua xi. 1 ; xii. 20 ; xix. 15 (in G[B] it is *Symoôn*, and in Josephus, *Vita*, 24, *Simonias*).

[1] Winckler, **MDOG**, xxxv, pp. 25 *ff*.
[2] TA(**K**), 299, 26 ; *cf.* **XII, LXXVI.**
[3] TA(**W**), 220 (**K**, 225), 4.

E

Under Tutankhamen, the successor of Amenophis IV, the latter's efforts towards religious reform were destroyed by a reaction in favour of the old order of worship. Profiting by these disturbances and the resultant weakening of the royal authority, the Hittites advanced into Syria as far as the district of Kadesh on the Orontes, while the raiding nomads, the *shasu*, evidently identical with the Habiru of Tell el-Amarna, continued " to revolt against the Asiatics of Palestine."[1] Hence the energetic Pharaohs of the nineteenth dynasty, among whom the most distinguished were Haremheb (1345–1321), Seti I (1319–1300), Ramses II (1300–1234), were confronted with the double task of recovering Canaan from the nomads, and central and northern Syria from the Hittites. The first of these undertakings was successfully carried out, proof of which is furnished by the two steles of Seti I and Ramses II found at Beisan by the American expedition led by Dr. Fisher,[2] but they failed in the second. After numerous arduous campaigns, Ramses II considered himself fortunate to be able to conclude an alliance at last with Ḥattusil II, the text of which has been preserved in two copies, and in which neither victor nor vanquished is recognized. The Hittites kept their conquests while Egypt had to be content, apparently, with Palestine (1279).

It may be noted in passing that Seti I and Ramses II mention a district which they call '*A-sa-ru* in the interior of southern Phenicia, that is, in the region in which, according the books of Joshua and Judges, the Israelite tribe of Asher settled.

Peace, as far as Egypt was concerned, reigned once more in Canaan, a relative peace, no doubt, similar to that in the time of Tell el-Amarna. At the beginning of the reign of Merneptah, the successor of Ramses II (1233–1224), Gezer and Ascalon were the scene of outbreaks which required military intervention and possibly the personal presence of the Pharaoh.[3] The quelling of this outbreak is mentioned

[1] *Cf.* **VII**, iii, § 101.

[2] **MJ**, 1923, pp. 227–48 ; Alan H. Gardiner, **JEA**, 1924, p. 93 ; Gressmann, **ZATW**, 1924, pp. 347–8 ; Moret, **REA**, i, pp. 18 *ff.* ; Dussaud, **SY**, 1926, pp. 16–17 ; Vincent, **RB**, 1926, pp. 124, 468–71 ; Mallon, **SY**, 1928, p. 124.

[3] **VII**, iii, pp. 258 *ff.* ; **CIII**, pp. 77 *ff.*

in the famous stele discovered in 1896 by Sir W. Flinders
Petrie, the first epigraphic monument in which Israel is
mentioned. We shall refer to this text again later.[1]

This inscription celebrates the victory of Merneptah and
the repulse of an attack on Egypt by a confederation of
Libyans and various European peoples. This attack was
only a wave of the general upheaval of the Ægean world
caused by the great migration of Aryan peoples of which the
Trojan war, no doubt, was an episode. The inhabitants of
the sea-coasts and of the Ægean isles, driven out by the
invaders, descended on the neighbouring countries, seeking
fresh homes for themselves in Asia, Africa, Italy, Sicily and
Sardinia. "The peoples of the north and the sea," in the
reign of Ramses III, again attempted the invasion of Egypt
by way of Libya (1195), and, three years later, tried to break
into her from the side of Syria and Palestine, spreading
desolation on their way (1192). Ramses III conquered them,
but could not prevent several of their tribes, especially the
Zekal and the Pulestiu (Philistines), from settling, the former
in the district of Dor, to the south of Carmel, the latter in
the coastal plain and in the Canaanite seaports as far south
as Gaza : this was the origin of the Philistine confederation
which was to give its name to Palestine and to play so
important a part in the history of Israel.

In the course of his subsequent campaigns Ramses III
was able to recover the rest of southern Syria as far as Shab-
tuna, near Kadesh on the Orontes, receiving the submission,
among others, of Leviel.[2] A statue of Ramses III was set
up at Beisan.[3] He boasts of having penetrated as far as the
Euphrates.[4] Shortly after, however the Egyptian domination of Palestine finally collapsed. Three-quarters of a
century later, even the official envoys of the Pharaoh were
unable to command respect in the ancient Egyptian provinces
of Asia. This fact appears in the autobiography of Wen
Amon, the envoy of Ramses XI (1117), who, mocked and
threatened by the King of Byblos, once the most loyal of
Egypt's vassal cities, was obliged to pay dearly for the cedar-

---

[1] *Cf.* pp. 186–9.   [2] **LXVIII**, p. 395.
[3] **MJ**, 1923, pp. 227–48 ; Gressmann, **ZATW**, 1924, p. 347.
[4] Concerning the historicity of this campaign, *cf.* **XVI**, i., pp.
43–4.

wood which he had come to seek in order to build a sacred
bark for the god Amon.[1]

The Hittite empire, on the other hand, already severely
shaken by the inroad of the " sea-peoples," fell to pieces
beneath the shock of another wave of barbarians driven
southward by pressure from the north, namely those whom
the Hebrews called Meshech, the Greeks Moschoi and the
Assyrians Mushkaya.

Thus fell in succession the three great powers who, during
the preceding centuries, had sought to establish an empire
embracing the whole of western Asia, namely, Babylon,
Egypt and the Hittite kingdom.   Since Assyria, as yet in the
early stages of its rise, only interposed occasionally in the
affairs of Canaan up to the ninth century, Tiglathpileser I
being the only king to reach the Mediterranean, the small
states of the Syrian coast had a breathing space of about 400
years in which they were free to develop without being
crushed by the superior might of the great empires.

Such a combination of historical circumstances is rare and
was not destined to recur again until the time of the Macca-
bees.   It enabled David to build up Israel into an independent and even conquering state.   This fact was of great
importance for the development of Israel's national consciousness.   If its beginnings had taken shape under an alien
yoke, it would never have been marked by that optimism,
that serene confidence in the nation's future which survived
through its darkest hours in the form of the Messianic hope.

[1] **LXVIII**, p. 398.

CHAPTER II

THE PEOPLES OF PALESTINE AT THE TIME OF THE ISRAELITE SETTLEMENT

IT is very difficult to offer an exact date for the entry of the Hebrew tribes into Palestine. Let us say about a period between 1500 and 1200. The population of the country at this time was far from homogeneous, as it could hardly fail to be in a region so often invaded.

According to their own traditions, the Israelites found there the remains of an ancient race of giants, known as Anakim in the region of Hebron and in Philistia, Emim (the terrible ones) in Moab, Zamzummim among the Ammonites, and, more or less throughout the country, Rephaim, which means, perhaps, "the weak ones," the shades, the dead.[1] In these legends, resembling those current in many other countries, there is, perhaps, as we have already suggested, the dim remembrance of a race earlier than the Amorites, who had erected the megalithic monuments.[2] In any case the name Anakim is the name of a people whose presence in the country is attested by pottery fragments of the eleventh dynasty.[3] At that time three of its chiefs appear to have had Semitic names, especially the second (Abima-'ammu).

Other more certain indications show that the Hebrews found on their arrival in Palestine several racial strata. In some texts the earlier inhabitants of the land are divided into Canaanites and Perizzites (Gen. xiii. 7; xxxiv. 30; Judges i. 4, 5). The Perizzites were no doubt the inhabitants of the *perazoth*, the unwalled villages. The *Kena'ani* would then be the city-dwellers. To explain how the term may have acquired this meaning, it must be supposed either that the Perizzites were nomad invaders who, like the Israelites when they first came in, were only able to occupy the open

---

[1] Joshua xi. 21; Gen. xiv. 5; Deut. ii. 10–12, 20–23.
[2] P. 42.   [3] P. 44.

country, or on the other hand, that the Canaanites were a
conquering people who, at the time when this phrase came
into existence, had seized the cities and driven the former
inhabitants into the country, somewhat as victorious Christianity compelled the old religions to seek refuge among the
pagani, i.e. among the peasants.

The Phenicians, who called themselves Canaanites—the
Phenician city of Laodicea assumed the name of " a mother
in Canaan "—felt that they were immigrants.[1] According
to Herodotus (vii. 98), they claimed to have come from the
shore of the Erythrean Sea ; it is irrelevant here whether
the expression refers to the Red Sea or the Persian Gulf.

Instead of the name Canaanites, preferred, for example,
by the narrators J and P, certain Hebrew writers, such as the
Elohist, the prophet Amos, and the Deuteronomists, used
the term Amorites to denote the collection of peoples who
together with Israel occupied the centre of Palestine. The
relation between these two names is still uncertain.

It is now generally admitted that these two names were
originally those of two distinct races[2] : the Amorites are
supposed to have been driven up into the mountains by the
Canaanites,[3] especially toward the north. This hypothesis
would explain how the Babylonians, who were in contact with
Syria from the third millennium, came to call the country,
including Palestine, by the name *Amurru*, land of the
Amorites ; the Amorites being at that time the principal
inhabitants of the district. On the other hand, the
Egyptians, who only came into active relations with Asia
from about 1600, kept the name *Emur* for central and
northern Syria and gave to Palestine proper, perhaps only to
southern Palestine,[4] that of *pa-Kana'ana*. Similarly in the
Tell el-Amarna tablets, about 1400, it is Palestine which is
called *Kinaḫḫi* ; while *Amurru* is the region of Lebanon.[5]
From this it has been supposed that about the middle of the
second millennium, the Canaanites, properly so-called, had
taken the hegemony from the Amorites in the southern part
of Syria.

While the possibility of this hypothesis may be admitted,

---

[1] **CXV**, pp. 46, 349.   [2] **CIII** ; Dussaud, **SY**, 1926, p. 343.
[3] Num. xiii. 29 ; xiv. 25 ; Deut. i. 7 ; xi. 30 ; Joshua v. 1 ; xi. 3.
[4] **XXVI**, p. 73.   [5] *Cf.* **XCIII**, p. 182.

it should nevertheless be observed that the Amorites were, in any case, like the Canaanites, Semites in the linguistic sense, which is the sense in which we understand the term today; for, judging by their proper names, they spoke a Semitic tongue.[1]

Moreover, excavations in Palestine have not established up to the present, that about 1500 a new and Canaanite civilization replaced an earlier Amorite civilization.[2] The essential difference between the two periods arises from the fact that from the middle of the second millennium, Egyptian and Ægean influences had exerted a more decisive effect upon Palestine. But the fundamental ideas, concerning death, for instance, and the gods, remained the same.[3] Hence if the terms Amorite and Canaanite originally denoted two distinct layers of population, there cannot have been any far-reaching difference between them, either in race or in degree of culture. Furthermore, the date of about 1500 assigned to the driving out of the Amorites would have to be pushed back half a millennium at least; for in the maledictory formulas of the eleventh dynasty (about 2000), *Amur* appears already merely as the name of one of the twenty-one small groups from the Phenician district of Palestine.[4]

It is equally difficult to give precise information concerning the relations between the Canaanites and Amorites on the one hand, and the various groups on the other hand, mentioned as being settled in Palestine before the Israelites.

Some of them were, or had been Bedouin tribes: for instance the *Avvites*, tent-dwellers in the neighbourhood of Gaza, who were exterminated (Deut. ii. 23) or driven out by the Philistines (Joshua xiii. 3), perhaps also the *Hivites*[5] settled in the district of Gibeon (Joshua ix. 7) and of Shechem (Gen. xxxiv. 2), if it is true that their name means " those who dwell in *ḥavvoth*," *i.e.* groups of tents (*douars*); but the etymology is not certain: the name Hivites might mean

---

[1] In the genealogy (Gen. x.), the Canaanites are connected with Ham, not with Shem. But it is not a question, in this text, of ethnological or linguistic classification.

[2] As M. Bertholet maintained, **IV**, pp. 53–129.

[3] M. Bertholet recognizes this, **IV**, pp. 77, 91, 111.

[4] **CLV**, f. 6.

[5] Related to the Kenites, according to **CXL**, p. 128, n. 3.

serpent-worshippers (*ḥevya* or *ḥivya* in Aramaic). We have no certain information about the Girgashites.

The Horites were the ancient inhabitants of the land of Seir, and became fused with the Edomites when the latter seized the country and gave it their name (Gen. xxxvi. 20–30). The Horites must have formed an important group, for the Egyptians gave their name to Palestine in general (*Ḥaru*), and the name Retenu or Lotanu by which they denoted the whole of Syria was perhaps that of the Horite clan of Lotan (Gen. xxxvi. 20, 22, 29), no doubt related to Lot.[1] The Horites, whose name can mean cave-dwellers,[2] but more probably meant " the free men,"[3] should not be identified with the inhabitants of the neolithic caves of Gezer : the latter were probably not Semites,[4] while the Horite clans bore definitely Hebrew names. For the same reason they should not be connected with the Harri, who are the Aryan people of Mitanni mentioned in the Boghaz-Keuoi tablets.

It is none the less true that the pre-Israelite population of Palestine contained non-Semitic elements. There must have been remains of the cave-dwellers of the third millennium, who had become Semitized. It has been suggested that these correspond to the *Iuntiu* of the Egyptian texts.[5]

In any case there were *Hittites* in Canaan. Doubt has often been thrown on the genuineness of this statement because it is chiefly met with in later Hebrew texts, one of which even calls the whole of Palestine " the land of the Hittites " (Joshua i. 4, M.T.), which is clearly an exaggeration, But the Tell el-Amarna letters have shown us that there was a king of Jerusalem named ARAD (Abd) -Ḫiba,[6] that is the servant of a goddess worshipped by the Hittites and their kinsfolk the Mitannites.[7] An inhabitant of the same city, Jerusalem, the Jebusite Araunah, bore a name related, no doubt, to those Hittite kings Arandas and Arnuanta.[8] Hence it is very probable that the Jebusite tribe to whom

---

[1] See however the objections of Ed. Meyer (**CCXVII**, p. 339) and the incompatible hypotheses of Eisler (**CXXI**, pp. 135–9) and Alt (**ZDPV**, 1924, p. 169). *Cf.* p. 16 and Lods, **RHR**, xcv, p. 215.

[2] **XXII**, p. 325. [3] **LXXVIII**, p. 210.

[4] *Cf.* p. 40. [5] **CXI**, p. 38

[6] **TA(W)**, 179–85 (**K**, 285–90).

[7] *Cf.* MDOG, 35, p. 48 ; **LXVIII**, pp. 337, 378.

[8] **XII, LXXXVI.**

Jerusalem belonged until David's time contained a strong Hittite element. This is why Ezekiel, in one of his invectives against Jerusalem, could say : " thy father was an Amorite and thy mother a Hittite " (Ezek. xvi. 3, 45).

The name of another ARAD-Ḥiba occurs at Taanach.[1] From this it may follow that there were Hittite elements in the population of the plain of Jezreel, especially if the names Sisera and Shamgar (Judges iv. and v.) are also of Hittite origin.[2] It is also possible that, as we find in P, there was a tribe of the same race in the neighbourhood of Hebron (Gen. xxiii. 20 ; xxvi. 34–35 ; xxvii. 46). The presence of Hittites in Transjordania is less certain.[3]

These islands of Asiatic settlement may have been left in the country by a Hittite inroad contemporaneous with their attack on Babylon about 1925, or by an expansion of the Mitannites in the time of the Hyksos.[4]

Beside these very various elements, the Israelites also found in Palestine three peoples with whom they were conscious of a close tie of kinship, the Ammonites, settled to the east of Transjordania, the Moabites to the east and southeast of the Dead Sea, and the Edomites to the south-east of the future territory of Judah. These peoples were, like the Israelites, nomads who had taken part in the Aramean migration, but who had left the desert earlier than their Hebrew kinsfolk ; hence Edom-Esau is represented in the early sources as the elder brother of Israel-Jacob. Moab is mentioned by Ramses II. Apparently, after having failed in the attempt to reach the interior of the country, they settled on the borders of the great steppes.[5]

Finally, about the time of the entry of the Hebrews into Canaan, or, according to another chronological system, two centuries later, there was added to all these racial elements,

[1] **CLII**, p. 39, ns. 7, 8.   [2] **XII**, pp. 76, 84, 113.

[3] R. Dussaud, *Les monuments palestiniens et judaïques* . . . , *Musée du Louvre*, Paris, Leroux, 1912, pp. 1–4 ; **SY**, 1926, p. 315 ; *cf.* **CXLI**, p. 164.

[4] See pp. 46–7.

[5] According to Benzinger (**III**, p. 56), these three peoples did not invade the Palestine region till after the Israelites, and it was the resistance of the latter that obliged them to settle on the borders. But there is no good reason for rejecting the unanimous testimony of the Hebrew tradition on this point (Num. xx. 14–21, 21–24 ; Deut. ii. 1–13 ; Judges xi. 14–27, etc.)

and widely differing from them, the new stock of the Philistines, a group of Ægean peoples who, as we have seen,[1] settled in the coastal plain between Carmel and the Syro-Egyptian desert in the time of Ramses III (1192).

[1] See p. 51.

CHAPTER III

PALESTINIAN CIVILIZATION AT THE TIME OF THE ISRAELITE SETTLEMENT

I

THE CHARACTERISTICS OF THIS CIVILIZATION

IN spite of their diverse origins, the Palestinian peoples possessed in common a culture that was fairly homogeneous. The excavations have shown that in northern cities like Taanach or Megiddo, the growth of civilization followed very much the same lines as in southern cities like Gezer or Lakish, and in an inland city such as Jericho. The Philistines themselves were very quickly " Canaanized " : about the middle of the eleventh century, less than 150 years after their settlement, one of their principal gods was Dagon,[1] undoubtedly the same as Dagan, the Canaanite corn-god.[2] Another Philistine deity bore the perfectly good Semitic name of Baal Zebub, " the lord of flies." This Canaanite civilization was already in an advanced stage. It had travelled far since the Neolithic Age.[3] The use of bronze had become general since the middle of the third millennium.[4] Iron seems to have come in about the end of the second. It may have been introduced by the Philistines,[5] or, more probably, the inhabitants may have learnt the art of iron-working from neighbouring peoples like the Hittites (*cf.* Jer. xv. 12), or the Arabs, who possessed important iron-mines, or they may already have found the mineral in their own soil, since deposits of it exist in various spots in the Lebanon and Transjordania.[6] An argument in favour of the derivation from Asia Minor is that Tubal, the eponymous ancestor of the Tibarenians of

---

[1] 1 Sam. v. 2–5 ; *cf.* Judges xvi. 23 ; 1 Macc. x. 83, 84 ; xi. 4.
[2] See pp. 127–8.   [3] Pp. 38–42.   [4] **IV**, p. 70.
[5] Belck, ZE, 1907, pp. 334–79 ; 1908, pp. 45–69.
[6] P. 32.

Armenia, was in Israel reputed to be " the father of all those who work in iron and brass " (Gen. iv. 22), and moreover, that there have been found at Byblos a quantity of bronze pins and rings displaying the same typical shape as that of similar objects found in great numbers in Russian Armenia, thus proving the existence of relations between Phenicia and the Caucasus about 2000.[1]

On the other hand, there were iron mines in the Sinai peninsula ; and the Kenites may possibly have been a race of smiths.[2]

The conquering Egyptians drew up lists of the spoil which they took from the cities of Canaan. These lists give us a picture of the wealth of the country and, if the objects mentioned were of native workmanship, of the skill of its craftsmen in working precious metals. For example, Thothmes III brought back from Megiddo, among other things, horses, chariots—one of which was plated with gold and fitted with a gold chariot-pole—breastplates of bronze, tent-pegs plated with silver, cups and vases of various kinds, one of which is described as " a great bowl of Syrian workmanship "—swords, litters, ivory couches, a gilded bed, a statue of gold, ebony, and lapis-lazuli, and in addition, more than 207,400 sacks of corn.[3]

The cultivation of the vine and the fig-tree, for which we already have evidence in Palestine in the time of Pepi I, about 2500, must have been highly developed : several oil- and wine-presses have been found, some of which were very skilfully contrived.[4] The enthusiastic descriptions of the tale of Sinuhe, of which the action takes place about 2000, may certainly be extended to Palestine, also those of the *Annals* of Thothmes III, about 1450. These sources tell us of the fertility of Retenu or of Zahi, *i.e.* of central Syria, that " wine is more plentiful there than water,"[5] " also the soldiers of His Majesty were drunk and rubbed with oil every day, which only happens in Egypt on feast-days." [6]

We have already said that the Canaanites were highly

---

[1] **SY**, 1925, pp. 16–29 ; **CXI**, pp. 69 (fig. 19), 157–9.
[2] Bertholet, **ZE**, 1907, pp. 945–6 ; 1908, p. 241–53 ; **IV**, p. 105. See, however, p. 205.
[3] **XXIII**², i, pp. 86–7.   [4] **CLIX**, pp. 77–8.
[5] **LXVIII**, p. 267.   [6] **LXVIII**, p. 319.

skilled in the art of fortification.[1] In order to secure for their fortresses, which were usually perched upon a rocky eminence, the necessary supply of water for a siege, they had carried out feats of engineering which were the more remarkable in that some of them seem to have been entirely wrought with stone implements : at Gezer, for instance, there was a tunnel 70 metres long, going down by 80 steps to a depth of 28 m. 80, in order to reach a subterranean spring.[2] Again, at Jerusalem, a tunnel cut in the rock brought the water of the " Virgin's Well " to a reservoir sunk in the old citadel of Zion. This may have constituted the mysterious *ṣinnor*, by which, as it would seem, Joab gained access to the impregnable stronghold.[3] Similar works existed, no doubt, at Gibeon,[4] Ibleam [5] and Megiddo.[6]

The Canaanites knew the art of dyeing threads of many colours and of weaving them into patterns, if we may suppose that the variegated stuffs worn by the Asiatics, depicted on the tomb of Beni Hassan (about 1900), were the work of native weavers.[7]

The Egyptian Government, at least during the period of its ascendancy, took measures to safeguard commerce and facilitate travel throughout the country. In one of the Tell el-Amarna letters an unnamed person undertakes to repair all the King's highroads as far as Busruna (Bozrah).[8] The " kings " of Canaan were responsible for the safe conduct of the royal caravans through their territory.[9] In fact, as we find later in the days of Solomon, commerce was, in a great measure, the monopoly of the sovereign. The Palestinian princes were also responsible for the safety of the envoys who were constantly passing to and fro between the courts of the various oriental states and that of the Pharaoh. Indeed, diplomats were actually furnished with passports drawn up in almost the same terms as those employed today.[10]

---

[1] **CLIX**, pp. 29–65. See also the gate of Bethshan, flanked by four separate towers (**RB**, 1929, pp. 90–1, and pl. ii).

[2] **IV**, p. 67.

[3] 2 Sam. v. 8 ; *cf.* **CLIX**, 27, n. 1 ; **CLXIII**, pp. 8–13, 48–49 ; **CLX**, i, pp. 146–60.

[4] Schick, **PEF**, **QS**, 1890, p. 23.   [5] **PEF**, **QS**, 1910, p. 107.

[6] **CLI**, pp. 161–2.   [7] **LXVIII**, p. 283 (fig. 22).

[8] **TA(W)**, 145 (K, 199), ll. 13–15.

[9] **TA(W)**, 256 (K, 255), ll. 12–19 ; **TA(K)**, 194, ll. 20–24.

[10] **TA(W)**, 14 (K, 30) ; *cf.* 11 reverse, ll. 1–10 (K, 8, 25–34).

This again presupposes that the " kings " of Canaan
were able to read the contents of these documents, and that
consequently, the art of writing was not unfamiliar in Palestine.   Each prince must have employed one or more scribes,
responsible not only for his correspondence with the court
of his Egyptian overlord, but also for that with his Canaanite
colleagues, and for the preparation of material for the archives
(lists of those liable for forced labour, etc.).   This is proved,
not only by the Tell el-Amarna correspondence, but by a
very similar diplomatic dispatch discovered at Tell el-Hesy
in 1891, and various similar letters found at Taanach [1]
and Megiddo. [2]

At Jericho, twenty-four unused tablets were discovered. [3]
It must not however be inferred from this that the knowledge
of writing was widespread among the population of Palestine
about 1400.   It is very likely that at this time the princes
themselves were unable to read, for occasionally the writer
of a dispatch will address it, not to the " king " for whom it
was intended, but to his scribe : " thou shalt say to the king,
etc." [4]   The knowledge of the script must have been, as in
Egypt, the privilege of the small minority of the learned.
Nor is this difficult to understand, for, until the introduction
of the alphabetic script, writing in Palestine was dependent
on the cuneiform script, a most complicated system, requiring
long study for its mastery.   Moreover, communications were
in Babylonian, a foreign language, Hebrew being the speech
of the country.   This last point, of considerable importance,
is proved by the fact that the scribes of Canaanite kings vary
considerably in their knowledge of the language which they
wrote, and that some of them slipped into the texts which
they were drawing up, either hebraisms, or marginal glosses
in Hebrew.   For instance the Babylonian *elippu*, a ship, is
explained by *anay*, Hebrew *oni* ; *shadu*, mountain, by *ḫarri*,
Hebrew *har* ; *qatu*, arm, by *zuruḫ*, Hebrew *zeroa'* ; *me*, water,
by *mema*, *mime*, Hebrew *maim* ; *niru*, yoke, by *hullu*, Hebrew
'ol ; *abulli*, gate, by *shaḫri*, Hebrew *sha'ar*, etc. [5]

  [1] **XXIII**[2], i, pp. 370–1.   [2] **SY**, 1929, p. 305.
  [3] **IV**, p. 107.   [4] **XIII**, p. 325.
  [5] **XCIII**, p. 652 ; **CXXXIV**, pp. 1545–9 ; **CIV**, p. 80.

II

FOREIGN RELATIONS

This relatively advanced civilization, for whose existence in Palestine in the middle of the second millennium we have abundant evidence, was largely due to the close contacts which had been established during the long course of centuries between the people of this land and the two chief centres of Oriental civilization, Babylon and Egypt.

A most striking witness to this fact is a seal found at Taanach. On it there is engraved a Babylonian scene with Egyptian hieroglyphs and a cuneiform inscription which reads : " Atanaḫili, son of Ḫabsi, servant of Nergal " ([1] and fig. 7). No more typical example could be imagined of the

FIG. 7. SEAL OF ATANAḤILI

mixture of influences prevailing in this country than this Canaanite, who declares himself in the Babylonian tongue a worshipper of a Babylonian god, and adorns his seal with Egyptian symbols.[2]

We must suppose that the influence of Babylonia was predominant in the things of the spirit. The scribes in order to learn the language which it was their business to write, were obliged either to visit the country in which it was spoken, or at least to study its literature. At Tell el-Amarna tablets have been found containing the myth of Adapa which the Egyptian diplomats used for scholastic purposes : we can still see the red-ink strokes dividing the words.[3] The scribes of Palestine must also have made translations of classical

[1] **CLIII**, p. 28 (fig. 12) ; **PEF**, 1906, p. 117 ; Jean, **SY**, 1928, p. 289.
[2] According to H. Zimmern, this seal dates from the Hammurabi epoch (**CLIII**, p. 28).
[3] **CXXXIV**, p. 25.

Babylonian texts. The educated Canaanites, who were necessarily more or less the spiritual guides of their people, in this manner came to be initiated into the religious beliefs of the Babylonians, and no doubt also into its science and its law.

The seals found in Palestine are often of Babylonian origin or copies of Babylonian models.[1]

The measures, weights and coinage in use in Canaan from the sixteenth century were those of the cities of the lower Euphrates; also the tribute levied by the Pharaohs were calculated on this system.[2]

In the science of fortification, as we have already remarked, the Canaanites seem to have been the pupils of the engineers of lower Mesopotamia. Perhaps they learnt the art of building the arch from the architects of the same region; at Megiddo an arch was found supporting a weight of 135 tons.[3]

As a symbol of authority, the Canaanites used the sickle-shaped scimitar which the Greeks called *harpé* and which was one of the characteristic weapons of the Assyro-Babylonian rulers and deities ([4] and fig. 8). Several were found at Byblos in the sarcophagi of princes contemporary with Pharaohs of the twelfth dynasty; one of them—another example of Syrian electicism—was ornamented with an Egyptian uræus ([5] and fig. 9); another bears, in Egyptian hieroglyphics, the name of its owner, Ipshemuabi, a Semitic name.[6] There is a specimen in the Louvre which may be from the same source.[7] Several examples of *harpés* have been found in Palestine proper: at Gezer ([8] and fig. 10)— probably fourteenth century—and at Nablus.[9] This weapon is represented on cylinder-seals from Gezer; [10] and it is no doubt a *harpé* that the Canaanite god Resheph is holding, who is depicted side by side with Ramses II on a cylinder found at Beisan.[11]

[1] **MN**, 1905, p. 20; 1906, pp. 10, 29.
[2] **III**, p. 195; Dalman, **ZDPV**, 1906, pp. 92–4.
[3] **CLI**, pp. 14–15. Assyro-Babylonian arches: **CLIX**, pp. 70 (fig. 40), 71 (fig. 41), 259 (fig. 175); **CXXXII**, p. 65 (fig. 50).
[4] **CXLV**, pl. 28. There are several specimens of them in the Louvre, for example **CIX**, p. 42 (fig. 10).
[5] *Cf.* **SY**, 1922, pl. lxv, pp. 282, 283, 286, 301–3.
[6] *Cf.* **CXI**, pp. 56, 154.   [7] Dussaud, **SY**, 1926, p. 254.
[8] **CLIX**, p. 231 (fig. 163); Dussaud, **SY**, 1926, pp. 253–5.
[9] **XIII**, p. 330.   [10] *Ibid.*   [11] **RB**, 1928, p. 529 (fig. 2).

Not only had Canaan close and fruitful relations with Babylonian culture, but also with the neighbouring empire of the Pharaohs. The great cedars of Lebanon were indispensable to the Egyptians, especially for the manufacture of coffins and for the building of sea-going vessels; hence they always attached great importance to the maintenance of friendly relations with the cities of middle Syria, especially with Byblos.[1] A tomb was found at Gezer containing scarabei of the twelfth and thirteenth dynasties.[2]

Commercial relations increased considerably after the

FIG. 8. BABYLONIAN HARPÉ.

FIG. 9. HARPÉ FROM BYBLOS.

FIG. 10. HARPÉ FROM GEZER.

sixteenth century, the beginning of the Egyptian conquest. In the time of Amenophis III (1415–1380), there were Haru, *i.e.* Palestinians, settled in Egypt, apparently for purposes of trade.[3] Wen Amon mentions a certain Birket-el, who seems to have been a well-known Semitic merchant living at Tanis.[4] Caravans crossed the desert of Gaza and Ægean or Phenician ships sailed up the Nile as far as Thebes, bringing merchandise of every kind. It is possible to reconstruct to some extent the fascinating list of those old-world imports.[5]

This influx of Semitic articles and customs, coupled with

[1] See pp. 43–5.   [2] **CLIX**, p. 217.   [3] **XXIII²**, i, p. 93.
[4] **XXIII²**, i, p. 73; *cf.* Eisler, **ZDMG**, 1924, p. 61.
[5] **LXIII**, ii, pp. 284–5.

the introduction of Asiatic vocabulary, religious practices and deities, became more pronounced during the nineteenth and twentieth dynasties.

The traders of Egypt, on their side, considerably increased the volume of trade with their Asiatic neighbours in the products of home industries. Amulets must have been the most coveted articles of trade, judging by the enormous quantities of these objects unearthed everywhere in the ancient soil of Canaan : there were scarabs engraved with Egyptian scenes and hieroglyphs, the stones called Horus-

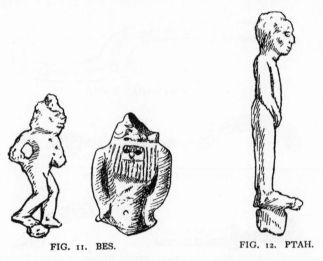

FIG. 11. BES.   FIG. 12. PTAH.

eyes, statuettes of Egyptian deities, particularly Bes, Anubis, Sebek, Ptah, Isis with the infant Horus, Bast, Sekmet, and even the *ushabtis*, little figures in the form of mummies, intended to assist the deceased in the underworld.[1] Along with these there were glazed porcelain beads, jewelry,[2] seals, vases, of which one very beautiful specimen found at Megiddo seems to have been used as an incense-burner.[3] The date of manufacture of these objects is even now still easy to determine owing to peculiarities of style or to the name of a contemporary Pharaoh engraved upon some of them, a king

---

[1] **IV**, pp. 97–101 ; **CXIV**, p. 96 ; **CLIX**, p. 171 (figs. 118 and 119) ; **RB**, 1928, pl. x, p. 3.
[2] Vincent, **RB**, 1909, pp. 110, 112.
[3] **CLIX**, p. 181 (fig. 131).

of the twelfth dynasty, a Hyksos ruler such as Hiyan [1] or Shesha,[2] or a Pharaoh of the nineteenth dynasty like Merneptah.[3]

At Megiddo an unusual number of Egyptian objects were found in the ruins of a building supposed to be a pharaonic fortress, perhaps the very one built by Thothmes III when he besieged the city (1479). At Byblos such objects abound in the royal tombs, of which several go back to the time of the twelfth dynasty. At Gezer they were found in a hypogeum, supposed at first to have been the burial-place of an

FIG. 13. CENSER FROM MEGIDDO.

Egyptian colony,[4] but which P. Vincent now inclines to regard as the necropolis of the native kings.[5]

Moreover, not content with importing Egyptian objects, the Canaanites themselves often imitated them. At Gezer there was found a mould which had been used to manufacture statuettes of the god Bes, a bearded dwarf of grotesque appearance, very popular in Egypt. He was one of those lesser divinities whose function was to amuse the gods by music and dancing, to guard their children and to fight against evil spirits; he was often represented armed or strangling

[1] **IV**, p. 59.   [2] Vincent, **RB**, 1909, p. 112.
[3] Vincent, *Ibid.*, p. 110.
[4] **CXXXVIII**, i, pp. 111–41; iii, pls. xxx–xliii.
[5] Vincent, **RB**, 1923, pp. 552 *ff.*; 1924, pp. 161 *ff.*; Gressmann, **ZATW**, 1924, p. 351.

serpents or lions.[1] Those objects in which are mingled Egyptian and Babylonian motives are apparently of native manufacture.

As is proved by many of the facts already quoted, the interpenetration of Egypt and Canaan extended to the field of religion, a point to which we shall return later.[2]

But Babylon and Egypt were not the only centres of culture with which the peoples of Canaan came into contact. We have already pointed out the discovery at Byblos of bronze objects bearing witness to the relations between Phenicia and the Caucasus about 2000.[3] At the same place have been found cylinders similar in style to those of Semites settled in Cappadocia between 2300 and 1800.[4]

From at least the fourteenth,[5] and perhaps even the

FIG. 14. EARLY CANAANITE POTTERY.

sixteenth century,[6] Palestinian pottery displays the very marked influence of Ægean art. About this time characteristic changes appear in the technique of the Canaanite potters. Previously the clay was usually impure, dried in the sun or hastily baked, sometimes burnished or incised; they had already learnt to paint their pottery, but the decoration consisted merely of geometric designs drawn at random on the sides of the vessel without attempt at symmetry ([7] and pl. i, 2); the figures of animals or plants were painted with various colours, but in flat tints ([8] and fig. 14). On the

---

[1] **XXI**, p. 78. It is possible, besides, that, originally, this god Bes was an Asiatic figure (**CXIV**, p. 96). Vincent (**CLIX**, p. 172, n. 4) believes him to be connected with the myth of Gilgamesh; cf. **CVII**, pp. 135 ff.

[2] Pp. 92–4; 117–8; 138–142.   [3] P. 59.

[4] **CXI**, pp. 156–7.   [5] Cf. Saussey, **SY**, 1924, pp. 173–4.

[6] **CLIX**, p. 304.   [7] For example, **CLIX**, p. 332, pl. ix, fig. A.

[8] So in **CLIX**, pp. 324 (fig. 213), 321–3.

other hand, from the period above-mentioned, it is clear that the shape has been modelled on the wheel; the clay is finer and better baked. The pottery assumes more graceful curves. New types appear, such as those the Arabs employed in the excavations have christened *bilbils*; these are small

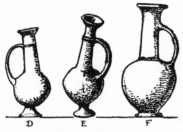

FIG. 15. BILBILS.

globular pots, with a slightly flattened handle and a long cylindrical neck which is sometimes tilted to one side by its weight as it dried in the sun ([1] and fig. 15). Several of these types are clearly akin to those beloved of the Mycenean potters, for example, certain bowls ([2] and figs. 16 and 17),

FIG. 16. MYCENEAN BOWL.

FIG. 17. PALESTINIAN BOWL.

or the stirrup vases ([3] and figs. 18 and 19). The geometric designs, which are symmetrically arranged on the surface of the pot ([4] and fig. 20) often exhibit the characteristic motives of Ægean art, especially the different varieties of spiral.[5] The animal figures are in monochrome, highly conven-

[1] **CLIX**, pp. 328–9, fig. 216 and pl. x, fig. 14.
[2] **CLIX**, pp. 332 (figs. 224, 225), 328, pl. x, fig. 1; **RB**, 1922, p. 103; Saussey, **SY**, 1924, pl. xliii, fig. 1.
[3] Saussey, *ibid.*, figs. 4, 5.
[4] **CLIX**, pp. 334 (fig. 227), 335 (fig. 230); pl. ix, fig. B.
[5] Saussey, **SY**, 1924, p. 185.

tionalized and drawn in fine lines ([1] and figs. 18 and 21).

It seemed at first natural to suppose that this Ægean technique had been introduced by the Philistines, since they had come, according to the Hebrew tradition, from Caphtor, *i.e.* probably, from Crete,[2] and were in any case imbued with the Ægean civilization. Hence several archæologists have bestowed upon this Ægeo-Canaanite pottery the name of Philistine ware.[3]

FIG. 18. STIRRUP VASE.   FIG. 19. STIRRUP VASE.

But, as has been shown by M. Dussaud,[4] P. Vincent,[5] and especially by M. E. Saussey,[6] there is good reason to believe that the influence of Ægean art began to be felt in Palestine long before the arrival of the Philistines in the land. Objects of Ægean pattern, possibly, it is true, sent by the Pharaohs, have been found in the royal graves of Byblos of

[1] So in **CLIX**, p. 324 (fig. 212) ; Saussey, **SY**, 1924, pl. xliii, fig. 5.
[2] E. Meyer, **SBA**, 1909, pp. 1022–3 ; **CLVII.**
[3] Thiersch, **AA**, 1908, cols. 378 *ff.* ; **ZDPV**, 1914, pp. 88 *ff.* ; **CLIV**, p. 135 ; **CXXXVII** ; Mackenzie, **PEF**, 1911, 1912, 1913, etc. Phythian-Adams, **PEF, QS**, April, 1923, pp. 60–78 ; **IV**, pp. 103–104.
[4] **CXX**, p. 302.   [5] **RB**, 1922, pp. 99 *ff.*, 103 *ff.*, 125.
[6] **SY**, 1924, pp. 169–85 ; Gressmann, **ZATW**, 1925, pp. 237–8.

the time of the twelfth dynasty (about 1900). Cuneiform tablets of the same age as the Tell el-Amarna letters, hence dating from about 1400, have been found at Tell el-Hesy (Lachish ?) and at Taanach, at the bottom of the layer containing fragments of Mycenean pottery.[1]   Consequently

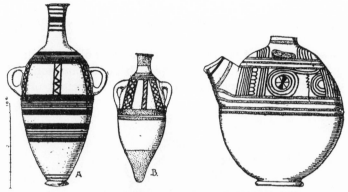

FIG. 20. PALESTINIAN POTTERY OF ÆGEAN TYPE.

it was by the end of the fifteenth century at the latest that Palestinian potters began to imitate Ægean models.

Nor is this surprising : the work of Cretan artists was highly valued in Egypt in the time of the twelfth dynasty.[2] And above all, from 1400, the period in which the hegemony

FIG. 21. ÆGEAN ORNAMENTATION.

of the Ægean passed from Cnossos to Mycenae, and commerce instead of being a Cretan monopoly was carried on by those whom Crete had taught, both on the mainland and in the isles, there poured, for two hundred years, a perfect flood of Mycenean trade into Egypt.   Thus, " At Tell el-Amarna

there were gathered up 1,345 potsherds with the cartouches of
Akhnaten and his family, all recalling the vases of Mycenæ,
Ialysos and Cyprus. . . . The vogue of this pottery was
so great that from the time of Amenophis III and on, the
Egyptians began to imitate it in their own ware."[1]   It was
natural that the Canaanites, who were at that time the vassals
of the Pharaohs, should have shared the tastes and imitated
the example of their contemporaries in the valley of the
Nile.

Furthermore, it is likely that the arrival of the Philistines
200 years later stimulated the growth of this fashion.   The
Ægean style of pottery reached its greatest height of popu-

FIG. 22. PALESTINIAN POTTERY OF CYPRIAN TYPE.

larity in Palestine immediately after the settlement there
of the " sea-people."[2]

Bronze objects of the same period also display Ægean
influence, for instance in the spiral decoration of needles
found at Gezer and Tell el-Ḥesy.[3]   The double axe found at
Gezer [4] is perhaps a copy of the sacred weapon of Crete,
although it is true that the double axe was also a sacred
symbol among the Hittites.

Palestinian craftsmen derived from the workshops of
Cyprus, to a notable extent, models which they continued
to imitate long after the general stream of Ægean influence
had ceased, up to the ninth or eighth century.   Mention may
be made, for instance, of the jars (fig. 22) shaped like a pil-

[1] **CXXVII**, p. 246.   [2] Saussey, **SY**, 1924, p. 183.
[3] **IV**, p. 104.   [4] *Ibid.*

grim's gourd,[1] of which the decorative motive consists of rosettes formed of concentric circles vertically applied ([2] and fig. 23). To such an extent do the cylinder seals of the second half of the second millennium found at Gezer betray Cypriote influence, that, according to a competent authority, " all this glyptic art from Gezer might be attributed to Cyprus, did we not already know its source."[3]

It is significant that this influence of Mycenean and Cyprian art should have become predominant in Palestine just at the time when the land had become subject to the great Pharaohs of the eighteenth and nineteenth dynasties, when the reappearance of Egyptian influence was more likely to be expected. It is evident that there was at that time a

FIG. 23. PALESTINIAN POTTERY OF CYPRIAN TYPE.

common civilization shared by all the advanced peoples of the eastern Mediterranean basin. From this common culture there arose almost simultaneously in various parts of the Mediterranean world changes in tastes and fashions causing currents of trade *totally independent of political changes.* Any advance in technical skill acquired in one region of this Oriental world quickly became available for the benefit of other regions thereof.

Naturally the contribution to this common stock of culture made by each of the racial groups which shared in it was very unequal. Those peoples more highly gifted or possessing a more ancient culture, such as the Ægeans, the Egyptians, the Babylonians or the Hittites, furnished the guiding impulse of the various cultural movements, the rest were mainly recipients.

[1] **CLIX,** p. 350 (fig. 249).
[2] **CLIX,** p. 349 (fig. 248).   [3] **CX,** p. 164.

III

ORIGINAL ELEMENTS IN THE CANAANITE CIVILIZATION

If we may judge by the results hitherto yielded by excavation, the Canaanites produced nothing in the field of art which can be compared, even faintly, with the amazing artistic creations of the peoples whom we have named above.

It must not however be thought that they were mere imitators. They had succeeded in attaining to or preserving a certain amount of originality along special lines. The imaginary letters written in the reign of Seti II (1209–1205), which are contained in the papyrus Anastasi IV, mention three cities in the plain of Jezreel as famous for the manufacture and export of war-chariots and their parts. These would be the famous " chariots of iron," that is, no doubt, chariots armoured with plates of the metal which was still new in that region. It was these, too, which so terrified the Israelites, and for many years prevented them from coming down into the plains, and in particular from settling in the plain of Jezreel.[1]

But a far better claim to the gratitude of posterity than that which rests on this warlike invention must be granted to the Semites of Palestine and Syria, if it be true that they were the inventors and first propagators of the alphabet. It is a matter of common knowledge that this method of writing differs from the infinitely more complicated cuneiform or hieroglyphic script in that its signs represent, not words (*i.e. ideas*) or syllables, but the fundamental elements of speech, namely, vowels and consonants. Thanks to this invention the number of characters, so excessive in the ancient systems of writing, was reduced to twenty or so.

Concerning the age and place of this invention classical tradition gives us no certain information, save that the Greeks had some dim remembrance that they owed their characters to the Phenicians, since they called them *phoinikika* or *phoinikeia* (Herodotus). They also credited Cadmus, a

[1] Joshua xvii. 16 ; Judges i. 19 ; iv. 3, 13 ; *cf.* **LXXI**, p. 153. A blacksmith's workshop with iron slag has been found at Tell el-Mutesellim (Megiddo) (**IV**, p. 105).

Phenician hero, with the introduction of writing.[1] The names which they gave to these letters, save for those which they modified the sound of or added, are in the main clearly derived from the Semitic names in general use among the Hebrews and Ethiopians. But scholars are still in disagreement on the question whether the Phenicians themselves invented the system[2] or borrowed it from the Syrians or the Egyptians.[3]

The hypotheses which were current until the recent discoveries at Byblos may be reduced to three :

1. According to the first hypothesis, the alphabet was invented by the Phenicians between the fifteenth century, when they were still using the cuneiform script (Tell el-Amarna tablets), and the ninth (the Moabite stone).

According to certain scholars, they borrowed the characters which they adopted from one of the forms of script which prevailed in Babylonia and Assyria [4] : the linear Sumero-Accadian script has been specially referred to in this connexion.[5]

A much greater weight of expert opinion favours the view that the Phenician inventor took his twenty-two signs from the Egyptian repertory of characters,[6] either in the hieroglyphic form,[7] or in the more cursive hieratic form.[8] The theory of an Egyptian origin seemed the more probable in that the Egyptians already possessed certain characters corresponding to single consonants, but not vowel signs. Nothing was needed, so it would seem, save for the inventors of the Semitic alphabet to take from the Egyptian script these mono-consonantal signs in order to produce their own system, which only uses consonants. Whereas, if their exemplar had been a Babylonian script, they would certainly have employed vowel signs, since the Mesopotamian system has simple vowel signs but no characters for the individual consonants.

[1] The Semitic etymology of the name Cadmus and his supposed Phenician origin have been recently challenged by R. Dussaud (**CXX,** pp. 390–1).

[2] Lucian, *Pharsalia*, iii, 220–2.

[3] *Cf.* Solomon Reinach, **An.** 1900, pp. 497–502.

[4] Lévy, Deecke.

[5] Ball, Hommel, Winckler, Burney.

[6] Champollion, Salvolini, Lenormant, van Drival, Saalschütz, Olshausen, Brugsch, Philippe Berger (**XCVIII**).

[7] De Rougé (**CXLVIII**).   [8] J. Halévy (**XXIX**, p. 168).

2. The second hypothesis is, in reality, a variant, although an important one, of that which assigns the invention of the alphabet to the Canaanites under the influence of Egyptian models. According to this view,[1] the first evidence for the existence of the alphabet is to be sought in the Sinaitic peninsula. At Serabit el-Ḥadim, the site of the turquoise mines worked by the Egyptians since the twelfth dynasty, in and around a temple of the goddess Hathor, there has been known since 1867, and more accurately reproduced since 1906, a series of inscriptions resembling on the one hand the Egyptian script, and on the other the Hebræo-Phenician alphabet (fig. 24). Some scholars would find here the documentary evidence that the signs of this alphabet were taken from the Egyptian script and that it was invented by Semites; in fact there is general agreement that a particular group of four signs represents the word *b'lt*, *i.e.* *ba'alath*, lady.

According to P. Butin, this simplification of the Egyptian script was worked out on the spot by unlettered Semites employed in the mines,[2] a thing which is hard to accept. Prof. Sethe holds that the invention was made in Egypt by the Hyksos, who were, according to him, Semites, the ancient " Phenicians " (*e.g.* *Fnḫu*); when they were driven out of Egypt in the sixteenth century, they took their alphabet with them into Canaan and definitely established it at Kirjath Sepher (Debir in Judah), the " city of writing."

Unfortunately, the age of these inscriptions is very uncertain; opinions vary between the time of the twelfth dynasty (about 1900) and that of the eighteenth (fifteen to fourteenth century). Very divergent modes of decipherment have been proposed. According to some the signs have been borrowed from hieratic,[3] others derive them from hieroglyphic.[4] The relation to Phenician is occasionally dubious. Moreover, it is not certain that the Serabit script

---

[1] **CXLIII**, p. 203; **CXLIV**; C.-I. Ball, **PSBA**, p. 243; Ch. Bruston, **RT**, 1911, pp. 177 *ff.*; 1912, p. 176; A. H. Gardiner, **JEA**, iii, pp. 1–16; Kurt Sethe, **NGG**, 1917, pp. 437–75; **CXXI**; **CXXXI**; **CLXII**; Völter, **NTT**, 1925, pp. 215–44; **CLV**; R. F. Butin, **HTR**, 1928. *Cf.* Charles F. Jean, **SY**, 1928, pp. 286–99; Kalinka, **Kl**, xvi, pp. 302 *ff.*; R. Savignac, **RB**, 1928, pp. 613–15.

[2] **HTR**, 1928, p. 30 (of the off-print).

[3] So Grimme. [4] Gardiner, Sethe, Butin.

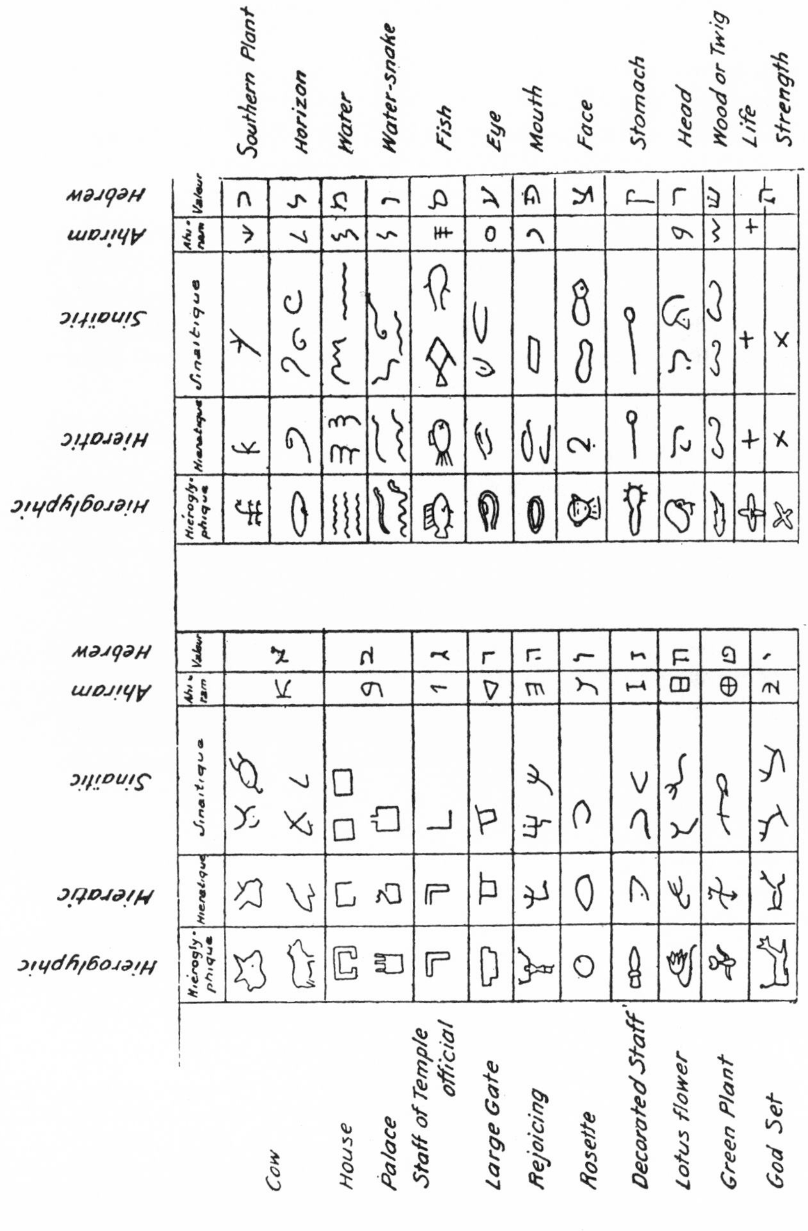

FIG. 24. SERABIT EL-HADIM ALPHABET, ACCORDING TO GRIMME.

is alphabetic, or at least purely so ; for not less than thirty-two signs have been distinguished, perhaps there are many more [1] ; the system may have employed ideograms and determinatives. [2]

3. According to Sir Arthur Evans,[3] the alphabet was of Ægean origin, a view adopted by S. Reinach,[4] H. Schneider,[5] and formerly, as a possibility, by R. Dussaud.[6] There have been found in Crete clay tablets covered with signs belonging, it appears, to several systems of linear script, not to mention documents in hieroglyphics such as the Phæstos disk. According to Sir A. Evans, it was one of these systems which gave birth, on the one hand to the archaic Greek alphabet, and on the other, to that of the Phenicians. M. Reinach thinks that it was brought into Syria by the Philistines in the twelfth century.

But the Ægean inscriptions have not yet been deciphered, so that it is not legitimate to assert either that the scripts in question are alphabetic, or that the signs alleged to be similar to those of the Greek and Semitic alphabets [7] represent the same sounds.

This was the state of the problem when, in 1923, M. P. Montet discovered in the necropolis of Byblos a sarcophagus inscribed partly on its lid, partly on the coffin itself, with Phenician characters closely akin to those of the Mesha stele, but presenting some letters in a clearly more archaic form. The inscription begins thus : " Ithobaal, the son of Ahiram, king of Byblos, made this sarcophagus for his father Ahiram." This Ahiram was perhaps contemporary with Ramses II (1300-1234) [8] ; for two alabaster vases were found with the name of this Pharaoh, one in the tomb itself, and one in the approach shaft, nor did any of the objects deposited in the hypogeum seem to be of a later date. In any case the inscription of Ahiram goes back at least to the eleventh century,[9] since the characters are evidently more archaic than those of two votive inscriptions of two other kings of

[1] SY, 1928, p. 286. [2] Ibid., p. 299.
[3] CXXIII, i, p. 273. [4] An. 1900, pp. 497-502.
[5] CL. [6] CXX, pp. 433-5. [7] CXX, pl. xii.
[8] Dussaud, SY, 1924, pp. 141-3 ; CXI, pp. 321-2.
[9] Spiegelberg, OLZ, 1926, p. 735 ; Lidzbarski, OLZ, 1927, p. 453 ; III, p. 176.

Byblos, Abibaal [1] and Elibaal, [2] engraved, one on a statue of Sheshonk I (945–924), the other on a bust of Osorkon I (924–895). To M. Dussaud is due the credit of having discovered the importance of these two certainly dated texts. By their help and that of other small texts, [3] we can carry back the history of the alphabet in Phenicia and Palestine at least two centuries, and perhaps four, earlier than the Moabite Stone (about 842).

M. Dussaud has shown further that in the case of certain letters the archaic Greek alphabet offers the older forms found in the inscriptions of Ahiram, Abibaal and Elibaal, while for others it presents the later forms of the Mesha Stele. This fact can only be explained on the view that the Greeks borrowed their alphabet from the Phenicians, and at a date which can be fixed exactly between the tenth century and the middle of the ninth. [4] Hence it follows that the Phenicians, who, since the collapse of the Ægean empire in the twelfth century, were supreme on the seas and held the effective monopoly of international sea-borne trade, must have been the main agents responsible for the diffusion of the alphabet.

Were they also its inventors ? The discoveries at Byblos have strengthened the presumption in their favour. However, the question remains open. It is possible to imagine that the Ægean, Phenician, Sinaitic, and perhaps the south-Semitic (Sabean and Safaitic), may be all different developments from an archetypal alphabet not yet discovered and of unknown origin. [5] It may also be acknowledged that in the second millennium, divers more or less independent attempts to simplify the old cuneiform and Egyptian scripts had been made in various parts of the ancient world. The discovery at Ras Shamra of a cuneiform script consisting only of twenty signs, and hence alphabetic, [6] tends to confirm this theory.

[1] CVIII, v, pp. 74–5 ; LIV, ii, p. 167 ; Dussaud, SY, 1924, pp. 145–6, pl. xlii ; 1925, p. 111.
[2] Dussaud, SY, 1925, pp. 101–7.
[3] Dussaud, ibid., pp. 327–38. An inscription of another king of Byblos, Yehimilk, has been discovered by M. Dunand in 1929.
[4] SY, 1924, pp. 149–50, 156.
[5] Praetorius, ZDMG, 1909, p. 191 ; CXX, pp. 434–5 ; CXI, p. 321.
[6] SY, 1929, pp. 304–10.

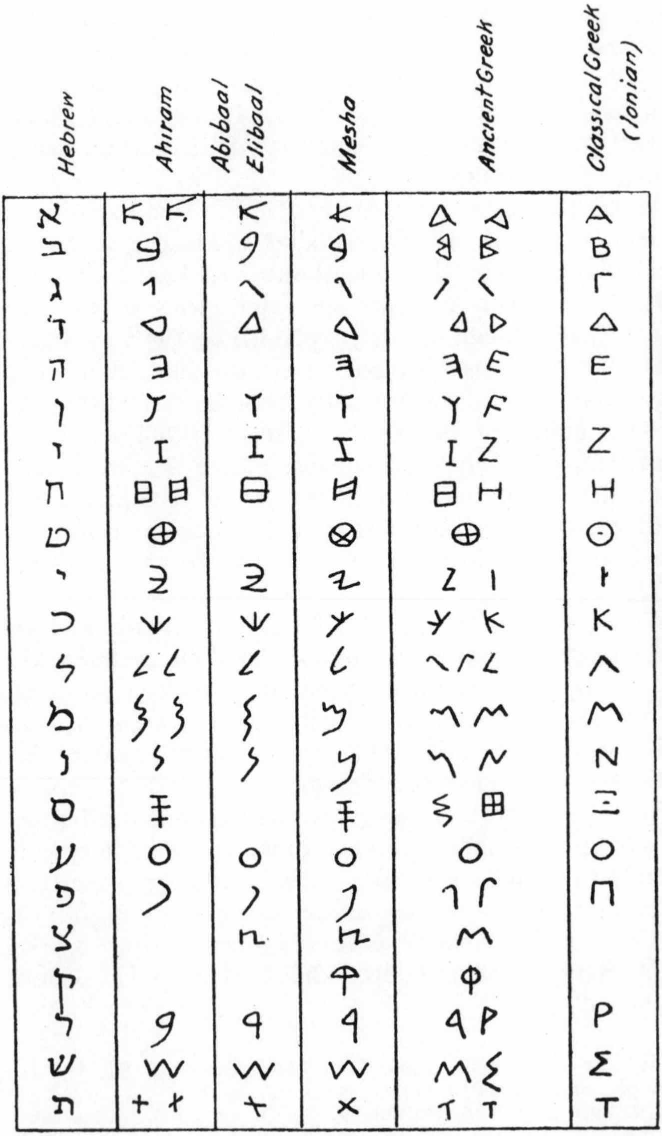

FIG. 25. HEBRÆO-PHENICIAN AND GREEK ALPHABETS.

The further question arises whether the inventors of this solution made use of other systems, as M. Glotz inclines to think,[1] or whether their system is entirely artificial and independent, as M. Dussaud now thinks.[2] The matter is however quite secondary, the essential thing being to know when and where the principle of the representation of consonants by single signs was first applied. The reliable decipherment of the Sinaitic and Ægean inscriptions will probably help us to settle the question.

The new script, by reason of its simplicity, no doubt spread rapidly outside the circle of professional scribes : on the wall of the shaft of the tomb of Ahiram, M. Montet has found an inscription of somewhat uncertain meaning,[3] but apparently the work of the master-mason responsible for closing the approach to the tomb.

The contribution of the early inhabitants of Syria and Palestine to the civilization of the ancient East would be much more important if Prof. Clay's claim could be established, that the great Babylonian creation myths were originally Amorite legends, composed in Hebrew, and carried by the Semites of Amurru from the west when they settled in lower Mesopotamia. This applies particularly to the flood story, the legend of Etana, the episode of Humbaba (Hobab) in the Gilgamesh epic. These poems have only been preserved to us in the languages of Assyria and Babylonia ; but according to Prof. Clay, they offer characteristic Hebraisms, and their gods are all " occidental " deities.[4] According to the same Assyriologist, the greater part of the code of Hammurabi originated in Aleppo.[5]

In reality, however, the evidence of excavations up to the present does not support the American scholar's theory

---

[1] **CXXVII**, pp. 421–38.

[2] **SY**, 1924, p. 155 ; *cf.* J. Halévy, *Revue sémitique*, 1901, pp. 356–70 ; Pilcher, **PSBA**, 1904, pp. 168–73 ; Lidzbarski, *Jew. Enc.*, i, 439 ; **LIV**, i, pp. 261–71.

[3] *Cf.* for example, Dussaud, **SY**, 1924, pp. 135–7, and Georg Hoffmann, **ZATW**, 1924, p. 350.

[4] **CVI**, pp. 5–55. Chiera has given the partial transcription of a text which he calls " A Sumerian version of the Amorite story of Creation " (in Crozier Theological Seminary Babylonian Publications). But the parts published hardly appear to justify this title ; *cf.* Erich Ebeling, **ZATW**, 1925, pp. 137–8.

[5] **CVI**, pp. 46–7.

that Syria, between 4000 and 2000, was the home of a sufficiently original and advanced civilization, not only to rival
that of the Sumerians and Egyptians, but also to exercise a
fertilizing influence upon the former. The interesting finds
at Tell el-Mishrifé (Qatna),[1] Djabbul,[2] Sheikh Sa'd,[3] give
reason to suppose that there was in *the second millennium* a
Syrian art prior to Hittite influence, " a vigorous art which
. . . acquired special characteristics indicating strong individuality," but which " was modelled on Babylonian examples, and drew from thence most of its motives." [4]
Perhaps the most ancient of these monuments, a cylinder
seal, assigned by M. Louis Delaporte to the age of Hammurabi,
displays " a scene borrowed from the Babylonian repertory,
combined with skilfully adapted Egyptian elements, and an
Ægean element, the spiral."[5]

But there is at least one realm in which the Canaanites,
in spite of foreign influences, seem to have kept their own
characteristic ideas and practices : the realm of religion.

[1] SY, 1926, p. 338 (pl. lxx).
[2] SY, 1926, pp. 340 (pl. lxxi), 342 (fig. 3).
[3] SY, 1924, p. 207 (pl. lii, 2).
[4] Dussaud, SY, 1926, p. 346, *cf*. pp. 336–46.
[5] Dussaud, *ibid.*, 1927, p. 24 (pl. xv, 1).

PLATE III

2. BRONZE FROM MISHRIFEH

1. BASALT HEAD, FROM DJABBUL

PLATE IV

1. CANAANITE
GODDESS.
BRONZE STATUETTE

2-4. CANAANITE GODDESSES. BAS-RELIEFS

5. BAS-RELIEF OF " SUN-RISE "

BOOK II

RELIGIOUS CONDITIONS IN PALESTINE AT THE TIME OF THE ISRAELITE SETTLEMENT

CHAPTER I

THE CULT

I

SACRED THINGS

MANY spots were regarded as sacred by the ancient Semitic peoples : such as mountains, springs and rivers, caves and stones.

In dealing with the Hebrews, we shall attempt to define the extent and the causes of this veneration.[1] For the present we shall content ourselves with establishing the fact that these beliefs were certainly shared by the Canaanites.

For them Hermon was a sacred mountain, as its name shows, being related to the Arabic *ḥaram* and the Hebrew *ḥerem* ; the fact is also borne witness to by the presence near the summit of the ruins of several temples and a thick layer of cinders and bones. On the summit itself is an oval enclosure called Qasr Antar, the *insigne templum* of which Jerome speaks (*Onomasticum, s.v.*), near which was found an inscription containing the commands of a θεὸς μέγιστος.[2] The sacred nature of the mountain is still further apparent in Jewish and Christian legends which represent it as the ill-omened scene of the fall of the angels, or the quasi-celestial abode of the Sethites.[3]

---

[1] Pp. 230 *ff*.

[2] Charles Warren, **PEF, QS,** v, 1870, pp. 210–15 ; **CVIII,** v, pp. 346–66 ; Franz Cumont in Pauly-Wissowa, **XV,** 1912, col. 893 ; **CXXXIX,** no. mli ; **XX,** pp. 389–90 ; **CXXXV,** pp. 42–3.

[3] See *Enoch,* 6–16, spec. 6, 5–6, and the fragment preserved by George Syncellus (ed. Dindorf, p. 47), and the studies of texts in **CVIII,** v, pp. 346 *ff*., and **CXXXV,** pp. 30–3.

Carmel was sacred during the same period, both for the Phenicians and for the Israelites ; we know from the narrative in 1 Kings xviii. 30 that an altar dedicated to the Baal of Tyre stood there side by side with one to Jahweh. Vespasian also offered sacrifice there and consulted the oracle of " the god Carmel " (Tac., *Hist.*, ii. 78 ; Suet., *Vesp.*, 5). The tradition that the Israelites regarded it as a place of refuge (Amos ix. 3) is perpetuated in the statement of Iamblichus that Carmel is " sacred above all mountains, debarred from profane approach " (*Vit. Pyth.*, iii. 15).

The rites practised by the Greeks and Romans in honour of Zeus Casius on Mt. Casius, to the south of the mouths of the Orontes, seem to have been the continuation of an extremely ancient cult. We know from the testimony of Philo of Byblos, in spite of his euhemeristic explanation, that Casius, Lebanon, Anti-Lebanon, and Brathy (Mt. Amanus ?) were sacred mountains for the Phenicians.[1]

The Canaanite town of Gibeon, which held a famous sanctuary, stood on a height, as its name (hill) suggests.[2] Moreover, the term commonly used to denote the Palestinian sanctuaries, either Canaanite, as certainly in the case of Bamoth-Baal (Num. xxii. 41), or Israelite, was *bamah*, a word of uncertain etymology, but whose meaning was at any rate " height " : it is accurately enough translated " high-place." The name shows that originally most of these sanctuaries were placed on hill-tops.

All waters were held sacred by the Phenicians, who were Canaanites. In the treaty which he made with Philip of Macedon, Hannibal swears by all the gods of Carthage, and invokes among others " the rivers, the meadows (or perhaps rather the ponds [λιμνῶν instead of λειμώνων]) and waters " (*Polyb.*, vii. 9.) Several of the Phenician rivers bore divine names, the Belus, beside which was shown the grave of the god, the Asclepius (the Greek name of Eshmun) near Sidon, the Ares (apparently identical with the Lycus, today Nahr-el-Kelb), the Adonis, whose entire valley was strewn with sanctuaries and which took its rise in the sacred lake of Aphaca, on the banks of which stood the most famous

---

[1] Frag., **II**, p. 7 ; *cf.* **CVIII**, 1903, p. 351 ; **XLIX**, p. 415.

[2] It follows from 2 Sam. xxi. 6 (G.) 9, that the holy place of Gibeah was on a " mountain."

temple of the country. We should add to the list the Kishon in Palestine if its name comes from that of the god Qais. The river of Tripoli is still called Kadishah (the holy).

An example of a tree held sacred by the Phenicians is the Diviners' Tree, near Shechem (Judges ix. 37.) At Aphaca in Phenicia there was a sacred wood above which, at the annual festival of the goddess, globes of fire were supposed to play.[1] Several sanctuaries have been excavated possessing grottos

FIG. 26. CANAANITE GODDESS, FROM TAANACH.

or pillars.[2] Another sacred object was the asherah, probably the trunk of a tree fixed in the ground. An Israelite account, one of the versions of the story of Gideon, relates the burning of an asherah which stood by the altar of Baal in the high place of Ophrah.[3] It is to be expected that such a perishable object should have disappeared. MM. Schumacher and du Mesnil du Buisson believe they have found remains of asherahs at Megiddo[4] and Qatna.[5] Another archæological document

[1] **LXXXIV**, pp. 175, 193. [2] *Cf.* pp. 87–97.
[3] Judges vi. 25 ; *cf.* Deut. vii. 5.
[4] **MN**, 1906, p. 13, fig. 16 ; **CLIX**, p. 97 (fig. 67).
[5] **SY**, 1928, pp. 8–9 and pl. vi, 2 ; **V.** 1.

gives us at least an idea of what a Canaanite asherah may
have been like. It is a little bronze relief (pl. iv, 5) found
at Susa by the de Morgan mission and now in the Louvre.[1]
It apparently represents an ancient Semitic high-place,
probably Babylonian, although made at Susa (*circa* 1100
B.C.). It depicts, as an inscription engraved in one corner
tells us, a " sun-rising," presumably one of the rituals performed in honour of the sun at its rising. In one corner on
the left is an alignment of four posts, one of which is a
stele, and the other three have the shape of tree-trunks
whose branches have been lopped off : these would be
asherim.[2]

The Canaanites had many idols. They have been found
in great numbers in all Palestinian excavations. There are
statuettes of Egyptian gods like Osiris, Ptah, Bes, Tueris,
Nephrit, Thoth ; above all there are images of the goddess,
the commonest of whose many names was Astarte. She is
represented in the round[3] (pl. iv, 1, and fig. 26), or more
usually in bas-relief ([4] and pl. iv, 2, 3, 4). At Beisan she is
seen at the door or the window of a little temple holding in
each hand an object like a bird.[5] It would appear that these
images, all of which are very small, were used in private
worship or as amulets rather than in public worship. It is
very likely that in the great sanctuaries the divinity was
represented rather by the shapeless fetishes of early times,
stone pillars or trees, natural or artificial. However, the
little monument of Beisan of which we have spoken, and
which should be a miniature representation of one of
the local sanctuaries, suggests that in this place at
least there was an image of the goddess placed in a sacred
chamber.[6]

[1] **CLIX**, p. 144 (fig. 93) ; **XXXIV**, *Bildermappe*, fig. 93.
[2] For the significance of this object, see p. 134.
[3] **CLIX**, pp. 163 (fig. 106), 164 (fig. 107), 165 (figs. 107–9).
[4] **CLIX**, pp. 158 (pl. iii), 160 (figs. 102, 103) ; **XLIII**, pp. 54–5.
[5] See p. 94.
[6] The model of the temple coming from Idalion in Cyprus (fig.
37, p. 300) implies a statue. Similar models are reported among
the finds from the excavations of the DOG in the archaic temples of
Ishtar at Asshur. (Andrae, *Die archaischen Ischtar-tempel*, p. 36,
fig. 5 ; **XXIII**, ii, figs. 442–3).

II

Sacred Places

The sacred things which have been described would naturally form the centre of a sacred place. Deuteronomy, with the command to destroy the Canaanite places of worship, gives an accurate description of them. " Ye shall utterly destroy all the places, wherein the nations which ye dispossessed served their gods, upon the high mountains, and upon the hills, and under every green tree : and ye shall overthrow their altars and break their pillars, and burn their groves with fire ; and ye shall hew down the graven images of their gods, and destroy the names of them out of that place " (xii. 2–3). From the Palestinian excavations we may gain an idea of some, at least, of these sacred places of the Canaanites.

They no longer consisted merely of a cup-marked rock like those of the Neolithic Age.[1] One of the best preserved of them has been excavated at Gezer ; [2] it contained at the time of its discovery an impressive alignment of eight monoliths, still standing, some roughly squared, some partly rounded (pl. v, 1). They are of unequal height : the tallest, viz. the first, the third and the fourth from the south end, are about three metres high, the fourth, which is the highest, is 3·28 metres high. With the exception of the second, they are all set in a stone-work platform.

This second pillar, fixed directly in the ground and much the smallest, being only 1·65 metres high, was probably the most sacred ; for its top is worn and polished by the kisses, the handling and the anointing of many generations of worshippers. The seventh menhir is made of a different kind of stone from the others, not found in the neighbourhood of Gezer, but, strangely enough, near Jerusalem. It has been supposed that it was the sacred stone of a conquered city, which the inhabitants of Gezer had brought back and erected in one of their sanctuaries.[3]

At some more remote period the alignment consisted of a

---

[1] See pp. 41–2. [2] **CLIX**, p. 112 (fig. 78).
[3] Just as the Philistines carried away the Ark of Jahweh (1 Sam. iv. 6) or as the Elamites removed the stele of Hammurabi and erected it at Susa, where it was found.

larger number of standing stones; for south and north of the eighth the sockets of two other steles have been found which have now disappeared. Further, near the first, in a lower layer, a fallen block was found resembling the most sacred stone of all. Hence there must have been at least eleven menhirs in all.

The sacred character of these pillars has been questioned : it has been maintained that they were simply monuments of a memorial or votive nature.[1] But this explanation certainly fails in the case of the second stone, polished by the adoring hands of worshippers. And many other indications suggest the presence of a sanctuary.

Between the fifth and sixth pillars, but somewhat outside the alignment, is a large stone cube (pl. v, 2) in the upper face of which a large rectangular cavity has been carefully hollowed out [2] : according to P. Lagrange [3] it is the pedestal of a statue, Prof. Macalister regards it as the socket of an asherah, it may be the base of a twelfth stele more sacred than the rest according to MM. Gressmann [4] and Bertholet,[5] while Prof. S. A. Cook [6] thinks that it may be a basin for lustrations. It is more likely some kind of altar, the cavity serving to receive the blood; it is noticeable, too, that the inner surface of the basin shows no marks of friction or wear such as would have been left by a block of stone or wood in close contact with it.[7]

Close to the alignment on the east is a double grotto which had been a human habitation at an earlier epoch, but which seems to have been transformed into a sort of *adytum* or sacred cave for the god : a small hole in the roof of the grotto probably served as a channel for the blood of the libations.

On the other side of the alignment on the west, that is, in the part of the sanctuary which was open to worshippers, is a pit for offerings in which was found, in addition to a great number of potsherds of the Cyprian period (twelfth to seventh century), a curious strip of bronze 15 cm. long in the shape of a serpent (fig. 27), very similar to an object found at Susa

[1] *Cf.* Thiersch, **AA**, 1909, pp. 375, 573 ; **ZDPV**, 1914, p. 67 ; Ed. Meyer, **AA**, 1918, p. 82 ; **LXV**, pp. 421, 423.
[2] **CLIX**, p. 114 (fig. 80) ; **XXIII**, ii, figs. 411 and 412.
[3] **XLIX**, p. 202.   [4] **CXXVIII**, pp. 26–7.
[5] **IV**, p. 115, n. 3.   [6] **CXIV**, p. 15.   [7] **CLIX**, pp. 131–5.

Plate V

1. The Mazzeboth in the High-place of Gezer

2. Altar before the Mazzeboth of Gezer

PLATE VI

FOUNDATION SACRIFICE
(*See* p. 99)

(fig. 28). It suggests at once the famous brazen serpent lifted up by Moses and still worshipped in the eighth century in the temple at Jerusalem.[1] The bronze serpent of Gezer must have been a votive offering to a serpent-god, quite in keeping with the idea of a chthonian divinity inhabiting the sacred grotto. The serpent also entered into the cult at Beisan and Beit-Mirsim.[2]

North and south-west of the alignment, a number of cup-holes have been cut in the rock, indicating that the new type of holy place, *i.e.* with pillars, was merely the ancient sanctuary with new features added.

Noteworthy also is the presence around the steles of

FIG. 27. BRONZE SERPENT FOUND AT GEZER.

FIG. 28. BRONZE SERPENT FOUND AT SUSA.

many jars containing the skeletons of new-born children, none of which, with about two exceptions, can have been more than eight days old. This uniformity in age suggests that the skeletons are those of first-born children sacrificed to the local divinity. As the bodies show no sign of mutilation (with the exception of the two older ones), it is supposed that the little victims were buried alive in the jars, which were then tightly packed with fine earth.[3]

---

[1] Num. xxi. 4–9 ; 2 Kings xviii. 4.   [2] See pp. 108–9.

[3] This use of earth may be compared with that of sand in burials, discussed by M. A. Canney (*Man*, 1926, pp. 14–17, 32–3). According to this writer " sand like salt is a life-giving substance, the source of fertility and prosperity. As life-givers sand and salt were employed by the ancient Egyptians in mummification. A magic power came to be attributed to them, perhaps in primitive times. If they could preserve the corpse, they might also create life or restore the vitality of the living."

Under a shelf of earth skulls were found which may have been also the remains of human sacrifices. If we may judge by the depth of the remains the sanctuary of Gezer must have been in use from about 2000 B.C. to 600 B.C., that is to say not only during the period of independent Canaanite occupation, but also during the whole of the Hebrew monarchy up to the exile.

Sanctuaries more or less resembling the one which we have described have been excavated both at Gezer and at other centres of exploration. No doubt caution is necessary : some archæologists may have taken for alignments of menhirs rows of pillars serving merely to support a roof ; [1] but scep-

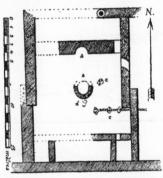

FIG. 29. PLAN OF THE CANAANITE SANCTUARY OF TELL ES-SAFY.

ticism is out of place when we find along with these pillars other characteristic features, such as a trench full of bones or a block which may have served as an altar. Further points of divergence or agreement will be furnished by those sanctuaries which have been most clearly identified as such.

The sanctuary, which is always open to the sky, is sometimes surrounded by an enclosure wall.[2] The grotto is occasionally replaced by a chamber, a *cella*, an incipient temple.[3] There are also other chambers, apparently for subsidiary purposes, a treasure house, a room for sacred meals, etc. In two cases the wall of the *cella* has a kind of apse opening on the court of the sanctuary (figs. 29–30).[4]

[1] So at Tell es-Safy, *cf.* **IV**, p. 83.
[2] Tell es-Safy (**CLIX**, p. 104, figs. 71–2) ; Gezer (p. 88).
[3] Tell es-Safy, **CLIX**, p. 104 ; Gezer.   [4] *Ibid.*

At Balata (Shechem), the sanctuary as it is believed to have existed in the thirteenth and fourteenth centuries, had

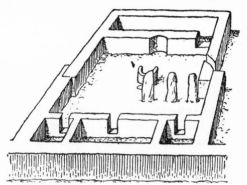

FIG. 30. ISOMETRIC VIEW OF THE SANCTUARY OF TELL ES-SAFY.

a more imposing appearance (fig. 31). The *cella* with its massive walls was entered from a narrow corridor and was divided into three naves by two rows of three pillars each;

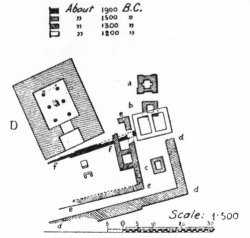

FIG. 31. PLAN OF THE TEMPLE OF BALATA.

a block of stone, still in its place in the centre of the building, served apparently as a base for the symbol of the divinity. This *cella*, before which the remains of an altar and a cistern have been recognized, rose from the midst of a great terrace bounded by a solid retaining wall; along this terrace were arranged various smaller buildings, serving perhaps as chapels for deities to whom the god of the town dispensed hospitality.[1] Such is the general plan of the Phenician temples [2] and of that of Jerusalem.

The sanctuaries of Beisan (Beth Shan) are not yet completely uncovered, hence it is impossible at present to give an opinion on their arrangement. It seems to have been much more complicated and irregular than that of Gezer. There were two temples side by side : that on the south belonged to the local god whose name we now know, Mikal ; that on the north was apparently reserved for the goddess. Mr. Rowe, on the strength of two biblical passages, thinks that the one on the north is the " temple of Ashtaroth," where the Philistines, after their victory on Mt. Gilboa, deposited the arms of Saul and his sons according to 1 Samuel xxxi. 10 ; and that the southern sanctuary is the temple of Dagon, where they nailed the head of the conquered king according to 1 Chronicles x. 10. But nothing in the passages suggests that it is a question of sanctuaries at Beth Shan, and one of Mr. Rowe's most recent discoveries shows that in the fifteenth century at any rate, the god of the southern temple was not called Dagon but Mikal.

The excavations have proved that the southern sanctuary, which existed under Thothmes III (1501–1447), has been rebuilt at least five times on the same site : in the time of Amenophis III (circa 1415–1380), of Seti I (1319–1300), twice under Ramses II (1300–1234), and finally in the Greco-Roman age.

The five oldest levels can be dated with certainty because in each of them objects have been found bearing the name or the cartouche of one of the above-mentioned Pharaohs. The most ancient of these temples (fig. 32) comprised, according to Mr. Rowe,[3] a cella of an asymmetrical shape (1 in the plan), enclosing a sort of stepped platform, styled an altar, but which was, perhaps, rather the base of the divine symbol (C) ; on the north, south and south-west of the sanctuary are

[1] Sellin, ZDPV, 1926, pp. 229–36 ; Vincent, RB, 1927, pp. 424–5 and pl. xii.
[2] CXI, pp. 162–71.
[3] RB, 1928, p. 512 (pl. xxi) ; 1929, p. 86 (fig. 1).

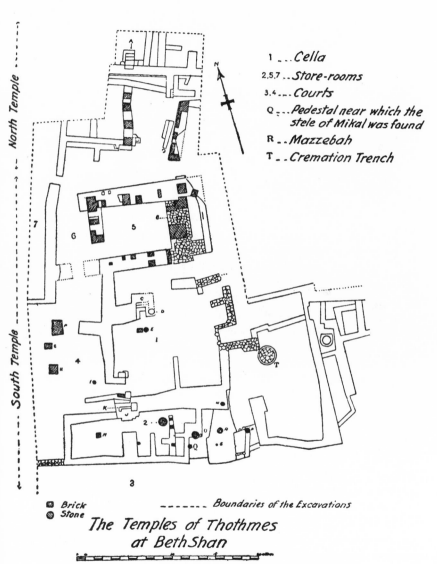

1 ...Cella
2,5,7 ..Store-rooms
3,4...Courts
Q...Pedestal near which the stele of Mikal was found
R..Mazzebah
T..Cremation Trench

Brick
Stone

------ Boundaries of the Excavations

The Temples of Thothmes at BethShan

FIG. 32. TEMPLES OF THOTHMES AT BETH SHAN.

chambers supposed to have been store-houses (2, 5, 7), on the
west was a court, only partly uncovered (4), where Mr. Rowe
would place the stone of sacrifice and the bases of the tables
for cutting up the victims ; to the south-west is a chamber
enclosing a conical block (R), which would be the *maṣṣebah*
representing the god, and close to it the votive stele, of
Egyptian style, which has preserved his name.   In a court
adjoining the platform of the *maṣṣebah* is a basin, containing
calcined remains of which we shall speak later.

So far only two small chambers of the southern temple
have been cleared and a pit (probably a pit for offerings).
Several small clay models representing a building of two or
three stories, at the windows of which the goddess appears,[1]
suggest perhaps that her temple contained a tower of several
stages, no doubt an imitation of the Babylonian *ziqqurat.*

One of the most characteristic features of the Canaanite
sanctuaries was, as we have seen, the standing stone ; there
were often several forming an alignment, and without doubt,
in two cases, a circle,[2] a cromlech, or what the Hebrews called
a *gilgal.* So far the discoveries hitherto made have not
yielded any decisive light on the meaning which the Canaanites attached to these standing stones.   Some archæologists
would give them a phallic significance ;[3] but the square
shape of many of these menhirs is not favourable to this
theory.   Other scholars hold that some of the stones represent a male divinity and others a female, because at Megiddo
two pillars were found containing on the summit of the one
and the wall of the other hollows whose arrangement might
be interpreted as representing the different sexes.[4]   But
these cup-marks, which are common enough on standing
stones, are differently arranged in all other cases.

It remains extremely problematic why these cup-marks
are for the most part cut in the side of the stones ;[5] they
could hardly have held liquids, and at the most it can only
have been possible to rub them with fat or oil.   According to
Father Vincent these hollows were put to no practical use :
they were simply the symbol of an offering ; and the standing

---

[1] See pp. 108–9.
[2] Tell es-Safy, **CLIX**, p. 105 ; Gezer, iii, 321–2 (fig. 408).
[3] **XXIII²**, ii (fig. 428) ; **III**, pp. 322–5, *cf.* p. 39 (fig. 6).
[4] So **III**, p. 324 (fig. 413).
[5] **XLVI**, pp. 126–9 (figs. 15, 16, 17).

stones were all, except one in each sanctuary, which was the dwelling of the god, simply memorial steles reminding the god of an offering which had been made to him. But this is doubtful, the most sacred stone of the Gezer alignment, the one which Father Vincent himself considers as the dwelling of the god, itself has two cup-marks.

It may then be possible that the Canaanites regarded all their sacred stones as the dwelling of their god, as the term *beth 'el*, baetyl, suggests. The fact that there were several in the same sanctuary does not imply that it was consecrated to several deities, each represented by one stone. For we find in Israel alignments or cromlechs of twelve *maṣṣeboth* dedicated to one god, Jahweh, as at Gilgal (Joshua iv. 20, *cf.* v. 2–15) or at Sinai (Exod. xxiv. 4). Among the pagan Arabs, the goddess al-Ouzza had in one of her sanctuaries three trees in which she dwelt.[1] Such a belief, no doubt, is an inheritance from the times when the personality of the local divinity was not yet fully differentiated : it was still uncertain whether several *elohim* or merely a single deity inhabited the spot in question.

The Altar. The Canaanites had passed the primitive stage of slaying the victim upon or beside the sacred object which was the abode of the god. In certain sanctuaries at least, one of the sacred stones served as the place of sacrifice, another as a table of offerings : that is, the Canaanites appear to have had altars (*cf.* Deut. xii. 3). One is supposed to have been found in Gezer,[2] in the form of a cube with a basin hollowed out in it. Other examples are reported from Megiddo[3] and from Taanach.[4]

In another sanctuary at Megiddo[5] the altar appears under the more ancient guise of a dolmen. None of the stones of this table nor the trench which surrounds it, with the exception of a basin for receiving the blood, has been touched by a tool. Hence this Canaanite altar corresponds exactly to the demands of Jahweh in the old book of the covenant embodying the ancient custom of Israel (Exod. xx. 25–6).

[1] **XC²**, pp. 36–7.   [2] Pp. 87–8.
[3] **CLIX**, pp. 133 (fig. 89), 187 (fig. 133, Israelite epoch).
[4] **CLIII**, pp. 34, 103.
[5] Schumacher, **MN**, 1905, pp. 11–12.

At Beisan, in the temple of the time of Thothmes III, Mr. Rowe has found against the south wall of what he calls the *cella* of the god, a brick platform (J in the plan, p. 93) which was approached by two steps, and in the surface of which were cut a basin and a channel leading out of it (K). Mr. Rowe with great probability regards it as a sacrificial altar ; he claims to have found the remains of the stake or hook to which the victim was fastened, the gutter in which it was placed for slaughter, and even the knife with which its throat was cut, together with the horns and shoulder-blade of the last bull slain on the spot. In the court on the west side of the *cella* he claims to have identified the socket of the stake to which the victim was tied to skin it (I), those of the tables on which it was cut up (F, G, H), in the *cella* itself the tables on which the flesh was laid (E) and the basin into which libations were poured before the god (D).

So far no example has been found of a Canaanite altar on which the victims had been burnt. However, we may infer from the presence of calcined bones of animals and charcoal in a pit of offerings at Megiddo [1] and of two partly burned bodies of children under the threshold of the great sanctuary of Gezer, [2] as well as from the thick layers of cinders found in the grottos of Serabit el-Hadim and on the summit of Mt. Hermon, [3] that the Canaanites had adopted at least to some extent the custom of burning the sacrifices. This would involve the abandonment of the old Semitic practice of merely sprinkling the symbol of the deity with the blood, leaving to the wild beasts such portions of the flesh as were not eaten by the worshippers or the priests.

At Beisan, a little to the north of the *maṣṣebah*, a pit was found, full of ashes, horns and calcined bones (T of the plan, p. 93). This pit has certainly served as a hearth, for its clay has been partly baked. What rite was celebrated here ? Mr. Rowe suggests holocausts of a special kind in which the animals were burnt alive, as at the feast of the funeral-pyre at Hierapolis, [4] or in the rites of Artemis at Patrai. [5] Or, as in the Hebrew holocausts, the animals may have been burnt after having been sacrificed, [6] the pit serving as an altar as in

---

[1] Schumacher, **MN**, 1905, pp. 11–12.   [2] P. 89.
[3] **CXIV**, pp. 41, 69–70.   [4] *De dea syria*, 49.
[5] Pausanias, vii, 18, 7.   [6] Barrois, **RB**, 1929, p. 87.

certain sacrifices to Hecate.[1] Again, it is possible that these were the remains of sacrificed animals which were burnt outside the sanctuary proper after the sacrifice, for fear of profanation, as was done in the case of certain Hebrew propitiatory sacrifices.[2] In any case it seems to be clear that, contrary to an older view, the burning of sacrifices was not introduced into Palestine by the Hebrews.[3]

Possibly the Canaanites may have borrowed the practice from the Ægeans.[4, 5] If the presence of the rite in Palestine is due to foreign influence, it may be that of Egypt, where " it appears that some of the food offerings were burnt on the fire altar,"[6] or of Babylon, where it was said to Nusku-Girru, the fire-god : " Without thee the gods would not smell the odour of sacrifice."[7]

The pre-Israelite inhabitants of Palestine had censers exactly like those which were in ritual use among the Egyptians and Assyrians.[8]

III

RITUAL ACTS

For the ritual of the Canaanite sacrifices we have only evidence of late date relating to the Phenician colonies in Africa : the tariff of Marseilles[9] and that of Carthage.[10] M. Dussaud, however, claims that the ritual supposed by these texts was in use among the Canaanites before the age of Solomon (tenth century), because, according to him, it is

[1] Apollonius Rhodius, iii, 1026–41.

[2] Lev. iv. 11–12, 21.

[3] It has been suggested that in one episode of the story of Gideon (Judges vi. 17–21) we have the account of the substitution of a new and specifically Israelite ritual (with cremation) for an earlier Canaanite ritual, with mere exposure of the victim (**XLVI**, pp. 99, 106, 108 ; cf. **LX**, pp. 95–6). As a matter of fact, this tradition, in its original form, was the ἱερὸς λόγος of the founding of the holy place of Ophrah and, like many similar stories, related the transformation of a simple meal into a sacrifice (**RHR**, lxii, pp. 367–8).

[4] **XLVI**, pp. 156–7 ; **LIX**, pp. 432, 435.

[5] Cf. **XXVII**, pp. 296–8.

[6] **CXLII**, pp. 110–11 ; **LIX**, p. 431.

[7] **XXXIV**, i, p. 297 ; cf. pp. 298, 317, 486–8.

[8] **CLIX**, p. 182 (fig. 132) ; **XXIII**², ii, figs. 466 and 467.

[9] **CIS**, i, p. 165 (translation in **XLIX**, p. 470), probably belonging to the third century B.C. (**CXI**, p. 135).

[10] **CXI**, p. 337.

identical with the levitical order, which proves that the Israelites borrowed it from the Canaanites after the building of the temple at Jerusalem.[1]

The Carthaginian tariffs distinguish three kinds of sacrifice :

First the *ṣewa'at*, where the offerer received a part of the flesh, as in the " peace-offerings " (*šelem* or *zebaḥ šelamim*) of the Israelites.

Second the *kalil*, in which the carcase of the victim belonged entirely to the priests, as in most of the propitiatory sacrifices of the levitical ritual (the *ašam* and, in some cases, the *ḥattath*).

Third the *šelem kalil*, where the animal seems to have been reserved for the god, as in the Israelite whole burnt-offering (*'olah* or *kalil*).

But, in reality the Carthaginian system and the levitical theory present, along with certain resemblances, important differences. For example, there is no agreement in the names of the various classes of offerings ; they vary in number, the levitical has four classes to the three of the Marseilles tariff ; they disagree in the perquisites of the priests.[2] Hence it does not seem in any way certain that the Carthaginian order furnished the model to the Jewish priests who drew up the levitical system and must be of extreme antiquity.

However, the comparative lateness of the theory does not prevent the practical regulations from being very early. It is also very likely that, as Dussaud holds, various sacrificial rituals, especially those corresponding to the three ideas of communion, propitiation and gift may have been practised by the Canaanites before the tenth century on the general ground that they exist in a rudimentary form even among the most backward of the Semites such as the pagan Arabs, and were certainly practised by the Hebrews before their entry into Canaan.[3] Hence it follows that the Israelites since they already knew these rites had no need to borrow them from the inhabitants of their new country.

[1] **XVIII ; XIX.**
[2] *Cf.* **RHR**, lxxvi, p. 230 ; lxxxvi, pp. 237–42 ; **RHP**, 1923, pp. 79–82 ; 1928, pp. 399–411.
[3] See pp. 276–82.

Human sacrifices, especially offerings of children, were one of the characteristic features of the Canaanite religion. On this point the evidence of the excavations corroborates that of Hebrew,[1] Phenician,[2] and classical writers.[3] Many skeletons of new-born children have been found under the sanctuaries,[4] probably of first-born. The bodies which show traces of cremation would probably also be the remains of sacrifices.[5]

Human victims were still sacrificed at the founding of a new house. The object may have been to secure a guardian spirit for the building, the spirit of the victim; or it may have been to appease the genius of the place, whose domain was being trespassed upon. These foundation sacrifices are, as we know, widely spread throughout the world. They are still found among the modern Syrians, except that the human victims are replaced by animals: sacrifices are offered at the foundation of a public or private building, at the repairing of a tent, at the entry of newly-married persons into their house, at the launching of a ship, even at the beginning of a railway line.

The Canaanites still practised the foundation rite in all its primitive horror. At Megiddo there was found under the fortress the body of a girl of fifteen: the body had no ornaments and rested on the first stones of the building to which it had been fastened by a layer of cement,[6] pl. vi. At Megiddo also was found in the middle of a wall a jar containing the body of an infant buried head first: the jar had been partly crushed by the stones of the wall;[7] hence it had not been buried in the wall after it had been built.

At Taanach, beside the gate of the fortress, was the body of a boy, protected by a stone of the same kind as those of which the wall was built.[8] At Gezer Mr. Macalister discovered, also built into the wall, the skeleton of a child and that of a woman, the latter showing signs of age and rheu-

---

[1] For example Deut. xii. 31 ; xviii. 9–12.
[2] Philo of Byblos, Fr. ii, 24.
[3] Diod. Sic., xx, 14 and 65, for Carthage.
[4] At Gezer, see p. 89 ; at Megiddo, **MN**, 1904, pp. 49–50 (fig. 14).
[5] At Megiddo, **MN**, 1906, pp. 60 (fig. 56), 61. On Carthage, **CXI**, pp. 137–8.
[6] **MN**, 1905, p. 11 (fig. 11) ; **CLIX**, pp. 196–8 (figs. 141–2).
[7] *Ibid.*, 1906, pp. 8–9 ; **XXIII**[2], ii (fig. 229) ; **XLIII**, p. 57 (fig. 9).
[8] Sellin, **NKZ**, 1905, p. 127 ; **CLIX**, pp. 53, 200.

matism.[1]　The last instance suggests that among the Canaanites the primitive custom gradually lost its rigour ; they ceased to offer the choicest victims. Occasionally they even replaced the living sacrifice by silver figurines [2] or, from the fifteenth century onwards, simply laid in the foundations the customary accessories, bowls, and especially lamps.[3] The lamp, whose original purpose was to give light to the dead in his subterranean abode, came no doubt later to be regarded as symbolizing, indeed as actually being magically the life itself (*cf.* Prov. xxi. 27).

The skulls buried under a shelf of earth in the great sanctuary at Gezer [4] were no doubt those of captured enemies sacrificed to the god of the city (*cf.* 1 Sam. xv. 31–3). Perhaps we should interpret in the same way the instances in which only parts of a skeleton, a skull or a few bones, were found in a grave.[5] However, the latter case may merely be an example of a widespread custom, that of dismembering the corpse before burial.

The religion of Canaan was a cruel one. It had preserved, in spite of a comparatively advanced civilization, the sanguinary rites of earlier days ; we learn that in the worship of Baal—although the specific reference is to the Baal of Tyre—the prophets, in order to obtain a reply from their god, struck themselves with lances and swords until the blood poured over them while they leaped and uttered loud cries (1 Kings xviii. 28). The object of the worshipper was to arouse the pity of the deity, or else perhaps to exercise upon him a sort of magic compulsion by establishing a blood-bond between himself and the god.

Not only were bloody sacrifices offered to the gods, but also libations, for many bowls have been found which had served this end.[6] Vegetable offerings were also made, especially of loaves or cakes which could be replaced by clay substitutes : hundreds of them have been found in the sanctuaries of Beisan, one in particular of the time of Seti I stamped fourteen times with the Egyptian hieroglyphic

---

[1] **PEF**, 1904, p. 17 ; 1906, p. 64 ; **CLIX**, p. 192, *cf.* pp. 117, 213 ; **XXIII**[2], ii (fig. 227).
[2] Gezer, **XXIII**[2], ii. (fig. 231).
[3] **XXIII**[2], ii (fig. 233) ; **CLIX**, p. 199.　　　　[4] P. 90.
[5] **CXIV**, pp. 38–9 ; **IV**, p. 86.
[6] **CLIX**, p. 180.

symbol *imenyt*, " daily."[1] Thus the Canaanites had already, at least in some of the great sanctuaries, not merely a custom similar to that of the " bread of the presence " which the Hebrew priest renewed each week before Jahweh,[2] but a daily baking of bread for the gods.

They also offered objects of various kinds. In some sanctuaries it seems to have been the custom to break them when they were offered. At Serabit the sacred enclosure was covered with pottery, tablets, bracelets, sistrums, all of them broken into small fragments ; at Gezer not a single one of the bas-reliefs representing the goddess was found intact.[3] In this connexion it may be recalled that there still exists in Syria, at Bludan, near ez-Zebedani, a holy place called " the mother of potsherds." When a woman has obtained an answer to the prayer which she had previously offered to the young girl who is supposed to represent the patron saint of the sanctuary, she brings a jar there and breaks it.[4] It is well known that the same observance occurs in the funeral customs of many peoples : the objects intended for the dead must be killed.[5] The purpose is doubtless the same in both cases : it is to place at the disposal of the dead the things which he needs by setting free their spirit.

IV

SACRED SEASONS

Since the Canaanites were an agricultural people it follows naturally that their religion was of the same nature. The only one of their feasts for which we have direct evidence is the vintage festival ; after they had gathered and pressed the fruit of their vines, the Canaanites of Shechem " kept *hillulim* : they entered into the house of their god Baal Berith ; they ate and drank and drank and cursed Abimelech (their Israelite tyrant) " (Judges ix. 27). The word *hillulim*, which was adopted by the Israelites (Lev. xix. 24)—clearly with the feast itself,—is derived, no doubt, from the joyous shouts which were raised in honour of the god (*hillulah* in

---

[1] **RB**, 1928, p. 132 ; **SY**, 1928, p. 126.
[2] 1 Sam. xxi. 5-7 ; 1 Kings vii. 48 ; Lev. xxiv. 5-9.
[3] **CXIV**, p. 45.   [4] **XV**, 19-20, 88-9, 300-3.
[5] P. 115.

Jewish-Aramaic).[1] One of the elements of the festival was
a sacred meal, when after the first-fruits of his bounty had
been offered to the god, men drank hugely, tongues were
loosed, and at times men betrayed their inward thoughts
by rash speech (Judges ix. 28–9).

By all indications, as is often the case with agricultural
religions, Canaanite religion was of an orgiastic nature : the
ritual tended to stir up in the worshippers a wild excitement ;
maddened by the cries, the dances, the wine, they gave themselves up by turns to unbridled merriment and to the bloody
practices which we have just alluded to, cutting themselves
or offering to the gods whatever they held most dear. For
the same reason ecstatic phenomena and sexual excesses
seem to have played a large part in the religious life of the
inhabitants of Palestine.

So far no documentary evidence has been found showing
that the mourning for the vegetation-god, who dies each year
and is re-born, was ever celebrated in the pre-Israelite period
in Palestine itself, nor even in Phenicia, at Byblos ; but it
is extremely probable that it was so.[2] Obviously, the wild
display of grief which characterized these ceremonies bordered
closely on licence.[3]

V

Sacred Persons

It is *a priori* probable that such of the principal sanctuaries
as possessed an image, a treasure-house or an oracle, had
also a regular and organized priesthood. However, the
existence of priests is not yet actually attested by the
monuments.[4]

On the other hand, the biography of Wen Amon, the

---

[1] Rather than from the purely Arab name of the new moon
hilal (**XC**, pp. 107–9 ; **IX**, *ad loc.* ; **LXXIV**, ii, pp. 138, 139 ; **LXXV**,
p. 90). Wellhausen has given up this etymology in **XC**[2], pp. 110–11.
Lagrange prefers the Assyrian *alalu*, to rejoice (**XLVIII**, *ad loc.*).

[2] See p. 131 ; *cf.* Ezek. viii. 14 ; Zech. xii. 11.

[3] Eusebius, *Vita Constant.*, iii, 55 (on Aphaca, the centre of the
worship of Adonis and Astarte).

[4] The only evidence available is that a letter from Tell el-Amarna
mentions a maid-servant of the Lady of Byblos (**TA(K)**), 84, 1,
42–3 ; *cf.* 86, 1. 25–6), and that, in the reign of Merneptah, a man
of Gaza is described as servant of Baal (**CXIV**, p. 33 ; Paton, **ERE**,
iii, p. 188*a*). See also p. 139.

Egyptian who journeyed through Palestine and Phenicia about the year 1117, describes in detail a scene of prophetic inspiration at Byblos.

> " As the king of the city was sacrificing to his gods, one of his noble pages was possessed by the god and fell on the ground in convulsions ; he cried : Bring hither the god. Bring the messenger of Amon who has entered into him. . . . Dismiss him. . . . Send him away."

The sequel goes on to show that the ecstatic seizure took place or was prolonged during the night.[1] The passage shows that the inspiration, as we see later among the Israelites,[2] might seize any of the persons present. It appears, however, that there were also professional ecstatics : the book of Kings mentions 450 prophets of Baal who were maintained at the court of Queen Jezebel.[3]

But the people to whom the title of sacred men and women belonged by special right (the *qedeshim* and *qedeshoth*) were the men and women who devoted themselves to sacred prostitution. We may gather from the Israelite story of Judah and Tamar that in Canaanite times in the villages of Palestine these sacred persons might often be seen. They importuned the passers-by, and no doubt paid their hire into the coffers of the sanctuary (*cf.* Deut. xxiii. 19). The Israelite historians also mention Canaanite sacred persons (1 Kings xiv. 24), and there were actually such persons who were officially listed under the name of " dogs " (*cf.* Deut. xxiii. 19) among the officials attached to the Phenician temple of Citium in Cyprus.[4] The original object of these customs, thought by some to be merely the survival of a very ancient form of marriage,[5] was, no doubt, either by an act of sympathetic magic to bring about the union of the invisible powers, thus securing the fertility of the soil, the procreation of the cattle, and the increase of the population,[6] or to secure for the worshipper in a highly realistic manner the closest union with the god or the goddess.

---

[1] Translation, **XXXVI**, ii, p. 365.　　　　[2] Pp. 442–8.

[3] 1 Kings xviii. 19. Four hundred prophets of Astarte were added afterwards, of whom no further mention is made in the story.

[4] **CIS,** i, p. 86, A, 1. 15, and B, 1. 10.

[5] **CXIX,** p. 25 ; **XVI,** p. 258, n. 2.

[6] *Cf.* Morris Jastrow, **AJSL,** 1917, pp. 116–18 ; **CXXV,** ii, pp. 98–9 ; **CXXVI,** p. 47, n. 2 ; Jérome Carcopino, **RH,** 1928, pp. 11–13.

CHAPTER II

BELIEFS

I

MAGIC

A S some of the facts already quoted suggest, those ancient
beliefs which underlie the practice of magic loomed
large in the minds of the Canaanites. They believed in a
" sympåthy," an interdependence between many kinds of
beings or facts which we should regard as quite unrelated.
For example, resemblance in their eyes denoted such a
relation ; they were convinced that it was possible tò control
by physical means those forces which we should call moral,
to confine a spirit or spiritual power in an object which thus
became an idol or a protective fetish.

In all the Palestinian excavations great quantities of small
objects have been found which had certainly been used as
amulets : bones pierced with a hole,[1] small perforated black
or white stones,[2] pearls like those to which Palestinian
peasants still attribute curative properties,[3] shell necklaces
such as are still worn by all Arab women and children and
are hung round the necks of mares and she-camels to guard
them against accidents,[4] earrings, often in the shape of rings
or crescents.[5]

The ornaments so found are nearly all coloured, either
red, coral or cornelian, or more often blue, pottery or glass.[6]
The preference for these two colours was not an arbitrary
one. Red, the colour of blood, has a sympathetic participation
in the many magical virtues attributed to the vital fluid : in
a tomb at Megiddo were found bones painted red ; the object
of this widespread practice was apparently to restore life to

---

[1] **IV**, p. 75.   [2] **CLIX**, p. 176.   [3] **CXIV**, p. 51.
[4] **IV**, p. 74 (cf. **LXXII**, iii, p. 314).   [5] P. 216.
[6] See, for example, **LXXX**, i, pp. 376–82.

the dead, and to strengthen him against the evil powers which threatened him.[1] Even today, coral pendants are supposed to give protection against the evil eye.[2] But blue is pre-eminently the colour which possesses this latter property ; the reason is obvious : blue eyes being rare in the East, are supposed to have a particularly evil influence. Hence, to carry about on one's person an object of the same colour is the homeopathic means best calculated to ward off their malign influence.[3]

The numerous statuettes of deities, usually Egyptian, discovered in Palestine were also amulets.[4] So too were the jewels in the form of an eye, called " Horus-eyes." In Egypt these objects were regarded as a most valuable gift, because, according to the myth, Horus restored his father Osiris to life by giving him one of his eyes to eat.[5] But in Canaan, as in the East today, a prophylactic value was also attributed to them.[6]

It has been supposed, with some probability, that a camel's skull, found at Taanach, was used to protect the house in whose ruins it was discovered. In Hebron, they still place a camel's skull near the door of a house with the same object.[7]

Possibly the bronze serpent in the sacrificial pit at Gezer [8] was used as a protection against the bite of real or imaginary reptiles, like the serpent of brass lifted up by Moses in the wilderness.[9] Glaser found in Arabia bronze serpents which had been used as amulets : since the head had been pierced to allow of the passage of a cord for suspension.[10]

An Egyptian story,[11] composed about the time of the twentieth dynasty, according to Maspero, represents the Canaanites, as believing that the sceptre of the King of Egypt contained, and could transmit to the possessor, the supernatural powers belonging to the Pharaoh, invincibility,[12] or

---

[1] Duhn, *Rot und Tot* (**AR,** 1906, p. 9). *Cf. Odyssey,* xi, 96–9.
[2] **CXIV,** p. 51.　　　　　　　[3] **IV,** p. 74 ; **CXXIX,** pp. 8–10.
[4] **LXXX,** p. 376.　　　　　　[5] **XXI,** pp. 37, 48.
[6] **CXIV,** p. 52.
[7] **IV,** p. 75. As at el-Kantara (Algeria) under a palm-tree " for the *baraka.*"
[8] Pp. 88 *f.*
[9] Num. xxi. 6–9 ; 2 Kings xviii. 4 ; **LVI,** pp. 184–5, 191.
[10] **IV,** p. 75.　　　　　　　[11] **LXIV²,** p. 151.
[12] *Cf.* Exod. xvii. 9–13 ; Joshua viii. 18, 26.

perhaps "life, health and strength," the privileges of the sons of Ra.[1]

The Canaanites made use of the formidable powers of magic not only to benefit themselves, but also to harm their enemies. The drinking-vessel found at Gezer, made of a piece of human skull,[2] may be interpreted in either sense: the possessor of this sinister cup may have wished, in drinking out of it, to imbue himself with the virtues of some revered relative or some brave foe, or, on the other hand, to perpetuate the sufferings of a dead enemy by keeping in his possession a portion of the wretched individual's corpse.

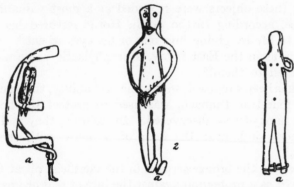

FIG. 33. BOUND FIGURINES FROM SANDAHANNA.

The sixteen lead figurines found at Tell Sandahanna, the probable site of the ancient Mareshah, are, on the other hand, clear evidence of sorcery, that is, black magic; these rude figures had the hands tied on the chest or behind the back with lead, iron, or bronze threads, and several of them had the feet tied in the same way ([3] and fig. 33). Clermont Ganneau was the first to see [4] that these figurines were intended to cripple the persons whom they represented: it was imagined that by binding a person's effigy he himself could be rendered powerless. The date of these objects is fairly late, apparently of the Seleucid era, but the practices

[1] Cf. XXXVI, ii, pp. 368–369; 2 Kings iv. 29–31; RHP, 1927, p. 14.
[2] Thiersch, AA, 1909, p. 360.
[3] CII, p. 154; PEF, QS, 1900, pp. 332–4; cf. RHP, 1927, pp. 12–14.
[4] CVIII, iv, pp. 156–8.

to which they bear witness must have been of ancient standing in Palestine. For binding has been practised in the East for many centuries : among the Hittites,[1] the Assyrians [2] and the Israelites (Ezek. xiii. 8–20). Moreover, Deuteronomy supposes the existence among the Canaanites themselves of a class of sorcerers called " binders of knots," *ḥober ḥaber* (Deut. xviii. 11).

The name of the city of Akshaph, dating back to the time of Thothmes III (1501–1447), suggests that magicians (*kashshaph, mekashsheph*) must have been numerous in Canaan.[3] Such a one may have been the possessor of the alabaster jar containing sixty-six little white pebbles, found at Taanach.[4]

II

ORDEALS AND ORACLES

The transition from magic to divination is very gradual. Among primitive peoples the ordeal has its own inherent efficacy, and an omen is thought of as being the cause of the event which it foretells, or rather as being already the event itself.[5] Only later, apparently, is the sign interpreted as the gracious revelation of a god concerning a future which is still shrouded in mystery. These different conceptions existed side by side among the Canaanites.

Near Shechem there was an oak, or terebinth, which the Canaanites held sacred under the name of the " diviners' oak " (Judges ix. 37), seemingly the same as the one which was known as the " oak which gives oracles " (Gen. xii. 6 ; *cf.* Deut. xi. 30). The diviners probably drew their omens from the rustling of the leaves (*cf.* 2 Sam. v. 24).

The heel-bones of men and animals have been found in great quantities at Taanach, sometimes in groups of four or six. It is possible that these were used for a game like the Arab *ki'ab* : a game in which winning or losing depended on the position in which the bone fell when it was thrown into the air. The game itself, however, may have arisen out of what was originally a means of divination.[6]

---

[1] **XXXIII**, p. 170. [2] **CXXIV**, pp. 78–80.
[3] *Cf.* Deut. xviii. 10 ; **IV**, pp. 76, 125.
[4] **CLIII**, pp. 42, 172 ; *cf.* **CLIX**, p. 178 ; **IV**, p. 76.
[5] **LII**, pp. 124–70. [6] **CLIII**, p. 112 (*cf.* **IV**, p. 76).

A passage from Deuteronomy already alluded to seems to attest the presence among the Canaanites not only of magicians, but also of diviners of various kinds which it is unfortunately difficult to distinguish : the *qosem*, who perhaps used arrows, as in the *istiqsam* of the Arabs ; the *me'onen*,[1] probably more of a diviner than a magician ; the *menahesh*, an interpreter of omens such as those derived from consulting a magic cup (Gen. xliv. 15) or from the first word spoken (1 Kings xx. 33) ; the necromancer, who consulted *obh* and *yidde'oni*, that is, apparently, the spirits of the dead who were supposed to possess a knowledge of the future (Deut. xviii. 9–15).

People also consulted the gods. A letter found at Taanach alludes to a direction given by the finger of Ashirath.[2] Possibly the expression may be taken literally, and refers to a statue of the goddess with a movable hand.[3]

III

Sacred Animals. Traces of Totemism

The Canaanites believed, or at an earlier period had believed, in the supernatural power or knowledge of certain animals or species of animals. Names of places such as " the city of the serpent (1 Chron. iv. 12), " the reptile's stone " (1 Kings i. 9), near the sacred well of the Fuller, the modern Job's Well to the south of Jerusalem, " the dragon's well " (Neh. ii. 13), suggest that certain local gods or spirits were conceived of under the form of a serpent, and chthonian divinities were often thought of as frequenting a spring or a cave.

At Beit Mirsim (probably the ancient Debir), Prof. Albright has recently found a fragment of a stele apparently belonging to the sixteenth century, and representing a great serpent coiled round the garment of what appears to be a god ([4] and pl. vii, 1).

At Beth Shan a serpent seems to have been closely connected with the cult of a local goddess. This animal occurs on many of the objects found in the temples,[5] especially on

[1] *Cf.* also Judges ix. 37.   [2] *Cf.* Exod. viii. 15.
[3] **CXIV**, p. 53 ; **XIII**, p. 346.
[4] Albright, **ZATW**, 1929, pp. 6–7 ; **RB**, 1929, pp. 105–6 and pl. iii.
[5] **RB**, 1928, p. 134 ; 1929, pp. 87–8.

Plate VII

1. Stele of Beit-Mirsim

2. Small Model of a Temple, found
at Beisan
(*See* p. 109)

3. Fragment of Uraeus,
found at Beisan
(*See* p. 109)

PLATE VIII

BULL SURMOUNTED BY A FISH, BAS-RELIEF FROM ER-RUMMAN

those small objects, some cylindrical in shape, others in the form of a house with several stories, in which a serpent is represented as going in and out at the windows of a building at whose openings figures of deities appear.[1] In these the goddess is represented as holding birds, possibly doves, in her hands (pl. vii, fig. 2).

On an Egyptian monument may be seen the Asiatic goddess Kadesh standing on a lioness and strangling a serpent.[2]

This raises the question of earlier theriomorphic divinities ; where the human representation of the gods prevailed, the animal was reduced, as often happened, to the level of an attribute of a god, or to that of an enemy vanquished by him. On one of the pottery plaques found at Beisan, the sacred serpent is represented with the breasts of a woman under which is placed a cup to receive the nourishing fluid ([3] and pl. vii). This suggests that the serpent was originally the goddess herself. Following Jirku,[4] Rowe and P. Vincent,[5] one is tempted to identify her with the serpent-goddess *Šaḥan, Shahan* or *Sha'an,*[6] mentioned in several Babylonian texts as the god or goddess of health, and to suppose that Beth Shan owed its name to the temple of this serpent-goddess Sha'an. The healing serpent is probably related to the sacred serpent of Eshmun-Asclepios and to the brazen serpent of the Mosaic tradition.[7]

The god of Ekron bore the title of Baal Zebub, the lord of flies,[8] perhaps because he was supposed to have the power of bringing or warding off these insects, conceived as the demons of certain diseases : at Elis in Greece, there was a god called Muiagrios, because he was supposed to possess the special power of driving away flies and thus of preventing

---

[1] **CXIII**, p. 262 (fig. 159). They were used, it seems, as censers and for tables of offerings : **XXIII²**, ii, pp. 127–8 and figs. 441–3.

[2] **LXVIII**, p. 379 (fig. 40).

[3] **RB**, 1928, pp. 137–8.

[4] **RB**, 1928, p. 128, pl. x, 4 (upside-down).

[5] **XXXVIII**, p. 135.

[6] " May thy god, the god Ša'an, make thee live," **CT**, ii, pl. 49, 1, 4 (**RB**, 1928, p. 138). *Ibi-Šaḥan* alternates with the spelling *Ibi-Ša'an* (**XXXIV**, i, p. 167).

[7] See pp. 138–9 ; 459–60.

[8] A Semitic divinity, to judge by his name : the Philistine rulers of the town had doubtless adopted him as they had Dagon.

epidemics ; [1] hence we can well understand why a king of
Israel should have sent to consult the above-mentioned god of
Ekron when he was sick (2 Kings i. 2–6). [2]

Elsewhere the old theriomorphic conception survived in
another fashion, in which the divinity assumed a half-human,
half-animal form ; Atargatis, for instance, to whom certain
fish were sacred : she is probably represented by a bronze
figurine found at Tell Zachariyeh (fig. 34), having the head
and bust of a woman, with the body and tail of a fish. [3]   The
baals of Arvad and of Ascalon were depicted on the coinage
in a similar fashion. [4]   This is probably the explanation of
the type of goddess whose head is adorned with the horns of

FIG. 34. ATARGATIS.

a cow or a ram : [5]   hence may have come the name of the city
of Ashteroth Karnaim, the horned Astartes. [6]

If the female divinity was represented under the form of a
cow, it was natural that the god should be conceived of as a
bull.   Such a god was doubtless represented by the little
bronze from Rihab (fig. 35), the bas-relief of er-Rumman
([7] and pl. viii), and the many statuettes in the shape of a
bull's head or fore-quarters, found in Palestinian excavations. [8]

[1] *Cf.* Pliny, H. N., x, 28, 75 ; Pausanias, viii, 14, 2 ; Clement of
Alexandria, *Protrept.* ii, 38.   Phylarch (*Fragm. Hist. græc.*, i, 147)
and Menander (iv, 447) according to the testimony of Lydus (*De
mensibus*, p. 171, ed. Wunsch), mention a Kronos, who allowed neither
woman, dog, nor fly in his sanctuary : *cf.* **XLIX**, p. 85.
[2] *Cf.* **LV**, p. 185.
[3] **CII**, pp. 148 *ff.*   This agrees with the description given by
Diodorus (ii, 4, 2) of the goddess of Ascalon.   *Cf. De dea Syria*, § 14.
[4] **XLIX**, p. 131.
[5] Macalister, **PEF, QS**, 1903, pp. 227–8 ; **CLIX**, p. 164 (fig. 107).
[6] Gen. xiv. 5.   The Greek version, however, gives " Ashtaroth *and*
Qarnaim."
[7] **XXIII** [2], ii (figs. 352 and 353).
[8] **CLIX**, p. 169 (fig. 116) ; the same at Byblos, **SY**, 1927, p. 98 and
pl. xxiv ; at Qatna ; **SY**, 1928, p. 93.

Possibly the bull here was simply the embodiment of certain attributes of the god : for agriculturists the bull represents strength and fertilizing power. Bull-gods or gods riding on a bull were common in western Asia.[1] It can hardly be doubted, as we shall see, that the Israelites, in this regard, followed the example of the earlier inhabitants of the land.[2]

The Canaanites had food tabus similar to those which were codified later in the Jewish ritual regulations. Perhaps the customs of the ancient inhabitants of Palestine may throw light on the original meaning of the practices of their Hebrew kinsfolk and successors.

These are the facts. The Canaanites, including the in-

FIG. 35. BRONZE FROM RIḤAB.

habitants of Syria in general, abstained from eating the fish which was sacred to Atargatis, in the belief that this food would cause ulcers ; on the other hand they sacrificed them to the goddess,[3] and the priests were said to eat them.[4]

The pig, which had been freely killed and eaten from pre-Semitic times, as is shown by the quantities of pig's bones found at Gezer in the neolithic stratum,[5] was tabu for the Semites of Syria in the historical period. Some of them, we are told, held it as unclean, while others regarded it as sacred.[6] The part played by the boar in the popular agrarian myth of Adonis is well known : hence we can understand how the Israelites came to refrain from the flesh of an animal of such

[1] **XIII,** p. 351 ; **XCIII,** pp. 448–9 ; **XXIII**[2], ii (figs. 355 and 356) ; **MOB,** 1910, p. 182.
[2] Pp. 319 ; 558–9. [3] Athen, 346. [4] **XLIX,** p. 131.
[5] **CXIV,** pp. 47–8 ; **CLIX,** pp. 188, n. 1, 202.
[6] *De dea Syria,* § 54.

dangerous potentialities, were it god or demon, and that, on the other hand, some of them, forsaking the national traditions, should have come to regard the sacrifice of the pig as particularly efficacious (Isa. lxv. 4; lxvi. 17).

The Canaanites, no doubt, believed that it was extremely dangerous to partake of the flesh of any living thing endowed with supernatural qualities : the epithet " sacred " applied to such animals implied that they were full of divine potency available under certain conditions ; they could also be called unclean from the point of view of other deities to whom, of course, these animals could not be sacrificed, or to show that they were debarred from common use. " Unclean " and " sacred," as Robertson Smith has shown, were for the Semites simply two aspects of the same idea, that which was tabu, forbidden. In practice the distinction was slight.

Whence, then, arose the veneration surrounding certain kinds of animals ? Was it because they were thought to possess power or knowledge more than human, or were they originally held to be ancestors ? (Totemism.)

Quite a number of peoples and clans of ancient Palestine bore names of animals or plants. For example, the sons of Hamor, i.e. the ass, at Shechem (Gen. xxxiii. 19 ; Joshua xxiv. 32 ; Judges ix. 28 ; cf. Gen. xxxiv. 2–26). The same may be true of the Hivites, if the name means the serpent-men.[1] Names of this kind are particularly numerous in the list of Horite clans [2] : Shobal, lion's whelp ; Zibon, hyena ; Ana, onager ; Dishon, gazelle ; Aya, kite ; Aran, ash or ibex ; Keran, sheep.[3]

Many cities in Canaan had names of animals or plants : for instance, Aijalon (cf. 'ayyal, a stag), Eglon (cf. 'egel, a calf), Shaalbim (which may be connected with shu'al, a fox), Ephron (cf. 'opher, a gazelle), Beth Hoglah (the house of the partridge ?), Beth Lebaoth (the house of the lionesses), Beth Nimrah (the house of the panther). It is quite possible that some of these cities may have taken the names of clans that settled there.

This was one of Robertson Smith's main arguments for the view that the ancient Semites had practised totemism. But as Nöldeke has shown, the proof is not conclusive ; a

[1] See p. 55.   [2] Gen. xxxvi. 20–30. Cf. pp. 55–6.
[3] LI, p. 21.

PLATE IX

LION, FROM SHEIKH SA'D

PLATE X

STELE OF MIKAL— THE GOD OF BETH SHAN
(*See* p. 129)

group might have taken the name of an animal because they desired the qualities which they thought it possessed, without believing that they were thereby related to every member of the species in question. We shall return to the question of Semitic totemism in dealing with the Hebrews.[1]

IV

THE DEAD [2]

Excavations in Palestine have given us copious information about the Canaanites' methods of burial, but unfortunately, much less about their beliefs concerning the after-life.

As we have seen, cremation [3] was practised by the ancient population of the country up to about the middle of the third millennium. From this date, the time when the first Semites are supposed to have arrived, burial seems to have been the only method of disposing of the dead, apart from exceptional cases like human sacrifices.

The passage from one mode of disposal to the other must have been abrupt : the cave which, for many centuries, had been used by the inhabitants of Gezer as a crematorium, at a definite moment became a cemetery ; the bodies of the dead were simply laid on the ashes of the old burnings.[4]

The bodies of children were often placed in a jar filled with finely sifted earth (pl. xiii), or enclosed in two urns placed mouth to mouth.[5] Most of the skeletons of adults which have been found were laid in natural or artificial caves in the hillside ; access was by a vertical shaft or a gallery, only partly blocked up. The bodies were generally laid on the side, regardless of orientation, with the knees drawn up under the chin in the fœtal position. They were often laid in a kind of hollow in the floor of the cave, whose purpose is not clear, or else on shelves running along the walls.[6] According to the Egyptian story of Sinuhe, the Asiatic inhabitants of the land of Tenu, *i.e.* Syria and Palestine, at the time of burial, placed the body in a sheepskin.[7]

---

[1] P. 40.
[2] **CLIX**, pp. 204–96 ; **IV**, pp. 85–91 ; **CXIV**, pp. 34–7, 55–60.
[3] Pp. 40–1.
[4] **IV**, p. 85. [5] **XXIII**[2], ii (figs. 226 and 228).
[6] **CLIX**, pp. 227–8 (fig. 159). [7] *Cf.* **XXXVI**, ii, p. 141.

In the royal necropolis at Byblos, the corpses were not laid side by side on the floor of the cave, but shut up with sumptuous funeral furnishings in massive stone sarcophagi, and as an additional precaution, on one of the coffins—that of Ahiram, the father of king Ithobaal—were engraved terrible curses against the profane person who should dare to open it.[1] But these luxurious burials were the privilege of a select few. In Palestine itself no similar burials have been found going back to pre-Israelite times.

In the necropolis of Beisan, however, there were found a number of pottery sarcophagi, of the " slipper " shape and anthropoid in form. In the place of the face was a large mask serving as a lid for the opening by which the body was introduced. Everything appears to indicate that these burials were those of the soldiers of the Egyptian garrison : they date from the reigns of Thothmes III, Ramses II and Ramses III, and contain purely Egyptian objects, such as statuettes of " sureties." Exactly similar sarcophagi have been found in Egypt from the eighteenth to the twenty-sixth dynasty.[2]

Where caves were lacking, arched vaults were sometimes used instead.[3]

Not everyone could afford to provide for himself a burial-chamber. Hence the Canaanites also buried the dead in the ground, either with or without stones to protect the corpse, and with or without a coffin. Near Gezer there were found great pits filled with the bones of men and animals (camels, cows, asses, horses) : these were no doubt public burial-places of the same kind as those " graves of the common people " into which the Israelite threw the corpses of criminals so that their punishment might continue after death (Jer. xxvi. 23), the dreaded penalty with which Jeremiah threatens king Jehoiakim when he declares that he shall have the burial of an ass, dragged through the streets and thrown outside the gates of Jerusalem (Jer. xxii. 19).

Beside the corpse were laid all his personal belongings : weapons, jewels, amulets, stone or metal knives, cups, dishes, jars, lamps.[4] Such a practice proves that the Canaanites

---

[1] SY, 1924, pp. 185–41 ; 1925, pp. 104–7.
[2] Dhorme, RB, 1927, pp. 100–1.   [3] CLIX, p. 223 (fig. 153).
[4] MN, 1905, pp. 10, 12–13 ; 1906, p. 55.

believed that the dead continued to live on in the grave,
" his eternal abode," as the inscription of Ahiram seems to
call it.[1] Sometimes the objects deposited with the dead were
" killed " by breaking them or boring them with a hole, no
doubt with the purpose, as we have seen, to enable the spirit
of the object to accompany the spirit of the dead ; [2] sometimes, with the same end in view, they made use of objects
left purposely incomplete, such as vases of animal form but
without a head.[3]

They thought of the dead as still subject to hunger and
especially to thirst. Some of the dishes laid in the tomb
still contained, when they were found, the remains of food
and bones of animals, the jars held what had once been milk.[4]
In a grave at Gezer there was found a bronze knife-blade
lying on a dish that had once contained a piece of sheep's
flesh, for the dead must surely be provided with means to
cut his meat. They even took care to cover the dish in order
to keep the meat hot. There was often a cup beside the
jar of water.

From the necessity of renewing these offerings of food
there arose a regular ritual practice. Some of the tombs
were provided with holes through which the dead could be
supplied with food and drink : for example, the keystone of
a funerary chamber at Megiddo was pierced with a funnel-
shaped passage 20 cm. wide.[5]

For the same reason, apparently, the grave was never
entirely closed. Access to it was made difficult, to keep off
beasts of prey or thieves ; a lateral passage was blocked
with stones, or a vertical one closed by a slab ; [6] but some
means of entrance to the grave was always provided, by steps,
for instance, cut in the wall of the shaft.[7]

It would also appear that animal victims were killed for
the dead, and hence that sacrifices were made to them as if
they were gods. In fact, pits have been found in several
graves, containing ashes, bones of animals, and cinders.[8]

[1] *Cf.* Eccles. xii. 5 ; Tob. iii. 6, the ἀΐδιους οἴκους of the Egyptians
(Diod. i. 51) and the *domus æterna* of the Roman inscriptions.
[2] See p. 101. [3] **IV**, p. 91.
[4] **MN**, 1906, pp. 9, 19.
[5] *Ibid.*, pp. 23, 60 ; **CLIX**, p. 223 (fig. 153).
[6] **CLIX**, p. 226 (figs. 157 and 159). [7] *Ibid.*, p. 226 (fig. 158).
[8] **MN**, 1906, p. 54 ; 1904, p. 53.

Prof. Sellin even thinks that he has found in the fortress at Taanach an altar reserved for the dead, since he considers that a channel leading from this *eschara* and running along a stairway carried the blood of the victims into a chamber below.[1] However, the funerary character of this chamber is uncertain.[2]

Nevertheless, the cup-holes often found near the grave are more probably intended to carry blood or libations [3] to the dead than to receive rain-water to quench his thirst or to contain flowers " symbolizing the mysteries of death and resurrection."[4]

Some cases are cited of the burial of adults inside the house. This fairly widespread Semitic custom [5] is perhaps a survival of an older ancestor-worship.

The children found buried within a house or city call for a different explanation. This would rather point to a Canaanite belief in the possibility of reincarnation, a belief common to many ancient peoples, and, it would seem, specially characteristic of the Semites. It cannot be maintained that all these children were first-born offered to a god, or victims of the rite of foundation sacrifice ; for there were found among them a number evidently still-born, incompletely developed embryos.[6] The purpose of burying them in a much-frequented spot was to give their supposedly restless and therefore dangerous spirits [7] every opportunity of entering the body of a woman who might afford them a reentrance to the world of men. The Egyptian fellaheen even now bury their still-born children under the house.[8] Moreover, another fact which suggests that the original reason for this custom was the hope of re-birth is that many peoples who usually practised cremation refused to burn the bodies

---

[1] **NKZ,** 1909, p. 127 ; **MN,** 1905, p. 35.

[2] **CLIX,** pp. 97–9. Hugo Gressmann regards the great temple of Byblos as a sanctuary dedicated to the cult of the dead kings of the city ; the *masseboth* are funerary steles (**ZATW,** 1924, p. 351); *cf.* Vincent, **RB,** 1923, pp. 552 *ff.* ; 1924, pp. 161 *ff.*

[3] **CLIX,** p. 214.   [4] **CXIV,** p. 36.

[5] *Cf.* 1 Sam. xxv. 1 ; 1 Kings ii. 34 ; *cf.* Isaiah xiv. 18 ; Ezek. xliii. 7–8 ; **LVIII,** i, pp. 182, 198–9.

[6] **MN,** 1905, p. 11 ; 1906, p. 55 ; **CLIX,** pp. 193–5, 222, 282–4.

[7] Thureau-Dangin, **RA,** 1922, pp. 81–2.

[8] Macalister, **PEF, QS,** 1906, p. 64.

of new-born infants and preferred to bury them by the side of a road, the Greeks and Romans for instance.[1]

We know little or nothing of the ancient Canaanites' beliefs concerning the conditions of life in the after-world. The Phenician inscriptions of Tabnith and Eshmunazar tell us that those who were buried with due rites and whose tombs remained unviolated were supposed to rest upon their beds among the Rephaim, who were, no doubt, the aristocracy of the dead. Although these texts are of late date,[2] it is not improbable that the belief in a common kingdom of the dead existed from a very early date, as it did among the Israelites, side by side with the idea that the tomb was " the eternal abode " of the dead.

It would clearly be illegitimate to generalize from the case of the Palestinian soldier whose grave was found at Tell el-Amarna in Egypt, and who had adopted the beliefs of this country as to the future life,[3] any more than from the case of a certain Heqab who, in an inscription found at Gezer, is declared " justified," according to the Osirian formula.[4] He would be a visiting Egyptian ; perhaps the very statuette upon which the inscription was engraved may have been imported from the land of the Pharaohs.

Amen-em-Opet, the architect of Beth Shan, for whom his son Pa-Ra-em-heb dedicated a stele to Mikal beseeching the god to grant his dead father " life, health, strength, provisions, favour, love, the privilege of mounting the throne and attaining honour in peace,"[5] would also be an Egyptian, to judge by his name and that of his son, as well as by their dress. The same may be said about Hesi-Nesht, who entreats the favour of Anath for his *ka*, that is, his double after death. The prayer runs : " May the king give a gift ! May Anath give life, strength and health to the *ka* of Hesi-Nesht ! "[6]

It is, however, significant that these favours beyond the grave should be asked of Canaanite deities, and it is well

---

[1] **LVIII,** ii, p. 117. According to M. van Gennep (**CXXVI,** p. 117) this was because the children had not yet a soul.

[2] Sixth (Th. Reinach), fifth (Dussaud, Contenau), or the fourth century (Clermont-Ganneau). *Cf.* **CXI,** pp. 243–7.

[3] **CXIV,** p. 76.

[4] " May the king give an offering and (the god) Ptah-Sokhar to the *ka* of the (royal) taster Heqab, justified," **PEF,** 1906, pp. 121–2.

[5] P. 129 ; *cf.* Mallon, **SY,** 1928, p. 127.

[6] P. 132.

within the bounds of possibility that Egyptian beliefs concerning the after-life should have impressed some of the inhabitants of Palestine, during the period of their constant contact with the subjects of the Pharaoh.

V

DIVINE KINGS

There are indications that some of the Canaanite kings may have claimed the right to receive divine honours after death and to live among the gods. Wen Amon, the envoy of the King of Egypt, attributes this belief to the King of Byblos. For he promises that if he will grant the wood needed for the barque of Amon, this god will give him " 10,000 years of life beyond his allotted portion " ; he undertakes to engrave the record of his liberality upon a stele, and adds : " In the future, when a messenger comes from the land of Egypt who shall read the inscription and recognize thy name upon the stele, thou shalt receive the water of Amenti (*i.e.* the libations of fresh water which were made to the dead), like the gods who dwell there."[1]

That the Egyptian author's attribution to a Canaanite of beliefs concerning the after-life proper to the subjects of the Pharaoh is not unwarranted, follows from the fact that the same suggestion occurs in greater detail in the inscription of Panammu : this King of Yaudi in the north of Syria expected after his death to be associated with Hadad and to share in the offerings and libations made to this great god.[2] It is true, the passage occurs in an Aramæan text of the eighth century.

But there is reason to believe that the ancient kings of Byblos claimed similar privileges at an earlier date, since their necropolis was in the immediate vicinity of the great temple.[3]

There is, however, no ground for supposing that the hope of such privileges as might be enjoyed by their kings in the

---

[1] Pap. Golenicheff, 2, 58–60 ; *cf.* **XXXVI**, ii, p. 369 ; **XXIII²**, i, p. 76.

[2] Inscr. of Hadad, ll. 15–24 ; *cf.* **XLIX**, pp. 492–4 ; **CXIV**, pp. 57–60.

[3] *Cf.* Gressmann, **ZATW**, 1924, p. 351.

future life was extended by the Canaanites to all their dead.
The king must have been for them, as for many other peoples,
a being apart, a kind of living god upon earth.

The Tell el-Amarna letters afford ample proof that the
Canaanites used the formulas and practised the rites of this cult
of the king in the centuries during which they were the subjects
of the Pharaoh, the son of Ra [1] : they addressed him as " my
god;" prostrated themselves seven times before him, styled
themselves his footstool, the dust under his feet and so forth.
It is extremely probable that either in imitation of Egyptian,
Babylonian, and Hittite kings, or as a result of the survival
of beliefs current among the non-civilized peoples of Canaan,
the kings of Canaan claimed similar honours from their own
people.

Tabnith, prince of Sidon, was a priest-king like his father
Eshmunazar I, [2] while Hebrew tradition preserved the legend
of Melchizedek, a Canaanite king of Salem, who was a priest
of the god El elyon (Gen. xiv. 18–20).

The ritual of anointing the king, which is found for the
first time in a Syrian State of the sixteenth century, was
possibly intended to transmit to the new king the divine
power for his future use. In the text referred to, one of the
Tell el-Amarna letters, the prince of Nuḥašši [3] mentions that
Thothmes III poured oil on his grandfather's head at his
coronation. [4] Since this text dates from the age of Egyptian
suzerainty, it would seem to have been customary for the
Pharaoh, the Sun-god of Egypt, to anoint his Syrian vassal-
kings.

It is possible that the rite, in this form, may have been
of Egyptian origin. [5] There appears to have been another
form in which the subjects " rubbed " their king, perhaps in
order to absorb some of the superior power or spiritual potency
which would henceforth reside in him by virtue of his
kingship. [6]

---

[1] P. 140.
[2] **XLIX**, p. 481 ; **CXI**, p. 145.
[3] In the region of Aleppo, according to **XCIII**, p. 181 ; **XX**, p.
109.
[4] **TA(W)**, 37 (K, 51), ll. 4–7.
[5] **XXI**, i, 317 ; Spiegelberg, **AR**, 1906, p. 144.
[6] Wellhausen, **AR**, 1904, pp. 33–41.

VI

THE GODS

1. *Traces of Polydæmonism*

The worship, in the strict sense, of the Canaanites, at the time when the Hebrews came into contact with them, was principally directed to those deities whom the Israelite writers usually describe as the baals and the Astartes (Judges x. 6 ; 1 Sam. vii. 4 ; xii. 10, etc.).

The " baals " were the numerous local divinities who were worshipped " on every high hill and under every green tree " in the land. Baal was not the proper name of a particular god, but an appellative meaning " master, lord," and applied to many divine beings : used alone it was always accompanied by the article, " *the* lord." Generally a determinative word was added to limit it to the particular one of the many " lords " whom it was intended to designate.

The defining word thus added to the title " baal," or to its feminine " baalath " in the case of a goddess, was often the name of the holy thing (mountain, tree, spring), or of the locality of which the designated deity was " lord " or " lady," as the case might be. For example, Baal Lebanon,[1] the lord of Lebanon ; [2] Baal Tamar,[3] the master or the spirit of the palm-tree ; Baalath Beer,[4] the lady of the well ; Baal Perazim,[5] the lord of the breaches, that is, perhaps, of welling springs ; Baalath Gebal, the lady of Byblos,[6] with her consort, Baal Gebal, the lord of the same city ; [7] Baal Meon,[8]

---

[1] **CIS**, i, p. 5.

[2] We do not include the title Baal Hermon, " Lord of Mt. Hermon," since the text of the passages in which it occurs is probably corrupt : Judges iii. 3 ; 1 Chron. v. 23.

[3] Judges xx. 33.   [4] Joshua xix. 8.

[5] 2 Sam. v. 20 ; 1 Chron. xiv. 11.

[6] For example, **SY**, 1925, p. 109 (pl. xxv) ; **TA(W)**, 55 *ff.* (K, 68 *ff.*).

[7] **SY**, 1924, pp. 145–7 ; 1925, p. 111 ; P. Montet, **AI**, 1921, p. 167.

[8] Num. xxxii. 38 ; Exod. xxv. 9 ; 1 Chron. v. 8. This name, like most of those which have been or will be cited, is only attested as a place-name ; but the variants Beth Baal Meon, " house (temple) of Baal Meon," Joshua xiii, 17, and Beth Meon, " house of Meon," Jer. xlviii, 23, prove that the form Baal Meon was an abbreviation in which nothing but the name of the local god had survived.

Baal Peor,[1] Baal Hazor,[2] Baal Hamon,[3] Baal Shalishah,[4] Baal Jehudah,[5] Baliras.[6]

Sometimes the local divinity was known by the same title of baal, accompanied by a word indicating the distinguishing rite of his cult, or some special power that was attributed to him. Such was Baal Marqod, the lord of the dance, who had a sanctuary with an " assistant priest " at Deir el-qal'a near Beirut, and whose real name was Megrin, *i.e.* perhaps, he who fills the threshing-floors.[7] Other instances are Baal Berith,[8] the god of the covenant, or better, perhaps, Bethel Berith, the Baityl, the sacred stone of the covenant [9] : these titles may have been given to the god of Shechem because it was his special province to guard the keeping of oaths taken before him, as the *Zeus Horkios* of the Greeks, the Roman *Jupiter Jurarius*, and doubtless the god of Hermon,[10] Baal Marphe, was a " lord of healing."[11] The name Baal Gad [12] means " the master of good luck," or " the lord Fortune." The sick consulted Baal Zebub, the lord of flies.[13]

Sometimes the addition to the title baal was merely a general

---

[1] Deut. iv. 3 ; Hos. ix. 10. Variant : Beth Peor (Deut. iii. 29 ; iv. 46 ; Joshua xiii. 20).

[2] 2 Sam. xiii. 23.   [3] Cant. viii, 11.

[4] 2 Kings iv. 42 ; *cf.* 1 Sam. ix. 4.

[5] Corrupted into Baale Yehudah, " the lords of Judah." But the city, Kirjath Jearim, was also called Kirjath Baal, " the city of Baal " (Joshua xv. 60 ; xviii. 14), or Baalah, " the lady " (Joshua xv. 9–11 ; 1 Chron. xiii. 6).

[6] That is, " the lord of the Cape," the name of the headland to the south of Nahr el-Kelb, where Shalmanezer III claimed to have erected his statue (**XXXVI**, ii, p. 301).

[7] **CVIII**, i, pp. 94–5, 103–4 ; *cf.* **XLIX**, p. 84 ; **RB**, 1896, p. 229.

[8] Judges viii. 33 ; ix. 4.

[9] Judges ix. 46, if we render " in the tower of Bethel Berith " (**RHR**, lxxxvi, p. 245).

[10] Hence, perhaps, the great number of " covenant " episodes assigned to Shechem by the Israelite traditions : a covenant of Jahweh with Abraham (Gen. xv.), the proposed treaty between Jacob and the sons of Hamor (Gen. xxxiv.), the treaty between Abimelech and the men of Shechem (Judges ix. 1–4), the attempted agreement between Rehoboam and the tribes of Israel (1 Kings xii. 1–19), and especially the great covenant rituals performed by Joshua, in the various holy places in the neighbourhood of Shechem (Deut. xi. 29–30 ; xxvii. 1–26 ; Joshua viii. 30–35 ; xxiv. 1–28). It seems hardly probable that the god of Shechem would derive his name from a particular treaty concluded in his sanctuary (**XVI**, pp. 171–2 ; Waterman, **AJSL**, vol. 38) or to a periodically renewed covenant between the people of Shechem and their god (Gressmann, **XXV**). It is still less likely that his title meant " lord of Beirut." It is equally futile to emend to " lord of the cypress " (Baal Beroth) or to " lord of the wells " (Baal Beeroth) ; *cf.* **IV**, p. 123.

[11] J Ph. 41.

[12] Joshua ii. 17 ; xii. 7 ; xiii. 5 ; it should also probably be restored in Judges iii. 3 ; 1 Chron. v. 23.

[13] Pp. 109–10.

name ; so, probably, Baal Zephon,[1] the lord of the north, if this name means " he who dwells on the mount of the gods in the uttermost north " (*cf.* Isa. xiv. 13) ; Baal Adon, master-lord ;[2] Baldir,[3] if this name is equivalent to the words *Baal addir,* " majestic lord." But even in this case the use of a specific title has the force of distinguishing a particular deity from the rest as having the right to be addressed as lord in some special connexion. Esarhaddon's treaty with the King of Tyre names together three Tyrian gods all bearing this title : *Baal sameme* (the lord of heaven), *Baal malagie* (perhaps the lord my king) and *Baal şapunu* (Baal Şaphon).[4]

How did these many gods bearing the title " lord " come into existence ? Some scholars say that they arose through the partition of a single supreme being, a great original Baal, whose local aspects gradually became differentiated. Renan compares the suggestion with what has happened in the case of the worship of the Virgin : Notre Dame de Lourdes, Notre Dame de la Salette, the black Virgin of Chartres, for the general body of the faithful, are almost separate individuals, although it is perfectly well known that only one person is indicated by these various titles. The same thing was true in Israel with reference to Jahweh before the reform of Josiah. P. Lagrange thinks it can be established that this original Baal was Baal Shamem, the lord of heaven, the great god of the Arameans,[5] also worshipped by the Phenicians, at least from the time of Esarhaddon (681–669),[6] and who is sometimes defined as the Baal of this or that city.[7]

It may be urged in support of this view that in certain texts, especially Egyptian texts, Baal seems to be exclusively, or at least chiefly, the name or title of a specific god, for the Egyptians identified him with their Sutekh, the god of thunder and war. Some Assyriologists think that in the Tell el-Amarna letters the names Baal and Hadad were inter-

---

[1] A Phenician god mentioned in the treaty between Esarhaddon and Baal, the King of Tyre (**XCIII**, p. 357), and whose cult had reached Egypt (Pap. Sallier, iv, pl. i, verso 6 ; *cf.* **XIII**, p. 348 ; Exod. xiv. 2, 9 ; Num. xxxiii. 7), also worshipped at Carthage and at Marseilles (**XLIX**, pp. 470–1). The mention of a Baalith Şaphon (**LXXI**, p. 315) seems to be based on a mistaken reading (**LXI**, p. 173).

[2] **CIS**, i, 155.　　　　　　　　[3] **CIL**, viii, 5279.

[4] **XCI**, ii, pp. 10 *ff.* ; **XCIII**, p. 357.

[5] **XLIX**, pp. 88, 92–4.

[6] Since the time of Yeḥimilk, King of Byblos (eleventh century ?), according to the newly discovered inscription of this prince.

[7] Altiburos, Cossura.

changeable,[1] which would suggest that for the Canaanites the storm god was the Baal *par excellence*.

It is, however, more likely that the process was reversed, and that a multiplicity of baals was the starting-point from which a unity or a tendency to unification developed later. The Arabs used to call a region watered by a spring and hence not in need of irrigation, "that which Baal refreshes."[2] Rabbinical Hebrew preserved a similar phrase. This usage would suggest that the Baal may have been primarily the genius of the spring which brought fertility to a province or an oasis. Hence he would be the patron deity of the agriculturists settled within his sphere of influence. It may be imagined that the peasants might come to look to him for other favours necessary to the success of their labours, the fertility of the flocks, or the seasonal rains essential to cultivation, and that thus earth-spirits, or at least some of them, might become "lords of heaven" and in particular givers of rain and storms.

Hence the religion of the great mass of the settled population of Canaan was from the first and must have continued to be very similar to that which still constitutes the essential and most living factor in the religious practices of the indigenous inhabitants of Syria and Palestine today, with the sole difference that the local divinities are no longer called "baals," but go by the names of Christian saints, Hebrew prophets or Moslem *welis*.

It can easily be believed that out of this dust of local divinities should arise in the course of the centuries the figure of a god of a more general nature, a single great Baal. The result would be the same whether we suppose that the Canaanites, and especially foreigners like the Egyptians, arrived at the conclusion that the various gods bearing the title of lord were all one and the same being, for many of the local divinities must have had almost the same attributes, or that the cult of one of these baals, possibly Hadad, under the title of Baal Shamem, "the lord of heaven," received at an early date a special expansion. But the most certain indication that the different "lords" were not all mere offshoots of a

---

[1] **XXXI**, pp. 220–1 ; **CXXXIII**, iv, pp. 320 *ff.* ; **XCIII**, p. 357 ; **XIII**, p. 348 ; **CXIV**, p. 89 ; *cf.* **CXXX**.
[2] **XC²**, p. 146 ; **LXXXIV**, p. 98.

great god of heaven presiding over the storms, is that the
baal of Harran, for example, was a moon-god,[1] that of Arvad
a sea-god with a fish's tail;[2] among the Arabs of the south
Athtar had the title of Baal,[3] etc.

The name Bethel is another divine title which seems to
have had a similar history to that of the word *baal*. Originally it was the name of the standing stone, the stele, the abode
of a god, " house of god," as its name implies.[4] But the
word came to denote the unseen being himself who dwelt in
the sacred stone : the guardian deity of the Canaanites of
Shechem seems to have been called both Baal-Berith and
Bethel-Berith.[5]

Then, no doubt by some such line of development as we
have supposed for Baal, Bethel became a kind of proper
name applied to a divinity of a more general character. In
the treaty between Esarhaddon and Baal of Tyre, *Ba-ai-ti-ile*
is named as one of the great gods of the " land beyond the
river," that is the land west of the Euphrates.[6] According
to Philo of Byblos, Baitylos was one of the great Phenician
gods, son of Heaven and Earth, brother of El, Dagon and
Atlas.[7] Jahweh himself was known by this title among the
Israelites, he said to Jacob : " I am the god Bethel."[8] At
the time of the return from exile we hear of a Jew named
Bethel Sherezer (Zech. vii. 2) ; and the Jewish settlers at
Elephantine, who still preserved in the fifth century many of
the ancient customs of pre-exilic times, assigned to Jahweh a
female consort, whom they called indifferently Anath-Jahu
or Anath-Bethel.[9]

Among the earlier Canaanites we find a sign of more
" primitive " conceptions of divinity than polydæmonism,
in the frequent occurrence of names of persons [10] and especially
of places,[11] compounded with the word *el*, if we may believe

[1] Fourth Sendjirli inscr., **XLIX**, p. 91.
[2] *Ibid.*, pp. 91, 131.   [3] *Ibid.*, p. 91.
[4] Gen. xxviii. 10–22.   [5] P. 121.
[6] **XCIII**, p. 437.   [7] Fr. **III**, 507.
[8] Gen. xxxi. 13, at least according to the Mas. text ; *cf.* R. Dussaud, **RHR**, lxxv, 1917, p. 133 ; **XIX**, pp. 231–43 ; R. Weill, **RHR**,
lxxxvii, 1923, p. 105.
[9] Pap. Sachau, Plates 17–20 ; *cf.* **XXIII**[2], i, pp. 453–4.
[10] So Ilimilki or Milkili in the Tell el-Amarna letters.
[11] Har-el (in the lists of Thothmes III), Yabne'el, Jizreel, Migdal'el,
Nahaliel, Ne'iel, Peniel, Qabze'el, Bethel, Yiphtah'el, Yrpe'el,
Eltolad, Elteqeh, Elteqon.

that in these names it had kept its early meaning of " power," a totality of still undifferentiated supernatural forces, something of the sense of *mana*.

However, it is certain that the Canaanites of the historical period had advanced beyond the stage of pure polydæmonism or animism. Some of their gods had the nobler outline, the wider sphere, the more definite personality which mark the gods of the polytheistic peoples.

Various elements in the environment tended to foster this development : first of all the conception held by the Canaanites, as by the Semites in general, of the relations between the local deity and the social group, clan or tribe, village or city, which resorted to his shrine and claimed him as their chosen patron. For since the god was in relation with persons he naturally tended to assume a personal character. This relation was at first thought of as a bond of kinship : hence those personal names in which the god appears as father ('*ab*), uncle or kinsman ('*am*), brother ('*ah*) : for instance, *Absha*, chief of the caravan of Asiatics that came down into Egypt about 1900, or *Ammienshi*, the Palestinian mentioned in the story of Sinuhe (twelfth or thirteenth dynasty).

When an urban civilization came to prevail in Palestine and the various cities became so many small city-states, usually under a king, the relation with the local god took on a political colour, he was called king, *Melek* ; [1] judge, *Dan* ; [2] lord, *Adon*.[3]

As time went on these titles were so constantly employed in the worship of certain gods that they came to be used as specific designations of those gods : one of the guardian deities of Tyre was usually called " the king of the city," Melqart.[4] The Ammonites called their national god Milkom. It is possible that the sacrifices of children practised in the valley of Hinnom near Jerusalem were originally made to a Canaanite deity called *ham-Melek*, " the king," a title better

---

[1] So in the names of Milkuru (**TA(W)**, 61, 53 ; 69, 85 ; 58, 43) or Urumilki (**XLII**, ii, p. 91) = " Uru is my king."

[2] So in the name of Addudan, " Hadad is judge " (**IV**, p. 123, n. 2).

[3] For instance in the name of Adonizedek (" Zedek is my lord "), King of Jerusalem (Joshua x. 1, 3).

[4] In a treaty with Esarhaddon, as read by Johns (**XCIII**, p. 357).

known under the debased form of Moloch.[1] It may have
been to him or to some other native god that " the valley of
the king " (Gen. xiv. 17 ; 2 Sam. xviii. 18) owed its name.
In the Tell el-Amarna age the names of certain Canaanite
princes bear witness to the worship of a god Melek [2] : Abdi-
milki (servant of Melek), Abimilki (Melek is my father),
Ilimilki or Milkili (Melek is my god).

The name of the tribe and the city of Dan was derived,
perhaps, from that of a god of the same name. Also it is
well known that Adon became a proper name under the
form of Adonis.[3]

It is especially among the Semitic peoples settled in
Canaan before the arrival of the Israelites that we find these
early Palestinian divinities whose political relations had over-
shadowed any previous connexion which they might have
had with natural phenomena : for instance, Milkom among
the Ammonites, Chemosh and Ashtar-Chemosh [4] among the
Moabites, perhaps Qosh among the Edomites.[5] It is, however, likely that among the Canaanites properly so-called
also, the chief deity of the city, at Byblos Baalath-Gebal,
or Baal Berith at Shechem, was for the members of these
little states, above all, the guardian and embodiment of their
country. But if this function imparted a more personal
character to the god, it hardly increased his sphere of influence, considering the narrow limits of the Canaanite states.

On the other hand, certain local deities had, no doubt,
always been credited with the power of controlling some
natural phenomenon such as the course of the sun, the moon
or a star, the incidence of storms, the lightning stroke. Such
an attribution did not prevent them from having their home
by a particular spring or on a special mountain—there was
a spring of the sun, 'Ain Shemesh ; a mountain of the sun,
Har Heres—nor did it preclude them from being the patrons
of a particular tribe ; for, to the mind of the primitive society

---

[1] Lev. xviii. 21 ; xx. 2–5 ; 1 Kings xi. 7 (without the article) ;
2 Kings xxiii. 10 ; Jer. xxxii. 35. In these passages the Massoretes
have vocalized the name *Melech* with the vowels of *bosheth*, to indicate
that this false god was a " shame " : *Molech*, whence the Greek
transcription Moloch.

[2] *Cf.* **XCIII**, p. 470.

[3] The Semitic derivation of this name appears certain in spite of
the objections raised in Pauly-Wissowa, *s.v.*

[4] The Mesha Stone, 1. 17.   [5] **XCIII**, pp. 472–3.

its own affairs take on a cosmic significance and cosmic happenings have a direct bearing on their little world. Nevertheless, those divinities gifted with universal attributes were most prone to assume the stature of great intertribal and even international gods.

2. Canaanite Polytheism

(a) *Native Gods.* There was no lack among the Canaanites of gods who ruled over a relatively wide realm, however acquired, and possessed a large circle of worshippers and a clearly marked individuality.

We have already mentioned Hadad, also known as Adad, Dad, Addu (*e.g.* in the name Rib Addi, a king of Byblos in the Tell el-Amarna epoch). He was worshipped alike by the Babylonians, the Arameans and the Edomites. The Canaanites knew him as the storm-god : Abimelek of Tyre calls the Pharoah " he who causes the thunder to resound in the heavens like Addu." [1]

We have also referred to Dagon, certainly the same as Dagan who had been worshipped in Babylonia since the time of the obelisk of Manishtusu,[2] of Idin-Dagan, of Ishme-Dagan, king of Isin (2297–2257),[3] and in Assyria from the time of Ishme-Dagan, the father of Shamshi-Adad I (about 1840).[4] He had a temple at Tirqa (the modern 'Ashara), on the middle Euphrates, from the time of the latter monarch.[5] In Palestine his cult is attested for the Tell el-Amarna period by the name of a prince Dagan-Takala.[6] It must have been common in the country, for at least two places bear the name Beth Dagon, " house of Dagon," one in the territory of Asher (Joshua xix. 27), the other in the region assigned to Judah (Joshua xv. 41). The latter occurs earlier in an inscription of Ramses III (about 1200) under the name of Bayti Dukuna,[7] and again in a text of Sennacherib under the name of Bet Daganna.[8] It is apparently the modern village of Beit Dedjan south-east of Jaffa. Eusebius mentions a Kefar Dagan (mod. Dadjun) between Diospolis (Lydda) and Jamnia ; and there is a Beit Dedjan to the south-east of Nablus.[9]

It is generally admitted that Dagan or Dagon was an autochthonous divinity in western Asia, and that his cult passed over from thence into Babylonia and Assyria. In any case he had been long worshipped in Palestine when the Philistines settled there

[1] **CXIV**, p. 91 ; *cf.* **XIII**, pp. 348–9 ; **V**, p. 43 ; **XLIX**, pp. 91–4 ; **XCIII**, pp. 442–51 ; Baudissin, art. *Hadad*, **HRE**[3].
[2] Scheil, *Elamite-Semitic texts*, i, obelisk A, col. v, 8 ; col. xi, 15, and C, col. xvi, 7.
[3] **XXXIV**, i, p. 219.   [4] **XXXVI**, ii, pp. 217, 225.
[5] Condamin, **ZA**, xxi, pp. 247 *ff.* ; Fr. Thureau-Dangin and P. Dhorme, **SY**, 1924, pp. 265–75 ; *cf.* Dhorme, **RB**, 1926, p. 541.
[6] **TA(W)**, 215 *ff.* (K, 317–18).
[7] **IV**, p. 80, n. 6.   [8] **XLII**, ii, p. 93.
[9] The existence of a temple of Dagon at Beth-Shan is, on the contrary, quite problematical, *cf.* p. 105.

(about 1192) and adopted him as the god of Ashdod, one of their principal cities, since he had a temple there or was represented by a statue (1 Sam. v. 2–5 ; 1 Macc. x. 83–84 ; Josephus, A.J. xiii. 4, 4–5). It may be inferred from the story of the death of Samson that at Gaza the Philistines had another temple dedicated to the same god, where they honoured him with games (Judges xvi. 23–30) ; but we cannot be certain of the locality of the incident, since the text seems to be composite.[1]

In Canaan Dagon was the god of corn, as his name signifies, the Hebrew word *dagan* meaning wheat. The Phenicians credited him with the invention of corn and the plough ; and Philo of Byblos adds that for this reason he was called Zeus Arotrios.[2] On a Phenician seal his symbol is a ear of wheat.[3] In Assyro-Babylonia he seems to have become the god of the earth in general, identified with Bel [4] and associated with Anu, the god of the heaven. It has been often maintained since the time of St. Jerome that Dagon was represented with the body of a fish,[5] and it is *a priori* possible that on account of the popular derivation of his name from the word *dag*, fish, some of his worshippers may have identified him with one of the ichthyomorphic gods of the coast, of Arvad for instance, or Ascalon : but so far this theory has no certain documentary support, since the Massoretic text of 1 Samuel v. 4 does not warrant the inferences which have been drawn from it ; the passage is also certainly corrupt. Further-more, it may be pointed out that none of the cities where Dagon is known to have been worshipped was on the coast.

The sun was worshipped under the names of Shemesh (or, according to the Babylonian pronunciation, Shamash) and Heres. An Asiatic prince of the time of the eleventh dynasty bore the name Shamshuili.[6] In the Tell el-Amarna letters Shamash is mentioned several times, along with Addu, as one of the greatest gods : the Pharaoh is " like Addu and Shamash." [7] He evidently had temples in the towns called Beth Shemesh, " house of the sun," [8] or Ir Shemesh, " city of the sun " ; [9] he had a sacred spring at 'Ain Shemesh,[10] a sacred mountain at Har Heres,[11] a temenos at Timnath Heres, " the portion of the sun." [12] It also remains probable, in spite of objections, that certain elements in the myth of this Canaanite god have helped to form the cycle of

---

[1] **LVII**, pp. 507–12.

[2] Fr. **II**, 16.   [3] **IV**, p. 80.   [4] **XXXIV**, i, p. 220.

[5] Thus **XLIX**, pp. 131–2 ; **XXXVII**, p. 285 ; **LXVI**, p. 28.

[6] **CLV**, n. 5, p. 51–2.

[7] **TA(K)**, 55 ; 108 ; 149 ; 159 ; *cf.* 151 ; 331 ; 323, etc.

[8] There was one of them in Judah (Joshua xv. 10 ; xxi. 16, etc.), the modern Ain Shems, where the English have made excavations ; another in Naphtali (Joshua xix. 38 ; Judges i. 33), and one in Issachar (Joshua xix. 22).

[9] Joshua xix. 41, probably identical with Beth Shemesh of Judah.

[10] Joshua xv. 7 ; xviii. 17, between Jerusalem and Jericho ; *cf.* also xix. 41 (Sept.).

[11] Judges i. 35.

[12] Judges ii. 9 ; *cf.* Joshua xix. 50 ; xxiv. 30, where the name has been intentionally altered.

Israelite traditions concerning Samson [1] : in fact, the pre-Israelite inhabitants of Hebron already knew of a giant called Sheshai,[2] a name which is merely a variant of Samson, and means " the solar one." [3]

Names of places like Jericho (derived from *yareah*, moon, month) and perhaps that of Hadashah, " new (moon)," suggest that the Canaanites had one or more lunar divinities.

A cylinder seal of Ramses II [4] found at Beisan and the name of the city Arsuf (the ancient Apollonia, a little to the north of Jaffa) [5] suggest that they also worshipped Resheph. This god, mentioned in several Phenician and Aramean inscriptions,[6] must have been a god of fire.[7] His name is found in Babylon as an epithet of the fire-god.[8] Judging from the various meanings of the word in Hebrew, he was perhaps specially regarded as the source of lightning [9] and burning fever [10] : this would explain why he was later identified with Apollo.[11]

His cult had reached Egypt, where he is represented wearing a conical cap with a gazelle's head coming out of it, and holding in his right hand a mace and in the left a buckler and a spear.[12] Hence it has been inferred that he must also have been a war-god.[13]

The god of Beth Shan is very similarly represented on the stele (pl. x) discovered in 1927 by Mr. Rowe [14] in an annex to what this scholar believes to be the chapel of the great temple at the time of Thothmes III.[15] The god is also wearing the high conical tiara with two streamers, one very long, attached to the top of the cap, the other, shorter and broader, to its base. On the front of the tiara, instead of the gazelle's head of Resheph, are two small horns, a characteristic attribute of the gods in Babylonian representations. The god is wearing Egyptian dress; he is holding in one hand the *ankh*, in the other " the sceptre of blessing " ; but his facial type is sharply Semitic, long and slightly aquiline nose, full lips, pointed beard. The great interest of this monument lies in the fact that it gives us the name of the god. According to the inscription the stele is an offering made by an individual named Pa-Ra-em-heb for his father Amen-em-opet, " to M.k.l. (or M.k.r.) god of Bethshan." This divine name or title perhaps pronounced Mikal or Mekal, occurs in several Phenician inscriptions from Cyprus (fifth and fourth centuries), where he is gener-

---

[1] **LXXXVII** ; Salomon Reinach, *Samson* (1912) ; Smythe Palmer (*The Samson-Saga and its Place in comparative Religion*, London, Pitman, 1913) ; **XII**, pp. 391–408.

[2] Num. xiii. 22 ; Joshua xv. 14 ; Judges i. 10.

[3] **LVII**, pp. 512–16.

[4] **RB**, 1928, pp. 528–32 and fig. 2.

[5] **CVIII**, i, pp. 676 *ff*.

[6] **XLIX**, pp. 456, 492–4 ; **XCV**, p. 50 ; **LV**, *s.v. rešeph*.

[7] *Cf*. Cant. viii, 6. [8] **XCIII**, p. 478.

[9] Ps. lxxvi. 4 ; lxxviii. 48.

[10] Deut. xxxii. 24 ; Hab. iii. 5 ; *cf*. **XXIV**, p. 85.

[11] **LIV**, i, pp. 150–1. [12] **CXIV**, p. 85.

[13] *Ibid.*, p. 84 ; **V**, p. 68 ; **XLIX**, p. 453.

[14] **RB**, 1928, p. 512 (pl. xxiii) ; **SY**, 1928, p. 127.

[15] See p. 94.

ally coupled with Resheph.[1] If the name is Semitic,[2] it might mean " he who devours " or " he who is able," the Powerful One. Several other objects more recently found at Beisan suggest that Mikal was later identified with Resheph on the one hand, and on the other with the Egyptian god Set-Sutekh.[3]

Baraq (lightning) was, no doubt, like Resheph, a name of the lightning-god ; a place near Jaffa, originally the name of a clan, bore the name of Bene Beraq.[4] Thence comes the name of the Israelite hero Barak (Judges iv. 5). Among the Babylonians Birqu was a god associated or coupled with Ramman, the storm-god.[5]

Shalem or Shalman is found as a divine name in Phenicia, northern Syria, Assyria, and Babylonia.[6] The cult of this god seems to be attested by the names of Jerusalem (Uru-Shalim) and of Solomon (Shelomoh). But we have no certain knowledge as to his attributes. A personal name on an Egyptian stele seems to identify him with Resheph.[7] Winckler connects him with Nebo,[8] Zimmern with Ninib, others with Ea.[9]

Gad, the god of Fortune, was worshipped by the Canaanites, as is proved by the names Migdal Gad, " the tower of Gad," in Judah (Joshua xv. 37), and perhaps Baal Gad.[10] We know that this god who was honoured by the Arameans, Phenicians [11] and Arabs,[12] was also persistently worshipped among the Israelites in spite of the exclusive nature of their natural religion ; it is for this reason, no doubt, that we find the name of the tribe of Gad and such personal names as Gaddiel,[13] Gadmelek.[14] About the time of the exile some of the Jews prepared a table[15] for him (Isa. lxv. 11) ; and again in the fourth and fifth centuries many Jewish houses contained, under the name of " the bed of Gad," a table decked with food for the guardian spirit of the house, sar habbayit [16] This would appear to suggest that this god is a product of the fusion of ancient local divinities.

It is possible that the Canaanites worshipped another god of Fortune, Asher or Ashir, the male consort of Asherah, and akin to Asshur the national god of Assyria ; there was indeed in Palestine, as early as the time of Seti I, a district with the name of Asaru, which is certainly closely connected with that of the Hebrew tribe of Asher.[17]

---

[1] CIS, i, pp. 86, 3 ; 89, 3 ; 90, 2 ; 91, 2 ; 93, 5 ; 94, 5. Perhaps also in the personal names of Amothmicar (CIL, viii, 12335) in Africa, and of Michal, daughter of Saul.

[2] A god of identical type is described as " lord of Kheta," that is to say, of the Hittites, cf. RB, 1928, pl. xxiv, n. 10.

[3] Cf. Vincent, RB, 1928, pp. 528–37.

[4] Joshua xix. 45 ; named also by Sennacherib, Banaibarqa (XCIII, p. 451).

[5] Ibid., pp. 446–7.　　　　[6] Ibid., pp. 224, 474–5.

[7] Ibid., p. 224.　　[8] Ibid.　　[9] Ibid., pp. 474–5.　　[10] P. 121.

[11] XCV, p. 96 ff. ; LV, s.v. gad.

[12] XC², p. 146.　　　　[13] Num. xiii. 10.

[14] Upon a seal, XCIII, p. 479.　　　　[15] Isa. lxv. 11.

[16] Talm. bab. Sanh. 20ᵃ ; Ned. 56ᵃ ; cf. XXVIII, p. 183 ; LVIII, i, p. 236, Upon these " beds," see XLIX, pp. 508–9.

[17] See p. 50.

According to Philo of Byblos, Phenician mythology assigned to the sun two sons, Suduq and Misor, that is, Justice and Equity, clearly personified abstractions.[1] It is strange that the first of these gods, Zedeq, whose characteristics are somewhat late, should already have been known to the ancient Canaanites : in the Tell el-Amarna letters occurs the personal name, Rab-zidqi,[2] " Zedeq is great." Hebrew tradition speaks of two pre-Israelite kings of Jerusalem named Melchizedek,[3] " Zedeq is my king and Adonizedek,"[4] " Zedeq is my lord."[5]

Possibly such names of cities as Jarmuth and Azmaveth, and personal names like Merimut[6] and Ahimiti[7] are an indication that the Canaanites worshipped the god Mut, another of the gods mentioned by Philo of Byblos in his Phenician theogony[8] ; this god was, no doubt, akin to Pluto, King of Hell, since his name means Death.

Hitherto the cult of the young vegetation-god who dies and is reborn each year, has not been found in Palestine proper in pre-Israelite times. This god seems to occur in the fourteenth century under the sumerian name of Tammuz, in a document coming from Byblos.[9] But it is difficult to believe that the cult practised in the sacred city in honour of the god who was known in the Greek period as Adonis (my lord), and especially the mourning for Adonis, could have been a foreign rite. Tammuz must have been assimilated to some native and analogous god.[10] In any case the myth of the young god and his sacred tree seems to have been known in Byblos from very ancient times ; for the *Ded*-tree, the old symbol of Osiris whose fate is in part connected with Byblos, seems to be a transformation of the cypress of Lebanon.[11] There are also reasons for believing that Pepi I (about 2500), refers to the tree-god of Byblos when, in his funerary inscription, he compares himself, shut up in his wooden sarcophagus, to the god Hay-Tau of Nega.[12]

---

[1] *Cf. Kettu* and *Mesaru*, sons of Shamash, among the Babylonians, **XCIII**, pp. 224, 370.

[2] **TA(W)**, 125 (K, 170), 37, Knudtzon's reading, **CXXXIII**, iv, p. 114.   [3] Gen. xiv. 18 ; Ps. cx. 4.

[4] Joshua x. 1, 3.

[5] It is not likely that in all these names *şedeq* should be the common noun " righteousness " (" the king is righteousness," " my lord is righteousness "), as Burney maintains (**XII**, pp. 41–3). For this does not explain the Phenician name *şdq dkr* : *şidqi dakar*, " Zedeq remembers " (**XCV**, p. 128).

[6] If this is how *mჳჳm(w)t* (**CLV**, e 15), should be read, *cf.* Meremoth Ezra viii. 33, etc.) ; but see Dussaud, **SY**, 1927, p. 227.

[7] Dussaud, *Ibid.* ; *cf.* 1 Chron. vi. 10.

[8] Fr. **II**, p. 24 ; *cf.* **XLIX**, pp. 424, 432.

[9] **TA(K)**, 84, 33 (according to **XIII**, p. 347).

[10] Eshmun, according to Damascius (*Vita Isidori*, 302) ; an identification which is adopted, for instance, in **CIX**, p. 115 ; *cf.* **XCVI**.

[11] **LXIX**, pp. 93–5.

[12] **CXI**, p. 117. In Palestine, during the Israelite period, we hear of " plantings " which are no doubt the " gardens of Adonis " (Isa.

It is not beyond the bounds of possibility that Jahweh was worshipped in Canaan before the Israelite settlement. Personal names compounded with *jah, jahu* or *jahweh* occur in Babylon from the time of Hammurabi, and Jahweh must certainly have been one of the gods of the kingdom of Yaudi in northern Syria in the eighth century.

However the evidence that the Canaanites worshipped this god are far from convincing. There is the name of the city of Batiya mentioned by Thothmes III, a name which may be interpreted " house of Jahweh," *beth-jah* ; also that of a correspondent of the prince of Taanach from whom a letter was found on a cuneiform tablet : this name may be read Aḫiyami or Aḫijawi : in the latter case it would be equivalent to the Hebrew Ahijah, " Jahweh is my brother (my kinsman)." In any case, Jahweh could not have been one of the principal gods of the Canaanites.

(*b*) *Native Goddesses.* Some of the goddesses worshipped by the Canaanites were clearly connected with definite localities : no doubt they had been originally, like so many masculine baals, the divinities of a particular sacred spot : for instance, Baalath Beer, the lady of the well (Joshua xix. 8), Baalath Gebal, the Lady of Byblos.[1] There was a place called Bealoth, " the ladies " (Joshua xv. 24 ; 1 Kings iv. 16).

Others, it is true, were called Baalath,[2] Baalah,[3] " the lady " [4]; but in this case the local determinative was probably understood : the complete name of the first of the above-mentioned places would have been " the Lady of Judah."[5]

Still, the Canaanites also possessed female deities of a more general character, Astarte, Asherah, Anath, Kadesh. And it would even seem that all these divine female figures, who were in reality various aspects of the fertility principle, tended to merge into a single great female deity, commonly called Astarte. This name, in turn, became, like the Babylonian Ishtar or the south-Arabian Shams,[6] a sort of general word for goddess. Thus arose the Hebrew expression " the baals and the astartes," denoting the entire Canaanite pan-

xvii. 10–11), and of women weeping for Tammuz (Ezek. viii. 14) ; when Jeremiah compares the nation, at the same time, to a woman weeping on the mountains for her lovers, and to a bird mourning in the cedars of Lebanon (Jer. xxii. 20–3), he is perhaps alluding to the myth of Astarte, the dove goddess of Aphaca in the Lebanon, who wept for her lover Adonis.

[1] P. 121.   [2] Joshua xix. 44.   [3] Joshua xv. 29.

[4] *Cf.* Har hab-Ba'alah, " the mountain of the Lady " (Joshua xv. 11).

[5] See p. 121, note 5.   [6] **XCIII**, pp. 420, 435.

theon ; a city of Bashan was called Ashtaroth, "the
Astartes."[1] The fact that Astarte thus tended to absorb
the other female divinities of the country suggests that she
was pre-eminent there.

She was worshipped among all the off-shoots of the Semitic
race : the Babylonians and Assyrians called her Ishtar, the
Arameans Atar (Atar-gatis = 'Atar'ate), the Moabites, Ashtar [2] ;
the Arabs, who regarded her as a male divinity,[3] called her Athtar
(whence *astar*, " god," in the Abyssinian inscriptions).[4]
In Phenician the pronunciation will have been Ashtart (whence
the Greek Astarte), in Hebrew Ashtereth. The Jewish editors of
the Hebrew Bible degraded it into Ashtoreth to suggest the word
bosheth, shame.[5] The question arises whether Astarte was originally a Babylonian divinity, whose name, derived from the root
asharu with the specific Babylonian meaning to assemble, pass in
review, denoted the planet Venus, who, in the evening passes the
stars in review, and whether her name together with her cult were
subsequently adopted by the rest of the Semitic peoples.[6] If so
the borrowing must have occurred at a very early date. On the
other hand her name may have belonged to the original common
religious vocabulary of the race ; since there are facts which
militate against the theory of borrowing : for instance the
unanimity with which the Semitic peoples, apart from the
Babylonians and Assyrians, begin the word with the strongest
of the gutturals, '*ain* and not with the weakest '*aleph* ; also the
masculine sex attributed to the goddess among the Arabs. It is
noteworthy that, except among the Canaanites, the word has no
feminine ending and that in Babylonia there are traces of a male
Ishtar.[7]
Be that as it may, the cult of Astarte among the ancient
Canaanites is borne witness to, not only by Israelite writers, but
by such place names as Ashtartu [8] and Ashtaroth,[9] also called
Be'eshterah,[10] that is, the temple of Astarte, *Beth Ashtereth*.[11]
Astarte, one of the chief deities of Tyre,[12] and Sidon, was also

---

[1] Deut. i. 4 ; Joshua ix. 10 ; xii. 4 ; xiii. 12, 31.
[2] The Mesha Stone, l. 17.
[3] It was the same perhaps with the Moabites (Dussaud, *Les monuments palestiniens et judaiques*, Paris, 1912, p. 15).
[4] *Cf.* XCIII, pp. 435, n. 8 ; 436, n. 5.
[5] *Cf.* p. 126, n. 1.   [6] XCIII, pp. 420–1.
[7] *Ibid.*, pp. 139, 420, 431.
[8] TA(W), 142 (K, 197), 10 ; 237 (K, 256), 21.
[9] N. 1 above.
[10] Joshua xxi. 27 ; but the text is not certain. The Syriac and
1 Chron. vi. 56 give Ashtaroth.
[11] On Ashteroth-Qarnaim, see above, p. 110.
[12] 1 Kings xi. 5, 33, 2 Kings xxiii. 13 ; treaty of Esarhaddon
(XCIII, pp. 357, 434). Tabnith, King of Sidon, was priest of Astarte ;
his wife, Amastarte, was priestess of the goddess ; Eshmunazar, their
son, was greatly devoted to her (CIS, i, 3, ll. 14–16, 18 ; *cf.* XLIX,
pp. 481, 483).

adopted by the Philistines.[1] At Ascalon, one of their principal cities, she was worshipped under her Aramean name of Atargatis.

In the Tell el-Amarna epoch, one of the most prominent of the Syrian princes was called Abd Ashirti or Abd Ashratu, that is, the servant of Asherah ; a king of Taanach was called Ashiraty-ashur.[2] The name of the goddess Asherah is also mentioned in the O.T. as a synonym of Astarte[3] ; and perhaps the two divinities are really identical, if it is true that Abd Ashirti is once called " servant of Astarte."[4] Asherah is frequently mentioned in cuneiform texts, but was apparently regarded by the Babylonians as a western goddess.[5]

The origin of the name and of the goddess who bears it is still much disputed. A derivation has been suggested from the Babylonian word *ashirtu, eshirtu*, sanctuary[6] : in that case the goddess would have reached the west from a foreign source. Others hold that Asherah was, like the god Bethel, a personified cult object[7] ; it is known that the sacred pole was also called asherah.[8] On the other hand, it is more generally agreed that the object took its name from that of the goddess, because she was usually represented by a tree-trunk with the branches lopped off.

It is perhaps more probable that there is only an etymological link between the proper name and the common noun. The plural was different : the sacred poles were *asherim*, while the goddesses were *asheroth*. Moreover, the artificial tree would seem in Canaan to have stood for a god at least as often as a goddess. For example, Jeremiah reproaches the back-sliding Israelites with saying to the wood, *i.e.* to the asherah, " thou art my father," and to the stone, *i.e.* to the stele, " thou hast begotten me " (Jer. ii. 27). According to Plutarch, *De Iside et Osiride*, 16, it was Adonis who was represented by the sacred pole which was still worshipped in his time in the temple of Isis at Byblos.[9] Both the proper name and the common noun may have been independently derived from the root *'ashar*, to be straight, whence the meaning to go straight, to be fortunate. The *asherah*, the sacred pole, would be that which is upright.[10] The goddess Asherah would be originally the giver of good fortune.[11]

The origin of the name of the goddess Anath is also obscure : according to some, Babylonian,[12] according to others Hittite.[13] In any case her cult was widespread in ancient Palestine.

---

[1] 1 Sam. xxxi. 10.   [2] **CLIII**, pp. 113 *ff.*

[3] Judges iii. 7, for example.

[4] If we suppose that *Abdi ashtati* (**TA(W)**, 40 (K, 63, 3) is a mistake for *Abdi Ashtaarti* .and denotes the same person ; see **XCIII**, p. 433.

[5] *Ibid.*, pp. 432–4.   [6] *Ibid*, p. 437.

[7] So **LXII**, p. 34, n. 3.   [8] See pp. 85–6.

[9] Dussaud, **SY**, 1923, p. 308.

[10] *Cf. te'aššour*, the name of a conifer, probably the cypress, and *maṣṣebah*, the " elevated thing," the stele.

[11] *Cf.* the god Asher, p. 130.

[12] Zimmern proposes, but with hesitation, to recognize here Antum, the female consort of Anu, the Heaven (**XCIII**, pp. 352–3).

[13] **LXXVII**, p. 259 ; E. Meyer, **ZDMG**, 1877, pp. 716 *ff.* ; **IV**, p. 81.

Thothmes III (1501–1447) found a city there called Beth Anath,[1] that is, the temple of Anath, apparently the one which the Israelite writers knew in the tribe of Naphtali.[2]

The name of Anati in the Tell el-Amarna period [3] shows that individuals might take the goddess as a guardian deity for their children. From a stele recently found at Beisan we learn that Anath was the chief goddess of this important city in the time of Seti I. She is there called " queen of heaven and mistress of all the gods." Bearing the usual Egyptian emblems of the sceptre of blessing and the ankh, she is receiving the offerings of an individual with an Egyptian name.[4] During the Israelite age, not only did the remembrance of the goddess survive in place names like Beth-Anath, Beth-Anoth,[5] Anathoth, *i.e.* the Anaths, the home of Jeremiah, and in personal names like Anath,[6] perhaps Ba'ana [7] and Anathothiah,[8] but her cult still persisted in the fifth century B.C. among the Jewish settlers at Elephantine in Upper Egypt.[9]

Hitherto the goddess Kadesh is only known to us from Egyptian monuments, but she was evidently borrowed from the Semites of Western Asia. She is called Lady of Heaven, Mistress of the gods, eye of Ra, and is depicted naked, standing on a lioness, holding in her right hand a lotus flower, and in her left a serpent. Her hair, arranged like that of the Egyptian goddess Hathor, falls about her shoulders in two large tresses. She is sometimes crowned with a disk resting on a crescent[10] representing either the sun with two horns,[11] or perhaps the old moon in the arms of the new. Judging by her general appearance, Kadesh must have been the goddess of love *par excellence* ; and her name closely resembles that of the temple prostitute in Hebrew (*kedeshah*).

On the other hand, Astarte and Anath, whose cult had gradually spread into Egypt during the times of the great invading Pharaohs, are usually represented by the Egyptians with warlike attributes : Astarte, who had a temple in Egypt [12] and whom a myth describes as entering the pantheon of Memphis by the side of Baal Zaphon, is entitled " mistress of horses and lady of chariots " ; she has the head of a lioness and urges her chariot over the bodies of her enemies. Anath, who had a priesthood at Thebes since the reign of Thothmes III and to whose protection Ramses II committed his favourite daughter, giving her the name of " daughter of Anath," is depicted clothed, seated on a throne, and holding in her right hand spear and shield and in her left a battle-axe.[13]

---

[1] *Cf.* **IV**, p. 81.   [2] Joshua xix. 38 ; Judges i. 33.

[3] **TA(W)**, 125 (K, 170), 43.

[4] See p. 117 ; *cf.* Gressmann, **ZATW**, 1926, pp. 72–3 ; Vincent, **RB**, 1926, p. 125.

[5] In Judah, Joshua xv. 59.   [6] Judges v. 6.

[7] That is to say the son of Anath ? 2 Sam. iv. 2, 5, 6, 9 ; xxiii. 29, etc.   [8] 1 Chron. viii. 24.   [9] See p. 124.

[10] **LXVIII**, p. 379 (fig. 40). [11] **CXIV**, p. 85.

[12] **XIII**, p. 348 and **CXIV**, p. 86.

[13] Elsewhere she is depicted standing wrapped in a panther-skin ; she holds the sceptre of papyrus and the emblem of life ; she wears a crown of feathers, ornamented at the base with a pair of horns (**CXIV**, pp. 85, 86 ; **XIII**, p. 347).

The Egyptians were apparently following the example of their Asiatic neighbours, the Canaanites, when they attributed a warlike character to these two goddesses. Nevertheless, among the many figures of female divinities found in Palestinian excavations, there are none with warlike attributes. This can hardly mean that none of them represent Astarte or Anath. It is more likely that these divinities were, like the Babylonian Ishtar, goddesses both of war and of fertility, and that the Egyptians of the periods of conquest, feeling the need of adding to their pacific national pantheon some deities of a more warlike character, were specially impressed by the warlike attributes of the Semitic goddesses, while to the Canaanites their most important function was, as the incarnation of female fecundity, to foster love and promote maternity.

The types of female divinities discovered in Canaan vary considerably : most of them are in the form of little pottery bas-reliefs.[1] There are also statuettes of the same material and of bronze, sometimes with two supports intended to fit into a pedestal,[2] or else with a pointed base. The execution often displays foreign influence, sometimes Babylonian, sometimes Egyptian, sometimes Cyprian or Hittite. The goddess is often represented with the heavy head-dress of Hathor, like the Kadesh of the Egyptian monuments,[3] or, especially at Taanach, with a Babylonian tiara,[4] or again she may be veiled.[5] Sometimes she wears jewels, necklaces, bracelets, earrings, arm- and ankle-rings ; or again she may be unadorned. Occasionally she carries a tambour, or, like Kadesh, a flower and a serpent, or she presses her breasts to make the milk start from them. Sometimes she is clothed in a clinging robe, sometimes she is quite naked. But always her sex-characteristics are emphasized, at times with a stark realism which leaves us in no doubt as to the nature of the benefits which the Canaanites, and especially the Canaanite women, expected from their goddesses. In some cases astral emblems have been found on these figures.[6]

Usually all these statuettes are called Astartes. In reality, we do not know which of the Canaanite goddesses these figures are intended to represent. An exception must be made in the case of Anath : the characteristic manner of

[1] See pl. iv, 2, 3, 4.
[2] Fig 26 (p. 85) and pl. iv, 1.
[3] **CLIX,** p. 160 (figs. 102–3), pl. iii, figs. 6, 9, 10, 11.
[4] **CLIX,** p. 161 (fig. 104).   [5] **IV,** p. 125.
[6] So **CLIX,** p. 460 (fig. 103).

representing the guardian goddess of Beisan is known to us from several small figures found there.[1]

3. Foreign Divinities

In addition to their native gods and goddesses, the Canaanites had adopted a certain number of foreign deities, such as Ḥepa or Ḥiba, a goddess of the Hittites and the Mitannites ; a prince of Jerusalem in the Tell el-Amarna age, and an inhabitant of Taanach, both named ARAD-Ḥiba, " servant of Ḥiba," had placed themselves under her protection.[2] But most of these foreign gods had been borrowed from the pantheon of the political over-lords of the country, the Babylonians and then the Egyptians. According to the ancient custom it was the vassal's duty to worship the gods of his suzerain.

(a) *Babylonian Divinities.* Palestinian place-names furnish the main evidence for the worship there of Mesopotamian gods.

A cylinder seal of the time of Hammurabi (about 2000) found at Taanach bears the inscription : " Atanaḥili, son of Ḥabsi, servant of Nergal." [3] Two cities [4] and a mountain [5] were dedicated to Nebo.

The adoption of certain Babylonian deities was facilitated by the fact that they were regarded as identical with similar native gods. The Babylonian thunder-god Ramman was regarded as interchangeable with Hadad the Syrian storm-god, as the compound name Hadad-Rimmon proves.[6] This god often appears in Palestinian place-names, under the guise of Rimmon, a name which had a familiar sound to the Canaanites, since *rimmon* in Hebrew means pomegranate. Thus we find Rimmon [7] or Ain-Rimmon—the spring of Rimmon [8] in Judah, Rimmon [9] or Rimmono [10] in Zebulon, Gath Rimmon—the wine-press of Rimmon,[11] Rimmon-Perez [12] Sela'-ha-Rimmon—the rock of the pomegranate.[13]

---

[1] See pl. vii, 2, and pp. 85, 108–9.
[2] **CLII**, p. 39, ns. 7, 8.   [3] See fig. 7, p. 63.
[4] The one in Moab (Num. xxxii. 3, 38 ; xxxiii, 47, etc.), the other in Judah (Ezra ii. 29 ; x. 43, Neh. vii. 33).
[5] Deut. xxxii. 49 ; xxxiv. 1.
[6] Zech. xii. 11, whether this be the name of a place or, what is more probable, that of the god himself, confused with Adonis.
[7] Zech. xiv. 10.
[8] Joshua xv. 32 ; xix. 7 ; 1 Chron. iv. 32 ; Neh. xi. 29.
[9] Joshua xix. 13.   [10] 1 Chron. vi. 62.
[11] Joshua xix. 45 ; xxi. 24 ; 1 Chron. vi. 54 ; *Giti Rimuni* in **TA(W)**, 164, 45 (K, 250, 46).
[12] Num. xxxiii. 19–20.   [13] Judges xx. 45, 47 ; xxi. 13.

Ninib, whatever may have been the real pronunciation of his name, has been identified with the god Shalem, if it be admitted that Bit-Ninib, in one of the Tell el-Amarna letters,[1] denotes the city of Jerusalem.[2] In any case the ideogram representing the name of this god is found in Palestine about 1400, not only in the name Bit-Ninib, but in another place-name Al Ninib [3] and in a personal name Abd-Ninib.[4]

It is possible that the name of Sin may be found in those of Mount Sinai and the desert of Sin. If this be so, it is likely that the Babylonian Moon-god has been assimilated to one of the native lunar deities.[5]

It has been supposed, but with even less certainty, that traces of the cult of Ṣalm, the god of shadows, or the image-god,[6] Sibitti, the god Seven,[7] Arba, the god Four,[8] Anu, the Heaven,[9] and Laḥmu,[10] have been found in Canaan.

At Beisan the seal of Manuum, the servant of Enki(Ea),[11] was found, but it may have been brought from Babylon.

(b) *Egyptian Divinities.* We have much better information concerning the influence of Egyptian religion upon that of the Canaanites. At certain periods this influence was much in evidence and widespread, but seems to have remained superficial.

We may leave out of account the effect of the religion of Egypt upon Byblos, very marked since the early dynasties as this city lies outside Palestine proper.

In the sixteenth century the country was conquered by the Pharaohs of the eighteenth dynasty. In agreement with ancient conceptions, the conquest involved the acquisition of the new provinces by the gods of the conquerors. Thothmes III consecrated to Amon three cities in the region of

---

[1] **TA(W)**, 55 (K, 74), 31.

[2] Sayce, Haupt (in Bennett, Joshua).

[3] **TA(W)**, 75 (K, 117), 41 (Knudtzon's reading).

[4] *Ibid.*, 53 (K, 84), 39.   [5] See p. 129.

[6] In the names of the mountain Salmon (Judges ix. 48), and of the cities, Salmona (Num. xxxiii. 41), and Buru-silim (**TA**, *cf.* Paton, **ERE,** iii, p. 181[a]).

[7] A prince of Byblos, in the time of Tiglat Pileser IV (eighth century) was called Sibitti bi'li (**XII**, p. 44). Beersheba might be the well of the god Seven (more probably "the seven wells") ; *cf.* the personal names Bath Sheba, Elisheba (Elisabeth) Jehosheba, and the names in Shua. See Paton, **ERE,** iii, p. 184[a] ; **IV,** p. 77, n. 3. On Sibitti, **XCIII,** pp. 413, 459, 620.

[8] If it is true that Qiryat Arba, the old name of Hebron signified " town of the four gods," as Arbela (Arba-ilu) in Assyria.

[9] Anharath (Joshua xix. 19) = Anuḥertu (list of Thothmes III).

[10] In che name of Bethlehem (more probably "house of bread ").

[11] **RB,** 1928, pp. 137 and 128 (pl. x, 6).

Lebanon;[1] later, Egyptian gods "dwelt" to the north of Tunip.[2] Seti I erected at Shihab, to the south of Tell Ashtarah in Transjordania, a stele on which he is represented offering a libation to Amon.[3] Yet again, under Ramses III (1200–1169) cities were set apart for Amon, and the king built in Canaan (or in the city of Canaan?) " a mysterious abode like the horizon of the heavens which is in the firmament " (that is to say, the abode of the sun); he erected there a great statue of " Amon of Ramses, chief (god) of Heliopolis " to which the natives were to bring offerings " for it was divine."[4]

A century later, after the fall of the Egyptian power, Wen Amon, a royal envoy, claimed the right to receive from the King of Byblos, free of cost, the cedars of Lebanon needed for the building of the barque of Amon : the Egyptian ambassador declares : " On the Nile there are no ships which do not belong to Amon ; his is the sea, and his is this Lebanon of which thou sayest—It is mine!—It is for the barque of Amon, who is lord of all ships." Wen Amon complains that the King of Byblos is bargaining concerning Lebanon with his master Amon, and goes on to say : " It is he who was lord of thy fathers who spent their time in sacrificing to Amon." It is true that the King of Byblos rejects these claims and demands payment : he is not the Pharaoh's servant and pays no regard to the supremacy of Amon : " I have," says he, " only to cry with a loud voice to Lebanon, and straightway the heaven will open and its trees will lie stretched upon the ground."[5]

Nevertheless, the speeches put into Wen Amon's mouth certainly express the official religious attitude of the Egyptian government ; and the Canaanites had been obliged to bow to it when they were not merely nominally but actually vassals of the Pharaoh. This is shown by the Tell el-Amarna letters, written at this period ; one of the correspondents of the Egyptian king attributes his victories to the gods of the King and to the Sun, that is, to Amon Ra identified with Shamash. Others invoke the god of gods of the King and

[1] **CXIV**, p. 77.
[2] *Ibid.*, The mod. Dunibeh, south-east of Hama (**XX**, p. 109).
[3] *Ibid.*, and **XIII**, p. 345.
[4] Harris Papyrus ; *cf.* **XXIII**[2], i, p. 98 ; **CXIV**, p. 77.
[5] **XXXVI**, ii, pp. 365–7.

acknowledge the power of Shamash.[1] A private letter found at Taanach contains a list of " men of Amon " together with others who are distinguished as " men of Addu," these are no doubt priests in the service of these two gods, one an Egyptian god, the other Canaanite.[2] In the Tell el-Amarna letters occur many personal names compounded with Amon ; [3] several of them were certainly native names : for instance Amanhatbi, the name of a Syrian prince ; [4] a servant of the King of Byblos bears the name of Pen-Amon,[5] " the (man) of Amon."

When Amenophis IV, the Pharaoh of the reform, attempted to replace the cult of Amon by that of Aton, the solar Disk, his Canaanite vassals sought to follow their lord in his religious developments : it is supposed that we have echoes of the " new teaching " in letters from the Kings of Tyre and of Jerusalem ; [6] some of the natives even changed their names to comply with the official doctrine.[7]

The worship of the king, the divine son of Ra, went hand-in-hand in Egypt with that of the Sun-god himself, while in Asia the vassals of the Pharaoh were likewise compelled to conform. In the Tell el-Amarna letters, the Canaanite princes address their sovereign as " my god," " my gods," " the Sun of the lands," " the eternal Sun,"[8] " my breath."[9] They say that they prostrate themselves seven times before him, on their backs and on their faces.[10] Ramses II erected a statue of himself at Tunip, and a city of southern Lebanon bore his name.[11] Ramses III placed an image of himself in the temple of Beth Shan.[12] In the Asiatic fortresses built by the same king in honour of Amon, annual offerings to the *ka* of the lord of gods were prescribed,[13] " the *ka* of the lord of

[1] **CXIV**, p. 79.   [2] **XXXVII**, p. 207.
[3] **XCIII**, p. 486, n. 5.   [4] **TA(W)**, 134 (K, 185).
[5] Voyage of Wen Amon. This was also the name of an officer in the service of Egypt (Anastasi Pap. III). *Cf.* Ranke, **XXIII**[2], i, pp. 75, 96.
[6] **TA(K)**, 147, 5 *ff.* ; 287, 60–1 ; 288, 5–7 ; *cf.* Weber in Knudtzon, 1025.
[7] **TA(K)**, 292, 36 ; 316, 13 ; 326, 1.
[8] **XIII**, p. 341.   [9] *Cf.* Lam. iv. 20.
[10] Asiatics are represented in these different postures, on a bas-relief of the tomb of Haremheb (see **LXI**, p. 33 (fig. 11).
[11] **CXIV**, p. 77.   [12] Now in the museum at Jerusalem.
[13] **CXIV**, p. 77.

gods " being a title of the Pharaoh who regarded himself as the " double " of his divine father.[1]

There was nothing in such claims to surprise the Canaanites. Many contemporary rulers, the Hittite kings, the Babylonian monarchs from the time of Hammurabi, and the Assyrian kings, called themselves the Sun of their country.[2] Several of the early kings of Babylon were worshipped in temples specially reserved for the purpose, and, as we have already seen, the Canaanite kings may have claimed similar honours.[3]

Moreover, it must not be thought that the worship of the gods of Egypt was a mere political obligation, confined to the official circle of princes and their courts. We have already pointed out the significance of the abundance in which statuettes and symbols of Osiris, Horus, Ptah, Isis and many other Egyptian divinities have been found in Palestinian graves ;[4] and the fact that Canaanite craftsmen themselves cast images of the god Bes, points to an extensive popular demand.

The cordial welcome given to Egyptian cults by the inhabitants of Palestine is partly explained by the extraordinary tolerance extended by the Pharaohs of the eighteenth and nineteenth dynasties to the gods of their Asiatic subjects. The usual policy of an oriental conqueror was directed to the humiliation of the gods of the conquered people : their images and their sacred vessels were carried off and placed as trophies in one of the temples of his capital.[5] A minor insult was to inscribe his name [6] and the might of his god [7] upon their statues, while at times he would go so far as to destroy the gods of the conquered with their temples [8] or to abolish their cult.[9]

In contrast to this, the Pharaohs of the New Kingdom

---

[1] **CXIV**, p. 62.   [2] *Ibid.*, p. 78.
[3] See pp. 118–9.   [4] P. 66.
[5] This was done by Mesha, King of Moab, with Israelite cult-objects (**II**, pp. 12–13, 17–18), just as the Philistines carried away the ark (1 Sam. v. 1–2), or David the gods of the Philistines : Tiglath Pileser I did the same with the gods of Songi, Sargon, with the gods of the Elamites, and the King of Elam with the stele of Hammurabi.
[6] As the Pharaohs did to the statue of Shamash at Qatna, at least according to Winckler (**TA(W)**, 138, Rev. ll. 18–31).
[7] So Esarhaddon did to the gods of Hazael, King of the Arabs (**XIII**, p. 345 ; **XXXVI**, ii, p. 306).
[8] As Asshurbanipal did in the land of Elam.
[9] As the Hyksos did according to the Egyptians.

paid lavish honours to the gods of their Syrian vassals. They filled the temples of Beth Shan and Byblos with their offerings. An officer of Thothmes III did sacrifice to a goddess of Lebanon.[1] The Egyptians of the eighteenth dynasty entreated the local gods of Beth Shan, Anath and Mikal,[2] for life, strength and health in the after-world. On the stele called " the stone of Job," Ramses II is represented in the act of worshipping a deity whose Semitic origin is indicated by his crown, horns and title.[3]

The Pharaohs even went so far as to admit several of these Syrian divinities into the Egyptian pantheon : they built temples for them and assigned priesthoods to them in various cities on the banks of the Nile ; for instance, to Baal Zaphon, Baal, Resheph, Astarte, Anath and Kadesh.[4]

Thus we frequently find the worship of Canaanite divinities accompanying, although in a subordinate rank, the cult of the gods of the ruling people. Occasionally the association is carried a step further by the identification of Asiatic gods with their counterparts in the Egyptian theology. Baal was assimilated to Set or Sutekh,[5] Shamash (the sun), to Amon-Ra or Aton, and the Lady of Gebal, as well as the Lady of the Turquoise, of Serabit el-Hadim, to Hathor.[6] Furthermore, as we have seen, Canaanite craftsmen often represented their goddesses with attributes borrowed from those of the latter divinity.[7]

However a sense of the difference between native and foreign gods persisted : the Taanach tablet already quoted seems to name along with Amon, not only Addu but Shamash, thus recognizing in him a second sun-god.[8]

It was no doubt by reason of the very respect paid to them by the Pharaohs that the local cults remained essentially unchanged in spite of the innovations introduced into them by the Egyptian overlords. Hence when Canaan became free from the political control of Egypt, after the death of Ramses III in 1169, the native religion seems quickly to have regained its ancient aspect, discarding almost completely the Egyptian veneer of the three preceding centuries.

[1] **XIII**, p. 345.   [2] See p. 117.   [3] **XCIV**, pp. 81–2.
[4] See pp. 139, 140, 148, 154–5. According to Dussaud (**SY**, 1926, p. 277), the temple of Bâl, built at Memphis under the Ramessides, was dedicated to the Baal of Tyre, Melqart.
[5] **CXIV**, pp. 83, 84.   [6] **XIII**, p. 345.   [7] P. 136.   [8] **CXIV**, p. 79.

CHAPTER III

RELIGION AND ETHICS

I

RELIGIOUS THOUGHT AND FEELING

IT has been suggested that here and there traces can be seen in Canaan, of a trend in the direction of monotheism. Special stress has been laid on a letter from an individual named Ahiyami or Ahiyawi to Ashiratwashur, King of Taanach. Here is the beginning of this tablet according to Hrozny's translation : [1]

> " May the Lord of Gods protect thy life, for thou art a brother and love dwells in thy bowels and in thy heart. . . . Are there still tears for thy cities or hast thou regained power over them ? Above my head is one who is above the cities. See then if he will not do thee good. If he shall shew his face, the enemies will be confounded and victory will be great."

The title " Lord of gods " given by the writer of this letter to his divine protector, has no great significance, for it was a conventional mode of address from the worshipper to his god, but the intense and somewhat mysterious way in which Ahiyami speaks of " one who is above the cities," the conviction with which he advises his correspondent to trust in him, bear the marks of an unusual personal piety.

Some have inferred from this that there was in the fifteenth century a sort of monotheism among the Canaanites, and that this type of religion had a deep influence upon the Israelites. It has been suggested that the idealizing picture of Abraham's piety, drawn by the author of Genesis, really refers to this pre-Israelite monotheism, and that the more advanced Canaanites were already calling their one god *Jahweh*, since Ahiyami may be interpreted as " Jahweh is my brother (or kinsman)." This is a somewhat far-fetched construction to

[1] **XCIV**, p. 57; **CLIII.**

build upon a phrase which, rightly interpreted, offers nothing which goes beyond the beliefs of a convinced and pious polytheist. Moreover, the translation of Ahiyami's letter is very doubtful. Another Assyriologist, Prof. Ebeling, reads it quite differently :

> " May the Lord of gods protect thy life ! Thou art a brother and love . . . and in thy heart it is that (*i.e.* perhaps, thou knowest well that) I interposed (?) at Gurra . . . Command thy cities that they do their work. On thy head is each man who . . . in the cities . . . See now that I have done thee good ! " [1]

It is true that some of the Canaanites may have claimed for one of their gods, especially Hadad or Shamash, supremacy over the rest ; the example of the hierarchy of Egyptian gods, the attempt of Amenophis IV to unite all the provinces of the empire in the worship of the one Solar Disk, may have fostered a tendency towards a monarchical polytheism. It is quite possible that, according to the tradition preserved by a Jewish midrash on Genesis xiv., a Canaanite city may have given to its god the titles of " El Elyon (God most high), Maker of heaven and earth."[2] Similarly, the Phenicians had two deities, one called Eliun, the other El, who were notwithstanding, only two of the many figures of their theogony.[3]

A matter of greater certainty is that the Canaanites possessed a knowledge of the great myths embodying the Babylonian explanation of the creation of the world and of the present state of mankind. It is well known that among the diplomatic tablets of Tell el-Amarna were found copies of the myth of Adapa, the first man, as well as that of Ereshkigal and of the descent of Nergal into hell.[4] The Palestinian scribes, like their Egyptian colleagues, must have studied the religious literature of the Babylonians in order to acquire a knowledge of their language. Moreover the glyptic art of Palestine shows that the ancient inhabitants of Palestine possessed a mythology closely akin to that of Babylon. For instance, a Gezer sealing depicts 19 objects resembling the signs of the Zodiac and especially the divine symbols engraved on the *kudurru*, the sacred boundary-stones of the Kassite

---

[1] **XXIII**[2], i, p. 371.
[2] Gen. xiv. 18, 19, 22.
[3] Philo of Byblos, Fr. ii, 12–14.
[4] See p. 63.

period.[1] Many seals display a conventional tree with seven branches, winged genii, heraldically opposed stags, etc.[2] It must, however, be pointed out that Syro-Hittite or Cypriote features are even more abundant,[3] and that Babylonian motives usually appear in forms peculiar to Syria.[4] Thus on a clay altar found at Taanach,[5] the very common motif of a hero strangling a serpent occurs as a child (pl. xvi, 3), a conception alien to Babylonian artists.[6]

A fact of fundamental importance for the explanation of the origin of the Israelite creation stories is the presence in Canaan of a body of myths essentially akin to those of Babylon, but bearing the peculiar impress of western Asia.

Thanks to the Tell el-Amarna letters, we can form some idea of the religious phraseology of the Canaanites, and consequently of their religious attitude. Indeed, the correspondents of the Pharaoh, obliged by convention to treat their suzerain as a divine being, must often have made use in addressing him, of the same formulas and metaphors as they employed in prayers or hymns addressed to their gods. Their religious language recalls in the most detailed way that with which we are familiar among the Israelites.[7] We find examples of parallelism, of strophical arrangement with refrains. The words with which a certain Tagi addresses the King : " If we mount up to heaven or if we go down into the earth, our head is in thy hands," [8] echo exactly the formula with which the prophet Amos (Amos ix. 2–3) and the author of Psalm cxxxix. describe the power of Jahweh :

" If I ascend up into heaven, thou art there :
if I make my bed in Sheol, behold thou art there ! "
—Psalm cxxxix. 8.

Among the Semites, personal names usually consisted of a short phrase indicating the relation of the bearer with his god, or proclaiming one of the attributes of the god. From these we learn what characteristics of the deity most strongly

[1] **CX**, pl. xxxix, n. 297 and p. 164.
[2] *Ibid.*, pl. xxxvi, n. 273, 264.   [3] *Ibid.*, p. 164.
[4] **CXLIX**, pp. 151 *ff.*
[5] Certainly, it is supposed to belong to the Israelite epoch, ninth–sixth centuries) ; **CLIX**, p. 185.
[6] **XXIII**[2], ii, pp. 115, 116 (fig. 397, *cf.* 400) ; *cf.* **CLIX**, pp. 183–5 (pls. iv-v).
[7] **XIII**, pp. 336–44 ; **CXIV**, pp. 98–102.
[8] **TA(W)**, 189 (K, 264), 15–19.

impressed the religious feeling of the Canaanites.[1] They were especially swayed by the majesty and power of their gods : we find such names as " slave of Asherah,"[2] " slave of Melek,"[3] "Adad is great,"[4] " Melek is exalted."[5] There are also names which declare the glory of the gods : " Adad is beautiful,"[6] " Ammu is full of majesty." [7] The Canaanites trusted in the care of their gods : " Adad will enlarge," [8] " El will build," [9] " Ammu is my keeper,"[10] " El is my hope,"[11] " Baal is with him."[12] They regarded children as the gifts of the gods : " Adad has given."[13] Like the rest of the Semites the Canaanites held that there was a bond of kinship between them and their gods : [14] hence the many names compounded with *abi*, father,[15] *aḥi*, brother,[16] *'ammu*, kinsman.[17]

The early inhabitants also regarded the gods as the guardians of justice and equity, but this aspect of their activities appears much less frequently in personal names : we have one example, that of a king named Addudayan, *i.e.* " Addu is judge."[18]

II

MORALITY

From the Tell el-Amarna letters we do not receive a very high idea of the truthfulness, loyalty or courage of the Palestinian princes.

On the other hand, the judgments passed by the Israelites

---

[1] *Cf.* **CXI**, pp. 132–3 ; **CLV** ; Dussaud, **SY**, 1927, pp. 216–33 ; Lods, **RHP**, 1927, p. 453.

[2] Abd Ašrat, **TA(W)**, 53–7, etc. (K. 60–2, etc.).

[3] Abd Milki, **TA(W)**, 77 (K, 123), 37 ; 252 (K, 203), 3.

[4] Rib Addi, **TA(W)**, 53–118 (K, 68–93 ; 95 ; 102–138).

[5] Milkiram, **CLV**, e. 27.

[6] Yapa 'Addi, **TA** (W), 61 ; 69 ; 72, etc.

[7] Yaqar 'Ammou, **CLV**, e. 27.

[8] Yapti 'Addi, **TA(W)**, 181, 44 (K, 288, 45) ; *cf.* **CLV**, e. 19.

[9] Yabni-el, **TA(W)**, 218 (K, 328).

[10] Omen 'Ammu, **CLV**, e. 12.

[11] Ilu miqwati, *Ibid.*, e. 22.

[12] Itho Ba'al, name of the son of Ahiram.

[13] Nathan Addu, **TA(W)**, 77, 37.

[14] See p. 143.   [15] **CLV**, e. 2 ; **TA(W)**, 149–56.

[16] **CLV**, e. 7, 24 (Hiqasin, " my brother is chief ").

[17] **TA(W)**, 128–30 (K, 141–3) ; **CLV**, e. 2, 8, 10, 12, 27 ; story of Sinuhe (Ammu-inši).

[18] **TA(W)**, 239–40 (K, 292–3)

on the moral condition of Canaanite society are not so entirely unfavourable as might have been expected. Their historians give an attractive picture of Tamar, the enterprising daughter-in-law of Judah (Gen. xxxviii.), of Araunah the generous Jebusite, of Uriah, the loyal Hittite officer in David's army (2 Sam. xi. 11). Abimelech, King of Gerar, is described by the Elohist as having behaved with integrity and uprightness : Abraham thought that in the country of this prince there was no fear of God, but events showed him to have been mistaken (Gen. xx.). A less flattering picture of Abimelech is given us by the Jahwist, who, moreover, makes him a Philistine : while the prince is scrupulous in his relation with Sarah (Gen. xxvi. 8–11), on the other hand, he exhibits bad faith in seizing the wells dug by Abraham and Isaac, and jealousy in driving out the latter patriarch. However, Isaac, like his father, made a permanent alliance with him (Gen. xxi. 25, 28–30, 32–3 ; xxvi. 12–33).

In the quarrel between the sons of Jacob and the men of Shechem over Dinah, it is the sons of Jacob who display treachery and cruelty (Gen. xxxiv.), and according to the most ancient Hebrew document, their father blames them publicly for it (Gen. xlix. 5–7). With very few exceptions, the patriarchs are represented as having maintained peaceful and even close friendly relations with the Canaanites : Judah was connected by marriage with the native clan of Hirah (Gen. xxxviii.) ; Abraham interceded for Sodom (Gen. xviii. 23–33) ; later texts describe him as summoning to his aid his Canaanite confederates and displaying the most friendly attitude towards the King of Sodom (Gen. xiv.). The men of Hebron vie with him in courtesy over the matter of the purchase of the cave of Machpelah (Gen. xxiii. P).

On the other hand, Israelite writers of every period agree that among the Canaanites, family ties were lightly regarded, the paternal authority was flouted, while in the matter of sexual morality, liberty was carried to the extent of licence. According to an ancient tradition the eponymous ancestor of the Canaanites had behaved shamefully to his father and had consequently been condemned to be a servant of servants to his brethren (Gen. ix. 20–7). Hence this story cites the moral shamelessness of the Canaanites as the cause of their subjection, on the one hand to Shem, that is to say, to the

Hebrews, and on the other to Japhet, that is to a northern people who had even encroached on the tents of Shem, possibly the Philistines.

The depravity of the Canaanites was notorious : witness the vices attributed to the inhabitants of Sodom and Gomorrah, the reason alleged for their destruction by the fire of Jahweh (Gen. xiii. 13 ; xviii. 20–1 ; xix.).

At the end of the Holiness code, edited in the exilic period, after the condemnations pronounced against those who curse father or mother, who pass their children through the fire, who practice unnatural vices or enter upon unions which the Jewish legislator regards as incestuous, the writer continues :

> " For all these abominations have the men of the land done, which were before you, and the land is defiled ; that the land spue not you out also, when ye defile it, as it spued out the nations that were before you." (Lev. xviii. 27–8 ; *cf.* xx. 22–4.)

No doubt the Elohist writer was thinking of corruption of this kind when he spoke of the iniquity of the Amorites as the reason why God would drive them out of the land, adding that, in the time of Abraham, it was not yet full (Gen. xv. 16).

In considering these judgments, allowance must be made for the narrower outlook of a people accustomed to the severity of desert morals and easily shocked by the greater laxity of city life. But there must have been a large residue of truth in these strictures : the very religion of the Canaanites, with its bloody ritual, its female deities, its frequent ceremonial orgies, the halo of sanctity with which it surrounded prostitution, all tended to foster licence rather than to eradicate it.

By means of the facts which we have cited it is possible to get some idea both of the moral and religious, and of the political and intellectual characteristics of the inhabitants of Palestine at the time of the Israelite settlement : we find brave and warlike peoples, incapable of concerted action by reason of their disintegration into rival city-states. In the interior of the country their living depended mainly on agriculture, while on the coast it was derived from fishing, but there was also a flourishing city life, sharing freely in the common civilization of the eastern Mediterranean, rather as receiving than giving. They were not gifted with any remarkable aptitude for the plastic arts, but were supreme

as traders : the Phenicians, as we know, came shortly afterwards to monopolize international commerce, and for the
Israelite, " Canaanite " was synonymous with " merchant."
In their religious rites agricultural forms of worship prevailed : the religion of the masses was still not far removed
from ancient polydæmonism, and was mainly centred on the
local Baals and Astartes. Nevertheless, out of this welter
of petty divinities there emerged a few gods and goddesses
with wider powers ; but in general we see a somewhat heterogeneous and undifferentiated pantheon, welcoming foreign
gods. A relatively high level of culture was accompanied
by a distinctly lower stage of morality.

We shall now go on to describe the state of the Israelites
at the time of their settlement in Canaan. After which the
consequences of the meeting of Canaanite and Hebrew will
occupy our attention.

PART II

THE HEBREWS BEFORE THEIR SETTLEMENT IN PALESTINE

BOOK I

HISTORICAL DATA AND SOCIAL ORGANIZATION

CHAPTER I

THE HISTORICAL FRAMEWORK

I

Origins. Patriarchal Traditions

AT first sight it might be thought that we possess fuller information about the origins of Israel than concerning those of any other people. Indeed Genesis has preserved for us a large body of Hebrew tradition about the " patriarchs." Even critics like Renan have been so impressed by the life-like nature of these old stories that they have not hesitated to base upon them a complete picture of the social and religious conditions of the ancestors of the Israel that was to be.

In order to form a judgment upon the historical value of such a picture, we must first consider the manner in which these traditions have been transmitted to us, and examine the nature of them.

The patriarchal narratives of Genesis are drawn from three of the sources which criticism has distinguished in the Hexateuch : the Jahwist (J) which appears to have been edited, in the main, between 850 and 760, the Elohist (E),

151

between 800 and 760, and the Priestly Code (P), between about 550 and 450.

Since, according to the chronology of Genesis, the events of the patriarchal history took place about 2000 B.C., there must be an interval of from 1,200 to 1,500 years between our documents and the period which they profess to describe, an interval as great as that which separates us from the Merovingian Age. Nor is there any indication that the earliest of these writers, the school of J, made any use of earlier written sources. It is impossible to imagine a serious historian undertaking to reconstruct the age of Jesus from documentary evidence of no earlier date than the time of St. Louis or Francis I.

No doubt the task of the writers who gave us the patriarchal narratives consisted simply in the faithful collection and arrangement of oral traditions which had been current long before their time. But experience proves that it is impossible for oral tradition to preserve with any degree of accuracy the memory of historical events for more than two or three generations. We have only to consider, for example, the shapeless mass of confusions and mistakes to which the traditions of the Rabbinical compilers of the Mishnah (about A.D. 150) have reduced the history of the Hasmoneans and the Herods, or even of a period so near their own time as the revolt against the Romans.

Moreover the transmission of the stories of the patriarchs presents the further complication that an immense break occurs in its continuity. Even on the evidence of the tradition itself, a gap of 430 years (Exod. xii. 40–1), the period of the sojourn in Egypt, interrupts the course of the transmission, a gap concerning which little or nothing has been preserved by any of our sources. It is absurd to assume that tradition has preserved an accurate and minute account of the trivial family events in the lives of the patriarchs, the places where they happened, and the very words which were spoken on each occasion, when it has forgotten the four succeeding centuries of the national life.

It is true that an economist of the school of Le Play, M. Champault, a few years ago, undertook to prove in a series of articles published in *La Science Sociale*,[1] the accuracy with

[1] **CLXXV.**

which the description of patriarchal life in Genesis corresponded with what must have been the mode of life of the
semi-nomads who led a half-settled existence on the borders
of Palestine ; from which he argued to the extraordinary
retentiveness of the Hebrew memory and hence to the
accuracy of the patriarchal narratives.   But the facts cited
by M. Champault, in so far as they are true,[1] are capable of
quite another explanation : namely, that these stories only
took on their present form after the final settlement of the
Israelites in Canaan.   The descriptions which the Israelite
writers give, both of social conditions and of the topographical
setting, are accurate because they reflect the actual experience
of the writers.   The conditions of life in Palestine have
remained unchanged.   In order to depict the state of the
semi-nomads who were their ancestors, the narrators had
only to watch such Bedouins as the Kenites, for example
(Judges iv. 11, 17–22 ; v. 24–7), who, then as now, used to
come at stated times, following their immemorial custom,
to pitch their tents and feed their flocks in the interior of
Palestine.

When we inquire into the nature of these traditions and
the manner of their growth, we find that they are made up
of a series of short stories, originally independent of one
another.   Each story is complete in itself, and has its own
peculiar character and point, instructive or humorous.   At a
subsequent stage of the transmission these separate pearls
were strung into a chain on the slender thread of an often
wholly artificial genealogy.   For example, it is clear that in
the mind of the first tellers of the story, the Cain who, after
the killing of Abel, is afraid that he may be slain by the first
person who meets him, is not the son of the first man and the
first woman, and hence the only man alive upon the earth
except his parents.

In order, then, to determine the primary intention of these
traditions, it is necessary to consider them apart from the
genealogies, the links, and the inferences which have been
drawn from the order of the narratives.   Each story must be
examined by itself in order to discover what was its point of
interest for the tellers and their listeners.   The answer is
obvious ; in most cases the centre of interest lay in the people

[1] See p. 203.

or tribe who traced their descent from the hero of the story.
The reason for the choice of the quarrels of Jacob and Esau
as the subject of their story was that the former represented
the *people* of Israel and the latter the *people* of Edom. In
the story of the jealousy between Isaac and Ishmael, we find
reflected the rivalry between the settled Israelite and the
nomad Arab.

Most of the persons who play a part in the patriarchal
narratives bear the names of peoples, clans, countries or
cities : for instance Jacob is also called Israel, Esau is known
both as Seir and Edom, we have the twelve sons of Jacob
representing tribes, similarly Ishmael, Moab and Ammon,
Midian, Cain, the eponymous ancestor of the Kenites, Hagar,
etc.

Even those who are not eponymous are none the less
ancestors, each of one or more peoples : Lot has two sons,
one named Moab, the father of the Moabites, the other
Ammon, the ancestor of the Ammonites. Abraham's sons
are not only Isaac the father of Israel, but Ishmael, Midian,
and Jokshan, the father of Sheba and Dedan.

Hence the first and by far the largest group of narratives
distinguishable among the patriarchal traditions may be
classed as *ethnic stories*.

Some are simply the transformation of an episode in the
history of a people or a tribe, into the adventure of an
individual.

Thus we learn from an early historical document that the
tribes of Simeon and Levi were scattered on account of an
act of cruelty which cast a stain on the whole nation (Gen.
xlix. 5–7). The patriarchal equivalent of this episode occurs
in Genesis xxxiv. : the patriarchs Simeon and Levi are disowned by their father, Jacob—Israel, on account of the
treachery and cruelty which they have shown towards the
Canaanite prince Shechem, who represents the city of
Shechem.

But more frequently we find that the adventures of an
ancestor, eponymous or not, are more than the mere reflection
of the history of the people sprung from him. Their purpose
is to explain by a word or an action of an ancestor, particularly
by a blessing or a curse or an oracle uttered by or concerning
him, the subsequent destiny or character of his descendants,

and their relations with the neighbouring nations. For example, the reason why the tribe of Ephraim had the supremacy over all the rest of the tribes of Israel after the death of Solomon, was because it was foretold in two dreams experienced by Joseph, the ancestor of this tribe (Gen. xxxvii. 5–11).

The patriarchal narrative, as this example suggests, might easily be used, not only to account for existing conditions, but also to establish a right, to validate a claim, the explanatory story might easily take on the guise of a legal justification. Thus the wells of the valley of Gerar, and that of Beersheba in particular, belong to Israel because Isaac, or according to another version now combined with the first, Abraham, dug them, and the right of the ancestors of Israel was formally recognized by the King of Gerar in a treaty sealed *by an oath*—Beer Sheba may mean " the well of the oath,"—or by the sacrifice of *seven* victims—Beer Sheba may also mean " the well of the seven."[1]

Very often, as in the tradition which we have just considered, an ethnological or legal explanatory story may be accompanied by an *etymological* episode explaining the meaning of a name. Of course such etymologies have no scientific value and merely represent the play of popular poetic or humorous imagination. The name Edom is supposed to be derived from the red hair of the ancestor of this people (Heb. *'admoni*), or from the colour (Heb. *'adom*), of the famous mess of lentils for which he bartered away his inheritance (Gen. xxv. 25, 30) ; the name Israel comes from the victory gained by the ancestor of the nation over a god at the ford of the Jabbok (Gen. xxxii. 29).

The purpose of other narratives or episodes is to account for the meaning and origin of some religious custom ; these we may call *cultual* explanatory stories. For instance, the question arises why unleavened bread was eaten during the spring festival. The modern prosaic explanation is that because this feast took place at the beginning of the harvest, it was the custom to eat bread hastily made with the first ears of corn, unmixed with any ingredient coming from the previous year's harvest. The far more picturesque expla-

[1] Gen. xxi. 22–4, 27, 31 (E) ; xxi. 25–6, 28–30, 32–3 ; xxvi. 19–33 (J).

nation given by popular tradition is that the Israelites, in the haste of their flight from Egypt, had no time to leaven the dough in their kneading-troughs (Exod. xii. 34, 39). We may also compare the three explanations given of the origin of circumcision in Israel.[1]

Many of these cultual explanatory stories gave the answer to questions of special interest to the Israelite settled in Palestine. If he desired to know why there were specially sacred holy places in certain localities, such as Shechem, Bethel, Hebron, Beersheba, Penuel or Mahanaim, tradition replied that it was because in this particular spot, under the shade of this tree, beside this spring, at this sacred stone, Jahweh appeared to one of the ancestors of Israel in a dream (Bethel), in bodily form (Hebron, Penuel), by a verbal communication (Lahai Roi), by a miracle (at the waters of Kadesh). These explanations had the immense value for the Israelites of authoritatively establishing as Jahweh's, since they had been founded by the fathers, the holy places of Palestine where the Canaanites had worshipped before the arrival of the Israelites.

We also find geographical explanatory stories accounting for the unusual appearance of certain districts such as the valley of the Dead Sea (Gen. xiii. 19).

Hence, to the Israelites the patriarchal stories had an essentially ætiological value, explaining the actual state of their land or the immediate historical conditions of their people or of the neighbouring peoples.

It is much more difficult to decide where the Hebrew writers got the original material of these stories.

The simplest solution would be to suppose that these stories were merely the product of folk-poetry. We should have to assume that, working with no other material than the historical facts, the political situation, the religious rites, and the proper names belonging to the period between the conquest and the monarchy, popular imagination built up out of these elements the adventures intended to explain them. It is very probable that in this way and at this time arose some of the stories in question; in any case it is clear that most of the patriarchal narratives did not receive their present form until the period referred to; the story of the

[1] Exod. iv. 24–6 (J); Joshua v. 9 (E); Gen. xvii. (P).

curse of Canaan (Gen. ix. 20–7) presupposes that the Canaanites had already been subjugated by Shem, which means, no doubt, by the Hebrews, an event which did not take place until the beginning of the Hebrew monarchy. The numerous stories about Esau and Jacob are intended to explain the subjection of the Edomites by the Israelites, which only took place under David and his successors. The dreams of Joseph presuppose the founding of the northern kingdom.

But this manner of explaining the growth of the patriarchal narratives will not account for all our stories. And even in the stories for which it does account there remain refractory elements. Even those critics who, like Stade, have most stoutly defended the solution described above, have nevertheless admitted the necessity for other lines of explanation. There occur names of patriarchs which are not, as far as we know, names of any tribes or peoples belonging to the time of the judges or the kings : Abraham, for instance, Sarah, Laban and Rebecca. It may naturally be asked why, if the heroes of the patriarchal stories were mere personifications of peoples who came into conflict with one another in the period between the thirteenth or fourteenth centuries and the eighth, they should usually be represented as shepherds, whereas the Israelites at this time were agriculturists, as nomads when the Israelites had become a settled people, and as peaceful and even generous (at least in the case of Abraham and Joseph), when the Israelites were warlike and vengeful. Why is Israel who had conquered Edom in open fight represented as a cowardly and deceitful shepherd (Jacob), and why should the Edomite people who were incontestably renowned for wisdom be [1] depicted under the guise of the brutal and stupid Esau ?

Such questions suggest that these stories did not arise by the simple method of idealizing events belonging to the times, or nearly so, of the writers. Other factors must have gone to their making.

The question then arises whether these factors were historical, whether they consisted of actual surviving reminiscences of the mode of life and varying fortunes of the ancestors of the Hebrew people before their final settlement

---

[1] Jer. xlix. 7 ; Bar. iii. 22–3 ; Job. ii. 11 (cf. Gen. xxxvi. 10–11); I, i (cf. xxxvi. 28 ; Lam. iv. 21).

in Palestine. To a certain degree this may be true. We
may grant, for example, that the wandering pastoral life
ascribed to the patriarchs is partly explained by a remembrance of the former life of the tribes, and that they actually
led, at one time, the life of nomads within a limited circle,
breeding sheep and goats, on the southern borders of Canaan
round the oases of Kadesh, Lahai Roi, and Beersheba, the
scenes of some of the traditions concerning Abraham and
Isaac. The Aramean origin which the Hebrews claimed for
themselves is probably a genuine historical tradition.

It is within the range of possibility that the names of some
of the patriarchs, Abraham, Isaac, and perhaps Joseph and
Jacob, may have been those of invividuals who actually lived
among these tribes. The names of Abraham (under the
form Abiramu,[1] " the father is exalted," or Aba(m)rama,[2]
" he loves the father "), of Nahor,[3] and of Jacob,[4] occur as
personal names in cuneiform inscriptions of the age of Hammurabi. The name of Jacob also occurs on Egyptian scarabs
of the Hyksos period, under the form y 'q b-hr, $i.e.$ perhaps,
Yaqobel.[5] It is true that those of Jacob, Joseph, Asher, and
perhaps of Simeon and Levi, occur in Egyptian documents as
names of Palestinian places or peoples under the eighteenth
and nineteenth dynasties.[6]

But the mere supposition that historical persons named
Abraham, Sarah, Isaac, actually lived among the Hebrews,
does not contribute much to the explanation of the growth
of the patriarchal *narratives*. For the adventures of which
they are composed are, as we have seen, mostly ethnic facts
presented as the story of an individual, tradition having used
certain ancient names as pegs on which to hang stories
originally unconnected with the lives of the persons in
question.

Certain critics, while agreeing unreservedly with this
conclusion, nevertheless think that it is possible in another
way to obtain from Genesis valid historical data concerning

---

[1] *Cf.* **XXVI**, p. 139.

[2] **CCXLIX**, vi, 5, p. 60 ; Gressmann, **ZATW**, 1910, pp. 1–4 ; *cf.*
Ball in **XII**, p. 250.

[3] **XCIII**, pp. 477–8.   [4] Pinches in **XXXI**, p. 95, **III**, p. 20.

[5] **CCXXVI**, pp. 68–9 ; **XII**, lxvi ; Gressmann, **ZATW**, 1910, p. 7,
questioned in **CV**, ii, p. 86.

[6] See pp. 7, 47, 48–50.

the pre-mosaic period. According to them it is only necessary to read the adventures of individuals and families as events in the history of tribes and peoples. Abraham, Jacob, and perhaps Isaac, represent so many successive waves of emigration from Aramean lands in pre-historic times ; [1] the wives of the patriarchs, Sarah, Rebecca, Leah, Rachel, represent Aramean clans which allied themselves to the Hebrew emigrants. For instance, according to Burney,[2] Rebecca is an Aramean tribe which united with the Hebrew group of Isaac ; thence sprang the peoples of Edom and Jacob. But Edom drove out Jacob, who then returned to the Aramean country, increased in numbers (a fact symbolized by his double marriage), and was again driven into Canaan by other Arameans (Laban). Steuernagel and Burney thus succeed in reconstructing an eventful and detailed history of the Hebrew tribes before the Mosaic era.

But the whole fabric seems somewhat insubstantial. It is largely based on the order in which the collected traditions present the patriarchs and the stories relating to each. Now the arrangement of the patriarchal narratives in cycles seems to be one of the latest achievements of the editors of the traditions. Originally each story had its own independent existence ; there was not always agreement as to which patriarch had been the hero of the story ; the same adventure is told twice in connexion with the wife of Abraham, and again in connexion with Isaac's.[3] The story of the going down of Abraham into Egypt seems evidently a doublet of the descent of Jacob and Joseph into the same country. The digging of the well of Beersheba is sometimes attributed to Abraham, sometimes to Isaac.[4] Hence the question arises whether the Aramean marriages of the three chief patriarchs are not variants of the same tradition, and if the same should not be said about the migration from Aram into Canaan attributed respectively to Abraham and to Jacob.

In short it seems best to acknowledge that the valid historical elements in the traditions concerning the past of the Hebrew tribes have only contributed in a very small degree to the creation of the stories about the patriarchs.

---

[1] Dillmann, *Genesis*.   [2] **XII**, p. cx.
[3] Gen. xii. 10–20 ; xx. ; xxvi. 6–11.
[4] Gen. xxi. 22–33 ; xxvi. 23–33.

In contrast to this we find a source upon which Israelite tradition has freely drawn in the making of these explanatory ancestral stories, namely, oriental folklore, especially that of Palestine. The adaptation of earlier material is obvious in the story of Esau and Jacob : we have here applied to the relations between Israel and Edom, a folk-story about the tricks played by a cunning shepherd on a fierce and somewhat stupid hunter (*cf.* Ulysses and Polyphemus).

In the story of Joseph we find the counterpart of several of the situations which arise in the Egyptian story of the Two Brothers.[1] G. Huet has also pointed out that it is a variant, and, curiously enough, a less primitive variant, of a story which appears for the first time in written form in the twelfth century A.D. in the Romance of the Seven Wise Men :

> " A child (or a young man) foretells a splendid future for himself, but one which involves the humiliation of his father and mother. The enraged father kills his son, or has him killed ; but the child survives in some way or other. After various adventures, the supernatural knowledge which had enabled him to foretell his future, achieves his fortune ; he becomes the son-in-law of a king, and finally king himself. The father, on the other hand, meets with misfortune. One day the father and mother find themselves in the presence of their son and abase themselves before him, without recognizing him ; but the son knows them. He reveals himself to them, points out the fulfilment of the prediction and provides for the future of his parents." [2]

The story of the uncompleted sacrifice of Isaac is akin to the Iphigenia legends. The account of the visit of supernatural beings to Abraham (Gen. xviii.) is related to the story of Philemon and Baucis and other similar stories. *A priori* it is more than likely that the traditions accounting for the origin of the various holy places in Palestine—Shechem, Bethel, Penuel, Mahanaim, Hebron, Lahai Roi—were but the adaptation of those which were already current in the very same sanctuaries before the arrival of Israel. These traditions show traces of the survival of Canaanite polydæmonism : as in the plurality of the divine visitors to Abraham and Lot (Gen. xviii. and xix.), the multiplicity of angels, originally gods, who haunt the holy places of Bethel and Mahanaim.[3]

---

[1] Orbiney Papyrus. Translated into French in **LXIV**, 4th ed., pp. 3–21 ; *cf.* **XXXVI**, ii, pp. 375–80.

[2] G. Huet, *les Contes populaires*, pp. 135–6.

[3] Gen. xxviii. 12 ; xxxii. 2–3.

These folk-stories, whether Canaanite or foreign, must have been of extremely varied origin. Some no doubt were simply tales having no other purpose save the entertainment of the listeners, others were explanatory stories, others, again, according to Gunkel's ingenious theory, were ancient ethnological myths referring to earlier extinct ethnic groups : on this theory Jacob, Joseph, Asher, might be eponyms of cities or tribes shown to have inhabited Canaan between the sixteenth and fourteenth centuries. Other stories may have been detached fragments of myths.

This brings us to a fourth element which, according to some critics, was a predominant factor in the growth of the patriarchal traditions of Israel, namely, mythology or the myths relating to the gods. Asher, Gad, Edom, were names of deities as well as tribal or racial designations. The story of Esau and Jacob recalls the Phenician myth of the rivalry between Ousoos the hunter and his brother (Sa)memroumos (the high heaven). Sarah (princess) and Milcah (queen) were the names, or rather the titles, of two goddesses of Harran. Nahor occurs as the god of the Abyss, under the form $Na\chi a\varrho$ on a maledictory tablet found at Carthage.[1]

Hence it is a plausible supposition that several of the heroes of the patriarchal narratives were originally gods and that some part of their adventures was consequently mythological in origin. Although the proofs are not very conclusive, we may admit with E. Meyer, B. Luther and Raymond Weill[2] that Abraham, Isaac, Jacob and Joseph, before being presented as founders of certain holy places, had been their gods or " baals " : Abraham at Hebron, Isaac at Beersheba, Jacob at Bethel, and perhaps Joseph at Shechem.[3]

But here we are on very uncertain ground, and it is necessary to beware of the unchecked imaginations of some scholars who, at every turn, discover astrological allusions [4] in the patriarchal narratives, or transform their most trivial incidents into myths of Egyptian gods.[5] One thing at least

---

[1] **L**, pp. 32–3 ; R. P. Molinier, **MAF**, lviii (1899), pp. 212–20.

[2] Gressmann, **ZATW**, 1910, pp. 1–34.

[3] **CCXVII**, pp. 267 ff., 533, etc. ; R. Weill, **RHR**, lxxxvii, pp. 69–120 ; lxxxviii, pp. 1–44. See also below, pp. 228–9.

[4] Stucken, *Astralmythen* ; **XCII**, ii ; **XCIII**, p. 365 ; **CCLVI** ; **XXXVII**, pp. 179–85, 209–49 ; **XCIV**, pp. 60–2.   [5] **CCLI**.

is certain, namely, that *for the Israelite writers*, the actors in the patriarchal stories were exclusively historical persons, human ancestors of real peoples and tribes. Whatever mythology there may be in them has already been transformed into a story of the adventures of men or at most, of heroes.

Moreover, these stories have the unmistakable impress of the national religion of Israel : save for a few faint traces, the gods who may perhaps have played a part in the original form of the narratives, have been displaced by Jahweh.

Taking all the facts into consideration, it is probable that many diverse elements have gone to the making of the patriarchal history : events and facts of the times of the Judges and the Kings idealized or explained by popular imagination, historical reminiscences, Hebrew or Canaanite folk-stories, fragments of mythology. The national consciousness has taken all this various material, fused and recast it and produced therefrom a cycle of explanatory stories, accounting for the present state of Israel and its neighbours.

Hence it follows that these traditions can only be used with great reserve as evidence for the pre-history of the Israelite tribes. We are only warranted in accepting this or that element in these traditions as a reminiscence of those far-off times, first, if the element in question can neither be explained by the transforming play of popular fancy, nor be more naturally accounted for by the influence of folklore or the local religious traditions of the Canaanites; second, if the element in question is consonant with what we can infer from other sources concerning the past history of the Hebrew tribes.

II

THE ORIGINAL HOME OF THE HEBREWS

The first question to arise is whether the statements concerning the original home of the ancestors of Israel can be regarded as historical.

In Genesis xi. 28 we read " Haran (the brother of Abraham) died in the presence of his father Terah in the land of his birth, in Ur of the Chaldees."

This item of information which recurs in two other passages of Genesis (xi. 31 and xv. 7), has always had the effect of stimulating the imagination of commentators. Early Jewish expositors, convinced that Kasdim could only mean the famous Chaldeans of the lower Euphrates, concluded from this passage that the ancestor of their race was an adept in the whole range of Babylonian knowledge. They placed Ur in Babylon without the slightest idea of its locality. Modern exegetes have generally identified Ur Kasdim with the ancient city of Ur in lower Babylonia, some distance south of the Euphrates, on the site of the modern el-Mugheir. On this foundation they have reared all sorts of theories about " Abraham the Babylonian " : the original nucleus of the Hebrew people will thus have been a group of highly civilized city-dwellers. Since Ur, together with Harran, was one of the chief centres of the cult of the Moon-god Sin, Winckler has inferred therefrom that the characteristic monotheism of Israel had been taught them by the priests of this god, and so forth.[1]

These hypotheses rest upon very slender foundations. It seems much more probable that[2] by Ur Kasdim the writers of the three passages of Genesis referred to above, understood a city or a country of *upper Mesopotamia*, and not a city on the Persian Gulf.

According to popular Israelite tradition the Aramean group constituted the original stock of the Hebrew people. Hence the stories of Rebecca, Leah and Rachel. The home of the patriarchs was Aram-Naharaim, Harran or the city of Nahor in J, Padan-Aram in P, and in E it was the region " beyond the Euphrates " (while Ur was on this side, *i.e.* from the Babylonian point of view). A summary of the national history which the Israelite was supposed to repeat on the occasion of paying his tithes began with the words " My father was a wandering Aramean " (Deut. xxvi. 5). This close kinship which the Israelites claimed with the Arameans is the more significant when we remember that during the historical period the two peoples were in a state of almost continuous warfare with one another from the time of David up to the Assyrian conquest, and spoke two lan-

[1] CCLVI.
[2] The grounds for this statement are given in an appendix (pp. 165-6).

guages whose divergence became more marked with the course of time.

We shall probably be safe, then, in accepting this claim as a piece of valid historical tradition, always provided that we remember that the term " Arameans," at the time when this tradition grew up, did not denote, as it came to do after the tenth century, a totality of organized states, with a settled population, with great cities and an advanced civilization, occupying northern Syria, but nomad tribes peopling the Syro-Arabian desert to the east and south-east of Palestine. This fact is established by the Israelite tradition itself.

The earliest form of the tradition, E, says that Jacob fled into the land of the Bene Qedem and took a wife from thence. Now the Bene Qedem are " the children of the East," that is, these very Bedouins of the deserts east of Palestine. Even the authors of J, although they have transferred Abraham and the wives of Jacob to the more northerly region of the city of Harran, which was in their time the centre of Aramean influence, in upper Mesopotamia, have nevertheless preserved the colouring of the original tradition : they depict Abraham's kin, not as true city-dwellers, but as wandering shepherds, gathering their flocks at evening round the well and ranging over immense pastures, for they could place a three days' march between their teeming flocks. The hill-country of Gilead which, according to the agreement between Jacob and Laban, was to be the border-line between them, is better suited to be a boundary between the Palestinians and the nomads of the east than between the Israelites and the settled Arameans of the north.[1]

There is no reason why the tribes which were to be the nucleus of the Israelite nation should not have been part of the wave of invading nomads comprised under the term Arameans. The differences between Hebrew and the various dialects spoken by these Bedouins must at the outset have been very slight. Moreover, it is quite possible that the Israelites did not adopt Hebrew until after their settlement in Palestine, since that language was, as we have seen, " the tongue of Canaan " (Isa. xix. 18).[2]

The problem of the original home of these Hebræo-

---

[1] For further arguments see **CCXVII,** pp. 239–42.
[2] See p. 62.

Aramean invaders is a highly controversial question. Most modern scholars believe [1] that the cradle of the so-called Semitic race must be sought in Arabia. Others adhere to the old theory that the Semites came from the north or north-east, from Armenia.[2] According to a third view the home of the Semites was on the shores of the Persian Gulf.[3] Prof. Clay, supported by M. Moret, would find the true cradle of the Semitic peoples in Syria, the region of Damascus, and Mesopotamia.[4] We shall not attempt here to dispose of a question which is probably, at any rate at present, insoluble, and possibly irrelevant.

APPENDIX

THE SITE OF UR KASDIM

It is extremely probable that the addition " in Ur Kasdim " was not originally found at the end of the first of the three passages of Genesis in which this place-name now occurs (Gen. xi. 28). We are there told that Haran " died *in the land* of his birth " ; now it is almost unanimously held that Ur was not the name of a country but of a city. The second passage of Genesis in which this place is mentioned is also editorial (Gen. xv. 7). Some scholars hold that the authors of these two glosses took their information from the third passage (Gen. xi. 31), which belongs to the priestly document. Others think that it came from a parallel account, now lost, the work of another J writer. But, in either case, it seems very probable that Ur Kasdim does not denote the famous city of lower Mesopotamia, but another city of the same name. In fact, it is certain that there were several cities of that name,[5] since, in order to distinguish one from the other it was necessary to add a defining epithet : " Ur of the Kasdim," just as they said " Bethlehem of Judah " in order to distinguish it from Bethlehem of Zebulon.

We maintain that if the statement came from a parallel J narrative, now lost, it must have referred to another of these cities of Ur. In fact, according to all the surviving forms of the J tradition, Abraham's birthplace was not in the lower Euphrates region but in upper Mesopotamia : when he sent his servant to seek a wife for Isaac " in his own country," he sent him to Aram-Naharaim, according to one version, and to the city of Nahor,

---

[1] So **CLXIV** ; **LXXXII**, pp. 452, 453 ; **XII**, p. lvi ; **LXVI**, pp. 19–21.

[2] **LXXVIII**, p. 518 ; **CCXXIX**, p. 11 ; John P. Peters, **JAOS**, 1919, pp. 243–60.

[3] **CXCV** ; **CCII**, p. 28 ; **IV**, pp. 54–5.

[4] **CLXXVI** ; **LXVIII**, pp. 226–7.

[5] So Uri to the east of the Tigris, **XXXII**, p. 469, n. 2 ; perhaps Urusalim (Jerusalem) " founded by Shalem " (**XIII**, p. 395) ; Urum (Rum Kaleh, north-west of Biredjik ?) ; **XX**, p. 450.

according to another (Gen. xxiv. 4, 10).   When Jacob went to the land of the family of Laban, the son of Nahor, it was to Harran near Edessa that he betook himself (Gen. xxvii. 43, 44 ; xxviii. 10). It is not *a priori* impossible that Ur Kasdim was originally, in one of the strata of J, the name of Nahor's city, now nameless in the text as we have it ; if so, it would follow that this Ur was in the Harran district.   In support of this suggestion it may be remarked that a J passage appears to place Kesed, the eponymous ancestor of the Kasdim, in this region—he makes him one of the sons of Nahor (Gen. xxii. 22)—and that the Kasdim or Chaldeans were for a long period nomads who led a plundering life in the Syro-Arabian desert and on the borders of Palestine (Job i. 17).   Ur is not mentioned among the cities which were the cradle of the empire of Nimrod, that is among the ancient centres of the civilization of lower Mesopotamia (Gen. x. 10 J).

The other hypothesis is that the Priestly writer was the first to mention Ur Kasdim.   In this case it seems difficult to believe that he should have placed it in lower Babylonia.   We know that in his account the ark rested on the Ararat range, *i.e.* in Armenia. Now the names of the patriarchs whom he assigns to Abraham as ancestors and who constitute the line of descent from Shem to Abraham, seem to point exactly along the route from Armenia to Canaan (Serug, Terah).   It is very unlikely that this doctrinaire historian should have taken the patriarchal line in a leap to the shores of the Persian Gulf only to take it back again to the point where the journey to the south-west had been broken.   It may further be pointed out that according to the Priestly writer, Terah, the father of Abraham, on leaving Ur, does not take with him his second son, Nahor (Gen. xi. 31).   This implies that the latter remained and settled at Ur Kasdim, and that consequently, according to P, it was the city of Nahor.   Now apparently for him, as for J, Nahor represented the Syrian Arameans.   Hence it is very probable that according to the Priestly writer Ur was in the neighbourhood of Harran.

A local tradition, only dating, it is true, from the fourth century A.D., placed Ur Kasdim ten stades east of Harran and five beyond Nisibis (The Itinerary of Etheria).   The reference may be to the fortress of Ur which Ammianus Marcellinus mentions about the same date as between Singara and the Tigris (xxv. 8, 7). According to E. Meyer, Ur or 'Awur was a transcription of the Babylonian Amurru : in which case Ur Kasdim would be the Chaldean part of the land of the Amorites.[1]

Whatever we may think of these traditions, it seems extremely doubtful that the idea of the Babylonian origin of the Israelites should ever have formed part of their *traditions*.   Certainly it was from Babel (Babylon), that according to a well-known story (J), the scattering of the peoples took place ; and in this sense the Hebrews came from Babylon, but neither more nor less than the other races of the world.   Moreover, this narrative was an explanatory story, accounting for the name and character of the great city (see **XXVI,** *ad loc.*).

---

[1] **LXV,** i², 2, p. 467.

III

The Sojourn of the Hebrews in Egypt and in the Desert

According to the Israelite tradition the family of Jacob, driven by hunger, sought refuge in Egypt. There Jacob's descendants were cruelly oppressed, escaped ' under the leadership of Moses, and after forty years of wandering in the wilderness, entered Canaan, the land promised to their fathers, and began to subdue it.

So far, no non-Israelite document has corroborated with any degree of certainty the tradition of the sojourn of the Hebrews in Egypt and their exodus, although some commentators have eagerly sought to give the texts the required interpretation.

Various inscriptions do indeed record the entrance of Asiatics into Egypt.[1] But none of them can refer to the descent of the Hebrews into the land of the Pharaohs : either the date or the context is against it.[2] They do, however, confirm the strong probability of the facts related by the Israelite tradition.

There is, besides, the problem of a people engaged in the labours needed for the building enterprises of the Egyptian kings, who are called '-p-r (read as apuriu). Several Egypt-ologists since Chabas (1862) and Hebraists such as Hommel, Skinner, Driver and Kreglinger,[3] have identified them with the Hebrews. But, to say nothing of the linguistic difficulties (p for b), the presence of these apuriu in Egypt is established by inscriptions dating from the reign of Ramses IV, a period later than any proposed date for the Exodus. Many other explanations of the word have been suggested, Ephraim, for instance, and Afri.[4]

We need only mention in passing the fantastic accounts of the Exodus given by certain Greek and Egyptian writers of the Alexandrian period, notably Hecatæus of Abdera, contemporary with Alexander the Great,[5] and Manetho, a Heliopolitan priest of the third century B.C.[6] It is easy to see

---

[1] See, for example, **LXVIII**, p. 283 (fig. 22) ; **LXI**, p. 33 (fig. 11).
[2] See p. 172.
[3] **XLVII²**, p. 48.
[4] **XIII**, p. 328.
[5] Diod. Sic. 40, 3.
[6] Josephus, c. Apion, i, 26–7.

that they do not depend upon Egyptian *traditions*.[1]   According to Manetho, the Hebrews were the descendants of lepers and other diseased Egyptians who had been placed by Amenophis in the quarries and then in a city of the land.   A priest of Heliopolis, also smitten with leprosy, by name Osarsiph (or Osarseph), surnamed Moses, taught them to despise all the gods and the sacred animals.   They summoned to their help the Hyksos who had previously been driven out of Egypt, and were then driven out with them.

But Manetho himself acknowledges that these are rumours, fables, μυθολογούμενα (§ 105), μυθευόμενα καὶ λεγόμενα (§ 229).   It is easy to see that his version is the product of the biblical accounts combined with reminiscences of the rule of the Hyksos and distorted by the anti-Semites of Alexandria.   In Egyptian texts foreign invasions, especially that of the Hyksos, are often called " plagues," and the Hyksos are styled " plague-bringers."[2]   Osarseph is the name Joseph with the name of Osiris substituted for the syllable *Yo*, which was supposed to represent the name of Jahweh.

It has been maintained that from the silence of the Egyptian sources we must conclude that the descent of the Hebrews into Egypt is a pure fiction without any historical foundation.   But it still remains necessary to explain how the legend could have arisen and become one of the most essential and best attested elements of the national tradition.

According to a very ingenious theory of Winckler's, the origin of the tradition was partly the result of an ancient confusion.[3]   He thinks that in the beginning the name Mizraim was not exclusively used to denote Egypt, but the region which the Babylonian geographers called *Miṣr* or *Muṣri*, *i.e.* broadly speaking, the north of Arabia, a region to which, in the minds of the inhabitants of Asia, the Nile valley also belonged.[4]   Winckler thinks that when the original tradition spoke of a sojourn of the fathers, especially Moses, in Mizraim, it was referring to the time when the ancestors of the Hebrews lived in the deserts of southern Palestine.[5]

We may admit that the gradual expansion of the conno-

---

[1] According to **XXXVII**, pp. 251–4 ;   *cf.* **XCIII**, p. 213.
[2] *Cf.* **LXVIII**, pp. 289, 290.   [3] **XCIII**, p. 213.
[4] *Ibid.*, pp. 145–8, 178.   [5] *Ibid.*, p. 213.

tation of the term Mizraim is a very plausible supposition : it would be perfectly natural for the inhabitants of Canaan, having first of all used the name for the southern steppes, to apply it also to Egypt itself, the country which, for them, lay behind the deserts.   This process of extension of meaning is of constant occurrence in the history of geographical terms (Palestine, Greece, Asia, Africa, Germany, etc.).   This hypothesis would explain satisfactorily why the wady near Gaza was called " the river of Mizraim," although it was three days' march from the Egyptian frontier.   It would also explain quite naturally why Ishmael, the perfect type of the pure Bedouin in the patriarchal tradition, was represented as the son of a *Miṣrith* and as having taken to wife a *Miṣrith*. Hence it is possible that in some Hebrew texts or traditions, Mizraim originally denoted the Egypto-Arabian desert and not Egypt proper.

But there are several reasons for doubting whether this theory explains the tradition with which we are occupied. This tradition does not merely speak of a *sojourn* in Mizraim, but of the *enslavement* of the fathers in this country.   Nor is it likely that a proud and warlike people like the ancient Hebrews would lightly have represented their ancestors as slaves, even with the end in view of exalting the power of the god to whom they ascribed their liberation.

It is also significant that certain Israelite personal names are Egyptian, among others that of Moses, which seems to be the same word which forms an element in the names Thut-*mosis*, Ah*mosis*, etc., and means " son," or that of Phinehas, which seems to mean " the negro."

The statements of the oldest form of the Israelite tradition (J) about the manner of life in the land of Goshen, and about the store-cities of Pithom and Ramses, agree with the facts observed on the spot or established by excavation.

It would appear therefore that, underlying the Israelite traditions about the sojourn in Egypt and the Exodus, there is a basis of actual reminiscence.   Moreover, it must be recognized that they have come down to us mingled with a mass of legendary features, some due to the desire of magnifying the power of Jahweh, the deliverer and creator of the nation, others arising from the fact that succeeding generations had lost contact with the actual conditions of nomad life—hence the stories about the manna, the forty years in the desert, etc. Furthermore, among the traditions of the Exodus, it is possible to distinguish various ætiological narratives similar to those which occur in the patriarchal history : popular explanations of a rite, such as unleavened bread (Exod. xii. 33, 34, 39), the Passover,[1] circumcision (Exod. iv. 24–26), or of an institution like that of the Elders (Exod. xviii ; Num. xi.), or again, of the origin of an object of veneration like the brazen serpent (Num. xxi. 4–9 ; cf. 2 Kings xviii. 4), or of a holy place, such as the sacred spring of Massah and Meribah, or that of Marah.[2] To the same source, perhaps, we owe the story of the burning bush (Exod. iii. 1–6) and that of the fight of Moses with Jahweh (Exod. iv. 24–26). The original purpose of the narrative of the Egyptian plagues may have been to account for certain unpleasant characteristics of the climate of that country. According to the Hebrew historian, the reason why the water of the Nile becomes red and insanitary at certain seasons, why, after the Nile-flood, the country swarms with frogs, and, after the waters have subsided, with mosquitoes, why Egypt,—for so the Israelites believed (Deut. vii. 15)—was the chosen land of epidemic and endemic diseases—Pliny calls Egypt " the mother of contagious diseases "[3]—was because these were all so many punishments for the obstinacy with which the Pharaoh of olden days held the ancestors of Israel in slavery. Other features have been borrowed from the common stock of Oriental folklore. For example, the charming story of the infant Moses, abandoned on the Nile and found by a princess, comes from this source, as is shown by a whole cycle of parallel traditions in which the same adventure is ascribed to the son of Nephthys found by Isis,[4] to Sargon of Agade, Gilgamesh, Bacchus, Semiramis, Cyrus, Ptolemy I, Cypselus, Perseus, Romulus and Sigurd.[5] It will suffice to quote the legend of Sargon as an instance.[6]

" I am Sargon, the mighty king of Akkad. My mother was a vestal . . . my mother the vestal conceived me, she brought me

---

[1] Commemorative rite according to D (Deut. xvi. 1) and R[d] (Exod. xii. 24–27 ; xiii. 11–16), apotropaic according to P (Exod. xii. 1–14) and R (Exod. xii. 21–23).

[2] Exod. xv. 23–25[a] ; xvii. 1[b], 7 ; etc.

[3] Hist. nat., 26, 1, 5.   [4] Cf. CLXII, p. 51.

[5] Cf. XXXVII, pp. 256–7.   [6] XLII, iii, 1, p. 101.

into the world in secret. She placed me in a basket of reeds, she sealed the lid with pitch, she put me in the river. . . . The river bore me to Akki the water-carrier. Akki the water-carrier took me out of the kindness of his heart (?). Akki the water-carrier reared me as his child. Akki the water-carrier made me his gardener. While I worked as a gardener, Ishtar loved me."

Sargon, moreover, is a wholly historical person who reigned in Akkad about 2850. His seal and several of his inscriptions have been found. It is equally possible for Moses to have become the hero of a legend without thereby ceasing to be an historical person.

In order to separate the prosaic reality from the legendary aura which surrounds it, the first step would be to give an account of the changes undergone by the tradition in the course of its written transmission, and if possible, from its oral stage. But this is a particularly difficult task in the case of this section of the Israelite national tradition which has been so much worked over. It has been attempted by Hugo Gressmann in an extremely suggestive, though sometimes too conjectural book.[1]

The following is a tentative reconstruction of the actual course of events.

A group of Hebrew nomads, of whom it is difficult to say whether they were merely the tribes who later on constituted the " house of Joseph," Ephraim, Manasseh and Benjamin, or whether other tribes or parts of tribes joined with them, obtained permission to settle on the borders of Egypt, in a pastoral district lying between the delta and the Arabian desert. They had been driven from their usual haunts either by a famine, the result of drought, or, according to another version of the tradition (the story of Joseph), by " their brethren," *i.e.* by other Bedouins.[2]

These temporary or seasonal admissions of nomads into an agricultural country are customary along the borders of the whole of the Arabian desert.[3] They had happened at all times on the Asiatic frontier of Egypt. Under the kings of Heracleopolis (ninth and tenth dynasties, 2360–2160), nomads had already " sought to go down into Egypt to beg

---

[1] CXCI ; XXV, pp. 1–27.
[2] The Edomites according to Isidore Lévy, REJ.
[3] *Cf.* CLXXX, p. 9.

for water *according to their custom* and to water their flocks."[1]
The well-known painting of Beni Hassan depicts a clan of
Bedouins, with women and children, thirty-seven persons in
all, apparently seeking permission to enter Egypt, about
1900.[2] A bas-relief on the tomb of Horemheb, the founder
of the nineteenth dynasty (1345–1321), represents Asiatics
driven from their towns in the desert by their enemies and
obtaining permission to " come to the land of the Pharaoh
according to the custom of your fathers' fathers since the first
time."[3] Under Merneptah (1233–1224), an official, warden
of the marches, at the Wady Tumilat, that is, apparently, in
the land of Goshen, says that he has allowed the tribes of the
shasu (Bedouins) of Edom to pass through the marshes of
Pithom " in order that they and their flocks may live in
the kingdom of the Pharaoh."[4]

These arrangements were to the advantage of the kings of
Egypt, since the nomads whom they admitted undertook to
defend their new pastures, and hence the frontiers of the
kingdom, from their kinsmen.

They preserved, moreover, their pastoral habits, and
undoubtedly their social organization, language and religion.
It is principally the later strands of Hebrew tradition (E and
P), that represent the Israelites as scattered in the midst of
the Egyptians,[5] living the life of fellahin,[6] or settled in the
capital itself (Exod. ii. 1–10).   On the other hand, according
to the more ancient version (J), they continued to form a
separate community occupied in breeding sheep and goats.
Since they were avoided by the Egyptians, both on account of
their occupation and for religious reasons (Gen. xliii. 32),
they were stationed, not in the Nile valley, but in a separate
district called the " land of Goshen." [7]

This region is usually identified, after Lepsius (1883),

[1] Petersburg Papyrus, Gardiner, **JEA**, vol. i, p. 105 ; *cf.* **LXVIII**,
p. 253.
[2] *Cf.* for example, **LXVIII**, pp. 283 (fig. 22), 284, 285 ; **LXI**, p. 32.
According to others, they came simply for trade, **CLIX**, p. 431.
[3] **VIII**, p. 312 (fig. 147) ; Bergmann, **ZAS**, 1889, p. 125 ; **LXI**,
pp. 33–4 (fig. 11).
[4] Anastasi Papyrus, vi, 4, 15.   *Cf.* Gardiner, **JEA**, 1918, p. 208 ;
LXI, pp. 34–5.
[5] Exod. iii. 21–2 ; xi. 2 ; xii. 35, 36.
[6] Exod. xii. 4, 7, 23 ; Num. xi. 5 ; xx. 5 ; xxi. 5.
[7] Gen. xlvi. 32, 34 ; xlvii. 3, 4, 6^b, 27 ; Exod. viii. 18 ; ix. 26.

Naville and Flinders Petrie, with the Wady Tumilat, a valley running east and west, from Zagazig (near the ancient Bubastis) to Ismailia.   This identification is not certain : according to Alan Gardiner, the Egyptian word which Brugsch and Naville read as *kes* or *qosem* (whence the Hebrew Goshen) and which they thought was that of the country, ought to be read *ṣesmet* (var. *shesem*) and was a name for Sinai.[1]   Various

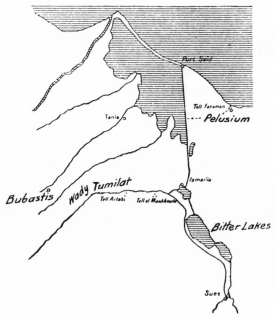

MAP II. THE LAND OF GOSHEN.

Jewish traditions placed the dwelling of the Hebrews further north, in the district of Tanis [2] and Pelusium.[3]

However, it remains likely that Wady Tumilat was at least a part of the land of Goshen : for the city of Pithom (Exod. i. 11) was certainly in this valley, as well as the city of Heroonpolis which the LXX version, made in Egypt, twice identifies with Goshen (Gen. xlvi. 28, 29). Now Wady Tumilat was a Bedouin country. It is crossed by a canal,

[1] **JEA,** 1918, pp. 218–23.
[2] Ps. lxxviii. 12.
[3] The Targum translates or explains the name of Ramses in this way. Gen. xlvii. 11 ; Exod. i. 11 ; xii. 37 ; Num. xxxiii. 3, 5.

fed by the Nile, maintaining a little herbage along its banks, while the whole of the region north and south is desert. Today, owing to agricultural development, the country supports a population of 12,000 peasants ; but, a century ago, it was only inhabited by about 4,000 nomads.[1] Such also must have been the nature of the population of this valley when Merneptah's warden allowed the Edomite *Shasu* to enter it.

A Pharaoh, failing to understand the independent spirit of his nomad vassals on the frontier, undertook to assimilate them to the native population. According to the Hebrew tradition the occasion of his attempt was the building of the store-cities of Pithom and Ramses (Exod. i. 11). This tradition seems to rest on an historical reminiscence : Pithom was in the Wady Tumilat, either on the site now called Tell el-Maskhutah (Naville), or at Tell Artabi or Rotab,[2] where there was also a Pithom, *i.e.* a temple of the god Atum, unearthed by Flinders Petrie ; on a column of this temple Ramses is represented as victorious over a Syrian. The inscription was found there of an " overseer of granaries."[3]

It is probable that the city of Ramses was not in the Wady Tumilat at all; for there is no proof, as is generally agreed, following Flinders Petrie, that Tell Artabi was ever called Ramses. The reference is rather, as Alan Gardiner has convincingly shown, to the most famous place of this name, the ancient city which stood at the mouth of the Pelusiac, or most easterly arm of the Nile, and which was first called Sin or Sain, then in the time of the Hyksos, Avaris. Restored, no doubt, by the Pharaohs of the eighteenth dynasty, and then by Ramses I,[4] it was transformed by Ramses II into a magnificent capital, which he used both as a residence and as a commissariat base for his Asiatic campaigns. At that time it received the name of Pi-Ramesseh. Later on it resumed its old name of Sin,[5] of which the Greek name of Pelusium (the muddy city) is a translation.[6]

It would be only natural that, for the purpose of rebuilding

---

[1] **CXCI**, pp. 400–2. See, however, Mallon's objections, **LXI**, pp. 97–8.

[2] Alan Gardiner, **JEA**, 1918, pp. 268–9.

[3] **LXI**, p. 108.

[4] Gardiner, **JEA**, 1918, p. 260.

[5] Annals of Asshurbanipal ; Exek. xxx. 15–16.

[6] *Cf.* Gardiner, *op. cit.*

the fortifications, the store-houses and the temples of these two strongholds of the Asiatic frontier, the Pharaoh should turn to the labour available on the spot, that of the Bedouins permitted to feed their flocks in the district.

Nothing could have more deeply roused the fierce pride of the Hebrew tribes. Moses was the heart and brain of the revolt. He was convinced, and succeeded in convincing his people, that they had on their side a more powerful god than all the gods of Egypt, Jahweh, the *Elohim* of Sinai, who wished not only to deliver the oppressed Hebrew tribes, but to make them into a nation. In spite of great difficulties which the tradition has magnified, Moses succeeded in leading the Hebrews into the steppes which lie to the south of Palestine.

There they remained a long time, according to the tradition for the space of a generation, or forty years. So long a stay in the desert seemed very surprising to the Israelites of a later age, for they thought of their remote ancestors as being equally numerous [1] and as having the same needs as the Israel of the monarchy ; on the other hand, they believed that Canaan had been predestined from all time for their nation, and promised to the patriarchs. Hence they related that Moses had from the first the intention of leading the new nation into Palestine, but that in punishment for an act of disobedience, God condemned a whole generation to perish in the desert. This is evidently an explanation after the event : the tradition itself recognizes elsewhere that Moses and the people wished to settle at the foot of Sinai, and would have stayed there if they had not been driven away by Jahweh (Exod. xxxii. 34 ; xxxiii. 15).

In reality, the Hebrew tribes, when they entered the Arabian steppes, found themselves in their ancient dwelling-place, a region, moreover, which cannot have differed much from the land of Goshen. On their arrival they did not live in the highly organized fashion of an army which advances or retreats as a whole,—the lists of marches with their many divergencies, depend in the main upon late editorial manipulations [2] of the tradition—but were scattered over wide

---

[1] See, on the contrary, Exod. i. 15 (two midwives for all the people).

[2] *Cf.* II, pp. 672-3.

stretches of country, to find the water and grass necessary for their flocks, and had only a rallying centre.

According to the tradition, this centre was for a time at " the mount of God," sometimes called Sinai (in J and P), sometimes Horeb (E and D), but for a much longer time it was at Kadesh, *i.e.* at the oasis which is still called today Ain Qudeis or Qedeis.[1]   Situated at the junction of several of the great desert trails coming from Ismailia, en-Nahleh, Akabah, Hebron and Gaza, it has four main springs, distant from one another from one to three hours' journey.   The most abundant of them, Ain el-Qedeirat, flows out of a rock in three jets, each as thick as a man's arm, and forms a stream by whose bank grow shady acacias and luxuriant vegetation. Explorers have found there the remains of a reservoir, of aqueducts, a village and a fortress, possibly going back to the tenth century B.C.   Such a spot which, on account of its springs, was not only suitable for cattle-rearing, but also to some extent for tillage, was admirably adapted to be the dwelling-place of the nucleus of the Hebrew confederation of tribes.

In the Pentateuch as we have it the importance of Kadesh is completely eclipsed by that of Sinai.   But it can still be discerned that once this oasis occupied a much larger place in the Israelite tradition, and it is there that most of the episodes of the wilderness sojourn are represented as happening.

It is most probable that, according to an earlier form of the J-tradition, " the Israelites went straight to Kadesh after the Exodus, and did not make the detour first of all to Sinai."[2]   Immediately after the story of the swallowing up of the Egyptians in the Red Sea we are told in a verse which apparently belongs to the Jahwistic tradition : " they went three days in the wilderness and found no water " (Exod. xv. 22).   Upon this there follows naturally the story of a miracle which enables the people to slake their thirst.   We find, in fact, a few pages further on, and before the account of the arrival at Sinai, a J-narrative of this kind : the story of the waters of Meribah (Exod. xvii. 1–7).   Now the waters of

---

[1] *Cf.* **CCXLVII** ; **LXXII**, pp. 175 *ff.* ; Woolley and Lawrence ; RB, Jan., 1922.

[2] **LXXXIX**, p. 348 ; *cf.* **LXXXVIII**, p. 13 ; **XXX**, pp. 112–13.

Meribah were undoubtedly at Kadesh (Num. xx. 1, 13, 24) ; their full name was " the waters of Meribah-Kadesh " (Num. xxvii. 14 ; Deut. xxxii. 51 ; xxxiii. 2 emend.). Thus the primitive J-account placed the arrival at Kadesh three days after the Israelites had entered the desert. The inference is that for this stage of the tradition, Kadesh was the goal, or at least the first halting-place, of the flight of the Israelites from Egypt, and the scene of their first formal meeting with Jahweh ; for the reiterated expression of their reason for wishing to leave Egypt had been : " Let us go *three days' journey into the wilderness* that we may sacrifice to Jahweh our God " (Exod. iii. 18 ; v. 3 ; viii. 23).

This view is confirmed by the fact that nearly all the episodes which in the present text intervene between the crossing of the Red Sea and the arrival at Sinai (Exod. xvi.– xviii.) were originally located in the neighbourhood of Kadesh. They are indeed actually related a second time in connexion with the stay which the Israelites were supposed to have made at this oasis after their journey to the holy Mount (Num. xi. ; xiv. 43, 45 ; xx.).

Nor is this all ; we have a passage of doubtful meaning, apparently a fragment of an ancient poem, inserted just after the description of the crossing of the Red Sea (Exod. xv. 25), which runs :

> " There he made for them a statute and an ordinance,
> and there he proved them."

The allusion contained in the last words shows that the scene took place at Massah (proving), *i.e.* at Kadesh. Hence, according to this ancient text it was Kadesh and not Sinai which saw the birth of the Mosaic legislation.

But we need not infer from this, as some critics have done, that in this form of the tradition Sinai had no place, and that the impressive episodes of Jahweh's meeting with his people at the holy mountain are merely the product of the poetic fancy of a later age.[1] It is certain that the J-narrative contained accounts of the sojourn at the foot of the mount of God and of the legislation there promulgated by Moses

---

[1] Certain features, especially the blowing of trumpets (Exod. xix. 16 ; xx. 18), suggest that this first meeting with Jahweh was pictured after the fashion of the characteristic ritual of the cult (**CCXX**, p. 128 ; **XIX**, p. 221 ; Lods, **RHR**, xcvii (1928), pp. 117–18).

(Exod. xxxiv.). Possibly the J-narrative, in its earliest form, may have described a lengthy stay in the steppes around Kadesh, together with a short and perhaps partial visit of the Hebrew tribes to Sinai.

It must also be acknowledged that we possess little certain information about this holy mountain of Jahweh. We do not know whether it was called Sinai or Horeb, nor whether these two names denoted the same mountain or two different localities, nor even the site of the peak, or peaks. The prevailing modern opinion [1] identifies Sinai with Djebel Musa

MAP III. THE DISTRICT OF SINAI.

(the mountain of Moses), in the granite *massif* which rises at the end of the peninsula, between the two arms of the Red Sea ; but the tradition upon which this identification rests does not go back beyond the sixth century A.D. Nor does the identification with Djebal Serbal, an imposing peak and ancient place of pilgrimage a little to the north-west of the same range, rest upon any more solid grounds. The most that can be alleged in favour of these two identifications is that the Priestly narrative and perhaps E before it, [2] seem to place the holy mountain in this peninsula.

On the other hand, the J-tradition apparently located

---

[1] Recently defended by Maurice Vernes, **CCL.**
[2] *Cf.*, for example, **XXX**, p. 112, n. 1.

Sinai in Midianite territory; for the revelation of Jahweh in the burning bush to Moses took place during the time when he was seeking asylum with his father-in-law, the priest of Midian. Now the mediæval Arab geographers bear witness that there were to be seen on the east of the Elanitic gulf (the modern Gulf of Akabah), near Makna, the ruins of a town of the name of Midian; Ptolemy mentions it under the names *Modiana, Madiama* (vi. 7, 2 and 27). In this case Sinai would be in Arabia proper. Along the coast there is a line of craters, now extinct, but one of which, Harrat al-Nar (crater of fire), near Medina, is attested to have been active during the historical period. There are also good reasons for supposing the mountain of Jahweh to have been a volcano. This would explain the fire, the earthquake, the clouds and the thunder in the theophanies of Jahweh, and especially in that described in Exodus xix.

According to Grimme and Völter, the problem of the site of Sinai has been settled by the inscriptions discovered at Serabit el-Hadim, on the west of the Sinai Peninsula. They believe that they have found the word *sny* used several times to indicate the site of the ruins.[1] But these readings are extremely uncertain.

A simplifying hypothesis finds Sinai in the immediate neighbourhood of Kadesh. This view, supported by Graetz (1878), Reuss, Holzinger and Cheyne, has the merit of dispensing with the antithesis between Kadesh and Sinai. It provides a natural explanation of the ancient poems assigning to Seir and Edom the dwelling-place of Jahweh:

> " Jahweh came from Sinai,
> and rose up from Seir unto them;
> He shined forth from mount Paran,
> he came from Meribah Kadesh." [2]

But on the other hand, various traditions scattered throughout the Pentateuch show that several days of journeying were necessary to reach the mount of God at Kadesh: three at least, according to E (Num. x. 33), eleven according to Deuteronomy i. 2, and twenty according to the list of stages in Numbers xxxiii. 16–36. Moreover, it would be difficult to explain why, if the holy mount lay at the very

---

[1] *Cf.* **CLXII**, p. 43.
[2] Deut. xxxiii. 2; *cf.* Judges v. 4, 5; Hab. iii. 3.

entrance to their land, the Israelites should so quickly have
entirely forgotten its site.   In fact, at a fairly early date the
belief was current in Israel that the mount of God was fabu-
lously remote : the story of Elijah, written probably before
760, relates how the prophet, starting a day's journey beyond
Beersheba, which is less than 100 kilos. from Kadesh, took
forty days and forty nights to reach Horeb (1 Kings xix.
3, 4, 8).

Dietlef Nielsen's identification of Sinai with Petra is open
to the same objections.[1]

These variations in the tradition have led some modern
commentators to the belief that Sinai was essentially a myth,
a real but invisible place,[2] " a mount of flame, where dwells
the god whom no man living has seen . . . to be reached by
no human pathway,"[3] like " the mount of assembly " of the
gods which the Babylonians placed in the far north.

This radical hypothesis is certainly attractive, but presents
difficulties.   That stage of the tradition in which the mount
of God was thought of as an invisible and inaccessible place
is only represented by the fairly late story of Elijah.   None
of the pentateuchal traditions belong to this type.

Hence the soundest view seems to be that Sinai-Horeb
was really an ancient holy place of Jahweh, but probably far
away from the borders of Palestine ; hence the vagueness of
tradition as to its site.   The eastern coast of the Gulf of
Akabah, the locality suggested by the earliest of the pentateuchal traditions, satisfies these conditions.

The period of the sojourn at Kadesh, culminating in the
journey to " the holy mount," seems to have been the decisive
moment when the Hebrew tribes formed themselves into a
nation, and adopted the worship of Jahweh as their national
religion.[4]

The new-born confederation could not long remain content
with their oases.   It is, as it were, a law of nature which
impels the nomads to an unceasing attack upon the cultivated
lands which lie along the borders of their steppes.   As soon
as the resistance of the organized states occupying the coveted

[1] CCXXII ; cf. RHR, xcix, pp. 294–8.
[2] CCLVII, iii, 3, pp. 360–80.
[3] R. Weill, REJ, 1909, pp. 54–5.
[4] See pp. 308–15.

territory begins to weaken, the nomads filter in, either as plunderers or as temporary sojourners, and often end by settling down.   Such was the history of the Israelites, as it had been[1] of their kinsmen the Moabites, the Ammonites and the Edomites before them, and as it was after them, of the Arameans, the Chaldeans, the Nabateans, the Itureans, and the Moslem Arabs.   This law provides the reason why Israel undertook the conquest of Canaan.

IV

THE CHRONOLOGY OF THE HISTORY OF THE HEBREW TRIBES UP TO THE TIME OF THEIR FINAL SETTLEMENT IN PALESTINE

In a previous chapter (pp. 37–52), a review, based on contemporary documents, was made of the events constituting the principal landmarks in the history of western Asia, and of Palestine in particular, up to the twelfth century.   We must now consider the place in the order of these events to be assigned to those facts in the pre-history of the Israelite tribes, which emerge from their traditions, namely, the sojourn in Egypt, the Exodus and the entry into Canaan.

Theories concerning the chronology of these events were already numerous in the time of Josephus.[2]   Those held today by historians of repute are also extremely varied. They may, however, be reduced to two main types.   Historians belonging to the first class agree in identifying the Habiru whose inroads are described in the Tell el-Amarna letters (about 1400) with the Hebrews who came out of Egypt.   The others oppose to this view what they regard as the incontestable fact that the Hebrews were oppressed in Egypt by Ramses II (1300–1234), since they helped to build the cities of Pithom and Ramses ; hence the exodus, coming after the death of the oppressing Pharaoh (Exod. ii. 23 ; iv. 19), could not have happened earlier than the time of Merneptah, the successor of Ramses II (1233–1224).

An example of the first type is H. R. Hall's reconstruction of the history,[3] according to which the descent of the Hebrews into Egypt coincided with the Hyksos invasion, the exodus

---

[1] See pp. 57–8.
[2] *Contra Apionem*, i, 14–16, 26–7, 32–5.   *Cf.* **LXXIX**, pp. 24–5, 27–34, 62, 87–8, 113, 117–20, 127, 302–3.   [3] **CXCVI.**

took place at the time of the expulsion of the Hyksos, while the conquest of Palestine by the Israelites was effected during the Tell el-Amarna period.

Hommel and Orr,[1] in support of a similar view, urge that it coincides exactly with the chronological data of the books of Exodus and Kings. According to these critics the arrival of the Hebrews in Egypt and the invasion of the Hyksos occurred in 1877 ; the departure from Egypt took place 430 years later, according to a passage in Exodus,[2] *i.e.* in 1447, under Amenophis II ; the invasion of Palestine began forty years later, that is, exactly at the beginning of the Tell el-Amarna period, and the building of the temple just 480 years after the exodus (967), as we are told in a passage in Kings.[3]

These reconstructions, at least Hall's, have the merit of offering a very simple explanation of how it is that contemporary documents mention the presence in Palestine of Jacobel and Josephel in the fifteenth century, of Simeon, Asher and Levi in the fourteenth, and in the beginning of the thirteenth ; it is that these were Israelite groups, called by these names, already settled in the land.

They would also explain—at least Hall's theory—how Jericho could have been destroyed " at the earliest about 1500 B.C.," as Sellin believes certain, according to pottery fragments which he found on the site,[4] or even shortly after 1600, according to a recent estimate of Watzinger, another explorer of the site of Jericho.[5]

But the chronological theories of this type also involve serious difficulties. There is no trace in the Israelite tradition of the presence of the Hebrews in Egypt as conquerors, or of Israelite kings of Egypt, as is the case with the Hyksos, but only of their having been first tolerated, then enslaved. Moreover, the details given in the books of Joshua and Judges concerning the settlement of the Israelites in Palestine disagree in general with the data of the Tell el-Amarna letters.

---

[1] **CCXXIII**, pp. 422–4.

[2] xii, 40–1, at least according to the Massoretic Text ; 215 years probably according to that of the LXX.

[3] 1 Kings vi. 1, according to the Massoretic Text ; the LXX version gives 440 years.

[4] **CCXXXVIII**, p. 82. His opinion is that it was not the Israelites who destroyed the city.

[5] **ZDMG**, 1926, p. 131. *Cf.* on this point J. Garstang, **PEF, QS,** April, 1927 ; Vincent, **RB**, 1927, pp. 470 *ff.* ; 1928, p. 318.

For example, the names of the Canaanite kings mentioned in the books of Joshua and Judges are not those of the princes who governed the same cities under Amenophis III and IV :

	Joshua-Judges	*Tell el-Amarna*
Jerusalem	Adonizedek or Adonibezek	ARAD-Ḫiba
Gezer	Horam	Yapaḫi
Hazor	Jabin	Abdi-Tirshi

If both documents refer to the same facts then the Israelite tradition has become hopelessly confused.

Even more perplexing is the fact that according to this theory, possibly the great campaigns of Thothmes III, and in any case those of Seti I, Ramses II and of Merneptah, occur after the final settlement of the Hebrews in Palestine. It is very difficult to explain the silence of the Hebrew tradition concerning the inevitable conflict with the Egyptian conquerors, and especially concerning the administration of the country by Egyptian officials, a fact whose significance is becoming more and more apparent.

On this theory it is also difficult to account for the fact that it is exactly between 1500 and 1200 that we have abundant evidence for the remarkable advance shown by Palestinian craftsmen in artistic methods and technique under Ægean influence ; since this is the golden age of Canaanite pottery.

It seems strange that this flourishing of art under western influence should have coincided with the invasion of the country by Bedouins who were certainly less civilized than the native inhabitants. It would be more natural that the arrival of these " barbarians " should coincide with the decline of which we have evidence after 1200.

It may be added that the chronological note in the first book of Kings, which indicates an interval of 480 (or 440) years between the exodus and the building of the temple is a very late element in the text : the LXX version places it elsewhere (after v. 30). It is probably the guess of a comparatively late chronologist, who inferred from the biblical records that a period of twelve generations lay between the two events, and assigned the somewhat high estimate of forty years to a generation : $12 \times 40 = 480$. The same is true in the case of the detailed chronological statements found throughout the books of Joshua, Judges and Samuel, which rest on the same estimate of forty years to a generation.

We shall now consider two examples of the system which takes as its point of departure the date of the building of Pithom and Ramses, apparently the most definite of the traditions preserved by the Hebrews concerning their sojourn in Egypt.

Prof. C. F. Burney, of Oxford, has written a monograph on the subject,[1] and has taken it up again in his commentary on the book of Judges.[2] He puts forward a theory of extreme chronological precision. Some of the Hebrew tribes settled in Egypt with the Hyksos and were driven out with them : this corresponds with the tradition of Abraham's descent into Egypt and his expulsion (Gen. xii. 10–20). One of these Hebrew groups, named Jacob (Yaqobel), was found in Palestine by Thothmes III, about 1479. After being driven out of Canaan by the Edomites (Jacob's flight from Esau), he again invaded the country (the Ḥabiru invasions about 1400), because Laban was pressing on his heels (i.e. the Aramean tribes, the SA.GAS of Tell el-Amarna). These Ḥabiru, who were already called Israel, directed their attacks specially on Shechem (cf. Gen. xxxiv.). A part of them, including Joseph, perhaps Simeon and probably Levi, went down into Egypt under Amenophis II (about 1435) ; for they stayed there 215 years (Exod. xii. 40, 41, LXX). But the main body of the Israelites remained in Palestine ; hence the mention of Asher by Seti I and Ramses II, and that of Israilu by Merneptah or during the period of anarchy which followed the death of that prince.

The special feature of Gressmann's hypothesis is that it compresses the events into the shortest possible space of time.[3] According to him the Ḥabiru belonged to a wave of Aramean invaders prior to that which brought the Israelites. The latter only reached the borders of Palestine about 1300. A part of them immediately went down into Egypt ; there they only stayed two generations, this being all the time that is required by the oldest form of the Israelite tradition (Exod. i. 6–8 ; cf. Gen. xv. 16 ; Exod. vi. 20), let us say fifty years. In the reign of Ramses II, the Pharaoh of the oppres-

[1] CLXXI.   [2] XII, pp. lv–cxviii.
[3] CXCI, pp. 399–400, 404–5.

sion, they fled from Egypt and settled in Canaan (about
1230); hence there is nothing surprising in the fact that
Merneptah, in 1229, should mention Israel among the peoples
whom he conquered during his campaign in Palestine.

Only with considerable reservations in matters of detail
would it be possible to accept these hyptheses, whose wide
diversity shows how plastic is the material they deal with,
and how uncertain the outlines of the picture which they
yield. To take a case in point, we could not, for reasons
which we have already given,[1] extract from the patriarchal
narrative so precise a chronological scheme of the pre-history
of the Israelite tribes as Burney has constructed.

But that need not prevent us from recognizing the advantages of the chronological system suggested by the two
critics whom we have just mentioned, namely the system
which places the oppression of the Hebrews under Ramses II,
and reduces the interval between the exodus and Solomon
to about 250 years. The ancient list of " the kings who
reigned over the land of Edom before a king of Israel reigned
there," only mentions eight kings between Bela, the son of
Beor—apparently to be identified with Balaam, the son of
Beor, a contemporary of Moses according to the tradition in
Numbers xxii.–xxiv.—and the time when David conquered the
land of Edom (Gen. xxxvi. 31–39). Allowing a mean length
of twenty-five to thirty years for each reign, we obtain the
necessary total of 200 to 240 years.

This theory also makes possible an explanation of the
occurrence in Palestine between 1400 and 1300 of the names
of Simeon and Asher : they might be the names of two
Hebrew groups that had not gone down into Egypt, or, more
probably, the names of Canaanite districts or cities which
were assumed later by the Israelite settlers. The same might
also be true in the case of Jacobel and Josephel.

But, on the other hand, we must not ignore the fact that
the foundation upon which these systems rest, namely the
identification of the Pharaoh of the oppression with Ramses
II, is by no means as certain as is commonly supposed.
Excavations have shown that while Ramses II adorned and
enlarged the fortresses of Pithom and Ramses, *he did not build
them*. On the two principal sites proposed for the latter city,

[1] See pp. 159–60.

Tell Artabi and Tell Faraman (Pelusium), prosperous cities had already existed long before.[1] Hence it is possible that the Hebrews of Goshen may have been commandeered for labour on the building carried out in the city *before it received the name of Ramses*, for instance, in the time of an eighteenth dynasty king. Nevertheless, the Israelite historians could still have related how their fathers in Egypt had built the city of Ramses, that is, the city which, in the time of the writers, went by that name. Everyone admits a similar case in Genesis xlvii. 11 P : there all commentators take the statement that the patriarch Jacob was allowed to settle in " the land of Ramses " to mean, " in the territory of the city which was later called Ramses."

Unfortunately, the stele of Merneptah does not decide the issue.[2] It is a triumphal ode celebrating the victory gained by this Pharaoh in the fifth year of his reign, 1229, over the Libyans, who had invaded Egypt from the west, helped by bands of Achæans, Tyrsenians (Etruscans), Siculians, Shardanians and Lycians, who had come over the sea. The poet describes the peace which reigned henceforth in all parts of the empire [3] :

> " The kings are overthrown and cry—Peace! None lifts up his head among the nine nations of the bow. Tehenu (Libya) is laid waste. Ḥatti (the land of the Hittites) is pacified. Canaan [4] is plundered with all evil. Ascalon is carried away, Gezer is led captive. Yanoam [5] is brought to nought. Israilu (Israel) is laid waste,[6] it has no more seed. Ḥaru (Palestine) is become as a widow before Egypt.[7] All the lands are made one ; they are pacified. The rebellious are bound by the king Merneptah."

---

[1] See pp. 173–4. [2] See pp. 50–1.

[3] Translation as given in **VII**, iii, p. 263 ; **XXIII**², i, pp. 24–5.

[4] According to Petrie, **CCXXVII**, iii, p. 12, this refers to a city named Kenan, three kilometres to the S.E. of Hebron.

[5] Mentioned also upon the stele of Seti I found at Beisan (*cf.* Gressmann, **ZATW**, 1924, pp. 347–8 ; Vincent, **RB**, 1924, pp. 424–8 ; 1926, pp. 124, 468–71 ; Dussaud, **SY**, 1926, pp. 16–17). It would be a question, according to some, of Yanoah, to the east of Tyre (**LXXI**, p. 394 ; Moret, **REA**, i, p. 29), according to others, of another Yanoah (Joshua xvi. 6–7), now Yanun, eleven kilometres south-east of Nablus (Dussaud), according to P. Vincent of Tell en-Na'ameh, to the north of Kedesh of Naphtali. Consideration might be also given to Yanum, a town on the heights of Judah (Joshua xv. 53), probably in the neighbourhood of Hebron.

[6] Or " his people are few in number " according to **XXIII**¹, i, p. 195.

[7] That is to say, without a protector, powerless.

It is not likely that this text merely describes in the language of hyperbole the panic which seized the vassals and neighbours of Egypt when they heard of the defeat of the Libyans (Maspero). Merneptah did inflict an actual defeat upon the city of Gezer, for he is elsewhere styled " subduer of Gezer."[1] Hence the allusion must be to a real victory over Israel. It is difficult to say whether the disturbance in Palestine was stirred up by the initial successes of the Libyans, or whether the defeat of Gezer took place in the third year of Merneptah.[2]

Unfortunately it is still more difficult to extract from this text any definite information about the Israel referred to in it. " Israel," we read, " has no more seed." From these words it has been inferred that the Israelites had already become an agricultural people, and hence were settled in Palestine. But, as a matter of fact, the words are simply a vague and conventional metaphor, applied in the official Egyptian texts to various nations, for instance to the barbarians of the north in the course of their migrations, in order to convey the idea that they have been conquered or raided.[3]

From the fact that Israel is mentioned, not only after Ascalon, but after Gezer, which is north-east of Ascalon and further inland, some critics have inferred that the Israelite territory lay still further in the same direction, and hence that the Israelites were already settled in the hill-country of Ephraim. But we have no right to suppose that the poet followed a geographical rather than a chronological order. If we admit that the devastation of the three Canaanite cities and that of Israel was carried out in one campaign, and by a single body of troops, for which we have no proof, the Egyptian army may still have smitten Ascalon, Gezer and Yanoam on their outward march, and Israel on their way back, in which case Israel might be in the south of the country.

The most that can be inferred with certainty from the stele is first, that the Israel under discussion, named along with Palestinian cities, between two general statements referring to Canaan and to Ḥaru (the land of the Horites, Palestine), was in Palestinian territory in 1229. Secondly, it is to be noted that the name Israel is accompanied by the determinative for " men," and not by that for " country," as in

---

[1] **VII,** iii, p. 258. [2] *Ibid.* [3] **VII,** iii, p. 257.

the case of Libya, the Hittites, Ascalon, Gezer and Yanoam.
Hence it might be inferred that Israel was still essentially a
tribe or group of tribes, and had not yet, like the Libyans or
the Hittites, a territory in which it had long been settled.
This fact would be better accounted for on the supposition
that Israel was still in a nomad or semi-nomad state than if
the people had been settled in the heart of the country already
for a century and a half.

A further question which the stele leaves unsolved is
whether " Israel " already included the tribes come out of
Egypt, or merely the Hebraic groups who had remained in
the extreme south of Palestine ; it is even possible that a
Canaanite community is denoted by this designation.

Thus we are led to the conclusion that the monuments
hitherto have not enabled us to arrive at any certain solution
of the chronological problem ; at the most they furnish
indications which seem to point in the direction of the theory
which assigns the entry into Canaan to about the reign of
Merneptah.

The following conjectural reconstruction may be offered
as a point of departure for further discussion. It is tenable
that among the Ḫabiru referred to in the Tell el-Amarna
letters were some of the tribes which later formed part of
the Israelite confederation. According to these texts the
Ḫabiru had apparently conquered the land of Lapaya, i.e.
the district of Shechem ; [1] on the other hand they were attacking Jerusalem. Now we shall see that a consideration of the
Hebrew tradition gives ground for the belief that, before the
final settlement of Israel in the heart of Canaan, Shechem
was temporarily occupied by the tribes of Simeon and Levi
(Gen. xxxiv. ; xlix. 5-7), and a region near Jerusalem by the
tribe of Reuben.[2] These first waves of the advancing tide of
Hebrew invasion were subsequently obliged to retreat ;
nothing remained of Simeon and Levi but scattered groups,
while Reuben left the country.

The main body of the Hebrews must then have led a
wandering life around the southern oases (Beersheba, Kadesh).
Those of them who went down into Egypt were there enslaved
either by Ramses II or by one of his predecessors. After a

---

[1] TA(W), 185, 8-11 ; cf. XIII, pp. 312-14.
[2] See pp. 331-2.

short time they escaped and pitched their tents in the oasis of Kadesh, where they seem to have united with the tribes who had remained in that region, and formed themselves into a nation.

It is possible that the stele of Merneptah refers to this confederation of the Bene Israel. The defeat of Israel of which it speaks may have been a reverse inflicted by an Egyptian force, or by a vassal of the Pharaoh upon the Hebrew tribes who were attempting to enter Canaan from Kadesh ; such a reverse is described by the Israelite tradition as having taken place to the north of Hormah.[1]

Scanty and uncertain as our information is about the movements of the Hebrew tribes before their settlement in Palestine, we are even worse off with regard to their social and religious conditions. However, we can derive some of the necessary information from the study of the civilization of better documented periods, since these yield certain features which seem to belong to an earlier age, because they recur in other Semitic communities which once led or still continue to lead the manner of life that must have been led by the ancient Hebrews. We shall have the more confidence in making use of these features for purposes of comparison, if we find that they are dissonant with the culture of later ages, or if their antiquity is confirmed by Hebrew tradition.

[1] Num. xiv. 39–45

CHAPTER II

SOCIAL ORGANIZATION OF THE HEBREW NOMADS

I

THE HEBREWS WERE ORIGINALLY NOMADS

IN the age of which we have historical records, the Israelites thought of their ancestors as having, prior to their settlement in Canaan, lived as Bedouins, breeding cattle and dwelling in tents.[1]

On this point tradition is certainly correct. Expressions remained imbedded in the language bearing the stamp of the wandering pastoral life which the Hebrew tribes had led for so many centuries. When he wished to express the idea of returning home, the Hebrew spoke of returning to his tent.[2] The word for " setting out," *nasa'*, meant " to pull up," because in preparing for departure the nomad pulls up his tent-pegs. The metaphor " their stake is torn up "[3] could also mean " they die." Conduct or manner of life were commonly indicated by the figure of the " way " (*derek*). A word meaning " pasturage " had taken on the sense of " abode " (*naweh*). The nomad's dream of a rich agricultural country was expressed in the phrase " a land flowing with milk and honey,"[4] where a peasant would say " a land of corn and must and oil." The Israelites did use the latter expression, but it belongs to a later epoch, to the time when they had become agriculturists.

Some of the oldest traditions of the Hebrews show that they had once known the meaning and the savour of the free, fierce life of the nomad, with his hand against every man, and every man's hand against him. Such, for instance, are the savage couplet of Lamech, boasting that he will be

---

[1] See pp. 203–6.
[2] 2 Sam. xviii. 17 ; xix. 9 ; xx. 1 ; 1 Kings xii. 16.
[3] Job iv. 21 emended.   [4] See pp. 34–5.

avenged seventy-seven times (Gen. iv. 23–24), the sketch of Ishmael, free and untameable as a wild ass (xvi. 12), or the story of Hagar, the proud Bedouin woman, who fled to the desert rather than submit to the ill-treatment of her mistress (Gen. xvi.).

II

PATRIARCHATE AND MATRIARCHATE

In historical times the Israelite thought of his nomad ancestors as possessing the same patriarchal organization as he himself was familiar with. Paternal authority, though not so absolute as it was at Rome, for instance, was nevertheless a potent factor in Hebrew society : a father could sell his sons and daughters for slaves.[1] Until the time when his right was limited by law (Deut. xxi. 18–21), he could put his children and his grandchildren to death ; an old story represents the head of a family condemning his daughter-in-law to be burnt (Gen. xxxviii. 24).

The wife was the property of her husband ; the word for husband was ba'al, master. If the wife was not a captive taken in war, the marriage was arrānged by the payment of a sum of money (mohar) to the father or the brothers of the young woman, as a purchase price ; the same was done in the case of fictive abduction (Judges xxi. 22)

Descent was exclusively in the male line. To such an extent did the Semite of historical times regard the patriarchal family as the norm of social organization, that he thought of all mankind under this form. For him, every nation was a family that had increased and multiplied, and traced its descent from a single father, to whom the name of the people whom he was supposed to have begotten was usually ascribed ; the Assyrians were the sons of a man named Asshur ; the Canaanites were the children of Canaan ; the Moabites traced their descent from an individual named Moab ; the Israelites were the sons of Israel. Each of the tribes was composed of the descendants of one of the sons of the eponymous ancestor of the nation. Each son of the tribal ancestor, in his turn, gave rise to one of the clans (mishpaḥah) of which the tribe consisted. Finally, each of

[1] Exod. xxi. 7 ; Neh. v. 1–13 ; cf. 2 Kings iv. 1.

the families or " fathers' houses " (*beth 'ab*) constituting the *mishpaḥah* sprang from a son of the ancestor of the *mishpaḥah*.

On the other hand, however, there are evidences in the Israel of the historical period, of an early stage of society in which descent was reckoned in the female line.[1]

For centuries the mother kept the right of naming her children : [2] not until the eighth century do we find the first certain cases of the choice of the son's name by the father.[3] In primitive society the sons belonged naturally to the group of the person who named them ; for it was in the power of the latter to give the children a name compounded with the name of the god of the namer's clan, thus placing them under the god's protection. It was also a common custom for the mother to give the child the name of her father or one of her uncles, thus securing the reincarnation of this relation in the new-born child.[4]

When descent is reckoned in the female line the children belong to their mother's clan ; hence it often happens that after her marriage the woman lives with her parents and brings up her children there. The husband only visits her at intervals. This form of marriage, which Robertson Smith proposed to call *ṣadiqa* marriage, existed among the ancient Arabs and the Assyrians.[5] The existence of such a custom among the Hebrews would explain the Jahwist's description of the union of the man with the woman, " a man shall leave his father and mother and shall be joined to his wife " (Gen. ii. 24) ; it would also explain why, among the Israelites,[6] as among the ancient Arabs,[7] the tent belonged to the wife ; it was the husband who " went in to his wife."[8] Although there are among the Hebrews, as among the inhabitants of

---

[1] *Cf.* **LVIII**, ii, pp. 8–23.   [2] *Cf. Ibid.*, p. 9, n. 1.

[3] Hos. i. 4, 6, 9 ; Isa. viii. 3. It is doubtless probable that it was Ahab and not his wife, the Tyrian Jezebel, who, already about 870, had given his children names compounded with Jahweh ; this, however, is not as certain as Sven Herner believes (**CXCIX**, pp. 140–1, : the picture of Jezebel, the persecutor of the worshippers of Jahweh, is a legendary one. (See below, p. 421.)

[4] *Cf.* **LVIII**, ii, 9, and the Arabian story Icd, iii, 272.

[5] **CCXXXII**, § 26–8, 33–4, 37. *Cf.* J. Morgenstern, **ZATW**, 1929, pp. 91 *ff.*

[6] Gen. xxiv. 67 ; xxxi. 33 ; Judges iv. 17 ; *cf.* Gen. xxiv. 28 ; Ruth i. 8 ; Cant. iii. 4.

[7] **CCLIII**, p. 445 ; Ammianus Marcellinus, xiv, 4, 4.

[8] *Cf.* **LVIII**, ii, p. 12, n. 3.

Palestine today,[1] other reasons for a woman remaining in the house of her parents after her marriage, it is no doubt the survival of *ṣadiqa* marriage that explains the relations of Samson with the Timnite woman whom he visited from time to time, bringing her a present,[2] the relations of Gideon with a woman who remained at Shechem,[3] and those of Moses with a Midianite woman who stayed in her own country with her sons.[4]

In communities where female descent prevails, the head of the family is the uterine brother or the maternal uncle of the wife. It is not without significance that among the Israelites, as among the ancient Arabs, in spite of the legal right of descent in the male line, an extremely strong feeling of solidarity persisted between the son and his mother's family,[5] and that the brothers, especially those born of the same mother, had the right to be consulted about the marriage of their sister, even if their father was still alive.[6]

It is also significant that in early times, a very close relationship on the father's side did not constitute a bar to marriage. Amram married Jochebed, his father's sister.[7] Abraham married his half-sister, Sarah, the daughter of the same father but not of the same mother.[8] Tamar could have become the legal wife of her blood-brother, Amnon.[9] When we realize that generally speaking there is a strict ban on marriages with relations among " primitive " peoples, this tolerance seems to indicate that kinsmen on the father's side were not regarded as relations.

In Jewish magical formulas the name of the person concerned was coupled with the name of his mother and not that of his father.[10] The same custom is still observed today by the Jews in the prayers which they address to the Patriarchs by placing the paper on which they are written in a hole by the stairway of the mosque of Hebron.[11] This, as well as similar customs found among the Mandeans, the Egyptians,

[1] Jaussen, *Chez les Arabes*, **RB**, 1910, pp. 237–49.
[2] Judges xv. 1.   [3] Judges viii. 31.
[4] Exod. iv. 18 ; xviii, 2ᵃ, 3–6.
[5] See the examples quoted **LVIII**, pp. 17–18.
[6] Gen. xxxiv. ; *cf.* Cant. viii. 8–10 ; Gen. xxiv. 50.
[7] Exod. vi. 20.   [8] Gen. xx. 12.
[9] 2 Sam. xiii. 13. See also Exek. xxii. 11.
[10] *Cf.* **LVIII,** ii, p. 19.   [11] **CCXV**, pp. 8–15.

the Greeks and the Romans, evidently points to " an ancient matriarchal mode of expression."[1]

Other customs point in the same direction, for example, the rite of suckling an adopted child (Ruth iv. 16–17), the use of such words as *reḥem*, " the mother's bosom," to signify " ties of kindred,"[2] *beṭen*, " the belly," [3] or *'umma*, from *'em*, " a mother," to designate a clan, or the common usage of representing a country or a city under the figure of a mother, " a mother in Israel."[4]

Hence it seems certain that, although the patriarchal system prevailed among the Hebrews in historical times, yet at an earlier stage of their development they had known and practised the matriarchal system.   On the other hand, since it is unlikely that the two systems should have existed side by side, save during the period of transition, we must admit that apparently among the Hebrews the matriarchal type of organization had preceded the patriarchal.   " It is perfectly natural that the relation of the child to the mother, obvious to the most superficial observation, should have impressed itself upon the primitive mind sooner than the much more mysterious tie which links the new-born child to its begetter."[5]

Moreover, there is reason to suppose that the transition from a matriarchal to a patriarchal form of social structure must have taken place among the Semites at a very early period, before the separation of the different branches of the race ; since certain terms belonging to the patriarchal system occur in all the Semitic dialects ; for instance, *ham* and *hamoth* to designate the parents-in-law of the wife, *kallah*, daughter-in-law and betrothed, *baal*, husband, *yathom*, a fatherless child, *mohar*, the price paid by the suitor to his future father-in-law, *'am* denoting both paternal uncle, relations on the father's side, and people.

The Hebrew organization into clans and tribes also suggests that among this people the patriarchal system was superimposed upon an earlier social stratum.

---

[1] Noldeke, **OMO**, 1884, p. 304.
[2] Amos i. 11.   [3] Job xix. 17 (?).
[4] 2 Sam. xx. 19 ; Hos. ii. 4 : *Cf.* Laodicea " mother in Canaan " (see p. 54).
[5] **LVIII**, ii. p. 25.

III

THE CLAN AND THE TRIBE

Throughout the whole of its history Israel preserved, at least nominally, its division into tribes (*matteh, shebet*), which were again subdivided into clans, each consisting of several families (*beth 'ab*). This organization is certainly a legacy from nomad times.

But the group to which we are accustomed to give the name " clan," and usually called *mishpahah* by the Hebrews, or sometimes *'am*, or *hay*, as among the Arabs,[1] was an institution of a peculiar kind, whose organization was in no way modelled on that of the patriarchal family. As in the case of the Bedouin tribe, there was no member of it who held a position of authority comparable to that of the father in his family. Neither the elders, *i.e.* the heads of the most important families, who usually guided the clan, nor the single chief who led it in war-time, possessed autocratic power. " The Bedouin sheikh only possesses a moral authority arising from his personal courage. Even when he acts as judge, which he is not obliged to do, he has no power to enforce his sentence. Even the poorest Arab takes orders from no one : he will only yield to the advice and intreaties of his kinsmen."[2] Early Hebrew tradition gives us just such a picture of the authority wielded by Moses : he can only enforce obedience to his decisions by his personal ascendancy.

An absolute equality of rights and duties held good in ancient times between the members of the *mishpahah*. This again is not patriarchal. The most sacred obligation of the *mishpahah* was the blood-feud. According to the custom of the Israelites settled in Palestine, this duty devolved only upon the nearest relative of the slain, the *goel*, and vengeance was confined to the murderer.[3] But in earlier times the number of persons involved in the vendetta or threatened by it was much larger : no distinction was made between near and remote kinsmen.[4]

---

[1] 1 Sam. xviii. 18 ; 2 Kings iv. 13.
[2] LVIII, ii, p. 34, according to CLXX, iii, pp. 84–9.
[3] 2 Sam. iii. 27 ; Num. xxxv. 9–34 ; Deut. iv. 41–3 ; Joshua xx.
[4] 2 Sam. xxi. 1–14 ; Gen. iv. 14–15, 23–4 ; Judges viii. 18–21 ; 2 Sam. xiv. 7.

" Similarly, among the Bedouins, even if the prevailing modern custom limits the liability of the kin of the victim and the murderer to those of the fourth remove, there are tribes which do not observe this limitation."[1] The same held good among the ancient Arabs : Imrulquais, after the murder of his father, swore to kill 100 men of the Banu Asad ; Amr slew 100 men to expiate the death of his son who was accidentally slain.[2]

It is probable that in early times the clan as a whole inherited the property of each of its members : moslem law still preserves traces of this ancient practice.[3] The *mishpahah* migrated[4] and made war as a unit.[5] It must have had, like the Arab tribes, its own special customs, religiously observed by its members. It constituted a small closed religious community ; even in the time of Saul it had an annual sacrifice in which it was an imperative duty for all its members to take part.[6]

The *mishpahah* was no doubt originally the group created by the rigorous necessity of desert life ; it had to be large enough for the purpose of effective defence against enemies, and small enough, on the other hand, to be able to find sufficient water and pasturage within a common circle of territory.

The *mishpahah* of Abiezer numbered 300 men of war,[7] that of Dan 600.[8] Others could place a thousand men in the field ; in fact, the word for " thousand," *'eleph*, was equivalent to *mishpahah* in current usage.

It is probable that this group constituted the social unit upon which the organization of the Hebrews in their nomad stage was built. It is true that the members of the clan considered themselves as all of the same blood and called each other " brother," and they also placed a high value upon purity of blood. But this belief in no way implies that the clan consisted of descendants of the same father. It is even more compatible with descent in the female line ;[9]

[1] **LVIII,** ii, p. 35 ; **CLXX,** iii, pp. 107–13, 232 ; **CCXL,** pp. 262–3 ; *cf.* **CCIV,** pp. 220–2, 433.
[2] **CCXL,** p. 53 ; **LXXXIV,** p. 420 ; **CCI,** pp. 144–5.
[3] **CCXL,** p. 54.   [4] Judges xviii.
[5] Judges viii. 2, 18–21.   [6] 1 Sam. xx. 6, 29.
[7] Judges vii. 16–22 ; viii. 4 ; *cf.* vi. 34 ; viii. 2.
[8] Judges xviii. 11, 16–17.
[9] See the discussion of this question in **LVIII,** ii, pp. 33–6.

for the child clearly partakes of its mother's blood, but its participation in its father's blood is much less evident. Moreover artificial fraternity, usually effected by exchange of blood, was regarded as absolutely equivalent to natural kinship.

The belief in the blood bond between members of the same *ḥay* threw a special emphasis on the fundamental solidarity which the Semite regarded as existing between himself and his " brothers " of the same group. " The members of the same clan," says Robertson Smith, " consider themselves as one and the same living being, like a single mass of living flesh, blood and bones, no member of which can be affected without all the members suffering. . . . In the case of homicide, the folk of an Arab tribe do not say : the blood of such a one has been shed, but : our blood has been shed."[1]

These small, closely-knit groups amalgamated to form the larger groups called *tribes*. According to the later Israelite belief, the tribe consisted of descendants of the same ancestor. But that this is merely a theory is even clearer in the case of the tribe than in the case of the *mishpaḥah*. The tribe was a temporary confederation of earlier social groups.

The tribal grouping of Hebrew clans certainly dates from nomad times; but there is every reason to suppose that the list of those which existed at that time did not wholly coincide with the twelve so familiar to us.[2] Like the similar aggregations among the Bedouins of today, they would easily have disintegrated, and their members would then pass into other confederations. This will explain how it is that the same clans appear in turn in the list of the sons of Midian, in that of the Bene Edom, in the list of the Horites, in the genealogy of the sons of Judah, and in that of the sons of Reuben.[3]

Two groups of different origin might come together and form a single " people," on the condition of adopting common rites such as circumcision (Gen. xxxiv. 9–10, 14–16, 21–23).

---

[1] **LXXXIV**, p. 274. [2] See pp. 391–3.

[3] Shobal and Manahath belong to the Horites (Gen. xxxvi. 20, 23, 29) and to Judah (1 Chron. ii. 50, 52, 54 ; iv. 1, 2) ; Kenaz to Edom (Gen. xxxvi. 11, 15, 42, etc.) and to Judah (1 Chron. iv. 13, etc.) ; Zerah to Edom (Gen. xxxvi. 13, 17) and to Judah (Gen. xxxviii. 30 ; xlvi. 12, etc.) ; Core to Edom (Gen. xxxvi. 14, 18) and to Levi (Exod. vi. 21, 24, etc.) ; Chanoch to Midian (Gen. xxv. 4) and to Reuben (Gen. xlvi. 9 ; Exod. vi. 14).

IV

AFFILIATION WITH THE CLAN

The clan consisted of adult males in whose veins flowed the blood of the group, either by birth, or by virtue of the performance of a treaty-rite. But, in accordance with primitive modes of thought, no one believed that a child became an adult by the natural process of growing up. It was necessary that certain acts should be performed which had the power of making the child into a real man, capable of carrying out all the functions of an adult. It was to such ceremonies of initiation that circumcision originally belonged. Its main object seems to have been the making of the youth into a male fit for marriage.

The close relation between circumcision and marriage is plain to be seen in the Israelite traditions. According to Genesis xxxiv. the son of Jacob compelled a Canaanite prince who wished to marry their sister, to undergo this rite. The word for bridegroom, *hathan*, means literally "circumcized";[1] and the term for father-in-law, *hothen*, means "he who circumcizes." In early times the ceremony was carried out when the boy reached the stage of puberty, between the age of six and fourteen among the Egyptians, and between six and fifteen among the Arabs; this explains why the Priestly writer represents Ishmael, the father of an Arab group of tribes, as being thirteen years of age when circumcision was instituted.[2] The circumcision of children is a relaxation of the rigour of the primitive custom; and the strange tradition preserved in Exodus iv. 24–26 seems intended to justify this relaxation.

Since circumcision was an initiation ceremony, it naturally came to be interpreted in a wider sense as an act of admission to a group. Even in Sheol the uncircumcized may not lie with his people; separated from them, he lies in the "pit," with the "slain" who have not received burial.[3]

In any case, circumcision was not in early times, and could not have been, as is sometimes maintained, one of the

---

[1] *Cf.* Exod. iv. 26.
[2] Gen. xvii. 25; *cf.* Josephus, A.J., i, 12, 2 (214).
[3] Ezek. xxviii. 10; xxxi. 18; xxxii. 18 *ff.*

distinctive marks which the members of a tribe or the devotees of a cult used to tattoo on their bodies.[1] For this custom was practised by all the peoples of the Near East, Egyptians, Arabs, Phenicians, Edomites, Ammonites, Moabites (Jer. ix. 24–52). The Philistines, new-comers from Asia Minor, were the only uncircumcized people known to the ancient Israelites.

The rite was clearly very ancient, older than the Bronze Age ; since the Hebrews made use of stone knives to perform the rite,[2] just as the pre-Islamic Arabs did in the case of their old custom of the blood-covenant.[3] The worshippers of Attis used stone implements to carry out their sacred mutilations,[4] the Romans in sacrificing pigs and sheep,[5] the ancient Cretans and certain American Indians for sacrificial purposes, and the Hottentots for sacrifices and circumcision.[6]

However, it is probable that the rite was not native to the Semites, but had been borrowed by them from outside. Herodotus tells us that " the Phenicians and the Syrians who live in Palestine, themselves acknowledge that they learnt the custom of circumcision from the Egyptians."[7] According to the Elohist, it was after the entry into Canaan that Jahweh, at Gilgal, commanded Joshua to circumcize the Israelites [8] in order " to roll away the reproach of Egypt from the people," that is to say, in order that the Israelites might no longer be despised by the Egyptians on account of their uncircumcized state (Joshua v. 2–3, 8–9).

According to the Jahwist, the first case of the circumcision of a Hebrew took place on the borders of Egypt, shortly before the exodus, and was performed by a Midianite woman (Exod. iv. 24–26).

On the other hand, the Priestly writer represents circumcision as having been already delivered to Abraham, the common ancestor of Edom, Israel, Ishmael and Midian, and the Jahwist and the Elohist themselves, forgetting their account of the recent introduction of the rite, describe it

[1] So in **IV**, p. 128. [2] Joshua v. 2–3 ; Exod. iv. 25.
[3] Herodotus, iii, 8.
[4] Catullus, lxiii, 5 ; *cf.* Plutarch, *Nic.*, 13 ; Ovid, *Fast.*, iv, 237.
[5] Titus Livius, xxi, 45, 8.   [6] **CLXXXV**, i, pp. 272–3.
[7] **II**, p. 104.
[8] The present text reads : " to circumcize the people again the second time " ; but the words " again " and " the second time " (in v. 2), as well as vv. 4–7, have been added by later editors, to bring the story into some kind of agreement with the other versions.

elsewhere as already practised by the sons of Jacob (Gen. xxxiv.).

The variations in the tradition may, perhaps, be explained by the assumption that the African custom of circumcision was spread by the Egyptians at an early date among the Semites of Syro-Arabia, including some of the Hebrew tribes, but did not become general in Israel till fairly late. In any case the introduction of this rite among the Hebrews cannot be ascribed to Jahwism. No tradition exists which attributes its origin to Moses ; according to Exodus iv. 24–26, the latter was and remained uncircumcized.

Throughout the history of Israel up to the exile, circumcision remained a social rite, devoid of religious significance. According to Joshua v. it was a mark of civilization, much as the use of linen or soap is today : Israel adopted circumcision for cultural reasons, to avoid the contempt of the Egyptians. To the Hebrews the uncircumcized Philistine was a barbarian, a savage. The early religious codes, the Book of the Covenant, the second Decalogue and Deuteronomy, know nothing of this practice. Circumcision was not even essential for participation in the worship of Jahweh : there were uncircumcized ministrants in the temple at Jerusalem (Ezek. xliv. 7–9). It would appear from Jeremiah iv. 4 that there might be at that time a circumcision of the flesh which was not a " circumcision to Jahweh."

No doubt this custom, like all the national usages, was referred to the God of Israel. He commanded it to be adopted (Joshua v.). According to Exodus iv. 24–26, the circumcision of Gershom appeased Jahweh when he was angry with his father Moses ; hence, no doubt, some kind of protective power, or curative virtue, was attributed to it, which may help to explain why the rite was transferred to infancy.[1] But it was chiefly considered as a utilitarian practice, without special religious value, putting the physical organ into the necessary condition to fulfil its functions. A man who is " uncircumcized of lips " is not eloquent (Exod. vi. 12, 30) ; to have " an uncircumcized ear " is to be incapable of listening (Jer. vi. 10) ; to " take away the foreskin of the heart," is to enable it to understand (Jer. iv. 4).

It was during the exile, when the Jews came into close

[1] **LXXXV,** p. 147.

contact with peoples like the Babylonians and the Persians, who did not practise the rite, that circumcision took on in the eyes of the Israelites the character of a symbol of nationality and religion. Its distinctive nature was the more marked in that the rite had fallen into disuse about the same time among the Phenicians [1] and no doubt among the other peoples of Palestine ; [2] then it was that circumcision became the sign of the covenant between Jahweh and his people (Gen. xvii. 11 P), and was required of all, stranger or slave, who partook of the Passover (Exod. xii. 44, 47–9).

V

THE SLAVE, THE *GER*, AND THE GUEST

Side by side with the members of the clan, there lived slaves and dependents, who were affiliated to the group by initiation ceremonies, such as circumcision.

The slave was his master's property, but could be attached to his master's " house " by a ceremony of a magico-religious nature : he was brought to the *elohim*—no doubt, his master's household deity—and his ear was bored to the door-post, in ancient times probably to the curtain which served as the entrance to the tent (Exod. xxi. 6).

The dependent or client (Heb. *ger*),[3] was a man who belonged by birth to another clan, but had either fled from his own people as a protest against some injustice of which he considered himself the victim, or had been driven out on account of a crime. The story of Cain well describes the miserable plight of the man compelled to live alone in the desert : " Whoever findeth me will slay me," is the cry of the banished (Gen. iv. 14) : the murderer is assured, however, that his victim will not be avenged. Hence the man without a clan usually seeks the protection of some member of another clan capable of defending him, and becomes his client (*ger*). The client's life was safe, but his status was inferior and often wretched (Exod. xxiii. 9) ; he had no legal rights (Gen. xix. 9 ; xxiii. 4) ; although he was obliged to serve the gods of the clan under whose protection he lived (1 Sam. xxvi. 19 ;

[1] Herodotus, ii, 104.
[2] Josephus, *A.J.*, viii, 10, 3 (§ 262).
[3] *Cf.* **CLXIX.**

Ruth i. 16 ; ii. 12), the tie of dependency which bound him to the group might at any time be severed.

An equally temporary, but much closer, relation existed between the nomad and the passing guest whom he received into his tent. The man who has touched the cord of an Arab's tent, or partaken of his food, even though he were his personal enemy, is regarded by the Arab, and treated by all the members of his clan, as a " brother." For instance, Zaid al-Khalil refused to kill a wanderer who had stolen his camels because, before committing the theft, the robber had drunk of his father's cup.[1] By the act of partaking of food belonging to a member of the clan, the stranger has absorbed some of the life of the group, he has become a part of it. The relationship thus established was, quite logically, only deemed to hold good during the time that the nourishment of which the guest had partaken was supposed to remain in his body. According to the Arabs consulted by Burckhardt, this period lasted three days and a third, two nights and the intervening day according to Doughty's informants, and only twenty-four hours among the Esquimaux.[2] The community resulting from a common meal might have more lasting effects ; hence the ceremonial meal constituted a part of the ritual of a treaty : [3] the Hebrew word *berith*, " alliance or covenant," may be derived from *barah*, to eat.[4] In any case, these ideas illustrate the fact that the Arab regards hospitality as the most imperative of duties and prides himself on the most generous exercise of it possible.

The Israelites had certainly shared these ideas and practised these customs in nomad days ; for they long continued to observe them (Gen. xviii.) : it was the duty of the host to risk his own life and the honour of his family in order to protect those who had come under " the shadow of his roof " (Gen. xix. 6–8 ; Judges xix. 23–24). Any breach of the duty of hospitality was regarded as the worst of crimes ; indeed, it was such a crime that justified the destruction of Sodom and the almost complete extermination of the tribe of Ben-

---

[1] Aghani, xvi, 51.

[2] *The Private Journal of Capt. G. F. Lyon*, London, 1824, p. 350 (according to **CXXVI**, p. 40).

[3] Gen. xxvi. 30 ; xxxi. 54.

[4] **CCXVII**, p. 558 ; Johs. Pedersen, *Der Eid bei den Semiten*, Strasburg, Trübner, 1914, p. 45, n. 1.

jamin (Gen. xix. ; Judges xix–xxi.). The first step in the abandonment of the nomad point of view in this regard is indicated by the approval of Jael's action in slaying her guest because he was the enemy of her nation (Judges v. 24–27 ; cf. iv. 17–22).

VI

MODE OF LIFE

There are many varieties of nomads,[1] from the nomads of the great deserts, whose main occupation is rearing camels, and who live either by escorting the passing caravans, or by plundering them, to those who breed buffaloes and live close to cultivated districts where they can find the abundant summer herbage which they need. The ancestors of the Israelites belonged, no doubt, to the intermediate class of the Bedouins who breed sheep and goats. They are expressly described as such in most of the Hebrew traditions, especially in the story of Jacob and Laban, and in the J-version of the descent into Egypt : [2] " Thy servants are shepherds, both we, and also our fathers." The district of Kadesh and of Beer-sheba, where the most reliable of the Hebrew traditions place the Israelites, is best suited to this class of cattle-rearing.

For beasts of burden they had asses, but no horses.[3] The camels,[4] the oxen,[5] the silver and gold,[6] sometimes enumerated among the wealth of the patriarchs, can at most have been only a small part of their property, unless we should regard these details as anachronisms. It is not possible that the Hebrews should have been breeders of camels to any great extent, since their language does not even possess a special word for a female camel.[7]

---

[1] See L. Febvre, *La Terre et l'évolution humaine*, L'Evolution de l'Humanité, n. 4, see index : *Nomadisme*. *Cf.* Baldensperger, **PEF, QS**, 1901, pp. 169, 171, 173, 252 ; **CLXVII** ; Schumacher, **MN**, 1904, p. 78 ; A. Jaussen, **RB**, 1902, pp. 87–93 ; **CLXXXII**, ii, p. 38 ; G. A. Smith, **EX**, 1908, pp. 269 *ff.* ; Eerdmans, **EX**, 1908, pp. 350 *ff.* ; **XCVI**, p. 63.

[2] Gen. xxxvii. 2, 12, 14, etc.

[3] Gen. xii. 16 ; xxii. 3 ; xxxii. 6, 16 ; xlii. 26, 27 ; xliii. 18, 24, etc.

[4] Gen. xxiv. 10, etc. ; xxxii. 8, 16.

[5] Gen. xii. 16 ; xiii. 5 ; xxiv. 35 ; xxvi. 14 ; xxxii. 6, 8, 16.

[6] Gen. xiii. 2 ; xx. 16 ; xxiii. 15 ; xxiv. 35 ; xlii. 25 *ff.*

[7] Gen. xxxii. 16. The *bikra* (Jer. ii. 23) is the *young* camel.

As certain accounts presuppose, it is possible that from their nomad period the Israelites occasionally practised cultivation.[1] The Bedouin is always ready to sow some kinds of grain when the season of the year enables him to harvest them before his migration. It is the planting of fruit trees which binds a man to the soil.

The rearing of small cattle made extended migrations necessary, since the desert grass was soon scorched, save in the immediate neighbourhood of springs. But in normal times these migrations had their appointed limits. Each nomad group has its own range, where it is conceded sole grazing rights ; such rights constituted a kind of communal landed property. Some such common property in land existed, no doubt, for a long time in Israel.[2]

The limits of the range of a nomad group are determined by the position of the watering-places of which it has the right to avail itself. It is certainly a proof of the reliability of the Hebrew traditions, that, in the patriarchal narratives, they should give such prominence to the finding of springs, the digging of wells, and to disputes and agreements connected with the possession or use of these most valuable of all properties to the Bedouin. A tribe will only leave its territory— as in the case of the descent into Egypt [3]—when it is forced to do so, especially by a drought which dries up the springs.

The Hebrews, like the modern Bedouins, derived most of their nourishment from their sheep and goats, not that they were great meat-eaters, for like most pastoral people they disliked killing their animals and only did so on ceremonial occasions, such as feasts or the arrival of a guest, and then, no doubt, as a sacrifice ; but they made great use of the milk, especially for butter.[4] To this staple food they added game as they were able,[5] the wild fruits of the oasis, and locusts.[6] When the Bedouin needs flour and oil he buys them from the settled population, but it is, no doubt, by an anachronism that the tradition represents corn as the main source of food for the nomad patriarchs, as it was, of course, for the agricultural Israelites in the time of the writers (Gen. xlii.–xlv.).

[1] Gen. xxv. 29–34 ; xxvi. 12 ; xxxvii. 7.
[2] See p. 396.
[3] See p. 171–2.   [4] Isa. vii. 21–2 ; Judges iv. 19 ; v. 25.
[5] Gen. xxv. 27 ; xxvii. 1–33.
[6] Lev. xi. 22 ; Matt. iii. 4 ; Mark i. 6.

For clothing and shelter the ancient Hebrew also had recourse to his flock. The garment which he girt about his loins (Gen. iii. 21), like the " hairy mantle " of the prophets of later times, was, no doubt, made from the skin of his animals. From the same material he made leather bottles for his milk, and his table consisted merely of a skin stretched out on the ground (*shulḥan*). Later on he learnt to make garments of woven goat's hair, the " sackcloth " which became the distinctive garb of mourning, and sometimes of the " man of God " (Isa. xx. 2). The same coarse material served then, as now, for tents. It is black like the hair of the eastern goat ; hence the spouse of the Song of Songs says " I am black as the tents of Kedar " (Cant. i. 5), and the darkened heaven could be compared to sackcloth (Isa. l. 3).

From the wool of the sheep were made the tunic and the mantle which, later on, took the place of the apron, also the carpets which together with the lamp and the camel's saddle constituted the principal furniture of the tent.

Apart from weaving, the women's occupation, metal-working is almost the only industry of the desert. Moreover, it is not carried on by the tribes of aristocratic descent, but is left to special communities, like our Bohemians, at once despised and feared. According to an old Hebrew tradition, evidently belonging to nomad times, mankind was divided into three classes : the sons of Jabal, who dwelt in tents with their flocks ; the sons of Jubal, who played the harp and the flute ; and the sons of Tubal (also called Cain), the half-brother of the two former : these were the workers in bronze and iron (Gen. iv. 20–22). The description exactly reflects modern Bedouin society, except that it is the members of the same group, the Nowar or Sunna, of Indian origin, who travel round among the tribes, and combine the trade of smith and tinker with that of singing, dancing and also sorcery.[1]

It has often been maintained that the Kenites, immemorial allies of Israel, were one of these communities engaged in metal-working, since Cain, the name of their eponymous ancestor, may mean smith, and has been identified with Tubal

---

[1] *Cf.* Burckhardt, *Bemerkungen*, 1831, pp. 52, 88 ; **CLXXVIII,** i, pp. 137, 278, 309 ; ii, 696 ; B. Stade, **ZATW,** 1894, p. 255 ; C. R. C. in **PEF, QS,** 1901, pp. 269–72 ; **CCV,** p. 34 ; R. Eisler, *Monde Oriental,* 1929, pp. 48–112. The same organization exists in the Sahara and the Soudan : *cf.* **CCXLVIII,** i, pp. 182–5 ; **CCXXXIX,** pp. 159, 249.

(Gen. iv. 22). In that case, however, it seems surprising that we are not told of Cain's slaying his brother with a weapon forged by him.

VII

RELATIONS WITH NEIGHBOURING PEOPLES. CHARACTER AND CULTURE OF THE NOMAD HEBREWS

The relations of the nomad Hebrews with their neighbours, especially with their settled neighbours the agricultural Canaanites, were apparently not so idyllic, so wholly peaceful, as the patriarchal narratives would have us believe.[1] Certainly the Bedouin does not live in a state of constant warfare with the fellah : many nomad tribes make agreements with some village or other (khouwweh), giving them the yearly right to come and pasture their cattle after the harvest, when the desert grass is withered.[2] Such must have been the nature of the proposed " covenant " between the Bene Jacob and the city of Shechem (Gen. xxxiv.). But there are early texts which show clearly that the ancient Hebrews rejoiced in raiding and plunder :

> " Benjamin is a ravening wolf ;
> in the morning he devours the prey ;
> in the evening he divides the spoil." [3]

It is evidently with approval that the story is told of how Jacob stole the flocks of Laban the Aramean, or of how the Danites raided not only the Canaanites of Laish, but also the Israelite Micah.[4]

When the Hebrews entered Canaan, they were warlike, fierce,[5] vindictive,[6] of unrestrained passions when it was a question of avenging a kinsman's honour or life,[7] utterly contemptuous of those who acquiesced in servitude.[8] These characteristics, clearly belonging to the desert life, long persisted among them.

This raises the highly controversial question of the degree

---

[1] Except Gen. xxxiv ; xlviii. 22 ; *cf.* chap. xiv.
[2] **CLXXX,** p. 4. [3] Gen. xlix. 27.
[4] Gen. xxx.–xxxi. ; Judges xviii., spec. v. 22–6. See pp. 336–7.
[5] Gen. xlix. 5–6, 8–9, 16–17, 19, 23–4.
[6] Judges i. 6.
[7] Gen. xxxiv. ; *cf.* above, pp. 195–6. [8] Gen. xlix. 14–15.

of culture attained by the nomad Hebrews. Later Israelite documents, especially the most recent, the Priestly Code, ascribe to them as highly developed a technical skill, as extensive a use of writing, institutions as elaborate, and moral and religious conceptions as refined, as those of Israel under the monarchy, or even of the Jews of the post-exilic period. Critical examination of the sources shows how constantly the ancient compilers were guilty of anachronism. At the same time, it is certain that the Hebrews were not, as some scholars have too confidently asserted, on a wholly uncivilized level, any more than the modern Bedouins. Without going so far as to assert, with some pan-Babylonists, that the original Hebrews were city-dwellers who adopted the nomad life,[1] or with Winckler, that the " astral knowledge " of the Babylonians, with all its subtleties, had penetrated to the heart of Arabia, there are good reasons for believing that the nomad Semites, both in early times as in the pre-Islamic age or today, were imbued to some extent with the general culture of their settled neighbours.[2]

Unfortunately, in the absence of evidence, it seems impossible to obtain accurate information as to the extent and depth of this cultural influence. The few short poetic fragments which can with certainty be assigned to the Israel of nomad times, such as the song of Lamech, Miriam's couplet on the cī ˉsing of the Red Sea, the invocation of Jahweh at the departure and return of the Ark, and perhaps the prayer to the Well,[3] bear witness to a finished poetic technique, a lively and colourful imagination, and strong emotions. But it is a very simple poetry, capable of no extended flights. Although these short pieces were, no doubt, composed by professional poets, the *moshelim* (Num. xxi. 17), similar to the arab *sha'ir*, they merely give expression to rudimentary group emotions. Nothing in them denotes the wider experience, the greater individuality of thought which mark the literature of a society with an advanced culture.

[1] **CCLVI ; XXXVII.**   [2] *Cf.* **III**, p. 57.
[3] Gen. iv. 23–24 ; Exod. xv. 21 ; Num. x. 35–6 ; xxi. 17–18. *Cf.* **CLXXIV**, pp. 9–26.

BOOK II

THE RELIGION OF THE NOMAD HEBREWS

HEBREW tradition is unanimous in asserting that when the Israelites finally settled in Palestine, they were worshippers of Jahweh. Certain modern critics maintain that this god only became the common national god of the tribes after they had been unified into a nation under Saul and David.[1] But this opinion is not supported by the texts. The ancient song of Deborah bears witness that, long before the first kings, when the trumpet sounded for war against the kings of Canaan, Israelite warriors of every clan and tribe were bound, under pain of public disapproval or of curses, " to come to the help of Jahweh among the mighty " (Judges v. 23).

The fact that the most fanatical followers of Jahweh persisted in regarding the nomad pastoral life in tents, without fields or vineyards, as the ideal state of the worshippers of Jahweh,[2] suggests that the cult of Jahweh had been the religion of nomads before it was adapted to the mode of life of a people who had become settled agriculturists.

One of the strands of Hebrew tradition naïvely carries back the beginnings of the worship of Jahweh among the ancestors of Israel to the creation of the world [3]; another, with a little more modesty, refers it to the third generation of mankind.[4] But it was the prevailing opinion that the tribes had only adopted this cult shortly before their entry into Palestine, as the result of certain definite historical events : the exodus and the work of Moses. Then it was that Israel became the people of Jahweh and that Jahweh became the God of Israel. This must be regarded as the memory of an actual fact, persistently preserved in spite of many causes

---

[1] **XLVII²**, p. 189.　　　　　　[2] See pp. 399–400; 410–1.
[3] J¹ (Gen. iv. 1).　　　　　　[4] J² (Gen. iv. 26).

which tended to obscure it, particularly the growth of the patriarchal narratives.

Several of the prophets, especially Hosea and Ezekiel, recall as a fact known to all, that Jahweh has been the God of Israel " from the land of Egypt," [1] that he " found Israel " in the wilderness.[2] When Ezekiel goes over the history of the relations of Jahweh with Israel, he usually begins with Egypt or the desert.[3] In two of the main streams of tradition (E and P) it is explicitly taught that Jahweh only made known his name, *i.e.* revealed himself to Moses.[4] These two writers reconcile the divergence between this conception and that of J and the patriarchal narrative, by maintaining that Jahweh was indeed the god of the fathers, but that, prior to Moses, he let himself be worshipped, not under his own name, but under the vague title of *elohim* (deity), or *El Shaddai* (almighty god ?). We shall see later on what historical basis there is for this explanation, but it remains clear that Israelite tradition held it to be the fact that Jahweh was not the god of Israel until Moses.

Hence we must distinguish two stages in the nomad life of the Hebrews : the one prior to the beginning of the national cult of Jahweh in the time of Moses, the other starting from this event.

[1] Hos. xii. 10 ; xiii. 4 ; Ezek. xx. 5.
[2] Deut. xxxii. 10 ; *cf.* Hos. ix. 10.
[3] Chapters xx. and xxiii. According to chap. xvi. the Covenant only dates from the sojourn in Egypt (v. 8).
[4] Exod. iii. 13–14 (E) ; vi. 2–3 (P).

CHAPTER I

BELIEFS OF THE HEBREWS BEFORE THE MOSAIC AGE

LACKING contemporary documents, we can only attempt by the method of induction to reconstruct the religious condition of the Hebrews before the Mosaic period, by collecting the numerous traces which exist in Israelite institutions and beliefs of the better documented periods. It is not difficult to recognize those customs and beliefs which go back to early times; since they are those which were common to all Semites, or at least to the Israelites and the nomad Semites—the pre-Islamic Arabs or the Bedouins of today;—an additional indication is afforded by the mistrust or hostility with which the official representatives of the national religion of Jahweh regarded them.

I

MAGIC

It may be safely asserted that the religion, as indeed all the other spheres of social and individual activity, must have been, as it still is among the modern Bedouins, saturated with magic, that is to say, with the belief in human ability to control invisible powers, gods, demons, spirits, the souls of things.

Among the very numerous ideas and practices of a magical character prevalent among the Israelites during the historical period,[1] there are not a few of which it can be said with certainty that they go back to pre-Mosaic times. One example is the fear of the evil eye, very common in

[1] *Cf.* **CCXXXVI**; **CXCII**; **CXCI**; **XXV**, pp. 1, 2; Hans Duhm, *Die boesen Geister im A.T.*, Tübingen-Leipzig, Mohr, 1904; **CCVI**; **CCVII**; **CLXXXVII**; **LIX**; **LXX**, i; **XLVII²**, pp. 151–4; **CLXXII**; **LVIII**; **CCLXXI**; **LVI**; **CCXXI**; Ad. Lods, **JP**, 1926, pp. 239–64; in the same way **RHP**, 1927, pp. 1–16; and **LXXVI**, pp. 55–76.

ancient Israel,[1] and which plays a great part in the life of the Arabs today.[2] The gesture of pointing with the finger was regarded by the Israelites as maleficent.[3] The Arabs attributed dangerous potency [4] to it, hence it was forbidden by Islam.[5]

Magic was not merely employed secretly by individuals with intent to do harm to another, which is sorcery, but was publicly used by the tribe in its official activities. For instance, before a campaign the King of Israel consulted a prophet; and the divinatory arrows of the man of God not only served to predict the issue of the war, but had a direct influence upon it; the number of arrows that the king shot into the ground would be the number of his victories (2 Kings xiii. 18–19). Similar customs are common among un-civilized peoples.[6] Divination by arrows was also the main method of divination in use among the pre-Islamic Arabs.[7]

Another means of securing the victory beforehand con-sisted in shooting an arrow in the direction of the enemy's country. This was done by King Joash after the man of God had imparted to him some of his own spiritual power by laying his hands upon those of his visitor (2 Kings xiii. 15–17). Elsewhere we are told that the Israelites succeeded in taking the city of Ai because Joshua had, *throughout the whole of the fight*, kept his spear directed against the city (Joshua viii. 18, 26), and Moses enabled his people to conquer the Amalekites by keeping his hands raised, or, according to another version, by keeping his rod stretched out during the engagement (Exod. xvii. 8–13). This particular pro-cedure of imitative magic, common among various uncivilized peoples,[8] is also familiar to the Bedouins. "All the Arabs know the story of Eben Rumman at Teima." Wishing to avenge himself upon his enemy Mur'y who, by means of the

---

[1] Num. xxiii. 13 ; 1 Sam. ii. 29 and 32 (G) ; xviii. 9 ; Prov. xxiii. 6 ; xxviii. 22 ; Cant. vi. 5 ; Matt. vi. 28 ; xx. 15 ; Mark vii. 22.
[2] For example CCV, pp. 57–8.
[3] Isa. lviii. 9 ; Prov. vi. 12–14.
[4] B. Hišam, pp. 272, 285 (**XXX**, p. 90).
[5] Guidi, *L'Arabie préislamique*, 1921, p. 40.
[6] For example, among the Dakotas, **CCVIII**, p. 94.
[7] **XC²**, pp. 132–3.
[8] For example among the Indians of the Thomson River, **CLXXXV**, i, pp. 29, 30 ; *cf.* pp. 27–32 ; among the Central Aus-tralians, **CXXVI**, p. 10.

evil eye, had killed one of his camels, Eben Rumman " fixed an angry eye upon him *while he pointed a sharp stick at his face.* Mur'y uttered a loud cry and put his hand to his right eye which had just been struck." [1] Mohammed, at the battle of Bedr, threw a handful of pebbles in the direction of the enemy, and pronounced a curse. [2]

Another well-known method of conquering the enemy in advance was to utter a curse against him before the fight. Like the blessing, the curse was regarded as a word of power, capable of attaining its end by its own inherent virtue, without the intervention of a god : it was a magic weapon. Thus it was that David and Goliath cursed each other before coming to blows (*cf.* 2 Sam. xxi. 21). The oracles of the prophets against " the nations " are an outgrowth of these maledictions of war. [3] The very ancient story of Balaam suggests that this practice had long been familiar to the Hebraic inhabitants of the Palestinian region, and that it was a kind of regular institution among them. Balaam, who is depicted as a real Arab *sha'ir,* was a renowned magician, Aramean, Edomite, Ammonite, or Midianite, according to various versions of the tradition, [4] who had made a speciality of these curses : those whom he blesses are blessed, and those whom he curses are cursed (Num. xxii. 6). Balak, King of Moab, brought him from another country to pronounce one of his formidable anathemas against Israel. The Israelite tradition revels in the story of how Jahweh saved his people in their extremity : he compelled Balaam to bless Israel instead of cursing them. It may be said in passing that this last point bears witness to the faith which the Israelites had in the irrevocableness of the malediction : if Balaam had uttered it, Jahweh himself, apparently, would not have been able to annul it (Num. xxii–xxiv.).

The *ḥerem, i.e.* the vow of utter destruction upon the enemy and all that he possesses, leaving nothing for spoil, was no doubt magical rather than religious : it would have been originally a kind of reinforced curse. [5]

---

[1] CCV, pp. 57–8. The underlining is ours.
[2] B. Hišam, pp. 439–45 (XXX, p. 91).
[3] *Cf.* Num. xxi. 29.
[4] *Cf.* Num. xxii. 4, 5 ; xxiii. 7 and ii. *ad loc.*
[5] See pp. 288–9.

The oath was also an essentially magical act, a conditional curse, capable of acting, even without the intervention of a god. It continues to play as great a part in the life of the Bedouin today, as it did formerly among the Israelites and ancient peoples in general.

Another essentially magical practice is the ordeal,[1] although it came to be regarded very early as the arbitrary decision of a god. The primitive nature of the ceremony is apparent in a form of ordeal which was in use in the temple at Jerusalem and was sanctioned by the Jewish law: the woman suspected of infidelity by her husband was brought to the sanctuary: there she was not only obliged to swear that she was innocent, but to drink holy water; if she was guilty, the water would without fail cause her belly to swell and her thigh to rot. This rite was reinforced by another, perhaps a later addition: the curses pronounced against the accused by herself in the event of her guilt were committed to writing, then the ink of the writing was washed off and the water drunk by the suspect, who in this way actually absorbed the curse.[2]

Practices of this kind must have been current already among the nomad Hebrews, judging by the names of the sacred springs of Kadesh, the oasis which was for so long their rallying centre: these were " the waters of Massa," *i.e.* the waters of testing or the ordeal,[3] " the waters of Meribah," *i.e.* of litigation,[4] " the well of Judgment." [5] Throughout the Semitic region there were many springs and rivers which had the reputation of exposing and even of punishing the guilty. They gave decisions either by throwing up to the surface the offering of the guilty (as at Aphaca, at the Stygian waters, near Bostra, and probably at Daphne near Antioch), or by rejecting the guilty person (as at Hadramaut), or, on the other hand, by drowning him, as in Babylonia.[6] At the Ashbamean springs (*i.e.* " the springs of the seven waters,"—*shab'a, maya*) near Tyana, the water was sweet and harmless to those who swore truly, but per-

---

[1] See the excellent chapter in L. Lévy-Bruhl, **LII**, pp. 244–93.
[2] Num. v. 11–31. The same procedure is employed for magical remedies in Egypt, **CCLXXX**, p. 26.
[3] Exod. xvii. 7; Deut. vi. 16; ix. 22; xxxiii. 8.
[4] Exod. xvii. 7; Deut. xxxiii. 8; Ps. lxxxi. 8.
[5] Gen. xiv. 7. [6] *Code of Hammourabi*, § 2.

jurers were smitten in the eyes, the feet and the hands ; they were afflicted with dropsy and consumption.[1]

Chiefs were regarded as endowed with magical power. A very old Hebrew poem represents them as digging a well with their staves (Num. xxi. 18), no doubt like the sorcerer with his wand.[2] We shall see that the Israelite cultus was full of practices usually regarded as magical ; this was certainly already the case in pre-Mosaic times. For instance, sacred objects, and in particular the sacred stone, the abode of the god, were rubbed with blood, this being the normal form of sacrifice among the pre-Islamic Arabs, and the central rite in the sacrificial act among the Israelites. The original reasons for this were magical, such as the purpose of establishing the tie of blood-relationship between the clan and a god, or the intent of giving or restoring life and strength to the sacred things and to the god himself, just as Ulysses gave the shades blood to drink in order to enable them to speak to him (Od. xi. 96–97).

Certain prohibitions which seem to have been originally pastoral and hunting taboos belonging to the order of sympathetic magic, probably go back to nomad times. Such are the prohibition to seethe a kid in its mother's milk [3] : this would cause double suffering to the goat which had produced the milk and given birth to the kid, and might possibly dry up its milk.[4] The regulations prohibiting the sacrifice on the same day of an animal and its young,[5] or of taking the mother-bird with its brood,[6] are probably of the same kind. The practices thus forbidden threatened the danger of causing by sympathy the destruction of the flock or the game, which might perish 'em 'al banim, " the mother with the children," [7] as the saying was, that is to say entirely.[8]

The original reason why it was forbidden to break the bones of the pascal lamb was perhaps the belief that if this were done, the cattle or one of the guests would break a limb during the year.[9] In the East today the same sacrificial

---

[1] Cf. **LXXXIV**, pp. 178–81.   [2] See p. 304.
[3] Exod. xxiii. 19 ; xxxiv. 26 ; Deut. xiv. 21.
[4] Mauss, **AS**, 1904–5, p. 190 ; **CLXXXVIII**, pp. 151–67 ; Sir James Frazer, **AI**, 1907, pp. 578–86 ; **CLXXXVII**, iii, pp. 111–64.
[5] Lev. xxii. 28.   [6] Deut. xxii. 6–7.
[7] Gen. xxxii. 12.   [8] Ad. Lods, **RHP**, 1927, p. 7.
[9] **CLXV**, p. 16 ; cf. Kohler, **AR**, xiii, pp. 153, 154.

rule is observed,[1] and when the sacrifice is made on behalf of a new-born child the reason alleged for the custom is that otherwise the bones of the child will be broken.[2]

The use of " mandrakes " (Gen. xxx. 14–16) and of philtres,[3] of charms and talismans against snake-bite or the evil eye are certainly practices which go back to nomad times. The Arabs make philtres,[4] especially with mandragora which they call " the apple of the jinns." [5] The women and children of Bedouin tribes are bedecked with jewels which serve at the same time as amulets. The traditions about the exodus rightly suppose that the same was true of the Hebrews in the wilderness : the story was told how Aaron obtained enough gold to make the golden calf by asking them to give him their ear-rings (Exod. xxxii. 2–5, 24). The use which was made of these jewels shows clearly that, for the Israelites too, these objects were not mere secular ornaments, but " holy things," [6] possessing mysterious potencies : Aaron, Moses, Gideon used them to make images of gods or sacred objects [7]; Jacob, fearing to destroy them or to use the metal for another purpose, buried them in a sacred spot (Gen. xxxv. 4). In one passage we find that the nomads —for that is the meaning of the word " Ishmaelites " here— not only wore rings of gold themselves, but hung round the necks of their camels " little moons," that is jewels in the form of disks or crescents [8] : these objects must have had a prophylactic value, perhaps against " moon-stroke," [9] that is against diseases attributed to this planet ; similarly it is to protect themselves against the evil eye or demons that the Bedouins, as the Arabs did formerly, place about their persons, or hang round the necks of their beasts of burden, shells and metal necklaces.[10]

When the Israelite fell sick, he seldom made use of rational methods of healing, based on observation, but generally employed propitiatory rites addressed to Jahweh, or had recourse to magic, such as the transference of the disease to

---

[1] **XV**, pp. 201, 242.   [2] **XV**, p. 201.
[3] *Test. XII Patr., Joseph*, 6.
[4] **CCV**, p. 15 ; talismans, p. 56.
[5] Dalman in **LXXVIII**, p. 173 ; *cf.* Wetzstein in **XLI**, iv, 4 (*Hohesl.*), pp. 439–45.   [6] See pp. 272–3.
[7] Exod. xxxiii. 5–6 ; Judges viii. 24–7.   [8] Judges viii. 21, 26.
[9] Ps. cxxi. 6.   [10] **XC²**, p. 165 ; **IV**, p. 74.

an animal or to the water of a river, the removal of the
individual supposed to be the cause of the malady, etc.[1]
The same was certainly true òf the nomad Hebrews, as it is
of the Bedouins today.[2] The regular method of driving
away the cholera, for example, consists in leading round the
tents an animal which is then killed [3] : the disease concentrated in the animal is removed when the victim is slain.

Mourning rites which evidently go back to a very remote
past, also, as we shall presently see, seem to have consisted
largely of magical means of acting on the soul of the dead,
or on the influence emanating from him.

Moreover, it was inevitable that the early Israelites should
both believe in and make use of magic. Their general mental
outlook was and remained throughout their entire history,
with the exception of a few choice spirits at certain epochs,
wholly similar to the " primitive mentality " so profoundly
studied by M. Lévy-Bruhl.[4] The Israelites, like the " primitives," explained nearly all phenomena by the direct action
of superhuman and invisible persons or powers, resembling
the human spirit. Like the " primitives " they recognized
no essential difference between the spiritual and the material.
Like them, too, they conceived of a solidarity, or more accurately, a practical identity, between many beings, events and
things which we regard as absolutely distinct.[5]

From the facts which have been enumerated it seems to
follow clearly that the magical beliefs and practices whose
existence in Israel during the historical period has been
established cannot be accounted for as mere borrowings,
more or less superficial, from foreign peoples, especially the
Canaanites.[6] As far back as we can go, the magical state of
mind was one of the constituent elements in the Israelite mentality, as it is in the case of all early peoples. We shall understand better the work of the protagonists of religious progress
in Israel, if we remember that they had to struggle against
this deep-rooted tendency. We shall also understand better
how it was that they could never destroy it entirely, and
why the Jewish law sanctioned so many survivals of it.

[1] **LVI.**   [2] **CCV,** pp. 47, 56.
[3] **CCV,** pp. 46–7.   [4] **CCX, LII, CCIX.**
[5] On these three points, cf. Ad. Lods, **LXXVI,** pp. 65–72
[6] See pp. 104–8.

II

THE DEAD

Nothing persists like funerary rites. As might be expected, the funeral customs of the Israelites of the historical period have preserved the traces of the beliefs of their distant ancestors in pre-Mosaic times.

We must first of all touch briefly on the historical aspect of the study of Hebrew eschatology.

Theologians were long agreed that the Old Testament writers held the same beliefs and hopes concerning the future life as the early Christians or the Jews of the rabbinical period.

But since the seventeenth, the eighteenth and especially the nineteenth century, criticism has discovered and proved conclusively that the doctrines of the resurrection of the body and of the immortality of the soul, upon which rests the belief in future retribution, only became current in Jewish circles from the second century B.C. and onward. With regard to the Israelites of earlier periods, up to about 1875 the evidence was thought to be decisive that they believed in an almost complete annihilation after death, and that they attributed to the dead a vague shadowy existence in Sheol, the ultimate goal of all : " A living dog," wrote the author of Ecclesiastes, " is better than a dead lion. For the living know that they shall die, whereas the dead know nothing " (Eccles. ix. 4–5).

It was agreed that this attitude towards death, which certainly is the prevalent view of the post-exilic parts of the Old Testament, had always characterized the Hebrews. Renan explained it by the genius of the people : the Semitic mind, prone to humiliate man before God, tended to regard mortals as poor transitory creatures, while the Aryan, who held that the soul could exist apart from the body, regarded his ancestors, the *Pitris*, as gods.   In this complete denial of any survival Renan found one of the chief claims of the Semites to superiority.[1]

This theory has been rendered untenable by the evidence of Semitic epigraphy and the study of comparative religion.

[1] **LXXXI**, pp. 41–2, 130–1.

Aramean, Nabatean, Phenician and Babylonian inscriptions have shown that many of the Semites shared the general beliefs of mankind with regard to the survival of the dead and their divine character.

On the other hand, comparative religion, by demonstrating the importance among widely differing peoples of animism and the worship of the dead, made it necessary to revise the opinions held about the Semites. It was felt that if primitive man in general believed in a continuation of life after death, the Semites could hardly be an exception.

Those who first ventured on these untried paths did not escape a tendency to exaggeration.[1] Since then the questions which they raised have been thoroughly sifted by competent Hebraists.[2] Sir James Frazer has re-examined the interpretation of funeral rites.

But after the necessary reservations have been made, and various pertinent criticisms, particularly those of Grüneisen, have been taken into account,[3] we are left with the following well-grounded results :

1. The Israelites, up to the exile, believed in the survival of the individual after death.

2. Before the advent of Jahwism, and even after, during the period that Jahwism held sway, in the popular belief the dead were regarded as beings endowed with supernatural power and knowledge, as *elohim*.

3. The Hebrews, in the remote past, carried on an organized cult of the dead, especially of their ancestors.

1. *The belief in an after-life.* With regard to the first of these points, certain narratives show that the Israelites, like most of the peoples holding animistic beliefs, thought that there was in man, as in all that lives, a double, the cause of his life and its activities. This double could leave him during his life, as in ecstasy, for instance,[4] or in panic :

---

[1] **XXIX**, pp. 7–9, 30–2, 146–68 ; J. Halevy, **AI**, 1883, pp. 210–13 ; **XXVIII**, pp. 365–75 ; *cf.* R. Dussaud, **RHR**, 1906, p. 424 ; **CCXLII** ; **CCXI**.

[2] The following are the most important works : **LXXXVI, CCXXXV, CLXVIII** ; R. H. Charles, *A Critical History of the Doctrine of a Future Life*, London, Black, 1899, pp. 19–50 ; **CLXVI**, pp. 3–29 ; **LVIII** ; **CCLXV**.

[3] **CXCIV.** See also Joh. Frey, *Tod, Seelenglaube und Seelenkult im alten Israel*, Leipzig, Deichert, 1898 ; **XLIX**, pp. 314–41.

[4] Ez. viii. 11 ; 2 Kings v. 26 ; Isa. xxi. 6.

hence, when they wished to say that any one was seized with astonishment or fear, they used the expression " there was no more spirit left in him."

The double also persisted after death, and preserved the traits of its possessor at the moment of his decease. Under such a form it could appear to the living on being summoned : the ghost of Samuel wore the guise of an old man covered with a mantle (1 Sam. xxviii. 14). Under such a form it lived on in Sheol : there kings still kept their thrones (Isa. xiv. 9) ; the old man might be known by his grey hairs, the bereaved still wore mourning, the slain displayed his wounds.[1]

The customs and beliefs connected with burial can only be explained on the assumption that, in the opinion of the early Hebrews, the dead retained consciousness and perception after death. Hence the immense importance attached by the Israelites to burial : not to be buried or to be cast out in some future time from their graves, was the worst threat which the prophets could pronounce against the enemies of Jahweh. Tobit risks his life in order to bury his fellow-countrymen who had been slain by the King of Assyria (Tobit i. 17*ff*.). The unburied dead is a homeless wanderer.

The double, or soul, feels all that is done to the corpse. Hence enemies and criminals were stripped and mutilated. David cut off the head of Goliath and took it as a trophy, as the Philistines did later with Saul and his sons (1 Sam. xvii. 54 ; xxxi. 9–10). David it was, too, who caused the hands and feet of Ishbaal's murderers to be cut off after they had been put to death (2 Sam. iv. 12), no doubt in order to prevent the dead from pursuing and overtaking their executioners. It was regarded as the most terrible of punishments to burn a corpse, and cremation seems only to have been practised in the case of criminals.

It was because the Hebrews believed that the double of the unburied dead hovered about the corpse and might do all kinds of harm to the living, that they were careful not to leave the body of a man who had been hanged upon the gibbet after sunset,[2] and that murderers themselves often took pains to bury their victims (2 Kings ix. 34).

---

[1] 1 Kings ii. 6, 9 ; Gen. xxxvii. 35 ; xlii. 38.
[2] Deut. xxi. 22–3 ; Joshua viii. 29 ; x. 26–7.

The life of the dead in his tomb was mainly one of calm and rest, but was none the less real. Hence the Hebrews, like many other peoples, deposited in the tomb everything that they thought might be useful to the dead : warriors were buried with their swords and shields (Ezek. xxxii. 27) ; the dead were clothed in their most gorgeous apparel ; the last abode of kings like David or Solomon often contained treasures of immense value, which excited the greed of their successors.[1]

Within his tomb the dead guards his own repose inviolate, and is also interested in the fate of the living, especially of his own descendants. We have an echo of this ancient belief in the well-known passage of Jeremiah which describes the disasters of the Babylonian invasion (Jer. xxxi. 15) :

> " Hark ! A funeral lament is heard in Ramah,[2]
>   bitter tears :
> It is Rachel weeping for her children ;
>   she refuses to be comforted."

While the Israelite thus believed that the dead lived on in the grave, he also held—apparently without attempting to reconcile the two conflicting ideas—that all the dead lived together in Sheol, an underground abode. Life in this land of the shades was gloomy, but in the mind of the ancient Hebrews it was anything but annihilation. The inhabitants of this realm might be feeble (this is, perhaps, the meaning of the name *Rephaim*, given to the dead, at least to the famous dead) : but if they lacked physical strength, —for they were only shadows,—they could, nevertheless, move and speak ; they could follow with intense interest the events of the world of the living. When the shade of the King of Babylon comes down among them, they greet him with an ironical and vindictive funeral chant (Isa. xiv. 9 *ff.*). Samuel complains that the peace of his subterranean life has been disturbed by Saul ; but his answer shows that he has forgotten nothing of the past, and still preserves all his prophetic foresight.

It is only in the later texts that the dwellers in Sheol are represented as devoid of all activity, of memory, and even of the consciousness of their own attenuated condition.

---

[1] Josephus, A. J., xiii, 8, 4, etc. *Cf.* perhaps Job iii. 15.
[2] The place of Rachel's sepulchre.

According to the earlier belief, life in Sheol was a continuation
of the present state of existence, with the same family and
national divisions, the same social distinctions, and, it is
hardly necessary to add, *without any moral retribution.* The
places of honour in Sheol are occupied by " the valiant who
spread terror among the living " (Ezek. xxxii. 27). This
last characteristic, which reflects very early social conditions,
suggests, although the question is still very uncertain, that
the Hebrews' conception of Sheol was prior to their settlement in Palestine. It may also be pointed out that similar
conceptions may be found, not only among the Babylonians,
but among many of the non-civilized peoples of all countries,[1]
and perhaps among the pre-Islamic Arabs.[2] The Babylonian[3] and Egyptian[4] etymologies which have been proposed for the word *sheol* are very uncertain. Sheol was
perhaps originally the realm of chthonian spirits, that is,
the realm of the most ancient Semitic gods.[5]

Further evidence of the belief in survival after death
in the form of a double lies in the suggestion, for it is still
nothing more, that at a very early period the Hebrews
believed that in certain cases the double might be rein-
carnated ; this is borne out by the custom of calling a child
by the name of his grandfather, a custom which among
many peoples is directly due to the belief that the spirit of
the dead ancestor has taken up its abode in the body of the
new-born child. We may also mention the beliefs concerning the Earth-Mother.[6] The idea that all men are born
from the earth is, indeed, closely allied to the belief that the
dead who return to the bosom of the universal Mother may
there be reborn.

Be that as it may, the body of stories and customs to
which we have referred prove, in spite of all philological
arguments, that the ancient Hebrews believed, like the
great majority of peoples, that the individual survives
after death.

[1] *Cf.* **CCLXVIII**, ii, pp. 85–9, 99 ; **LVIII**, i, p. 210, n. 1.
[2] **XC¹**, p. 217 ; **XC²**, p. 185.
[3] **XCIII**, p. 636 ; Jensen in **CLXVI**, p. 15.
[4] Devaud, *Sphinx*, xiii, 1910, p. 210 ; Gressmann, **AAW**, 1918,
p. 34, n. 1.
[5] **CLXVI**, pp. 7–19.
[6] Ps. cxxxix. 13–15 ; Job i. 21 ; Sirach xl, 1 ; Isa. xxvi. 19.

Moreover, a careful examination of the passages and phrases in which the words *nephesh* (soul) and *ruach* (spirit) occur will show that two periods must be distinguished in the use of these words, as in the beliefs concerning survival : in the early period these two terms, then almost synonymous, usually denoted the double in the animistic sense ; at that time it was held that the *nephesh* with its individuality persisted after death, since in exceptional cases it might return to the body of the deceased (1 Kings xvii. 21–2), and it went down into Sheol (Ps. xxx. 4 ; xvi. 10). On the other hand, after the exile, the spiritual part of man, the *ruach*, is rather thought of as a sort of impersonal substance or effluence which God resumes at the moment of death, so that logically, after the body has returned to dust, nothing should remain of what was once a man. Hence, instead of a single conception of the constitution of the human personality, there were two Israelite anthropologies which predominated in turn, and which corresponded, the one to the primitive animistic point of view, with its cult of the dead, the other to Jahwist monotheism, the determined foe to all worship addressed to the dead.

2. *The dead are " elohim."* For a long time the Hebrews regarded the dead as beings endowed with supernatural power and knowledge. This is shown by the study of their mourning customs. By the very fact of their extreme antiquity these customs are, unfortunately, capable of ambiguous interpretation. We may, however, call to our aid the striking similarity which the Hebrew customs present with those of widely differing peoples : hence the explanation of these rites should be sought, not in the modes of thought peculiar to the Israelites, but in the realm of those very simple ideas common to primitive man.

Earlier interpreters preferred to see in these customs the natural expression of the grief of the survivors. This explanation must be abandoned : such specific customs as that of putting on sackcloth, for instance, or of placing ashes on the head, cannot be regarded as spontaneous expressions of grief.

Among the numerous explanations which have been proposed, two in particular seem worthy of acceptance : one which regards these customs as actually religious, or propitiatory rites, intended to render the dead favourable to the living,[1] the other which explains them as acts of an apotropaic character, aiming at the protection of the living from the harm which might be done to them by the spirit of the dead.[2] In our estimation, these two explanations should be combined in order to account for the Israelite funerary customs ; since there are among them some propitiatory rites and many apotropaic practices.

The protective character of most mourning customs has been brought out by Sir James Frazer : this scholar has shown that they belong to the category of taboos, that they exhibit a close relationship, and often an absolute identity, with the regulations imposed upon kings, sorcerers, pregnant women, on young men at the time of their initiation, on warriors, avengers, on those who wish to enter a holy place, or to approach one of these persons who are under a taboo. Now the various forms of taboos are essentially intended for a protection against the spirits or spiritual powers with which these classes of persons, by reason of their condition, may be in special relation. The invisible power from whose contact protection is sought in mourning customs, is presumably the spirit of the dead, or an influence emanating from him.

> The purpose of *closing the eyes of the dead* was originally to prevent his spirit from coming out and wandering about before the body was borne to the grave.
> In bereavement the Israelite's first act was *to rend his garments* or to *take them off*, then to *clothe himself with* the coarse material called *sackcloth* ; this was because the dangerous emanation from the dead might attach itself to the clothes which were being worn at the time when the death occurred. The practice presents a striking analogy with the Semitic custom on entering a holy place ; in both cases the motive was the fear of a spirit attaching itself to the clothes—in the one case the spirit of the dead, in the other spiritual influences emanating either from the secular environment, or from the " holy ground,"—and this fear led to a series of wholly similar acts [3] : *e.g.* taking off the clothes usually worn, and then either remaining naked, which was sometimes done in mourning as in worship (Isa. xx. 2–4), or putting on a special garment, sackcloth in mourning, or again putting on the usual garment after it had been torn, *i.e.* rendered useless.
> For the same reason, from fear of contagion, the mourner, like the worshipper, *took off his sandals.*

---

[1] Stade, Schwally, Bertholet, Valeton, etc.
[2] Frazer, Grüneisen.   [3] See pp. 270–1.

Veiling the face, as in the presence of a god, was intended to put a barrier between the mourner and dreaded contact with the wandering spirit. The same end was served by *covering the head of the dead* (Jubil. xxiii. 1).

The purpose of *placing the hand on the head* was probably to protect this important part of the body, the abode of the spirit, from the same wandering spirit. By *covering their mouths* those present at the time of death sought to prevent the spirit of the dead from drawing out their spirits through the mouth or nose.

Other customs were to *roll in earth or ashes*, or *to put earth or ashes on the head*. These practices were probably intended to render the mourner unrecognizable by the spirit of the dead.

The custom of *sitting or lying on the bare ground* probably goes back to the time when it was usual to destroy the furniture of the house where the dead was, for fear of the spirit which haunted it. In many countries it is the custom to abandon the house itself.

It was also the rule that *the first meal eaten by the mourners* should be *brought from outside* by neighbours.[1]   Originally this was because the spirit of the dead might have entered into the food which was in the house. For the same reason, probably, a strict fast was kept until the evening.

Finally, the *purifications* prescribed by the Jewish law at the end of the seven days of mourning must be explained by the same motives. It is not necessary to regard them, as has often been done, in the light of late evidence of Jahwist hostility to the cult of the dead, for similar ceremonies are found among the most widely differing peoples, but as very ancient customs intended as the final severance from the spirit of the dead.

These various protective rites show how dreaded was the supernatural power which the remote ancestors of Israel ascribed to the spirits of the dead, and they alone suffice to prove that the spirits of the dead were placed in the same category as demons and gods.

But along with these apotropaic rites were others which originally possessed or had acquired in the course of time a propitiatory character.

Such was the *lamentation*, consisting of the *misped*, or mourning wail, and the *qinah*, or lament, the *vocero*, a kind of ode sung by a soloist in praise of the dead. The Old Testament shows clearly that the lamentation was made *on behalf of* the dead, for whom it was a terrible disaster to be deprived of it.

The practice of *cutting off a lock of hair* or *part of the beard* for the dead, as also the custom of *making incisions* in, or mutilating the body, in honour of the dead, were likewise of a religious nature. For these two customs were forbidden by the Law, which added that Israel must be holy to Jahweh (Deut. xiv. 1–2): hence these two practices were looked upon as acts of consecration to another god. The former of the two customs, the tonsure, seems originally to

---

[1] 2 Sam. iii. 35 ; Jer. xvi. 7 (present text).

have been an offering of hair to the dead.[1] The purpose of the incisions was probably an offering of blood to the dead in order to establish a bond of communion with his spirit, or to restore strength to him.

Finally, actual *sacrifices* were made to the dead in the form of funeral feasts of which the dead received a portion,[2] or of offerings laid on the tomb or libations poured on it,[3] or of bloody sacrifices intended to appease the unquiet spirit of the slain who had not been and could not be avenged.[4]

The displeasure of the dead was greatly feared ; it was a wide-spread belief that they were able to grant or withhold the fertility of the soil so necessary to both pastoral and agricultural peoples. Two ancient stories suggest that the Israelites shared this belief. One is the account of a famine which happened in the days of David, and which had been sent, according to the present form of the story, *because of* the Gibeonites slain by Saul, but no doubt the original version represented it as sent *by* the spirits of the slain Gibeonites (2 Sam. xxi. 1–14). The other is the story of Cain, in which Jahweh says to the murderer :

" And now art thou cursed from the earth which hath opened her mouth to receive thy brother's blood from thy hand ; when thou tillest the ground, it shall not henceforth yield unto thee her strength." (Gen. iv. 11–12).

Originally it would not have been the Earth which took up Abel's cause, but the slain man's spirit, which, having entered the soil in the form of blood, denied to the murderer the fruits of that soil.[5]

The fact that the dead were consulted, that oracles were sought from them as from a god, shows that they were supposed to possess supernatural knowledge ; moreover, evidence of this was found in the foreknowledge displayed by the dying.[6] There were various ways of consulting the dead, as was the case with the gods. It might be done by means of an individual possessed by an '*ob* [7] or a spirit of

[1] See p. 284.

[2] Deut. xxvi. 13–14, and perhaps Jer. xvi. 7 (original text).

[3] Tobit iv. 17 ; Sirach vii, 33 ; Gen. xxxv. 8, 14.

[4] Deut. xxi. 1–9.

[5] *Cf.* **CCLXV**, pp. 150–2, *cf.* p. 135 note ; **LVIII**, i, pp. 172–4.

[6] Predictions attributed to Isaac, Jacob, Joseph, Moses and Joshua just before their death.

[7] On the meaning of this term, which has been very much discussed, see (besides the hypotheses indicated **LVIII**, i, p. 250, n. 5). **CCLXV**, p. 69 ; **CLXVIII**, pp. 36–7 ; **CCVI**, pp. 5–11 ; **CCXXXIII**.

the dead (Lev. xx. 27), by incubation (Isa. lxv. 4), by evoca-
tion, with or without a visible apparition (1 Sam. xxviii.;
Isa. xxix. 4). The scene of the consultation might be a
grave, or certain spots which were held to be entrances to
Sheol (Isa. lvii. 9). No feature of the ancient cult of the
dead persisted with greater tenacity than necromancy. It
is a piece of unexpected good fortune that the Old Testament
itself should have preserved the account of an act of evoca-
tion. In the story, the dead is rightly called *elohim*, a god
(1 Sam. xxviii. 13). The same appellation is probably
found in another passage describing the consultation of the
dead : the prophet is there denouncing those who say :
" Consult the spirits of the dead . . . should not a people
seek unto its *elohim*, unto the dead on behalf of the living "
(Isa. viii. 19).

This was, in truth, the most suitable term to describe
the attitude of the early Israelites toward the spirits of the
dead : they were *elohim*, of a much lower rank no doubt,
but still *elohim*, powerful spirits capable of help at need.

3. *Traces of Ancestor-worship.* "Whenever an Arab
pitches his tent near the grave of a member of his family
or clan, he slays a victim for the dead." [1] It would appear
that in early times there must have been among the Hebrews
also some form of organized ancestor-worship.

In the historical period, the Israelite attached the greatest
importance to being buried with his fathers. The chief
reason for this desire must have been the same among the
Hebrews as among the Babylonians : for a man to be torn
from the grave of his fathers was, according to a text of
Asshurbanipal, " to be deprived of sacrifices and libations."
The family grave was the sanctuary where the ancestors
received the worship of their descendants. Hence arose
the custom of erecting on the tomb a *maṣṣebah*, or a stele,
intended not only to represent or to embody the spirit of
the dead among the living, but to receive the libations which
should be made to him (Gen. xxxv. 8, 14 E).

There is reason to suppose that the anniversary of a
death was kept with fasting and mourning. This is suggested, on the one hand, by the analogy of public mourning
ceremonies which were apparently copied from private

[1] **CCV**, p. 77, n. 1 ; *cf.* pp. 76–7 and **CCIV**, pp. 253, 371 *ff.*

mournings, and on the other hand, by the fact that the *qinoth*, or laments for the dead, were " learnt," evidently with a view to their recital on some similar occasion.

Another proof of the early existence of ancestor-worship among the Hebrews is that mourning was only obligatory for a father, a mother, or members of the family in the patrineal line. The Law, which only permitted a priest to take part in obligatory mourning, did not allow him, for instance, to mourn for his wife, who did not, in fact, belong to the circle of the ancestral cult.

While the organization of the Hebrew patriarchal family was not entirely the creation of ancestor-worship, as Stade, under the influence of Fustel de Coulanges' theory of the Græco-Roman family, maintained, nevertheless, it owes more than one of its features to this cult, and thus bears witness to its existence at a very early period.

For example, the reason why the Israelite longed for sons was not merely the usefulness of sons as sharers of labour and defenders against raiders ; the supreme misfortune was not to live without children but to die without leaving a son.

Adoption was practised, as in Greece and Rome, to avoid this last dishonour (Gen. xv. 2–3 ; xxx. 3–8).

Even if the Israelite died without having taken this precaution, he still had one last chance of keeping his name alive : an ancient custom, the levirate, provided that the nearest relative of the deceased should marry the widow, and that the first son born of this marriage should be regarded as the dead man's son and should inherit his property.

Lastly, let us mention a group of facts which indicate that in very early times the Hebrew must have worshipped, not only the ancestors of his family, but also those of the larger group to which he belonged, the clan. These facts consist of the religious rites with which, even in the Jahwist Age, the Israelite honoured the burial-places of those who were reputed to be the ancestors of a clan or of the whole Israelite people.

There was a *maṣṣebah*, a pillar, apparently intended for libations, on the grave of Rachel (Gen. xxxv. 19–20). Joseph's coffin was kept in a sacred enclosure with a pillar dedicated to Jahweh and an oracle-giving tree. The cave of Machpelah, where Abraham and Sarah were buried, was, according to the P-narrative, within the sacred enclosure which also contained the trees of Mamre. The Hebrew historians carefully indicate the locality of the graves of individuals otherwise entirely unknown and probably fictitious, but who are the eponymous ancestors of a group or of a clan : these monuments clearly occupied the same place in the pious regard of the people as the local sanctuaries of Jahweh. Each *mishpaḥah* made a point of having its own ancestral shrine. No doubt these ancestors were invoked and summoned to help in time of need. We learn this from the very protest of a prophet who will not hear of an appeal to any save Jahweh, the only father of Israel (Isa. lxiii. 16) :

> Thou art our father.
> For Abraham knows us not,
>   and Israel is not mindful of us.
> Thou, Jahweh, art our father,
>   who from the beginning hast been called our *go'el*.[1]

Even now, in Palestine, the Jews write out prayers to the patriarchs and place them in the crevices of the wall of the burial cave of Hebron.[2] Hence there was, in the Jahwist period, a cult of the national ancestors, as well as of the ancestors of the smaller groups.

It is not entirely certain that all such cults go back to the earliest stages of Hebrew history. As in the case of the Catholic saints or of the Moslem *welis*, the ancestor whose tomb was venerated by the Israelite may have been, in several cases, one of the old local gods or demi-gods, reduced to the rank of a mere mortal, a servant in his time of Jahweh the God of Israel. But in order to account for the fact that the Hebrews should have transformed a Canaanite god or hero into an Israelite *ancestor* whose worship was an accepted custom, we must assume that before their entry into Palestine the Hebrews had been accustomed to address similar worship to ancestors of their own.

From such a mass of evidence it would seem that we are warranted in the conclusion that before their entry into Canaan the Hebrew tribes must have possessed a fully organized cultus of the ancestors of families and clans.

In concluding, it is necessary to add one important

---

[1] Avenger and near relative.   [2] See p. 193, n. 11.

remark. This worship addressed to the ancestors, *i.e.* in the male line, was neither the only nor the earliest form which the cult of the dead assumed among the Hebrews. Another guise in which this cult always held an important place in Hebrew religion was the worship of heroes. Deborah, on whose funeral pillar they were wont to pour libations, was not an ancestor, neither was Miriam who was buried in the holy place of Kadesh ; the same may be said of Joshua, Gideon, Jephthah, Samson, certainly of Samuel, the place of whose burial is named, and of Elisha whose bones worked miracles.

Now the veneration of certain special individuals, endowed with particularly powerful *mana*, is one of the oldest forms of the cult of the dead. It may have existed among the prehistoric ancestors of the Hebrews in the remote period when they still reckoned descent in the female line,[1] and when, consequently, they still had neither ancestors in the patriarchal sense, nor family in the strict meaning of the word.

III

Powers and Spirits of Nature

1. *Facts relating to the worship of trees, springs, caves and mountains.* The Israelites settled in Palestine worshipped a great number of trees, springs and rivers, caves and mountains.

Examples are the terebinth or ever-green oak " which was in the sanctuary of Jahweh " in Shechem, and was called *'elon moreh*, " the (sacred) tree which gives oracles," [2] that of Mamre,[3] the tamarisk of Beersheba,[4] the terebinth of Ophrah,[5] the thorn-bush of Sinai,[6] the oracle-giving balsams (?) of the valley of Rephaim [7] and other objects of wood which were consulted for oracles, Aaron's rod,[8] the sceptres of the chiefs,[9] perhaps the pomegranate of Migron [10] and the tamarisk which was at Gibeah in the high-place [11] ; *cf.* Hos. iv. 12, " the (sacred) tree of weeping "

---

[1] See pp. 192–4.
[2] Gen. xii. 6 ; xxxv. 2–4 ; Joshua xxiv. 26, 32.
[3] Gen. xiii. 18 ; xiv. 13 ; xviii. 1, 4 ; xxiii.
[4] Gen. xxi. 33. [5] Judges vi. 11 *ff*.
[6] Exod. iii. 2–5 ; Deut. xxxiii. 16.
[7] 2 Sam. v. 22–4 (text questioned by XCI, iii, p. 215 ; III, p. 316, n. 4). [8] Num. xvii. 16–24.
[9] Num. xxi. 17–8. [10] 1 Sam. xiv. 2. [11] 1 Sam. xxii. 6 (G).

which was by the grave of Deborah, Rebecca's nurse, probably the same as " the palm-tree of Deborah " the prophetess,[1] the tamarisk of Jabesh-Gilead.[2]

There were the springs of En Giḥon (the modern Virgin's Well) and En Rogel (probably the modern Job's Well), at which the Israelites in the time of David, probably imitating the Jebusites before them, consecrated their kings,[3] the " waters of Dan " (one of the sources of the Jordan), one of the great sanctuaries of early Israel,[4] the wells of Beersheba, another place of pilgrimage,[5] the miraculous springs of Lahai Roi,[6] of En haq-Qoreh,[7] of Kadesh,[8] of Beer,[9] of Jericho,[10] of Marah,[11] the "holy water" of the temple at Jerusalem.[12]

There was the " cave " of Horeb, where Moses and Elijah met Jahweh face to face,[13] the grotto, venerated by the Moslems as by the Jews before them, under the sacred rock on which stood the altar in the temple at Jerusalem.

There was the " mountain of God " in the desert, known as Sinai or Horeb, Mt. Zion with its two sacred eminences, " the city of David " and the threshing-floor of Araunah,[14] Carmel with its altar built by Elijah,[15] the Mount of Olives on the summit of which was " a place of worship," [16] the mountain of Gilead where Jacob and Laban made a covenant by a sacred meal,[17] the high-places of Ramah whose name means " high-place," of Gibeah (hill), also called Gibeath-elohim (hill of god), of Mispah (watch-tower),[18] of Gibeon (little hill).

The Israelites regarded these places as sacred and practised religious rites there until the revolutionary reforms of Josiah forbad the offering of sacrifices anywhere save on the one holy mountain of the temple at Jerusalem, and condemned as displeasing to Jahweh, the immemorial rites hitherto carried on " on every high hill and under every green tree " (622 B.C.).

Most of these mountains, caves, springs and trees were already sacred for the Canaanites, a fact of which we have occasional documentary evidence.[19] The newcomers merely took over the holy places with the beliefs which were attached

---

[1] Gen. xxxv. 8 ; Judges iv. 5.

[2] 1 Sam. xxxi. 12.   [3] 1 Kings i. 9, 38.

[4] Amos viii. 14 ; Judges xviii. 29–31 ; 1 Kings xii. 29 ; cf. Enoch xiii. 7.

[5] Amos v. 5 ; viii. 14 ; cf. Gen. xxi. 28–33 ; xxvi. 23–33.

[6] Gen. xvi. 7–14.   [7] Judges xv. 18–9.

[8] Gen. xiv. 7 ; Num. xx. 1–13 ; Exod. xvii. 1ᵇ–7.

[9] Num. xxi. 16–18.

[10] 2 Kings ii. 19–22 ; Josephus, B. J., iv, 8, 3.

[11] Exod. xv. 23–25.   [12] Num. v. 11–31.

[13] Exod. xxxiii. 22 ; 1 Kings xix. 9, 13.

[14] 2 Sam. vi. ; xxiv. 16–25.

[15] 1 Kings xviii. 30–8.   [16] 2 Sam. xv. 32.   [17] Gen. xxxi. 45–55.

[18] Judger xi, 11.   [19] See pp. 83–5 ; 344 ; 406.

to them and the rites which had been celebrated there from time immemorial.

But it is equally certain that from their nomad days the Hebrew tribes had carried on entirely similar rites in the desert. The tamarisk of Beersheba was already for them a sacred tree, regarded, perhaps, as the same tree under which Ishmael, the father of a powerful confederation of Arab tribes, according to the tradition had almost perished of thirst (Gen. xxi. 15). The traditions relating to the burning bush of Sinai belong to nomad times; for in the historical times the Israelites seem to have almost abandoned the pilgrimage to "the mount of God," and ended by forgetting its site.[1]

From the same period come the stories accounting for the holiness of the wells of Lahai Roi and Beersheba, of the springs of the Kadesh oasis, watering-spots necessarily frequented by the Hebrew nomads, and hence far more significant to them than they could be to the Israelite peasants of later ages.

A typical example of both a holy mountain and a sacred cave is furnished by Sinai with its cave which were most certainly regarded as sacred in nomad times.

A strong confirmation of the existences of these practices among the pre-Mosaic Hebrews lies in the fact that the same practices occur throughout the whole Semitic area, especially among the ancient[2] and modern Arabs : in the cult of the *welis* (protectors), *i.e.* the Moslem saints, the customs and beliefs of the nature-religion of the ancient Semites have persisted almost unchanged among the peasants and Bedouins of today.[3]

[1] See pp. 179–80.

[2] Sacred trees on which were hung clothing and jewelry : **LXXXIV**, p. 185 ; **XC²**, p. 104. Sacred waters, like the *zemzem* well at Mecca (**LXXXIV**, p. 118 ; **CLXX**, i, pp. 192–3 ; **CLXXXIX**, pp. 71–101), the pool of Dhu l'Shara (B. Hisham, p. 253 ; **XXX**, p. 106), the Stygian waters of Bostra which accepted or rejected the offerings of worshippers, the healing springs of Phoinikon (Agatharchides, in Diod. Sic. iii, 42–3) ;—sacred caves or *ghabghab* ;—sacred mountains, like the Nabatean high-places of Petra or Mt. Arafa (**CLXXXIX**, pp. 241–55).

[3] Examples of sacred trees : **XV**, pp. 163–4, 222, 287 ; **CCIV**, pp. 333 *ff.* ; **CCV**, pp. 55, n. 3, and 56 ; **CLXXXVII**, iii, p. 143 ;—of sacred springs : **XV**, pp. 95, 113, 114, 231 ;—of wonder-working caves, **XV**, p. 100 ;—of sacred mountains in nomad regions : Nebi Harun above Petra (**XV**, pp. 86, 158, 206, 307, and figs. 4 and 5) or Gebel Serbal.

2. *Reasons for the Cults.*   The question next arises of the origin and primitive significance of the veneration with which the Semites regarded these various natural objects.

According to the earliest explanations prevalent in Israelite traditions as in those of modern Syria, trees, springs or mountains were merely venerated as memorials, as historical monuments, so to speak, marking the place where some noteworthy event of religious history had taken place, such as the tree of Shechem, the palm-tree of Deborah, the terebinth of Mamre and Ophrah.   Or the tree might have been planted or the spring discovered by some holy person, as, for instance, the tamarisk and the well of Beersheba, according to Genesis xxi. 25–33.   But this is evidently a rationalizing interpretation of later times, and which does not account for the sacred rites connected with these objects.

For the same reasons we cannot accept the explanation of the veneration given to a tree, a spring or a mountain as being due to the fact that they had been at some time or other the abode of a god or spirit, as, for instance, the balsams of the valley of Rephaim, the bush of Sinai, doubtless also the sacred trees of the shrine of Aphaca in Phenicia, on which the goddess descended on the annual feast-day in the form of balls of fire,[1] the lake of the same holy place, or the pool of Bethesda according to John v. 4.   Or, if a spring was in question, the reason assigned might be that a god had given, revealed or healed it, as in the case of the waters of Massah, Meribah, Beer, En haq-Qoreh, Marah, Jericho, or Hagar's well according to E (Gen. xxi. 8–19).

A third type of explanation alleging the permanent abode of a god or a spirit in the sacred object, no doubt brings us nearer to the original significance of these practices.

In modern Syria and Arabia the sacred tree is usually thought of as the dwelling of a supernatural being, who is a *weli* buried under its roots.   It is supposed that the tree is permeated with the life and supernatural power of the saint. Hence the common custom of hanging fragments of clothing to its boughs (Pl. xi).   According to one of the native interpretations,[2] the purpose of the suppliant is " to bind his

---

[1] Zosimus, *Hist.*, i ;   *cf.* Eusebius, *Vita Constantini*, iii, 55 ;   *Laud. Const.* 8.

[2] **CCXLIV**, pp. 171 *ff.* (according to **CLXXXVII**, iii, p. 45).

suffering to the spirit of the *weli*," that is to transfer his disease to the saint who, naturally, can no longer suffer from it ; often, too, the sick person seeks to make his cure more certain by taking from the tree one of the rags hanging on it, and wearing about his person this relic permeated with the living potency of the *weli*.[1]

> " The hot springs of Kallirhoe (the modern Zerka Ma'in) are, in the popular mind, under the guardianship of a saint (*weli*) or a spirit (*jinn*). The latter lights the fire and maintains it. The natives who repair thither for the healing of their rheumatism, entreat the spirit to keep up the fire so that the water may be hot, and to this end they offer sacrifices,"[2] whose blood must flow into the water.[3]

The Israelites, no doubt, shared this belief in the spirits of the waters. For the mysterious opponent who assailed Jacob at the ford of the Jabbok, was probably in the original of the tradition the spirit of the brook.[4] Among many peoples it is the custom for travellers when they wish to cross a river to give presents or offer sacrifices to appease the spirit of the stream, otherwise he will do them harm. It was so in Jacob's case. Owing, however, to his extraordinary strength, the hero was able to conquer the god, whence his name of Israel. It would even appear, according to the E-form of the narrative, that he dislocated the god's thigh.[5] In any case he forced the god to bless him, and perhaps, in the primitive form of the story, to reveal the rites necessary for crossing the ford in safety.[6]

But it would seem to be possible to penetrate even further into the past history of the cult of trees, springs, caves and mountains among the Semites. For the question naturally arises why, among the Semites, gods, genii or the spirits of dead heroes chose such objects as their abode. It is clear, in the last analysis, that the tree was considered as the dwelling of a spirit on account of the life which it displays. This life has in it something animal, almost human, most likely to impress primitive minds. The tree grows, its branches are supple,

---

[1] *Cf.* Acts xix. 11–12 ; xv. 96–7. *Cf.* **CLXXXVII**, iii, p. 46.
[2] **XV**, p. 95. [3] **XV**, p. 230.
[4] Gen. xxxii. 23–33 ; *cf.* **XXVI**, pp. 363–5.
[5] *Cf.* **LXXI**, p. 163 ; Luther, **ZATW**, 21, p. 66 ; **CCXVII**, p. 57 ; **XXVI**, p. 361.
[6] *Cf.* **CLXXXVII**, pp. 410–25.

Plate XI

Sacred Tree with Offerings of Pieces of Cloth

PLATE XII

ALTAR OF ZOREAH
(*See* p. 268)

like an animal's limbs; more favoured than the animal the tree grows again after it has been cut down (Job xiv. 10). Its leaves, rustling or moaning in the wind, seem to laugh or lament. There are plants which bleed when they are wounded.

Running water, or, in the Hebrew phrase, " living water," moves like an animal; it has its rages and its whims; it spreads fertility wherever it passes. In the desert there is little life save in the neighbourhood of the watering-places. Certain springs have healing powers. Such qualities were enough to convince the Semite that " living water " has 'a spirit like a man, an animal or a tree, and that this spirit is divine.

There are in modern Syria, springs which are addressed as persons. Thus the Bedouin woman, as she dips herself in the spring of Abu Selim, exclaims : " O hot spring of Abu Selim, if I have a child, I will offer a sacrifice."[1] Among the ancient Arabs, " when the water failed (at the spring of Ilabistan), they organized a feast by the spring, with music and dancing to induce the spring to flow again."[2] It was probably in the same circumstances and with similar rites that the ancient Israelites invoked the sacred well at Beer with the old prayer :

> " Spring up, O well ! Sing ye unto it,
> Well which the princes digged,
> Which the chiefs of the people digged
> with their sceptre, with their staves." [3]

According to another view this was an ode sung by the workmen as they dug some well.[4] It is easy to imagine an invocation addressed by the sick to an intermittent healing spring.[5] In any case we have here a *prayer to a spring*, one of the most ancient and typical examples of the cult of waters among the Semites.

The *holy cave* was not originally a mere receptacle for offerings. It was the custom also to shed the blood of victims there : hence it was the dwelling of a god. The preference for these underground shrines may, no doubt, be partly

---

[1] **XV**, p. 115 note ; *cf.* pp. 94, 113, 114.
[2] Rob. Smith, *Die Rel. der Semiten*, p. 140.
[3] Num. xxi. 17.
[4] **XI**, pp. 22–3 ; **IV**, p. 140 ; **CCXIII**, p. 12 ; *cf.* **CLXXIV**, pp. 15–7.
[5] *Cf.* John v. 4.

explained as a survival from the times when the inhabitants of these countries who were themselves living a troglodyte existence, likewise lodged their gods and their dead in natural caves. But it is probable that the cave itself, full of shadow and mystery, the haunt of reptiles and wild beasts, was enough to awaken the awe of the supernatural.

We might be tempted to think that the reason why the Semites preferred *mountains* or hills as sites for their holy places was that, on a lonely summit, the soul can more easily retire from earthly things and rise toward God. But this would be to ascribe to early peoples an entirely modern mode of thought : what primitive man sought in a sanctuary was not a place suitable for meditation, but the presence of a god in as tangible a way as possible.

Another view is that the Semites worshipped on the mountain-tops because there they were nearer to the sky, and that the numerous " high-places " show that the Semites must have regarded the astral or celestial deities as pre-eminent objects of worship from a very early date.[1]

There are, however, various grounds for thinking that the mountain was regarded as sacred, not because its summit was nearer to the abode of the gods, but because it was itself the abode of a god, or—a still more primitive conception—because it was entirely permeated with divine energy. Sinai was impregnated with it to such an extent that Moses was obliged to put a boundary round its foot so that no one might touch even its extreme limit. Any living thing, man or animal, that touched it was to be put to death, and that at a distance, by means of arrows or stones.[2] This was to prevent the victim from communicating the sacred fluid, fatal to the profane, to the rest of the people.

Moreover, it can be understood that the mountain with its imposing height, its wild gorges, its springs, the luxuriant forests or thickets which clothe its sides, the mountain which by drawing down the clouds seems to spread rain around it and cause the thunder, should have early inspired the Semites with holy " terror," and that they should have spoken of " mountains of God."[3]

---

[1] **CLXXXIV**, p. 23, n. 3 ; **CXXVIII**, pp. 23, 24 ; **CXXIX**, pp. 24, 25.
[2] Exod. xix. 12–3, 21–4 ; xxxiv. 3.
[3] Ps. xxxvi. 7.

3. *The Stars.* The stars, although they were not the only or even the principal object of the worship of the ancient Semites, must nevertheless have been worshipped also by the nomad Hebrews as the seat of supernatural powers. The Israelites of the historical period still attributed to the moon a direct influence on the fertility of the soil (Deut. xxxiii. 14) and on certain diseases (Psa. cxxi. 6). They regarded the stars as personal beings. Joshua commanded the sun and moon to stand still, and they obeyed (Joshua x. 12–3). The stars fought for Israel against Sisera (Judges v. 20), probably by sending the rain which swelled the torrent of Kishon and either bogged the chariots of the enemy or carried them away. The Babylonians similarly ascribed to certain stars an influence on the rain.[1] The Hebrew poets hymned the sun as a bridegroom coming out of his chamber, or as a hero advancing to battle (Ps. xix. 6–7). And the book of Job shows us how the Jew, even after he had become a monotheist, was tempted when he saw the sun shining or the moon proceeding majestically through the sky, to raise his hand to his mouth for a kiss of homage (Job xxxi. 26, 27).

The moon and certain stars seem at all times to have played an important part in the religion and in the magical beliefs of the nomad Semites, which perhaps accounts in part for the fact that in the desert journeys are undertaken by preference before sunrise, under the protection of the stars of the night. And we have seen that the Midianites hung " little moons " about the necks of their camels. The southern Arabs worshipped Athtar, the masculine form of Astarte, the god of the planet Venus,[2] and Sin, the moon-god. The Saracens of the fourth century offered bloody sacrifices to the morning-star.[3] About the first century A.D. the Arabs worshipped it under the title of Kabir, the Great star,[4] and in the time of Mohammed under the name of Al-Uzzah,[5] they attributed to the stars the power of affecting the weather and especially of bringing the rain.[6] The modern Bedouins ascribe to the moon and to various constellations all kinds of

---

[1] **XXXV**, p. 280, according to P. Dhorme, **RA**, viii, pp. 41–63; *cf.* Jubil. xii, 16–18.

[2] **XLIX**, pp. 133–6.   [3] *Nili opera,* **PG**, 79, p. 611.

[4] Cumont, **SY**, 1927, p. 368.

[5] **XC²**, pp. 31–45.   [6] *Ibid.,* pp. 210 *ff.*

lucky or evil influences on their life ; certain stars in particular
control the rain.[1]

That the Hebrews must have had similar beliefs and
practices is confirmed by the fact that certain feasts whose
origin can be traced back to them had a lunar character.
Such, perhaps, was the Passover, a pastoral rite which was
kept on the night of the first full moon of spring ; in any case
there was the feast of the new moon at the beginning of
each month.[2]

4. *Other spirits and demons.* Moreover, the nomad
Hebrews, like their Arab kinsmen, must have believed in
many other spirits manifesting themselves in the most various
phenomena. The ancient Arabs were convinced that the
desert was peopled with jinns :[3] the apparently causeless
rustlings and chatterings which the traveller sometimes
thinks he hears are caused by them. They specially haunt
places which have once been inhabited, also cemeteries.
But they are everywhere, and they may be disturbed when
a field is cleared, when a well is dug, and when a house or a
bridge is built. They often appear under the form of animals ;
" the zoology of Islam is also a demonology."[4] They take up
their abode especially in wild beasts, birds of prey and most of
all in serpents, lizards and scorpions. Sometimes they take
on a hybrid form. On account of their half-animal nature
they are hairy. They cause all kinds of diseases, and especially madness. They are dangerous to the newly-married.[5]

These beliefs are still alive among modern Bedouins.
When the Arab, for example, passes near a ruin, he stops his
nose to prevent the jinns from entering his body. The whirl-
wind of sand which may be seen revolving like a great pillar
moving across the desert, is the passing of a jinn.[6] The
Bedouins of the desert of Tih believe in the existence of flying
serpents, *haiye taiyara* :[7] an ancient Arab fable, which had
travelled as far as Egypt, where Herodotus said he had
seen the bones of one of these marvellous creatures,[8] and even

---

[1] **CCV**, pp. 65–7 ; **CCIV**, pp. 323 *ff*.
[2] See pp. 290, 293.
[3] The same belief existed among the Babylonians, **CCVI**,
pp. 37–9.
[4] **XC**[2], p. 151.   [5] *Ibid.*, pp. 148–59.
[6] *Ibid.*, p. 151.   [7] **CVIII**, iv. p. 319.
[8] **II**, p. 75 ; *cf.* Josephus, A. J., ii, 10, 2 (245–7).

to Rome. A griffin was called in Egyptian *sefr* or *serref* [1] and Lucan (Pharsalia, vi, 677) mentions the *Arabum volucer serpens* among the grim ingredients employed by a sorceress in raising a dead man. According to the Arabs these jinns are everywhere : " every place has its (supernatural) inhabitants."[2] For this reason anyone who settles within their sphere of influence must sacrifice a victim to them, or they will avenge themselves upon the intruders (dedication sacrifices).

We find wholly similar ideas and practices among the Israelites of the historical period ; [3] there is accordingly every reason to think that they go back to nomad times. The Israelites believed that the caravans crossing the desert were attacked by formidable winged serpents [4] called *seraphim* (burning ones). The only way of escaping their fatal bite was to make a bronze image of them, which had the double virtue of a magic control over them and of a means of appeasing them by sacrifices (2 Kings xviii. 4). These hybrid creatures were certainly not ordinary animals, for, according to Israelite belief, they were the seraphim who proclaimed Jahweh's glory in the Temple ; they always retained something of their half-animal origin, being naked and winged.[5] The traveller on arriving at his halting-place, perhaps a waterhole, might be attacked by a supernatural being, as Moses was by Jahweh on his way from Midian to Egypt (Exod. iv. 24–6).

Deserts and tombs are the chosen haunts of demons.[6] The desert of Judah was the abode of Azazel, the mysterious being to whom the inhabitants of Jerusalem sent the goat laden with the sins committed during the year ; it may be that originally Azazel himself was driven out in the form of the goat.

Desert places which had once been inhabited were regarded by the Israelites, as by the ancient and modern Arabs, as specially haunted. Such places were the dwelling of *Lilith*,[7] a female demon also dreaded by the Assyrians ; she probably

---

[1] **LXIII**, i, p. 83. [2] **XV**, p. 265.
[3] *Cf*. Marcel Cohen, *Sur la définition et le nom des sirènes* (*Donum natalicium Schrijnen*, Chartres, Durand, 1929, pp. 228–39).
[4] Isa. xxx. 6 ; Num. xxi. 4–6 ; Deut. viii. 15 ; *cf*. Isa. xiv. 29.
[5] Isa. vi. 2–7.
[6] Matt. xii. 43 ; Luke iv. 1–2. [7] Isa. xxxiv. 14.

corresponds to the succuba, and plays an important part in Jewish folklore ; she would seem to have been identified with the great horned owl. There, too, danced the *se'irim*,[1] " the hairy ones," goat-like demons resembling fauns or satyrs, to whom, according to the accusation of the later orthodox writers, an accusation probably founded on fact, the common people were in the habit of offering sacrifice.[2] To the same category belong the *'iyyim* and the *ṣiyyim*, also dwellers in the desert.[3] The ancient site of Sodom and Gomorrah was perhaps called " the valley of demons."[4] Any-one who dared to dwell among ruins was reckoned an impious person, a despiser of the invisible powers.[5] A man could only avert their vengeance by sacrificing his own offspring. When Hiel wished to rebuild Jericho :

" He laid the foundation thereof in Abiram, his firstborn,
and set up the gates thereof in his youngest son, Segub." [6]

From this example we learn that the Israelites, like the modern Syrian Bedouins and peasants, were in the habit of offering foundation and dedication sacrifices.

They referred the cause of various pathological conditions, especially madness, leprosy and plague, to " evil spirits " who smote the sufferer, or entered into his body.[7] Other diseases, no doubt, were attributed to demonic animals, such as the *seraphim*, or flies.[8]

They also attributed to special invisible powers the mysterious facts of sexual life ; hence the many taboos imposed upon men and women in whom the various phenomena connected with sex occurred.[9] Since they were under the influence of special *elohim*, such persons were declared unclean by the Law, that is, debarred from the worship of Jahweh. Hence also the sacredness of the organs of generation ; with

---

[1] Isa. xiii. 21 ; xxxiv. 14.
[2] Lev. xvii. 7 ; 2 Kings xxiii. 8ᵇ ; 2 Chron. xi. 15.
[3] Isa. xiii. 21 ; xxxiv. 14 ; Jer. l. 39 ; *cf.* **CCVI**, pp. 36–7.
[4] If it is true that *śēdim* should be read instead of the enigmatic *siddim* (Gen. xiv. 3) ; *cf.* **LXXXI**, p. 116, n. 4, **LXXXVIII**⁵, p. 105.
[5] Job xv. 28 ; *cf.* Strabo, 13, 1, 14–2 (Ilion) ; Appian, *Punica*, 8, 135–6 (Carthage) ; Wetzstein in Delitzsch, *Job*, 1864, p. 165, n. 1.
[6] 1 Kings xvi. 34.
[7] 1 Sam. xvi. 14–23 ; Exod. xii. 23 ; 2 Sam. xxiv. 15–7 ; 2 Kings xix. 35 ; Job. ii. 7 ; Lev. xiii. 14.
[8] **LVI**, pp. 184–5.
[9] Lev. xii. 1–5 ; 1 Sam. xxi. 5–6.

his hand touching them a man might take an oath in the same way as if he laid his hand on a sacred stone.[1] Sanctity and uncleanness were, as we know, two divergent aspects of the same conception.

The Hebrews, in short, peopled their world, in pre-Mosaic times, with powers and spirits whom they regarded in much the same way as the Canaanite countryfolk seem to have thought of their baals. And this comparison helps us to understand why the Israelites, when they settled in Palestine, found it so easy to adopt the religious practices of the natives : it was because these practices corresponded to the ideas and the needs which had been those of their own ancestors.

There was, however, a shade of difference between the beliefs of the Canaanites and those of the pre-Mosaic Hebrews : the baals of the settled inhabitants of Palestine were pre-eminently local and agricultural divinities, controlling the fertility of their respective spheres of influence, while the *elohim* worshipped by the Hebrews in their nomad period must have been rather the protectors of those human groups —clans, tribes, confederations—of which they were the patrons.[2]

IV

CLAN CULTS. KINSHIP WITH THE GODS

We have already seen that the *mishpahah*,[3] even in the Jahwistic period, constituted a cultual unit. Originally each clan and each tribe must have had its own particular *elohim*, who were, no doubt, usually the spirits or gods of one of the sacred trees, or of one of the sacred springs, mountains or caves, situated within the range of the group, as was often the case among the Arabs of pre-islamic times.

Many of these gods must have been regarded as related to members of the group of which they were the protectors. This was a common idea in the Semitic world. The Moabites are called the sons and daughters of Chemosh.[4] A heathen woman is " the daughter of a strange god."[5] Jeremiah accuses the Jews of his time of saying to the wood " thou art

---

[1] Gen. xxiv. 2, 9 ; xlvii. 29.
[2] *Cf.* Albrecht Alt, *Der Gott der Vater*, Stuttgart, Kolhammer, 1929.
[3] See p. 195.   [4] Num. xxi. 29.   [5] Mal. ii. 11.

I.

R

my father " and to the stone " thou hast begotten me."[1]
Many Arab tribes hear the name of a deity whom they claim
as an ancestor : for instance, the Banu Hilal, sons of the new
moon; the Banu Badr, the sons of the full moon; the Banu
Shams, the sons of the sun. Similarly among the Israelites
and related peoples there is no lack of eponymous ancestors
who are certainly ancient gods, such as Gad, Asher, Edom,
Cainan, perhaps Dan, Uz, Jeush.[2] To the same conception
are due such personal names as Benhadad, son of the god
Hadad ; Barlaha, son of God ; Barate, son of the goddess Ate ;
Barqos, son of Qos; Bardesanes, *i.e.* Bardaisan, son of the
river-god Daisan; Abiyahu, Jahweh is my father; Ammiel,
God is my fellow-tribesman, or more definitely, my uncle ;
Ammishaddai, the Almighty is my uncle ; Ahijah, Jahweh is
my brother ; Ahimelech, Melek is my brother.[3]

The idea of kinship with the god was so common that the
titles " father," " uncle," " brother," were used in many
proper names as synonyms of " god," [4] *e.g.* Abiram, my father ;
i.e. my god is exalted ; Amminadab, my uncle is generous ;
Hammurabi, the uncle is great ; [5] Ammuyakun, Yaqarammu.[6]
According to M. Rene Dussaud, the last three names may
suggest that the title Ammu had become a sort of proper
name denoting a particular god.[7]

This manner of regarding the relations between the god
and his worshippers must be extremely ancient ; since, if the
title of " father " given to the god presupposes a patriarchal
organization of society, the title " brother " must go back to
the time when descent was reckoned in the female line,[8]
and the same may be true of 'am, fellow-tribesman.

Since these expressions are used indifferently to denote
either the relation of Israel [9] or of its king [10] with Jahweh,
one might be led to suppose that the term " father " in these
phrases was nothing more than a metaphor for the care of a
god for his own people.[11] For, according to the conception

[1] Jer. ii. 27.　　　　　　　　[2] *Cf.* **LVIII**, ii, p. 120.
[3] See p. 146.　　　　　　　　[4] **XCIII**, pp. 480–4.
[5] Pognon, **JA**, 1888, i, p. 543 ; **XCIII**, p. 480.
[6] In the texts of curses of the eleventh dynasty (**CLV**, e. 10, e. 27).
[7] **SY**, 1927, p. 220.　　　　　　[8] **LVIII**, ii, p. 121.
[9] Isa. lxiii. 16 ; Ps. lxxxix. 27 ; *cf.* Isa. i. 4, etc.
[10] 2 Sam. vii. 14.
[11] Interpretation adopted for the Babylonian names by **XXXIV**,
p. 212, and Ch. Jean, *Sumer et Akkad*, 1923, Introd., ch. 1.

which prevails in Hebrew traditions, Israel could, at most, only claim to be the *adopted* child of Jahweh, who had " found him in the wilderness " ; and the same was true for the national king.[1] But according to the first-named conception, which long persisted, the bond of a physical relationship between the god and his group was certainly involved in the titles mentioned. The worshippers of Jahweh themselves regarded the marriage of " *sons of elohim*," i.e. divine beings, or gods, with the daughters of men, as perfectly possible.[2] Conversely, the Assyrians and Babylonians believed that a woman could give birth to a guardian demon (*shedu* or *lamassu*) : this contingency is provided for in a list of fatal omens.[3] Their kings, like the Egyptian Pharaohs, used to relate in detail how they had been brought forth and suckled by a goddess.[4]

These beliefs still persist in Arabia and Syria. " There is in Medina," says the traveller C. M. Doughty, " a family of three generations which traces its descent to a jinniah, a female jinn."[5] Curtiss quotes the case of an inhabitant of Nebk " who is regarded by the common people as the son of a jinn." " A jinn may have an earthly wife, or a man may have a spirit-wife who will brook no rival."[6]

It is not necessary to suppose the influence of ancestor worship,[7] or of totemism to explain the rise of these ideas : " We need only remind ourselves that the sole tie known to the nomads was that of blood-relationship. When two men wish to make an alliance, they form an artificial blood-bond between them. It was hence natural and almost inevitable that, at this stage, the Semite should regard the god to whom he looked for help and protection as a member of his clan, a being of the same blood as himself, a kinsman,"[8] a brother.

V

THE PROBLEM OF SEMITIC TOTEMISM. DIVINE ANIMALS

Although the belief in the relationship of the clan with its divine protectors does not *necessarily* presuppose totemism,

[1] Ps. ii. 7.   [2] Gen. vi. 1–4.   [3] **XXXIV**, ii, pp. 905–6.
[4] So Lugalzaggizi, Gudea, Asshurbanipal (**XCIII**, p. 379).
[5] **CLXXVIII**, ii, pp. 191–3.
[6] **XV**, pp. 121–4 ; *cf.* pp. 100, 112–5, 118, 119.
[7] **LXXXVI**, i, p. 406 ; *cf.* on the contrary **LVIII**, ii, pp. 119–24 ;
XCVI, pp. 45–6.   [8] **LVIII**, ii, p. 123.

it is nevertheless an essential element in the totemic form of organization. Hence it is a problem of great importance to determine whether, as has been maintained by many competent scholars since Robertson Smith,[1] the nomad Hebrews and the ancient Semites in general practised totemism at a certain stage of their development.

The reply to this question depends largely on our definition of totemism. According as our definition is broader or narrower the answer will be affirmative or negative.

It is well known that ethnologists and students of comparative religion are far from being in agreement on the specific characteristics and the nature of totemism.[2] Without entering into this discussion, it seems possible to state what are the most characteristic features of a totemistic society. They are, first, a belief in the relationship between a human group and an animal or vegetable species ; second, the co-existence in the same tribe of several groups having each special relations with a different totem-species.

Now the first fact that forces itself upon our notice is that there is no certain evidence of the presence of either of these characteristic features among the ancient Hebrews.

As far as the second of the two essential features mentioned above is concerned, a totemic tribe must comprise at least two closely associated clans, who co-operate in the magical practices necessary to secure the perpetuation of the animal or vegetable totems, or to assist the functioning of certain natural phenomena : these clans are so far indispensable to one another that very often the members of the one are compelled to take a wife from the other clan. As far back as we can go there is nothing resembling this among the Semites. The Semitic group usually called a clan, the *mishpahah* or *ḥay*, is, as we have seen, a local unit, originally the body of men whom the slender resources of the desert permitted to live together in the same spot, *the essence of the ḥay is to be self-sufficing.* No doubt it can unite with other similar groups to form a tribe ; but the Semitic tribe is only a later and temporary confederation of local *ḥay*.

With regard to the other characteristic of totemism, the

---

[1] **JPh**, 1880, pp. 25–100 ; **CCXL**, pp. 186–240 ; **LXXXIV** ; Wilcken, Stade, Joseph Jacob, G. A. Barton, Stanley A. Cook.
[2] **CXC.**

belief in a relation with an animal species, the only direct evidence for its existence is found among the Arabs in certain tribal names.[1] The members of one of these groups call themselves " panthers " or " sons of panthers." A member of the tribe of " the sons of the dog, or dogs," may be known either as " a dog " or as " a brother of dogs." There was also a tribe of " lizards " or " sons of lizards," a tribe of " sons of asses," one of " oxen " and one of " scorpions." But names of this kind are very rare.

Although the specific characteristics of the totemistic organization of society are wanting or only slightly attested among the Semites, there is evidence for the presence among them of a number of traits which occur among many totemistic peoples, but whose origin is not necessarily totemistic. Their presence constitutes at the most a presumption of ancient totemism.

1. Certain Hebrew, Edomite and Arab groups have animal or vegetable names,

> for instance, the sons of Leah (antelope), and Rachel (ewe), those of Beker and Gemal (camel), Caleb (dog), Arod (wild ass), Tolah (worm), Zimri (antelope), Kor (wasp), Shaphan (rabbit), Sus (horse), Hamor (ass), Akbor (mouse), Elon (terebinth or ram), Shumath (garlic).

The names of animals or plants borne by certain individuals or localities may be derived from ancient clan-names.

However, it should be noted that such names are comparatively rare, and that the communities or persons in question might have received them merely as the expression of a wish that they might possess the pride of the wild ass or the speed of the antelope. The Arabs give their children names for various reasons : for instance, they may call a boy Kelab, because there was a dog in the tent at the moment of his birth ;[2] or they may call him " tick," " flea " or " thorn," because they hope that he may be as troublesome to his enemies as these insects or these plants,[3] or again, they may hope to avert the jealousy of the invisible powers by these depreciatory epithets.

2. The Semites, and especially the ancient Hebrews, as

[1] **CCXL**, pp. 189–91. See, however, the reservations and objections of Noldeke, **OMO**, 1884, pp. 300–4 ; **ZDMG**, 1886, pp. 163–6.
[2] Burckhardt, Notes on the Bedouins, 1831, p. 97.
[3] **XC¹**, p. 200.

we have seen, believed in the existence of a relationship
between themselves and their gods.

3. On the other hand, they attributed to certain kinds of
animals a supernatural or divine character.

For them, as for primitive peoples, animals in general
were at first much more akin to man than the modern mind
will admit. The animal has a soul.[1] Its vengeance is to be
feared : hence the blood of a slain animal must be covered
like that of a man.[2] Animals are treated as responsible by
the law.[3] They are individuals with whom treaties may
be made.[4]

There are animals which are endowed with superhuman
power or knowledge. Balaam's ass saw the angel of Jahweh
long before his master, who was a seer, perceived the presence
of the mysterious being. The early Arabs too were persuaded that the cock crows and the ass brays when they see
spirits who are invisible to men.[5] This is a widespread
belief : the dogs of Telemachus were the first to perceive
Athene ; [6] Jews, Moslems and the peasants of our countryside,
like the ancient Scandinavians, are convinced that dogs can
see the dead at the moment of passing, and announce the fact
by their mournful howling.[7]

The serpent was regarded as the most cunning of all
animals : according to the story in Genesis, he had recognized
before man the magical properties of the tree of knowledge.[8]
We have mentioned the stories which were current about
the winged serpents of the desert, the *seraphim* ; at Jerusalem
it was the custom to offer sacrifices to the bronze image of
one of these creatures. By the same city there was a Dragon's
Well (*'en hat-tannin*, Neh. ii. 13), and beside the sacred spring
of the Fuller there was a " Reptile's stone " (*zoheleth*, 2 Kings
i. 9) : it was apparently recognized that the spirit of the
waters usually appeared under the form of a serpent.

Similar beliefs are met with in great numbers among the
ancient and modern Arabs, the Babylonians the Phenicians.
Philo of Byblos calls the serpent " the most intellectual of
the reptiles."

[1] Lev. xxiv. 18 ; Prov. xii. 10.   [2] Lev. xvii. 13.
[3] Gen. ix. 5 ; Exod. xxi. 28–32 ; Lev. xx. 15–16.
[4] Gen. ix. 10 ; Hos. ii. 20 ; Job v. 23.
[5] **XC²**, p. 151.   [6] Odyssey, xvi, 160–3.
[7] **CCXLVIII**, ii, p. 256   [8] *Cf.* p. 302.

The animals which the prophets describe as haunting the ruined palaces of Nineveh or Babylon, side by side with recognized demons such as Lilith and the satyrs (se'irim), were evidently invested by them with superstitious terror.[1] They were the ostrich, said by the Bedouins to be ridden by the jinns; the owl, of which one species is regarded as sacred by the Palestinian peasants;[2] the viper, the vulture, the hedgehog, and other animals whose identification is uncertain, such as the ṣiyyim (wild cats ?), the 'iyyim and tannim (jackals and wild dogs), the qa'ath (pelican or little owl).

Perhaps a more striking testimony to the supernatural character which the ancient Hebrews attributed to certain kinds of animals, is the fact that some of them were forbidden to be used as food. The systematic distinction which the Law sets up between clean and unclean[3] is of late origin : the priests endeavoured to lay down certain general physiological characteristics by which unclean species might be recognized, and this quasi-scientific attempt no doubt largely increased the number of forbidden species ; but the basis of the distinction is certainly much older, being known to the Jahwist.[4] Similar restrictions are observed by the Syrians and the Arabs, and the common occurrence of food-taboos among non-civilized peoples is well known.

The motive of these prohibitions was neither concern for health,[5] a motive almost unknown to primitives, nor a dislike to food that was not traditionally familiar : for the restrictions observed by the Hebrews and by their Arab kinsfolk were entirely different. The locust, which was eaten by the Hebrews, as it is by the Moslem Bedouins,[6] was, on the other hand, forbidden to the pagan Arabs. Conversely, the camel, the chief food of the Arabs, was unclean to the Israelites.

What we really have to do with here is a taboo, a protection from the dangers of the world of spirits. An unclean thing, which may not be used in the worship of a particular god, is a thing which is permeated by the influence of another god or spirit. The animals forbidden as food were " spiritual " animals, the dwelling-place of a superior spirit

---

[1] Isa xiii. 21–22 ; xxxiv. 14–15 ; Jer. l. 39 ; li. 37 ; Wisd. ii. 14–15.
[2] **PEF**, 1901, p. 272.   [3] Deut. xiv. 3–20 ; Lev. xi.
[4] Gen. vii. 2, 3, 8 ; viii. 20.   [5] **LXXXI**, pp. 122–3.
[6] See, for example, **CCV**, pp. 86–7.

to man's, divine or demonic, whose entry into a man was much to be dreaded.

For example, the pig was considered by several of Israel's neighbours and kinsmen as a sacred animal, that is, as possessed by *divine* influences : among the Babylonians it was sacred to Ninib, among the Syrians to Tammuz : the month of Tammuz was called by them Ḥeziru.[1] In Egypt the pig, which was usually forbidden (taboo), on a certain full moon was sacrificed to deities identified by Herodotus with Selene and Dionysus, and was eaten by the worshippers.[2]

The original reason for the taboo placed on certain animals was doubtless not so much their more or less close connexion with some of the great anthropomorphic gods, as the fact that they themselves were regarded as the abode of formidable spiritual powers.

The prohibition of " unclean " animals belongs to the same class as the rest of the Israelite food taboos, such, for instance, as the restriction on eating with the blood, intended to prevent the entrance of a strange spirit, or the prohibition against eating the sciatic nerve. The traditional reason for the latter prohibition was that a god had hallowed it on the occasion of his wrestling with Israel, the ancestor of the nation (Gen. xxxii. 33), but the primitive reason was, no doubt, because this sinew was held to be the seat of the procreative force.

According to Robertson Smith, the reason for certain animal taboos was because these animals were the kinsmen, the totems of certain clans : the list of animals proscribed by the Law as unclean would correspond to that of the ancient totems of the Hebrew clans. This hypothesis is neither necessary nor probable : the ewe ought to appear in the forefront of the list of animals forbidden to the " sons of Rachel," the ram should be forbidden on account of the clan of Elon or Aijalon ; but this is not the case.

There would be less objection to an inversion of this connexion of the facts : unquestionably the ancestors of Israel regarded certain kinds of animals as " demonic " and this would suffice to render them taboo. From this it would be a imple step to take one of these superhuman species as the patᵣon of a group, and consequently to look upon it as an

[1] **XCIII**, pp. 409–11.   [2] **II**, pp. 47–8.

ally, and finally as related to the clan, in short, as a totem.

There is, however, no proof that the ancient Hebrews ever took this step. No doubt the Semites had a great number of theriomorphic gods ; but the animal form may be merely a symbol of the attributes of the god—as seems to be the case for the bull-gods—or else the god might be thought to be embodied in a particular individual of the species, in a certain fish, for instance, and not necessarily in the entire species. However, there are a few cases among the Syrians and the Philistines where a whole species seems to have been regarded as divine and worshipped : such were the species of fish at Ascalon and Hierapolis, the doves, bulls, horses, eagles, bears, lions, and perhaps pigs, in the same sanctuary of Hierapolis.

We may neglect the other features stressed by Robertson Smith, such as the communal sacrifice, tatooing and exogamy, since these are not peculiar to the totemic organization.

The following conclusions may sum up the discussion of totemism :

1. Nearly all the constituent elements of the totemic system were present among the Semites : clan or tribal cults, belief in the relationship of the group to the gods whose names it often bears, belief in the supernatural nature of certain kinds of animals, and in the possibility of making alliances with them.

2. It is possible that occasionally among the Arabs, the Syrians and the Philistines, these elements combined in such a way as to give rise to a cult resembling that which certain totemistic peoples (not all) render to their totem. But, on the other hand,

3. There is no actual evidence among the Semites of the social organization characteristic of totemistic peoples.

VI

DYNAMISM AND ANIMISM. POLYDEMONISM AND POLYTHEISM

Let us now attempt to sum up the results of our inquiry into the religious beliefs of the Hebrew tribes before their acceptance of the new religion.

The first conclusion that forces itself upon us is that when this event took place these tribes had already passed through

a long period of evolution. Some of the features which we
have endeavoured to reconstruct only existed in a fragmentary state, as survivals of a remote past.

Hence it is necessary to define the stage of development
reached by the Hebrew tribes at the moment when the cult
of Jahweh welded them into a single people.[4]

Some of the phenomena which we have met with belong
to a stage which it has been proposed to call *dynamism*, in
which supernatural powers are thought of rather as impersonal
forces than as invisible persons. In fact, although for the
primitive mind these two conceptions are not mutually
exclusive,[1] it has been necessary to emphasize, now one
aspect and now the other, according to the periods under
consideration. Now, many of the magical practices, the
beliefs relating to the contagious nature of holiness and uncleanness, and to the way in which the influence of the dead
could attach itself to clothing and hair, show how far, at a
certain period, superhuman powers were conceived as a fluid,
as an impersonal force.

According to certain critics, the very ancient term which
is found in all Semitic languages to express the idea of " god "
under the various forms of *'el* (Hebrew), *ilu* (Babylonian),
ilah (Arab), originally denoted the vague force which is the
source of all strength and life, the divine rather than a god or
a divine personality : it would have had a meaning similar
to that of the term *mana* among the Polynesians, the Indian
brahman, and the Latin *numen*.[2] Certainly we can best
explain in this way phrases by which the Hebrews denoted
specially striking mountains, or a particularly fine cedar : thus
harare 'el, *'erez 'el*, would designate mountains or a cedar,
permeated with *'el*, with divine force.

However, the dominant idea in the beliefs which we have
been studying is that the invisible powers are spirits similar
to the vital principle whose existence in himself man recognizes, the soul, beings capable of willing, thinking, feeling like
himself : this is the stage of *animism*, taking the term in its
widest sense. But in its turn, animism comprises many
different manifestations of the religious spirit : polydemonism, polytheism, monotheism.

Most of the religious phenomena whose existence among

[1] *Cf.* pp. 224–5 ; 461.   [2] **XLVII**[2], p. 71.

the ancestors of Israel we have recognized seem to belong to the category of polydemonism. There is a somewhat vague but real distinction between this stage of belief and polytheism. In polytheism each divine being has its personality sharply defined ; each god has his own name, attributes and sphere of action ; moreover he is related to the other deities ; the gods constitute an organized hierarchy, with more or less clearly defined distinctions of rank, and reciprocal obligations.

On the other hand, in the polydemonist stage, man feels himself surrounded by mysterious powers, with ill-defined personality, whom he cannot always even name. Sometimes he does not know whether he is dealing with one of these beings or with several. He thinks of them somewhat as the Arab thinks of his *jinns*.

This the state of mind which underlies the simplest forms of that cult of trees, springs and mountains which we found among the ancestors of the Hebrews. It also underlies that reverence mingled with fear which was aroused by the dead, by taboos, and sometimes by the sacred esteem in which they held certain animals. Wherever he met with some unusual manifestation of energy, in the luxuriant oasis springing out of a parched desert, in the magic power of a chief or in the ecstasies of a seer, the early Hebrew recognized the presence of supernatural spirits, of δαίμονες.

It would also seem that the simplest explanation of the very peculiar use of the *plural elohim* to denote *a* god lies in this early lack of differentiation between the various supernatural powers. In Hebrew, the word *elohim*, literally meaning *gods*, in the plural, may be used to denote either several divine beings, or in speaking of a single god or goddess. And even when it has a singular meaning it may be construed with plural adjectives and verbs The Phenicians used the plural *elim* in the same way, while the Babylonians also applied the plural *ilani* to a single god. Sin was called *ilani ša ilani*, " god(s) of gods." Hence the interchange of *Babili*, Babel, with *Babilani*, Babylon. Doubtless, the worshipper, uncertain whether, in any particular place, he had to do with one or several supernatural beings, used the expression *elohim*, in the indeterminate sense of " the divine powers."

We have next to ask whether the Hebrews were still at this stage of pure polydemonism when they came into contact with Jahwism, and whether, as Stade maintained, they passed immediately from this elementary religious stage into the national religion. There are various grounds for thinking that before the Mosaic Age, Hebrew polydemonism was moving towards polytheism ; this appears especially in the fact that they were beginning to recognize the different divine beings as possessing distinct personalities.

In the religions of the tribes and of the clans the divine being was gradually ceasing to be the vague spirit of a spring or a mountain, and becoming more and more the chief of a human group, the god of the " fathers " of this group,[1] and hence a *person*. This is apparently the force of the word *'el* in the various names of tribes and peoples with which it is compounded : *Ishmael*, the god (of the tribe) hears ; *Jerahmeel*, the god is merciful; *Israel*, the god strives ; *Jacobel*, the god is cunning.

The objection is often made that if the gods of the pre-Mosaic Hebrews had been individualized they would have borne personal names. But, it is said, we know of none that can be referred with certainty to this epoch. The reason for this may be that these names were intentionally omitted by the Jahwist tradition. Besides, there is at least one pre-Mosaic divine personal name which has come down to us, and which proves that the gods were sometimes endowed with a clearly marked individuality : it is that of Jahweh, who, as we shall, was the god of Sinai, and very probably the god of a Hebrew group before the time of Moses.

It should also be remembered that the Hebrews, like the rest of the Semites, seem to have worshipped certain stars, and the moon in particular. Now the astral cults, being common to several tribes, tended to break through the particularism of tribal religions ; moreover, since the heavenly bodies are related to one another of necessity, the stellar gods inevitably tend to have relations with one another also, and to form a hierarchical society.

It is further objected that the Hebrews had no special term for " goddess." But the Phenicians also applied to female divinities the masculine term *elim* : but that did not prevent them from having goddesses. The pre-Mosaic

---

[1] Exod. iii. 13, 15 ; *cf.* Gen. xxxi. 5 ; Exod. iii. 6; etc. See A. Alt, *Der Gott der Vater*, 1929.

Hebrews may, too, have had a feminine of *el* analogous to the Phenician *Elath* or *Eloth*, or have employed a circumlocution like the phrase used by the pre-Islamic Arabs, " daughter of Allah."

But if, as seems probable, there were tendencies towards polytheism among the early Hebrews, we must not go to the opposite extreme and, like the Assyriologist Hommel or Baentsch the Hebraist,[1] attribute to them a monarchical polytheism bordering on monotheism, with a supreme god exalted above the rest. If the pre-Mosaic Hebrews had possessed an organized polytheism, the latter would have offered to Jahwism a resistance of which we should certainly find traces in the apostasies of which the prophets so often accused Israel. But Israel's main temptation in the early centuries of their settlement in Canaan was, not the practice of an astral religion or some kind of polytheism, but the cults of the local *baals*, the gods of the green trees and the high hills : this apparently was the basic element of their traditional religion, as it is still today under their veneer of Mohammedanism or Christianity, the indestructible basis of the religion of the peoples of the Near East.

We shall probably not be far from the truth if we define the religious state of the Hebrews at the time of the inauguration of Jahwism as a polydemonism tinged with polytheism.

APPENDIX

THE HYPOTHESIS OF A PRE-MOSAIC HEBREW MONOTHEISM

Certain scholars, whose point of view we must briefly define and discuss, maintain that the tribes of which Israel was ultimately composed were, at the time of the founding of the national religion, at the far more advanced stage of monotheism.

There is no inherent impossibility in the view that the stages of religious development whose traces we have demonstrated were preceded by a different religious level such as monotheism. Another possible hypothesis is that the early Hebrews, after having passed through the stages already referred to, arrived at monotheism, either by the spontaneous development of certain racial tendencies, or by the process of borrowing from a more advanced civilization. Hence the three forms under which the hypothesis of a pre-Mosaic Hebrew monotheism has been advanced.

1. *Primitive Monotheism of Mankind*

It was long the universal belief that mankind began with the worship of the one true God, and that Israel alone had remained

---

[1] Bruno Baentsch, *Altorientalischer Monotheismus*, Tübingen, Mohr, 1906.

faithful to its ancient trust, while all the other nations degraded and distorted it, thus giving rise to the infinite variety of cults, polytheism, nature-worship, fetichism, and other forms of idolatry. The elements of fetichism and polytheism which are to be found in Israel, are regarded by the defenders of this position, when they do admit the truth of the facts, as temporary declensions from the faith of the fathers, or as foreign intrusions.

We shall not stop to argue with those who rely upon the dogmatic *a priori* assertion that such is the teaching of the Bible or the Church. It is the less necessary in that the Israelite traditions collected into the book of Genesis differ widely on this very question of the religion of the ancestors : according to E, the fathers worshipped many gods.[1]

But the attempt has also been made, as by P. Lagrange for instance, to prove the existence of a primitive monotheism by evidence drawn entirely from the comparative study of religions.[2]

P. Lagrange brings forward first of all the pheonomenon known as henotheism or kathenotheism : " The individual in the presence of his god, as in prayer, whether the god be nameless or whether his genealogy be set forth, heaps upon him all the epithets proper to divinity and unhesitatingly places him above the other gods."

The same writer also goes on to state that among many savages " there is taught the existence of a supreme being who is just and good, who has created everything, and who cannot die." He also appeals to the existence of cosmogonies, and finally maintains that " it is impossible to find a single case in history of a monotheism which has developed out of polytheism," while " on the contrary, the multiplication of gods is a fact abundantly established by the evidence of history."

None of these arguments support the conclusion drawn from them. Henotheism, that is, the use of monotheistic expressions in utterances inspired by religious feeling, is a well-established fact, but one which is associated with definitely polytheistic beliefs. It proves, perhaps, that religious feeling only finds full satisfaction in entire dependence upon a single object of worship : but it does not prove that from the beginning man was *conscious* of such an answer to his inmost needs. If we grant that man is " naturally monotheistic," it does not therefore follow that he was *originally* a monotheist. Henotheism may just as easily be a vague feeling after monotheism, as a survival from a monotheistic age.

The same must be said about the vague belief in a good and just supreme being which is found among certain savage peoples, and which may have been shared by the pre-Mosaic Hebrews : this figure *who is never worshipped* does not seem to be the remains of an ancient religion, of the cult of an early sky-god, for instance,[3] for it is the rites, not the beliefs, of ancient religions which persist the longest—but rather the product of speculation : this being is " the all-Father " (Lang), " the primal scource " (Söderblom) demanded by logic.

The prevalence of cosmogonies is of even less value as a proof of an original monotheism : in these old myths the creator is not necessarily the supreme god, nor the oldest of the gods, still less

---

[1] Joshua xxiv. 2, 15 ; *cf.* Gen. xxxv. 2, 4.
[2] **XLIX** ; *cf.* **CCXXXIV**.   [3] **CCXXIV** ; **CCXXV**, pp. 77–81.

the sole god. For instance, in the Babylonian cosmogony the world exists long before the divine pairs ; Marduk, who brings order into the universe, is one of the youngest of the gods, and remains subordinate to the supreme god. In many cosmogonies the creation is ascribed to a human couple.

P. Lagrange is also contradicted by the facts when he maintains that " it is impossible to find a single case in history of a monotheism which has developed out of polytheism." It would be more accurate to say that, apart from Hebrew monotheism which has arisen from the deepening of a monolatrous religion, all the monotheistic speculations of antiquity sprang from definitely polytheistic religions, either by the elevation of one of the gods to the supreme position (Mazdeism, Egypt), or by the fusion of the members of a polytheistic pantheon (Egypt, Babylon, Greek philosophy, ancient Rome).

2. *Semitic Monotheism*

The most distinguished supporter of this theory was Renan. In his view, the monotheism of the ancestors of Israel was not the heritage of the past, but a conquest, a position won by age-long conflict. Animists at first, like the rest of mankind, the Semites attained to a belief in " the supremacy of a common lord of heaven and earth " by " the fusion of nameless gods." [1] The main " cause of Semitic monotheism," according to Renan, must be sought in " the habits of the nomadic life," where ritual necessarily plays but a small part, and where " philosophic speculation working with intense activity in a limited range of experience leads to the formation of extremely simple ideas."

Renan further maintains that another cause of the monotheism of the primitive Semites lay in their language. " The essence of mythology," he writes, " lies in the living force of words. But the Semitic languages do not readily lend themselves to this kind of personification." [2]

However, these ingenious theories have not stood the test of facts. Babylonian discoveries have shown that the poverty of the Semitic languages did not prevent the Babylonians and Assyrians from developing a very rich mythology. Moreover, Max Müller's hypothesis, that myth is the fictitious life of metaphor, is now almost universally abandoned.

Furthermore, the continually increasing body of evidence yielded by excavation goes to prove that the belief in many gods prevailed not only among settled and civilized nations like the Babylonians, Assyrians or Phenicians, but also among the inhabitants of the desert and its borders : the Moabites, the Nabatæans, the Safaites, and especially the pre-Islamic Arabs.

It may be added that the figure of the nomad Semite inspired by the deepest religious feelings and possessing an exalted conception of the deity, is a purely legendary one, if at least we may judge by the Bedouins as they appear in history, and as they are to-day. Before Islam the mental outlook of the Arab was non-religious and sceptical. The modern Bedouin is utterly careless of the most elementary duties of the Moslem religion, and often speaks of Allah in the most irreverent fashion : all his reverence, his vows,

---

[1] **LXXXI**, i, pp. 59, 45. [2] *Ibid.*, pp. 46–9.

his sacrifices and his prayers are addressed to the *weli*, who is the successor of the petty gods and the manifold spirits of primitive polydemonism.

The facts upon which the theory of a primitive Semitic monotheism is supposed to rest do not merit more than a cursory remark : they are—

(*a*) The etymology of the word meaning god, '*el*. It is suggested that the ancient Semites connected it with the preposition '*el*, meaning " towards," in the belief that it was towards God that the heart of man yearned. But grammatically the derivation is doubtful, and its abstract character makes it still more improbable ; it is more likely that the word comes from a root meaning " to be strong."

(*b*) The frequent occurrence of names compounded with '*el*, God, and not with the proper name of *a* god.

(*c*) The use of this same term '*El* to denote a particular god.

But in the two latter cases '*el* merely denotes the one or the chief god of a tribe, a people or a particular locality, the one who was *the* god of the group or place in question. These names no more prove the existence of a Semitic monotheism than do the names Thucydides or Timotheus prove the prevalence among the ancient Greeks of the belief in a single god. In short, this monotheism of the ancient Semites appears to be a mere phantasy of the imagination.

3. *Monotheism the Product of the Culture of the Ancient East*

A fresh theory has recently been advanced by Prof. Winckler of Berlin and his followers, commonly known as the Pan-Babylonist school. It is that the source of Israelite monotheism must be sought in the amazingly advanced civilization which had developed in the ancient East and especially in Babylon thousands of years before the settlement of the Hebrews in Canaan.

According to A. Jeremias, one of the followers of Winckler, this borrowing took place before the advent of the national religion of Jahweh. His version of the facts is as follows.[1]

In the civilizations of the Ancient East there had already arisen religious movements tending to monotheism : that of Amenophis IV in Egypt, about 1400 ; Melchizedek of Jerusalem was a monotheist (Gen. xiv. 15–20). Abraham was the author of a similar monotheistic reform. From Ur of the Chaldees he led a propagandist mission through Mesopotamia, before arriving at Harran (Acts vii. 2). Then he brought " the souls which he had gained to Harran " in Canaan, that is beyond the authority of Hammurabi, who had just founded a new religion, that of Marduk. Abraham conquered the land of Canaan, " but in the most peaceful fashion "—so Jeremias assures us.[2] The patriarchs, at least Abraham and Jacob, were religious sheikhs, leaders of a sect (here Jeremias borrows, no doubt unconsciously, an idea from Renan).

It is useless to discuss at length this phantastic reconstruction of the history of the ancestors of Israel.[3] We have already pointed out how the historicity of the patriarchal narratives should be regarded. The romance of Jeremias is, moreover, much more

[1] **XXXVII.**   [2] *Ibid.*, p. 182.
[3] *Cf.* **RHR**, 1906, pp. 218–30.

improbable than the Hebrew tradition. The picture of Abraham, the preacher, founding a religion by propaganda after the manner of Mohammed, is obviously an anachronism. The religions of remote antiquity were national religions : membership was automatic, by the accident of birth, not by free choice. For centuries the religion of Israel was the most exclusive of these national religions.

The argument from the passage which speaks of " the souls which Abraham had gained in Harran " (Gen. xii. 5) is a mere play on words, the reference is to the *slaves* whom the patriarch had *bought* in Mesopotamia.

Finally there is one fact which puts out of court the theory of a pre-Jahwistic Hebrew monotheism, in whatever form it may be advanced. It is that the Israelites, when they emerge into the full light of history and up to the time of the great prophets, although Jahwists, were not monotheists. They only worshipped one national god, Jahweh ; but they believed in the existence and power of other gods : they were monolaters. But monolatry is a form of polytheism. Israel only attained to monotheism in the eighth century and to a clear and conscious monotheism only in the sixth, and that by a slow process of internal development whose stages we can trace.

The most that can be admitted is that the Hebrews before Moses had a vague belief, like that of many savage peoples today, in the existence, side by side with other gods or spirits, of a supreme being, the creator of all things, to whom no worship was addressed, and whom they called elohim, God. It is possible that Moses may have taken this belief as a point of departure, just as Mohammed presented his monotheistic message as a development of the belief of the Arabs of his time in Allah, whatever might have been the origin of that belief.[1] However, it is far from probable, for the god to whom Moses sought to win over his people was not a universal god like that of Islam : he had a proper name, Jahweh, local centres of worship, and an essential national character, he was and chose to be the God of Israel.

---

[1] *Cf.* **XC²**, p. 217 ; **CCXXII**, p. 24.

CHAPTER II

RITUAL PRACTICES

I

Holy Things

THE Hebrews' places of worship in the pre-Mosaic times, as we have seen, must often have consisted of a tree, a spring, a cave or a mountain, regarded as the abode or the body of the god. But in many of the holy places, beside these natural objects or instead of them, might be seen a mere stone or a group of stones.

In the oasis of Kadesh there was a rock, evidently very sacred, whence there flowed a sacred spring, the spring of Massah or Meribah ; according to the Israelite tradition it was Moses who had caused the water to gush out by striking the rock with his rod.[1] At the foot of Sinai there were twelve standing stones or steles (Heb. *mazzebah*), also an altar. It was Moses, again, according to the Hebrew stories, who had set them up, in order that the youths of Israel might offer burnt offerings and slay peace-offerings there (Exod. xxiv. 4–8).

Plainly it could not have been Moses who *introduced* the use of stones into the ritual of the Hebrew tribes, since it was a common custom among the nomad Semites.

" The Arabs," said Clement of Alexandria, " worship the stone." [2] Some of the sacred stones of the pre-Islamic Arabs were masses of rock having a more or less vague resemblance to the human form.[3] Others, like that of Dusares, at Petra, or the two sacred stones of the Ca'abah at Mecca, were merely cubes.

The sacred stone of the Arabs was usually an upright

---

[1] Exod. xvii. 1–7 (the localization near Horeb is due to a later editor) ; Num. xx. 1–13.
[2] **PG,** vii, col. 133.   [3] **XC,** pp. 45–8, 51–4.

258

monolith ; it was called *nuṣb*, a thing set up (a word of the
same root as the Hebrew *maṣṣebah*) or *ghari*, that is, rubbed
with blood. It stood either in the centre or on the boundary
of the sacred enclosure, and the blood of the victims was
poured upon it. They spoke to it, caressed it and even
clothed it with garments.

Sacred stones occur among all the branches of the Semitic
race : steles, ziqqurats (stepped pyramids), and kudurrus
(boundary-stones or dedication-memorials) among the Babylonians and Assyrians, the black stone of Emesa in the
Aramean country,[1] the sacred cones of Byblos (fig. 36) and

FIG 36. COIN OF MACRINUS, THE TEMPLE OF BYBLOS.

Paphos among the Phenicians, boulders with cup-marks,
and standing stones among the Canaanites and Israelites
settled in Palestine,[2] the " *weli* of Job's rock "—a stele of
Ramses II worshipped at Sheikh Sa'ad,[3]—and other sacred
stones of the modern Syrians.[4]

In many of the Semitic sanctuaries there were not only
one sacred stone but several [5] ; they were sometimes arranged
in alignments, as at Gezer,[6] at Tell es-Safy,[7] in the bed of
the Jordan according to one of the traditions concerning
the miraculous crossing of that river,[8] perhaps in the Israelite

---

[1] Herodian, v, 3.   [2] See pp. 41-2, 87-97.   [3] **XV**, p. 92.
[4] **CCV**, p. 56, n. 1.
[5] **CLXX**, i, p. 183 ; **CLXXXIX**, pp. 27, 38 *et passim* ; **LXXXIV**,
p. 201.
[6] See p. 87.   [7] **CLIX**, pp. 104–5 (figs. 71–2).
[8] Joshua iv. 4, 5, 7ᵇ, 9 (E).

holy place of Ophrah, if, as we suggest, the word *ma'arakah* in the text may be understood in the sense of " alignment." [1]

Elsewhere they were arranged in circles, as in one of the holy places of Gezer, for instance,[2] and no doubt in the many palestinian holy places called hag-Gilgal, which means " the circle." There is the one, for example, where Joshua is supposed to have erected the twelve stones taken from the dry bed of Jordan, a circle which this tradition referred to the Gilgal near Jericho,[3] the modern Tell Djeldjul, or to the locality of the same name (the modern Djaledjil) near Shechem.[4]

Often two high colonnades of pillars, either detached or

FIG 37. MODEL OF A TEMPLE, FROM IDALION (CYPRUS).

connected with the building, were erected at the entrance of the sanctuary : as at Byblos (fig. 36), at Paphos,[5] and on the model of a temple found at Idalion in Cyprus [6] (fig. 37), at Tyre, in the Island of Gozzo, on Mt. Lyceus, at Hierapolis, at Petra and in the temple of Solomon.

Instead of a monolith it was permissible to raise a cairn or heap of stones, called in Hebrew a *gal*.[7]

Most of the stones of which we have spoken stood in the centre of a holy place and constituted its most sacred object. But the stele or cairn might serve many other purposes.

As we have seen, the standing stone might be a boundary-stone, marking the limits of a sacred enclosure or of a private estate. There was the votive stele, reminding the god of

---

[1] Judges vi. 26 ; see **VI.**
[2] According to **III**, p. 322 (fig. 408).
[3] Joshua iv. 1–3, 8, 20–4.
[4] Deut. xi. 30 ; *cf.* **CCXXXVIII.**
[5] Herodotus, ii, 44 ; fig. in **XLIX**, p. 211.
[6] **III**, p. 317 (fig. 403).   [7] Gen. xxxi. 46–8, 51–3.

the accomplishment of a vow, the offering of a sacrifice or the completion of a pilgrimage. Steles and cairns were also used to mark burial places.[1]

Among these many uses of the stone, it is hardly probable that the memorial or votive use was the earliest. It is not likely that the block of stone standing in the centre of a sanctuary could ever have been a mere ex-voto or memorial.

Neither is it permissible to suppose that the earliest use of the sacred stone was as an altar. The oldest Israelite code, the so-called Book of the Covenant, forbids the building of altars to Jahweh made of hewn stone, because the use of the chisel on the stone would profane it (Exod. xx. 25; cf. Deut. xxvii. 5; Joshua viii. 31): it was an ancient regulation, already violated by Solomon, but showing that in certain Israelite circles it was still felt that an altar was a heap of sacred stones. The right of asylum was still a special privilege attached to the altar: whoever seized its horns became inviolable. Hence, apparently, it is not the altar which becomes a deified sacred stone, it is rather the sacred stone which, somewhat specialized and fallen from its high estate, becomes an altar.

On the other hand, there is a conception whose extreme antiquity is incontestable, it is the idea, influential in all the periods of Semitic history and in all parts of the Semitic world, that the stone was the dwelling-place, the body of a god, a spirit or an invisible power. The worshippers embrace the stone, they kiss it,[2] they anoint it with oil,[3] they burn incense to it, they rub it with the blood of victims, they dress it, they erect it in the centre of the holy place and address it by the name of the god.[4] The Jews of Jeremiah's time were in the habit of saying to the stone: "thou hast begotten me" (Jer. ii. 27). In order to denote the sacred stone, the Semites seem to have employed the significant term beth-'el, house of God, a word from which the Greeks in the beginning of the Christian era took the name βαίτυλος, βαιτύλιον, "baityl," which they used to describe all kinds of sacred stones reputed to possess magical properties, and

[1] Gen. xxxv. 8, 14, 19–20; 2 Sam. xviii. 18; Joshua vii. 24–6; 2 Sam. xviii. 17; cf. III¹, 1894, p. 59 (fig. 6).
[2] As at Mecca, for example; cf. Hos. xiii. 2; 1 Kings xix. 18.
[3] Jacob, Tiglath Pileser I.
[4] At Shechem; Gen. xxxiii. 20.

which Philo of Byblos very accurately calls " living stones,"
λίθους ἐμψύχους.[1]

The union between the divine presence and the object
which embodied it was so close and so vital that the Semites
sometimes used the name of this object as the equivalent
of the name of a god.[2]

We are next faced with the question of the reason which
induced the Semites to choose a stone to become, or to be
recognized as, the abode of a god or a spirit. This is an
exceedingly difficult problem.

According to P. Lagrange the sacred stone, usually conical
in shape, was a miniature of the *ziqqurat*, the huge stepped
pyramid which was erected in the temples of Babylon and
Assyria. P. Lagrange, like many other assyriologists, regards
this pyramid as itself a small image of the earth, which the
Babylonians represented as a mountain. But the earth
itself is the abode, the body of the deity.[3]

This idea seems far too abstract, too theological, to be
the *original* meaning of a religious object such as the sacred
stone, which is found even among the most backward peoples.

The phallic significance sometimes ascribed by the Semites
themselves to their pillars and their steles [4] is also unlikely
to have been the primitive meaning of all the sacred stones.[5]
The pillar, indeed, might equally well represent gods or
goddesses; [6] to the stone it was said : " thou has brought
me forth " (Jer. ii. 27). Hence it was not the specific symbol
of the male principle.

It was believed that the " baityls " had fallen from the

---

[1] Frag. ii, 19 ; *cf.* Photius, *Vita Isidori, Biblioth.*, 242, **PG,** vol. ciii,
cols. 1292 *ff.* ; **XLIX,** p. 195.

[2] The Phenicians also : **XCI,** ii, p. 10 ; **XLIX,** p. 196 ; **CCXXXI ;**
the Canaanites ; Judges ix. 46 (see p. 121) ; the Israelites ; Gen. xxxi.
13. Dussaud interprets in the same way Jer. xlviii. 13 ; Hos. x. 8 ;
Amos viii. 14 ; iii. 14 (**XIX,** pp. 231–43) ; *cf.* **RHR,** lxxiii, pp. 330–1.
See also the names of Bethelsar'eser (Zech. vii. 2), Betheldillani
(**XLIX,** p. 196, n. 2), Bit-ili-nuri (*ibid.*), Bethelnathan, Bethel'aqab,
Betheltaqim (?) (*Sachau Pap.* 33, 17, 25), Anat-bethel (*Sachau Pap.*
32) Ašam-bethel (*Sachau Pap.* 18).

[3] **XLIX,** pp. 192–4 ; W. Baudissin, **ZDMG,** 1903, p. 829 ; **CLIX,**
p. 127 ; *cf.* I. Benzinger, **III,** pp. 321–2.

[4] *Cf.* p. 94, n. 3.

[5] As is maintained by Louis-Germain Levy, for example, **LI,**
pp. 46–7, and Benzinger (**III,** pp. 322–5) who combines this explanation with the preceding one.

[6] Byblos ; Paphos.

sky.[1] This was supposed to have been the origin of the conical stone of Emesa, and of the Heliopolitan baityl. Orthodox Moslems believe that the black stone of the Ca'abah came from Paradise.[2] Some scholars are inclined to see in this belief the explanation of the sacredness attributed to these stones by the Semites.[3] But only a few of the cases can be explained in this way.

The theory is more attractive which would derive the cult of these stones from that of mountains.[4] But the objection to this view is that there are examples of these stones being erected beside a sacred mountain (Sinai) or on a summit (Petra); moreover, the standing stone has hardly the appearance of a mountain.

Another suggestion is that the veneration was due to the resemblance which the Semites found in the stone to the form of a god, especially to the human form which they sought. Also the stone might have served as a rudimentary statue in a time when sculpture was unknown. But the objection to this view is that the same deity might have in one and the same place several sacred stones.[5]

Hence the most probable explanation seems to be that advanced by Robertson Smith : the purpose of the sacred stone was to provide the god who had manifested himself in a particular place, with an abode, a body, and to enable the worshippers to establish permanent relations with him. The reason why a stone was selected for this purpose was because it was the most suitable object to receive the sacrificial blood. Doubtless the choice of a particular stone might be determined by its form, colour or supernatural origin, such as blocks of a regular shape, the black stone of the Ca'abah, rocks resembling the human form, aeroliths, etc. ; the magical value attached by savages to pebbles of an unusual shape is a commonplace.[6] But it was not *necessary* that the stone should have any peculiarity.

There is every reason to believe that the pre-Mosaic

---

[1] βαίτυλος, according to Philo of Byblos, was the son of Ouranos (Frag. ii, 14).

[2] **CLXXXIX**, p. 43, n. 4 ; Lammens, **BIA**, 1920, pp. 39 *ff*.

[3] **XXXVII**, p. 133, n. 1 ; **CCXXVIII**, pp. 19–20.

[4] Thus **CXXVIII**, p. 26 ; **CLXXVII**.

[5] **LXXXIV**, pp. 208, 211 ; **XC²**, p. 102.

[6] **CCXLVIII**, ii, pp. 188–212 ; **CLXXXVII**, ii, p. 62.

Hebrews did not use statues, at least in public worship.
We know that the same was true in the most sacred shrines
of ancient Egypt,[1] among the Ægeans,[2] in ancient Greece,
among the early Romans,[3] and perhaps among the Canaanites.[4] The pre-Islamic Arabs had few statues and regarded
the custom of representing the gods by images as one of
late and foreign origin : the Arabic words for statues are
borrowed from other languages.[5]

Hence the prophetic religion of Israel, when it prohibited
the making of an image of anything in the heavens, on the
earth or in the abyss under the earth, only gave an absolute
sanction to an ancestral custom. There was nevertheless
a profound difference between the two attitudes : the prophets
and the prophetic legislators of the Jahwist school laid down
the condemnation of idolatry as a principle, while the nomad
Hebrews had probably no more hesitation than the Canaanites
in making use of statuettes of the gods as amulets or objects
of private worship.

II

THE HOLY PLACES

1. *The Sacred Enclosure.* According to Semitic custom,
the holy things were surrounded by a well-defined area which
partook of the sanctity of the cult-object and which the
Hebrews called " holy ground," " a holy place," or merely
" the place," *maqom* (Gen. xxviii. 11), a word whose Arabic
equivalent, *maqam*, is still in use in Palestine to denote a
plot of ground sacred to a *weli*.

The Israelites settled in Canaan possessed certain sacred
enclosures : such were " the mount of Jahweh " (*i.e.* the
temple precincts) at Jerusalem, " the portion of the field "
constituting the sanctuary of Shechem,[6] or that which
surrounded the cave of Machpelah.[7] There were some among
the Canaanites, Carmel, for example, and Hermon ; among
the Phenicians, such as the valley of the River Adonis or

---

[1] See, for example, Tiele, *Kompendium der Religionsgeschichte*
(3rd ed., Söderblom), 66.
[2] Karo, **AR**, vii, pp. 155–6.
[3] Tiele, *op cit.*, pp. 381, 385.
[4] See p. 87.
[5] According to **XC²**, p. 102.
[6] Gen. xxxiii. 19–20.
[7] Gen. xxiii. 11, 13, 17, 18–20.

" the field of Narnaka " [1]; in Babylonia and Assyria, among others the island of Icarus or the parks surrounding the temples of the great cities [2]; among the Nabateans, at Petra ; among the other pre-Islamic Arabs, who called them *haram* or *hima* [3]; there are also inviolable territories, sometimes very extensive, surrounding the sanctuaries of the *welis* in Syria.[4]

The Israelite traditions represent the Hebrew tribes, doubtless correctly, as possessing these " holy grounds " in their nomad period of existence. It was related that when Moses saw the burning bush, he heard a voice saying to him : " Draw not nigh hither ; take thy sandals from off thy feet : for the place whereon thou standest is holy ground " (Exod. iii. 5). When the people encamped at the foot of the mount of God, Moses was commanded to put a boundary round the mountain (Exod. xix. 12-13, *cf.* 21-5). None were permitted to ascend the mountain except those who were personally summoned by God ; and even these were to be " prepared," to be " sanctified " by certain rites of which we shall speak later ; otherwise Jahweh would " make a breach among them."

To explain the beliefs connected with the sacred enclosures of the Semites and the rites which were practised there, it is not sufficient to suppose that these areas were regarded as the private property of a god, his garden or his park, whence arose the prohibition to take anything whatever from such an enclosure, or to enter it without permission, under pain of incurring the dreaded anger of the divine owner of the place.

As Robertson Smith has shown, this explanation will not do, first of all because it implies the existence of private landed property among the ancient Semites, an institution unknown among the nomad Arabs, and secondly, because certain rites observed within the sacred enclosures assume that the presence of the divine is thought of after the manner of a dangerous fluid active throughout the entire soil of the " holy place " and in all that it contains, especially the trees and the animals. This fluid is capable of being trans-

[1] **XLIX**, p. 182. [2] *Ibid.*, pp. 181-2.
[3] **XC¹**, pp. 105-8.
[4] For example, **XV,** pp. 107, 108, 109, 161-2.

mitted by contact. This conception appears clearly, as we have seen, in the case of Sinai.[1] In Arabia, a man who Ḵad broken into the *ḥima* of Wadj to cut wood, was deprived of his axe and his garments. The reason for this strange regulation was because the objects in question had been in contact with the dreaded fluid, and were consequently fraught with danger to all who might come in contact with them.

If strayed or stolen cattle enter the sacred precincts they become impregnated with the divine fluid and are henceforth lost to their owner ; it would be fatal for him to touch them. For the same reason a fugitive slave or a man-slayer are safe from pursuit as soon as they have crossed the boundary of the sacred enclosure.

On the other hand the worshippers of the god have comparative freedom to pasture their flocks, to walk about, and even to live in the *haram*, because, being regarded as allies and often as actual kinsmen of the god, they are, to a certain extent, always permeated by the mysterious fluid.

Hence these primitive ideas concerning the sacred enclosure are not based on the conception of property as we understand it today, but on the magical idea of contagious sanctity and taboo.[2]

According to P. Lagrange, ancient man had a double purpose in thus marking out these enclosures ; on the one hand he wished to have " God's dwelling " near him, and on the other, he wished to secularize the part of the country which he desired the free use of. " By reserving a portion for God, usually the best portion, he could henceforth enjoy the rest without scruple." [3]

But it is very doubtful whether the Semites ever thought of things in this way. In most of the stories which have come down to us concerning the founding of sanctuaries, it is not man who chooses the site of the future holy place, but the deity who indicates it, usually by manifesting himself there ; that is to say, for this is doubtless the earliest conception, he reveals the fact that he inhabits the spot in question by appearing there. Jacob was not aware of the sanctity of the place where the holy place of Bethel was to stand in later days, until he had a vision there. Then,

[1] See p. 236.
[2] See pp. 112, 240, 250. [3] **XLIX**, pp. 186–7 ; **CLIX**, p. 146.

full of awe, he exclaimed : " Surely Jahweh is in this place, and I knew it not ! " (Gen. xxviii. 16). Similarly it was God who indicated to Abraham upon which of the mountains he was to sacrifice his son (Gen. xxii. 2–4, 9) ; it was he who marked the sites of the holy places of Shechem, Lahai-Roi, Mamre, Beersheba, Mahanaim, Penuel, Sinai, Gilgal, Ophrah, and Jerusalem,[1] by appearing there, either in person or by his angel. The only cases in which the initiative seems to come from the patriarch are those of Jacob's field at Shechem, and the cave of Machpelah.[2] Nearly always the place is " holy ground " before man marks it out, or even suspects its sacred character.[3]

Hence it is most probable that the sacred enclosure, by some characteristic of its own, acquired the veneration with which it comes to be regarded. According to Robertson Smith's attractive hypothesis, it was the natural phenomenon of the oasis which served as the prototype of the holy place. Springing out of the midst of the desert, the sharply defined region of the oasis, with its plants, trees, streams and animals, seems to the nomad full of the power of supernatural life.[4]

A fact which suggests that the oasis was really at the outset the primitive type of the holy place, and remained as its remote ideal, is that we often find plants and free wild animals playing an important part, even in the urban sanctuaries of the Semites, as at Curium in Cyprus, at Narnaka, in the Island of Icarus and in various Babylonian temples.[5]

The custom of ascribing to the god the ownership of sacred territories of varying size may have extended to sanctuaries which centred round a mountain, an isolated tree or a block of stone. This process would be facilitated by the fact that it was clearly to man's interest to know exactly where he ran the risk of coming into contact with the divine fluid.

2. *The Altar.* It is probable that among the nomad Hebrews, as among the pre-Islamic Arabs and in the cult of the Moslem welis, it was customary to rub the blood of the

[1] 2 Sam. xxiv. 18–25.   [2] Gen. xxxiii. 19–20, 23.
[3] Exod. iii. 5 ; Joshua v. 15.
[4] LXXXIV, p. 103.
[5] *Ibid.*, p. 160, n. 1 ; XLIX, pp. 181–2 ; *cf.* Ps. lii. 10 ; lxxxiv. 3–5 ; xcii. 14.

victims directly on the sacred stone or tree, or to pour it
into the sacred spring or cave.[1]

In certain sanctuaries, however, beside the sacred object
regarded as the abode of the god, there may already have
existed certain stones devoted to the preparatory acts of the
sacrificial rite. One of them, or several piled in a heap,[2]
may have served as the place where the victim was slain.
The Saracens of whom St. Nilus speaks, used to sacrifice
their young captives upon a heap of stones prepared for the
purpose.[3] In the holy places of the modern Bedouins there
is often a point of rock, a flat or rounded stone, where they
cut the victim's throat before sprinkling its blood on the
tomb of the weli. Sometimes this sacrificial stone is provided
with holes to receive the blood.[4] No doubt at a very early
date, another stone of the sanctuary was used as a kind of
table on which certain offerings were placed.

It was apparently from these various sacred stones with
special uses that there arose the several types of " altars "
met with among the Semites : the table of offerings, slaughter-
stone, basin-stone. To the latter class, for instance, belong
those of Zoreah (pl. xii,) and of Gezer,[5] perhaps those of
Megiddo and Taanach,[6] and very probably the " altars "
of Zib Atuf at Petra which are only accessible by narrow
stairs and hence could not have been the place where the
victims were slaughtered.[7]

Elsewhere a certain amount of interchange seems to have
taken place between the uses of the various stones of the
sanctuary. The stone of sacrifice (mizbeaḥ) entirely super-
seded the sacred object as the receptacle for the blood of
the victims [8] and for the food offerings ; on the other hand
it ceased to be the place where the victims were killed :
in the temple at Jerusalem the victims were not slain on
the altar, but on tables near the doors, at least, according

---

[1] Cf. Gen. xxviii. 18 ; xxxi. 13.
[2] Exod. xx. 24–5.
[3] Nili opera, PG, 79, p. 611.
[4] The same custom at Beth Shan according to Rowe's interpretation (see p. 96).
[5] See pp. 88–9, 96 and pl. i, 2.
[6] CLIX, pp. 132–4 (fig. 89).
[7] Pl. xi, 1 ; cf. XXIII², ii, figs. 446–8 ; iii, pp. 318–9.
[8] So at Jerusalem (Deut. xii. 27 ; Lev. i. 5 ; etc.) except in the
ritual of certain sin-offerings (Lev. iv. 5–6, 16–17).

to Ezekiel xl. 39–43. Unfortunately it is not yet possible
to give any detailed account of this development.

It seems equally impossible to say when the Hebrews
introduced the use of altar-hearths. As among the Arabs,
it was probably the original custom among the Hebrews
for such portions of the flesh of the victims as were not
eaten by the worshippers in the sacred meal, to be thrown
to the wild animals which inhabited the holy place and
which were themselves sacred.[1] Later, however, it became
the custom to burn the remains of the victim, both to preserve
them from profanation, as is shown by the ritual of the
expiatory sacrifices where the burning of the victim did
not take place on the altar, and to convey the essence of
the victim in the form of smoke, to the gods, who were
thought of as dwelling in the sky or the upper air.[2] In
view of the light which this custom throws on their conception of the gods, it would be interesting to know whether
it belongs to the pre-Mosaic period, or whether the Hebrews
adopted it at the time of the founding of the national religion,
or only after their settlement in Canaan.

Israelite tradition states definitely that the burning of
the victims was practised by the earliest ancestors of the
nation.[3] On the other hand, it is a fact that the use of
fire in the sacrifices is unknown among both ancient and
modern Arabs.[4]

In any case it does not appear that the custom of burning
the victims was, as has sometimes been maintained,[5] a rite
peculiar to the religion of Jahweh, and that the Israelites
were the first to practise it in Palestine. There are, as we
have seen, reasons for believing that this custom was not
unknown to the Canaanites.[6]

III

The Sacred Acts

1. *Purification and Entry into the Holy Place.* The essentially conservative nature of ritual is well known. Many

---

[1] See p. 279.
[2] See the ritual of the burnt-offerings.
[3] Gen. viii. 20–21 (J) ; xxii. 1–18 (E) ; Exod. x. 25 (R) ; xviii. 12
(J) ; xxiv. 5 (E) ; *cf.* p. 111.
[4] **XC²**, p. 116.　　　[5] See p. 97, n. 3.　　　[6] See pp. 96–7.

of the ritual acts which the Israelite of the historical period performed before entering, or in the act of entering, a sanctuary, were the same as those which his nomad ancestors used prior to the founding of the national religion.

It was the duty of the Hebrew, before presenting himself in the presence of his god, " to sanctify himself," or, in the equivalent expressions, " to purify himself " or " to prepare himself " during a time which varied, no doubt, according to the place and nature of the ceremony to be performed. Preparatory rites might begin two days before the ceremony (Exod. xix. 10), or the day before (Joshua iii. 5 ; vii. 13), or even immediately before it (1 Sam. xvi. 5). The rites of sanctification, as known to us, consisted in washing, in changing or washing the garments, and refraining from sexual intercourse.

These practices were certainly very ancient, for entirely similar regulations were observed during the sacred seasons among the Arabs,[1] the Phenicians (according to 2 Kings x. 20), and in a cult, doubtless of Syrian origin, for which we have evidence at Delos,[2] as in Vedic India before the sacrifices,[3] among the Peruvians before the mysteries, among Buddhist pilgrims, and sometimes in Catholic pilgrimages.[4]

At first sight it might be thought that the regulations relating to washing and to the changing of garments were merely due to a sense of what was fitting, the worshipper being supposed to make himself clean and to array himself suitably before entering the presence of his god, just as he would in appearing before a powerful chief, but the variations in the rule relating to the change of garments, among different Semitic peoples, show that this was not the original motive of the regulations.

The worshipper might either wear special garments for the sacred acts, or wash his ordinary [5] garments before [6] and,

---

[1] **LXXXIV**, p. 451 ; **XC²**, p. 122 ; **CLXXXIX**, pp. 168–91. They confer a positive " sanctity " ; the pilgrim is taboo (**CLXXXIX**, p. 280 ; cf. p. 281 n. 2).
[2] Pierre Roussel, *Mélanges Holleaux*, pp. 265–70 ; cf. **XIX**, p. 324.
[3] **CC**, pp. 49–50.   [4] *Cf.* **CXXVI**, p. 264.
[5] So the Jewish priests (Exod. xliv. 19 ; Exod. xxviii. ; xxix. 5–9 ; Lev. viii. 16), ordinary worshippers in ancient Israel (Gen. xxxv. 2), the Phenicians according to Silius Italicus (iii, 23 *ff.*) and Herodian (v, 5, 10).
[6] Exod. xix. 10, 14 ; Num. viii. 7.

for greater safety, after the ceremony,[1] or again, he might borrow for the occasion a garment which remained in the holy place ; the latter practice was observed in pre-Islamic times at Mecca and in the sanctuary of Al Djalsad,[2] in the cult of the Tyrian Baal at Samaria (2 Kings x. 22), and perhaps at Jerusalem, if the ephod which David wore to dance before the ark was a priestly dress (2 Sam. vi. 14). Finally, the sacred rite might be celebrated without wearing any clothing : This was the custom of certain Bedouins at the Ca'abah [3] ; and both the Israelites [4] and the Babylonians [5] seem to have been familiar with the practice.

If he had omitted to take any of these precautions, the Arab, on leaving the sanctuary, was obliged to abandon his garments, which he was no longer entitled to wear or to sell.

The idea behind these various precautions was clearly the conception, so common among primitive peoples, that clothing is particularly liable to be impregnated by the spiritual influences with which it may be surrounded. Hence there is always the danger that it may either bring hostile influences into the sacred precincts, or, an equally dreaded possibility, that it may carry a portion of the sacred fluid into profane surroundings. The Jews of the sixth century were still clearly aware of this motive : Ezekiel lays down the rule for the priests that they must remove, in the inner court, the dress in which they have officiated, " in order that they may not sanctify the people by their garments " (Ezek. xliv. 19).

The prohibition of sexual intercourse might be due to the belief that everything relating to the act of birth was under the control of special gods or spirits : hence it was necessary to avoid all contact with these powers on approaching any other divinity or the spirits of the dead ; many peoples observe the same taboo during mourning,[6] as long as the slain remains unavenged,[7] or during a campaign.[8] Perhaps

---

[1] Lev. xvi. 26–8. [2] **LXXXIV**, p. 451.
[3] **LXXXIV** ; **CLXXXIX**, pp. 171, 172, 283.   [4] 1 Sam. xix. 24.
[5] **CCIII**, p. 340, pl. 28 ; **XXXIV**, *Bildermappe*, figs. 81, 84, 93.
[6] So among the Jews, Rabbinowicz, *Der Todtenkult*, pp. 44, 47, 48, 60 ; and among the Burgondes, **LIX**, p. 143.
[7] For example, among the Arabs, **XC²**, p. 122.
[8] So in ancient Israel, 2 Sam. xi. 11.

the idea was also present that the female was a source of weakness for the male, and that it was necessary for those taking part in sacred rites to preserve their strength unimpaired, "the magic virtue by which the success of their undertaking was secured." [1]

Hebrew tradition related, no doubt on good grounds, that the ancestors of the nation, especially the women and children, on setting out for the holy place, adorned themselves with all the jewels which they possessed or could procure. [2] Later on this practice seems to have been condemned (Gen. xxxv. 4). The original purpose would not have been merely that of honouring the deity by appearing before him in rich array. For the oriental a jewel is primarily an amulet, an object possessing supernatural powers. In Hebrew a crown is called *nezer*, "consecration." An ear-ring in Syriac is *qedosho*, a holy thing. [3] When Jacob commanded the members of his family to "put away their strange gods," he also made them take off their ear-rings, which he buried under a sacred tree (Gen. xxxv. 4) : he would not have dared to destroy them or put them to a secular use. [4] Hence in adorning himself with jewels of gold and silver to approach a sanctuary, the Hebrew must have had a religious object. Either he wished to make himself in advance as holy as possible, or (the one motive does not exclude the other) to recharge with the sacred fluid the amulet which was his protection in ordinary life.

When the Hebrew, thus "prepared," entered a sacred enclosure, such as Sinai, for example, [5] his first duty was to take off his sandals. It was essential to avoid all contact between the sacred environment and the influences emanating from profane ground. Hence this rule also was based on the same principle as those relating to clothing ; an assumption which is confirmed by the various forms in which the regulation occurs. It was permissible, in order to enter the sanctuary, to put on special shoes,—the sacred clothing of the Phenicians included some kind of linen stockings, [6]

---

[1] **LIX**, pp. 39–41.
[2] Exod. iii. 21–22 ; xi. 2–3 ; xii. 35–6 ; xxxiii. 5–6 ; *cf.* Hos. ii. 15.
[3] *Cf.* also **CCXXXVI**, p. 37, n. 1 on *nezem*, ring.
[4] See p. 216.
[5] Exod. iii. 5 ; *cf.* Joshua v. 15 (Gilgal) ; **CLXXXIX**, p. 285, n. 8.
[6] Herodian, v, 5, 10 ; *cf.* **LXXXIV**, p. 453.

—or they might be borrowed from the sanctuary—as in the cave of Trophonius in Greece,[1] or, today, in the mosques.

The worshippei might then advance, but slowly (Exod. xix. 21, 24), with his face covered (Exod. iii. 6 ; 1 Kings xix. 13). It might be fatal, indeed, for him to meet the god unawares face to face : for no mortal can live after having seen an *elohim*. We have evidence that these two rules were in force in the desert sanctuary of Sinai. In the Arab sanctuary of Al Djalsad, similarly, it was necessary to approach the sacred stone slowly and with bowed head.[2]

On reaching the sacred object, the Hebrew of nomad times would kiss it, as the Arab kisses the black stone of the Ca'abah,[3] aș the modern Syrian kisses the sacred trees of Abu Zeituni or Imam Ali,[4] and as the Israelite settled in Canaan used to kiss the sacred bull of Jahweh (Hos. xiii. 2) or the Baal of Samaria (1 Kings xix. 18), and sometimes may have allowed himself to kiss his hand to the sun or the moon (Job xxxi. 27). It is probable that the worshipper also embraced the sacred object, as the Arabs used to do to their gods and especially to their household idols. This would seem to be the meaning of the attitude of supplication which consists in stretching out the palms of the hands toward God.[5]

Prayer necessarily began with the mention of the name of the god who was being invoked, often accompanied by some adulatory epithet or by the grounds on which the suppliant expected an answer to his prayer. This exact mention of the name of the deity was necessary, first because a prayer was an appeal intended to arouse the attention of the unseen divinity.[6] Hence prayer was usually made aloud, the Israelite in distress " cried to Jahweh." Silent prayer was so far an exception that the priest Eli, seeing Hannah moving her lips without speaking, thought that she was drunk (1 Sam. i. 12–14). For the same reason the Moslem pilgrims, during the *wuquf* of Arafa, call out with a loud voice the names of the men and women whom they wish to associate with the pilgrimage by uttering their names before Allah.[7]

---

[1] Pausanias, lx, 36.   [2] **XC²**, p. 55.   [3] **CLXXXIX**, pp. 48–6.
[4] **XV**, pp. 164, 287.   [5] Exod. ix. 29 ; Isa. i. 15.
[6] *Cf*. also Num. x. 9–10 ; Sir. 50, 16.   [7] **CLXXXIX**, p. 248.

A second reason why the exact mention of the name of the god invoked is necessary is that to the mind of the early Hebrew the utterance of the name had the power of compelling the god to be present. Hence the reluctance displayed by supernatural beings, in the early traditions, to reveal their true names.[1] This also explains why the special title by which the God of Israel was worshipped in each holy place is, usually, carefully mentioned in the story of the founding of the holy place in question.

Two other features of the Israelite ritual which, because of their close resemblance to ·the rites of Arab paganism, may be referred to pre-Mosaic times, are the shout of praise and the dance.

On feast-days, when the Israelites visited the sanctuaries of Jahweh, or when the ark was brought into their camp, they uttered shouts so loud that at a distance they sounded like shouts of battle, and the earth shook with them.[2] The word denoting this shout was *hillel*, akin to the verb *yalal*, to howl. The moment when the congregation was supposed to utter a sacred cry was marked in the liturgy by the formula *hallelujah*, " praise ye Jahweh ! " which we have changed into " alleluia."

An Arabic word of the same root, *tahlil*, denotes the shout which used to accompany the sacrifices in pre-Islamic times, and which has persisted in the Moslem ritual, where they cry unceasingly *labbaika*, " in thy service ! "[3]

These shouts must have been long accompanied by dances, or at least by a procession round the sacred object, the altar or the victim. We are told that they danced with shouting round the golden calf (Exod. xxxii. 6, 17–19) : such was probably the ritual of the sanctuary of Bethel which has given its form to this story. At the vintage festival in Shiloh, the women came out of the city with dances (Judges xxi. 21–23). When they brought the ark to Jerusalem, David " returned and danced with all his might before Jahweh " (2 Sam. vi. 5, 14, 16). The custom of circular

[1] Gen. xxxii. 30 ; Exod. iii. 13–14 (*cf.* pp. 373–4) ; Judges xiii. 17–18.

[2] Exod. xxxii. 17–18 ; Lam. ii. 7 ; Ezra iii. 12–13 ; Zech. iv. 7 ; 1 Sam. iv. 5.

[3] **XC²**, pp. 110, 111 ; **CLXXXIX**, pp. 249, 250.

processions round the altar persisted in certain Temple
ceremonies,[1] particularly in the Feast of Tabernacles. These
dances must have played an important part in early Hebrew
religious ceremonies ; for the Hebrew word for a feast, *ḥag*,
means literally a dance.[2]

It is the same word as the Arabic *ḥadj*, which in pre-
Islamic times denoted the processional circuit round the
Ca'abah, a rite which was preserved by the Prophet. The
term was extended to cover the whole pilgrimage, including
a visit to the various shrines of the district. St. Nilus,
who lived in the convent of Sinai about A.D. 400, in his eye-
witness's account of a Saracen sacrifice tells us that these
Bedouins, before slaying the victim, " went three times round
it, in a vast circle." [3]

The same rite was practised among the Canaanites, in
Greece, and among many other peoples.[4] On Mt. Carmel
the priests of the Tyrian Baal performed a limping dance
before the altar (1 Kings xviii. 26). Near Beyrut there was
a god called Baal Marqod, the lord of the dance.

The circular procession is, among certain peoples, undoubtedly regarded as a "*rite de passage*," of the type
described by van Gennep, although he does not quote
it.[5]

Various explanations of this custom have been offered.
According to Robertson Smith the cries uttered in the
sanctuary were originally lamentations for the victim, others
regard them as intended to drive away evil spirits, or as
supplications addressed to the god.

Elsewhere the same rite is intended to describe, around
the sacred or magical act which is to be performed, a kind
of enchanted circle (Joshua vi. 3–20). Still more often the
dance claims to re-enact the adventures of a god, but in
reality the original purpose was by magic action to help or
compel him to accomplish the act of beneficence expected
of him.

According to some historians, cries and dances were
originally ecstatic phenomena—manifestations of the presence

---

[1] Ps. xxvi. 6–7 ; xlii. 5, and perhaps cxviii. 27.
[2] *Cf.* 1 Sam. xxx. 16 ; Ps. cvii. 27.
[3] *Nili opera*, **PG**, 79, p. 613.
[4] See, for example, **CCVIII**, pp. 261–2.
[5] *Cf.* Goblet D'Alviella, **RHR**, lix, p. 239.

of the god who enters his worshippers [1]—and at the same
time, a means of bringing on the ecstatic state, as we know
from the example of the whirling dervishes, or the old Hebrew
nebi'im.[2]

It would be necessary to have more precise information
about the ritual of the sacred dances of the ancient Semites
in order to know which of these explanations is the most
satisfactory. Possibly the meaning of the ritual varied
according to the different sanctuaries and according to the
nature of the ceremonies in which they occurred.

2. Sacrifice

(a) *The Rites.* In certain respects, for instance, as far
as the frequency of obligatory sacrifices was concerned, the
sacrificial order of the pre-Mosaic Hebrews must have been
very much simpler than the imposing public service of the
post-exilic Jews contained in the levitical code. The latter
comprised, in addition to many voluntary offerings, the
provision of victims in minutely prescribed numbers to be
offered each day on behalf of the community by a hierarchy
of priests.

This view is supported by the analogy of the pre-Islamic
Arabs, whose order of sacrifice must have been almost the
same as that of the nomad Hebrews. Among the ancient
Arabs there seem to have been only two annual seasons of
sacrifice : one in the month of Radjab at the local sanctuaries,
the other at the pilgrimage to Mecca.[3] Moreover, the sacrifices which took place during a pilgrimage must have been,
as among the Arabs, individual and optional offerings, the
fulfilment of a vow.[4]

Similarly among the modern Bedouins the few fixed sacrifices are either those signalling the occasion of a visit to the
sacred cities—a survival from the pagan period which
Moslem custom has faithfully preserved [5]—or those which
are offered, usually once a year, to the *weli*, or local saint.

Seasonal sacrifices cannot have been much more frequent
among the nomad ancestors of Israel. Such rites as that
of the " Bread of the Presence," renewed every week,[6] and

[1] **LXXXV**, pp. 123, 149.
[2] 1 Sam. x. 5–6 ; 2 Kings iii. 15 ; *cf.* **LXX**, ii, p. 112.
[3] **XC²**, pp. 98–101, 118.
[4] **XC¹**, pp. 121–2.   [5] *Cf.* **CLXXXIX**, pp. 277–91.
[6] Already in 1 Sam. xxi. 7.

especially that of the daily burnt offering, can only have come in after the settlement in Palestine, in imitation of the practices of the centralized states, such as the royal Canaanite [1] or Phenician cities, and the Egyptian or Babylonian empires.

On the other hand, there is no need to exaggerate the paucity of the sacrifices offered by the nomad Hebrews. Their system must already have contained, even if in a somewhat barbarous and elementary form, *the greater part of the rites which were later codified in the levitical law.*

No doubt the pre-Jahwistic Hebrews, like the pre-Islamic Arabs, possessed traditions concerning the right age and the suitable species of sacrificial victims. The regulations concerning these matters laid down by the Moslem teachers are, in fact, a heritage from the pagan period. [2]

In further resemblance to the ancient Arabs, the nomad Hebrews must have been in the habit of offering, not only compulsory sacrifices (*qodashim*), and votive offerings (*nedarim*), [3] but also individual offerings and sacrifices made by the whole clan or tribe. [4]

Moreover, all the evidence would lead us to suppose that *the ritual slaying of victims must have taken many forms.*

It is true that the pre-exilic Hebrew texts only mention two categories of bloody sacrifices, the *zebah shelamim*, or peace-offering, also called *zebah* or *shelem*, in which the greater part of the flesh of the victim was eaten by the worshippers in a sacred meal, and the *'olah*, or whole burnt offering, also called *kalil*, or total (gift), where the whole animal was given to the deity. Hence many of the historians of the religion of Israel have been inclined to depict the sacrificial ritual of pre-exilic times as of an extreme simplicity.

But, as a fact, when we look at the matter more closely, we see that the Israelites of that period, like other ancient peoples and savages today, practised the ritual slaughter of living beings with very various objects, by reason of very diverse mental processes, and hence also with very different rites. They practised ritual slaughter, not only to win the

[1] See p. 101.
[2] CLXXXIX, pp. 278–79 ; *cf* XC², p. 115.
[3] XC², pp. 121–2.
[4] For example, that which St. Nilus describes or that of the Anaza (XC², pp. 119–21.)

favour of their god, to appease his anger, to feed him, to enter into communion with him, either by the communal meal or by a blood bond (Exod. xxiv. 6, 8), but also to make a curse efficacious by the magic identification with a divided victim, of the individual who passed between the severed portions (Gen. xv. 9–12, 17–18 ; Jer. xxxiv. 18 [1] ; *cf.* 1 Sam. xi. 7), to obtain an oracle, probably given originally by the victim itself (Num. xxiii. 1–6, 14–15, 29–80 ; *cf.* Ezek. xxi. 26), to remove a disease by transferring it to an animal (Lev. xiv. 4–5, 49–50 ; *cf.* xvi. 20–22), to preserve a house by means of the blood of an animal (Exod. xii. 13, 21–23), etc.

The living being buried under the foundations of a city, apparently to preserve it from the wrath of the genius of the place (1 Kings xvi. 34), was not slain according to the same rites as the heifer intended to avert the vengeance of a murdered man (Deut. xxi. 1–9).

There were also many local differences : the *zebaḥ* was not practised at Ophrah,[2] at Shiloh,[3] or at Ramah [4] in exactly the same way as at Jerusalem.

The cult of ancient Israel, before its priestly codification at the period of the exile, must have been, like that of Greece or Rome, a confused mass of very various customs, some of the most ancient of which evidently bordered on magic. The term *zebaḥ* and *'olah*, used to denote the totality of bloody sacrifices, were no doubt in the main very general categories into which the great variety of ritual slayings were conveniently divided.

Among these sacred or semi-magical acts practised by the Israelites after their settlement in Palestine, there are several which can with more or less certainty be relegated to the pre-Mosaic nomad period.

(i.) The sacrifice accompanied by a meal (*zebaḥ*) was certainly practised by the Hebrews of this time. This is suggested on the one hand by the evidently very ancient ritual of the Passover, and on the other by the analogy of the pre-Islamic Arabs.[5] Among the modern Bedouins also the victims are often eaten in a ceremonial meal, or distri-

---

[1] Where one should doubtless read ka'égel, " as the calf."
[2] Judges vi. 19–21.   [3] 1 Sam. ii. 13–16.
[4] If it is this high-place which is referred to in 1 Sam. ix. 24.
[5] See the description by St. Nilus of a Saracen sacrifice (*Nili opera*, 613) ; *cf.* **XC**[2], pp. 118–20, n. 3.

buted to the guests or the poor. In spite of objections [1]
it seems certain that the original idea of these meals following
the sacrifice was to establish communion with the god by
means of a communal meal. [2]

(ii.) The pre-Islamic Arabs had another type of sacrifice
where the bodies of the victims were thrown out around
the sacred stones over which their blood had been poured. [3]
The original belief was, no doubt, that the flesh was eaten
by the deity represented by the wild beasts of the holy
place. This custom has been preserved by the Moslem
pilgrims, at least as far as the compulsory sacrifices are
concerned. [4] We have here a form of the *kalil*, or total
(gift), a prototype of the holocaust as the nomad Hebrews
must have practised it before adopting the less barbarous
practice of burning the victim in order to convey it to the
deity.

(iii.) The practice of sacrifice to atone for a fault or to
remove some evil cannot have been unknown to the pre-
Jahwistic Hebrews; and in this case it was, no doubt,
necessary that the person on whose behalf the sacrifice was
offered should refrain from eating the flesh of the victim.
The pilgrim on the way to Mecca was obliged to offer an
expiatory victim (*dam*) if he should happen to omit certain
of the rites of his pilgrimage. [5] In which case, as in that of
compulsory sacrifices in general, " the prevailing teaching
is that the pilgrim has no rights in the victim. It seems
that even the poor have none. [6] Among the Fuqara Bedouins,
they usually slay a goat to cure a sick person; they pour
the blood over the part affected, and then bury the victim,
which must not be eaten. [7] We can see here the germ of the
ritual of the Levitical atonement sacrifices which prescribed
that the flesh of the victims should be burnt in a special
place or eaten by the priests, two methods of disposing of
the flesh without danger of profanation. [8] *The guilty person,*

---

[1] For example, by Curtiss, **XV**, pp. 254, 255 and P. Lagrange,
XLIX, p. 272.

[2] **LIX**, pp. 450–3.   [3] **XC²**, pp. 61, 121.

[4] **CLXXXIX**, pp. 289–90. Cf. Ezek. xxxix. 17–20 ; Jer. xxxiv.
18–20 (imprecatory sacrifice.)

[5] **CLXXXIX**, pp. 262, 278.

[6] *Ibid*., p. 290, n. 2 ; cf. pp. 289–91.

[7] **CCV**, p. 70. •   [8] Lev. iv.–v. ; vi. 17–7, x.

even if he were a priest, *was forbidden to eat any of it*.[1] We might even add that the very various ideas current in Israel, in the historical period, concerning the way in which expiation is effected by the sacrifice, must previously have been current among the nomad Hebrews, as among the ancient and modern Arabs. For instance, the removal of evil (sickness, sin, uncleanness) by the transference of it to an animal which is thereupon driven out or put to death,[2] the sprinkling of blood on sacred beings or things in order to restore to them their vitality or their virtue affected by the evil—to give blood is to give life [3]—the ransom of a life by a life.[4]

(iv.) Very often among modern Bedouins, the blood of the victim is used as a protection : it is put on the door of houses which they wish to protect, or on the forehead of cattle or of a child as a preservative from disease. In addition, some of the blood is often sprinkled on the sacred object representing the *weli*. Whatever might have been the manner in which the blood was supposed to exercise its protective force, the custom was certainly well known to the nomad Hebrews, as is proved by the ancient ritual of the Passover, with its sprinkling of blood on the door-posts of the houses to be protected against the plague.

(v.) Israelite tradition also refers back to the period of desert life a very similar rite consisting in sprinkling part of the victim's blood upon the altar and part upon assembled worshippers (Exod. xxiv. 4–6, 8). According to this story it was thus that the alliance between the Hebrew tribes and Jahweh was established. The blood shared between the people and their god established communion between the two parties.

The pre-Islamic Arabs performed similar ceremonies to seal an agreement between two men or two clans : the contracting parties dipped their hands into the blood of the same victim,[5] or, according to a more ancient rite recorded

---

[1] Lev. x. 19–20.

[2] Lev. xiv. 4–7, 49–53 ; xvi. 20–22 and **LVI**, p. 190. *Cf.* **CCLIII**, p. 454 ; **CLXXXVI**, p. 33 ; **CCV**, pp. 46–47, 70, 210 ; **LIX**, pp. 313–14.

[3] Deut. xii. 15–16, 22–23 ; xv. 22–23 ; **XC²**, p. 117. *Cf.* **LIX**, pp. 205–7.

[4] Lev. xvii. 11. *Cf.*, among the modern Arabs, the sacrifices called *fédou*, ransom (**XV**, pp. 256–8 ; **CCIV**, pp. 357–63)); on the ancient Arabs, see **XC²**, p. 127.   [5] **XC²**, p. 128.

by Herodotus, some of their own blood was placed, by means
of a thread drawn from their garments, upon seven stones,
with a prayer to Dionysus and Urania.[1] This variant suggests that these various covenant rites are based on the
" blood-covenant," as it is practised in various parts of the
world : the two partners each drink some of the other's
blood : they are henceforth brothers with the same blood
in their veins.

It is evident, in short, that nearly all the forms of sacrifice
which we find practised by the Israelites of the historical
period,[2] must have existed, at least in germ, among the
pre-Mosaic Hebrews.

There only remain the divinatory sacrifice, the sacrifice
intended to render a curse efficacious, and the sacrifice after
a murder by an unknown person (Deut. xxi. 1–9), which we
cannot carry back to the same early period in the history
of the Hebrew tribes, although the archaic nature of the
rites makes such a reference not improbable.

It follows that the Israelite system of sacrifice, in its
essentials, does not seem to have been either a Jahwistic
innovation, as in the priestly narrative, which represents
it as having been revealed to Moses by Jahweh (P intentionally records no example of sacrifice before the Mosaic period),
nor a borrowing from the Canaanites, as Dussaud has recently
maintained,[3] nor a creation of the Jewish priests at the time
of the exile. In the main, it comes from the old pre-Mosaic
Semitic stock of religious practices.

To the Canaanites the Hebrews need not have owed
more than agricultural rites, perhaps the use of fire, a greater
frequency of sacrifice in the important urban sanctuaries,
and the rituals peculiar to the various Palestinian high
places.

The work of the priestly editors of the levitical legislation
in the exilic period consisted, on the one hand, in *the authoriza-
tion and development of the changes* which had grown up during
the course of centuries in the sacrificial customs of Israel.
These changes mainly concerned the priests' part in the
ceremonies, their revenues, their order of rank, the nature

---

[1] Herodotus, iii, 8.
[2] On the foundation sacrifices, see pp. 285–7.
[3] **XIX**, see pp. 97–8.

of the cult, which had gradually been transformed into a public ceremony, and the place of the ritual of atonement in this public worship.

On the other hand, it may be said that in certain directions their work *constitutes a retrogression* towards the past ; for instance, in their ideas concerning the value of sacrifice : they represented sacrifices as working *ex opere operato*, as so many magical acts, whereas the Israelites as a whole, before the exile, had come to regard sacrifice to some extent from an ethical point of view, as being mainly a gift offered to God, which he could accept or refuse at his pleasure.[1]

As far as *the theory of sacrifice* was concerned, the legislators of the exile *introduced a richer terminology*, dividing the sacrifices into four classes [2] instead of two.[3] But as far as *the rites themselves* are concerned, and this is the subject which interests us at present, they do not seem to have added much. Indeed it is probable that *they may rather have reduced the abundant variety* of the sacrifices in their attempt at systematization.[4]

These observations tend to confirm one of the main conclusions of Loisy's great study of the history of sacrifice in the various religions of mankind [5] : in the beginning we find complexity and variety both in the rites and in the conceptions underlying the rites. At the end of the period of evolution we find uniformity, either relative, as in Greece, Rome, Israel, India, or ancient Egypt,[6] or complete, as in Catholicism.

(b) *The Material of the Sacrifices.* In the cult of Jahweh the usual content of the sacrifice was an animal from the small or large cattle, rarely a dove or a pigeon. But in the historical period, especially before the exile, many other things might be offered ; flour, uncooked or cooked in various ways, wine, oil, flax, wool, clothing, arms, horses, hair, human victims.

---

[1] On the history of this notion of gift-sacrifice among the Israelites, *cf.* Buchanan Gray, *Sacrifice in the O.T.*, Oxford, 1925.

[2] The burnt sacrifice ('ôlâh), the peace-offering (zebah), the sin-offering (hatta'th), the trespass offering ('asam).

[3] 'ôlâh and zebah.

[4] See Ad. Lods, **RHP**, 1928, p. 411.

[5] **LIX** ; *cf.* **RHP**, 1921, pp. 483–506 ; **CCXII.**

[6] **LXIX**, p. 451.

Prior to the settlement in Palestine, wine, the special product of the agricultural districts, was probably forbidden in the cult.[1] The *elohim* of the nomad Hebrews must have been among those gods " who do not drink wine," like Shai al-Qaum, a god of the Nabatean Arabs, who is thus described by one of his worshippers in an inscription found at Palmyra.[2]

Among the Israelites in Palestine oil was offered either mixed with flour,[3] or, at least before the exile, in the form of a libation.[4] It was a food, the food of a settled people, offered to the god.

But the nomad Hebrews must already have used oil, like the Arabs in certain ceremonies connected with oaths,[5] to anoint sacred stones,[6] perhaps also to consecrate objects or persons,[7] to cleanse (originally to heal) a leper,[8] whatever may have been the primary intention of this rite.[9] It has been supposed, not without probability, that this rite should be compared with the custom of the Australians who kill a man in order to anoint themselves with his kidney-fat and thus to absorb the " soul," the strength which resides in this organ : oil would have been substituted for human or animal fat.[10]

In the historical period the Israelite used to offer to Jahweh clothing and weapons.[11] The purpose might have been to establish communion between the deity and the owner of these things, as is the case with the fragments of cloth hung by the Arabs and the Syrians on a sacred tree or to the grating of the cenotaphs of the patriarchs in Hebron,[12] for a man's garment and his regular tool are regarded by the " primitive " as part of the man himself, permeated by the

---

[1] See pp. 399, 410–1.

[2] Littmann, **JA**, 1901, pp. 374 *ff.* ; **CVIII**, iv, pp. 382 *ff.* ; **XLIX**, pp. 506–7 ; R. Dussaud, **RHR**, xcv, pp. 200–1.

[3] Lev. ii. 1–15 ; Num. xv. 4 ; *cf.* Ezek. xlv. 24.

[4] Gen. xxxv. 14 ; Mic. vi. 7 ; Isa. lvii. 9 ; Ezek. xvi. 18 ; xlv. 14, 17 ; *cf.* Gen. xxviii. 18 ; Judges ix. 9.

[5] **LXXXIV**, p. 233.

[6] *Cf.* Gen. xxviii. 18 ; xxxv. 14.

[7] 1 Sam. x. 1 ; xvi. 1–13ᵃ ; 1 Kings i. 9 ; xix. 15–16 ; Exod. xl. 9–16, etc.

[8] Lev. xiv. 15–18.

[9] *Cf.* Wellhausen, **AR**, 1904, pp. 33–9 ; **XVII**, pp. 242 *ff.* ; **XIX**, p. 118.

[10] A. E. Crawley, art. *Anointing*, **ERE**, i, p. 550ᵇ ; **CXIV**, p. 42.

[11] Ezek. xvi. 18 ; 1 Sam. xxi. 10.   [12] See pp. 233–4.

spiritual fluid which is in him. .A man who wishes to "bind his soul" to that of his friend gives him his clothing and his weapons (1 Sam. xviii. 1, 4).

Elsewhere weapons and clothing seem to have been laid up before the god for his personal use. The sword of Goliath deposited at Nob will have been Jahweh's share in the spoil taken from the Philistines (1 Sam. xxi. 10). The Arabs invest the Ca'abah with garments made to measure for the stone. In pagan times they used to make two garments, it would appear, for this monument, one for winter and one for summer.[1]

Offerings of hair to the gods and to the dead must have been a Semitic custom from the earliest times; for they occur among the Syrians of Hierapolis,[2] in Phenician territory, —at Citium where barbers were attached to the sanctuary,[3] —and in ancient Arabia,[4] as also among the modern Bedouins,[5] and Syrians.[6] This practice also existed, no doubt, among the Hebrews, for a persistent funerary rite, which Jahwism was never able to destroy, required the making of "a tonsure for the dead," that is the cutting of a lock of hair from the forehead or the temples,[7] apparently for the purpose of throwing it into the grave. It was no doubt in order to offer it to Jahweh that Absalom cut off his hair "at the end of each year" (on the occasion of the feast of Jahweh) and had it weighed.[8] For a man to give his hair was in a way to give himself to the god or to the dead; since the hair is, in the estimation of primitive peoples, an essential part of the individual: whoever omits to destroy his hair after it has been cut off is at the mercy of any sorcerer who may get hold of it.

The cutting off and destruction of the hair of the head and the beard, when performed at the beginning or end of a period of taboo—such as leprosy (Lev. xiv. 9), the Nazirite-

---

[1] **CLXX**, pp. 186–7; **XC²**, p. 73.
[2] *De dea Syria*, § 60.   [3] **CIS**, i, 86, **A**, l. 12.
[4] *Cf* Goldziher, *Le sacrifice de la chevelure chez les Arabes*, **RHR**, xiv, p. 50; **XC²**, pp. 181–2.
[5] Goldziher, *ibid.*
[6] So **XV**, pp. 189–91; *cf.* pp. 173–218.
[7] Deut. xiv. 1; Lev. xxi. 5; Isa. xv. 2; xxii. 12; Jer. xvi. 6; xlviii. 37; Ezek. vii. 18; xxvii. 31; Amos viii. 10; Mic. i. 16; *cf.* Lev. xix. 27.
[8] 2 Sam. xiv. 26; *cf.* Herodotus, ii, 65; and **LXXXIV**, p. 484.

Plate XIII

Funerary Jars containing the Bodies of Infants, from Megiddo

Plate XIV

1. The Kubbet es-Sakhra Rock at Jerusalem, seen from above
(*See* p. 413)

2. Laver on Wheels, found
at Larnaka (Cyprus)
(*See* p. 415)

3. Fragment of a Laver on Wheels,
found at Enkomi (Cyprus)
(*See* p. 415)

ship (Num. vi. 18), the pilgrim's vow (*XC*,[2] pp. 122-3), the priesthood (Num. viii. 7)—spring from a related conception, though slightly different : we shall return to the subject.[1]

Child-sacrifices were often practised by the Israelites after their settlement in Canaan : this is proved, not only by the little skeletons discovered in the foundations of buildings belonging to the Israelite age,[2] but by many texts, such as the story of the double foundation sacrifice offered by Hiel, the rebuilder of Jericho (1 Kings xvi. 34), or the indignant protests of Jeremiah, Ezekiel, Deuteronomy, the Holiness Code (Lev. xviii. 21 ; xx. 2), the editor of the book of Kings and the author of Isaiah lvii. : there was near Jerusalem, in the Valley of the sons of Hinnom, a high place known as Tophet, reserved for these grim rites. It is certain that the Israelites ascribed great virtue to these sacrifices. The book of Kings relates that it was owing to the sacrifice of his eldest son that Mesha, the King of Moab, was able to avert the wrath of his god Chemosh from himself, and turn it upon his Israelite, Jewish, and Edomite foes (2 Kings iii. 27).

It is also certain that child-sacrifices were often performed in honour of Jahweh. It must have been to him that Jephthah, Ahaz and Manasseh offered their children as burnt-offerings.[3] The author of Micah vi. 1-8 depicts a Judean offering to give his first-born to appease Jahweh. Jeremiah is obliged to protest that such a demand was never even thought of by his god (Jer. vii. 31 ; xix. 5 ; xxxii. 35). Ezekiel goes even further : he admits that Jahweh had once demanded such sacrifices, but adds that it was a fatal commandment, intended to destroy a guilty people (Ezek. xx. 25-26). There stood, in fact, in the old Book of the Covenant, the explicit command : " Thou shalt give to me the first-born of thy sons. Thou shalt do the same with thy great and thy small cattle " (Exod. xxii. 28-29). Ezekiel, like most of his contemporaries, believed that this text contained a stringent command to sacrifice all the first-born.

In spite of Stade's authority, it seems difficult to believe

---

[1] P. 305 ; *cf.* LVIII, i, pp. 124-36, 268.

[2] At Megiddo, at Gezer (Macalister, PEF, QS, 1903, p. 224), at Jericho (CLIX, p. 199 ; H. Vincent, RB, 1909, p. 275).

[3] Judges xi. 39, *cf.* vv. 30, 31, 36 ; 2 Kings xvi. 3 ; xxi. 6.

that this interpretation was correct. So stern a demand as the slaying of all the first-born sons is too incompatible with the spirit of Jahwism, with the importance of the first-born in the Israelite family, and with those cases of child-sacrifice of which we know the details : Jephthah, Mesha, the individual who apostrophizes the prophet in Micah vi. 1–8, suggest that the offering of a child to God is an extraordinary thing, and not that they are fulfilling an obligation. Hence it is probable that already at a very early date it was customary to ransom the first-born of men (Exod. xxxiv. 20 ; Gen. xxii.). It is none the less true that early Jahwism admitted the possibility and even, in principle, the obligation of sacrificing children to the god of Israel.[1] This theoretical obligation is probably a softening of an earlier actual obligation.

The question here arises whether it was after their entry into Canaan that the Israelites borrowed these ideas and practices from the Canaanites who attached so much importance to them.[2] It has often been asserted that they did, but the truth of the assertion is doubtful. Traces of the same custom are found among the Babylonians[3] and, more significant still, among the ancient Arabs up to a period shortly before Mohammed. We are told that

" Abd al-Muttalib vowed that if he brought up ten sons he would sacrifice the tenth ; he ransomed him afterwards for a hundred camels."

To this legendary instance may be added an historical case :

" A woman vowed to sacrifice her son in case of the success of a certain undertaking : when it fell out thus, she consulted Ibn al-Abbas, who decided that she ought, like Abd al-Muttalib, to sacrifice a hundred camels in place of her son ; but Marvan, at that time governor of Medina, declared that the vow was invalid."[4]

The evidence might be considerably increased if we regard the very common Arabian custom of burying new-born daughters alive as examples of an early sacrificial custom.[5]

Hence it does not seem safe to assert, as Renan does,[6]

[1] Cf. Exod. xiii. 12[b] ; Gen. xxii. 2.
[2] See pp. 89–90 ; 99–100.   [3] XCIII, pp. 434, 599.
[4] XC[2], p. 116.
[5] LXXXIV, p. 370, n. 3.   [6] LXXXI, pp. 120–2.

that this barbarous custom was entirely unknown to the nomad ancestors of Israel. It may simply have been intensified by contact with the natives of Palestine.

Many theories have been propounded concerning the original meaning of these child-sacrifices. It is clear that the Semites in general regarded them as a gift made to a god or a spirit, either to win his favour, or to avert his possible enmity ; there are a few indications that these sacrifices may sometimes have involved the idea of communion. But there are no proofs that this second conception is more primitive,[1] or was more widespread in ancient times than the other.

It was also the custom from very early times, to slay adults, especially prisoners of war and criminals, with rites more or less resembling those of sacrifice. Among the pagan Arabs, captives were slain under every form of sacrifice : Theodulus, the son of St. Nilus, narrowly escaped this fate.[2] Long after the slaughter of prisoners had become a purely secular act in Arabia, the term *hadij*, sacrificed, still denoted the slain captive.[3] Similarly, the Carthaginians, after the defeat of Agathocles in 307 B.C., slew the prisoners of rank " before the altar, in front of the sacred tent." [4]

Among the Israelites, on the other hand, the conquered were only occasionally slain in a sanctuary (1 Sam. xv. 32–3), more usually on the battlefield, but before Jahweh nevertheless. The Deuteronomist uses the term *kalil*, holocaust, to describe the destruction of a rebel city (Deut. xiii. 17).

Various motives may have given rise to these ritual slayings : sometimes the purpose was to prolong the life of a chief : for instance Amenophis II and Ramses II slaughtered their prisoners in order that their name and person " might live for ever." [5] According to a suggestion of Robertson Smith, the conqueror may have occasionally substituted a captive for one of his own children whom he had vowed to his god.[6] More commonly, the slaying of the captive (as in the case of the son of St. Nilus), was the means of conveying to the god his share of the spoil, instead of the

---

[1] As Rob. Smith has upheld, with great ingenuity.
[2] *Nili opera*, **PG**, 79, p. 611.
[3] **XC**[1], p. 112.　　　　[4] **CXIV**, p. 39.
[5] **CXIV**, p. 44.
[6] *Cf.* the example quoted in **LIX**, pp. 440–2.

alternative procedure of placing the captive as a slave in the service of the temple.[1]

These motives, however, do not completely explain the earliest and most striking of these ritual slayings, the *herem*, in Greek, ἀνάδεμα. This rite, which was also practised by the Moabites,[2] corresponds exactly to the Roman, Gallic and German custom denoted by the Latin word *consecratio*, which is, moreover, the etymological meaning of the word *herem*. In war, when Israel specially desired the help of Jahweh (Num. xxi. 2–3), or sometimes even by his command, the enemy and all his belongings were dedicated to Jahweh by the ban (*herem*). In this way the enemy·and all his property became *herem*, a consecrated thing, removed from secular use. The houses were usually destroyed, and the cattle burnt. No quarter might be shown to the inhabitants. To spare one of them would be to withold his due from Jahweh, who would thereupon avenge himself by taking life for life.[3] Whoever kept back any part of the *herem*, himself fell under the ban which had been uttered : Israel became *herem* because Achan had " stolen " some of the spoil of Jericho which was *herem* ; Jahweh smote Israel until the guilty person had been destroyed (Joshua vii.).

The Romans explained the rite of *consecratio*, and its accompanying slaughter, as the devotion of the enemy to the infernal powers, the gods of the dead.[4] But this explanation cannot be primitive, since it does not account for the Semitic practice where the enemy was dedicated to the national gods.

In the historical period, no doubt, the prevailing view among the Semites was that the *herem* was intended to satisfy the anger of the god against his enemies. " I slew," said Mesha, King of Moab, " all the men of the city for a spectacle to Chemosh and to Moab." [5]

These two explanations seem to put us on the track of the original meaning of the rite : the effect of the *herem* is to release a fatal power. But the blind working of this force, which may destroy friends as well as foes, suggests

---

[1] Ezek. xliv. 7–8 ; *cf.* Num. xxxi. 25–47 ; Isaiah viii. 20.
[2] The Mesha Stone, ll, 16–7.
[3] 1 Kings xx, 38–42 ; *cf.* 1 Sam. xv. 32–3.
[4] *Dis manibus Tellurique*, Titus Livius, viii, 19.
[5] The Mesha Stone, ll. 11–12 ; *cf.* Titus Livius, viii, 9–10.

that originally it was not conceived of as personal. The *ḥerem*, no doubt, was at first regarded as a particularly efficacious curse, which, like the other curses, entered into the people and things against whom it was directed, and by its own power brought about their destruction : after the completion of the seventh magic circle drawn round Jericho—the city which had been devoted to the *ḥerem*,— the wall fell of itself. The deity, who derived no profit from this vow, only appeared at first, when the narrator brought him in, as the means by which the curse was rendered effectual.

Hence the *ḥerem* seems to have been originally a magical rite, one of the many forms of war-magic.[1]

The execution of criminals, in Israel, was conceived of more or less under the guise of the *ḥerem* (Exod. xxii. 19). It could also be thought of as a satisfaction given to Jahweh's anger, which had been aroused by the breach of some obligation of which he was the guardian. At an earlier period, no doubt, the matter was thought of somewhat differently. When some member of the tribe, by violating tribal custom, threatened the whole group with supernatural disasters, for the sake of its own safety the group was obliged to remove him from its midst, for the same reason that compelled it to remove the person who had touched the *ḥerem*. But exactly on account of those same mysterious forces by which the violator of the taboo is either threatened or already infected, the group is obliged, in removing him, to take precautions which give to his execution a character more or less resembling the rites of an apotropaic sacrifice. However, in Israel, during the historical period, the assimilation of execution to sacrifice was not complete.[2]

IV

Sacred Seasons

1. *The Feasts.* Among the feasts kept by the Israelites after their settlement in Palestine there are three whose origin can be traced back with comparative certainty to the pre-Mosaic nomadic times.

---

[1] See pp. 213–4; *cf.* **LX**, pp. 134–5.
[2] 2 Sam. xxi. 6, 9–10, 13 ; *cf.* Num. xxv. 4 ; Deut. xxi. 1–9.

(i.) *Sheep-shearing* was accompanied by feasts to which relations and friends were invited ; [1] consequently there were sacrifices, since in ancient times cattle were never killed save ritually. It was no doubt on this day that the first-fruits of the shearing of sheep and goats were brought to the *elohim*, or in historical times to Jahweh. [2]

(ii.) *The New Moon Festival.* Nearly all peoples celebrate the re-appearance of the moon. Such ceremonies must have been of special significance among the Bedouins, in whose beliefs the moon plays a great part. [3] Among the Israelites in Palestine the feast of the new moon long held an important place. [4] But the fact that it is entirely ignored by the oldest Hebrew codes [5] suggests that its non-Jahwistic character was still realized. Hosea names it among the " days of the Baals " (Hos. ii. 13–5). Apparently it was originally celebrated in honour of a lunar deity. [6] The Phenician inscription of the " accounts of Citium " speaks of the " gods of the new moon." [7] Possibly the ancient Hebrews cele-brated also a feast of the full moon, a feast which, no doubt, originally bore the name of sabbath. [8]

(iii.) *The Passover*, save for one allusion, of doubtful authenticity, in the second decalogue (Exod. xxxiv. 25), is without attestation until about the seventh century. [9] Never-theless, there can be no doubt concerning the great age of this feast. The Passover rites, as described by the Priestly Code (P), are not innovations introduced by the ritualist school of the exilic period, for they are obviously incom-patible with the tendencies characteristic of this group.

In order to find parallels to the Passover ritual as des-cribed in the Priestly Code, it is necessary to go back to the earliest forms of Semitic sacrifice, and in particular to the

---

[1] 1 Sam. xxv. 2–13 ; 2 Sam. xiii. 23–7.

[2] Deut. xviii. 4 ; Hos. ii. 7.

[3] CCV, p. 53, n. 1.

[4] 2 Kings iv. 23 ; 1 Sam. xx. 4–6, 26, 27–9 ; Amos viii. 5 ; Hos. ii. 13 ; Isa. i. 13.

[5] Book of the Covenant (Exod. xxi.–xxiii.), second and first Decalogues (Exod. xxxiv. and xx.), Deuteronomy.

[6] See pp. 238, 252.   [7] A, 3 ; B, 3.

[8] See pp. 437–440.

[9] Exod. xii. 21–3 (R[1] or R[2]) ; Deut. xvi. 1–8 ; 2 Kings xxiii. 21–3 ; Ezek. xlv. 21 ; and the texts from P (Exod. xii. 1–20) 43–9 ; Lev. xxiii. 5 ; Num. ix. 1–14 ; xxviii. 16 ; Joshua v. 10–12, etc.).

picture drawn by St. Nilus of such a ceremony as practised among the half-savage Saracens of Arabia Petraea.

The date on which the Passover was celebrated suits the conditions of a very ancient Semitic festival. The month of Radjab originally fell in the spring ; this month was one of the two sacred seasons of the pagan Arabs,[1] and also the period of great festivals among the inhabitants of Harran, and in Cyprus and Hierapolis.[2]

The fact that the meal took place within the *bayith* (house or tent) and that the circle of guests was in principle strictly limited to the family, is an almost unique feature of this feast, and sets the Passover in a class by itself among Semitic rituals.

Another very ancient feature of the Passover is the sprinkling of blood on the door-posts and the lintel—among the Bedouins, on the curtains serving as the " door " of the tent.[3]

The feast of Passover is no doubt one of the best preserved of those relics of the ancient Semitic religion which have been adopted and perpetuated by Jahwism.

Concerning the original meaning of this ceremony, before it came to be explained as a memorial of the exodus from Egypt, many divergent hypotheses have been advanced, several of which must be rejected.[4]

---

[1] **XC²**, pp. 97–9. [2] **LXXXIV**, p. 406. [3] **XV**, p. 208 ; *cf.* p. 280.
[4] The Passover could not have been either a solar festival marking the " passage " (a possible meaning of the Hebrew word *pesach*, whence are derived the Greek πασχα and the French Pâques) of the planet into the sign of the Ram (von Bohlen, *Genesis, Einl.*, pp. 140–1 ; Vatke, *Bibl. Theol.*, pp. 492 *ff.* ; Lengerke, *Kenaan*, i, pp. 381, 422)—since it was held at night,—neither was it a fertility ritual whose principal activity consisted in leaping (another meaning of the word *pesach*) in imitation of the ram leaping upon the ewes (**CLXV**, pp. 13–4), a purely hypothetical custom—neither is it an expiatory rite borrowed from the Babylonians by way of the Canaanites, and intended to " appease " (Babyl. *pasahu*) the heart of the gods (**CXCVIII**, p. 61 ; **CCLVIII**, p. 92 ; **XCIII**, p. 610),—since the victims, in the case of expiatory sacrifices, were never eaten by the worshippers. Neither could it have been an initiatory rite, as van Gennep thought (**CXXVI**, p. 56), nor the reduced form of an early human sacrifice, when the Hebrews were accustomed to offer up their first-born male children, in spite of Sir James Frazer's vivid reconstruction of the horrible scenes enacted on such an occasion (**CLXXXV**, ii, pp. 59–60 ; *cf.* **CXXVIII**, p. 37 ; **CXXIX**, pp. 32–3 ; Gressmann suggests a foundation sacrifice). For the Passover sacrifice was essentially an " eaten sacrifice," while the children offered as a sacrifice were burned among the Israelites, and buried among the Canaanites (*cf.* **LIX**, p. 231).

The most probable theory is that which regards the Passover of pre-Mosaic times as the day on which the first-born of the flock was sacrificed. In fact, in almost all the Hebrew codes, the command to offer the first-born occurs in connexion with the regulations for the Passover or the feast of unleavened bread.[1] According to the earliest tradition, the Israelites wished to go out of Egypt in order to keep a feast to Jahweh. If this feast was that on which the first-born were offered to God, it yields a satisfactory explanation of the tenth plague : Jahweh takes the first-born of the Egyptians and of their cattle in exchange for those of the flocks which the Hebrews are prevented from offering to him. It is true that the Book of the Covenant excludes even the possibility of a feast at which all the first-born of the year may be sacrificed together, since it prescribes that each first-born is to be offered eight days after its birth (Exod. xxii. 29). But the same code also ignores the Passover. Hence we may assume that the old custom of holding a feast at which the yearly produce of the flock was offered, had, by the ninth century, lapsed into a local custom, only preserved in certain districts, such as Judah, where the pastoral mode of life had survived, and that it did not regain its character of a national religious ceremony until the Judæan code of Deuteronomy.

There are grounds for believing that among the pagan Arabs the festival rites of the month of Radjab included the offering of first-born.[2] Even today, among the Amur Arabs the slaying of the first-born of the flock is the occasion for a great feast.[3] Moreover, they do not eat the first-born of each animal, but the first lamb of each flock of sheep and the first kid of each flock of goats.[4] This may also have been the practice of the nomad Hebrews.

In any case, the blood of the victim was used to protect the house against misfortune, especially, no doubt, against epidemics.[5] A similar rite is practised with the same purpose in Arabia, Syria, Palestine,[6] and also among many peoples

---

[1] Exod. xxxiv. 18–20 ; Deut. xv. 19–20 and xvi. 1–8 ; Exod. xii. and xiii.

[2] **LXXXIV**, pp. 227, 228, 465.

[3] **XV**, p. 205.   [4] **CCIV**, p. 366.

[5] *Cf.* for example, **LXII**, p. 49.

[6] See, for example, **XV**, pp. 201, 206, 229 ; **CLXXVIII**, i. p. 499.

of Africa and America.[1] This is the idea, so strikingly expressed by the priestly narrative when it depicts Jahweh as going through the land of Egypt and slaying the first-born in every house on the door of which he did not see the blood (Exod. xii. 12–3). It is probably this apotropaic rite which has given its name to the feast, since the verb *pasaḥ*, from which *pesaḥ* is derived, may mean " to spare."

This use of the blood of the victim as a protection would in no wise prevent the feast from being also the day of the offering of the first-born. On the contrary, the slaying of the first-born is in essence also a rite of preservation : its purpose was to avert the vengeance of the *baal*, the divine owner of the flock, or—the more ancient conception—to guard against the discharge of divine energy displayed in the life of the cattle. In any case, the combination of the slaying of the first-born and the apotropaic use of the blood seems to occur among certain modern Bedouins.

" The Beni Hamide . . . say that the first-born of the sheep belong to Nebi Musa. . . . He who is able brings the victim himself to the sanctuary ; otherwise it is slain in the tent in the name of the saint. . . . Usually some of the blood of the slain animals is sprinkled on the flock for ' the blessing,' in order to protect the offerer from all evil." [2]

It has been supposed that the Passover sacrifice was originally offered to a lunar deity,[3] because the victim had to be slain at sun-down and wholly consumed before the morning, because the feast was observed, at least before the exile, on the night of full moon (the 14th of Nisan), and because all ancient peoples ascribed to that planet a decisive influence on birth (Deut. xxxiii. 14). It should be noted, on the other hand, that the feast was held *inside* the house —or tent—and that *it was expressly forbidden to go out of the house until the morning* (Exod. xii. 22) ; it was not held, as might have been expected if its object was a lunar deity, in the open air, in the light of the moon. This consideration would rather lead us to suppose that the sacrifice was offeerd to a household god, to the genius of the house.

However, it seems more probable that originally the Passover was not a *propitiatory* rite, intended to appease

---

[1] *Cf.* Marillier, **RHR**, xxxvii, pp. 222, 351 ; Epiphanius, *Haer.*, xviii, 3.

[2] **XV**, p. 204.

[3] **LXXXV**, p. 173 ; **CLXV**, pp. 14–5 ; **IV**, p. 152.

some divinity. Its purpose was, no doubt, as in the case of all the rites relating to firstfruits, to enable the possessor to partake freely and without danger of the new produce— in this case, of the young lambs and kids—without offending or driving away the spirit of the flock, which causes it to multiply. To this end the usual procedure is followed : it is assumed that this spirit is concentrated—or it is concentrated by means of certain rites—in the first animal of the season to be born : this animal is then killed in order to remove the spirit from the rest of the new brood, hence the necessity of eating it entirely. But it is slain with infinite precautions, with a certain anxiety, gathering all the members of the group, as though to share the responsibility of the fatal act. The blood is kept with special care and none of the bones may be broken, in order that the spirit may be reborn and the future fertility of the flock be secured.[1] In this sense we may agree with Mowinckel [2] when he says that in its origin Passover seems to have belonged to the class of rites concerned with a dying and rising god.

It will easily be understood that to these rites, magical rather than expiatory, others similar to them came to be added, intended to protect the flock and the house from all possible disasters in the course of the new year. Hence we have, not only the blood on the door, but also, perhaps, the eating of bitter herbs (Exod. xii. 8 ; Num. ix. 11). At the festival of the dead, in ancient Greece, it was customary to chew buckthorn and bay leaves to prevent demons from entering.[3] Even in the eighteenth century modern Greeks thought of the plague as a horrible spectre which, during the night, marked with an indelible sign the houses which it would enter ; but they believed that the one means of warding off its visit was the eating of garlic.[4]

2. *War-time*.[5] For the Jahwist Israelite of historical times, war-time was a sacred season in the strictest sense of the term. On the battle-field the Israelite felt that he was in the presence of Jahweh quite as much as when he entered a holy place.[6] Before and during a campaign he

---

[1] **LIX,** pp. 229–31.   [2] **LXX,** ii, p. 37.
[3] Beer, **ZATW,** 1911, pp. 152–3.
[4] Guys, *Voyage littéraire de la Grèce*, 1771.
[5] *Cf.* **CCXXXVI.**   [6] See pp. 462–3.

was obliged to observe those forms of abstinence which were
connected with sanctification (1 Sam. xxi. 2–7 ; 2 Sam. xi. 11).
Hence the warriors were called " the sanctified ones " of
Jahweh (Isa. xiii. 3). The Hebrew expression for " to
begin a campaign " was " to hallow a war." The camp
was treated as a sacred enclosure : those who were ritually
unclean had to leave it, nor was it permissible to satisfy
the needs of nature there, for, as the Deuteronomist explains
" Jahweh thy god walketh in the midst of thy camp . . .
therefore shall thy camp be holy : that he see no unclean
thing in thee, and turn away from thee " (Deut. xxiii. 14).
The list of the assembly of the servants of Jahweh was
indistinguishable from that of the men of war who could
bear arms : a man might be excluded from the latter for
ritual reasons and from the former for military reasons.

But there are grounds for thinking that these rules are
not all the product of Jahwism, based on the fundamental
principle of that religion that the will of the national god is
identical with the interests of his people. In fact, many of
these customs present a detailed resemblance to those of
widely differing peoples. Among uncivilized tribes the
warrior is surrounded by a network of the most intricate
and meticulous taboos.[1] And the purpose of these prohibitions seems to be not so much to fit him to live in contact
with the god or gods of the tribe present in the camp, as
to protect him against the hostile spirits and magical powers
set in motion against him by the enemy, or against the
wrathful spirits of the warriors whom he has slain ; it is
also necessary to protect the rest of the tribe from the contagion of the perilous influence emanating from the warrior.
He is forbidden, for instance, to touch his own body with
his hands, even for the purpose of scratching himself,
since the hands are soon contaminated ; he must eat out of
special vessels, refrain from sexual intercourse, like the
Hebrews, and observe rules of cleanliness entirely similar to
theirs.

It is possible that taboos of this nature may explain the
remarkable exemptions from military service laid down in
Deuteronomy xx. 1–9 ; xxiv. 5. They have often been
regarded as ideal provisions inspired by a sentimental

[1] *Cf.* **CLXXXV**, i, pp. 251–60.

humanitarianism; but they may be ancient Hebrew or Canaanite prescriptions whose original intention was to remove from the army those who were specially threatened by invisible powers. It is well known that among many peoples it is believed that evil spirits haunt the betrothed and the newly-married [1]; the man who has planted a vine is under the power of the spirit of the vine, so long as the latter has not been secularized, *i.e.* in the fourth year. Possibly the fearful were sent out of the camp because they were believed to be bewitched by the enemy.

According to the Priestly Code, at the end of a campaign the men who have slain anyone must purify themselves, their prisoners and their spoil, on the third and the seventh day; metal objects must be passed through the fire (Num. xxxi. 19–24). Similar customs are found among many non-civilized peoples, especially among the Basutos, who say that otherwise " the ghosts of their victims would haunt them incessantly and disturb their sleep." [2]

V

SACRED PERSONS

1. *Priests.* It is probable that the Hebrew tribes already possessed priests before the founding of the national religion. Indeed, the institution of the priesthood is found among all the ancient Semitic peoples, including nomads like the Midianites [3] and the pre-Islamic Arabs. [4] There was a priest among the Saracens of Sinai, [5] a priest and a priestess at Phoinikon [6] and also at el-Ela. [7]

The Arab priest was called *sadin* or *hadjib*. His duty was to supervise the sanctuary. His presence was not essential for the offering of sacrifices. The priesthood was hereditary. It was often held by nobles who owned the sanctuary; sometimes even by princes of the nation (among

---

[1] Tobit vi. 8; on the Arabs, **CCXLI**, pp. 2, 123; **XC²**, p. 155, n. 4.
[2] **CLXXIII**, p. 273; *cf.* **CLXXXV**, i, pp. 260–7.
[3] Exod. iii. 1.
[4] **XC²**, pp. 130–4; **XXX**, pp. 100–7.
[5] *Itinerarium beati Antonini Martyris*, 1640, p. 28, *Acta Sanct.*, Mai, t. ii.
[6] Agatharchides (about 130 B.C.), in Diod., Sic., iii, 42–3.
[7] *Minean Inscriptions. Cf.* p. 442, n. 1.

the Itureans and the Palmyrenes). There is evidence to show that among the ancient Arabs the priests were in the habit of giving oracles. Their chief means of consulting the deity was the *istiqsam* (a word derived from *qasam*, meaning, in Hebrew, to divine); blunt arrows, perhaps of different colours, were used for this purpose [1] : by the arrow which came out it was decided whether the god's answer was in the negative or the affirmative, or which of two courses he favoured. At Mecca it was the priest who kept the sacred arrows ; in order to consult them it was necessary to pay 100 dirhem and to sacrifice a camel. Elsewhere the oracle was given by a voice which was heard by the priest or by the consultant, who spent the night in the holy place for the purpose. [2]

The Arab *sadin* closely resembles the Israelite priest, not as he is depicted by the Levitical law, that codification of the rights and claims of the Jewish priesthood in the age of the second temple, but as he appears in the earliest documents of Hebrew history. In those early days the priest was a person of no social standing and without political influence ; sacrifices could be offered without him ; his two chief duties were to supervise the sanctuary and to consult the god ; it was no doubt in virtue of his office of adviser that he bore the title of "father." [3] He asked counsel of Jahweh by a procedure very similar to the Arab *istiqsam* : by the drawing of the lot the priest asked Jahweh to give *urim* or *thummim*. [4] The oracle given by the priests was called *torah*, a word apparently derived from the Hebrew *yarah*, to throw—cast the lot —rather than from the Babylonian *tertu*, omen. [5] The Israelites were also familiar with revelations by means of *incubatio*, [6] and it must have been the special prerogative of the priests, since they slept in the sanctuary, to receive the divine communication in this way. [7]

The priestly functions were often hereditary, but the rule was by no means absolute. [8]

The close similarity between the early Israelite *kohen*

[1] B. Hisam, p. 94.   [2] **XXX**, p. 105.
[3] Judges xviii. 10, 19 ; *cf.* **LXII**, p. 54.
[4] 1 Sam. xiv. 41 (Sept.).   [5] Haupt, Zimmern.
[6] Gen. xxviii. 10–22 ; 1 Kings iii. 4–15 ; Gen. xxvi. 24–5 ; xlvi. 1b–5a ; Strabo, *Geogr.*, xvi, 35 ; *cf.* Isa. lxv. 4.
[7] 1 Sam. iii. 1–18.   [8] See p. 441.

and the Arab *sadin* is a strong argument in favour of the extreme antiquity of the priesthood among the Hebrews.

Similarly in the East today the *welis* are actual priests, called *sheikhs* or servants of the saint. Their title is hereditary. They receive a quarter of the victim and various dues differing according to the locality. It is not their duty to slay the sacrifices, although they will do it if the offerer desires it. Their principal functions are to supervise the sanctuary and to preserve the legends concerning the origin of the holy place and the life of the *weli* : the sheikhs, too, like other holy persons, practise the rite of exorcism.[1]

The primary object of the priesthood was, no doubt, to provide the god with a permanent attendant. This would be the literal meaning of the word *kohen*, if we may regard it as related to the verb *kun*, which means " to stand," be present at. The priest's office was called *'abodah*, a slave's service.

Such an individual, continually at the disposal of the god, was at the same time extremely useful to the tribe. All the evidence goes to show that his chief duty was originally to communicate the will of the god to the tribe. The priest was regarded as a kind of " diviner " ; he was a diviner attached to a sanctuary. In Arabic the word *kahin*, corresponding to the Hebrew *kohen*, denotes the diviner, the seer. Among the Babylonians, the various types of divination were practised and even, apparently, monopolized by the priests. In Israel, the priest obtained oracles, not only by use of the ephod for *urim* and *thummim*, but also by inspiration : there were inspired priests even after the exile.[2] Moses,[3] Aaron[4] and Samuel[5] are represented as having been both priests and prophets or seers. Even in the Jewish period and up to the Christian era, it was believed that the priest, especially the high priest, often received divine revelations, particularly when he officiated.[6]

[1] **XV**, pp. 165, 173.
[2] *Cf.* **LXX**, iii.
[3] Deut. xxxiii. 4, 8–10 ; Judges xviii. 30. Num. xii. 6–8 ; Deut. xxxiv. 10 ; Hos. xii. 14.
[4] Exod. iv. 14 ; Num. xii. 2.
[5] 1 Sam. i.–iii.
[6] John Hyrcanus (Josephus, A. J., xiii, 299–300 ; B. J., i, 69) ; Zacharias (Luke i. 11, 22) ; Caiaphas (John xi. 51 ; xviii. 14) ; Josephus (B. J., iii, 352–3, 400–1 ; iv, 625) ; *Cf.* **CCLII**, p. 134.

It was originally supposed, no doubt, that the priest was naturally possessed of divine knowledge, because living as he did, in daily contact with the deity, he necessarily became permeated by supernatural powers. It was for this reason that the person of the priest was inviolable, his blessing or his curse were specially efficacious, and that he was capable of interceding with the god or driving away evil powers.[1]

2. *Ecstatics, Diviners and Magicians.* In addition to the priests, the Hebrews must also have had, from pre-Mosaic times, other " men of God," whose superhuman power and foresight were regarded as belonging, not to the place where they exercised their activities, but to their own individuality. The ancient Arabs possessed the *kahin,* or diviner, as well as the *sadin,* or priest.

In Israel, during the historical period, these privileged possessors of supernatural power or knowledge constituted three classes, sharply differentiated in theory : ecstatics, interpreters of omens, and magicians. Ecstatics and interpreters of omens merely professed to make known the divine will, the former having learnt it by a direct revelation, being what the Greeks called τὸ ἄτεχνον καὶ ἀδίδακτον γένος (μαντέιας), while the latter acquired their knowledge of the secrets of the future by the observation of certain omens —τὸ τεχνικὸν γένος. Magicians, on the other hand, claimed to be able to act, by a kind of irresistible compulsion, either directly on the course of things, or indirectly, by influencing the gods or the spirits who control the course of things.

In practice the boundaries between these different classes were much less sharply marked than in theory. From the end of the monarchy, inspiration was the only mode of communication of the divine will recognized as legitimate by the official representatives of Jahwism ; [2] but it must not be supposed that prophecy was confined to Jahwism. The Edomites, Moabites, Ammonites and Phenicians all possessed ecstatics who were described as prophets (Jer. xxvii. 9). Balaam, the Ammonite or Aramean diviner is depicted as an ecstatic (Num. xxiv. 4, 16). Wen Amon (twelfth century) relates that at Byblos, that is, in Phenicia, during the per-

---

[1] The Babylonian *asipu* ; the modern sheikh ; *cf.* Lev. iv. 4–7, 49–53 ; xvi. 20–2.

[2] For example, Deut. xviii. 9–19.

formance of a sacrifice, a young nobleman was possessed by the god, fell into a trance and began to prophesy.[1]

The important part played in the history of Israel by inspired women [2] also suggests that prophetism was not the product of Jahwism, a religion whose active membership was entirely composed of warriors.

It is often supposed that it was not until after they came into contact with the Canaanites in Palestine that the Hebrews learnt and adopted this method of consulting the deity.[3] But it is hardly likely that so universal a phenomenon as " inspiration " should have been unknown to the Hebrews before their entry into a civilized country. The manner in which the Israelites conceived of inspiration (possession by a spirit or permeation by an impersonal spiritual force), the manner in which they explained visions (the carrying away of the seer, either in or out of the body, or second sight), the practices employed to induce the spirit to enter the inspired person (sacrifices, *incubatio*, music, dancing, fasting, the use of intoxicants) all resemble those found among many " primitives." Among the ancient Arabs the *kahin* was supposed to be instructed by a demon whom they called a companion (*sahib*). He was the supernatural being who spoke by the mouth of the *kahin*. The Arab seers uttered their revelations in verse, this being the language of the ecstatic state.

The most that can be admitted is that certain forms of prophetism, especially the phenomena of collective inspiration, were developed in Israel in imitation of the Canaanites : the Phenician Baal of Tyre had bands of prophets (1 Kings xviii. ; 2 Kings iii. 13 ; x. 19). Yet even examples of this kind of inspiration are related by the Israelite tradition to have already occurred in the wilderness (Num. ii. 25–30). The dances performed in the holy places, and the cries uttered before the god, as we have seen, can best be explained as the phenomena of possession : it is the god entering into the worshippers.[4]

Moreover, the Israelites believed in signs and omens. A favourable or unfavourable omen might be drawn from the

[1] See p. 103.
[2] Miriam (Exod. xv. 20–1 ; Num. xii. 2–15), Deborah (Judges iv.–v.), Huldah (2 Kings xxii. 14–20). *Cf.* **LXXXV**, p. 125.
[3] **XXX**.   [4] See p. 276.

first word uttered by a person whom one expected to meet,[1] or from a chance occurrence happening at a critical moment,[2] especially if such an occurrence had been asked for or announced beforehand.[3] Still more were unusual events regarded as divine forecasts of the future (Judges vi. 36–40), especially those which preceded or accompanied births,[4] these formed the subject of a highly developed branch of the science of divination among the Babylonians and the Romans. Dreams partook of the character, both of visions, since the same explanation was given of them (cf. Gen. xx. 3), and of signs, since both often required to be interpreted. They could be induced, for instance, by sleeping in a holy place.[5] There were professional dreamers.[6] There were also men who specialized in the interpretation of dreams : among the Israelites, however, this was not, as among the Egyptians or the Assyrians, a science which could be learnt, but a personal gift from God.[7]

The lot was supposed to give information concerning the divine will.[8] We read in Proverbs xvi. 33 :

"The lot is cast into the lap :
    but the whole disposing thereof is of the Lord."

We do not know exactly the mechanical method by which the Israelites consulted the lot : the nature of the *ephod*, the *teraphim*, and the *urim* and *thummim*, is, in fact, an obscure and controversial matter.[9] Arrows seem to have been used.[10]

Other means of foretelling the future consisted in the use of the divining-rod [11] and the cup (Gen. xliv. 5). The manner of using the latter was, no doubt, by observing the patterns formed by oil dropped into water, as was the custom in Babylonia.[12] Perhaps the Israelites, like certain natives of

---

[1] 1 Sam. xiv. 8–12 ; 1 Kings xx. 32–3.
[2] Gen. xxvii. 20 ; 1 Sam. xv. 27–8.
[3] Gen. xxiv. 12–14 ; 1. Sam. x. 2–10.
[4] Gen. xxv. 22–3, cf. 25–6 ; xxxviii. 27–30.
[5] Cf. p. 297.
[6] Deut. xiii. 2, 4, 6 ; Jer. xxiii. 25 ; cf. Gen. xxxvii. 19 ; 1 Sam. xxviii. 6.
[7] Gen. xl. 8 ; xli. 15–6 ; cf. Dan. ii. 30.
[8] Joshua vii. 16–8 ; 1 Sam. x. 20–2 ; Jonah i. 7 ; Acts i. 23–6 ; Josephus, B. J., iv, 3–8.
[9] See pp. 429–31.
[10] Ezek. xxi. 26 ; cf. 1 Sam. xx. 20–2 ; 2 Kings xiii. 14–9.
[11] Hos. iv. 12 ; Num. xxi. 18.   [12] **XXXIV,** ii, pp. 749–75.

New Guinea, observed the manner in which the water poured out of a boiling cauldron (Jer. i. 13–6) in order to forecast the result of a campaign.[1]

Animals were supposed to be more sensitive than men to the presence and desires of unseen powers (Num. xxii. 22–33 ; 1 Sam. vi. 7–12). In early times many animals were considered to be divine beings.[2] Hence their actions were observed in order to obtain oracles. This was no doubt one of the reasons for charming serpents. The usual word meaning " to divine," *niḥesh*, seems to be related to the word for " serpent," *naḥash*. The Israelites knew and probably practised [3] to some extent the inspection of the entrails of victims, the method of divination raised by the Babylonians into a kind of science, and borrowed from them by the Hittites, the Greeks, the Etruscans and the Romans. In any case the Israelites considered the liver as one of the abodes of the soul, and they had tokens by which they knew whether a sacrifice was acceptable or not ; [4] they drew omens from incidents which happened during the ceremony (Gen. xv. 11–4).

They possessed at least the rudiments of astrological lore. Eclipses, and any unusual appearance of the sun or the moon were regarded as sinister omens.[5] According to Genesis i. 14, the stars were created to serve as " signs " for man. A dangerous influence was ascribed to the planet Mars if the poet's metaphor in Canticles vi. 10 should be read " terrible as Nergal." [6]

In the historical period these signs were usually regarded as the manner in which Jahweh revealed his purposes. But in several of the recorded instances it is clear that the presage was originally regarded as the cause of the event foretold, or more accurately, as a part of the event itself. Hence, by rendering a dangerous omen abortive, it was supposed to be possible to avoid the misfortune which it presaged. By driving away the birds of prey which descended upon the victims, Abraham averted the disaster which threatened his posterity (Gen. xv. 11–14).

---

[1] LII, pp. 215–16. [2] See pp. 246–9.
[3] Ezek. xxi. 26. [4] Gen. iv. 4–5 ; Ps. v. 4 ; xx. 4–7.
[5] Joel iii. 3–4 (ii. 30–31).
[6] Reading *kenergal* or *kenergálôth* (XCI, i, pp. 3, 293 ; CLXXIX, pp. 50, 98).

There are numbers, such as the number seven, which are inherently lucky. There are fortunate days and days which are cursed.[1] The left side is "sinister" and the right is favourable.[2]

The ordeal is not merely an oracle by which God reveals the guilty person: it is the unleashing of a power which automatically smites the criminal.[3]

The arrows of Elisha served to foretell the issue of the campaign, but at the same time they served the more important end of a propitious influence on the future.[4]

These examples show how closely omens were allied to magic among the Israelites, as among other peoples. This explains why Jahwism ultimately condemned the use of divination as derogatory to the sovereignty of God.

This belief in signs, and many of the practices in which it was expressed in Israel during the historical period, must go back to pre-Mosaic times. For similar facts are common among the modern Bedouins as among the ancient Arabs. We know the use which the latter made of divinatory arrows.[5]

There was no great difference between the interpreters of signs and magicians. After what has been said about the diffusion of magical conceptions among the ancient Hebrews,[6] it is unnecessary to multiply proofs that the magicians were people who were regarded as having the power to influence the course of events, and who made use of this power, either to do harm—as the sorcerers, who were dreaded and regarded with disapproval—or who used their power openly for the benefit of the community, as Balaam, for instance, is represented as doing.

3. *The Chiefs.* Among peoples who have this belief in "men of God," the political and military leadership of the tribe or nation is usually in the hands of one of these individuals endowed with a particularly powerful *mana*.[7] Almost everywhere the chief controls the sun and the rain. Rules of etiquette are the outcome of taboos which surround this being

---

[1] For example Jer. xx. 14 ; Job. iii. 3–10.
[2] Ps. cx. 1 ;. 1 Kings ii. 19 ; Matt. xxv. 33–4, 41 ; Deut. xi. 29–30 ; xxvii. 11–13 ; Joshua viii. 33 ; Gen. xxxv. 18.
[3] See pp. 213–4.
[4] 2 Kings xiii. 18–19 ; see p. 212.
[5] See p. 297.   [6] See pp. 211–17.
[7] *Cf.* **CLXXXV**, i, pp. 145–86.

whose slightest act may shake the world. Hence arises the deification of monarchs, and the class of priest-kings.

Among the Hebrew tribes chiefs were regarded as possessing supernatural powers of this kind. The emblem of their rank was a rod (Judges v. 14), the prototype of the royal sceptre (Gen. xlix. 10). This object was so significant, that the usual designation of a tribe was by the words for " rod " or " staff " (*maṭṭeh, shebeṭ*). The sceptre was supposed to have supernatural powers ; with their staves the chiefs " digged the well," like sorcerers with their wands (Num. xxi. 18). Moses and Joshua secured victory for their armies, the former by stretching out his rod, the latter by extending his spear, in the direction of the enemy ; [1] the spear, too, might serve as a sign of royalty.[2] It was Joshua also who commanded the sun and the moon and they obeyed him.[3]

The chief possesses knowledge above the lot of common men. Joseph, having become vizier of Egypt, says to his brethren : " Wot ye not that such a man as I can certainly divine ? "[4]

Moreover, similar beliefs and practices are found among the other nomad Semites. The Bedouins will take as war-chief a child rather than an experienced elder, if the former belongs to a family possessing the *barakah*.[5] Certain Arab tribes have priest-kings : the Nabateans had deified kings. We are told of an Arab chieftain who tore his garments every night lest anyone should incur the extreme risk of wearing them.[6]

Hence we must dismiss the still very prevalent idea that one of the permanent characteristics of the Semitic race was that it had created an impassable gulf between the deity and man. Such a conception is neither true of remote antiquity, with its divine men and its deified kings and dead, nor of the popular religion of the modern Orient, which obliterates the dividing-line between the divine and the human spheres, in its worship of dead welis and living marabouts. The sharp, absolute distinction between God who is all and man who is nought, is above all a product of the monotheism of the

---

[1] Exod. xvii. 9–13 ; Joshua viii. 18–26 ; see p. 212.
[2] 1 Sam. xxii. 6. [3] Joshua x. 12–13 ; *cf.* **CCXXX.**
[4] Gen. xliv. 15 ; *cf.* Jer. xviii. 18 ; Ezek. vii. 26 ; Lam. ii. 9.
[5] **CLXX,** iii, pp. 214–19. [6] **LXXXIV,** p. 452.

Israelite prophets ; whence it has passed into the three great religions sprung from this common source, Judaism, Christianity and Islam, in which, however, it has found a very unequal expression.

4. *The Nazirites.* When the ancient Arab was under the obligation of a blood-feud, he might neither comb his hair, wash, nor drink wine until his vow was accomplished.[1] During a period of pilgrimage, that is, when he had made a vow to offer a sacrifice, he might neither shave his head, nor pluck a hair from his body, nor cut a nail. This rule is still observed by the Moslem hadji.[2] Even now, when the Fuqara Bedouins undertake a campaign or a raid, they undo their hair ; it is said of anyone who is preparing to take part in an expedition : " he has untied his hair."[3] We may infer from the first verse of the ancient poem on the victory of Deborah, according to the most probable interpretation, that the Israelites observed the same custom, evidently an inheritance from nomad times (Judges v. 2) :

" Because, in Israel, (the warriors) have let down their hair ;
    because an army of volunteers has offered itself, bless ye Jahweh."

There seems to be evidence for the existence of similar practices among neighbouring peoples.[4]

The *Naziriteship* of the Israelites, after their settlement in Palestine, was probably a particular application of these ancient rules, but, unfortunately, we possess little information concerning the stages through which this institution seems to have passed.

The early fragment which forms the first part of the story of Samson, although it was not part of the original tradition concerning the hero,[5] suggests that, at the time when the story was taking shape, the *Nazirite* was a man who had dedicated himself to Jahweh for life—he might even have been dedicated thus before his birth,—in order that Jahweh might take possession of him, impart his spirit to him,[6] and perhaps endow him with a special share of his own supernatural power in view of struggles in which the tribe or

---

[1] **XC²**, p. 122.   [2] **CLXXXIX**, pp. 185, 186 ; **XC²**, p. 122.
[3] **CCV**, p. 73.   [4] Deut. xxxii. 42 ; Ps. lxviii. 22.
[5] **LVII**, pp. 505, 511–12.
[6] Similarly in the case of Samuel (1 Sam. i. 11) and John the Baptist(Luke i. 15).

I.   X

the nation might be engaged. If the Nazirites were men who placed themselves at the disposal of Jahweh, to be possessed by him, the warrior god of Israel, it is easy to understand that their presence in an army constituted a pledge of victory, and that men might well praise Jahweh for having raised up his " consecrated ones " with their flying hair.[1]

This primitive type of Nazirite has been rightly compared with the Norse berserkers, those " men of Odin," who " charged without breastplate," who " raged like dogs and wolves, bit their bucklers, were stronger than bears and bulls ; they smote down their enemies, but neither fire nor steel could harm them."[2]

The abstinence imposed upon the Nazirite is best explained by the presence in him of a divine power : similar restrictions are everywhere imposed upon those who are in special contact with supernatural powers. The prohibition relating to the hair—the favourite abode of spirits and magical influences[3] —is often laid upon those who are in mourning,[4] because they are in contact with the spirit of the dead ; in Israel it was enforced in the case of the leper and the woman undergoing the ordeal, since both were possessed by an evil power.[5]

The reason why the Nazirite was forbidden to drink wine was, no doubt, because drunkenness was regarded as a form of possession,[6] and that by another spirit than Jahweh's, the god of the desert.[7] The same restriction was imposed upon the avenger of blood among the Arabs,[8] upon the Jewish priest when he was about to officiate,[9] upon the Flamen Dialis at Rome,[10] and upon the kings of Egypt.[11] Hence the taboos observed by the Nazirite must originally have been simply the result of his consecrated condition.[12]

[1] Amos ii. 11 ; cf. Judges v. 2.   [2] CCXXXVI, pp. 101–2.
[3] CXCVII, iii, pp. 112 ff. ; CLXXXV, i, pp. 295–315 ; LVIII, i, p. 131 ; CCLXXI, pp. 272–3.
[4] So in Israel, Lev. x. 6 ; xxi. 10.
[5] Lev. xiii. 45 ; Num. v. 18 ; cf. LVIII, i, pp. 133–6 ; CCXXXVI, pp. 69–74.
[6] Cf. Prov. xx. 1.   [7] See pp. 283, 410–1.   [8] XC², p. 122.
[9] Lev. x. 9 ; Ezek. xliy. 21.
[10] Plutarch, Quaest, rom., c. 112.
[11] Plutarch, De Iside et Osiride, 6.
[12] It is often stated that the reason why the Nazirite refrained from cutting his hair was because he had made a vow to sacrifice it to Jahweh (e.g. III, pp. 357–8). But this is to deny the historicity of the lifelong Naziriteship. If the man who had become a temporary

Subsequently the connexion of the Naziriteship with war disappeared ; then the practical value of such vows for Israel, still recognized by Amos (eighth century), was forgotten. In the priestly code (sixth and fifth centuries), the Naziriteship had come to be regarded simply as a mode of life pleasing to Jahweh, without any ostensible reason : it was a pious and meritorious act to become a Nazirite for a time ; it was a vow like any other (Num. vi.).

CONCLUSION

It appears from our inquiry that, in spite of the scarcity of contemporary documents, we are better informed than we might have expected concerning the religious condition of the Hebrew tribes before the foundation of their national religion. Indeed, many of the beliefs of these remote times persisted down to better documented periods, either incorporated in the new religion, or as survivals, tolerated or resisted by it. As for the religious practices, they continued almost unchanged : the forms of Israelite and Jewish worship are almost all the heritage of primitive Semitism. This gives us a clue to the work of the founder of the national religion : it did not consist in the introduction of new rites, but in the infusion of a new spirit into immemorial customs. On the other hand, it was to be anticipated that in spite of the efforts made to change their meaning, these practices involved the persistence in the new religion, of many ideas and feelings belonging to earlier stages.

Nazirite cast his hair into the fire of the altar (Num. vi. 18), it was rather to ensure the complete destruction of the " sacred thing " in order to prevent it from being defiled (cf. **XIX**, p. 203). On the completion of his pilgrimage, the Moslem hadji is supposed to bury his hair which he has cut off (**CLXXXIX**, p. 294). A more usual explanation is that the Nazirites, like the Rechabites, refrained from wine in order to protest against Canaanite culture and to proclaim a return to nomad customs (**IV**, pp. 157, 207, 263, 399 ; **XLV**, p. 250). The Nazirite rule may have been interpreted in this way (Amos ii. 12) ; but it cannot have the original meaning of the institution. There is no indication that the Nazirites ever formed an " order " like the Rechabites (**XLV**, p. 250).

CHAPTER III

THE JAHWISM OF THE NOMAD PERIOD

. I

THE WORK OF MOSES

WE have no certain evidence concerning the activities
of Moses. It is true that some scholars claim to
have found his name, together with biographical information,
in the inscriptions discovered at Serabit el-Hadim, in the
Sinai peninsula.[1] But their readings vary considerably, and
their interpretations of them still more so. The decipherment
of these signs is, for the present, too uncertain to rest any
conclusions upon such hypothetical data.[2]

Sellin claims to have found in certain passages of Hosea,[3]
the traces of a tradition differing widely from the accepted
version; according to this tradition Moses died a martyr,
slain by the priests who destroyed almost entirely the religion
which he had founded.[4] In order to arrive at these para-
doxical conclusions, it is necessary to subject passages which
are in any case very obscure to extensive and wholly conjectural emendations.[5]

The narratives of the Pentateuch relating to the most
distinctive period of the national religion have been, even
more than the rest, recast, idealized and enlarged in the
course of the centuries, as each successive generation of
historians referred back to the founder those principles, laws
or institutions which they considered essential to the national
religion.

[1] For example, **CXXXI** ; **CLXII** ; D. Völter, **NTT**, 1925, pp. 215–44.
[2] See pp. 76–7.
[3] iv. 4–9 ; v. 1–4 ; vii. 3–7 ; ix. 7–11 ; xii. 15–13, 1.
[4] **CCXXXVII** ; **ZATW**, 1928, pp. 26–33.
[5] *Cf.* L. Bauer, **NKZ**, 1927, pp. 817–18 ; J. Weill, **REJ**, 1929,
pp. 89–93.

No part of the Pentateuch can be carried back with certainty to the Mosaic age, not even the Decalogue.[1]

Owing to the lack of contemporary documents it is very
hard to say with any certainty who Moses was and what
he did. It is impossible to escape the conviction that at the
beginning of the age-long process of idealizing the tradition
there must have been a dominant personality. As soon as
we rise above the lower levels of civilization we find that
forceful individuals have usually been the determining
factors in the religious life of the peoples. The attempts
which have been made to dissolve the figure of Moses into a
purely mythical supernatural personage [2] have not been
successful.

But the greater the strength and originality of a personality, the more difficult, not to say impossible, it becomes to
reconstruct it by inductive methods. In such a case nothing
can take the place of contemporary evidence. Unless we
are willing to step outside the realm of certainly attested
facts, all that can be done is to reconstruct those parts of his
work whose consequences can still be traced in the age to
which our first reliable documents belong. This is the task
which we shall attempt in the case of Moses, but we must not
hide from ourselves the fact that the picture which will emerge
from our efforts may be extremely imperfect, as it would be,
for example, in the case of the figure of Jesus, if we possessed
no other material on which to depend for its reconstruction
save the evidence for the beliefs and practices of the Christians
of the third or fourth centuries.

The earliest considerable fragment of Hebrew literature,
the poem describing the victory of Deborah and Barak over
Sisera the Canaanite (Judges v.), gives us a picture of the state
of the Israelite tribes shortly after their settlement in Palestine : we see them living in a condition of almost complete
anarchy ; each tribe does what it pleases, takes part in the
campaign or remains neutral. Nevertheless, in spite of this
entire absence of any visible unity, they are conscious of being
one people. This national consciousness could not have
arisen in the course of, and as a result of, their settlement
in Canaan ; for there was no united conquest of the country,

[1] See appendix, pp. 315-6.
[2] For example, CCLI, pp. 65-95.

but a gradual infiltration of isolated tribes (Judges i.). Hence the national consciousness of Israel must have been the product of an earlier time, of the Mosaic age.

Another point brought out by the poem is that this intense national feeling was closely linked up with the belief in Jahweh. It is Jahweh whom the poet praises as he celebrates the victory of Israel. Jahweh himself came from Seir ; it is he who makes war ; Sisera and his army are his enemies ; the Israelites who volunteered in answer to the appeal of the prophetess came " to the help of Jahweh among the mighty " (Judges v. 23).

Hence we find a very real national consciousness, although it had not taken shape in any central political organization, and on the other hand, a religion which is essentially national. These two facts are naturally explained by the events of the Mosaic period, and especially by the personal activity of Moses, as far as they can be seen through the poetic mist of the tradition.

Before he arose, the various Hebrew tribes felt, no doubt, that they belonged to one race, but did not yet constitute a people. Then came the Egyptian bondage. The tradition represents Moses, even before the liberation, as a patriot, deeply touched by the afflictions of his brethren (Exod. ii. 11, 15). There grew up in him the conviction that, in their distress, his oppressed people could rely on the help of a stronger power than Pharaoh and all his armies : a God who had revealed himself to him at Sinai, and whom he called Jahweh, had declared to him that he had heard the cry of his brethren and had commissioned him, Moses, to deliver them. He succeeded, in spite of the difficulties which the tradition does not conceal, in imparting his conviction to his people. In spite of the formidable power of Egypt, the promise was fulfilled.

Out of the tribes thus delivered, united, no doubt, to some of their kinsmen of the Sinai deserts, and, perhaps, some Midianite and Kenite elements, it was the task of Moses to build a people, by which we must naturally understand a confederation of tribes. And in spite of the disintegrating effect of desert life, in spite of the absence of any fixed central authority within this voluntary association, he succeeded in his undertaking by reason of his personal ascendancy, by reason of the solidarity created by a long period of trials and successes shared in common, above all, by reason of the close tie which the worship of the God who had delivered them had created between the confederated tribes, and finally by reason of the victories over Amalek and the conquest of Canaan, fresh witnesses to the power of the God who had already vanquished Egypt.

Hence the work of Moses seems to have been above all a practical work : the creation of a people by the founding of a national religion. Jahweh would be Israel's god and Israel Jahweh's people. This often repeated formula seems to express the guiding idea of the activity of Moses.

But a question now arises. Other Semitic peoples had national religions. Their god, too, was not merely the chief of the nation, but in a manner its spirit, almost identified with it. Such was Chemosh, among the Moabites ; Mesha slaughtered the population of a conquered city to please Chemosh and Moab (Moabite Stele, ll. 11–12) ; by his oracle Chemosh guided the armies of Moab (*id.* ll. 14 and 42) ; it was he who put to flight the enemy before the Moabite king (l. 19 ; *cf.* Judges ii. 24) ; when the Moabites conquered a country Chemosh was said to take up his abode there (ll. 8, 9, 33). Among the Assyrians Asshur played the same rôle ; they spoke of the enemies of Asshur, his forces, his weapons.[1] Hence the question arises, whether the national religion instituted by Moses was in all respects similar to these other tribal, federal or state cults which existed among the Semites, or whether it was distinguished from the first by some essential feature. This is one of the most difficult questions with which criticism is confronted.

It seems very probable that the religion founded by Moses did not contain any specific *doctrines* promulgated by him, which differentiated it from the religions of other Semitic peoples. Moses could neither have taught monotheism,[2] nor the spiritual nature of God ; the ark, which was, perhaps, adopted by Moses, to whom its construction was ascribed at a very early date, was identified with Jahweh in the most literal fashion ; since the ancient Israelites, like their kinsmen, held the naïve belief that the deity could dwell in, and express himself through a stone (Bethel), a tree or an image.

[1] For example, **XXXIV**, i, pp. 205–14.   [2] See pp. 257, 454–6.

Neither can the originality of Israel's religion, as we have already said, be sought in the realm of ritual observances.

That which, from the beginning, seems to have distinguished Jahwism from other national religions was rather, on the one hand, its *intensity of life*, and on the other, certain features not yet prominent, but which contained *the germ of future developments*.

Israel possessed, and that no doubt from the first, a particularly keen sense of *the power of its god*. None among the *elohim* could be compared to him. Nothing was impossible to him who, according to a very ancient poem (Exod. xv. 21),

> " has cast into the sea
> horse and rider,"

who vanquished Pharaoh and humbled the redoubtable gods of Egypt, the most powerful empire then known to the Hebrews.

Another specially marked feature of the belief of the ancient Israelites was their deep certainty of *the care of Jahweh*, manifested in all departments of national life, but especially in war and the maintenance of justice.

We must also apparently ascribe to Moses the source of the lofty *moral inspiration* which in " the prophets " constitutes the unique glory of the religion of Israel. Doubtless, it is possible to exaggerate here. Not merely the morality but the morals of ancient Israel left much to be desired.[1] However, the tendency to seek a less barbarous conception of justice and a more effective protection of the weak, which is clearly found in the old collections of Israelite laws, must go back to the very beginnings of Jahwism. For it was the priests who were the chief depositaries of the law of custom, and who enforced it by their oracles or *toroth*. But the authority of *Torah* is always referred back to Moses. Certain traditional narratives give us a very vivid and probably reliable picture of this side of the work of the founder of the nation. He sat from morning to night dispensing justice. Those who had cases to be decided came to him to inquire of God, and he gave decisions, teaching the people the directions of God and his oracles (Exod. xviii. 13–16). In order to do this he went into a tent pitched outside the camp and guarded

[1] See pp. 466–70.

by his servant Joshua, which was known as " the tent of
meeting " ; there he consulted Jahweh and conversed with
him as a man talks with his friend (Exod. xxxiii. 7–11). The
decisions which he gave concerning cases, established, supple-
mented or corrected traditional custom. Moses apparently
promulgated no code, since Jahweh's abiding presence among
his people, to be inquired of at all times, made such a proceeding unnecessary. But there is no doubt that he inaugurated the tradition of that humane and equitable
jurisprudence which survived throughout the centuries in the
living and oral *torah* of the priests before it gave birth to the
written *torah*, that is to the successive collections in which
the scribes enshrined these decisions.

A still more characteristic feature of primitive Jahwism
is the *exclusivism* which it had already attributed to the
national god : Jahweh insists on being the sole god of his
people, at least as far as its national life is concerned.
This exclusivism, however, involves no denial of the existence
or of the rights of the gods of other peoples. It did not even
necessarily involve the prohibition of cults practised by individuals, especially by women—Leah, Rachel, even David
himself, had their household images, their *teraphim*.[1] An
important question concerning which, unfortunately, we
lack information, is whether from the first Jahweh took the
place of the special *elohim* belonging to each tribe and clan,
and how early the principle was laid down that whoever
sacrificed to other *elohim* should be put to the ban (Exod.
xxii. 20). In any case, the principle of national *monolatry*
must have been one of the essential features of primitive
Jahwism.

Cases of divine intolerance and " jealousy " occur also,
and more frequently than we are always told, in other religions
of antiquity. In Egypt, under Amenophis IV, Aten violently
drives out Amon. A statue of the god Nebo, set up under
Adadnirari III (812–783), bears these words : " Trust in Nebo ;
trust not in any other god."[2] Marduk punishes the introduction of strange gods into his city by the destruction of the
Chaldean empire.[3] Chnum, the ram-god of Elephantine,
cannot suffer the presence in his city of Jahweh, the *elohim*

---

[1] See p. 431.   [2] **XXXVII**, pp. 44–5.
[3] **XXXIV**, i, pp. 254–5.

of the Jews, to whom they sacrifice rams.[1] In this exclusivism of a god who insists on being all that there is of the
divine, all the *elohim*, for his worshippers, there lay the germ
of immense religious advance. But it is a fact of history
that this germ only attained its full development in the
soil of Jahwism : prophetic monotheism grew out of the
monolatry of ancient Israel.

Finally, there is one feature of the national religion which
also led to important consequences. It is what we way call
its *historical character*.

While the majority of the other Semitic peoples, worshipping their gods from time immemorial, regarded themselves
as linked to them by a natural tie, and often by a bond of
actual physical kinship, Israel, on the other hand, had established relations with Jahweh at a particular point of time,
by the intervention of a personality the memory of whom
persisted among them

Hence there is no reason to doubt, as many critics have
done, that the new religion was introduced under the form
of a covenant. Among the ancient Semites, no undertaking
was binding unless the parties concerned bound themselves
by the proper rites to observe it. Hence the important part
played by covenants in the public and private life of the pre-
Islamic Arabs. This procedure persisted in Israel throughout
the monarchy.[2] Hence we may assert with practical certainty that the worship of Jahweh was established among the
confederate Hebrew tribes by a *berith*, although we may not
be able to define the exact terms of this covenant : it may
have been a covenant between Moses and the people in the
form of a mutual undertaking to observe the new cult or
covenant between Jahweh and the people,[3] or it may have
been a covenant between the various tribes under the sanction of the common god adopted as the patron-deity of the
confederation.[4]

The first conditions of this agreement were not preserved ;
hence the wide variation in the tradition. The content of

---

[1] Elephantine Papyrus, letter to Bagoas.

[2] 2 Kings xxiii. 1–3 ; Jer. xxxiv. 8 ; 2 Sam. v. 3 ; *cf.* Joshua ix. 15,
16.

[3] For example, **XXXIX**, p. 66.

[4] So Eerdmans, *Theol. Tijdschrift*, xxxvii, 19 *ff.* ; **CCXXXVI**, pp. 2–3 ;
CCXX, pp. 136–7.

the covenant was perhaps simply that which Jeremiah suggests : " Obey my voice, and I will be your God, and ye shall be my people : and walk ye in all the ways that I shall command you (by my successive oracles) " (Jer. vii. 23).

It is well, moreover, to emphasize the fact that, prior to the eighth century, no one seems to have inferred from the remembrance of this initial act its logical consequences, in which alone lay its religious value : the people did not believe that this formal bond, established at a definite point of time, might also one day be broken if its conditions were not observed, nor that Jahweh, before entering into a covenant with a particular people, might have been more than a national god, namely, a god of all nations. Amos, as far as we know, was the first to draw these conclusions.

To sum up, it is probable that to an outside observer the religion established by Moses among the Hebrew tribes could not have been distinguished from the rest of the national Semitic cults. It was the emphasis laid on certain points, there were certain tendencies, as yet only faintly discerned, in which alone lay the promise of future potentialities.

APPENDIX
THE DATE OF THE COMPILATION OF THE DECALOGUE

If we take this document in the form in which we find it in our Bibles, it is clear that it could not have been edited in the Mosaic period : it presupposes a people who make use of oxen for the labour of the fields, who possess houses, " gates," which imply walled cities, and hence a settled community, whose principal means of subsistence is agriculture. It contains ideas and forms of expression which are characteristic of the Deuteronomic outlook (seventh century) or even of the Priestly Code (sixth or fifth century). It is true that these obviously late features are specially found in the explanatory comments which must have been later additions. But even if we eliminate these and reduce the Decalogue to the few and pithy commands of which it must have originally consisted, it still does not seem possible to ascribe it to Moses, as some independent critics would do (**XLV**, i, pp. 653 *ff.* ; **CCXXXVII** ; Hans Schmidt, *Mose und der Decalog* in *Gunkelfestschrift*, i, 78 *ff.* ; P. Volz, **LXXVI**, pp. 29–36, and art. *Decalog* in **RGG**, i, cols. 1816– 19). Originally this document did not appear in the early narratives J and E, each of which gives a different list of the divine words which are supposed to have constituted the basis of the covenant between Jahweh and his people at the holy mount. (In J : Exod. xxxiv. 14–26, except the expansions which have been added. In E : Exod. xx. 23–6 ; xxii. 28–9 ; xxiii. 10–19.) A critical analysis of the texts shows that our Decalogue was inserted at a later date, on the one hand in E, and on the other in

Deuteronomy. Hence it only appears in Israelite literature about the seventh century. But a consideration of its contents shows that it is this very period whose ideas and institutions it reflects. It condemns on principle the cult use of any kind of images, as do Deutero-Isaiah and the post-exilic Psalms, whereas their use had been regarded as legal in early times ; Elijah in the ninth century, and even Amos himself in the eighth, had not protested against it, and the most strenuous upholders of Jahwism had only condemned molten images of gold and silver (Exod. xxxiv. 17 ; xx. 23), or those of animal form (Exod. xxxii. ; Hos. viii. 5–6 ; xiii. 2). The Decalogue seems to suppose the regular Sabbath as already established (see p. 440) ; it ascribes to this holy day, the only one which it mentions, a central importance which it only assumed after the exile, when an increasing number of the Jews of the Dispersion ceased to be able to take part in the Temple worship. Finally, the Decalogue, while it presupposes the existence of ritual (e.g. the laws relating to images and the Sabbath), does not mention it among the fundamental requirements of Jahweh, in contrast to the ancient decalogues contained in J and E, most of whose regulations are concerned with sacrifices and feasts. The Decalogue of of Exodus xx. and Deuteronomy v. is wholly occupied with moral and social responsibilities. We have no proof that such an attitude was ever characteristic of early Israel, whereas it is one of the distinguishing features of the prophetic movement, especially in its beginnings : Jahweh desires justice and mercy, not sacrifices (Amos v. 21–5 ; Hos. vi. 6 ; Mic. vi. 1–8). The Decalogue is, like Deuteronomy, a faint echo of the message of the prophets of the eighth and seventh centuries (cf. CCXX).

II

THE ORIGINS OF THE WORK OF MOSES

Since we know so little concerning the work of Moses, it is obviously impossible to determine with any certainty the influences which may have shaped it. We must content ourselves with a brief mention of the theories which have been propounded.

According to the tradition, Moses was brought up by a daughter of the King of Egypt. From this it was natural to infer that he was " learned in all the wisdom of the Egyptians."[1] At a very early date the explanation of his entire work was sought in his Egyptian training. Manetho had already represented him as a former priest of Heliopolis in revolt against the traditional teaching of his people.

This manner of explaining the work of Moses no longer receives the favourable recognition which it once had. Most critics are of the opinion that Egyptian influence played a

[1] Acts vii. 22 ; Philo, De vita Mosis, i, 15.

very limited part in the formation of the national religion
of Israel.[1] There are, on the other hand, grounds for believing that the Midianites, a nomad group living in the
neighbourhood of Sinai, and no doubt worshipping there,
exercised a very direct influence on the early stages of the
religion of Israel. According to the tradition, Moses lived
among them for a long period before beginning his work ; he
even became the son-in-law of " the priest of Midian."
According to J, it was a Midianite woman who introduced
circumcision into Israel. The institution of " elders " or
sheikhs, was established by Moses on the advice of his father-
in-law (Exod. xviii.).

With one of these tribes, the Kenites, Israel continued
throughout its history in the closest political and religious
relations. According to some forms of the tradition, Moses'
father-in-law was called Hobab, the Kenite (Judges i. 16,
LXX ; cf. iv. 11, 17 ;' v. 24) ; it was related that he and his
group had guided the Israelites through the wilderness
(Num. x. 29–32). The Kenite tribe entered the land of
Canaan with the Israelites, but adhered to their nomad mode
of life (Judges i. 16, etc.). When Saul destroyed the Amalekites, we are told that he was careful to spare the Kenites
who were living among them (1 Sam. xv. 6).

Now the tradition represents this nomad Midianite tribe
as having known and worshipped Jahweh from time immemorial. One narrative explicitly states that the Kenites
worshipped Jahweh *before the Israelites* : when Jethro, the
father-in-law of Moses arrived at the camp of the Israelites,
we are told [2] that he offered a burnt-offering and sacrifices to
Jahweh, and that the nobles of Israel took part in the sacred
meal. Hence it was a Kenite priest who offered the first
sacrifice to Jahweh in which the Hebrew tribes who had come
out of Egypt took part. According to the story of Genesis,
Cain, the eponymous ancestor of the Kenites, already bore
" the mark of Jahweh " (Gen. iv. 15). Even as late as the
ninth century, the Kenites [3] produced one of the most ardent

---

[1] See appendix, pp. 318–20.

[2] Exod. xviii. 12. The Massoretic Text has simply " he took,"
but it is evidently an attenuation : the Syriac and Latin versions,
and the Targum, have preserved the original reading.

[3] At least according to the corrupt and mutilated text of 1 Chron. ii.
56.

upholders of Jahwism, Jonadab, the son of Rechab, the founder of the Rechabite community, who bound themselves to observe strictly all the customs of nomad life (2 Kings x. 15–16 ; Jer. xxxv.).

It is an interesting question whether, as has frequently been suggested, the Kenites were one of those groups of smiths who wandered about the Arabian desert, like our gipsies, outcasts who were both despised and feared, protected by a kind of taboo because mysterious knowledge and magical powers were ascribed to them. If this were true it would help to explain the influence of their cult upon the tribes of the Hebrew confederation. There are, however, as we have seen, reasons to doubt it.[1]

Leaving aside this point, it seems certain that the Kenites had long been worshippers of the god who, through the intervention of Moses, became the national god of Israel ; it is also true that the Hebrew tribes took over more than one of their traditions, for example the tradition that all the classes constituting (desert) society, shepherds, musicians and smiths, were descended from Cain (Gen. iv. 17–24 J).

APPENDIX
THE THEORY OF THE EGYPTIAN ORIGIN OF THE WORK OF MOSES

According to the upholders of this point of view, the religion of Egypt will have influenced the founder of Hebrew religion in two opposite senses ; positively, in the sense that he may not only have tolerated certain customs which the Hebrew tribes had adopted during their sojourn in the land of the Pharaohs, such as the abstention from the flesh of certain animals,[2] but may also himself have adopted certain of the conceptions of the Egyptian priests, such as in particular, monotheism, or certain features of the ritual system. Max Lohr would explain in this way the division of the sanctuary into the holy and the most holy place, the use of the term " house " to denote temples, the importance attached to ritual cleanliness, the institution of an " assistant priest " to the high priest, the wearing of a breastplate by the chief priest.[3]   According to Ed. Montet, " The ark of the covenant, the cherubim covering it with their wings . . . the shewbread . . . are so many features borrowed from similar customs in the Egyptian cult." [4]

On the other hand, the Egyptian religion may have exercised a negative influence on Moses in the sense that he may have sought in certain of his laws to guard his people against the customs and beliefs of Egypt. Hence, for instance, the prohibition of images, directed against such a practice as the worship of the golden calf,

---

[1] See pp. 205–6.   [2] **CCXLIII.**   [3] **CCXIV**, pp. 34, 35.   [4] **LXVI**, p. 47.

a survival in the wilderness of the worship of the bull Apis at Memphis.[1] Certain critics in the middle of the last century [2] explained in a similar way the silence of the Pentateuch concerning the future life : it was the disgust inspired by the worship which the Egyptians paid to their dead that caused Moses to abstain from all mention of the subject.

This conception of a deep Egyptian influence on the origins of the religion of Israel has appeared recently in a new form. Völter, in 1907, undertook to prove that the whole of Jahwism is nothing but a transposition of Egyptian mythology : the god of Sinai corresponds to Khepera, the young sun who rises from the winter solstice to the spring equinox. The god of the ark, according to this critic, originally distinct from the god of Sinai, is Osiris ; the ark is the coffin of the god. Moses is Thoth, the god of the new moon, legislator, judge, and great magician, etc.[3]

The fact that Moses, Phinehas, Hur, Hophni, bear names which evidently seem to be Egyptian, proves, no doubt, that the influence of Egypt was a real one. It is impossible for nomads to escape entirely from the influence of the civilization of the countries which border the desert ; but in ancient times, this civilization was almost entirely Babylonian and Egyptian. The shrine of Serabit el-Hadim, in the heart of the desert of the Sinai peninsula, is a concrete example of the influence of the Egyptian religion on the cults of the neighbouring nomads : the " Lady of the Turquoise," a Semitic goddess, was worshipped there under the form of Hathor.

But on the other hand, in the first place, most of the customs and beliefs which critics have claimed to explain by the positive or negative influence of Egypt, turn out, on closer examination, to be genuinely Semitic ; for instance, the ancient Hebrew ideas concerning the state of the dead, the food taboos, the absence of images of the deity. In the second place, Moses did not borrow monotheism from the Egyptian priests for the simple reason that the founder of the national monolatry of Israel was probably not a monotheist, and for the further reason that the speculations of the priestly colleges of Thebes or Memphis concerning the unity of the divine, and the attempted reform of Amenophis IV, spring either from pantheism or from monarchical polytheism, and hence are of an entirely different character from the *moral* monotheism of the Israelites, which, moreover, does not appear until about the eighth century. In the third place, Egyptian influences in points of detail, which may be disclosed by various religious institutions of Israel, need not necessarily go back to the Mosaic epoch : they may have been mediated by the Canaanites, who had long been vassals of Egypt and had assimilated the cult of their overlords, or they may belong to the time of Solomon and his successors. Bull-worship, in particular, called by the prophets in derision the worship of the golden calves, seems more Canaanite than Egyptian, for in Egypt living bulls were the object of worship. In Israel, as among the Canaanites, they worshipped bull-images, which were simply symbols of the power of the god. The story of the making of the golden calf in the wilderness (Exod. xxxii.), seems to be, at least in its present form, a satire on the activities of Jeroboam I. Its original intention was probably a cult myth whose object was

---

[1] **LXVI**, p. 47. [2] Von Cölin, Hengstenberg. [3] **CCLI**.

to *legitimise* the borrowing of bull-worship from the Canaanites by taking it back to the period of the origins of Jahwism.

For the division of the Israelite sanctuary into a holy and most holy place, in which Lohr would see an Egyptian borrowing, there is no certain evidence until the time of Solomon ; at Shiloh, the child Samuel slept in the same chamber as the ark (1 Sam. iii. 3).

In short, it does not appear that the cults of Egypt had any deep influence on the half-nomad Hebrew tribes of Goshen, at the time when their national religion took shape : the divergence between the two peoples was too great.

III

Jahweh before the Mosaic Epoch

It has been maintained that in pre-Mosaic times Jahweh was exclusively the patron *elohim* of the Kenites, in which case the treaty made by Moses with the nomads of Sinai would have had as its implication and result the adoption by the Hebrew tribes of the religion of their new confederates, the religion of Jahweh. We should have here the earliest example of the acceptance of a new religion by a whole people.[1]

It is difficult to believe that Moses could have succeeded in inducing the Hebrews to leave Egypt by the promise of the aid of a god who was absolutely unknown to them, one who was exclusively the *elohim* of another people. According to the tradition, Moses announced himself as sent by " the God of their fathers," and it is *a priori* likely that there is a measure of truth in this statement. Jahweh might have been, not only the god of the Kenites, but also the god, or one of the gods, of some Hebrew tribe, of Levi, for instance ; the mother of Moses was said to have been called Jochebed, a theophorous name, compounded with that of Jahweh.[2]

We find in cuneiform documents of the pre-Mosaic age, a great number of personal names compounded with the syllables *ya, yau, yami* (or *yawe*), and even *jahveh*.[3] If these elements represent the name of Jahweh, it would be proved that the worship of this god in pre-Mosaic times extended far beyond the narrow circle of the Kenites to Canaan and Babylonia. We might add Syria ; for, in a couple of inscriptions coming, one from the petty kingdom of Yaudi [4] and the other from Hamath,[5] although, it is true, they are not

---

[1] So **X**, pp. 12, 13.
[2] Exod. vi. 20 ; Num. xxvi. 59.   *Cf.* for example, **IV**, p. 154, n. 3.
[3] **CCXVI**, pp. 322–4 ;   *cf.* Sayce, *CT from Babylon*, I, iv, 27.
[4] **XCIII**, pp. 54, 262.   [5] *Ibid.*, p. 66.

earlier than the eighth century, we find a mention of individuals named *Azri-ya-u* (*cf.* Azariahu) and *Ya-u-bi-'-di*, the latter also being called *Ilu-bi-'-di*, proving that *Yau* certainly represents here the name of a god, since in Babylonian *ilu* means god. Hence it would not surprise us if the worship of Jahweh had been practised by one or other of the Hebrew tribes.

Provisionally, however, it will be wiser to use these documents with considerable caution.[1]

None the less it remains very probable that the *elohim* of the celebrated mountain which Sinai was later to become was known and worshipped, not only by the tribe which lived on its slopes, but by all the nomads who, like the ancient Hebrews, may have pastured their flocks in the neighbouring steppes.

The name of this god, unfortunately, tells us little that is certain about his original character.

Even its pronunciation is far from certain. Of course it was never read as Jehovah : this name arose from a gross blunder of the first Christian Hebraists who, in the thirteenth century,[2] read the consonants of the divine name *jhwh* with the vowels of *adonai* (lord), the word which the Jews, from reverential motives, substituted for it in the reading of the sacred text. The latter indicated this substitution by writing these vowels under the consonants of the tetragrammaton, in accordance with their usual method of marking a variation between the written and the spoken text : thus *JeHoWaH*.

It is very probable that the pronunciation of the divine name, in the official religion of Israel, at least from the eighth century (E), that is, the pronunciation familiar to the biblical

---

[1] The syllable *ya* at the end of names is regarded by competent Assyriologists as merely a suffix of Mitannite origin (Ungnad, **BA**, vi, 5, pp. 10 *ff.* ; Tallquist, *Assyrian Personal Names*, p. 286 ; *cf.* Otto Schroeder, *Studia Orientalia*, i, Helsingfors, 1925, pp. 266–7 ; G. R. Driver, **ZATW**, 1928, p. 9 ; **LXXVI**, p. 20). According to Prof. Langdon, the syllable *yau* at the beginning of a word is a common noun meaning " someone," and representing a divine name ; it has been established that, in pre-Mosaic texts, this syllable is not accompanied by the determinative sign for divinity. (*Cf.* König, **ZATW**, 1915, pp. 45–52.) According to G. R. Driver, the Syrian Arameans who bear names compounded with *yau* may have been Jewish settlers (**ZATW**, 1928, pp. 8–9).

[2] *Cf.* **CCXVIII**, pp. 145 *ff.* ; **AJSL**, XXVIII, i, 1911.

writers, was *jahwe(h)*, which is attested by the transcriptions *Iaβε* (Theodoret), *Iaove* and *Iaovaι* (Clement of Alexandria), *Iaωovηε* (Jewish-Egyptian magical papyri). But it is open to question whether this was the original pronunciation.[1]

As for the etymological meaning of the name, nothing is more uncertain, even if we grant that *jahweh* was really the original pronunciation. This is the interpretation given by the elohist historian in Exodus iii. 13–14 :

> " And Moses said unto God, Behold, when I come unto the children of Israel, and shall say unto them, The God of your fathers hath sent me unto you ; and they shall say unto me, What is his name ? what shall I say unto them ? And God said unto Moses, I AM THAT I AM [2] : and he said, Thus shalt thou say unto the children of Israel, I AM hath sent me unto you."

The usual translation, " I am he who am," means : " I am he who subsists of himself " or " he who exists for ever," hence the usual translation of Jahweh by the Eternal One. But if this had been the intention of the author, he would certainly have used the correct construction : " I am he who *is*," the more so that the word " is " (*yihyeh*) was much more akin than " am " (*ehyeh*) to the name Jahweh which he was explaining. But it can hardly be doubted that in God's answer to Moses we have an expression very commonly used in Hebrew when an intentional vagueness was desired.

---

[1] In extra-biblical documents, side by side with the spelling *jhwh* (Mesha Stone, *circa* 842), we find the forms *yhh* (Aramaic papyrus, 447 B.C.), *yhw* (Elephantine papyrus, 465–408, jar-handles of the fifth and fourth centuries, Phenician or Philistine coins, 405–380), *yh* (jar-handles of the fifth and fourth centuries ; *cf.* *yah* in biblical passages). Among Greek transcriptions we find *ιαω* (Diodorus, Origen, Theodoret, Macrobius, and gnostic writers), *ιενω* (Porphyry). It has also been maintained that the original vocalization was *yahoh* (A. L. Williams, **JTS**, 1926–27, pp. 273–83 ; F. C. Burkitt, *ibid.*, pp. 407–9). G. R. Driver supposes that the original form of the name has been preserved in the theophorous names of persons placed under the patronage of this god (**ZATW**, 1928, p. 19) and that, whatever may have been the spelling adopted, the original pronunciation was *ya* ; Jahweh will have been a specifically Israelite lengthening (*ibid.*, pp. 24–25). This hypothesis creates several difficulties, and the general view is more probable, that the longer form of the divine name is the earlier, and that it was shortened in forming compounds as in popular speech.

[2] The original text possibly read " He is " (*Jahweh*). In any case this is the author's meaning, correctly interpreted in the commentary in v. 15 : " Thus shalt thou say unto the children of Israel : It is Jahweh . . . who hath sent me unto you."

Similarly Jahweh says elsewhere : " I will be gracious to whom I will be gracious, and will show mercy to whom I will show mercy " (Exod. xxxiii. 19) ; " I will speak what I will speak " (Ezek. xii. 25) ; David says : " I go whither I go " (2 Sam. xv. 20) ; Moses : " Send whom thou wilt send."[1] God intentionally evades the question which is put to him, as is the custom of divine beings when a mortal ventures to ask their name, for that is an attempt to penetrate the secret of the god's nature.[2] The essential nature of the God of Israel is and must remain inscrutable. According to our account, the word Jahweh is merely a formal title which the God of Horeb revealed to Moses in answer to the practical needs of the cult, but it was intended to be a continual reminder of the phrase of which it was the epitome : " He is that he is," the Being whom none may know. While such an explanation is a lofty one, it seems too theological, too artificial to convey the original meaning of the name of the Midianite god.

The same must be said about other modern interpretations, such as, " he causes to exist " (he creates), " he causes to live," " he causes (events) to happen." More plausible are such etymologies as " he blows," " he destroys," or " he causes to fall." These designations would suit a god of storm and lightning, such as the *elohim* of Sinai seems to have been.

If the original pronunciation of the name was *ya*, it may have been an ancient, pious exclamation transformed into a divine name, like Ἴαχχος, Βάχχος or Εὔιος among the Greeks : [3] *ya*, accompanied it is true by the divine name, is a common ejaculation in various Semitic languages, especially in Arabic and Aramaic.

Others again have attempted to prove that Jahweh was originally the name of a Babylonian or even of an Aryan deity.

Amidst all these uncertainties one thing at least seems sure, namely, that this name did not appear for the first time in the Mosaic epoch, as E and P suggest, representing it as having been revealed, for the first time, to Moses. If this were its true origin, it would have an intelligible meaning in

---

[1] Exod. iv. 13 ; *cf.* xvi. 23 ; 1 Sam. xxiii. 13 ; 2 Kings viii. 1.
[2] *Cf.* Gen. xxxii. 30 ; Exod. xxxviii. 18–23 ; Judges xiii. 17–18.
[3] G. R. Driver, ZATW, 1928, p. 24.

Hebrew, the remembrance of which would have been preserved by the Israelites. It is apparently a much older name whose meaning the Israelites had already forgotten, and to which they attempted later to give a meaning conformable to their own religious conceptions.

The god of Sinai was naturally a mountain-god. His cult must have included the various features which we have already described in dealing with the pre-Mosaic Hebrews. Hence it is not necessary to repeat what has already been said. When the Israelites adopted Jahweh as the guardian of their federation, they doubtless made no changes in the ritual of his religion. There is not a single ritual custom or sacred object whose origin can with certainty be traced back to the Mosaic period, not even the ark.[1]

On embracing his religion, the Israelites must have taken " the mark of Jahweh." Just as each Bedouin tribe has its mark (wasm) branded on its cattle, so each deity must have had special marks borne by his worshippers. There might be, for instance, a certain way of cutting the hair, as among the ancient Arabs,[2] perhaps, too, among the Babylonians and the Assyrians,[3] or else tattooings, στίγματα, like the βαρβαρικὰ γράμματα stamped on the wrists and necks of the Syrian worshippers of the great goddess of Bambyke, near Hierapolis,[4] or the sacred stigmata which rendered inviolable the slaves who sought asylum in the temple of Hercules at the Canopic mouth of the Nile.[5]

The Kenites bore a mark of this kind. According to the story, Jahweh had once marked their ancestor, Cain, with this mark, in order that no one who met him should slay him, and had declared :

" Whosoever slayeth Cain, vengeance shall be taken on him sevenfold " (Gen. iv. 15).

This mark, in fact, was a protection, in the desert the only efficacious one, for the life of each member of the tribe, impressing upon possible aggressors the fear of the vengeance

[1] See pp. 425-9.
[2] Jer. ix. 25 ; xxv. 23 ; xlix. 32 ; Herodotus, iii, 8 ; whence the Jewish prohibition. Lev. xix. 27.
[3] Code of Hammurabi, § 127 ; **CCXXXII**, § 1 ; cf. P. Dhorme, **RB**, xxx, pp. 519, 522.
[4] De dea Syria, 59 ; Paris Papyrus, 10, p. 178.
[5] Cf. **LXXXIV**, p. 334, n. 1.

of the kinsmen of the victim. This divine mark could also protect its wearer from spiritual dangers : Jahweh ordered the cross (*tau*) to be put upon the foreheads of the inhabitants of Jerusalem who were to be spared by the destroying angels.[1] In the East today tattooings are supposed to possess magical protective powers.

The marks of Jahweh were worn on the hand and on the forehead, between the eyes.[2] They were known as *ṭoṭaphoth*. The custom long persisted, at least among the prophets.[3] It fell into disuse about the period of the exile : Leviticus xix. 28 forbids every kind of tattooing. By that time, through the force of circumstances, circumcision had come to be regarded as the mark of the covenant between Jahweh and his people.[4]

The ancient custom survived, however, in a spiritualized form ; the author of one of the exhortations which constitute the Deuteronomic framework (vi. 8 ; ii. 18) requires that instead of branding a mark or a name in his flesh, the worshipper of Jahweh should place upon his hand and between his eyes, the essential demands of his God. Hence the custom of the leather cases containing passages of the Scriptures, which the pious Jew fastens with straps to his left arm and his forehead, and which the Hellenistic Jews used to call " phylacteries," that is to say, protections. It is a survival from the remote past of the protective mark of the clan of Cain.

But the links which the figure of Jahweh possessed with an older ethnic group or with certain natural phenomena, seem to have had but a secondary importance in the work of Moses. The past gave him nothing but materials. The true origin of his work must be sought in his remarkable conviction that his God was almighty and paramount, that he would deliver the Hebrews and make them his people : its origin lies in an inward illumination, which tradition, and perhaps Moses himself first, depicted in the form of the vision of the burning bush.

---

[1] Ezek. ix. 4, 6 ; *cf.* Apoc. vii. 3 ; xiv. 1.
[2] Isa. xliv. 5 ; Exod. xiii. 9, 16 ; *cf.* Apoc. xiv. 9.
[3] 1 Kings xx. 41 ; *cf.* Zech. xiii. 6 (emend : " between thine eyes and upon thine hands ").
[4] See pp. 200–1.

PART III

ISRAEL IN PALESTINE FROM THE SETTLEMENT IN CANAAN UP TO THE ASSYRIAN INVASIONS

BOOK I

HISTORICAL DATA AND SOCIAL ORGANIZATION

CHAPTER I

THE HISTORICAL FRAMEWORK

I

THE SETTLEMENT OF THE ISRAELITES IN CANAAN

ACCORDING to the narratives of the books of Numbers, Deuteronomy and Joshua, as we have them today, the Hebrew tribes under the leadership, first of Moses and then of Joshua, made a swift and complete conquest of the whole country. Save for the inhabitants of Gibeon and three other small cities, which succeeded in tricking the Hebrews into an alliance, in accordance with the command of Moses all the Canaanites were put to the ban (*ḥerem*), and the land was divided by lot among the invading tribes : hence there was a sudden and violent displacement of the old population by the new.

But this purely idealistic picture of the course of events is the creation of the latest historians, the Deuteronomists (eighth century) and the Priestly writers (sixth and fifth). On several important points it is contradicted by the earlier documents, especially by an ancient account of the settlement

in Canaan (probably J), a large part of which has been preserved in the first chapter of Judges, and a few fragments in
Numbers and Joshua.[1]

According to this earliest account of the facts, there was
no united invasion, at least of Canaan in the strict sense :
after having seized Transjordania and taken Gilgal and the
city of Palm-trees (*i.e.* Jericho), the Israelites separated. The
first wave of invasion consisted of the tribes of Judah and
Simeon who conquered the King of Jerusalem and shockingly
mutilated him. The two tribes took the city of Hormah, in
the far south of Palestine : Caleb, who marched with them,
took Hebron and Debir ; the Kenites occupied a district
south of Arad.

A second wave of invasion was formed by the house of
Joseph, that is, by the future tribes of Ephraim, Manasseh
and probably Benjamin ; since the latter tribe, even in the
time of David, still regarded itself as belonging to the " house
of Joseph " (2 Sam. xix. 21). We are told how Bethel fell
into the hands of the invaders through treachery. As this
place was close to Ai, there are grounds for thinking that
both these places were taken in the course of the same campaign, consequently that the conquest of the whole of Canaan
ascribed to Joshua by the later tradition is an exaggerated
version of this expedition of the house of Joseph against the
" hill-country of Ephraim." It may be surmised that
Joshua, if he is an historical personage, was merely the chief
of the house of Joseph.

The account of the book of Judges does not state the
chronological order in which the rest of the tribes settled in
their respective territories, since it is confined to a list of
them in the geographical order which they occupied from
north to south in the time of the monarchy, with a note in
each case of the places which they failed to conquer. But

---

[1] Since these fragments partially supplement Judges i., we may
attempt to reconstruct the original form of this important document.
The following may have been its arrangement : Judges i. 1–3 (except
the first four words of v. 1), 5–7, 19, 21 (emend acc. to Joshua xv. 63) ;
Joshua xiv. 12 (end) ; xv. 13 ; Judges i. 20, 11–15 (parallel to
Joshua xv. 14–19) ; Judges i. 16–17, 36 (?), 23–26 ; ii. 1ᵃ–5ᵇ ;
Joshua ix. 6*, 7, 14, 15ᵃβ, 16* ; Judges i. 29 (parallel to Joshua xvi. 10),
27–28 (parallel to Joshua xvii. 11–12) ; Joshua xvii. 14, 16–18ᵃ–15ᵇ ;
Num. xxxii. 39, 41–42 ; Joshua xiii. 13 ; ii. 18ᵃ (?) ; Judges i. 30–34 ;
Joshua xix. 47 ; Judges i. 35 ; ii. 23ᵃ ; iii. 2ᵃ, 5ᵃ,–6.

we can gather from these accounts that the settlement of these tribes also was the result of individual enterprises ; for they are represented as meeting with varying success, evidently according to their respective strength. Of the tribe of Zebulon we read : " the Canaanites dwelt in the midst of them " ; on the other hand it is said of Asher : " they dwelt in the midst of the Canaanites," and the same is said about Naphtali : in the north the immigrants were minorities subject to the natives. The tribe of Dan fared still worse : " The Amorites forced the children of Dan into the mountain," so much so that, according to the original account, they were compelled to abandon the district and emigrate (Judges i. 34 ; Joshua xix. 47).

We also gather from these ancient traditions that the settlement, thus carried out in isolated detachments, was only very gradually completed. Up to the beginning of the monarchy, the Israelites were only able to occupy the open country in the mountainous districts. Accustomed to fight on foot, with no weapons but sword and spear, bow and sling, they were helpless in pitched battles in the plains where the formidable iron chariots could manœuvre. Neither were they equipped for siege operations : and it was only by surprise attacks that they were able to take a few cities such as Ai and Bethel, Hebron, Debir, Laish and Shechem. Up to the time of the monarchy the Israelite settlement only consisted of four somewhat compact groups : on the highlands of the Transjordanian plateaux, in the hilly parts of Galilee, in the hill-country of Ephraim and in that of Judah. These groups were separated by lines of fortresses which remained in the hands of the Canaanites, especially those which lay along the valley of Jezreel, forming a barrier between Galilee and Ephraim, and on the other hand, those which, extending from Gezer to Jerusalem, controlled the routes between Judah and the central tribes.

Another important point in which the early texts enable us to correct the conception which became prevalent later on, is that the task of conquest, far from being completed in a single generation, or even in five or seven years (Joshua xiv. 10, 11), continued throughout the whole period of the judges : during this time Laish (Judges xviii.) and Shechem (Judges ix.) passed into the hands of the Israelites. The

process did not come to an end until the time of the early
kings, with the conquest of Jerusalem, the subjugation of
Megiddo, Taanach, Bethshan and the district of Dor, and
the annexation of Gezer.

Moreover the earlier historians considered this slow
process of conquest as providential ; according to J', it was
the purpose of Jahweh by this means to teach the succeeding
generations the art of war (Judges iii. 2) ; while according to
E', he wished to prevent the land from becoming a desert,
with the consequent increase of wild beasts (Exod. xxiii.
29–30 ; Deut. vii. 22).

In the course of this slow progress, the conquered, generally speaking, were neither exterminated nor driven out :
at the most they became tributary. The early account in
the book of Judges states expressly : " And it came to pass
when Israel was strong, that they put the Canaanites to
tribute, and did not utterly drive them out " (Judges i. 28).
The savage ḥerem was only enforced in special cases, when,
for certain reasons, the help of Jahweh was desired (Num.
xxi. 1–3 ; Judges i. 1, etc.). Similarly, the general slaughter
of conquered enemies appears to have been a measure very
rarely resorted to (Judges xviii. 27 ; Gen. xxxiv. 25–6).

Hence there is no evidence in the earliest Hebrew tradition
for the ritual extermination of the ancient inhabitants of
Palestine. Such an appalling massacre is a creation of the
fancy of the Deuteronomist historians. It is merely, if one
may use the expression, " a pious wish " on the part of these
fierce opponents of heathenism, and reveals the intensity of
their fear of pagan influences. It is the expression of a regret
that Israel had not preserved its purity by the extermination
of the contaminating influences.

Finally the old accounts reveal the fact that periods of
bitter warfare alternated with peaceful intervals during which
the immigrants entered into close relationships with the
natives, and frequent intermarriages took place between the
two peoples (Judges iii. 5, 6).

This ancient narrative gives us, no doubt, a picture,
accurate in its main outlines, of the settlement of the nomad
Hebrews in the midst of Canaanite civilization. In reality,
however, the advance of the newcomers was more diversified,
irregular and unorganized than the accounts would lead us

to suppose. Even the earliest Israelite tradition has already begun to idealize and simplify the story of the conquest, as, for example, when it depicts the whole of the Hebrew tribes as entering Canaan together by way of " the city of Palm-trees," apparently after a united conquest of Transjordania. We see no ground for the doubt which has been cast on the tradition[1] that one section of the invaders actually entered by the east, either by the ford of Jericho, or by that of Adam, as one version of the tradition seems to assert.[2] For these lines of approach were used later by other nomads, such as Midianites (Judges vi. and vii.) and Arabs. But there are reasons for supposing that at least the southern portion of the future people of Israel entered Canaan directly from the south. This was certainly true of the Kenites, the Kenizzites (Caleb), and the Jerahmeelites, semi-nomad tribes who were only absorbed by Judah in the time of David ; it was probably also true of Judah and the remnant of Simeon, since the conquest of Hormah which is ascribed to them (Judges i. 17) is represented in another version as having taken place from the south (Num. xxi. 1–3). These Hebrew groups must have moved northwards from Kadesh and have been stopped by the chain of Canaanite fortresses which stretched from Gezer to Jerusalem.

On the other hand, the account in the first chapter of Judges assumes that the conquest took place according to a preconceived plan after the land had been divided by lot (Judges i. 3). This again must be a simplification of the facts. We learn from an ancient tradition that Simeon, before settling in the extreme south, had attempted, together with Levi, which was then a warrior tribe, to seize Shechem, in the heart of the territory which was later occupied by " the house of Joseph " (Gen. xxxiv. ; xlix. 5–7) : the attempt was a disastrous one and resulted in the almost complete disintegration of the two tribes. At some period Reuben must have occupied the region later settled by Benjamin : for on the border between Benjamin and Judah there was a place called " the stone of Bohan, the son of Reuben " ;[3] tradition

[1] Bernhard Luther, ZATW, 1901, p. 45.

[2] Joshua iii. 16 ; Deut. xi. 29–30 ; xxvii. 2–7. Cf. LXXXVI, i, pp. 138–9 ; CCXXXVIII ; Ad. Lods, RHP, 1923, pp. 575–9.

[3] Joshua xv. 6, xviii. 17 ; cf. CCLXXVII, pp. 15 ff. ; CCLXXV, p. 334 ; LXXVIII, p. 266.

assigned the transgression of the eponymous ancestor of the tribe to a spot near Jerusalem (Gen. xxxv. 21–2), and an " altar " connected with the tribes of Reuben and Gad was shown on the west bank of Jordan (Joshua xxii. 10). Early poems represent Dan, Asher and Zebulon as originally settled by the shore of the sea or a lake (Judges v. 17 ; Gen. xlix. 13). Hebrew tradition itself had preserved the memory of the northward movement of Dan[1] and of the crossing into Transjordania of the half-tribe of Manasseh.[2] These migrations may have been much more numerous. The tribal divisions of territory with which we are familiar were the result of a settlement which was not completed until the time of the monarchy.

Moreover, there can be little doubt that the Hebrew tribes found other means of entering Canaan than the sword's point. They must often have been hired by some Canaanite king to help him in a campaign against a neighbouring city, just as in the Tell el-Amarna period various Palestinian princes had each " his Habiri." Arrangements such as these may be the historical basis of stories like those of the treaty with Gibeon which Joshua is obliged to defend against a coalition of Canaanite cities (Joshua ix.–x.), or of the agreement between the Israelites and Rahab's clan at Jericho. Elsewhere the Hebrews may have gradually gained a footing in the country, after the manner of nomads, as allies and protectors of the peasants.[3]

As we have already said, tradition indicates that there were intervals of peaceful relations between the Israelites and the Canaanites. The results of recent excavations leave no doubt on this point : they show that there was no sharp break between the new civilization and that of the Canaanites which it should have replaced. We find, not two civilizations, but one : the continuity is unbroken, or at most there is a slight confusion apparent about 1200 B.C.

Hence the Israelites must have adopted the arts, industries and technical methods of the Canaanites, and this could only have resulted from a long period of peaceful relationship.

More than this, the Hebrew tribes not only lived side by

---

[1] Joshua xix. 47 ; Judges xvii.–xviii.
[2] Joshua xvii. 14–18 ; Num. xxxii. 39, 41–42.
[3] See pp. 181, 206.

side with the Canaanites, but in the end the two populations merged into one another. This is the inevitable result as soon as we admit that the Canaanites were not exterminated. On no other theory is it possible to explain what became of the old inhabitants when, under the first three kings, Palestine became to all intents an Israelite country. We are told, it is true, that Solomon put the remnant of the ancient population under forced labour (1 Kings ix. 20-1) : but after his time we hear no more of the Canaanites. If we ask what had become of them, there is only one answer : they had been assimilated. There is no other explanation of the numerical discrepancy which we find—allowing for the un-reliability of figures in the Hebrew tradition—between the Israelite fighting force in the time of the judges (40,000 men of war for all Israel in the age of Deborah, Judges v. 8) and that of the monarchy (1,300,000, according to 2 Sam. xxiv. 9). In the period of the monarchy *the Israelite people was a mixture of Hebrews and Canaanites.*

In this fusion of peoples the Canaanites constituted the majority, as the figures show. Moreover, since they were the more civilized, they naturally imposed their culture upon the newcomers : in this sense we may say that the Canaanites conquered their conquerors. But, on the other hand, the Hebrews always preserved the consciousness of being con-querors : they succeeded in imposing their social order, their name and their God upon the whole population of Palestine. When we come to study the social organization and the religion of the period, we shall attempt to form an estimate of the nature and results of this interpenetration of the two peoples.

II

The Period of the Judges

1. *The Sources.* " The days when the judges ruled." These are the words in which a Jewish historian, shortly after the exile, characterizes (Ruth i. 1) the period of national history which lies between the settlement of the Israelites in Palestine and Saul's accession to the throne. According to some commentators, the Israelite leaders of this period were called " judges " because they executed judgment on the

oppressors of their people, and delivered them. The phrase of the author of Ruth suggests rather that the word *shophet* is used here in its common sense of " magistrate " : it was often applied to the king (Amos ii. 3 ; Mic. iv. 14 ; Deut. xvii. 9, 12) ; the Latin " *suffete* " represents the same title as borne by the political rulers of Carthage.

At all events, the judges, according to the preface of the book which constitutes the sequel to Joshua (Judges ii. 11–21), were, in a sense, rulers by divine right, raised up by Jahweh to deliver and govern his people after they had fallen into heathenism, had been sold into the hand of the oppressor as a punishment for their apostasy, and had repented. According the present form of the books of Judges and Samuel, this situation occurred no less than fourteen times between the death of Joshua and Saul's accession.

But this theoretical manner of presenting the facts is only characteristic of the latest editors of these books (E^2 and R^D). Fortunately they have confined themselves to a statement of their interpretation of the history in a general preface and in a formula added to the beginning and end of the history of each " judge " ; but they reproduced these narratives substantially as they appeared in the earlier sources. In order to reconstruct the real history of the period, we must, of course, detach it from this later framework. There are also other late and unreliable elements which must be discarded, such as the wholly idealized story of Othniel (Judges iii. 7–11), the accounts of the six deliverers usually called " the lesser judges," because of the brevity of the narrative dealing with their exploits, most of them being merely eponymous ancestors of clans of whom nothing is known but their place of burial, probably fictitious.[1] We may also ignore the story of the shocking incident at Gibeah, a compilation of three versions, none of which seems to be early (Judges xix.–xxi.).

Setting aside these portions of the book, there remain six narratives belonging apparently to the early sources J and E : with the exception of the story of Samson, which both in its original form and in its later modifications, seems to belong entirely to the J-cycle, it is still possible to detect in these narratives the parallel versions of the two sources which

[1] Judges iii. 31 ; x. 1–5 ; xii. 8–15.

have come down to us, either standing side by side (Judges iv. and v.), or fused into a single narrative.

Now, an examination of these early accounts shows that the general nature of the traditions was picturesque and popular, each dealing with a particular tribe or district, for no judge is represented as ruling over the whole of Israel. The traditions vary widely, some being of first-rate historical importance, such as the poem on the victory of Deborah, or the story of Abimelech, others having a more or less legendary character, while one, the story of Samson, belongs to the region of folk-story, and is probably mythical in origin.[1] The heroes of these tales or sagas never appear as religious reformers ; Samson is not even a chief.

These narratives were entirely independent of one another. It is no longer possible to say with certainty what was the chronological order of the events recorded. Possible conjectures[2] are that the event related in the story of Othniel should be placed in the third generation after Moses (about 1150–1125), and Gideon's achievements in the fourth (about 1125–1100). The former conjecture depends upon the supposition that the name Cushan-rish-athaim, King of Aram, the adversary of Othniel, is a corruption of Husham *rosh teman* or *rosh ittayim*, *i.e.* Prince of Teman or, following a conjecture based on the LXX, Prince of the city of Ittaim, the third King of Edom,[3] while the latter conjecture supposes that the Midianite raids repulsed by Gideon were contemporary with the victory over Midian gained by the fourth King of Edom, according to Genesis xxxvi. 35.[4]

In spite of the uncertainty as to the chronological sequence of events, the early narratives of the book of Judges disclose the fact that during the period with which we are dealing, the history of the Hebrew tribes was not one of stagnation, marked only by alternations of adversity and prosperity : they show us a development in the course of which the increasing pressure of historical circumstances led at last to the creation of a national monarchy.

2. *Advances and Reverses in the Occupation of Palestine.*
Several of the episodes referred by the Israelite historians to

---

[1] *Cf.* **LVII.**   [2] **CCXVII**, p. 381.
[3] Gen. xxxvi. 34, 35[b] (G).   There is frequent confusion in the texts between Aram (Hebr.'rm) and Edom ('dm).   [4] See p. 185.

the period of the " judges " belong to the story of the fortunes of the " conquest " of the land, which lasted, as we have seen, during several generations. The only events of which the memory has survived are, as might be expected, desperate struggles.

It does not seem that the immigrants met with any serious checks from the great powers which claimed, at least nominally, the suzerainty of the country at the beginning of our period. Tradition has preserved no record of a clash with Merneptah (1235–1224) or Ramses III (1200–1169), both of whom invaded Palestine,[1] nor with Ramses IV, who claims to have received tribute from Retenu (Syria),[2] nor with Tiglathpileser I, King of Assyria (1115–1110), who, moreover, does not seem to have advanced further south than the Nahr el-Kelb, near Beirut. Some commentators have identified one or other of these sovereigns,[3] or else a Kassite King of Babylon,[4] with the mysterious Cushan-rishathaim, King of Aram-naharaim (Judges iii. 8–10). But these conjectures rest on very slender foundations. The story of Wen Amon shows that about 1110, at least, the authority of the Pharaoh was not only destroyed but had become an object of derision in Syria.[5]

It was the Canaanites whom the Israelites found themselves confronted with. An early narrative[6] gives us a picture of the little group of Danites, so small that it is sometimes called a tribe, sometimes a clan, driven into the hill-country of Ephraim by the Amorites, who were themselves probably being pressed by the newly arrived Philistines. Unable to hold their ground the Danites decided to emigrate and made a surprise attack on the unwarlike Phenician city of Laish or Leshem (probably pronounced Lesham), near the sources of the Jordan ; they gave no quarter, burnt the city and settled in the land. This historical fragment, in reality the story of the origin of the famous sanctuary of Dan, throws much light on the religious conditions of the period. It also furnishes us with a concrete example of the extent to which the nomad habits of brigandage were still held in esteem

---

[1] See p. 51.   [2] Cf. **XVI**, pp. 42–46.
[3] Ramses III ; **LXVII**, p. 85 ; Tiglath Pileser, **XLIV**, i, 2, p. 70.
[4] Ball, **ET**, 1910, p. 192.
[5] See p. 51.
[6] Judges xvii.–xviii. ; cf. i. 34–5 ; Joshua xix. 47.

among the Israelites in Palestine : on their march the Danites carried off the images and the priest of one of their Ephraimite fellow-countrymen, named Micah. The form of the story shows the sympathies of the narrator are with the clever thieves and not with their victim. There is also an old proverb which celebrates the adherence of Dan to the ancient customs of Israel (2 Sam. xx. 18, LXX).

Much more vague and confused is the tradition of a victory over Jabin, King of Hazor, in Upper Galilee. In one version this achievement is ascribed to Joshua (Joshua ii. 1–15), in another to Barak, the conqueror of Sisera : in one form of the story of Barak, indeed, Sisera merely appears as the general of Jabin's army (Judges iv.). The tradition probably relates to a local success of the tribe of Naphthali, Barak's tribe (Judges iv. 6).

On the other hand, when we come to the defeat of Sisera, we are on the firm ground of history. The book of Judges has preserved a poem evidently composed by an eye-witness of the events and still breathing the passion of the fight. It is not, strictly speaking, an account of the battle, but rather a kind of address to the victorious army, dealing out praise and blessing to those who have contributed to the victory, blame and reproach to the cowards and the conquered. However, it gives us a fairly clear picture of the course of events. The poem, corrupt in places, as might be expected from its antiquity, was not composed *by* Deborah and Barak, as was believed later (already in Judges v. 1), but *concerning* them, since they are addressed in the course of the poem (Judges v. 7, 12). The error may have arisen from the fact that the poem was entitled " the song of Deborah and of Barak."

Together with this poem we have a prose narrative of much later date in which some of the facts have clearly been distorted (Judges iv.), but from which it seems possible to obtain some supplementary information.

The following is a possible reconstruction of the events. A league of " the kings of Canaan," apparently the rulers of the cities of the plain of Jezreel, led by Sisera, the Prince of the city of Harosheth hag-Goim (Judges iv. 2), possibly el-Haritiyeh, to the south-east of Haifa, had cut the communications, as it would appear, between the Israelite tribes

in the north and those of the hill-country of Ephraim. Panic
prevailed, and all labour in the fields ceased.

None of the Hebrew tribes dared to confront in battle the
terrible war-horses of the Canaanite princes.

> " In the days of Shamgar, the son of Anath,
>   the highways were deserted ;
>   Travellers went by the by-ways ;
>   the villages in Israel were deserted, they were deserted . . .
>   Not a shield nor a lance was to be seen
>   among the forty thousand men of Israel."

The tribe of Issachar, most directly affected by the
renewal of Canaanite hostilities, and recognizing the advantages of united action, took the lead in forming a counter-
coalition. Deborah, a woman of this tribe,[1] " uttered the
songs," that is, either passionate appeals for united action
against the oppressors, or, perhaps, curses directed against
the enemy : the parallel has been cited of those Arab tribes
who begin hostilities by reciting songs against one another.[2]

Barak was among the first to respond to her appeal : he
had a personal injury to avenge, since he had been taken
prisoner by Sisera. He assumed the leadership of the
movement.

> " Awake, awake, Deborah ;
>   awake, awake, utter a song !
>   Be of good cheer, arise, Barak ;
>   take captive those who captured thee, son of Abinoam ! " [3]

Six tribes sent volunteers. These were, in addition to
Issachar, the neighbouring groups, also threatened by the
Canaanite offensive, Zebulon, Naphthali, Machir (the future
tribe of Manasseh), and, no doubt owing to kinship with the
latter group, the other sections of the house of Joseph,
Ephraim and Benjamin.

On the other hand, four tribes whose interests were not
threatened, stood aloof, after long deliberation. The poet
pours scorn on their indolent selfishness :

[1] Judges v. 15. The prose account makes her reside in Ephraim
(iv, 5), in order to reconcile the story with the popular tradition which
attributes to Deborah " the prophetess " the tree of Deborah, the
nurse of Rebekah, between Ramah and Bethel (cf. Gen. xxxv. 8).

[2] **XXX**, pp. 91–2, according to B. Hišam, p. 273. See p. 213.

[3] V. 12, text emended according to the Syriac.

" By the water-brooks of Reuben
   there were great deliberations.
Why didst thou remain among the sheepfolds,
   to listen to the pipe calling the flocks ?
Gilead [1] stayed beyond Jordan ;   ·
   and why does Dan go in foreign ships ?
Asher stayed by the sea-shore ;
   he remains peacefully in his harbours."

On the actual scene of the fighting, an Israelite city, which has not been identified,[2] refused to come to the help of Jahweh, and incurred a curse which was, perhaps, effectively enforced.

It is remarkable that neither Judah, Simeon, nor Levi were even summoned. The two latter tribes were already scattered ; Judah was so isolated as not to be reckoned among the Israelite tribes.

The Israelite forces may have assembled at Mt. Tabor, in the north-east corner of the plain (Judges iv. 6, 14). But the battle took place further south, between Taanach and Megiddo, on the banks of the Kishon. A violent storm, it would appear, contributed largely to the Israelite victory ; the chariots could not manœuvre on the sodden ground : the Kishon, usually an almost dry water-course, became a raging torrent which swept away large numbers of the defeated enemy, a situation which was repeated on the occasion of the battle of Mt. Tabor, on April 16, 1779.[3] At the sight of the storm-clouds, regarded by the Israelites as the chariot of their God, and hearing the rolling of the thunder, the " voice of Jahweh," the Israelites were convinced that their divine leader had come from the desert to overwhelm their enemies.

" Jahweh, when thou camest forth from Seir,
   when thou didst march forth from the fields of Edom,
The earth trembled, the heavens shook,
   the clouds poured down their waters :
The mountains streamed down before Jahweh,
   before Jahweh, the God of Israel."

---

[1] Later, Gad.

[2] Meroz according to the Massoretic text, Mazor (G⁴), Marod (S). The reference may be, perhaps, to Merôn, near Dothan, or to Rimmon, between Taanach and Megiddo ?

[3] Lortet, *La Syrie d'aujourd'hui* (*Tour du monde*, 1881, *ist sem.*, p. 58).

The poet goes on to recount the aid given to his people by the stars and the torrent Kishon. We may recall that among the Babylonians and even still among the Arabs, certain stars are regarded as the cause of rain.[1]

> " The stars fought from heaven ;
> in their courses they fought against Sisera.
> The torrent Kishon swept them away,
> the sacred (?) torrent, the torrent Kishon."

Sisera fled alone on foot. Trusting to the Bedouin custom of hospitality which regarded even an enemy guest as inviolable,[2] he sought refuge in the tent of a Kenite, Jael, whose clan were nomads in the country. But in the heart of the woman, even the sacredness of a guest gave place to hatred of the foe of the allies of her people. While Sisera was drinking the milk which she had given him, she crushed his forehead with the tent-peg. And the poet extols her savage deed :

> " Blessed be Jael among women . . ."

No sentiment was more foreign to the mind of an Israelite in that barbarous age than generosity towards a conquered enemy. This is still more evident from the final strophe of the poem, which gloats over the growing anxiety of Sisera's mother, as she waits in vain for her son :

> " The mother of Sisera looked forth from the window ;
> she watched through the lattice :
> ' Why doth his chariot tarry ?
> why is his train so slow in coming ? '
> The wisest of her princesses answered her,
> yea, she made answer to herself :
> ' Doubtless they are gathering and dividing the spoil ;
> a maiden or two for each warrior ;
> A piece of dyed stuff or two for Sisera,
> a garment, two embroidered garments for his neck.' "

However, we must not judge the ruthlessness of the early Israelites too harshly. The same motive recurs in the literature of many peoples, in the *Persæ* of Æschylus, for instance, and, to come nearer home, in our own folksong on the death of the English general Marlborough.

Concerning the results of this victory, or whether it brought one of the cities of the plain of Jezreel into the

---

[1] See pp. 237–8.　　　[2] See pp. 202–3.

possession of the Israelites, we are ignorant. Its historical importance arises from the fact that, for the first time, the Hebrew mountaineers were victorious on the open plain over the war-chariots of the city-dwellers, and for the first time, as far as we know, since they came out of the deserts, the Israelites manifested, even if only in a temporary and partial fashion, that unity of action as members of the people of Jahweh which ultimately led to the final unification of the tribes around a national king, the Anointed of Jahweh.

In the stories of Gideon and Abimelech we shall find other episodes illustrating the relations, now friendly and now hostile, between the Israelite invaders and the Canaanite city-dwellers.

3. *The Struggle with the Nomads and the Founding of a Kingdom in Manasseh : Gideon and Abimelech.* By reason of its lack of cohesion, the mixed population which now occupied Palestine was the natural prey of plundering nomads. The Midianites, following the example of the Habiri and of the Israelites themselves, began to make daring raids on the west side of the Jordan.

In the Israelite tradition the credit for the deliverance from this scourge is connected with the name of Gideon, also known as Jerubbaal,[1] of the Manassite clan of Abiezer. His figure lingered long in the popular imagination (*cf.* Isa. x. 26). In the present text of the book of Judges it is still possible to distinguish two parallel cycles of tradition in which the story of Gideon has been preserved. Each of these again consists of various layers of narrative in which the popular imagination of successive ages has glorified the national hero. We have stories of a supernatural call, which are at the same time variant traditions concerning the origin of sanctuaries (Judges vi. 11–24 and vi. 25–32), and tales of wonder intended to emphasize Jahweh's part in the miraculous deliverance, etc.

The following appears to be the order of events according to the oldest part of the earliest cycle.[2] When the scene opens, we see Gideon with 300 men crossing the Jordan in pursuit of two Midianite kings, or sheikhs, Zebah and Zal-munnah. Needing food, Gideon and his men sought to procure it from the two Israelite (or Gileadite) cities on their way, Succoth and Penuel, but met with a mocking refusal.

[1] See p. 408.   [2] Judges viii. 4–10*a*, 11–27*a*, 29–32.

On the edge of the desert, near the Bedouin highway, that is, no doubt, the main caravan route from Damascus to Arabia, they surprised the camp of the freebooters, possibly by means, of the stratagem of torches concealed in jars, an episode which should be transferred to this part of the narrative. Gideon captured the two sheikhs.

On his way back, he severely punished the two cities which had insulted him. Then, probably on his return to Ophrah, he asked his captives : " What manner of men were they whom ye slew at Tabor ? " " They were as thou art," replied the sheikhs, " each of them looked like the son of a king." " They were my brothers, the sons of my mother," answered Gideon. This incident shows us the motive of the daring expedition of the hero : it was not, as the later narratives represent it, a divine call to save the nation, but the private duty of avenging his kinsmen. Gideon orders his son to slay the murderers that he may learn the sacred duty of the vendetta. But the child shrinks from the task and the two sheikhs excuse his reluctance ; without reproaches they request Gideon to kill them himself, so that it might not be said that a child slew them. The proud sense of personal prestige so simply expressed by the two Bedouin chiefs, the importance attached to the vendetta, the exclusive pre-occupation with the responsibilities and interests of the narrow group constituted by the clan or the city, are all characteristic traits of this period of Israelite history.

After this achievement, the " Israelites "—the sequel of the narrative shows that only the Israelites of the district of Ophrah were in question—asked Gideon to become their hereditary chief, or, in other words, their king. According to the present form of the story, he refused with the words, " Jahweh shall be your king." But this reply, breathing the spirit of a later age which regarded the rule of Jahweh as incompatible with that of a man, is certainly not historical. In reality, Gideon accepted and exercised the power of a king, for at his death we find his sons disputing about the succession, the only question being whether it shall be divided among them, or whether one of them shall inherit the whole (Judges ix. 2).

Anticipating David and Solomon, Gideon's first thought was to create a royal sanctuary : he made and set up in

Ophrah an *ephod*, probably some kind of image,[1] which the people came to seek oracles from.

In further resemblance to David and Solomon, he consolidated his power by forming a numerous harem, in order to form links with the chief families of the communities whom he wished to conciliate. One of his wives was from Shechem. But this city, as we see from the story of Abimelech, was still a Canaanite city at that time : hence this powerful native city had voluntarily accepted the rule of Gideon, the famous defender of the settled population against the Bedouins.

The territory ruled by Gideon and his son, with the exception of the city of Shechem, can hardly have comprised more than the country of Manasseh and, no doubt, the districts of Succoth and Penuel beyond Jordan : Ephraim was hostile to him (Judges viii. 1–3), and Beer lay outside his authority (Judges ix. 21).

Such would seem to be the basis of historical fact underlying the stories of Gideon, the founder of a petty local kingdom. It is, moreover, probable that his struggle with the nomads included other episodes than the one which we have cited, and possibly the other traditions concerning the deliverer may have preserved some trace of them.

The fate of Gideon's line was a tragic one. It is related in one of the most restrained and credible chapters of Israelite history (Judges ix.). Such difficulties as the story presents arise chiefly from its fragmentary character.

On the death of Gideon one of his seventy sons, Abimelech, came to Shechem and persuaded his uncles on his mother's side to say to the men of the city : " Whether is better for you, either that all the sons of Jerubbaal, which are threescore and ten persons, reign over you, or that one reign over you ? remember also that I am your bone and your flesh " (Judges ix. 2). This Abimelech was the son of the Shechemite woman whom Gideon had married. Since, even after her marriage, she continued to live in Shechem (Judges viii. 31), it has often been inferred from the words of Abimelech that this marriage was of the matriarchal type where the children belonged to the mother's clan.[2] This is not likely : Abimelech considers himself as a member of his father's group, since he claims his

[1] See p. 430.　　　　　　[2] See p. 193.

inheritance. But he makes use, however, of the feeling of
close relationship which existed between the son and his
" mother's brethren," no doubt a survival from the old custom
of tracing descent through the female line.

The Shechemites gave him financial assistance from the
treasure-house of their god Baal-Berith, " the lord of the
covenant." [1] With this money the young man hired a band
of adventurers and led them to Ophrah to slaughter the
seventy sons of Gideon " upon one stone."   Then the men of
Shechem and the inhabitants of Beth-Millo made him king
" by the sacred tree of the pillar that is in Shechem "—apparently the same tree and the same pillar, the former of which
was believed later, when Shechem had become an Israelite
city, to have been consecrated by Jacob, and the latter to
have been set up by Joshua under the tree (Gen. xxxv. 4 ;
Joshua xxiv. 26).[2]

The Shechemites, no doubt, expected that a king who
owed them so much would be obliged to leave the supremacy
of the state in their hands, but in this they were disappointed ;
Abimelech did not even live in their city.

By the end of three years the misunderstanding was
complete.   The men of Shechem received a man by the name
of Gaal, probably a Canaanite, who aspired to replace Abimelech, and who appealed, apparently, to the local pride of the
Shechemites : " Who is Abimelech ? " said he, " and what is
Shechem that we should be subject to this man ?   Does it
not rather become the son of Jerubbaal and his captain Zebul
to serve the men of Hamor, the son of Shechem ? " [3]   Abimelech took the city by surprise, razed it to the ground and
strewed salt on its site.   He also took the fortress, which
constituted a separate city called the Tower of Shechem, and
burnt the temple of the god together with all those who had
taken refuge in it.   But during the siege of another rebel city,
Thebes, the modern Tubas, a woman threw a millstone on to
his head, and he was only just able to ask his armour-bearer
to run him through with his sword, lest it should be said of
him that a woman slew him.

The story of Abimelech is proof positive that the Canaan-

---

[1] See p. 121.   [2] See pp. 230–1, 406.
[3] That is to say, the native nobility ; *cf.* Gen. xxxiv.   The text of
ix. 28 is slightly emended.

ites had not been exterminated, that certain of their cities preserved civil and religious independence, and from time to time formed with the neighbouring Israelite groups alliances in which they might claim to have the preponderating influence.

The experiment of monarchy in Manasseh does not seem to have survived the death of Abimelech. The foreign situation was not yet sufficiently serious to force upon the native and Israelite clans and cities the 'necessity of abandoning their isolation and concentrating the political power in one hand. The kingship, even when confined to a single district, was still too distasteful to the majority of the Israelites : they considered that royalty was a useless institution, even if it was not actually harmful. This is the point of the parable which the historian has put into the mouth of Jotham, the son of Jerubbaal, but whose relation to the case of Abimelech and the men of Shechem is evidently forced : it is the parable of the trees who desired to set a king over them. The olive, the fig-tree, the vine, all the useful trees, refuse :

" Should I," said the latter, " cease to yield my wine which rejoices gods and men, to go and reign over the trees ? "

Only the thorn-bush accepts the proposal :

" Come and take shelter under my shadow ! "

But the thorn-bush set fire to the whole forest (Judges ix. 8–15).

This fable, which bears so hardly on the monarchy, is somewhat out of place in the mouth of the son of a king. But its point of view must have been that of many Israelites at that time : although they had become agriculturists, growers of fruit-trees, they still held to their Bedouin anarchism tempered with aristocracy.

4. *Struggles with Neighbouring Hebraic Peoples, Moabites and Ammonites. The Gileadite Monarchy : Jephthah.* Even the kings of Israel found the Moabites no mean adversaries, and they must have been far more formidable to the disunited groups of the period of the Judges. During this time the territory of Moab must have included, not only the high plateau north of the Arnon, a much-contested region, but also the east bank of the Jordan, opposite Jericho ; for this

part of the valley was called *Arboth Moab*, the portion of the *Arabah* (*i.e.* of the Plain of Jordan) belonging to Moab.

Under a king named Eglon, the Moabites even invaded the west bank, took the city of Palmtrees (Jericho) and exacted tribute from the Benjaminites. A barbarous story tells how one of these Benjaminites named Ehud, under the pretext of bringing tribute, or, according to another version, claiming to have a " word of God," an oracle, to impart to the King, obtained a private audience of Eglon and assassinated him, after which there was a general massacre of all the Moabites who had crossed the Jordan.

The historicity of Ehud has been called in question because, in one of the genealogies in Chronicles (1 Chron. vii. 10), he appears as the great-grandson of Benjamin. But it is not necessary to regard every person who is mentioned in a Hebrew genealogy as an imaginary eponymous ancestor ; he may be an historical figure who later on has been claimed by a family as an ancestor. The story of Ehud, with its typical savagery, its restraint, its entire probability, and its two versions standing side by side, offers every appearance of historical credibility.

It must be acknowledged that the same cannot be said about the story of Jephthah. The famous incident of the sacrifice of the hero's daughter has been regarded on good grounds as mythical in origin. Seasonal periods of mourning such as that which the daughters of Israel celebrated annually for the young victim are found among many peoples and are based upon the myth of the death or disappearance of a god. Usually it is a vegetation god, sometimes an astral divinity : we find mourning for Adonis-Tammuz, Kore, Linus, Hyacinthus, Hylas, etc.[1] These ceremonies are often accompanied by human sacrifices. The object of the ceremony was to slay or remove the spirit of the harvest, in order that the fruits of the earth may be partaken of without danger. To this end the spirit was embodied in a human or animal victim which was then slain ; as a consequence it was necessary to bring about the resurrection of the vegetation-spirit by another ritual.

The most striking parallel is found in the story of Iphigenia. Iphigenia was originally a name of the god-

[1] *Cf.* **CCXVII**, p. 472.

dess Artemis Tauropolus, who was worshipped with human sacrifices. Popular tradition made her the daughter of Agamemnon, one of the heroes of the Iliad. Similarly we have here the transformation of the myth of an ancient Gileadite deity into an Israelite heroic legend of Jahwist character. This supposition is rendered more probable by the fact that the period of four days during which the funeral rites for the young heroine lasted, was not the customary period of mourning for the dead in Israel, three or seven days being the usual duration of such rites.

Epiphanius says that in his time " the daughter of Jephthah was honoured in Palestine, at Shechem, under the name of Kore, which is the same as Persephone."[1] Philo of Byblos gives a place in the Phenician theogony to a goddess, the daughter of El-Kronos, whose head was cut off by her father [2] and whom P. Lagrange rightly connects with Persephone; [3] the truncated head of the goddess entered into the ritual of several of the shrines of Persephone and Demeter.[4]

Stade went further and relegated to the realm of myth the figure of Jephthah himself, chiefly because he is represented as a bastard son of Gilead : this was interpreted to mean that he was the personification of some obscure and despised clan of the tribe of Gad.

The discovery, partly divined by Reuss, Kittel and Frankenberg, and established by Holzinger (1897), of two parallel versions within the frame of the present narrative, rendered invalid some of the objections against the historicity of Jephthah. Critical analysis shows that the two most suspicious features, the story of the illegitimate origin of Jephthah, and the episode of the vow, did not form part of the original nucleus of the tradition concerning the hero, since the first of these features is wanting in one version and the second in the other. Moreover, the passage which makes Gilead himself, the eponymous ancestor of the inhabitants of the country beyond Jordan, the father of Jephthah, is, as the language shows, a very late addition (Judges ii. 1^b).

The accounts given by the two versions differed widely. According to the one Jephthah was the son of a harlot ; cast

---

[1] *Panarion, Haeres.*, 55 and 78.
[2] Fr. ii, 17.　　　　　　　　[3] **XLIX**, pp. 430–1.
[4] Mayer, **JAI**, 1893, pp. 200–1.

out by his brethren, he became a freebooter. When the
Ammonites invaded the country, the elders of Gilead, his
birthplace, summoned him to their aid. He agreed on the
condition that if he were victorious they should make him
their permanent ruler. He conquered the Ammonites and
was then attacked by the Ephraimites who were jealous of
his prestige.

According to the other version, the Moabites were the
invaders. The inhabitants of the country agreed that the
man who was willing to lead them against the enemy should
become the ruler of the whole of Gilead. Here Jephthah is
represented as a prominent citizen of Mizpah where he lives.
He attempts at first to induce the King of Moab to retire
by diplomacy. When this fails he joins battle, but only
gains the victory by making a vow to sacrifice to Jahweh the
first living being that comes out of his house to meet him
when he returns in triumph : it is his daughter who comes
out to meet him.

These two versions, however, have a common nucleus,
which may be regarded as historical fact. Jephthah, as the
reward of the victorious defence of Gilead, became permanent
ruler of the country. He was successful in a struggle with the
Ephraimites, who claimed a kind of hegemony over the rest
of the tribes. It is even possible that there are historical
elements in the story of the vow, and that the memory of
this tragic sacrifice was combined with some ancient local
religious rite.

III

THE NATIONAL MONARCHY. SAUL, DAVID AND SOLOMON

1. *Israel under Philistine Domination.* We have already
pointed out that the Philistines,[1] as Champollion had recognized, were the remains of the " sea-peoples " whom Ramses
II had succeeded in repulsing from the borders of Egypt about
1192. They retained some of their customs ; their armour
and weapons (1 Sam. xvii. 5–7) recall those of the peoples of
Asia Minor ; they rejected the custom of circumcision, practised by all their new neighbours. But otherwise they
adopted as quickly as the Hebrews, and even more com-

pletely, the customs of the Canaanites, no doubt as the result of free mingling with the native population.[1] All the Philistine deities known to us are genuine Semitic divinities : Dagon, the corn-god;[2] Atargatis-Derketo, the goddess of Ascalon, a form of the ubiquitous Semitic Astarte;[3] a Palestinian or Philistine Astarte mentioned in an inscription discovered at Delos;[4] Baal Zebub, " the lord of flies," the god of Ekron.[5] Most of the personal names of Philistines known to us are Hebrew; they are an indication that the newcomers quickly adopted the language of the country.

Judging by the narrow limits of their territory, the Philistines must have been much less numerous than the Israelites, especially when the latter began to absorb the Canaanite population. But they were far more united than any of the other peoples of Palestine. They were divided into five principal cities, Ekron, Ashdod, Ascalon, Gaza and Gath, each governed by a *seren* ; this term, which in Hebrew is only used in connexion with the Philistines, was evidently a word of their own language, perhaps akin to the Greek τύραννος : the Syriac Bible renders it *truno*, and the Targum *turono*.[6] These princes, at least in our period, usually acted in concert.[7] One of them, the prince of Gath, is sometimes styled " king," but only King of Gath, and not of the Philistines. The five cities apparently constituted a federation possessing abundant resources. The plain which extends along the coast is one of the most fertile regions of Palestine ; Gaza, the starting-point of several caravan routes, was always an important trading centre. The port of Dor belonged to allies of the Philistines, the Zekal, another " sea-people."[8]

The Philistines were warlike and heavily armed ; they numbered among their ranks many of those giants who were so formidable in those days of hand-to-hand encounters :[9] on the bas-reliefs of Ramses III the Philistines are usually represented as taller than the Egyptians. The newcomers quickly subjugated the coastal plain and found themselves

---

[1] *Cf.* **XIII**, pp. 379–80.   [2] See pp. 127–8.   [3] See pp. 133–4.
[4] **AI**, 1909, pp. 297–8, 307–15 ; *cf.* **RB**, 1911, p. 156.
[5] See pp. 109–110.   [6] *Cf.* **XII**, p. 62.
[7] 1 Sam. v. 8 ; vi. 4, 12, 16, 18 ; xxix.
[8] *Golenischeff Pap.*, i, 8–9 ; ii, 63, 71 ; *cf.* **XIII**, p. 380.
[9] 1 Sam. xvii. ; 2 Sam. xxi. 15–22.

confronted by the Israelite hill-folk. The tribes of Dan and Judah were, no doubt, the first to succumb to their attacks. The spirit of this depressing time has been preserved in the stories of Samson, even though none of the facts related can be regarded as definite historical events. Samson was, no doubt, originally a solar hero, already popular among the Horites ; for his father Manoah seems to be the eponymous ancestor of the Horite clan of Manahath,[1] and Samson himself (Shimshon) is apparently a form of Sheshai, the pre-Israelite giant of Hebron.[2] But in the local Danite and Judæan tradition (Judges xvi. 1–3), he became the half-heroic, half-comic embodiment of those small groups of frontier Israelites, who, in the struggle against the Philistines, performed prodigies of strength, cunning and refinement of vengeance, but, ill-armed, often betrayed by their own people, were crushed in the end.

But the situation grew worse : the Philistines conquered the territory of Ephraim and Benjamin, that part of the country in which the Israelites were most firmly entrenched. This is attested by an Israelite tradition of which we possess two versions which have been intimately interwoven (1 Sam. iv. 1[b]–vii. 1) ; it appears to have been a " sacred legend " which the priests of Jerusalem were in the habit of relating to pilgrims in praise of the ark, the centre of temple worship.[3] Incidentally it has preserved for us a memorial of certain important facts of general history.

When the story begins, the Philistines had already " enslaved " the Israelites (1 Sam. iv. 9). But the latter, probably those of the house of Joseph, had rebelled. The Philistines attacked them.[4] The encounter took place at Eben ha-ezer, the Stone of Help, a sacred, perhaps a miraculous, stone, which must have been near Mizpah (perhaps en-Nasbeh, to the north of Jerusalem). After the first defeat the Israelites persuaded themselves that it was due to the fact that their God was not in their camp. They sent to Shiloh to fetch the ark of Jahweh. When it reached the camp the Israelites, filled with joy, uttered ritual salutations.[5] The Philistines, on learning the cause of the shouts, were ex-

---

[1] Gen. xxxvi. 23 ; 1 Chron. ii. 52–4.
[2] LVII, pp. 512–15.   [3] XXV, ii, p. 12.
[4] iv. 1 (G).   [5] See p. 274.

tremely alarmed : " A god is come into the camp of the Hebrews," said they, " such a thing has not been before. Woe unto us ! " However, they did not allow themselves to be daunted by the thought of having to fight against a divine adversary,—like the homeric heroes,—and fought with more determination than ever. Israel was utterly defeated, and to crown the disaster, the ark fell into the hands of the enemies.

The historians, who were exclusively interested in the fate of the sacred object, relate with delight the dreadful plagues which the captive ark inflicted upon the conquerors until they were compelled to send it back. But they tell us nothing of the results of the defeat for Israel. But we can gather the gravity of the situation. It was no doubt at this time that Shiloh, whose temple had hitherto housed the ark, was destroyed,[1] for the sacred chest, on its return, was not replaced there, and the priests of Shiloh emigrated to Nob. Moreover, the Philistines placed a *neṣib* in Gibeath Elohim (1 Sam. x. 5 ; xiii. 3–4), probably the same city that is else-where called Gibeah of Saul and Gibeah of Benjamin, twenty or thirty stades north of Jerusalem.[2] Whether the word *neṣib* denotes here a governor, an outpost, or, as seems most probable, a stele of victory, the Philistines asserted thereby their mastery over the most distinctively Israelite part of Palestine.

Desperate diseases require desperate remedies. The hopeless situation into which the Hebrew tribes had fallen forced them to gather round a single leader, as soon as one was found daring enough and strong enough to organize a national revolt.

2. *Saul becomes King of Israel.* No events in the whole of the history of Israel were current in more numerous and more divergent forms than those which led up to the accession of Saul to the kingship. Nor is this difficult to understand : the monarchy was very differently regarded in different periods and in different environments ; moreover, the figure of Saul was presented under colours which varied according to the degree of sympathy which the narrator possessed for the line of David.

[1] Jer. vii. 12–15 ; xxvi. 6 ; Ps. lxxviii. 60.
[2] A.J. v, 2, 8 ; B.J. v, 2, 1.

In the narratives concerned with the institution of the monarchy (1 Sam. vii.--xv.), critics are usually content to distinguish two main strands, one favourable,[1] the other inimical [2] to the monarchical principle. We have elsewhere attempted to prove that in the strand favourable to the monarchy two parallel series of stories can be discerned,· each constituting a complete and connected whole.[3] Hence we possess, with the anti-monarchical account, three .versions of the events.[4] Moreover, each of these cycles consists of traditions of very different value and origin.

The reality seems to be that Saul drew attention to himself by a victory over the Philistines occupying Gibeah, his native city, and as a result of this achievement he was hailed as king by the tribes.

APPENDIX

The Three Versions of the Founding of the Monarchy

i. According to the most reliable part of the oldest of the two main strands, Saul overthrew the *neṣib*, the stele which the Philistines had erected in his native town of Gibeah. It was an act of overt rebellion. Saul blew the trumpet to summon the patriots to his aid, but only 600 warriors gathered round him. The Philistines assembled a powerful army which the text estimates, with true oriental exaggeration, at 30,000 chariots, 6,000 horsemen, and foot-soldiers like the sand of the sea. They encamped at Michmash, only separated from Geba (the modern Djeba), where Saul was posted, by the deep gorge of the wady es-Sueinit. Saul hesitated to attack, but Jonathan, his son, precipitated matters. Without telling his father, and followed only by his armourbearer, he crossed the ravine, attacked the enemy outposts and slew twenty men. The entire Philistine camp was seized with panic. The Israelite sentinels reported to Saul that the enemy's camp was in confusion. Saul did not wish to act without guidance from Jahweh : but the ritual of consulting the *urim* and *thummim* was long. The uproar increased, and Saul was obliged to break off his inquiry and fall upon the Philistines. In his zeal he bound his men to eat nothing until the evening.

The pursuit ended with a tragic incident. Jonathan, who was not aware of the impetuous oath imposed upon his troops by Saul, ate a little honey. In the evening, when Saul asked Jahweh if the pursuit should be continued through the night, the oracle was

---

[1] 1 Sam. ix. ; x. 1–16,' 27^b ; xi. 1–11, 15 ; xiii. ; xiv.

[2] 1 Sam. vii. 2–8, 22 ; x. 17–25^a ; xii. ; xv.

[3] **CCLXXII.** Budde's objections (**KHC,** *Samuel*) do not appear decisive.

[4] This is also, in spite of numerous differences of detail, the general conclusion of Ch. Bruston (**RTP,** 1885, pp. 511–21) ; R. Kittel (in **XL**) ; Ed. Montet (**LXVI,** pp. 70–1).

silent. Saul perceived that some serious fault had been committed. The sacred lot disclosed that Jonathan was the guilty person. He confessed without hesitation, and Saul swore that he must die. But the warriors ransomed him, that is, either one of them or a captive of rank [1] was executed in his stead.

According to the version which we are following it would appear that as the result of this brilliant success Saul was proclaimed king. The passage relating the event has not been preserved ; but the break is visible, for the text continues : " Therefore when Saul had taken the kingdom . . ." (1 Sam. xiv. 47). According to this tradition it was, perhaps, at Gibeah that Saul assumed the royal authority, and the prophet Hosea seems to refer to a similar tradition (Hos. x. 9).

In the same version this story was preceded by a fragment equally noteworthy for its vivid simplicity, but which is, nevertheless, undoubtedly at bottom only one of those poetical legends with which popular fancy loves to invest the beginnings of great men (1 Sam. ix. 1–10, 12). Saul, sent to find the lost asses of his father, despairing of success, has recourse to a seer who lives in a little town through which he passes. This seer, named Samuel, has been previously warned by Jahweh : " Tomorrow about this time I will send thee a man out of the land of Benjamin, and thou shalt anoint him to be captain over my people Israel, that he may save my people out of the hand of the Philistines." Samuel disclosed to Saul the high position to which he was destined and secretly anointed him king. According to this account it was the seer who gave Saul the idea of attacking the triumphal stele of Gibeah by telling him that when he arrived at this spot he would meet the " prophets," and would be possessed by the spirit of Jahweh : " Do as occasion serve thee ; for God is with thee."

It is possible that this charming story contains a nucleus of historical fact. Saul does actually seem to have been seized by the ecstasy of the *nebi' im*, those wandering ecstatics similar to the Moslem dervishes, who may have been then, as in the time of Elisha, the preachers of Israelite patriotism. It is also possible that a seer of the name of Samuel may have had some part in arousing the revolt and hence in preparing the way for the kingdom. But the arrangement and the whole atmosphere of the story betray the influence of popular fancy. Saul comes before us here as a retiring and modest young man, about whose prolonged absence his father is anxious, and not as we find him in the previous narrative, a grown man, the father of a hero of Jonathan's stamp. This amazing story is the expression in literary form of the profound belief of the great majority of Israelites from the tenth century to the exile,[2] that the national monarchy was an institution designed and prepared by Jahweh, and not created by the mere act of the people or of the first king. Hence the part assigned to the seer, the instrument of the national God.

ii. According to the second monarchical version, Saul first distinguished himself by an encounter, not with the Philistines, but with the king of the Ammonites, Nahash, whom he compelled

---

[1] **XXV**, ii, 1, p. 44.
[2] *Cf.* for example, 2 Sam. iii. 18 ; xix. 10 ; Deut. xxxiii. 5 ; Judges xvii. 6 ; xviii. 1 ; xix. 1 ; Lam. iv. 20.

to raise the siege of the town of Jabesh in Transjordania. Following this exploit he was proclaimed king at Gilgal,—probably the ancient circle of sacred stones near Jericho [1]; for it was a Benjaminite sanctuary. He then undertook the great task for which he had been chosen, the struggle with the Philistines. According to this version it was Jonathan who overthrew the stele of Gibeah. Then follows another account of the battle of Michmash. The Philistines were thrown into confusion by an earthquake. The Hebrews whom they had compelled to join them went over to the conquerors, together with the countryfolk who had taken refuge in the mountains of Ephraim. In this account, similarly, the pursuit ends with an incident which illustrates Saul's piety. He had uttered a solemn vow : " None of the people shall taste food until I am avenged of my enemies." Hence, after the victory, the famished Israelites threw themselves upon the cattle taken from the enemy and began to eat them without first pouring out the blood ; this was a serious breach of national custom.[2] Saul ordered a great stone to be rolled into place on which his men might slay their victims. " And Saul built his first altar to Jahweh."

This second version, like the first, must contain genuine historical material. There can be no doubt that Saul delivered the besieged town of Jabesh, since it displayed, ever after, a special attachment to him (1 Sam. xxxi. 11–13 ; 2 Sam. ii. 4–7). But the story of this exploit presents serious improbabilities : is it credible that Nahash should have granted to the besieged townsmen a delay of seven days before surrendering, in order to allow them to send messengers for help throughout all Israel ? Further, it is extremely difficult to place the expedition against the Ammonites in a time when the Philistines were unquestioned masters of the country and of Saul's own town : they would hardly have allowed the Israelites to assemble troops and create a united nation. The other version, according to which Saul's first efforts were directed against the people which held his own town in bondage, is much more natural.

It is possible that the history of Saul, both in the Jabesh story, and in the other, was preceded by a sort of poetic prologue describing the boyhood of the future " anointed of Jahweh." There are, indeed, reasons for supposing that the charming story of the birth and childhood of Samuel (1 Sam. i.) was originally told about Saul. In no other way can we account for the explanation given by the mother for the name which she has chosen for her son. We read in the text as it is at present : " She called his name Samuel, saying, because I have asked him of the Lord." The popular mind certainly did not shrink from fanciful derivations : but it is difficult to see how she could have got *shemuel* from the verb *sha'al*, to ask. On the other hand, we should have a perfectly good etymological derivation if the original text read : " she called his name *Saul*," since *sha'ul* means " asked for." The whole story, moreover, is a series of particularly ingenious variations on the theme given by the name Saul : the child is first of all " asked for," whence we get the classic story of the barren wife

---

[1] Rather than the place of the same name in the district of Shechem (**CCXXXVIII**, pp. 18, 20).

[2] See p. 248.

praying that a son may be given to her ; then he is " borrowed " by Jahweh, " lent " to Jahweh (another meaning of the word *sha'ul*), whence we get the vow by which his mother consecrates him to Jahweh.

It may seem strange to us that a fierce and gloomy warrior king like Saul should have been pictured by the popular imagination as having begun life as a sort of choir-boy, a little priest attached to a sanctuary. But such an association of ideas seems to have been a natural one in the Hebrew imagination ; for we find it again in the traditions relating to Joshua : there it is related how the future conqueror of Palestine was once an assistant to Moses, the priest, " Joshua . . . departed not out of the tabernacle " (Exod. xxxiii. 11). Moreover, in reality, Saul's kingship possessed a distinctly religious character. In any case, this second version is marked by a complete and unreserved sympathy for Saul.

iii. The third version, whose tendency is anti-monarchical, is also very interesting, but mainly as a witness to the conceptions of a much later age.

Occasionally Israel and Judah had some very bad kings. On the other hand, the eighth century was marked by the appearance of prophets who advanced entirely new ideas concerning the demands of Jahweh : these announced that Jahweh cared little for the greatness or even the existence of Israel ; justice and mercy were what he sought ; further, he required trust in him alone, not in war-horses and foreign alliances. But the monarchy, by its very nature to some extent, existed to promote the greatness of the state by war and diplomacy. Hence it is not surprising to find in a prophet of that period, Hosea (about 760–22), a condemnation of the very principle of monarchy. " O Israel, thou hast sinned from the days of Gibeah " (Hos. x. 9). According to him Israel will not be free from " prostitution," that is, from unfaithfulness to her God, until the day when she has no king (Hos. iii. 4 ; *cf.* xiii. 9–11).

It was natural that among the disciples of this prophet, the ancient accounts which magnified the kingship should not have found favour, and that they should have re-edited the narratives to bring them into accord with what they considered the right point of view. This point of view also has been preserved for us in the first book of Samuel. They inserted, before the account of Saul's accession, a brilliant victory over the Philistines (1 Sam. vii.), in order to show that the monarchy was in no wise indispensable for the deliverance of Israel. This victory, gained, moreover, entirely by supernatural means, such as prayer, fasting and thunder, was ascribed to Samuel, who from a mere seer was magnified into a " judge," a religious reformer whose authority in Israel was absolute. They transferred to him the story of Saul's childhood.

Then they related that one day the Israelites came and asked him to appoint a king over them. This request, actuated, according to the present account, by the evil conduct of Samuel's sons, perhaps originally by the attack of the Ammonites (1 Sam. xii. 12), was, in the opinion of the narrators, arbitrary and unreasonable, and a proof of the basest ingratitude towards both the judge and Jahweh. The latter however ordered Samuel to grant the guilty demand of the people. In an assembly gathered at Mizpah, the sacred lot indicated Saul, who was hidden among the baggage. According to an ingenious theory of Gressmann's, this last feature of the story is the remains of another method of selection by which the possible candidates hide themselves, and the first one found is considered to be chosen by the deity.[1] After this the aged judge laid down his office, having first by a fresh miracle induced the people to acknowledge that in asking for a king they had added another sin to all those which they had previously committed.

Samuel went on to say that he would, however, continue to teach the people and their king the right way. A final story, which is perhaps the modified form of an ancient tradition, relates that he commanded Saul to exterminate the Amalekites as a punishment for their enmity during the Mosaic period; Saul spared the king of the Amalekites and part of the cattle, in consequence of which Samuel announced to him that Jahweh had rent the kingdom from him and given it to another, David.

These imposing scenes, perfectly reflecting the theocratic point of view, profoundly influenced the mediæval Papacy. But they are valueless as evidence for the founding of the Israelite monarchy. At that period there was no opposition between the civil and the religious power: the King, and Saul in particular, was himself Jahweh's instrument. He owed his authority, like Gideon or Jephthah, to a military achievement, and his exploits were ascribed, not without motive, to the direct influence of the spirit of the national God.

3. *The Reign of Saul.* Saul's reign was principally occupied with the struggle against the Philistines (1 Sam. xiv. 52). In this war there would seem to have been very few pitched battles; it was mainly a frontier warfare in which small parties attempted to raid the threshing-floors of the enemy, or to take one of the enemy towns by surprise.

In order to carry on the struggle, Saul does not seem to have created any machinery for the raising of taxes or the levying of troops. He continued to live on his farm. He had no palace or sumptuous court. Once a month, at the new moon, he held a feast at his house to which he invited his officers and at which he presided, sitting on a seat against the wall with his spear beside him. Or else he held a council of war under the sacred tamarisk of Gibeah.

The nucleus of Saul's forces was probably constituted by the warriors of Benjamin, his own tribe. At their head he had placed Abner, his first cousin (1 Sam. xiv. 50–1). It was to Benjaminite chiefs that Saul gave the choicest of the vineyards and fields taken from the enemy (1 Sam. xxii. 7; *cf.* 2 Sam. iv. 2–3). His rule was still in many respects a tribal kingship. However it was an advance on the days of Gideon

[1] **XXV**, ii, 1, p. 35.

and Jephthah. Round the Benjaminite nucleus Saul gathered " strong and valiant " men from every tribe (1 Sam.
xiv. 52) : such as David, who belonged to the tribe of Judah.
Moreover, he felt himself responsible to place his forces at
the disposal of all who bore the Israelite name. Not only
did he deliver Jabesh-Gilead, but he must have intervened
successfully, on other occasions, on behalf of the Israelites
dwelling beyond Jordan ; for after his death, this district was
the most loyal supporter of his son's claims. It was in
defence of Transjordania that he undertook his campaigns
against Moab.

He intervened on behalf of the northern Israelites against
the Kings of Beth Rehob and Zobah,[1] that is, against the
Arameans, a new adversary, of whom we have here the first
certain mention. The Arameans, hitherto nomads, were at
this time beginning to break through into Syria, and to found
flourishing states. Beth Rehob was probably in the neighbourhood of Hermon (Judges xviii. 28). According to some
authorities the kingdom of Zobah marched with the territories
of Israel, Damascus and Hamath,[2] according to others it lay
to the south of Damascus.[3]

If it is true, as the anti-monarchic historian (1 Sam. xv.),
and the author of a gloss inserted in 1 Samuel xiv. 28, relate,
that Saul fought with the Amalekites, it would naturally be
in order to defend the tribes of the extreme south, Judah,
Caleb and the Kenites, from the raids of these plunderers.
In any case, it is highly significant that Saul had already
brought these groups, hitherto strangers to the Israelite
commonwealth, within the sphere of his influence ; for when
David lost favour at court, his parents deemed it wise to
leave Bethlehem Judah ; the men of Ziph and Keilah were
on the point of delivering up their fellow-countryman to
Saul ; and David, although, no doubt, the sympathies of most
of the inhabitants of these regions were with him, could not,
in the long run, hold his ground there against the will of the
king, and was compelled to pass over to the Philistines.

Saul's efforts were also directed towards the annexation
of those Canaanite cities which remained independent. It

[1] 1 Sam. xiv. 7 to be completed according to G[r].

[2] **XX**, pp. 233–4, according to 2 Sam. viii. 3–12.

[3] **XCIII**, pp. 61, 97, 135, 186 ; **XXVII**, p. 108, according to Assyrian
texts.

was probably in the pursuit of this end that he treated the Gibeonites with severity (2 Sam. xxi. 1–14). Perhaps he was pursuing the same policy towards the Canaanite cities of the plain of Jezreel, and it was in defence of the threatened or revolting natives that the Philistines engaged Saul in this district in his last and fatal battle.

On the other hand, Saul's rule had a strongly marked religious character. The most ancient sources agree in recording his strict observance of religious obligations, as for instance in the case of Jonathan and the altar-stone of Aijalon, and in depicting him as possessed from time to time by the spirit of Jahweh. That he was able to impose himself upon the people as the authentic representative of the " God of Israel " must have been of the greatest assistance to Saul in his work of unification. On his campaigns he took with him a priest who was expert in the use of the ephod, and did not fail to consult him. An entirely probable tradition relates that he proscribed those who consulted the dead and familiar spirits (1 Sam. xxviii. 3, 9) ; if he condemned these practices, it must not be supposed that he considered them fraudulent, on the contrary,[1] it was because he regarded the spirits of the dead and the spirits of the *elohim* as rivals of Jahweh, the sole God of Israel.

The close of his reign was darkened by the attacks of a mental disorder which afflicted the heroic king. He had fits of melancholy in which depression alternated with mad rages : he saw traitors everywhere. His contemporaries naturally explained his condition as the result of possession. But it is a striking proof of the deep affection which Saul had inspired in his people that this misfortune was not regarded as a mark of divine displeasure and did not deprive him of their reverence and obedience.

The hatred of the unhappy king was specially directed against a young Judean, named David, whom he had attached to himself as a musician, as a means of soothing his attacks of depression, and whom he had also made his son-in-law and one of his principal captains. Concerning the relations between Saul and David, tradition, so sparing in information on the general history of the reign, provides us with a rich store of anecdotes, some tragic, some comic, some marked

[1] See the account in 1 Sam. xxviii. 7–25.

by the savagery of early times, some pandering to the idealizing and sentimental tastes of later times, some evidently mythical, but all displaying an exclusive sympathy for David. The latter, with a company of 600 adventurers, attempted to carve out for himself some kind of kingdom in the extreme south of Judah, but was at last obliged to emigrate to the Philistines. He placed his sword at their disposal against his former countrymen. No doubt Saul's ill-timed persecution of the brave Judean had the effect of loosening the links which the King had succeeded in establishing between the southern groups and Israel.

Saul and three of his sons met a heroic death fighting on Mt. Gilboa against the Philistines. Their mutilated bodies were hung on the walls of Beth Shan. The Israelite minorities who had settled here and in other cities of the plain of Jezreel were obliged to emigrate. Central Palestine, no doubt, fell back again under Philistine domination [1]; we hear nothing of war with them in the following period of history.

The work of liberation and unification accomplished by Saul was wiped out. However, it is a noteworthy fact proving the extent to which the Israelites had been impressed by the success of the first king, that there was no thought of abolishing the institution of monarchy.

4. *The Reign of David.* Ishbaal,[2] the fourth son of Saul, probably a minor, was proclaimed king at Mahanaim beyond Jordan. But at the same time David, while displaying deep and sincere grief for the death of Saul and Jonathan, for whom he composed a touching lament,[3] set up an independent state in the south, consisting of the half-Israelite, half-Canaanite tribe of Judah (Bethlehem) and the non-Israelite groups of Caleb, who belonged to the Kenizzites and occupied Hebron, together with the Kenites and the Jerahmeelites. The capital of the new community was Hebron, but it called itself Judah, and corresponds to the tribe of that name as it is known to the genealogists of the classic era.[4]

This step was a violation of the claims of Ishbaal. The

---

[1] *Cf.* 2 Sam. iii. 18, where " I will deliver " should be read.

[2] 1 Chron. viii. 33 ; ix. 39 ; 2 Sam. ii. 8 (G⁹³, Aq., Sym., Theod., L). His name, which means "the man of the Lord " (Baal), is generally travestied into Ishbosheth, " the man of shame," in hatred of the word " Baal," which was accounted heathen.

[3] 2 Sam. i. 19, 27.   [4] See p. 391.

Philistines must have favoured the undertaking, the more so that David remained their vassal. There followed a war which lasted about seven years between Israel and Judah. Its course turned in David's favour. Two assassinations contributed largely to this result ; Abner, the mainstay of the house of Saul, was treacherously killed by Joab, David's nephew and general, in order to avenge the death of one of his brothers ; and Ishbaal himself was murdered by two of his Benjaminite captains, who brought his head to David. The latter emphatically disowned responsibility for these murders ; he lavished funeral honours on the victims and ordered the murderers of his rival to be executed. But he skilfully availed himself of the fruits of these opportune deaths : the elders of the whole land assembled at Hebron and anointed David king over Israel.

His first task was to free the country from the foreign yoke. The initiative was taken by the Philistines. The union of all the Israelite forces under a vigorous rule was too obvious a threat to their domination. The struggle must have been long, but consisted mainly of petty frontier fights, marked by many acts of individual prowess, and in which David's paladins, the " thirty " and the " three," slew a number of giants.[1] The war ended, not only with the expulsion of the Philistines from Israelite territory, but with the complete humbling of their power ; we even hear of an encounter at Gath, one of the five principal cities of the league ; on the other hand, David kept and handed down to his posterity the city of Ziklag, which had been given to him as a possession by the King of Gath (1 Sam. xxvii. 6). Gath itself became an Israelite city (2 Chron. ii. 8), no doubt under David.

It was only after he had repulsed the first attacks of the Philistines, and not immediately after his acknowledgment as king by all the tribes, as the present biblical order of the narrative seems to suggest (2 Sam. v. 4–25), that David was able to undertake the attack on Jerusalem. This city, which had remained in the hands of the Canaanites, interfered seriously with the communications between the north and the south of his states and hence hindered the unification of Judah and Israel, which was one of the central aims of his policy.

[1] 2 Sam. v. 17–25 ; xxi. 15–22 ; xxiii. 9–17.

Moreover, it was his intention to make Jerusalem his capital. Renan expresses his surprise that David should have chosen this paltry Canaanite fortress instead of retaining Hebron as his capital, an ancient city full of associations with the past, famous for its sanctity, and possessing important public buildings. On the contrary, the King's choice is a clear indication of his political sagacity and foresight. By retaining Hebron as the capital he would have incurred the risk of appearing to the mass of the nation as a mere tribal king who was attempting to impose upon " Israel " a foreign rule, so to speak. On the other hand, if he had chosen a city from Benjamin or Ephraim, he would have risked offending Judah, his strongest support. It was a stroke of genius to choose a neutral city, conquered by the united effort of all his people, and yet in the neighbourhood of Judah.

Furthermore, Jerusalem was no petty fortress, but one of the oldest and most illustrious royal cities of the land.[1] Its citadel, Zion, was supposed to be impregnable (2 Sam. v. 6) ; it is practically certain that it is the walls of this ancient citadel which have been discovered on the spur which runs out from the south of the Haram between the Tyropoeon valley and that of the Kedron ; hence Zion was not situated on the western hill as is commonly believed.[2] Joab took it by direct assault, perhaps by means of the aqueduct which the Canaanites had driven through the hill in order to utilize the spring of Gihon, the modern Virgin's Well,[3] for their water-supply.

David took up his residence in Jerusalem, but permitted the native population to remain there. Henceforth the citadel was known as " the City of David." With the aid of Phenician workmen the King built himself a palace on it.

The only thing still lacking to the new capital was religious prestige. It is true that Canaanite Jerusalem possessed its own holy places, which were, according to the custom of that time, adopted by the cult of Jahweh : there was the spring of Gihon, where Solomon was to be consecrated ; the Fuller's Well (En Rogel), where Adonijah offered sacri-

---

[1] See pp. 44, 48.
[2] The localization is upheld however by Benzinger, III, pp. 29–30.
[3] See p. 61.

fices by the Stone of Zoheleth, *i.e.* the serpent's stone ;
Nehushtan, the brazen serpent, still worshipped in the
eighth century (2 Kings xviii. 4) and which was related by
tradition to have been made by Moses ; doubtless, too,
there was the rock on which later stood the altar of Solomon
and, still later, the " Dome of the Rock," the Moslem holy
place ; for the story of the purchase of the rock by David
(2 Sam. xxiv. 18–25) is probably intended, like the similar
traditions concerning the sacred enclosure of Shechem
(Gen. xxxiii. 19–20 ; Joshua xxiv. 32) and the cave of
Machpelah at Hebron (Gen. xxiii.), to prove that the natives
had no right to this holy place, and this supposes that they
did lay claim to it.

But these Jerusalem sanctuaries had too recently become
Jahwist holy places to have any great attraction for true
Israelites. David set on foot a search for the ark, the
most authentic symbol of Jahweh, long the palladium of
the house of Joseph, but which had fallen into the hands of
the Philistines. A possibly ancient tradition relates that the
King had sworn not to sleep until he had recovered it (Ps.
cxxxii. 1–8). Finally there was found at Kirjath Jearim
a sacred chest which was asserted to be the very ark of
Shiloh, brought back in triumph from the land of the Philistines, and then inexplicably fallen into oblivion. David
caused it to be borne with great ceremony into his citadel
of Zion, where he had prepared a tent for its reception.

The administrative machinery was still very simple, but
the royal power was already predominant.

The army consisted of two elements : (i.) the *ṣaba'*, the
militia, a gathering of the able-bodied men of the tribes,
called together by the sound of the trumpet, by the raising
of standards, or by the kindling of fires on the hills, troops
without uniform equipment, whose number, punctuality of
assembling, and length of stay under arms depended entirely
on individual good will.[1] Joab knew how to get the utmost
out of this very imperfect instrument. (ii.) A body of permanent troops, whose nucleus consisted of the 600 adventurers
who had gathered round David when he was banished by
Saul. They were called the *gibbore David*, " David's mighty
men," or simply the *gibborim*, sometimes the *Kerethi* and

[1] 2 Sam. xix. 8–10 ; 1 Kings xxii. 17, 36.

Pelethi, from the names of two Philistine peoples ; many of the members of this bodyguard of David were, as a matter of fact, recruited from foreign peoples : notably there was a contingent of *Gittim, i.e.* Philistines from Gath, who had joined David's forces with their chief named Ittai. This standing army, wholly devoted to David, was commanded by Benaiah.

In order to feed and pay these men, and to meet the expenses of the court, especially the maintenance of the king's sons, who lived in great splendour (2 Sam. xv. 1 ; 1 Kings i. 5), financial resources were necessary. David seems to have obtained them principally by successful wars followed by plunder and by tribute imposed upon the conquered. Adoram, who was over the conscript labour, was responsible for the levying of tribute. It does not appear, in the disturbances which marked the close of the reign, that the Israelites had to complain of being forced to pay taxes, an intolerable imposition in the eyes of nomads.

In addition to the heads of the army and the treasurer, the court included a *mazkir,* doubtless a kind of *vizier,* whose duty it was to " remind " the King of business to be dealt with, a *sopher,* or scribe, responsible for official correspondence, and the priests—among whom were several of David's sons—whose function it was to consult Jahweh, and who therefore doubtless assisted the King in the administration of justice. The King's counsellors were accused, probably not without good grounds, of partiality, especially in favour of Judah (2 Sam. xv. 2, 3, 6).

The establishment by David, in the centre of Palestine, of an organized state with a formidable army, trained and accustomed to live by plunder, appeared,—it must be confessed, with justice,—to the neighbouring peoples as threatening their power or even their very existence. If we may judge by the account of the struggle with the Ammonites (2 Sam. x. 1–5), this was the cause of the wars which David was obliged to undertake on his eastern and southern frontiers (2 Sam. viii. 2–14). There is no reason to doubt that he fought with the Moabites, conquered them and treated them with extreme severity. In any case, he defeated the Ammonites, as well as the Arameans of Zobah, Beth Rehob and Maachah, whom the King of Ammon had summoned to his

aid. The Edomites were crushed by Joab in the Valley of
Salt (still called the Wady-el-Milh, to the south of Hebron) ;
the royal family was exterminated ; a young prince named
Hadad alone succeeded in escaping to Egypt : the land
became an Israelite province ruled by governors.

Compared with the great Babylonian, Egyptian, Hittite
or Assyrian empires, the kingdom of David was only a modest
principality. It only comprised Palestine proper [1] without
the coast-line, with a ring of small dependent states, either
conquered, as Edom, vassals, as Moab and Ammon, tributary,
like the Arameans, allies, as Tyre and the Arameans of
Geshur, or held in restraint, like the Philistines. But in
Syria nothing of the kind had been seen for two centuries.
To the Israelites, above all, David's achievements seemed
incomparably magnificent. Long after the fabric of his
kingdom had decayed, poets continued to sing of the glories
of the " star " of Jacob (Num. xxiii.–xxiv.). The expectation of a return to the golden age of the reign of David was
one of the classic forms, doubtless the earliest, of the Messianic
hope in Israel.

In reality, this golden age was anything but a time of
unmingled happiness. The second half of the reign was
heavily shadowed by tragic rivalries between the various
pretenders to the succession of the aged King.

One of the great weaknesses of oriental dynasties is that
they have no fixed and recognized principle of succession.
No doubt, in Israel the eldest son had a presumptive right ;
but the rank of the mother, the King's partiality, the choice
of the people, and the manifested approval of Jahweh, might
cause the selection of one of the younger sons. In fact,
all the sons of the ruler might hope to succeed him. Hence
arose shady intrigues instigated by the women of the royal
harem, each eager to promote the fortunes of her own son.
Hence, too, developed increasingly bitter jealousies between
the young princes, hot with the headstrong passions of
youth.

The dramatic events which followed are related in 2
Samuel ix–xx and 1 Kings i–ii, with an accuracy, vividness
and psychological insight which are the marks of a great

[1] See the list of the districts of which the census was taken by
Joab (2 Sam. xxiv. 5–7).

writer recording firsthand experience. To this account we may refer the reader, confining ourselves here to a brief summary.

Amnon, the eldest son of David, was assassinated by his half-brother, Absalom, in order to avenge an assault on his sister Tamar, but also, no doubt, with the purpose of removing a rival. Absalom, banished for this crime, was soon restored to favour, owing to his father's partiality. By clever exploitation of the defects of David's administration, especially in regard to justice, he then succeeded in stirring up a general revolt against his father, who was obliged to escape into Transjordania, with hardly any followers save his *gibborim*. Absalom was defeated and slain by Joab. But the undying enmity between " Israel " and Judah, and the rankling hatred of the Benjaminites against the successful despoiler of the house of Saul, led to the secession of all the provinces north of Jerusalem : David was compelled to reconquer them.

Ten years later the court was divided into two factions : the old retainers of the King, Joab, Abiathar, upholders of the principle of legitimacy, supported Adonijah, the eldest of the princes, who assumed the role of heir to the throne with the knowledge, and hence with the tacit approval, of his father. The ".new " men, Benaiah, Zadok, as well as the *gibborim* and the prophet Nathan, were supporters of Solomon, who was only the tenth son of David, but whose mother, Bathsheba, was the King's favourite wife, a woman of extraordinary beauty whom he had acquired at the cost of adultery and assassination. Adonijah thought that he was strong enough to proclaim himself King before his father's death. But Bathsheba, learning his intentions, prevailed on the aged King to give orders for Solomon's immediate consecration and installation on the throne. Adonijah sought asylum at the altar of Jahweh and received a provisional pardon.

David died shortly afterwards. His was a character rich in contrasts. A chivalrous courage was set off by a cunning that often bordered on duplicity. Cruel when reasons of state demanded it, he showed a tender affection for his sons to the point of weakness. Poet, musician, orator of persuasive eloquence, he cast the spell of his charm

upon all who came in contact with him. While he loved
power, he made use of it above all to increase the greatness
of his people : it was he who made Israel into a powerful
state. In later days he came to be depicted as a kind of
saint, composing psalms by the hundred. But the picture
of him which we can create from the oldest sources, stands
out in a more engaging vividness. His piety was deep and
sincere, but did not rise above the level of his time, a level
which was still almost wholly material and naïvely selfish.
He had a very lively respect for Jahweh's commands, but
thought that a little ingenuity would enable him to get
round them ; since they were concerned rather with external
acts than with inward feelings and moral sentiments. This
is shown with all possible clearness by his last instructions,
which it was his son's first care to carry out on his accession.

5. *Solomon, King of Israel.* Shortly before his death,
David had advised Solomon not to allow Joab's grey hairs
to go down to Sheol in peace, because he had shed the blood
of Abner and Amasa in time of peace, and had stained
David's girdle and his shoes with murder. The King had
never dared to punish Joab for these crimes, which, moreover, had been extremely serviceable to his master's cause ;
but if no vengeance were taken for this innocent blood there
was the danger that Jahweh might one day demand a reckon-
ing for it from the house of David, as he had avenged the
slaughter of the Gibeonites on the house of Saul. In his
anxiety, David casts the responsibility upon his son of
finding a way in his wisdom of slaying the old servant of the
royal house. Horrible as it seems, it was logical. He also
recommends to his good offices the son of Barzillai, who had
rendered him a service, and advises him to have Shimei
put to death, a Benjaminite who had followed David with
curses at the time of Absalom's revolt, but whose life he
had sworn to spare, in a moment when generosity was
policy.

Solomon faithfully carried out his father's instructions,
and completed them by the satisfaction of his own grudges.
When his brother Adonijah asked for the hand of one of
David's concubines, Solomon pretended to see in this step
a proof that he was seeking the throne : since it was indeed
the custom for the harem of a dead king to pass to his suc-

cessor.[1] Hence Solomon had his brother executed. Joab also, accused of complicity, was put to death. Shortly afterwards, Shimei too was executed for having left Jerusalem without permission.

Some historians of repute [2] think that it is possible to clear David of the stigma of having instigated these acts of vengeance. According to them it would be a later historian who, in order to acquit Solomon, the founder of the temple, threw the responsibility for these executions upon his father. This is not likely : if it had been the intention of the narrators to clear the character of Solomon, they would also have attributed to David the blame for Adonijah's death. There is an antique flavour about the words of the old King which is entirely lacking in the Deuteronomic interpolations : he said exactly what he should have said under the impulse of his feelings of gratitude, his desire for vengeance, his remorse and his crude ideas of justice. On the other hand, Solomon acts as he might have been expected to act, both as a dutiful son assuming the responsibility for his father's quarrels, and as a politician ruthlessly pursuing his own interests.

Here, unfortunately, we come to the end of the extracts which have been preserved to us of that valuable firsthand history of the court which we have followed, at least from the beginning of David's reign. For the rest of Solomon's biography, the information of the book of Kings seems to have been drawn chiefly from a " chronicle of Solomon," compiled in the ninth century, and which contained reliable official data concerning the fortunate or disastrous events of the reign, together with anecdotes of a popular nature. The present book of Kings has also collected a number of more or less marvellous legends which were current concerning the wealth, power and wisdom of the King. Finally the Deuteronomic editor, divided between his partiality for the founder of the Temple and the reprobation which he felt for certain of his actions, conceived the idea of dividing the reign into two periods : in the first period he was pious and fortunate ; in the second he was unfaithful to Jahweh and experienced nothing but misfortune. But as the editor has

[1] *Cf.* 2 Sam. iii. 7 ; xvi. 20–2.
[2] Stade, Cornhill, Kamphausen (**XL³**).

reproduced his sources verbally, we can see that the lights
and shades are, as a matter of fact, spread over the whole
of his reign.

As soon as he heard of the death of David and Joab,
Hadad, the Edomite prince who had found shelter at the
court of the King of Egypt,—probably one of the last
pharaohs of the twenty-first dynasty,—took in hand the task
of reconquering the former kingdom of his line ; according
to the biblical narrative he partly succeeded : " he became
King of Edom." [1] Since we learn later on that Solomon
had unrestricted access to the port of Eziongeber, at the
head of the Elanitic gulf, we may assume that he finally
made peace with Hadad—possibly through the intervention
of another Pharaoh, the father-in-law of Solomon,—but
conceded Hadad's title to Mt. Seir.

Another kingdom whose establishment belongs to the
beginning of his reign was the new Aramean kingdom of
Damascus, founded by Rezon, the former general of Hada-
dezer, King of Zobah : " he was an adversary to Israel all
the days of Solomon " (1 Kings xi. 25).

These examples show that the new ruler of Israel was
not able to preserve intact the boundaries of the kingdom
which he had received from his father.

He succeeded, no doubt by means of diplomacy, in bringing Israel, as we should say today, into the circle of the
great powers. He strengthened the friendly relations already
established by David with Hiram, the son of the founder
of the line of the Kings of Tyre.[2] Even the Pharaoh, who
must have been the last [3] or the last but one of the kings
of the twenty-first dynasty,[4] although related by marriage
to Hadad, King of Edom, gave Solomon one of his daughters
(we know from the Tell el-Amarna Letters that this privilege
was greatly coveted, and was seldom granted by the Pharaohs,
even to their most powerful neighbours). The Egyptian

[1] 1 Kings xi. 25 ; read, with G and S. " Edom " instead of
" Aram."

[2] According to Menander of Ephesus (Josephus, c.*Ap.*, i, 113–7 ;
A. J., viii, 144).

[3] **XLV**, p. 219, n. 2.

[4] According to Alt (in **CCLX**, vi, 1909, pp. 32 *ff.*), this would be
Sheshonq, the founder of the twenty-second dynasty. It is less probable ; we should have to explain why this Pharaoh afterwards wel-
comed one of the rebellious subjects of Solomon (1 Kings xi. 40).

princess actually brought with her a dowry for Solomon, namely, the city of Gezer, which the Egyptian king had recently seized from the Canaanites. It was perhaps on the occasion of this expedition against the south-western inhabitants of Palestine that the Pharaoh had realized the value of an alliance with the King of Israel.

Certainly one of the principal objects of Solomon's policy was to surround his kingdom with all the external signs of a great power. Nothing impressed the imagination of his contemporaries so much as the measures which he took to attain this end.

His harem was extremely numerous, even though the traditional figures may be exaggerated and incompatible with one another (1 Kings xi. 3 ; Cant. vi. 8).

The complex of luxurious palaces which he built constituted a new royal city to the north of the gloomy " city of David," probably occupying a part of the modern site of the Haram es-Sherif. The precincts of this royal city included a temple, a kind of royal chapel, vieing in magnificence with the wealthiest shrines of Phenicia or Egypt.

Solomon also embarked upon enterprises more immediately connected with public needs. He created the first body of cavalry and war-chariots hitherto possessed by the Israelites ; since they had previously been in the habit of hamstringing the horses which they captured.[1] He fortified certain towns of strategic or commercial importance : Hazor and Megiddo on the route from Egypt to Damascus, Beth-Horon and Gezer (probably also Baalath) situated on the approaches to Jerusalem, Tamar, belonging to Judah, at the entrance to the caravan-route leading to the Red Sea.[2] In Jerusalem he built or completed the Millo, a block of fortifications intended to " close up the breach of the city of David " (1 Kings xi. 27), that is perhaps to fill up the ravine which originally divided the hill of Zion from that upon which had been erected the new royal palaces and the temple.

---

[1] Joshua xi. 6–9 ; 2 Sam. viii. 4. There is no need to question, as Budde does (**KHC,** *ad loc.*), the historicity of this statement.

[2] 1 Kings ix. 18 (*kethib*). An ambitious scribe has changed the name of Tamar into that of Tadmor (reading of *qere*, the versions and of 2 Chron. viii. 4), thus attributing to Solomon the foundation of Palmyra.

Stimulated by the example of the Phenicians, Solomon seems to have grasped the immense source of wealth contained in commerce. It is true that Canaan was an agricultural country, devoid of industries : when the temple came to be built, Solomon was obliged to fetch a metal-worker from Tyre for the metal-work (1 Kings vii. 13–51), and workmen from Byblos for the woodwork.[1] Hence the Palestinian trader possessed no articles of export upon which to build up a profitable foreign trade, but he was in a position to act as a middleman. Solomon seems to have realized this fact, for to him is ascribed the building up of a trade in horses, which his servants collected from Musri and Queh,[2] *i.e.* from the Taurus and Cilicia, a great horse-breeding country (Ezek. xxvii. 14), and which they sold throughout the whole of Syria, even to the Kings of the Hittites. In these commercial activities Solomon was, according to his usual custom, following the example of the great foreign monarchs. We know from the Tell el-Amarna letters that the exchange of " presents " between princes constituted real commercial transactions, consisting of orders, and complaints when the articles delivered were not satisfactory.[3]

Solomon also saw, like Peter the Great, that his country could not develop without an outlet to the sea. Hence he secured the route across the Arabah to the Red Sea. In alliance with Hiram he built at Eziongeber [4] a fleet which made voyages every three years, it was said, to the mysterious land of Ophir, possibly southern Arabia, whence it brought back articles which the merchants of that country had, apparently, collected from Africa and India : almug-trees, precious stones, gold, silver, apes, ivory and peacocks(?) [5] : the Hebrew names of several of these articles seem to be derived from Sanskrit or Tamil words.[6]

---

[1] According to the ingenious emendation proposed by Dussaud, **SY**, 1923, p. 315, for 1 Kings v. 32 : " and the Giblites hewed the wood, and the masons of Solomon and those of Hiram raised the stones for the construction of the Temple."

[2] This is the probable reading of the corrupt text of 1 Kings x. 28–9. *Cf.* **CCLXXXIII**, pp. 168 *ff.*, **CCLXVII**, p. 94 ; Alt, *Israel und Aegypten*, 1909, pp. 23–4.   [3] *Cf.* **XIII**, pp. 329–30.

[4] The modern Ma Ghadyan, about 30 kilometres to the north of the present head of the gulf. (*Cf.* **XXXII**, p. 631, n. 3.)

[5] 1 Kings ix. 28 ; x. 11–2, 22.

[6] **LXXXI**, ii, p. 122 ; **CCLXVII**, p. 93.

But, strange as it may seem to us, the attitude of the Israelites of that time was opposed to commercial activities on a large scale. Solomon's great undertakings were viewed with suspicion. Moreover, they seem to have yielded little in the way of profits. It was not in gold of•Ophir that Solomon contracted to pay for the materials and labour furnished by Hiram, but in oil and wheat. There even came a time when, in order to obtain the sum of 120 talents of gold from his Tyrian ally, he was obliged to cede twenty towns in Galilee (1 Kings ix. 10–14). From this we may learn how much importance should be attached to the passages describing the fabulous wealth enjoyed by the Israelites under this king (1 Kings x. 27).

As a matter of fact, in order to meet the heavy expenses entailed by his public works and by the administration of the State, Solomon was obliged to impose upon his subjects a system of levies and forced labour similar to that of Egypt.

For this purpose he divided the country into twelve districts, each in charge of a prefect whose duty it was to furnish a month's supplies for the maintenance of the court and the war-horses (1 Kings iv. 7–19). It is noteworthy that, with the exception of four or five instances, the boundaries of these provinces did not coincide with the ancient limits of the tribes : with the definite intention of centralization, Solomon, like the Constituent Assembly of 1790, aimed at destroying the structure of autonomous provincial government. It also appears from this list that the remaining independent Canaanite cities were at this time incorporated in the Israelite kingdom, namely, Dor, Megiddo, Taanach and Bethshan. It is also significant that the territory of Judah—at least the hill country of Judah—does not seem to have formed part of any of the twelve provinces.[1] Hence it would seem that Solomon exempted the royal tribe. This fact would help to explain the increasing hatred which grew up in the northern tribes against the King of Jerusalem and which broke out for the first time during Solomon's reign when forced labour was imposed upon the men of " Israel " for the fortifications of the capital. The revolt was suppressed, and its leader, Jeroboam, was obliged to

[1] On this text, *cf.* Alt (in **CCLX**, p. 13).

flee into Egypt to Shishak (Sheshonq), the founder of a new dynasty, the twenty-second (about 943).

But the final break occurred immediately after Solomon's death. And it is he who must be held in a great measure responsible for the schism by reason of his partiality for Jerusalem and Judah, and on account of the harsh and heavy burdens which he imposed upon his subjects for expenditure which was often purely sumptuary.

Solomon was interested in the arts, as we know by the sculptures which he ordered to be executed for his palace and his temple. It is possible that he had literary leanings : a tradition ascribes to him the composition of 1,005 lyrics (shîr) and 3,000 proverbs, among which there may have been fables like those of Jotham or of Ahikar ; for we are told that Solomon spoke of plants and animals (1 Kings v. 12–3). It has often been maintained, with some probability, that he caused the first collections of the national songs to be made, as Charlemagne did for the Teutonic sagas. However, caution is necessary in speaking of the wisdom of Solomon : it is a subject which later ages have most freely embroidered, attributing to the illustrious king that which each age held to be the highest form of wisdom : the sagacity of the judge, skill in solving riddles, the composition of moral maxims, books of philosophy, love-songs, psalms and sacred lyrics, magic spells. According to the most ancient documents, Solomon's wisdom consisted in political craft, by means of which he was able to rid himself of Joab and Shimei (1 Kings ii. 6–9).

IV

The Two Kingdoms. Israel and Judah

1. *The Schism* (*about* 935). When Solomon died, as in France at the death of Louis XIV, there must have been a great sigh of relief among the northern tribes : they seized the opportunity when the dead king's son Rehoboam came to Shechem, the capital of Ephraim, to be proclaimed king, to present a demand for relief.

Some historians have found it surprising that a king who, like his father and his descendants, held his throne by hereditary right, should have been willing to submit his right of succession to popular ratification. Hence they infer that the assembly at Shechem was a revolutionary gathering, which the King attended with the object of attempting to recover the Israelites who had already revolted,[1] not in order to be made king, as the biblical account has it.

But the principle of an autocratic hereditary rule had never been so securely established in Israel as to enable the King to dispense with the ratification of his subjects, either in the matter of his succession, especially in troubled times,[2] or even in the matter of important legislation.[3] Hence it is quite within the bounds of probability that Rehoboam, conscious of the disturbed state of public feeling, may have thought it a wise stroke of policy to show his regard for his northern subjects by coming to be proclaimed king among them. Moreover, if we are to see in the assembly at Shechem an encounter with the rebels, we must reject almost the whole of the rest of the narrative : Rehoboam was surprised by the demands of the Israelites ; for he deliberated two days before replying. And when, finally, he gave an arrogant refusal, and the infuriated people had slain the royal plenipotentiary—a most unfortunate choice, the superintendent of the levies—the King fled in his chariot, a clear proof that he had brought no troops to quell a revolt.

At all events, the assembly decided to break with the house of David and to proclaim Jeroboam who had returned from Egypt. The tribe of Judah alone remained faithful to Rehoboam : the ten other tribes—for in spite of the traditional belief, there were at that time only eleven tribes—seceded.[4]

In addition to the errors of Solomon and his son, recognized even by the Judean editor of the narrative of Kings, the causes of the breach were the deep-seated antagonism between the " Israelites " and the half-foreign peoples of the south, and, no doubt also, a revival of the old spirit of independence and simplicity which had been sorely wounded by Solomon's despotic policy and by the extent of his borrowing from the civilization of the " nations."

[1] **LXXXVI**; **XXVII**; **XLV**, pp. 219–20.
[2] 2 Sam. xvi. 18 ; 1 Kings i. 40 ; ii. 15 ; 2 Kings xi. 4–20 ; xxiii. 30.
[3] 2 Kings xxiii. 3 ; Jer. xxxiv. 8–22.
[4] 1 Kings xi. 29–39. Hence there is no imperative necessity to correct the figures of this text, with Kittel (*Biblia Hebraica*) and Eissfeldt (in **XL**).

The consequences of the schism were very serious. The Israelites, divided into two rival or hostile groups, carried on henceforth the precarious existence of petty states which are no longer masters of their own fate, but are compelled to maintain themselves by a predatory mode of life among the more powerful states by which they are surrounded.

2. *The Dynasties of Jeroboam and Baasha. A period of Weakness for the Two Kingdoms.* Rehoboam, his son Abijah or Abijam, and his grandson Asa, were in a state of continual warfare with the kings of Israel who were contemporary with them (1 Kings xiv. 30 ; xv. 6, 16), apparently without any decisive success on either side. It is, however, possible that Rehoboam may at one time have threatened Shechem, the capital of Jeroboam, if this was the event which compelled him to remove his residence to Penuel, beyond Jordan.[1]

These internal conflicts brought about a disastrous foreign intervention. Sheshonq I, in Hebrew Shishak, a Libyan mercenary who had founded the twenty-second dynasty with his capital at Bubastis, descended on Jerusalem, and seized the treasures of the temple and the royal palaces, including the golden shields made by Solomon. As it was this Pharaoh who had received the exiled Jeroboam, and who might well have been unfriendly to Rehoboam on account of the latter's relationship through his father to the previous Egyptian dynasty, it is natural to suppose that Sheshonq's campaign was directed against Judah, and had been undertaken at the request of the King of Israel. But there was found on the south wall of the Temple of Amon at Karnak a great bas-relief depicting the god and goddess of Thebes leading to Sheshonq more than 150 chained captives, representing so many cities whose names, unfortunately often obliterated, are inscribed in a crenellated cartouche forming the body of the individual representing the city. Now in this bas-relief, side by side with about a hundred names of cities of Judah, there are also to be found the names of fortified cities of Israel, such as Taanach, Megiddo, and possibly Penuel.[2]

---

[1] 1 Kings xii. 25 ; *cf.* **XLV,** pp. 223, 229. According to Stade (**LXXXVI,** pp. 351–3) this would have been at the time of the invasion of Sheshonq ; a less probable view, because the Pharaoh appears to mention Penuel among the conquered towns.

[2] *Cf.* **CCLXVII,** p. 121.

It is not likely that these names of northern towns should have been added gratuitously by the royal sculptors from earlier lists in order to flatter the monarch,[1] nor that they would have mentioned side by side all the places, hostile or friendly, which paid tribute to the Egyptians,[2] nor that Sheshonq should have reconquered the whole land, city by city, from Rehoboam, supposing that the latter had seized it :[3] if the King of Judah had recovered, even temporarily, the northern kingdom, it is strange that the book of Kings should be totally silent concerning a success which was never repeated by any of the Kings of Judah.

The most probable hypothesis is that perhaps Sheshonq was called in by Jeroboam against Rehoboam, but that, after having conquered and plundered Jerusalem and the rest of the cities of Judah, he seized the opportunity to restore, either by treaty or by arms, that suzerainty over Palestine which the glorious Pharaohs of the eighteenth and nineteenth dynasties had formerly enjoyed and which their successors had never ceased to claim in theory.[4] It does not appear that Egypt was able to maintain a permanent hold over the early kingdoms of David and Solomon. Certainly Osorkon I was still recognized as overlord by Elibaal, the King of the faithful city of Byblos.[5] Osorkon II, too, boasts, in an inscription at Bubastis, of having conquered " the upper and lower Retenu." It has been maintained that a reminiscence of an expedition of either Osorkon I[6] or II[7] against Judah underlies the narrative of Chronicles which ascribes to Asa an overwhelming victory over Zerah, the Ethiopian (2 Chron. xiv. 8–14 ; xvi. 8). But Zerah is not Osorkon and the dynasty of Sheshonq was not Ethiopian : it is impossible to draw any certain conclusions from so late and confused a tradition, and one so evidently characterized by a definite editorial tendency.

In any case, the Egyptian intervention under Sheshonq gives a clear indication of weakness of the Israelites.

[1] *Cf.* **XLV**, p. 223.   [2] **LXIII**, ii, p. 773, n. 3.   [3] **L**, pp. 70–2.
[4] **XLV**, pp. 222–3 ; Alt, *Israel und Aegypten*, pp. 27 *ff.*
[5] *Cf.* the statue of the Pharaoh with a Phenician inscription, **SY**, 1925, pl. xxv.
[6] Champollion : J. Jéquier, *Histoire de la civilisation égypt.*, p. 249 ; R. Dussaud, **SY**, 1925, pp. 114–15.
[7] Naville, *Bubastis*, pp. 50–1.

Another sign of this weakness is that the Philistines, who had been so completely crushed by David, once more became dangerous foes for their Hebrew neighbours : twice within a period of twenty-five years we find Israel warring with them over the same little place, Gibbethon, in the territory of Dan, west of Jerusalem.[1]

One of the main reasons for the weakness of the northern kingdom was the instability of the royal power. Nadab, the son of Jeroboam, came to his end during the siege of Gibbethon, assassinated. in the second year of his reign by Baasha, who exterminated the entire family of Jeroboam and seized the throne. He made Tirzah his capital (probably Talluzeh, to the north of Nablous).

The only event recorded in the reign of Baasha yields a fresh example of the disastrous consequence of the division between the two kingdoms. Already Abijah, the King of Judah, to defend himself against Israel had appealed for help to the Arameans of Damascus, and had made an alliance with their King Tabrimmon (1 Kings xv. 18). Baasha succeeded, evidently at the cost of heavy concessions, in detaching their powerful ally from the Judeans. He seized the opportunity to fortify Ramah, the modern er-Ram, barely ten miles north of Jerusalem, and actually threatened the capital of the southern kingdom. In his distress, Asa sent all his treasures to Benhadad I, the son of Tabrimmon, thus inducing him to break off his alliance with Baasha and to make an inroad into the north of the kingdom of Israel. Baasha was obliged to abandon in haste the fortification of Ramah. The Arameans seized Ijon, Dan, Abel-Beth-Maachah and the district of the lake of Chinnereth, that is, the northern part of the Israelite territory, which the traders of Damascus wanted in order to secure their communications with the coastal cities.[2]

The dynasty of Baasha came to an end in the same way as that of Jeroboam. His son Elah, after a reign of two years, was assassinated during a feast by an officer of inferior rank named Zimri, who proclaimed himself king. The army which was engaged in the siege of Gibbethon, did not ratify his *coup d'état*. The general-in-chief, Omri, besieged the capital. Zimri shut himself up in the palace, set fire to it

[1] 1 Kings xv. 27 ; xvi. 15.　　　[2] *Cf.* **XLV**, pp. 225-6.

and perished in the flames after a reign of seven days.   Omri only succeeded, however, in securing the throne after a struggle of four years with another claimant, named Tibni, who was supported by half the country.   It is a probable supposition [1] that the individualism of the tribes, revived as a reaction from the centralizing policy of Solomon, and which the kings of Israel had been obliged to tolerate, played some part in these recurrent disturbances : whereas Jeroboam relied on Ephraim, Baasha belonged to Issachar ; it is very likely that Omri, the general-in-chief of this king's son, was of the royal tribe ; the more so that the kings of the house of Omri had estates at Jezreel in the territory of Issachar, where they preferred to reside.

3. *The Dynasty of Omri.   Beginning of the Great Struggle with the Arameans.*   The book of Kings tells us almost nothing concerning Omri.   It is from external evidence that we learn the importance of this king's reign.   Assyrian documents call the kingdom of Israel " the land of Omri " or " the land of the house of Omri " ; even when the dynasty had been overthrown, the King of Israel to them was still the " son of Omri."   This may be partly due to the fact that the Assyrians first came into contact with the Israelites during the period of the dynasty of Omri, perhaps in Omri's own reign, for he may have been the king who sent presents to Asshurnasirpal III (880–860), when the latter advanced as far as Nahr el-Kelb, near Beìrut.   In any case, the Assyrian inscriptions quoted presuppose a reference to Omri.   On the other hand we learn from the stele of Mesha that Omri " oppressed Moab " in the time of King Chemoshgad (?), the father of Mesha, that is to say that he compelled him to pay tribute ; the same source also tells us that he took from Moab the district of Medeba.

Omri was less successful in his encounters with the Arameans of Damascus : he was obliged to cede several cities to them, probably on the east side of Jordan, and to grant them the privilege of " streets," that is, a special quarter with a bazaar, in Samaria (1 Kings xx. 34).

It was Omri who founded the latter city, or at least made it the capital.   According to the tradition he bought the site from a certain Shemer, from whom the city received its

[1] **XXVII**, p. 159.

name of Shomron. In reality, perhaps, the name meant
" watch-post." [1] In any case, Omri's object was to place
the royal residence in a city which was not, like Shechem,
attached to a particular tribe, and was not at the mercy of
a sudden attack, as Tirzah seems to have been, since Omri
had taken it in less than a week. The choice of the site of
Samaria does credit both to the political wisdom and to the
military judgment of Omri. The city stood on a hill forming
a promontory joined on one side only to the adjacent plateau :
we shall see that the Arameans twice besieged it in vain, and
the Assyrians themselves were obliged to invest it for three
years before they succeeded in taking it. The excavations
carried out by an American mission from 1908 to 1910 have
made it possible to gain some idea of the strength of the
city's fortifications, especially of its single gate, as well as of
the importance of the royal palace which was built by Omri
and enlarged and adorned by his son Ahab. [2]

Administrative districts were created (1 Kings xx. 14–5)
either by Omri or by Ahab : hence the Omride dynasty
probably undertook, as Solomon did earlier, to destroy the
old tribal organization and to strengthen the centralizing
influence of the royal power.

For the reigns of Ahab and his two sons, Ahaziah and
Joram, who succeeded him, we have once more abundant
material from Hebrew sources (1 Kings xvi. 29–2 Kings x.) ;
but its value is very unequal. The most reliable elements
seem to be extracts from a popular history of the house of
Omri and its fall, a source which in spite of its episodic
tendency and occasional mixture of legendary material, is
on the whole of genuine historical value (1 Kings xx. ; xxii. ;
2 Kings ix.–x). It must have been compiled about 800 B.C.
On the other hand, the extracts taken from the biography
of the prophets Elijah and Elisha, in spite of their great
value for the history of religion, must be used with extreme
caution. [3] The extracts from the life of Elijah (1 Kings
xvii.–xix. ; xxi.) may justly be reckoned among the most
magnificent portions of the Old Testament ; but they are
epic poetry not history. This biography must have been

---

[1] LXXXI, ii, p. 254 ; R. Dussaud, SY, 1925, p. 314, n. 3.
[2] LXXX ; R. Dussaud, SY, 1925, pp. 314–38 ; 1926, pp. 9–29.
[3] See pp. 420–3.

written between 800 and 760. In the traditions relating to Elisha, apparently compiled between 800 and 722, it is possible to distinguish an early stratum containing very valuable information (2 Kings iii.; vi. 24-7, 20), and later additions, at times recalling the most puerile monkish legends and containing evident doublets with the life of Elijah. In addition, the stele of Mesha and Assyrian documents provide contemporary evidence of first-rate historical value.

Ahab understood that in order to save Israel he must be free to concentrate all his forces against the Arameans of Damascus, his more dangerous enemies. Hence he established close relations with the King of Tyre, Ethbaal or Ithobaal, which enabled him to close his enemies' access to the sea by way of Phenicia; the Tyrians, on their side, found the alliance extremely advantageous; for the corn and other products of northern Palestine were indispensable to the coastal cities.[1] On the other hand, it was to the interest of the Phenician traders to prevent their Aramean competitors from reaching the Mediterranean by way of Acco through Israelite territory.

To cement this "brotherly covenant" (Amos i. 9), Ahab married Jezebel, the daughter of the King of Tyre. As a pledge of the closeness of this tie, Ahab erected in Samaria a temple to Baal, that is, to the Baal of Tyre, Melqart, who must have been the guardian of the agreement, conjointly with Jahweh, to whom a temple may similarly have been erected in the Phenician city. This very prudent measure of Ahab's aroused among certain of the prophets, ardent upholders of the rights of Jahweh, indignant protests and before long an organized opposition which finally brought about the downfall of the dynasty. We shall deal with this important movement when we come to discuss the religious history of the period.

In pursuance of the same policy, Ahab also took steps to free his kingdom from anxiety concerning its southern frontier and, with this end in view, endeavoured to put an end to the disastrous and barren feud with Judah : an alliance whose conditions we are ignorant of, was concluded between Ahab and Jehoshaphat. The sequel shows that Judah was responsible, in the event of any warlike enterprises, to assist

[1] Acts xii. 20 ; cf. Ezek. xxvii. 17.

Israel with all its available forces, hence the southern kingdom, being the weaker, was the vassal of the northern kingdom. In this case the alliance was still further secured by a marriage : Jehoram, the son of Jehoshaphat, married Athaliah, the daughter of Ahab, and perhaps on this occasion also a temple in Jerusalem was built for Baal, the god of the King of Tyre, the third member of the triple alliance (without detriment, however, to the reputation of Jehoshaphat for piety).

The alliance was profitable to both parties. Jehoshaphat was enabled to maintain or restore his suzerainty over the Edomites, to the extent of being in a position to build a fleet at Eziongeber which would have resumed the trading expeditions of Solomon if the ships had not, unfortunately, been wrecked in harbour. Ahab, on his side, was able to keep the King of Moab in subjection.[1] During his reign the country seems to have enjoyed a very real measure of prosperity ; it was at this time that the rebuilding of Jericho was undertaken (1 Kings xvi. 34).

In his wars with the Arameans Ahab gained several brilliant successes. Five years before the end of his reign, when he was closely blockaded in Samaria, he haughtily rejected the humiliating conditions of surrender which Benhadad would have imposed upon him, made a sortie and completely routed the besiegers (1 Kings xx. 1–21). In the following year he again defeated the Arameans in a pitched battle at Aphek (perhaps Fiq or Afiq),[2] on the plateau to the east of the Sea of Tiberias, and even captured their king. With a generosity for which he was severely blamed by a prophet of Jahweh, Ahab spared Benhadad's life, and contented himself with demanding the restoration of the

---

[1] Only during the first half of his reign, if we translate line 8 of the Mesha Stone : " Israel abode there (at Medeba) during his days (Omri's) and half the days of *his son*." But as the text goes on to add " for forty years," we should probably read " of *his sons* " (Nordlander, Winckler, Lidzbarski, Dussaud), *i.e.* the reigns of Ahab, Ahaziah and Jehoram (*circa* 876–842). The revolt of Moab will have taken place, in agreement with 2 Kings iii. 5, at the death of Ahab, an event which apparently ought to be placed forty years after the accession of Omri (35 years, according to the chronology of the book of Kings, *circa* 887–853) and about the middle (the last third, according to Kings) of the combined reigns of the last three Omrides.

[2] Yakut, iii, p. 932.

cities which had been taken, and the privilege for Israel of having " streets " in Damascus (1 Kings xx. 22–43).

The reason for Ahab's clemency may have been that he foresaw a time when all the small states of Syria would need to combine against a peril which was about to threaten them all, the advance of Assyria. Indeed it would seem to be during the truce of three years which followed the victory of Aphek that we must place the date of the battle of Qarqar (854), when Shalmanezer III (859–825), on his march southwards, was met by a coalition at whose head was Bir-Idri (Benhadad II) of Damascus, and which included twelve kings, among others some Phenician princes and Ahabbu Sirlai, that is, Ahab of Israel ; according to the obelisk of Shalmanezer, the latter's force consisted of 10,000 footmen and 2,000 chariots. The Assyrian king claims the victory ; but as he gained nothing by it, it is probable that the Arameans and their allies on this occasion succeeded in repulsing the invader.

After three years of peace, war broke out again between Israel and the Arameans. The latter had apparently refused to fulfil the conditions of the agreement and to restore the city of Ramoth-gilead, perhaps er-Remteh near Irbid. Before beginning the campaign, Ahab, at the request of his ally and vassal Jehoshaphat, inquired of Jahweh : 400 prophets promised him success ; a solitary prophet, Micaiah, the son of Imlah, who always foretold evil for him—he was probably a member of the organized opposition—announced his defeat and death. It was the latter's oracle which was fulfilled. The King, although he had disguised himself, was wounded by a chance arrow and died in his chariot ; upon which his army disbanded.

Ahab, than whom no King of Israel has been more severely dealt with by the historians, deserves, as we can see, some measure of rehabilitation. No doubt he had, like Solomon, a tendency to despotism, as in the case of Naboth, and to luxurious tastes ; he did not understand the peculiar characteristics of his people's religion ; but he was brave, energetic, beloved by his subjects, feared by his enemies, generous toward the conquered. Above all he displayed a remarkable grasp of the political interests of his people.

His two sons succeeded him in turn : first Ahaziah, who

died as the result of a fall after a reign of two years, and then Jehoram.

Mesha, King of Moab, had taken advantage of the defeat and death of Ahab to declare his independence by refusing tribute. The King of Israel, probably Jehoram, with his vassal Jehoshaphat, King of Judah, and the latter's vassal, the King of Edom, organized an expedition to bring back Moab to its allegiance. The allies attacked by the way of the south of the Dead Sea, in order to turn the flank of the fortresses with which Mesha had guarded his northern frontier, and to avoid being taken in the rear by the Arameans. Mesha, finding himself defeated and shut up in his capital, Kir Haresheth (the modern Kerak), saw no other means of escape than to offer up his son as a burnt offering, on the wall of the city in order to recover the favour of his god Chemosh. A reverse inflicted on the Israelites was interpreted by them as a sign that the anger of the god was kindled against the invaders of his country (2 Kings iii. 27) : they accordingly retreated.

The Edomites, encouraged, doubtless, by the victory of the Moabites, threw off the yoke of Judah : Jehoram, the son and successor of Jehoshaphat, attempted to reduce them to submission, but was utterly defeated. He also lost the city of Libnah, which became independent.

His namesake, Jehoram, King of Israel, carried on the policy of his father Ahab toward the Arameans. He took part, either as a voluntary ally or as a vassal, in the campaigns which Benhadad II conducted against Shalmanezer III in 849 and 846 ; for the King of Assyria says that he had to fight against the same twelve states as in 854. These struggles seem to have resulted in no decisive successes for either side.

On other occasions Jehoram was at war with the Arameans. It was perhaps in his reign—according to others, in that of Jehoaz,[1]—that the second siege of Samaria took place, the account of which is related with somewhat legendary colouring in the biography of Elisha (2 Kings vi. 24–7, 20).

In any case the Israelites succeeded in recovering the city of Ramoth-gilead, aided, perhaps, by the disturbances accompanying a change of dynasty which took place at that

[1] Kuenen, Kittel (**XLV**, pp. 258–9).

time at Damascus. Benhadad's general, Hazael, a usurper, whom an Assyrian document describes as " a no man's son," slew his sick master by suffocating him under a wet bed-covering. As soon as his power was established, Hazael undertook the task of recovering their conquest from the Israelites. Jehoram was severely wounded and was obliged to go to Jezreel to be nursed. Elisha, the leader of the prophetic group hostile to the house of Ahab, judged the opportunity favourable for the overthrowing of the hated dynasty.

He sent a young prophet to anoint Jehu, one of the generals in command at Ramoth, secretly. Jehu, with a few followers, galloped to Jezreel, and when the King came out to meet him, shot him through the heart with an arrow. The new King of Judah, Ahaziah, the son of Jehoram, happened to be there on a visit to his uncle. He fled and was pursued by the servants of Jehu, who wounded him mortally at Jibleam; he reached Megiddo and died there.[1] Meanwhile Jehu had entered Jezreel. There Jezebel awaited him, painted and adorned to go down as a queen to Sheol. He ordered her to be thrown out of the window of the palace, and trampled her under his horses' hoofs. He proceeded to massacre forty-two princes of the house of David who had come on a visit to Jezreel. The nobles of Samaria, intimidated, at his first request sent him the heads of the seventy sons of Jehoram entrusted to their care.

He then made his entrance into the capital, accompanied in his chariot by Jehonadab, the son of Rechab, a zealous upholder of Jahweh, the founder of a kind of brotherhood dedicated to the nomad life. By this gesture he proclaimed himself the vindicator of the rights of the national god. He destroyed the temple of Baal and massacred all those who had taken part in his worship. According to the book of Kings, in order to accomplish this he resorted to the trick of proclaiming himself to be an even more devoted worshipper of the foreign god than Ahab himself. But it is difficult to see how Jehu could have expected his ruse to

---

[1] A town situated on the road to Jerusalem would be more probable. The reference might be to Migrôn (mod. Makrun, near Michmash), which the Greek version calls Mageddo (Isa. x. 28 ; *cf.* 1 Sam. xiv. 2, G^L) ?

succeed while he was openly allying himself with Jehonadab.

The extermination of Omri's glorious dynasty is an important turning point in the religious history of Israel to which we shall return later.[1] The immediate political consequences of this event were disastrous for Israel.

4. *The Dynasty of Jehu. End of the Aramean Wars* (*about* 843–743). The nation found itself surrounded by enemies. The alliance with Tyre was, of course, broken. In Judah the power had been seized by the mother of the King, who had been killed by Jehu, Athaliah, the daughter of Ahab. At Dibon, Mesha, King of Moab, set up the stele on which he celebrated his triumphs over Israel : " I rejoiced to see the destruction of Ahab and his house, and Israel perished for ever."

Jehu initiated a new policy against the hereditary enemies, the Arameans of Damascus, and attempted to gain the support of the Assyrians. When Shalmanezer III undertook a fresh campaign against Damascus in 842, not only did Jehu send no troops to the aid of Hazael, who was defeated at Mt. Saniru, that is, in Anti-lebanon, and was obliged to retire into his capital, but he sent his tribute to the conqueror, an incident which is depicted on the obelisk of Shalmanezer.[2]

Jehu's hopes were disappointed. Assyria certainly sent another expedition against Damascus, in 839, but, either by reason of weakness or on account of wars on other frontiers, she did not make her presence felt again in the West for more than thirty years. As soon as the flood of invasion had withdrawn, Hazael exacted a heavy penalty from Jehu for his desertion. He laid waste the land of Israel, burning the cities, slaughtering the youth, dashing out the brains of infants, and ripping up women with child (2 Kings viii. 12 ; Amos i. 3). Jehu lost the whole of Transjordania (2 Kings x. 32–3).

The relations between Israel and Judah doubtless improved when Athaliah, after a reign of six years, was overthrown and put to death, either by a conspiracy of the

---

[1] See pp. 421–3.
[2] In the British Museum ; *cf.* **LXXXIII,** pp. 533 and 535 ; **XXXVII,** pp. 295 (fig. 98) and 296 (figs. 99 and 100) on the texts **XCIII,** pp. 208–9 ; **XLV,** p. 268.

army, or by a popular rising against the worship of Baal
which was supported by the queen (the two accounts are
given side by side in the book of Kings). The whole story
of Athaliah is, moreover, somewhat mysterious. According
to the tradition she began her reign by slaying all the princes
of the royal family, that is to say, all her grandchildren.
One of them, unknown to Athaliah, had been saved from the
massacre and hidden in the temple. No satisfactory motive
for these slaughters has been alleged, since Athaliah could
only hold power in the capacity of queen-mother and guardian
to one of her grandchildren during his minority.[1] The
tradition may possibly be a popular and distorted reminiscence of Jehu's massacre of the forty-two princes of Judah.
The ambition of some of the nobles, humiliated by the rule
of a woman who was not even a native of Judah, would
sufficiently explain the plot which resulted in the overthrow
of Athaliah.

Under Jehoahaz, the son of Jehu, the condition of Israel
became more critical than ever. Hazael apparently conquered the whole land, for he entered upon a campaign
against the southern kingdom : he took Gath, on the south-
west frontier of Judah, and would no doubt have attacked
Jerusalem if Joash, the grandson and successor of Athaliah,
had not induced him to retreat by giving him all his treasures.

A turn of fortune took place at last under the son of
Jehoahaz, King of Israel, who also bore the name of Joash.
Adadnirari IV, King of Assyria (812–783), compelled Benhadad III, the son of Hazael, whom he calls in his inscription
Mari (an Aramean title meaning " my lord "), to pay him
tribute (between 806 and 803). At the same time he received
presents, which he of course describes as tribute, from Tyre,
Sidon, " the house of Omri " (i.e. Israel), Edom and the
Philistines. Joash, King of Israel, profited by the weakness
of the Arameans of Damascus to defeat them three times
at Aphek. He recovered the cities which had been lost by
his father Jehoahaz.

During the same period Judah also recovered some of
its ancient power. Amaziah, who had come to the throne
after the assassination of his father Joash, defeated the
Edomites in the " Valley of Salt," took from them the city

---

[1] Cf. **XIX**, pp. 300–2.

of Sela, which has often been identified with Petra, and
re-opened for his country the approach to the Red Sea,
as is proved by the fact that his son Azariah, also called
Uzziah, rebuilt and fortified Elath. Elated by a sense of
recovered power, Amaziah ventured to provoke a quarrel
with Israel, whom he supposed to be weakened by her
struggle with the Arameans. Amaziah was defeated and
made prisoner at Bethshemesh. Joash, King of Israel,
entered Jerusalem and broke down part of its wall, but
allowed Amaziah to retain the throne, probably as his
vassal.

During the reign of Jeroboam II, the son of Joash, the
northern kingdom gained a still more striking success : the
long struggle with Damascus ended at last in the victory of
Israel. Assyria does not seem to have played any important
part in the subjection of the Arameans. Shalmanezer IV
certainly made an expedition against Damascus in 773, but
during this period the Assyrians were engaged in their struggle
with the Medes and especially with the powerful Chaldean
kingdom of Urartu (the Hebrew Ararat), that is, Armenia.

Jeroboam II restored the ancient boundaries of the
kingdom in the time of Ahab, and even of Solomon : from
the entering in of Hamath (that is, from the district of
Hermon) to the Wady of the Arabah, to the south of the
Dead Sea.[1] Hence he must have apparently again subdued
the Moabites. This was the most brilliant period of the
history of northern Israel. There would seem to have been
at this time an outburst of literary activity breathing a
spirit of national pride, a sense of security and of confidence
in Jahweh.[2]

It proved to be a short-lived prosperity. Six months
after the death of Jeroboam II his son Zechariah was assassinated by a usurper named Shallum (about 743). From
that time on the history of the northern kingdom was a
succession of revolutions and civil wars which aided the
Assyrians in their work of destruction. From 734 the
Assyrians carried on their dismemberment of the unhappy
kingdom until its final annexation in 722.

---

[1] Amos. vi. 14 ; 2 Kings xiv. 25 ; cf. pp. 17–18.
[2] The last edition of J and the first form of E ; Deut. xxxiii. ;
Num. xxiii.–xxiv.

THE ECONOMIC CONDITIONS AND POLITICAL AND SOCIAL ORGANIZATION OF THE ISRAELITES IN PALESTINE

I

TRANSFORMATION OF THEIR MODE OF LIFE

THE far-reaching changes which the settlement in Canaan brought about in the mode of life of the Israelites were not accomplished suddenly. They were the result of a series of imperceptible transitions. As we have seen, the Israelites, even during their desert life, did not range widely, but were semi-nomads who might sow and gather in some kind of grain crop in the interval between one stage of their wandering and the next. The oasis of Kadesh and the region of Transjordania were particularly suited to this mixture of a little agriculture with an essentially pastoral mode of life.

Hence, when the newcomers entered Canaan, either as conquerors or as allies, mercenaries or privileged settlers (*ger*) among the natives, an agricultural life was neither hard nor distasteful to them. They easily exchanged the tent for the house. The settlements of the " sons of Jair " in Transjordania kept the name of " the encampments of Jair," but we learn from certain texts that they were " great cities with walls " ; [1] clearly the tent-circles of the newcomers had gradually developed into fortified towns.

The change was certainly complete by the time of the Judges. In a dream related in the story of Gideon, a barley cake symbolizes the Israelite, while his foe the Midianite freebooter is represented by the tent (Judges vii. 13–14). In the parable of Jotham, which is certainly Israelite and prior to the monarchy, the useful members of the community

[1] Num. xxxii. 41 ; Deut. iii. 14 ; Joshua xiii. 30 ; Judges x. 4 ; 1 Kings iv. 13 ; 1 Chron. ii. 23.

are symbolized by the olive, the fig-tree and the vine (Judges ix. 8–13). Hence the newcomers had become addicted to that form of agriculture which binds the peasant irrevocably to the soil : they had begun to grow fruit-trees.

This change of occupation naturally brought with it profound changes in the mental outlook of the Israelites. Their point of view was no longer that of the plundering Bedouin bent on raiding the settled inhabitant of the land, but that of the peasant defending the fruits of his labour against invaders.

The Kenites, who had long been closely connected with the Israelites, were almost the only people who retained in its ancient purity the nomad mode of life. Whether they remained in their own territory, on the borders of the Edomit' desert, or whether they wandered in Israelite territory [1] to feed their flocks at certain seasons of the year, or perhaps to carry on their craft of smiths, [2] they still lived in tents, sowed no crops and above all cultivated no vines. But it is significant, as showing how strange this mode of life had come to be regarded by the Israelites as a whole, that they felt it necessary to explain the existence of such unusual customs. This was the purpose of the story of the divine curse which had condemned Cain, the eponymous ancestor of the Kenites, to the life of a wanderer (Gen. iv. 2–16). One of the traditions about Hagar [3] and those which were current about the wilderness sojourn of the patriarchs similarly show how completely the attraction and even the very conditions of the nomad mode of life had been forgotten.

In some districts the principal means of subsistence continued to be the rearing of sheep and goats, involving that limited form of nomadism which consists in the periodic change of pasture-grounds. This was the case in the south of Judah (e.g. 1 Sam. xxv.) and in Transjordania (Judges v. 16), hard by the land of Moab which, in the days of Ahab, paid a tribute of 100,000 lambs and the wool of 100,000 rams (2 Kings iii. 4). But, even in Judah, tillage rather than a pastoral life would seem to have been prevalent : the peasant who sold his goats would buy a field with the profits of the transaction (Prov. xxvii. 26).

---

[1] Judges iv. 11, 17–22 ; v. 24–7 ; 2 Kings x. 15.
[2] See, however, pp. 205–6, 317–8.   [3] Gen. xxi. 6, 8–20.

The population of Israel became a purely agricultural one. The exports of the country consisted of corn, honey, wax (?), oil and spices.[1] Solomon paid his debts to Hiram in corn and oil.[2] Flour and oil formed the staple food of the country.[3] The cultivation of the vine was so general that the poets often represented the nation under the figure of a vine.[4]

Technical activities unknown to the nomad Hebrews were carried on by the Israelites, especially after the absorption of the Canaanites. " Industry," however, seems to have played a very small part in the social life of the people. This fact is borne out by the small number of crafts mentioned in Hebrew literature.

In the villages and the fortified towns, almost the only craftsmen were the wandering smith,[5] unskilled in art; [6] the carpenter, who was at the same time furniture-maker, inlayer, carver and woodman, and who combined, no doubt, in early times, the craft of metal and stone working with his own trade of woodworker; for there is only one word, *harash* (lit. " hewer "), to designate the workman who was engaged in any one of these three occupations; in order to distinguish them it was necessary to add a defining epithet : " a worker in iron " (2 Chron. xxiv. 12), " a worker in wood " (Isa. xliv. 12–13 ; 2 Sam. v. 11), " a worker in stone " (2 Sam. v. 11 ; 1 Chron. xxii. 15) or " a maker of a wall " (1 Chron. xiv. 1).

In addition to this general craftsman and the smith, there was the potter, who imitated foreign models in a somewhat crude fashion. There were settlements of potters in Jerusalem, in the lower city (Jer. xviii. 2–4). But the districts round Hebron and Beit Jibrin seem to have been specially favoured by the potters, since they abounded in potter's clay, and still supply the markets of Jerusalem.[7] Many vase-handles, apparently belonging to the seventh century,[8] are stamped with the names of Hebron, Ziph, Socoh and Mareshah (?), and the words " for the King," suggesting that there

---

[1] Ezek. xxvii. 17 (emended text).
[2] 1 Kings v. 35.
[3] 1 Kings xvii. 12–16 ; *cf.* 2 Kings iv. 2.
[4] Isa. v. ; Ezek. xv. ; xvii. ; *cf.* Gen. xlix. 11–12 ; etc.
[5] See p. 205.
[6] 1 Sam. xiii. 20–21. See p. 370.
[7] P. Schwalm, *La vie privée du peuple juif*, pp. 233–4.
[8] 650–500 according to **CII**, p. 116, and H. Vincent, **JPOS**, i, p. 64 ; 727–643 according to R. Dussaud, **SY**, 1925, p. 338.

were royal potteries in these places.[1]   Other potters stamped
their own names upon their goods.[2]

In the cities it was natural that there should be a much
greater degree of specialization of crafts than in the country,
a state of things which was, no doubt, a legacy from the
Canaanite period.   In Jerusalem, bread was supplied by
professional bakers who lived in a special street (Jer. xxxvii.
21), or as would be said today, in a *suq*.   There were fullers,[3]
weavers,[4] jewellers, locksmiths,[5] barbers,[6] probably too,
although the texts which mention them are later than the
exile, there were seal-engravers.[7]   Such seals as the beautiful
intaglio of " Shema' the servant of Jeroboam," with its
mixture of Babylonian (the lion), Egyptian (the *ankh*), and
Palestinian (the inscription) elements, must have been of
native workmanship.[8]   Spices, which were at first made at
home, at least for kings (1 Sam. viii. 13), were in the seventh
century prepared by a corporation of professional perfumers
(Neh. iii. 8).

In spite of the efforts of such kings as Solomon,[9] Ahab
(1 Kings xx. 34), Jehoshaphat, Azariah (2 Chron. xxvi. 2),
the bulk of international trade seems to have remained in the
hands of the Phenicians and the Arabs ; the usual designation
of the trader was " the Canaanite," *i.e.* the Phenician.   The
commercial activities of the Israelites in Palestine seem to
have been limited almost entirely, during the whole of the
monarchy and even to the close of the Jewish state (in A.D.
70), to the sale or purchase of agricultural produce, cattle and
land (Amos viii. 5 ; Hos. xii. 8–9), and to the exchange of
such products for what a poet calls " the abundance of the
seas, and the hidden treasures of the sand," that is to say, for

[1] *Cf.* 1 Chron. iv. 23.
[2] **IV**, p. 242, n. 1.   On jar-handles, *cf.* **III**, p. 150 ; **CLIX**, pp. 357–
60 (fig. 255) ; R. Dussaud, **SY**, 1925, pp. 337–8 and pl. xliii.
[3] 1 Kings i. 9, etc. ; Isa. vii. 3 ; xxxvi. 2 ; Mal. iii. 2 ; Mark ix. 3.
[4] 1 Sam. xvii. 7 ; *cf.* Exod. xxviii. 32 ; xxxv. 35, etc. ; 1 Chron. iv.
21.
[5] 2 Kings xxiv. 14, 16 ; Jer. xxiv. 1 ; xxix. 2 (translation a little
uncertain).
[6] Ezek. v. 1.
[7] Exod. xxviii. 9–11 ; Sir. xxxviii. 27.
[8] **XLIII**, pl. vi (80).   On the date of this seal, *cf.* **LIV**, ii, p. 140
(under Jeroboam) ; **CLI**, p. 99 ; R. Dussaud, **SY**, 1925, pp. 108,
336–7 (under Ahab).
[9] See pp. 369–70.

articles imported by sea or manufactured by the peoples of the coast, such as glass or purple (Deut. xxxiii. 18–19).

II

CHANGES IN THE POLITICAL ORGANIZATION

1. *Clans and Tribes.* When the Hebrews arrived in Palestine they were organized, like all the nomadic Semites, into tribes and clans ; but as the result of the settlement in Canaan this organization underwent profound changes.

The tribes, formed from groups of federated clans, were not always able to settle in a compact group in a single district, as we learn from the cases of the tribes of Manasseh and Dan.[1] Some tribes, like Simeon and Levi, were completely scattered ;[2] others, like Reuben, diminished ;[3] others, again, like Machir and Gilead, which were tribes in the time of the Song of Deborah (Judges v. 14–17), fell back into the rank of clans, mere *mishpaḥoth* in the traditional genealogy (Joshua xvii. 1–2).

On the other hand, Judah increased considerably. We learn from the documents the significant fact that this was due to fusion with Canaanite elements (symbolized by Judah's marriages with Canaanite wives, Gen. xxxviii.), and, later on, as the result of David's alliances, to the admission into the confederation of Kenites, Jerahmeelites and Kenizzites,[4] who are similarly represented in the genealogies as descended from the patriarch Judah.[5]

The tribe of Joseph increased to such an extent that it divided and gave rise to the tribes of Ephraim and Manasseh. Benjamin, " the son of the right hand," *i.e.* of the south (a name which has the same meaning as Yemen, the " south " of Arabia), was, no doubt, only the southern offshoot of the powerful " house of Joseph " ;[6] it would seem that the division did not take place until after the settlement in Palestine, since the eponymous Benjamin was, according to the tradition, represented as a late-comer, *born in Canaan* (Gen. xxxv. 16–20).

---

[1] Joshua xvii. 14–18 ; Num. xxxii. 39, 41, 42 ; Judges xvii.–xviii.
[2] Gen. xxxiv. ; xlix. 5–7.   [3] Deut. xxxiii. 6.
[4] 1 Sam. xxvii. 10 ; xxx. 14, 29 ; *cf.* pp. 359*f.*
[5] 1 Chron. ii. 9, 18–20, 25–7, 33, 42 *ff.*, 55 ; Num. xiii. 6, etc.
[6] 2 Sam. xix. 21 ; *cf.* Judges v. 14.

The supposition that some of the tribes in the traditional lists did not come into existence until after the settlement in Palestine is confirmed by the fact that several of them are named after the district which they occupied : for instance, Gilead, Benjamin, Ephraim (the name of a " mountain," exhibiting the ending characteristic of many place-names, such as Mizraim, Mahanaim, Naharaim).

The names of Asher, Joseph, and later of Simeon and Dan,[1] mentioned as existing in the country in the time of Thothmes III, Seti I and Ramses II,[2] were perhaps those of ancient Canaanite peoples or places.

But it was not only the number, distribution and relative importance of the clans and tribes that underwent changes. The entities denoted by these terms soon acquired an entirely new character. The early groupings, based originally on consanguinity (natural or artificial), tended to become territorial aggregations.[3] The clan finally became synonymous with the population of a town : " And thou, Bethlehem, Ephratah, art the least of the thousands—i.e. the clans—of Judah " (Mic. v. 1). Membership of a tribe consisted, not in descent from a particular individual, but in belonging by birth to a particular locality. An ancient writer says of a certain Rechab of Beeroth : " he was of the children of Benjamin, *for Beeroth also is reckoned to Benjamin* " (2 Sam. iv. 2). Once settled in Canaan, the Israelites soon reached the stage of the peasants of Khorassan, of whom the Arabs say contemptuously : " their villages are their pedigrees." Caliph Omar urged his Arabs to preserve their pedigrees and not to become like the peasants of Iraq, who to the question, " Whence art thou (*i.e.* from what tribe) ? " were wont to reply, " From such and such a village."[4] Now the Israelite, when he met a stranger, no longer asked him, like the Bedouins, " From whom art thou ? "[5] but " Whence comest thou ? "[6]

---

[1] Stanley A. Cook (**XIII**, p. 388) gives the name of an Addu-Dani in what was later the Danite region in the Tell el-Amarna period (**TA(K)**, 292–5).

[2] See pp. 46, 49–51.   [3] *Cf.* B. Luther, **ZATW**, 1901, pp. 11–53.

[4] Th. Nöldeke, **ZDMG**, xl, p. 183.

[5] Gen. xxxii. 18 and 2 Sam. xxx. 13 have another meaning : " To whom do you belong (as a slave) ? " Ruth ii. 5 signifies : " To what father or to what master does this young girl belong ? "

[6] Gen. xxix. 4 ; Joshua ii. 4 ; Judges xiii. 6 ; 2 Sam. i. 13 ; xv. 2 ; xxx. 13 ; *cf.* Jonah i. 8.

Most of these territorial groupings, however, were not, as might have been expected, a legacy from the regional subdivisions of Canaanite times, since Palestine was then divided, not into a dozen states of moderate size, but into a large number of petty rival city-states. The Israelite tribes of historical times arose out of the gradual transformation of the ancient nomadic Hebrew tribes, and long continued to be characterized by the nomadic tendency to individualism. This spirit occasionally expressed itself in open warfare, nor were the kings ever wholly successful in breaking it.[1] The tribes also retained their faith in genealogies, however fictitious these might be, and in their rival claims to pre-eminence, as exemplified, for instance, in the arrangement of the sons of Jacob in the official genealogy (Gen. xxix. 30 to xxx. 24), and in the jibes directed against various tribes in certain early poems (Gen. xlix.; Judges v.).

Hence it appears that the Hebrew settlers imposed their own social framework upon the population of the country, but the requirements of a settled mode of life brought about profound changes in the nomadic social organization.

2. *The Monarchy.* We have seen that the pressure of political necessity forced the tribes to accept the institution of the monarchy. At the same time they adopted those beliefs and customs which had been associated with the kingship from time immemorial, among the Canaanites as throughout the ancient East, especially the belief in the sacred and semi-divine character of the person of the King.[2] The fact that they recognized in their sheikhs similar supernatural powers facilitated this transition.[3]

The King is the " consecrated one " (*nazir*), the anointed of Jahweh; it is sacrilege to lift a hand against him.[4] It is as much a breach of the commandment to curse the King as to curse God himself (Exod. xxii. 27). He was believed to have the power, like the god-men of primitive peoples, of controlling the rain and the sun, since it was he who was supposed to cause famine.[5] He was addressed as " the breath

---

[1] Solomon (see pp. 371–2), perhaps the Omrides (see pp. 377–8).
[2] See pp. 118–9.   [3] See pp. 303–4.
[4] 1 Sam. xxiv. 7, 11; xxvi. 9–11, 23; 2 Sam. i. 14–16; iv. 12.
[5] 2 Kings vi. 26–7; Isa. viii. 21; Ps. lxxii. 3, 16; perhaps iv. 3, *cf.* 8 (Duhm, **KHC**, p. 14).

of our nostrils," [1] " the lamp of Israel " (2 Sam. xxi. 17) ;
his wisdom is compared to that of the angel of God (2 Sam.
xiv. 17). He may even claim the title of son of God (2 Sam.
vii. 14), for on his accession Jahweh makes him the object of
a special decree of adoption : " The Lord said unto me :
Thou art my son, this day have I begotten thee " (Ps. ii. 7).
Possibly some kings even went so far as to accept the title of
" gods."[2] But Jahwism had already set up too sharp a
distinction between *elohim* and ordinary mortals for such
claims to be taken seriously.

On the other hand, the King was very distinctly a priest.
David danced a sacred dance before the ark, wearing the
priestly dress of a linen ephod (2 Sam. vi. 14). Solomon
blessed the people (1 Kings viii. 54–61). We have seen that
there are grounds for believing that a tradition existed that
Saul, in his childhood, had been " lent " to Jahweh, and
thus attached to the sanctuary at Shiloh.[3] The King could
appoint priests and deprive them of their office at his pleasure,
and could alter the temple furniture.

The sacred power of the King was conferred upon him
by the rite of anointing, a rite of which there seem to have
been two forms, one theocratic, the other more democratic.
The theocratic form of this rite was in use in the region of
Syria from the sixteenth century [4] : an ancient text suggests
that the custom of anointing the King was prior to the age
of Saul.

The earliest insignia of royalty were the spear, borne by
the ancient sheikhs, and the bracelet (2 Sam. i. 10 ; *cf.* 2 Kings
ii. 12) : it is possible that the crown was not adopted until
the time of David.[5]

Court etiquette became increasingly elaborate, evidently
in imitation of the practice of neighbouring peoples : in the
time of David anyone who entered the King's presence to
present a petition was obliged to prostrate himself (2 Sam.
xiv. 4 ; 1 Kings xvi. 23 ; *cf.* ii. 19).

Since it was believed to be of divine origin, the royal power
was theoretically absolute. But in practice there were only a

---

[1] Lam. iv. 20 ; *cf.* p. 140, n. 9.
[2] Ps. lxxxii. 1, 6.   [3] See pp. 355–6.   [4] See p. 119.
[5] 2 Sam. xii. 30—2 Sam. i. 10 is not very certain. *Cf.* IV,
p. 274, n. 6.

few kings like Solomon or Ahab, who by reason of their power or their prestige were able to impose their will upon the people.

There were several limits to the King's power. In the first place, the absence of any fixed rule of succession often enabled the people to choose their own king, or to lay down conditions which the new king was forced to accept.[1] Moreover, the kings allowed the traditional tribal organization to persist : the elders, that is, the heads of the principal families, continued to meet at the gate of the city, to dispense justice and to discuss the affairs of the city.[2] Ahab consults " the elders of the land " (1 Kings xx. 7). The kings merely placed over this communal aristocracy officials of their own appointment (*sarim*), whose main duty was to levy taxes, raise troops and hear appeals from the decisions of the elders ; litigants were also entitled to appeal directly to the King.[3] But law-abiding people might spend the whole of their life " in the midst of their people," that is to say, within the circle of their clan, without ever having anything to do with the King or his *sar ṣaba'* (2 Kings iv. 13).

There was, of course, no constitution defining the rights of the sovereign, the clans or the individual. The " law of the kingdom " (Deut. xvii. 14–20) is not so much a political charter as a moral and religious dissertation ; it belongs, moreover, to a very late stage of the redaction, since it has clearly been added to the already existing Deuteronomic code (*v.* 18–20). The anti-monarchic source describes Samuel as writing the " manner of the kingdom " in a book which he lays up before Jahweh, that is, in a sanctuary.[4] This consisted of a satirical description of the tyrannies practised by kings, and which, according to the writer, constituted " the custom," the normal functioning of the abhorred institution of the kingship. We learn, moreover, from this document what royal encroachments upon the ancient Bedouin individualism were most strenuously resisted. Some of these restrictions of individual liberty seem to be the natural consequence of the organization of the people into a state : taxation (the tenth), military service, requisitions for

---

[1] See pp. 364–5, 372–3 ; 2 Kings xiv. 21 ; xxiii. 30.
[2] For example, 1 Kings xxi. 8–14 ; 2 Kings x. 1–5.
[3] 2 Sam. xiv. 4–11 ; xv. 2–4 ; 1 Kings iii. 16–28.
[4] 1 Sam. viii. 11–18 ; x. 25ᵃ.

the needs of the army, the establishment of a hierarchy of officials.[1] But there seem better grounds for regarding some of the other restrictions as " bondage " : the commandeering of Israelite maidens for the needs of the court (" he will take your daughters to be perfumers, and to be cooks, and to be bakers "), and above all the seizure of fields and vineyards to provide rewards for the King's officials or estates for his sons,[2] practices whose existence is attested by Ezekiel's anxiety to prevent their return.[3] However, even Ahab was obliged to resort to a false accusation followed by the semblance of a trial in order to obtain possession of the vineyard of a single recalcitrant private citizen, Naboth (1 Kings xxi.) : hence the arbitrary power of the King was forced to bow, in appearance at least, to the prescription of immemorial custom by which a man's ancestral inheritance was inviolable.

III

SOCIAL CHANGES

According to the nomad custom, pasture-lands and springs are the indivisible property of the whole *douar*. In the early period of their settlement in Canaan the Hebrews may have attempted to preserve this custom. But in historical times nothing remained of it but gradually disappearing traces : it would seem that there were here and there, as in Palestine today,[4] common lands which were periodically assigned by lot to the inhabitants of the city ; [5] the ideal state of the post-exilic legislators, in which lands returned to their original owner every fifty years (Lev. xxv.), is doubtless a faint reminiscence of these periodical allotments. From the same source also arose the right of the nearest relation to redeem the property of a man who had been compelled to sell his ancestral inheritance,[6] and the custom which required heiresses to marry *within their own clan* (Num. xxxvi.). The object of these practices was to prevent land from going out of the *mishpaḥah*.

[1] 1 Sam. viii. 12 should probably read " to establish over them captains of thousands, etc. . . ." and not " to make of them captains . . .," which would not be at all tyrannical.
[2] *Cf.* 1 Sam. xxii. 7.   [3] xlvi. 16–18.   [4] **CCLXII,** p. 57.
[5] Jer. xxxvii. 12 ; Mic. ii. 5 ; Ps. xvi. 5 ; Prov. i. 14.
[6] Jer. xxxii. 7–16 ; Ruth iv. 3–12 ; Lev. xxv. 23–5

But facts such as the bitter resentment stirred up by the seizure of Naboth's vineyard show how deeply rooted in the minds of the people was the principle of individual ownership of the land. Only the possessors of a plot of ground had the full rights of citizenship.[1]

A further consequence of the attachment of the Israelites to the soil was the growth of sharply marked social divisions. Among nomads the poorest is actually the equal of the richest ; all alike partake of the same simple food, wear the same coarse clothing, and inhabit the same primitively furnished dwelling, the tent. " Wealth carries with it neither influence nor power. At most it involves the privilege of a more lavish hospitality." The reason for this is that tomorrow the richest, like Job, may see all his cattle carried off by a hostile tribe, and similarly, the poorest may suddenly find himself enriched by a fortunate raid.[2]

But this state of things underwent a complete change when the Israelites became sedentary agriculturists. Thanks to the increasing security of tenure which prevailed in the land, skilful cultivators were able to save their profits and use them to enlarge their property. It was possible to amass wealth by shrewd dealings in land and crops.[3] On the other hand, there grew up, after the institution of the monarchy, a military aristocracy enriched by the spoils of war or by royal favour. The exercise of power was a source of profit for the " elders " and for royal officials, since it is a custom in the East that the person who seeks a favour should not appear before his superior with empty hands.[4]

The absorption of the Canaanites, who had already long reached the stage of urban civilization, and especially the adoption by the court of Solomon of a mode of life increasingly removed from primitive simplicity, accentuated the division of Israelite society into more and more sharply differentiated grades. The rich demanded palaces modelled on those of the King, with winter and summer houses, a luxury which appears to have been introduced into Asia in the eighth century,[5] feasts in which meat was a daily dish, and where

[1] 2 Kings xv. 20. [2] **III**, p. 138. [3] Amos viii. 5 ; Hos. xii. 8-9. [4] Gen. xxxii. 14–22 ; xxxiii. 8–11 ; xliii. 11 ; 1 Sam. x. 27 ; xvii. 18 ; xxv. 18–19 ; Mal. i. 8.

[5] Amos iii. 15 ; *cf.* inscr. Barrekub, l. 18–19 (**XLIX**, p. 498). See pp. 28–9.

wine was drunk in bowls to the sound of music, and where they reclined on divans instead of squatting on the ground after the ancestral fashion.[1] The women came to regard an enormous quantity of toilet articles and cosmetics as indispensable; Isaiah has preserved an amusing catalogue of such requisites (Isa. iii. 16–24).

In order to satisfy these suddenly acquired needs of a more complicated life, the rich made use of those weapons which their very wealth made available, with increasing harshness. By right of their rank they were judges, and used their position to oppress the litigants. Especially widows and orphans, who had no natural protectors, were the prey of their rapacity. From small proprietors, who were compelled by misfortunes to borrow from them, they exacted ruinous interest, and in the end sold the insolvent debtor and his children as slaves, and seized his land.[2]

> " They covet fields, and seize them ;
>   and houses, and take them away.
> They oppress a man and his house,
>   even a man and his heritage " (Mic. ii. 2).

In this way small holdings gradually disappeared, and the country was covered with *latifundia*. Isaiah exclaims :

> " Woe unto them that join house to house,
>   that lay field to field,
> till there be no more room and ye dwell
>   alone in the midst of the land " (Isa. v. 8).

Thus there grew up a minority of nobles opposed to an ever increasing peasant proletariat. We can understand the bitterness which was aroused in the mass of the people by such a complete subversal of the old equality of nomad times.

IV

First Attempts at Reaction

In civilized societies, laws are made to protect the rights of the weak against the encroachments of the strong. Hammurabi declares that he has engraved his code upon a pillar

---

[1] Amos vi. 4–6. [2] Amos ii. 6, 8 ; viii. 6.

" in order that the strong may not harm the weak, to give security to orphans and widows."[1]

The legislators of Israel, whether they were the kings, or more probably the priests, understood that it was their duty to intervene in the social conflict which was dividing the people. The collection of civil laws embodied in the "bock of the covenant," which was edited, apparently, about the ninth century, requires the liberation after six years of the Hebrew who has become a slave on account of debt (Exod. xxi. 2–6) ; a similar enactment already existed in the code of Hammurabi, actually limiting the period of service to three years (§ 117). The Israelite legislator exhorts the creditor not to be harsh [2] and not to keep overnight the garment which has been taken in pledge (Exod. xxii. 25–7). He lays it down as a rule that the produce of fields left fallow belong to the poor [3] : in fact, the fields were to be left fallow every seventh year.[4]

But these measures were only palliatives. There were some who entertained the much more radical idea that it was necessary to restore the nomad mode of life, that ever since the settlement in Palestine Israel had gone astray, and that her only hope lay in the total rejection of that civilization, borrowed with such disastrous consequences from the foreigner. Such was the belief of Jonadab, the son of Rechab, the Kenite, who in the middle of the ninth century, imposed upon his clan the religious duty of a perpetual observance of those nomad customs which they had hitherto followed as a matter of tradition.[5] By way of parallel the case may be recalled of the Nabateans of the Dead Sea, who for similar reasons, no doubt, laid down the same rule, under penalty of death.[6] The mass of the people evidently regarded this unambiguous and vigorous attitude of Jonadab with marked approval, for Jehu was glad to shelter himself and his attack on the " civilizing " dynasty of the house of Omri under the prestige of the authority of this sacred individual.[7]

---

[1] Epilogue (**CCLXXXII**, p. 40).

[2] Exod. xxii. 24 (25) : The end of the verse, which forbids the taking of interest, appears to be a later addition.

[3] Exod. xxiii. 10–11.   [4] See p. 402.

[5] 2 Kings x. 15–16, 23 ; Jer. xxxv. 6–10.

[6] Hieronymus de Kardia in Diod. Sic., **XIX**, 94. *Cf.* **XXX**, pp. 172–3. See pp. 283, 410–1.   [7] See pp. 383–4.

Most of the Israelites, however, did not take such a trenchant view of the matter; they had too completely absorbed the habits and tastes of a sedentary life to be able to divest themselves of it. Nevertheless, many of the simple folk felt in a confused way that it would have been better to have adhered to the austere life of their fathers, that the troubles of Israel were due to adoption of foreign culture, and of Canaanite culture in particular, and that civilization itself brought in its train more disadvantages than it was worth.

These ideas which played an important part in the early stages of the prophetic movement, were not exclusively the product of the religious spirit : they were due in part to the suffering entailed by the sudden transformation of the social order of Israel.

BOOK II

THE RELIGION OF THE ISRAELITES IN PALESTINE

CHAPTER I

EFFECT OF THE POLITICAL, ECONOMIC AND SOCIAL CHANGES ON THE RELIGION OF ISRAEL

I

THE CRISIS CAUSED BY THE SETTLEMENT IN PALESTINE [1]

1. *THE Causes of the Crisis.* On entering Palestine, Israel left the desert, the sphere of Jahweh's authority, and passed into the domain of other gods, the *baals*, the owners of the land. Now, according to ancient conceptions, it follows as a matter of course that the act of settling in the territory of a foreign god carries with it the duty of rendering to him the worship to which he is entitled. For immigrants to provoke the hostility of the unseen powers holding sway in the new country would be an act of insane temerity. Such also was the belief of the Israelites. David regards it as self-evident that to banish a man is the equivalent of saying to him : " Go, serve other gods ! "[2]

On the other hand, his new duties did not involve for the immigrant the necessity of forsaking the god of his fathers, for, although his ancestral god may be attached to a certain locality, he is also bound to the tribe or people whose guardian deity he is, and can protect his clients even in the territory of other gods.[3] A princess contracting a foreign marriage might bring with her the statues of the gods of her own country [4] and might even be allowed to build temples for them.[5]

---

[1] **XVI**, i, pp. 268–94.
[2] 1 Sam. xxvi. 19 ; *cf.* Jer. xvi. 13.   [3] See pp. 455–6.
[4] **TA(W)**, 20.   [5] 1 Kings xi. 7–8 ; xvi. 31–2.

But it was at least an obvious precaution to add the worship of the *elohim* of the land to that of the ancestral god. Thus did the foreign settlers whom the King of Assyria introduced into Palestine after the destruction of the northern kingdom : ravaged by wild beasts, and believing that it was the god of the country, namely Jahweh, who was punishing them, they learnt the " manner " of this god, and at the same time continued to worship their respective deities (2 Kings xvii. 25–33). Hence Jahweh was in danger of being compelled to share the worship of the Israelites with the baals of Canaan.

Nor was this all. In changing their abode the immigrants also acquired a new mode of life. For, while there was no traditional connexion between Jahweh, the thunder-god of Sinai, and the fertility of the harvest, the conception of the baals and their ritual was intimately bound up with those agricultural activities of which Israel now began to acquire the knowledge under the tutelage of the Canaanites. Convinced, like all early peoples, that their traditional agricultural methods were the result of a divine revelation, the Canaanites of Phenicia worshipped Dagon as the god of crops and tillage, the inventor of corn and the plough.[2] It was, no doubt, from their Canaanite teachers that the Israelites learnt to leave unharvested a corner of the field, and to allow some grapes to remain in the vineyard. From them, too, they learnt to refrain from using for any purpose, sacred or profane, the produce of a fruit-tree during the first three years of its life[3] : for the original object of these practices was to conciliate the spirit of the field,[4] the vine or the tree, that is to say, the baal who permeated them with his own supernatural life.

Hence it is clear that the cult of the local gods threatened, not only to rival the worship of Jahweh, but to eclipse it ; for it was the baals who seemed to be the givers of the agriculturist's greatest desire, an abundant harvest. Even as late as the eighth century, Hosea reproaches Israel with not recognizing that it was Jahweh who gave her corn, must and

---

[1] *Cf.* Isa. xxviii. 23–9.
[2] Philo of Byblos, Fr. ii, 16 ; *cf.* **XLIX**, pp. 132, n. 1 ; 423.
[3] Lev. xix. 9–10, 23–5 ; xxiii. 22 ; Deut. xxiv. 19–22.
[4] *Cf.* Lev. xxvi. 34–5.

oil, blessings which she regarded as gifts from the baals (Hos. ii. 10, 14).

Lastly it must be remembered that the settlement of the Hebrews in Palestine involved the establishment of close relations and finally of complete fusion with the native population. Now in ancient times religion was so closely interwoven with all the activities of life that it was impossible to avoid participating to some extent in a neighbour's cult. Meals were preceded by libations and often by sacrifices; contracts were confirmed by oaths or by the rite of a common meal which placed the agreements entered into under the sanction of the gods of the two contracting parties.[1] Markets, as among the ancient Arabs or in our own provinces, were held in the neighbourhood of a sacred place at the time of a festival which brought pilgrims together,[2] and those who were present would, doubtless, participate in the traditional rites, as, in the third and fourth centuries of our era, Jews, Christians and pagans were wont to do on the occasion of the market which was held round Abraham's oak.[3] Marriages were another specially fertile source of religious contamination; for the wife, according to Semitic custom, did not enter her husband's cultual group, but remained free to worship her own gods.

It can be understood that the rigid Jahwists ascribed to Moses the prohibition against any kind of matrimonial alliance with the Canaanites,[4] and that they should have seen in the breach of this prohibition one of the chief causes of the tendency of the Israelites, after their settlement in Palestine, to slip into the religion of the native population (Judges iii. 6).

Hence the settlement in Canaan brought about the most serious crisis which Jahwism encountered before the exile.

2. *The Consequences of the Crisis.* The attitude of the immigrants towards the gods of Canaan seems to have varied in different times and in different environments.

There may have been Israelites who simply adopted the cults of the Baals and the Astartes and *forgot their national*

---

[1] Gen. xxxi. 53–4 ; Exod. xxxiv. 15.

[2] Deut. xxxiii. 19.

[3] See references in LVIII, ii, pp. 98–9.

[4] Exod. xxxiv. 15–16 ; Judges ii. 2 ; *cf.* Gen. xxiv. 3, 37 ; xxvi. 34–5 ; xxviii. 1–2 ; xxxvi. 2.

god. This would not have been of frequent occurrence : the earliest text of importance in which the Hebrew tribes emerge upon the stage of history, the song of Deborah, shows that the appeal to " come to the help of Jahweh among the mighty " could be counted upon to awaken a universal and heart-felt response.

It was more often the case, and was probably the rule from the early days of the settlement, that *the worship of Jahweh and of the baals was carried on simultaneously.* Jahweh, the god of Sinai, remained the sole guardian deity of the nation ; but the baals of the various districts also received the worship which was necessary in order to obtain from them abundant harvests and rich vintages.

The early poem about Deborah preserves, perhaps, a reminiscence of this attitude when it represents Jahweh as coming from Mt. Seir, marching from the land of Edom to lead the Israelite warriors and to smite the Canaanite. Jahweh comes from Seir, hence he is not yet thought of as having taken up his abode in Canaan ; he is still the warrior-god of the wilderness.

According to the compiler of the present book of Judges, those generations of the Israelites who came after the conquest worshipped Jahweh when they were in trouble, and the baals when they were prosperous. Possibly this theoretical interpretation of the history [1] contains a measure of truth : in the early days of the settlement enthusiasm for the worship of Jahweh may have burned with a more intense flame during the periods of warfare, while in the intervals of peace the Israelites may have directed their adoration mainly to the baals who guarded their fields.

It is also significant that the inhabitants of Jerusalem, as late as the eighth century, associated with the cult of Jahweh in the temple that of a brazen serpent which was probably an ancient Jebusite idol (2 Kings xviii. 4), and perhaps, also, at some period, the worship of a goddess Asherah. [2]

Finally there are grounds for supposing that the Jews of Elephantine, in Egypt, in the fifth century, side by side with Jahweh, worshipped several consorts whose names have been preserved, *e.g.* Anath-bethel, Ashim-bethel, Anath-jahu,

---

[1] *Cf.* pp. 333–4.
[2] At least according to 1 Kings xv. 18 ; 2 Kings xxiii. 4, 7 (?).

Haram-bethel, Mesgid.[1] Anath is the name of a Canaanite goddess. The same is apparently true of Ashim, for, according to Melito, a goddess Sime, the daughter of Hadad, existed at Beirut,[2] Emesa,[3] probably at Hierapolis[4] and, under the name of Ashimath, at Samaria (Amos viii. 14) ; a god by the name of Simi is found at Kefr Nebo.[5] Hence it is permissible to suppose that this association of Canaanite goddesses with the God of Israel among the Jews of Elephantine was a survival from the early days of the settlement in Palestine. Apostasy from the national religion among the Israelites commonly took the form of worshipping other gods together with Jahweh.[6]

However, natural as this attitude may have been, it was not the predominant one. It gave place at an early date to a new point of view which is reflected in all the early documents which we possess. *Jahweh was the sole object of worship, but all the titles and attributes of the baals were transferred to him.* Jahweh replaced the local divinities by absorbing them.

This usurpation of the place of the ancient deities by Jahweh seems to have begun by his appropriation of their places of worship. Only rarely was transition accompanied by violence.[7] What usually happened was that the Israelite immigrants became convinced through some resemblance in detail, that the baal of their new abode was the same as the god of their fathers. Or else the Canaanites declared that their god had voluntarily admitted the god of their new neighbours to a place in his sanctuary, just as we see, in the inscriptions, the gods of Teima solemnly receiving the god Salm,[8] or the gods of Thebes assigning temples and revenues to the gods of the new Asiatic provinces of the Empire.[9] In the same way Jahweh himself, in the time of Manasseh, received the astral gods of Assyria into his temple at Jerusalem. But when once he had obtained a footing, Jahweh soon came to be regarded by the Israelite as the true and only master of the land.

---

[1] **XXX**, p. 160.   [2] **CIL**, iii, 159 and suppl. 6669.
[3] Perdrizet and Fossey, **BCH**, 21, p. 70.
[4] *De dea Syria*, 33.
[5] V. Chapot, **BCH**, 26, p. 182 ; *cf.* **CCLXXIV**, p. 58.
[6] 1 Kings xviii. 21 ; Jer. vii. 9, 10, 16–18 ; xliv. ; **XLIV** ; Soph., i, 5, etc.
[7] Judges vi. 25–32.   [8] **XLIX**, pp. 502, 503.   [9] *Cf.* pp. 141–2.

However almost all the sanctuaries dedicated to Jahweh in Palestine had previously been Canaanite holy places. Even when this is not explicitly stated, as in the case of the sacred enclosures of Shechem [1] or Ophrah,[2] it may be inferred from the fact that the sanctuaries of Jahweh generally contained the spring, the terebinth or the oak of the locality (large trees are extremely rare in Palestine), or were situated on the summit of a neighbouring mountain : all of them places which were naturally sacred for the Canaanites, as they still are for the Moslem, Christian or Jewish successors of the Israelites in these countries.

A circumstance which greatly facilitated the usurpation of the ancient sanctuaries of the baals by clothing it with the semblance of a rightful title, was the creation of the patriarchal traditions. One of the main objects of these stories was to explain the origin of the various holy places of the land, their foundation being ascribed to the remote ancestors of Israel, Abraham, Isaac and Jacob. Hence it could be claimed that when the Israelites on their return from Egypt began to worship Jahweh in these holy places, they were only restoring them to the use for which they were originally intended : the baals had been merely temporary usurpers.

There may be an even closer connexion between the patriarchal traditions and the appropriation of the Palestinian sanctuaries to the worship of Jahweh. We have already seen [3] that there are reasons for thinking that some of the individuals who figure in the patriarchal narratives of the Israelites were originally divine or semi-divine beings worshipped by the Canaanites. The Israelites will have aided the transference of the local sanctuaries to their national religion by transforming the ancient supernatural possessors of these places into mere mortals, actual Israelites, worshippers of Jahweh and ancestors of the Hebrews. The process would be similar to that which happened in the case of many of the Greek heroes, Æsculapius, Trophonius, Amphiaraus, Erechtheus, ancient local gods who were reduced to the rank of attendants on the new gods. Many Oriental Christian or Moslem saints have similarly inherited the sanc-

---

[1] *Cf.* Judges ix. 6, 37 with Gen. xii. 6–7 ; Joshua xxiv. 26.
[2] Judges vi. 25–32.   [3] Pp. 229–30.

tuary, the rites and sometimes even the name of the ancient local baals.

Having entered into possession of the sanctuaries, Jahweh soon became *the* god of the land. Palestine was soon regarded by the Israelites as the land of Jahweh.[1] They looked to him for the success of the labours of the field ; it was he who dispensed at will drought or fertilizing rain. The transference of these functions to Jahweh may have been facilitated by the fact that he was originally a storm god. He was believed to have revealed the technical methods of agriculture (Isa. xxviii. 23–9).

Hence the nature of his worship underwent a change. To him, as to the baals, were brought offerings of grain, fruit, oil and wine. His three chief feasts were henceforth agricultural festivals [2] ; the chief was the vintage festival, which was also a religious occasion among the Canaanites : at Shechem the native inhabitants of the land celebrated it in the temple of Baal Berith (Judges ix. 27). The pastoral festivals of nomad Jahwism, sheep-shearing and Passover, were relegated to obscurity. The Passover only recovered its place of honour in Judah, in the seventh century.

The worship of the God of Israel took on that character of joyous and often licentious revelry which marked that of the baals. Sacred prostitution was practised in his honour.

He was freely represented, like Hadad, under the form of a bull.[3]

In each sanctuary, Jahweh was worshipped according to the traditional rites of the place ; he was distinguished there by a special title which will usually have been that of the ancient local baal : El Roi, *i.e.* " God of Vision " (Gen. xvi. 13), " God of Dan " (Amos viii. 14), " God of Eternity " (Gen. xxi. 33) or " Beloved of Beersheba,"[4] " God of Bethel " or perhaps " the God Bethel," *i.e.* " the Pillar-God."[5] This identification with the ancient genius of the place was carried to such an extent that Jahweh was in danger of being divided into as many gods as there were originally local Canaanite deities, and a Deuteronomic commentator, in the seventh

---

[1] Hos. ix. 3 ; *cf.* pp. 451–2. [2] See pp. 435–6.
[3] See pp. 457–8. [4] Amos viii. 14 (read dôdekâ).
[5] Gen. xxxi. 13 ; xxxv. 7 ; *cf.* pp. 124, 261–2. The text of these passages is, however, uncertain.

century, was obliged to utter the explicit warning : " Hear,
O Israel, Jahweh, our god, is one Jahweh."[1]   It was partly,
no doubt, to avoid the danger, thus threatened, of sub-
division, that the reformers in the time of Josiah laid down
the rule that there should be only one sanctuary.

Even the title of *baal*, " lord," was, in the times of the
judges and the early kings, frequently applied to Jahweh.
Saul himself, the anointed of the national god, called one
of his sons, Ishbaal, " the man of the Lord."[2]   One of Jonathan's sons was called Meribaal (1 Chron. viii. 34 ; ix. 40),
meaning, perhaps, " the beloved of the Lord "[3] :   A son of
David was named Beeliada (1 Chron. xiv. 7) ;   one of his
officers bore the name of Baal Hanan (1 Chron. xxvii. 28).
Gideon was also called Jerubbaal, the true meaning of which
is " may the Lord plead for him," and not " let Baal strive
with him," or " let Baal plead for himself," according the
popular etymology on which has been based the incident of
the destruction of the sanctuary of Baal (Judges vi. 25–32).
According to *ostraka* found at Samaria, many Israelites of
the time of Ahab bore names compounded with Baal : Abibaal, Baalzamar, Meribaal, Baalah, Baalazakar, Baalme' oni.[4]

The features borrowed from the baals became so completely identified with the figure of Jahweh that even those
prophets who were most hostile to everything which they
regarded as Canaanite retained them almost in their entirety.
It was related that Elijah arranged a ritual contest to prove
that Jahweh, and not Baal, was the dispenser of rain in
Palestine.   Hosea declares that Israel owes her corn, her
wine and her oil to Jahweh and not to the baals.   The prophets were accustomed to speak of Canaan as Jahweh's land
and of foreign countries as unclean.[5]

Hence there arose what was to a great extent a mixture
of the ancient Canaanite cults with the religion of the Israelite
immigrants.   But while, as among the Philistines for instance,
the native deities, Dagon, Astarte, Atargatis, seem in the end
to have absorbed the gods of the newcomers,[6] in Israel it was

[1] Deut. vi. 4 ; *cf.* William Frederick Bade, **ZATW**, 1910, pp. 81–90 ;
CCLIX, pp. 187–217.
   [2] See p. 359.   [3] Paul Humbert, **ZATW**, 1919–1920, p. 86.
   [4] D. G. Lyon, **HTR**, 1911, pp. 136–43.
   [5] Hos. ix. 3–5 ; Amos vii. 17 ; *cf.* Hos. viii. 1 ; ix. 15 ; Jer. xii. 14,
etc.   [6] P. 349.

the religion of the invaders which predominated in the resultant mixture of cults ; the national religion constituted the outline in which the elements derived from Canaanite custom fell into their place.

This result, no doubt, was partly due to the strong national feeling of the Hebrew settlers, to their greater measure of racial solidarity as compared with the disintegration of the Canaanites, to the untamed spirit of the conquering Bedouin, to the frequent wars—" wars of Jahweh," as they were called —which kept alive their enthusiasm for the national god, to the religious prestige surrounding the Levites, the members of the tribe of Moses, scattered even as far as the central and northern tribes,[1] and who were by tradition ardent supporters of Jahweh.[2]   But it must have been due above all to the fact that the founder of the Hebrew confederation had formulated and succeeded in instilling into his people the principle that Jahweh was and must be the sole *elohim* of Israel.[3]

The absorption of the baals by Jahweh brought into the religion of Israel an influx of heterogeneous elements.   It would not, however, seem that Jahwism suffered any essential loss or corruption in the crisis, but that it was rather, on the whole, increased and enriched.

Doubtless there were practices, such as sacred prostitution,[4] which were not in harmony with the spirit of Jahwism and which, in the course of time, had to be resisted and exterminated.   But such features seem to have remained rather on the surface of the religion.   For the mass of Israelites, Jahweh was always essentially a national god, whose relations with his people were of a moral nature.   He never became for them what the baals were, a being whose existence was practically indistinguishable from the life of nature, like Tammuz-Adonis, for instance, who died and was reborn each year with the vegetation.   Hence it may be maintained that the practice of sacred prostitution, by which the individual associated himself with the great divine procreative act supposed to effect the annual rebirth of nature, was never really assimilated by Jahwism.   It seems to be an inference from the vow which is forbidden in the Deuteronomic code (Deut. xxiii. 18–19) that this practice was interpreted as an offering

---

[1] Judges xvii.–xix.
[2] *Cf.* **X**, pp. 45–8.   [3] Pp. 313–4.   [4] *Cf.* p. 103.

to God of that which was regarded as most valuable : the money received as the price of this offering was wont to be paid into the sacred treasury.

As for such fetichistic, magical or barbarous practices as the worship of trees, springs, sacred stones, casting lots, human sacrifices, which the religious reformers of the seventh and fifth centuries branded as so many sinister borrowings from the Canaanites, we have already seen that entirely similar customs existed among the nomad Hebrew tribes at the time of the birth of Jahwism, as in earlier times.

Hence we must not exaggerate the seriousness of the deteriorating influence of Canaanite practices upon Jahwism. On the other hand there is reason to believe that as the result of the absorption of the attributes of the baals, the power of Jahweh was considerably increased ; it was extended over the whole of Canaan, and the agricultural life of the country was regarded as having its sole source in him. Another equally important circumstance was that the nation had been committed to an act of faith in the helping power of Jahweh, they had confessed that wherever they might settle and whatever new needs might arise, the power and providence of their God could never fail. By this very act of affirmation, Israel's faith in Jahweh became more confident, better prepared for fresh conquests.[1]

It must be added for the sake of completeness that this assimilation of the native cults was not carried through without meeting here and there opposition and even organized protests.

Those communities who, like the Kenites, consciously preserved the customs of the nomad mode of life, would also set themselves to guard the religion of their fathers pure from any contamination from the agricultural cults.[2] The shepherds of southern Judah were, no doubt, slower to become " Canaanized," and were more superficially affected by the religion of Canaan, than the cultivators and vine-growers of the centre and north.[3]

The use of wine, the special gift of the baals, in the ritual and at the periodic feasts, met with a stubborn resistance. It was wholly forbidden to the Nazirites, as well as to the Rechabites. The priest was forbidden to partake of wine or

[1] See also pp. 481–8.   [2] P. 399.   [3] *Cf.* **XXX**, p. 163.

any fermented beverage before officiating.[1] The custom, common in the ancient world, of using intoxicating liquors to produce the phenomena of inspiration,[2] was frowned upon by genuine Jahwists, although it was practised by some of the Israelite prophets.[3] Libations of wine became part of the ritual at a very early date.[4] Nevertheless, about 573, Ezekiel again attempted, although without success,[5] to exclude wine from the list of offerings to Jahweh.[6]

The ritual forms of early Hebrew religion were, no doubt, defended, to some extent at least, by the priests, especially those of the tribe of Levi, whose prestige[7] apparently rested on the profound knowledge which was ascribed to them of the traditions of their great ancestor, Moses. We may assume that they defended the exclusive authority of Jahweh, and thus prevented the assimilation of his cult to that of the baals. However, they did not go so far as to offer an organized opposition to the "Canaanization" of the ritual: we are told of Levites who officiated in sanctuaries where images were worshipped (Judges xvii.-xviii.), where cereals were offered,[8] where the sacred meal included wine,[9] and where the feast of vintage was kept.[10]

The vague yearning for the old nomad days which, in spite of everything, persisted among the masses,[11] however permeated they might be with civilization, extended also to religious matters. The prophets of the eighth and seventh centuries assume as a universally admitted fact that the sojourn in the wilderness had been the golden age of the relations between Jahweh and Israel.[12]

This persistence of the nomad ideal, especially in certain groups and by the help of certain institutions, was a ferment whose effects made themselves felt later on.[13] The reaction against Canaanite civilization was one of the special watchwords of the prophetic movement, even though, like many reform movements, it aimed at and achieved something very different from the mere restoration of the past.

[1] Lev. x. 9 ; Ezek. xliv. 21.   [2] Cf. **CCLXXIX.**
[3] Isa. xxviii. 7, 8 ; Mic. ii. 11.   [4] Judges ix. 13.
[5] See the Levitical laws.
[6] xlv. 24–5 ; xlvi. 7, 11, 14–15.   [7] See pp. 440–1.
[8] 1 Sam. xxi. 5–7 (4–6).   [9] 1 Sam. i. 13–15.
[10] 1 Sam. i. 3, 21 ; cf. Judges xxi. 19.   [11] See p 400.
[12] Amos v. 25 ; Hos. ix. 10 ; x. 1 ; Jer. ii. 2.   [13] Pp. 418–21.

II

THE INSTITUTION OF THE MONARCHY. THE BUILDING OF
THE TEMPLE. THE DIVISION OF THE KINGDOM

1. *The Institution of the Monarchy.* We have seen that
at the time of its institution, the national monarchy was
hailed as having been not only approved but prepared and
initiated by Jahweh.[1] This is easily understood. By
securing the independence and unification of the tribes, and
thus making Israel for the first time an actually existing fact,
the early kings completed the political part of the work of
Moses.

But the historians and legislators of the period following
the eighth century could see nothing but the disastrous effects
of the kingship upon the original purity and exclusivism
of the national cult. Actually, the kings had achieved the
incorporation of the Canaanites into the Israelite nation.
In the political interest of the country they had formed a
multiplicity of ties with other kingdoms, they had contracted
alliances and marriages with the royal houses of neighbouring
countries, and had even promoted intercourse with foreign
cults. At the same time they had endeavoured to imitate
the luxury of the " kings of the nations," and had imported
foreign craftsmen. The monarchy had largely contributed
to create a secular spirit in Israel and to introduce the people
into the main stream of oriental civilization.

But the influence of the monarchy on the ancestral
religion was far from being a merely negative one. The
growth of general culture benefited Jahwism ; for instance,
by the creation of a literature. It was owing to the unification achieved by the kings that the various traditions of
the local sanctuaries were fused into a single organized
national tradition (the patriarchal narratives). Some of the
kings exerted their authority to exterminate practices which
the loyal adherents of Jahweh regarded as corruptions of
the ancestral religion. Saul prohibited seeking after the
dead and familiar spirits (1 Sam. xxviii. 3, 9). Asa forbade
the use of sacred poles or *asherim* ; he and his son Jehoshaphat
proscribed sacred prostitution (1 Kings xv. 12–3 ; xxii. 47).

[1] Pp. 353, 356.

Josiah introduced the law of the central sanctuary (2 Kings xxii.–xxiii.). Finally, it is in the conception of the monarchy that we can trace some of the sources of the Messianic hope : on the one hand the yearning for the vanished glories of the early kings clearly helped to awaken the expectation of the glorious ruler of the future ; on the other hand, the titles and honours of the king were extended to Jahweh himself.[1] Thus arose the hope of a day when " the kingdom of God " would be finally set up over the whole earth.

2. *The Temple.* If the actual importance of the institution of the monarchy for the development of the religion of Israel was minimized by the biblical writers of a later date, they exaggerated, on the other hand, the importance of the building of the temple at Jerusalem. It was only in consequence of the destruction of the northern kingdom (722), and the check which the Assyrians received before Jerusalem in 701, that this sanctuary began to assume a special place in the national religion ; and it was wholly owing to the reform of Josiah (622) which declared the temple to be the sole legitimate sanctuary of Jahweh, that the temple became for Judaism up to the abolition of sacrifices in A.D. 70 the heart of the national religion and the object of the ardent affection of all the loyal worshippers of Jahweh.

When Solomon built the temple, he certainly had no intention of substituting it for the ancient high places— Gibeon, Hebron, Bethel, Gilgal, Dan or Beersheba—several of which, as we know, continued to exist for many centuries. He had not foreseen that a whole nation would resort to the new sanctuary : the brazen altar which he had erected was so small that it became necessary, on the days when sacrifices were liable to be at all numerous, to sanction the slaying of sacrifices in " the midst of the court which is before the Lord's house " (1 Kings viii. 64), that is to say, apparently, on the whole surface of the cup-marked rock which constituted the threshing-floor of Araunah (pl. xiv, 1). Another noteworthy fact is that the approaches to the temple seem to have had no gate on the west side, that is, toward the city, while there was direct communication with the royal palace, whose entrance was immediately opposite the entrance to

---

[1] Num. xxiii. 21 ; Isa. vi. 5 ; Jer. viii. 19 ; Exod. xv. 18 ; Ps. xciii., etc. *Cf.* pp. 435–6.

the temple.[1] The new sanctuary was primarily a royal chapel.

In building it, Solomon seems to have been influenced by political motives, as well as by religious aims : he wished to dazzle the eyes of the surrounding nations by the power and wealth of the Israelite State, which Jahweh's glory was pledged to maintain ; to perpetuate the splendour of the dynasty, and finally to enhance the religious prestige of the capital by erecting for the ark which David had placed there, an abode of unparalleled magnificence.

In respect of this last object, Solomon's hopes were destined to be disappointed. The attraction of a sanctuary does not consist in its wealth, but in the popular belief in its sanctity, and this halo of sanctity usually arises from the prestige of the immemorial traditions which are associated with it. Now Solomon's temple could only offer the beginnings of a sacred " legend."[2] Moreover, its sumptuous building, in the eyes of the northern tribes, stood for little more than an increase of levies and taxes.

Finally, the very splendour of the temple must have been an offence rather than an attraction to those Israelites who cherished the tradition of the simplicity of the genuine worship of Jahweh. No doubt, after the settlement in Canaan, the Israelites had followed the example of the Canaanites[3] in dedicating to Jahweh, in certain holy places, some kind of temple, with a *cella* for the emblem of the god, swinging doors,[4] and a chamber for the sacred meals.[5] But these buildings were probably simple and unadorned. The display of wealth in the sanctuary at Jerusalem, resplendent with gold and cedar, must have seemed to be a deliberate departure from the ancient customs.

The sight of the decorations and furniture of the new sanctuary could only have confirmed these suspicions. The building, constructed on the plan of the great Egyptian temples, by Phenician architects, was full of symbols expressing conceptions wholly foreign to Jahwism, directly derived

---

[1] Ezek. xliii. 8 ; the threshold is evidently not that of the royal tomb (CCLXI, *ad loc.*).

[2] 2 Sam. xxiv. ; perhaps Gen. xxii.

[3] Tell es-Safy, Shechem, Beth Shan.

[4] At Shiloh : 1 Sam. i. 9 ; iii. 3, 15.

[5] 1 Sam. i. 9 (emended) ; ix. 22.

from Tyre and Sidon, or even Babylon and Egypt. Before the entrance to the building, as at Tyre, Hierapolis, and Petra,[1] there stood two probably isolated columns ; like the obelisks, these were originally connected with the solar cult. Everywhere appeared carvings representing flowers and animals ; within the court was a great bronze reservoir, the " brazen sea," supported by four groups of three bulls apiece ; it was much too high to have been used for washing purposes,[2] and, as its name suggests, must have symbolized the celestial " sea." There were reservoirs of this kind in the Babylonian temples, called *apsu, tamtu,* " ocean," " abyss," and also in the temples of Karnak, Baalbek, and Samaria.[3] The ten " bases," heavy basins supported by bronze frames mounted on wheels, must also have had some symbolic meaning ; for it is clear from their size and weight that they could hardly have been used for carrying the water needed for the sacrifices. In any case they were foreign articles, almost identical objects having been found in Cypriote tombs of the last Mycenean age.[4]

The building of the temple must have seemed an attempt at syncretism, a fusion of Jahwism, represented by the ark, with foreign cults, especially Phenician cults.

It was owing to these diverse causes that Solomon's enterprise remained for several centuries without any appreciable effect upon the development of the national religion.

3. *The Schism between Israel and Judah.* According to the final redaction of the book of Kings (1 Kings xii. 26–31), the division of Solomon's realm into two kingdoms resulted in a religious schism. Jeroboam, fearing lest the northern tribes should return to their allegiance to their rightful king, Rehoboam, conceived the idea of making two golden calves, which he placed, one at Bethel and the other at Dan, saying to his people : " It is too much for you to go up to Jerusalem ; behold thy gods, O Israel, which brought thee up out of the land of Egypt." He set up high places, and appointed as priests men who were not of the tribe of Levi ; moreover (this has been added by the later editor who inserted c. xiii.), he

---

[1] See p. 260.
[2] According to later editor of 2 Chron. iv. 6.
[3] **III**, p. 329.
[4] At Larnaka and at Enkomi : **III**, p. 219 (figs. 227–8). See pl. xii, 1 and 2.

transferred to the eighth month " the feast " which was held in Judah in the seventh month (v. 32).

The facts which we have cited show very plainly certain points in which the cult of the northern tribes differed from that of Judah, but, be it noted, *the cult of Judah as it was practised after the reform of Josiah in* 622, in the time of the editor of the book of Kings. Our author has committed the anachronism of representing these features, which according to him were peculiar to the Israelite cult, as *innovations* introduced by Jeroboam. As a matter of fact, they were simply the old traditional customs which had persisted in Israel, while Judah, in the course of time, had come to abandon or modify them. The worship of Jahweh in the high places, that is to say, in other sanctuaries than the temple at Jerusalem, was not condemned in Judah until the seventh century. The admission to the priesthood of men who were not Levites was still a common practice in the time of David [1] : the prerogative of the levitical priests was first definitely sanctioned by the Deuteronomist (seventh century). The worship of the " golden calves," that is, the worship of bull-images representing Jahweh, was similarly not a real innovation. Image-worship, doubtless unknown, or only slightly practised among the nomad Hebrew tribes, had long been, in the time of Jeroboam I, a well-established practice in Judah (1 Sam. xix. 13–6) as among the northern Israelites.[2]

As for the date of the feast, that is to say, the great feast of Jahweh in the autumn, the northern tribes, when they kept it in the eighth month, followed the ancient custom which was still observed in Judah in the time of Solomon Indeed, we learn from an early text that the temple was finished in the month Bul, the month which was later on called the eighth month of the year (1 Kings vi. 38) ; another text adds that " the feast " was held immediately after the dedication of the temple (1 Kings viii. 65). Since it is extremely probable that the dedication took place as soon as the temple was completed, and not eleven months later, it would follow that the dedication and the feast of Ingathering took place in the eighth month, and not in the seventh (Etanim), as another passage has it, which has apparently been corrected according

[1] See pp. 440–1.   [2] Pp. 429–32

to later usage (1 Kings viii. 2). Hence it was not Jeroboam who changed the date of the " feast " ; the change was made after Solomon's time, in Judah. Nor is the reason far to seek. The " feast " was supposed to be held as soon as the last fruits of the year had been gathered in. As long as Israel and Judah were united, the feast was delayed until the ingathering was finished throughout the whole of the country, which could hardly happen in the north of Palestine until the eighth month. According to the agricultural calendar of Gezer, the fruit-gathering lasted two months, the sixth and the seventh, counting from the beginning of barley harvest, which is known to have begun about the fifteenth of Nisan (the first month of the official calendar of the post-Exilic period) ; hence in the centre of Palestine the ingathering would finish about the middle of the eighth month. When Judah became separated from the northern kingdom, the ceremony was naturally held earlier, since in the south of Palestine the fruits ripened distinctly earlier than in the north.[1]

If any concern for religion was mingled with the political motives which caused the secession of the northern tribes, it would have been the desire to defend the traditional simplicity of the worship of Jahweh, threatened by the heathen luxury of the temple at Jerusalem.[2] " We will leave nothing to Rehoboam but the temple which his father built," was the declaration of the Israelites, according to Josephus.[3] It was related that the prophet Nathan had deprecated the building of so sumptuous a temple (2 Sam. vii.), and that another prophet, Ahijah, had predicted and approved of the schism (1 Kings ii. 29–39). In any case, in respect of the cult, it was the northern Israelites who were the conservative party.

The political breach with Jerusalem was so far from being a religious schism that, up to the fall of Samaria (722), the more powerful northern kingdom, the only one which bore the name of Israel, continued to be the true home of Jahwism. It was the scene of the activities of Elijah, Elisha, Micaiah the son of Imlah, Hosea, and even a prophet like Amos, who came originally from Judah. The people of the

[1] Kittel, **CCLXVII**, pp. 111–12 ; Eissfeldt, **XL**, i, p. 513, n. 6.
[2] *Cf.* **CCLXV**, pp. 46–54 ; **XLV**, p. 218.
[3] A.J., viii, 8, 3 (219).

two kingdoms retained the consciousness of being still a single nation ; they desired the restoration of unity, although this was conceived of in very different ways. The southern legitimists hoped for the return of the Israelite rebels to the authority of " David," while the Israelites and even some of the Judeans thought that it was Judah who should " return to his people." In an Ephraimite poem there occurs this prayer :

> " Hear, Lord, the voice of Judah,
> and bring him in unto his people " (Deut. xxxiii. 7).

It is noteworthy that the traditions which specially concern Judah, such as the story of the relations between Jacob and Esau, that is between Israel and Edom, and the traditions which exclusively concern the northern tribes, such as the story of Joseph or that of the relations between Jacob and Laban, that is, between the Israelite and the Aramean peoples, occupy approximately as much space in the Jahwist history, which apparently comes from Judah, as in the Elohist narrative compiled in Ephraim.

It was the religion which kept alive this strong sense of national unity : Jahweh was the one god of the two kingdoms ; there was still only one people, Israel, the people of Jahweh. Hence, instead of resulting in a religious schism, the division into two kingdoms, on the contrary, intensified the sense of the deep ideal unity, in spite of political differences, existing between all Israelites by virtue of their religion.

III

The Defenders and Restorers of Genuine Jahwism

The resistance to the influx of Canaanite influences, somewhat wavering at the beginning of the settlement in Palestine,[1] gathered strength from the time of the monarchy and especially from the ninth century. The Rechabite movement belongs to about 850.[2] On the other hand, various forces were at work tending to maintain the national tradition, especially the traditional resistance to any foreign element in the religion, and to preserve and emphasize the characteristic features of Jahweh's " right."

---

[1] See pp. 410-1.   [2] Pp. 399-400.

The religious legislation of the " Book of the Covenant," while it sanctioned the transformation of Jahwism into an agrarian cult, nevertheless, attempted to restore in the sanctuaries the ancient simplicity of worship.[1]

The same code, in its civil legislation, aimed at maintaining or restoring, among the peasants and city-dwellers of Palestine, the spirit of comradeship which existed among the members of the nomad clan. It is not difficult to understand the reason for this conservative or reactionary tendency of the laws : justice was the special prerogative of the priests, who were the accredited guardians of the tradition of Israel, responsible for spreading " the knowledge of Jahweh," as Hosea says—that is to say, the knowledge of his will—by their oracular decisions (torah).

The story-tellers who, during the same period, collected and arranged the local traditions and whose narratives were gathered up into the great collections J and E (ninth to eighth centuries), assisted, in no small measure, to stir up among the Israelites a feeling of pride in their glorious origins, and of faith in Jahweh, to whom Israel owed everything in the past, and in whom lay all their hope for the present and the future. These traditions were united, in fact, into a " sacred history " of the nation, its guiding idea being that Jahweh had willed, from the beginning, and had carried into effect, in spite of all obstacles, the creation of a prosperous, powerful and innumerable people, and, centuries before had destined the land of Canaan for their undisputed possession.

One of these chroniclers, the Jahwist compiler, has sometimes been represented as " a partisan of the nomad ideal," who " in naïve and grandiose myths, perpetuates the undying patriarchal dream of his people and a despairing protest against culture."[2] Such a statement ascribes to the pious collectors of the traditions a greater degree of deliberate purpose than they possessed. Together with stories exalting or idealizing the wandering life of the patriarchs, depicting the building of Babylon as " a monument of ambition and folly,"[3] the Jahwist has collected many others in which the agricultural life is presented as man's natural state (Gen. ii. 5), and a wealth of corn and wine as his highest good (Gen. xxvii. 27–8, 39 ; xlix. 11–2, 20, 25, 26 ; cf. Gen. v. 29 ; ix.

[1] Pp. 413–4, 432–3.   [2] CCLXIII, p. 45.   [3] Ibid., pp. 46–7.

20–7 ; Judges ix. 8–15, etc.), others, again, exalting the kingship, or relating, without attaching any blame to its originators, the advance of civilization (Gen. iv. 17–22 ; v. 29). It is, however, true that the general tendency of these traditions was to exalt the past, especially that part of the past which was specifically Israelite.[1]

But the prime movers in this process of inward consolidation and growth in the national religion seem to have been the prophets.

There is, no doubt, a nucleus of historical fact in the story which depicts Nathan as condemning David for having " despised Jahweh " in causing Uriah to be slain in order that he might take possession of his wife (2 Sam. xii. 9). We are told that the prophet Gad announced to the same monarch the punishment of Jahweh because he had taken a census of the people, an act which is regarded by many peoples as sacrilegious.[2] Another prophet, Ahijah, the Shilonite, seems to have fostered the revolt of Jeroboam, no doubt because he believed that Solomon, by his despotic behaviour and his temple in the Phenician mode, had departed from the true Israelite tradition.[3]

A far more serious and significant conflict was that in which the prophets Elijah, Micaiah the son of Imlah, and Elisha were ranged against the last rulers of the house of Omri, Ahab and his sons. Unfortunately the stories which have come down to us concerning the beginnings of this struggle contain more poetry than exact history.

In that section of the book of Kings containing the life of Elijah, Ahab and his wife, Jezebel, are represented as endeavouring to abolish the worship of Jahweh, and to replace it by that of Baal : they overthrew the altars of the God of Israel and slew his prophets. Elijah alone escaped, after having announced that the land would be smitten with a drought which would not cease until he gave the word. At the end of three years, Elijah reappeared. Ahab, in his alarm, agreed to summon the 450 prophets of Baal to Carmel for a public ordeal in which it would be manifested whether Jahweh or Baal was the true god. For nearly the whole day the prophets of Baal vainly endeavoured to bring fire from

---

[1] Cf. Ad. Lods, **RHR**, lxxxv, pp. 198–201.
[2] See p. 463.   [3] 1 Kings xi. 29–39 ; cf. p. 417.

heaven to consume their sacrifice. But the moment Elijah offered up his prayer the miracle took place. The prophet of Jahweh then proceeded to slay his 450 opponents. The worship of Baal being thus extirpated in Israel, the drought could cease ; Elijah asked and obtained an abundance of rain.

But Jezebel threatened to slay the prophet, and he thereupon fled to Horeb. There Jahweh appeared to him and promised that the guilty should be punished ; he commanded him to anoint those who should be the instruments of the divine vengeance : Hazael, King of Syria, Jehu, King of Israel, and the prophet Elisha. There should only remain 7,000 men in Israel, all who had not bowed the knee to Baal and whose mouth had not kissed him.

These stirring pages are not history but the product of popular tradition which, according to its wont, has dramatized and simplified the facts, concentrating into a few episodes, of which a single hero is the central figure, all the reminiscences of the prophetic struggle against the house of Omri. To confirm the truth of this statement it is only necessary to consult the other documents preserved in the book of Kings. There it appears that, far from seeking to abolish the religion of Jahweh, Ahab and his wife were the first Israelite sovereigns, after David, to give their children names compounded with that of the national God : Ahaz*iahu*, *J*oram, Athal*iah* ; the ostraka found in the palace of Ahab in Samaria show that names of this kind were also common among the officials of this king.[1] The royal pair could not have slain all the prophets of Jahweh save one, since Ahab listened to them with respect, and, on the eve of his death he was surrounded by 400 of them, who all, with one exception, predicted his success (1 Kings xx. and xxii.). The worship of Baal was not abolished by Elijah in the time of Ahab, but years after by Jehu (2 Kings x.). Hazael, according to another tradition, and in any case Jehu, were made king by Elisha, not by Elijah.[2]

What we hear in the story of this prophet is above all the echo of the deep impression made upon the minds and hearts of the people by this stalwart defender of Jahweh, who, with

---

[1] CCLXXVI, pp. 20–7 ; Gressmann, ZATW, 1925, p. 148 ; G. R. Driver, ZATW, 1928, p. 8 ; D. G. Lyon, HTR, 1911, pp. 136–43.
[2] 2 Kings viii. 7–15 ; ix. 1–6.

his mantle of skin and leather girdle, so completely embodied the severity of the ancient customs as opposed to the effeminacy of the followers of a foreign civilization.

We can obtain some glimpses of the real nature of the conflict between Ahab and the prophets opposed to him.

For political reasons Ahab had built in Samaria a temple for Baal, *i.e.* the Baal of Tyre, Melqart, the god of his ally, Ithobaal. In so doing, the King no more intended to attack the rights of Jahweh than did Solomon when he set up for the gods of his foreign wives those high places in the neighbourhood of Jerusalem which still existed in 622.[1] But in Ahab's case a new and dangerous element made its appearance : the King, and therefore his courtiers also, offered sacrifices to the foreign god.[2] Hence Jahweh was no longer the sole *elohim* worshipped by the Israelites in Palestine. One of the fundamental rights of Jahweh had been violated by Jahweh's own anointed ; a rival to Jahweh had been set up in his own domain. Hence we can understand why Elijah was consumed with " jealousy " for his God.

The question arises whether deeper issues were at stake ; whether it was not more than an attempt to vindicate the limits of Jahweh's exclusive authority, and that for Elijah there was an essential difference of nature between Jahweh and Baal, the power of Jahweh being so infinitely greater that the title of God could rightfully be ascribed to him alone. It may be so. Certain passages in the idealized biography which we have just summarized seem to attribute such conceptions to the prophet.[3] However, it is quite likely that these passages should rather be interpreted in the light of the words of Elijah on Carmel : " Let it be known this day that thou art God in Israel, and that I am thy servant " (1 Kings xviii. 36). It is not a question of proving who is God in the absolute sense, but who is God in Israel. We cannot show that the conflict ever passed from the plane of monolatry to that of monotheism.

On the other hand, it seems to be certain, from an allusion in a document which is in the main very reliable (2 Kings xxv.–xxvi.), that Elijah predicted the death of Ahab and his

[1] 1 Kings xi. 7–8 ; 2 Kings xxiii. 13.
[2] 1 Kings x. 18–9, 24 (G), 25.
[3] 1 Kings xviii. 21, 24, 27, 37, 39.

family on account of the judicial murder of Naboth and his sons (1 Kings xxi.). This episode is noteworthy for several reasons. It suggests that the prophetic movement of the ninth century was social as well as religious. It also indicates a sensible deepening of the conception of the righteousness of Jahweh. It had certainly long been believed that the God of Israel was the avenger of innocent blood; but the belief was still more firmly held that he promoted the greatness of his people, and that he was, in spite of all, on the side of those who were "fighting the battles of Jahweh." But Elijah had other ideas about the moral requirements of his God: it mattered little to him if the guilty person were the anointed of Jahweh; he cared little for his political skill and military courage and his successes, which seemed to be signal marks of the divine favour: Ahab had treacherously destroyed a family in Israel, hence his house must perish.

It is a remarkable thing that the prophets of the ninth century should have thus entered upon a struggle to the death with one of the most energetic and successful of the representatives of the national idea. The defence of the endangered religion of Jahweh and of violated justice, in the minds of these men took precedence of the immediate interests of the nation. The attitude of Elijah and of Micaiah already foreshadows that of Amos and the other great prophets of the eighth and seventh centuries, who placed the demands of righteousness above everything, even above the existence of their nation.

There was still, however, a long road to traverse. In order to vindicate Jahweh, Elisha does not hesitate to make use of the cynical Jehu, while Hosea, no longer thinking that the end justifies the means, condemns as inexpiable crimes the cold-blooded massacres of Jezreel (Hos. i. 4). Moreover, Elijah, Micaiah and Elisha are only concerned with a guilty dynasty; they cannot see, as do the prophets of the eighth century, that it is the nation itself which is corrupt to the core and doomed to destruction.

RELIGIOUS OBSERVANCES OF THE ISRAELITES SETTLED IN PALESTINE

AMONG the Israelites, after their settlement in Palestine, religious observances remained, no doubt, in all essential respects, what they had been not only in early Jahwism, but in the period prior to the founding of the national religion.[1] Hence we shall confine ourselves here to pointing out the changes which seem to have been introduced after the entry of the tribes into Canaan, and which were mainly due to imitation of the Canaanites.

I

SACRED THINGS

The central object of an Israelite high place was usually a tree, spring, cave, hill-top, rock or pillar, which had been worshipped by the Canaanites in that place.[2] The new-comers had no hesitation in adopting these sacred objects, since they had long been accustomed to worship similar objects in their own holy places.[3]

But in certain sanctuaries, the Hebrews found certain sacred objects, unknown, or almost unknown, to them in their nomad state.

1. *The Asherah.* The *asherah*, or sacred pole of the Canaanites,[4] became one of the regular features of the Israelite holy places.[5] It was erected alongside the altar of Jahweh (Deut. xvi. 21). There was one of these poles at Samaria,[6] and another at Jerusalem.[7]

Our reason for believing that the *asherah* was unknown

---

[1] See pp. 258–307.   [2] Pp. 83–4.
[3] Pp. 258–264.   [4] Pp. 84–5.
[5] Mic. v. 12–13.   [6] 2 Kings xiii. 6.
[7] 2 Kings xviii. 4; xxi. 7 (?); xxiii. 6.

to the Israelites before their entry into Palestine, is that the equivalent of this object is not found among the pagan Arabs and that it seems to have become an object of condemnation to strict Jahwists long before the pillar : neither the Jahwist nor the Elohist narrative ascribes to the patriarchs the erection of an *asherah*. This aversion is best explained on the assumption that this object was not part of the ancient religious heritage of the patriarchs.

2. *The Ark*. While the asherah was condemned at an early date, the ark, on the other hand, continued to be an object of reverence to the faithful long after the sacred chest had disappeared from the temple at Jerusalem, either by reason of age, or during one of the spoliations of the temple.[1]

According to the tradition, it was a coffer which was carried to battle (at least up to the time of David) as a pledge of the divine presence ; oracles, it would seem, were obtained from it, and in the intervals between campaigns it was deposited in some sanctuary or simply in a tent.[2] Thus we find the " ark of God " at Bethel,[3] Shiloh, Bethshemesh, Kirjath-jearim,[4] in the same period, in Saul's camp, attended by a priest of Nob,[5] and finally at Jerusalem.

According to the view of the Deuteronomist (after 622) and priestly (sixth and fifth centuries) writers, the sanctity of the ark arose from the fact that it contained the tables of the Law. Hence the names *'aron berith* and *'aron 'eduth*, meaning, not " ark of the covenant " and " ark of the testimony," but " ark of the Law " : *berith*, contract, has often the meaning of law, while *'eduth* means attestation, declaration before witnesses, charter : it is the name which the priestly writer gives to the Decalogue.

[1] There is no trace known of its existence after Solomon : 1 Kings viii. 8 seems to say that the staves of the ark were still visible at the time of the editing of that section (ninth century ?). The text, however, is not certain (*cf.* **XXV**, ii, 1, p. 214 ; Kittel, *Bibl. hebr.*). 2 Chron. xxxv. 3 is too late a redaction to serve as evidence for the presence of the Ark in the temple under Josiah. In any case, it was no longer there in the time of Jeremiah (iii. 6) ; the way in which he speaks of it suggests that it had recently disappeared (in 597 ?).

[2] 2 Sam. vii. 6.

[3] At least according to Judges xx. 26–8 ; *cf.* ii. 1 (?).

[4] 1 Sam. iii. 6.

[5] At least according to the Masoretic text of 1 Sam. xiv. 18 ; some Greek exemplars (G^B) have " the ephod " instead of " the Ark."

But this is clearly a late interpretation, intended to spiritualize the old half-fetishistic beliefs attaching to this ancient sacred object. The usual method of preserving the knowledge of a legal text was not to shut it up in a chest, but to engrave it on a pillar which all could see (the code of Hammurabi), or on the walls of a temple.

According to the most ancient evidence, this early *palladium* of the Israelite hosts was practically identified with Jahweh himself; it was addressed as if it were God in person (Num. x. 35–6). When the ark was brought among the army, there was rejoicing because " God is come into the camp " (1 Sam. iv. 5–8). It exacts vengeance, as Jahweh might do, from those who are negligent in reverence towards it (1 Sam. iv.–vi.; 2 Sam. vi.). It guides the oxen attached to the cart which carries it (1 Sam. vi. 7–12).

Unfortunately in the history of the ark and of the beliefs which were attached to it, many points remain obscure, in spite of various learned conjectures concerning it which have been put forward in recent years.

According to the theory of a Greek scholar, Reichel, in 1897, which found wide acceptance,[1] the ark was a throne, apparently empty, on which Jahweh sat unseen : similarly, Xerxes had in his army " a sacred chariot of Zeus (*i.e.* the supreme god of the Persians), drawn by eight white horses. The driver, holding the reins, followed on foot, for no man might mount the throne." [2] In support of this view such passages are quoted as 1 Samuel iii. 10 (Jahweh comes and stands) ; Psalm xxiv, where the doors of the temple are commanded to lift up their heads that the king of glory may enter, when the ark is brought in procession into the temple ; the title " seated above the cherubim " given to the god of the ark. Hence, on this view, the ark would be a witness, not to the fetishism of the early Israelites, but to their extremely lofty conception of God.

Some biblical passages seem, indeed, to reflect this conception, especially Jeremiah iii. 16–17, where the prophet declares that in time to come no one will think of making

---

[1] This conjecture has been defended by Meinhold, Dibelius (1906), Gunkel (1906), Gressmann (**XXV**, ii, 1, pp. 15–19), Benzinger (**III**, p. 313).

[2] Herodotus, vii, 40.

the ark again, because " in that day Jerusalem (itself) shall be called the throne of Jahweh." But this is, no doubt, a weakened form of the earlier conception.

According to this, Jahweh was present *in* the ark.[1] This is the force of the name by which the object was known, and which signified à chest, or coffer ; it might be applied to a sarcophagus or an alms-box. The same thing is suggested by its shape. It was an oblong box without back or arms, and was carried with the narrow end in front : it would have been a most inconvenient seat. It may be added that, in the *cella* of Solomon's temple, the space above the ark was intersected by the wings of two colossal statues of cherubim, standing on either side of the sacred object : such an arrangement would never have been thought of if it had been supposed that this space was occupied by the divine being, seated on the chest. In Ezekiel's vision the throne of Jahweh is placed in its logical position, *above* the cherubim, which support it, and not below.

Hence the original idea was that Jahweh dwelt *in the ark*.[2] This would not prevent him, of course, from making his power felt through the walls of his abode, as is done, according to Palestinian belief, by holy persons who from their bier can direct the bearers at will, either to hasten or to stop, to turn to the right or the left. Hence the ark was a sacred coffer, similar to those in which the Egyptian gods were carried in procession, or to the shrines of Catholic saints.

Another highly controversial point concerns the contents of the ark. It has been suggested that it contained sacred stones, possibly coming from Sinai,[3] which would explain the origin of the Deuteronomic theory concerning the tables of the law ; however, there is no example among the Israelites of portable sacred stones.[4]

Another view is that the ark bore an image, which could be seen in some way by the worshippers,[5] representing

[1] See particularly the vigorous criticism of Budde, **TSK**, 1906, pp. 489–507.

[2] Gressmann and Mowinckel have accepted this view, although they previously supported the hypothesis of Reichel and Dibelius (Gressmann, *Die Lade Yahwä's*, 1920 ; **LXX**, ii, p. 114 ; iv, pp. 31, 51 ; **CCXX**, pp. 67–8.

[3] **LX**, p. 109 ; **LXII**, p. 81 ; **LXXXV**, 1, p. 117 ; Smend, *Lehrb d. altt. Rel. gesch.*, 1893, p. 42.

[4] **III**, p. 314. [5] Sevensma, *De Ark Gods*, 1908.

Jahweh, either under the form of a bull,[1] or, more probably, in the form of some more or less roughly carved human figure.[2] It may be urged in support that the worshippers came to the temple " to see the face of Jahweh," " to behold his beauty " (Ps. xxvii. 4). It has also been maintained [3] that the ark originally contained the sacred " lots," *urim* and *thummim* ; nevertheless the ancient texts are far from suggesting that the ark was a coffer which the priest could handle and open at pleasure.[4] It is more likely that the casting of lots took place *before* the ark. For the same reason it is not likely that the ark contained the " tablets of destiny," a Babylonian magical object.[5] Again, it has been suggested that the ark was originally the sarcophagus of a god, similar to the coffins of Osiris.[6] In this case it would be a sacred object whose source was entirely foreign to Jahwism ; for the God of Israel never seems to have been thought of as a god similar to Osiris or Adonis, who dies and is reborn annually.

There are grounds for believing that there existed in Palestine, not one but several arks of Jahweh.[7] The analogy of the shrines of Egyptian gods, indeed, and several references in the biblical texts themselves,[8] suggest that the sacred chest was intended for processional use at least as much as to accompany the armies ; from this it follows that the ark must have belonged to a definite sanctuary, and hence that each of the holy places where, according to the tradition, *the* ark sojourned, would in reality have had its own ark.[9] We possess no certain information as to the date when the Israelites adopted the use of the ark.

According to the Hebrew tradition, the ark which later on found a home in the temple at Jerusalem had been made by Moses, apparently to represent Jahweh in the midst of the people of Israel, at a time when Jahweh refused to accompany his guilty people.[10] If it really went back to nomad

---

[1] Mowinckel, **RHP**, 1929, pp. 198–9, 209.   [2] **CCXX**, p. 69.
[3] Sevensma, *op. cit* ; Arnold, *Ephod and Ark,* Cambridge (U.S.A.), 1917. Mowinckel returns to this hypothesis for the Ark for the period following the pillage by Sheshonq (**RHP**, 1929, pp. 215–16).
[4] 2 Sam. vi. 6–10.   [5] **II**, p. 314.
[6] **CCLI** ; **LX**, pp. 110–11.   [7] Arnold's theory.
[8] 2 Sam. vi.–vii. ; Ps. xxiv. 7–10.
[9] Gressmann, *Die Lade Yahwä's*, 1920 ; **CCXX**, p. 67.
[10] Exod. xxxiii. 1, 6 (mutilated account, see **VI**).

times this ark might perhaps have been a sacred object belonging to one of the confederated tribes, probably Joseph : Moses will have made a place for it in the worship of Jahweh, just as Mohammed incorporated in Islam the ancient black stone of the sanctuary of Mecca. But it is a very plausible supposition that various Canaanite sanctuaries may have had chests or sacred sarcophagi, and that one or several of these arks might have been assumed by the Hebrew invaders to be dwellings of the God of Israel.

3. *Images.* We have already seen that it is probable [1] that the early Hebrews, before their settlement in Canaan, possessed no statues of the deity in their holy places, but that this was due rather to loyalty to the traditions of a time when the art of sculpture was unknown, than to any theoretical hostility to a plastic representation of the deity.

Hence, after their settlement in Palestine, most of the Israelites had no scruples in adopting the customs of the inhabitants of the country, who made free use of divine images in their private worship, and must also have had images in some of the public sanctuaries. [2] Excavations in Palestine have yielded a quantity of statuettes of Astarte and Isis belonging to the Israelite period. [3] The women attached great value to these figurines of " strange gods." [4] David had in his house the statue (termed *teraphim*) of a household god, whether it was Jahweh or not. [5]

The Israelites also set up these representations of the deity in the principal sanctuaries of their national God. In the temple at Jerusalem, sacrifices were offered to a brazen serpent (the *nehushtan*) up to the end of the eighth century (2 Kings xviii. 4) : it is not likely that this was regarded as a representation of Jahweh [6] : more probably it was worshipped as a subordinate divinity, to whom the power of healing was ascribed (Num. xxi. 8–9), as in the case of Eshmun-Asclepios, the god of the caduceus. [7] But it was undoubtedly Jahweh who was represented by the silver image set up by the Ephraimite, Micah, in his private

[1] P. 264.   [2] See p. 86.   [3] **IV**, p. 383, n. 8.
[4] Gen. xxxi. 19, 30, 35 ; *cf.* xxxv. 2, 4.
[5] 1 Sam. xix. 13.
[6] **LX**, pp. 81–2 ; **III**, p. 327 (text).
[7] **III**, p. 327 (note). See pp. 109, 239 ; *cf.* **XCVI**, pl. ix, 1, 2, 3 ; pp. 299, 575.

sanctuary, and which, after being carried off by the Danites, became the centre of the high place at Dan.[1] Jahweh was also represented by the golden bull-images which Jeroboam I set up, one in the same high place of Dan, now become a royal sanctuary, and the other in the high place of Bethel (1 Kings xii. 28–9); these images were kissed by the worshippers.[2] According to some scholars, the ark was connected with an image of Jahweh,[3] and this was probably also the case with the *ephod*.

Indeed, it seems impossible to agree with the view, often maintained, that this word always denotes an oracle-bag which the priest wore attached to his girdle.[4] While in certain early passages, the *ephod* denotes the linen drawers which originally constituted the priest's costume,[5] and in other later texts, some kind of garment with a pocket for the sacred lots, worn by the high priest over his priestly costume, there is a third series of passages in which the *ephod* is clearly the name of a divine emblem, and, apparently, of some kind of image. Such were the ephod weighing 1,700 shekels which Gideon made out of the gold rings taken from the Midianites and after which the Israelites " went a whoring " (Judges viii. 24–7), which means, according to the regular use of this metaphor, that they offered illegal worship to it; the one which was in Micah's " house of God "[6]; the one in the sanctuary at Nob, behind which the sword of Goliath had been laid up,[7] and which was often brought before Saul and David by the priest for consultation. The most likely supposition is that, in these passages, *ephod* denotes some kind of fetish, overlaid, perhaps, with precious metal (*'aphad*, to cover, overlay) and from which the priest could obtain an oracle. Either the object

---

[1] Judges xvii.–xviii. appears to speak of four different objects made by Micah. This is the result of the mixture of sources and of the addition of a gloss (*massekah*, " molten image "). There was, no doubt, only one statue, called in one of the versions *pesel* (graven image), and in the other, *ephod*.

[2] Hos. xiii. 2. On this method of representing Yahvé, see pp. 457–8.

[3] *Cf.* p. 427.

[4] Theodore C. Foote, *The Ephod, its Form and Use*, Baltimore, 1902 ; **XXV**, ii, pp. 46 *ff.* ; **XVI**, p. 336.

[5] See particularly 2 Sam. vi. 14, 16, 20–2.

[6] Judges xvii.–xviii. ; *cf.* Hos. iii. 4.

[7] 1 Sam. xxi. 9–10.

might be set in motion and allowed to come to rest in various different positions, or it may have contained the sacred lots in some hollow place, or, again, the lots may have been enclosed in a bag forming part of the clothing of the image.[1]

It is doubtful whether, as is commonly supposed, the word *teraphim* denoted a sacred object of specific form or significance, the image of an ancestor, the statue of a guardian deity, or an object used as a sacred lot. It seems impossible to give a single meaning to all the passages in which the word occurs. Sometimes it denotes a household god (Gen. xxxi. 19, 30, 35 ; 1 Sam. xix. 13–16), sometimes an object used in the worship of Jahweh (Judges xvii.–xviii. ; Hos. iii. 4), sometimes a means of divination condemned by strict Jahwists (Ezek. xxi. 26–7 ; Zech. x. 2 ; perhaps 1 Sam. xv. 23 ; 2 Kings xxiii. 24). Hence it is a plausible supposition that *teraphim* may be, rather, one of those terms of reproach, like " shame," " abomination," " filth," which the Jews of later times substituted in the text for the names, abhorrent to them, of idols and false gods : *teraphim*, which is associated with such words in 2 Kings xxiii. 24, might be the plural of *toreph*, " rottenness." In any case, several of the texts in which the word occurs show that the worship of images was long regarded in Israel as legitimate.[2]

However, the evidence shows that even before the prophetic movement in the eighth century, the first signs of a reaction against this custom were appearing. In certain circles, mainly, no doubt, among the southern tribes, which had remained more attached to nomad traditions, there was a more or less sharply defined feeling that images were not a part of the original, genuine worship of Jahweh. The J and E narratives do not ascribe to the patriarchs the erection of any image of Jahweh.

However, the first prohibition was aimed at idols made of metal. " Thou shalt not make to thyself molten images," is the command of the Jahwist decalogue probably compiled in the ninth century (Exod. xxxiv. 17). " Ye shall not make other gods with me ; gods of silver or gods of gold, ye shall not make unto you " (Exod. xx. 23), is the ordinance

[1] **XXV**, ii, 1, p. 46 ; **CCXX**, p. 65 ; Budde, **ZATW**, 1921, pp. 1 *ff.* ; Hoffmann and Gressmann, **ZATW**, 1922, pp. 102–9.
[2] 1 Sam. xix. 13 ; Judges xvii.–xviii. ; Hos. iii. 4.

of Jahweh in the ancient Elohist decalogue. There was evidently no intention of forbidding every kind of plastic representation of the deity, since the old wood and stone images were still allowed, but of prohibiting the foreign fashion of images made of the precious metals, whose luxury contrasted strikingly with the simplicity of the genuine Israelite tradition.[1] Even this restriction seemed comparatively unimportant to the defenders of the rights of Jahweh : neither Elijah nor Amos himself condemned the worship paid to the golden bulls at Bethel and Dan.

As far as we know, Hosea was the first to protest against theriomorphic representations of Jahweh ; and the condemnation of any kind of image of the deity belongs to a still later date (Isa. ii. 8, 18 ; Exod. xx. 2–6 ; Deut. iv. 15–24 ; etc.).

4. *The Altar.*[2] According to the ancient Israelite custom,[3] when the altar was not identical with the sacred object (a rock, with or without cup-marks, a standing stone, tree, spring, etc.), it was merely a heap of earth or a pile of undressed stones (Exod. xx. 24–6) erected on the ground, upon which the victims were laid or burnt. After the settlement in Palestine these customs, no doubt, persisted among communities who were specially attached to the old ways, or in certain sanctuaries where the Canaanites had retained this old type of altar. Cup-marked rocks remained in use at Ophrah (Judges vi. 19–21), at Bethshemesh (1 Sam. vi. 14–15), even at Jerusalem [4] ; at Aijalon (1 Sam. xiv. 33–5) and probably at Gibeon (2 Sam. xx. 8), a " great stone " served as an altar ; the altar on Carmel was of unhewn stones (1 Kings xviii. 31–2), also the one which Joshua built, according to the Masoretic Text,[5] on Mt. Ebal, where P. Tonneau believes he has discovered its site,[6] but more prob-

---

[1] See also the account of the golden calf (Exod. xxxii.).

[2] Barton, *Jew. Encycl.*, i, 465[a] ; Kegel, **NKZ**, June, Nov., 1924 ; König, **ZATW**, 1924, pp. 337 *ff*. ; K. Galling, *Der Altar in den Kulturen des alten Orients*, 1925 ; Sellin, **ZDPV**, 1926, pp. 232–3 ; J. Touzard, **RB**, 1919, p. 71 ; Dr. J. de Groot, *Die Altäre des Salomonischen Tempelhofes*, 1924 ; **XLVI**, pp. 1–158 ; J. B. Harford, **ET**, Oct.–Dec., 1928 ; Gressmann, **RGG**, i, 371 *ff*. ; **CCLXXXI** ; **III** ; Dalman, **CLXXVII**, pp. 56 *ff*., 79 *ff*.

[3] See pp. 268–9.   [4] 1 Kings viii. 64 ; *cf.* p. 413 and pl. xiv, 1.

[5] Deut. xxvii. 4–7 ; Jos. viii. 30–1.

[6] **RB**, 1926, pp. 98–100.

ably, on Mt. Gerizim, the mount of blessing, according to the Samaritan Pentateuch.[1]

Usually, however, the appointments of an Israelite high place were of a less primitive nature : the altar which David had placed in the fortress of Jerusalem, in front of the tent in which the ark was lodged, had " horns," that is, some kind of cornice at each corner, which were grasped by suppliants seeking asylum in the presence of Jahweh.[2] It was elevated, since Adonijah was " brought down " from it.[3] The altar which Solomon erected in the temple was of bronze.[4] That of Bethel rested on a pediment [5] and had horns.[6] To the same type belonged the larger altar set up in the temple in Jerusalem by Ahaz, in the eighth century (2 Kings xvi. 10–16), the one described by Ezekiel (Ezek. xliii. 13–17), and the more magnificent altars erected in the second temple,[7] and in Herod's temple.[8]

This type of altar had so far prevailed by the time of the exile, that the writers of that period represented Moses as having already built an altar of this pattern, elevated,[9] with bronze horns and sumptuous bronze decorations, but of wood and of smaller dimensions, for convenience in carrying.[10]

Another innovation consisted in placing on the altar a hearth called *ar'el* or *ari'el*, which seems to have been removable.[11]

From time to time an attempt was made to reconcile these more elaborate practices with the ancient rules forbidding altars with steps leading up to them, and the use of hewn stones. Judas Maccabæus only used undressed stones.[12] Herod did the same. The practice was introduced of ascending to the upper platform of the altar by means of an inclined plane.[13] Harold Wiener, on the other hand, has recently maintained that the law which only permitted the use of altars of earth or unhewn stone was not intended to exclude

[1] Deut. xxvii. 4. [2] 1 Kings i. 50–1 ; ii. 28–34.
[3] 1 Kings i. 53.
[4] 1 Kings viii. 64 ; 2 Kings xvi. 14–15 ; Ezek. ix. 2.
[5] According to 1 Kings xii. 33. [6] Amos. iii. 14.
[7] Hecataeus in *c.Ap.*, i, 22 (198) ; cf. 2 Chron. iv. 1.
[8] Josephus, *B.J.*, v, 5, 6 (225) ; *Mishnah Middoth*, iii, 1.
[9] Lev. ix. 22 ; cf. Exod. xxviii. 42–3. [10] Exod. xxvii. 1–8.
[11] *Mesha*, 1, 2, 12 ; Ezek. xliii. 15, 16. [12] 1 Macc. iv. 47.
[13] Josephus, *B.J.*, v, 5, 6 (225).

I.

F F

altars with steps and horns; since it was merely directed against local sacrifices or private slaying of victims, not against the sacrifices offered at the religious capital.[1] But such a theory does violence to the passage which is addressed to Israel as a whole, and hence to every individual Israelite, expressly commanding him to offer " his burnt-offerings and his peace-offerings " on altars of earth or of unhewn stone (Exod. xx. 24). There can be no doubt that this law is a protest of the ancient Hebrew spirit against ritual innovations.

Such novelties had come in, no doubt, in imitation of the surrounding peoples. Stepped altars were in use at Beth-shan,[2] and Byblos,[3] as later at Petra[4] and at Baalbek.[5]

The origin of horns is still very doubtful. Up to the present not a single example has been found of a Canaanite altar belonging to the pre-Israelite period possessing this feature. The two altars of this type found at Shechem seem to belong to the Israelite period[6]; so does the one found at Gezer, whose date would be about 600.[7] On the other hand, the use of altars with horns occurs in non-Israelite Syrian cults belonging to earlier periods.[8] Perhaps this practice was borrowed from the Ægeans, among whom horns of consecration were a common religious symbol, being a frequent accessory of their altars.[9]

Some archæologists have supposed that these horns originally represented the points of the lunar crescent.[10] A view more commonly met with is that the purpose of the horns was to assimilate the altar to the divine bull,[11] or that the early practice was to hang the horns of the victims to the corners of the altar[12]; in support of this view it may be urged that an object found at Taanach, usually believed to be an incense-altar, is decorated with a spiral motive in the form of a ram's horn.[13]

In some Israelite sanctuaries, at Jerusalem, for instance (1

---

[1] CCLXXXI.   [2] See p. 96.

[3] Dunand, SY, 1929, p. 211 and pl. xxxviii.

[4] Pl. xv, 3; cf. XXIII², ii, figs. 446-9.

[5] XXIII², ii, p. 30 (fig. 42).   [6] Pl. xvi, 1 and 2.

[7] Pl. xv, 1; cf. CCLXXXI, pp. 16, 30.

[8] XXIII², ii, figs. 458-64.

[9] CXXVII, pp. 299, 304, 305, and fig. 48; CXX, pp. 338-9 and figs. 239-46.

[10] III, p. 320.   [11] Stade.   [12] Robertson Smith.

[13] CLIX, p. 180 (pl. iv); CCLXXXI, pl. 1, fig. 2.

Plate XV

2. Censer (?) from Taanach

1. Altar with Horns, found at Gezer

3. Altar at Petra

Plate XVI

1-2.   Horned Altars found at Shechem

3.   Child strangling a Serpent, Bas-relief on a Censer (?)
found at Taanach

Kings vii. 48), and earlier, no doubt, at Nob (1 Sam. xxi. 5–7), there was also a table on which loaves were placed before Jahweh, and renewed at regular intervals.[1]

There is no proof, on the other hand, that the Israelites, prior to the end of the fifth century, had adopted the custom of assigning a special altar to the burning of incense. The oldest parts of the Priestly Code, as well as Ezekiel, are not acquainted with the custom ; they only know one altar of Jahweh, the altar of burnt-offering ; the burning of incense, as in Egypt and Syria, was done in small spoon-shaped pans, held in the hand. It is only in the latest laws of the Priestly Code that this addition to the sacred furniture is prescribed. Hence it is probable that those passages of the book of Kings which seem to ascribe the introduction of the incense-altar to Solomon have been interpolated or emended.[2] The curious object found at Taanach decorated with mythological figures (pl. xv, 2 and xvi, 3) is possibly not Israelite ; moreover, it is not certain that it had a sacred use ; it may simply have been the censer or brasier of a rich inhabitant of the city.

II

SACRED SEASONS [3]

It must have been after their settlement in Palestine that the Israelites inaugurated their three main feasts, for all of them were of a distinctly agricultural character. They were :

1. The Feast of *Unleavened Bread,* held as soon as the sickle was put into the harvest (Deut. xvi. 9), and begun by the offering of the first sheaf of barley (Lev. xxiii. 10) ;

2. The Feast of *Harvest* (Exod. xxiii. 16), also called the day of *Firstfruits* [4]—the firstfruits of the wheat—or again, the *Feast of Weeks,*[5]—the seven weeks of the gathering in of grain,—whence the later name of Pentecost (the fiftieth day) ;

3. The Feast of *Ingathering* [6] or *Tabernacles,*[7] so named originally from the booths of greenery which were put up in

---

[1] *Cf.* the Canaanite custom of Beth Shan (pp. 100–1).
[2] 1 Kings vi. 20–2 ; vii. 48.   [3] See pp. 276–7 ; 289–96.
[4] Num. xxviii. 26.   [5] Exod. xxxiv. 22 ; Deut. xvi. 10, 16.
[6] Exod. xxiii. 16 ; xxxiv. 22.
[7] Deut. xvi. 13, 16 ; Lev. xxiii. 34.

the vineyards during the vintage. We can observe, however, even before the eighth century, a tendency to transform
these agrarian festivals into historical anniversaries, that is,
to bring them into relation with those events in the national
history about which the religion of Jahweh centred : " Thou
shalt keep the feast of unleavened bread . . . in the month
Abib (for in it thou camest out from Egypt)." [1]

The third and most important of these feasts, specially
designated as the " feast of Jahweh," must also have been
the feast of the New Year, for it was held at " the revolution
of the year " [2] which at that time took place in the autumn.
It is true that the feast of the " beginning of the year " is
not expressly mentioned until after the exile, at which
period it was at first kept five days (Ezek. xl. 1 ; Lev. xxv. 9),
and afterwards fifteen days (Num. xxix. 1), before the feast
of Tabernacles ; but its pre-exilic origin is indicated by
the fact that it continued to be held in the autumn, although
the Jews had adopted, about the time of the exile, the
Babylonian calendar, which then began in the spring.

It is very probable, as Volz and Mowinckel have shown,[3]
that this New Year feast, at least in the great sanctuaries,
such as the temple at Jerusalem, consisted of ceremonies
which celebrated the ascent of Jahweh to the throne. The
numerous psalms which hymn the inauguration of the reign
of the God of Israel, " Jahweh reigns," will have been
composed for these festivals. Like the coronation ceremonies, the Feast of Tabernacles was distinguished by great
processions and shouts of joy, while the New Year feast was
accompanied by the sound of trumpets.

Even today the Jewish liturgy prescribes the *malkiyyoth*,
that is, the passages dealing with the kingship of Jahweh,
to be read at the New Year feast, and also the recitation of
the prayer : " Our Father, our King." It is quite possible
that originally the procession accompanied the ark—that is,
Jahweh—as he made his royal entry into his palace (Ps. xxiv.).

Similarly, in Babylonia, the New Year feast was marked

[1] Exod. xxiii. 15 ; xxxiv. 18.
[2] Exod. xxxiv. 22 ; cf. xxiii. 16.
[3] Volz, *Das Neujahrfest Jahwes*, Tübingen, 1912 ; LXX, ii. On the
same subject, Hans Schmidt, *Die Thronfart Jahves*, 1927 ; F. M. Th.
Böhl, *Nieuwjaarsfest en Koningsdag* . . ., Groningen, 1927 ; Otto
Eissfeldt, ZATW, 1928, pp. 81–105.

by processions in which the statue of the god was carried into his temple by a special way (in Babylon and Erech). In Egypt, at the feast of the god, at Abydos, similar practices were carried out. There are grounds for supposing that the Israelites, when they adopted these customs, common in the great temples of the ancient East, only followed the example of the Canaanites. In any case, it was not until after their entry into Palestine that the Hebrews, who hitherto had been ruled only by sheikhs or elders, could have ascribed to their God the title of king and the honours due to monarchs.

They must also have adopted many other local Canaanite festivals. Only a few of these customs are known to us through the incidental mention of them in an early text, or by the sanction given to them in the Levitical law or post-exilic custom : such was the ceremony, a genuine piece of sympathetic magic, which consisted of drawing water from Siloam, bringing it in procession to the temple and pouring it out by the altar in order to ensure abundant rain during the new year [1]; such also was the mourning for the daughter of Jephthah celebrated by the Israelite women upon the mountains of Gilead. [2]

Similar inferences may be drawn from various other passages. For instance, that in honour of Deborah, origin-ally, perhaps, a bee-goddess,[3] it was the custom to pour out a libation of oil by the Tree of Tears, not far from Bethel ; that at Penuel a dance was performed in which the partakers limped like the hero of the mysterious adventure related in Geneses xxxii. 23–32 ; that at Rachel's Tomb, near Ramah, ritual lamentations took place (Jer. xxxi. 15) ; that in the holy place of Shechem, between Mt. Ebal and Mt. Gerizim, there was a ceremony, consisting of solemn blessings and curses, described in Deuteronomy xxvii. 11–26 and Joshua viii. 33.

The origins of the Sabbath still remain shrouded in mystery.[4] According to Eerdmans,[5] this institution goes

---

[1] Mishnah Succah, iv, 9 ; *Tosefta* (*cf.* Fiebig, *Mi. Roch hachchana*, p. 41.)

[2] *Cf.* pp. 346–8.   [3] **XXX**, p. 120, n. 1.

[4] *Cf.* Meinhold, *Sabbat und Woche im A.T.*, 1905 ; Webster, *Rest Days*, Univ. Studies, xi, 1–2, Lincoln, Nebraska, 1911 ; **CCXX**, pp. 75–98.

[5] *Der Sabbat*, in Marti-Festschrift, 1925, pp. 79–83.

back to the time when the Hebrews were nomads ; his view
is that it was at first a day of weekly cessation from work
observed by the Kenite smiths through fear of the dangerous
influence of Saturn or Kaiwan (*cf.* Amos v. 26) ; hence the
prohibition of the lighting of fires on that day (Exod. xxxv. 3 ;
Num. xv. 32). The Israelites will have borrowed this taboo
from them. But, in addition to the fact that it is doubtful
whether the Kenites were smiths,[1] it is very difficult to
believe that the Israelites, during the nomad period, could
have observed a weekly day of rest : the shepherd's " work,"
which must be done every day, consists in feeding and
watering his flocks. Moreover, the relation of the days of
the week to the planets does not appear until quite late.

On the other hand, it is certain that the sabbath was
kept by the Israelites in Palestine, before the eighth century.
But the early meaning of the term seems to have differed
from that which the Jews later on attached to the name.
The word *shabbath* was, apparently, derived from the Babylonian *shab'attu* or *shapattu*, which denoted the feast of the
full moon (the day when the planet " ceases " to grow) :
the original meaning of the Hebrew word seems to have been
the same. On their entry into Canaan, the Israelites would
have adopted this term to denote a festival which they no
doubt observed from nomad days [2] in honour of the planet.
This would explain the close connexion which we find in
early texts between the sabbath and the new moon,[3] as well
as the absence of this term—with its heathen associations—
from the early Jahwistic legislation,[4] and the hostility which
some of the prophets display towards this feast.[5]

About the ninth century, on the other hand, the early
Israelites were accustomed to observe a rest of one day in
seven during the arduous toil of ploughing and harvest
(Exod. xxxiv. 21) ; hence the name " feast of weeks "
given to the rejoicings which closed the gathering in of the
crops. Thus they were acquainted with the week, as is
further proved by the period of seven days assigned for
mourning and by the application of the name " week " to

[1] See p. 205.   [2] See p. 290.
[3] 2 Kings iv. 23 ; Amos viii. 5 ; Hos. ii. 13 ; Isa. i. 13.
[4] Second Decalogue, Book of the Covenant, Deut. xii.–xxvi.
[5] Hos. ii. 13 ; Isa i. 13.

the seven days of marriage festivities (Gen. xxix. 27). But there is nothing to show that the hebdomadal periods, at this time, formed an unbroken sequence through the months and years.

It would rather seem that the hebdomadal days of cessation from work observed by the Israelites should be connected with the " unlucky days," which were, among the Babylonians, the 7th, 14th, 21st and 28th of the months Elul II and Marcheswan—and perhaps of all the months,— days on which certain individuals, the King, the priest and the doctor, were obliged to abstain from certain acts.[1] The phases of the moon were evidently regarded as dangerous days, hedged in by taboos.

Hence the institutions of the sabbath, on the one hand, and of the week, on the other, seem to be of astral, and in part, of foreign origin. But they underwent profound changes, which seem to have been peculiar to Israel and are doubtless due to the fact that these customs were, like so many other customs of this people, taken over and assimilated by the national religion.

First, the *shabbath* (full moon), on the one hand, and the hebdomadal days of rest, on the other, became " days of Jahweh." The *shabbath* was a day on which people went to consult the man of God (2 Kings iv. 23); there seems to have been an assembly at the temple on that day.[2] Cessation from work on the seventh day was included among the demands of Jahweh.[3]

Secondly, the cessation from work on the seventh day was interpreted, in accordance with one of the tendencies of the national religion, no longer as a precaution against the supernatural dangers attaching to an unlucky day,[4] but as a humanitarian provision intended to allow slaves, workmen and cattle to rest from their labours.[5]

Thirdly, the name *shabbath*, originally reserved for the full moon, was extended to the other critical days of the lunar month, perhaps because the idea of *rest* had become

---

[1] Text in **XCIII**, p. 593 ; **XXXVII**, p. 90 ; **CXVIII**, pp. 380–1.
[2] 2 Kings xi. 5–8. Among the Babylonians already the *šapattu* was a " day of appeasing the heart " (of the gods), **XCIII**, p. 592.
[3] Exod. xxxiv. 21 ; xxiii. 12.
[4] The Israelites had them : Job iii. 8.
[5] Exod. xxiii. 12 ; Deut. v. 14.

the characteristic feature of the institution : it was, in fact, possible to interpret the term *shabbath* as referring to the day when man " ceases " (to work), and no longer as the day when the moon " ceases " (to grow).

Fourthly, the hebdomadal days of cessation from work were detached from the phases of the moon, and the weeks came to constitute a continuous sequence throughout the year. One feature of the ancient custom may have contributed to the change : the Babylonians also regarded as unlucky the nineteenth day of certain months, that is to say, the forty-ninth day from the beginning of the previous month [1] ; while, on their side, the early Israelites reckoned the seven weeks of harvest as a continuous period. Hence, from a very early date, there were periods of two months of which the second had its days of rest determined independently of the moon's cycle. The earliest passages in which we find the unambiguous occurrence of a *periodically* recurring seventh day of rest with the name of *shabbath* belong to the end of the pre-exilic period or to the beginning of the exile.[2] It was not till then that, as the result of the exile, this day became the most important and the most distinctive of the sacred seasons of the religion of Jahweh.

In short, it is clear that, while the sabbath and the week were perhaps of foreign origin, it was in Israel that the rest of the seventh day assumed the characteristics from which it derives today its social and religious value.

III

SACRED PERSONS

1. *The Priests.* After the settlement in Canaan the priest's status remained essentially what it had been from nomad times : his principal functions were to look after the sanctuary and especially to consult the god who dwelt there, by methods the knowledge of which was his special possession.[3]

Here it is necessary to point out the increasing importance

---

[1] **XCIII**, p. 593.

[2] Ezek. xlvi. 1 ; Lev. xxiii. 3 and the first Decalogue (Exod. xx. 8–10 ; Deut. v. 13–14), which was probably compiled a little earlier.

[3] See pp. 296–9.

then assumed by the priestly families which claimed descent from Levi. Before the seventh century a real or fictitious descent from Levi was not considered essential for the exercise of the priestly functions : sons of David (2 Sam. viii. 18) and of Nathan (1 Kings iv. 5), a son of Micah (Judges xvii. 5), a son of Abinadab (1 Sam. vii. 1), the Ephraimites Samuel and Joshua (Exod. xxxiii. 11), Ira, the Jairite (2 Sam. xx. 26), were priests. In the northern kingdom this unrestricted state of affairs continued to exist till the end (722).[1]

However, the Levitical priests possessed a special prestige : the Ephraimite Micah counted himself fortunate in securing for the care of his private sanctuary the services of a Levite descended from Gershom, the son of Moses, who subsequently became the ancestor of the priestly family of the high place at Dan.[2] The priests of Shiloh also must have been Levites : one of them bore the characteristic name of Phinehas, which was also that of a grandson of Aaron.[3]

From the middle of the ninth century it would appear that this primacy of the Levites tended to pass into a monopoly. A poem which seems to belong to this period claims for " the men of the faithful one of Jahweh," that is, for the fellow-tribesmen of Moses, the sole privilege of the *urim* and the *thummim* (the sacred lots), the right of teaching the Torah to Israel and of causing the smoke of the sacrifices to ascend before Jahweh (Deut. xxxiii. 8–11). We can see, however, that these claims of " Levi " met with strenuous opposition, for the poet ends with this prayer :

" Smite through the loins of them that rise up against him,
    and of them that hate him, that they rise not again."

There is, no doubt, an echo of these rivalries in the narratives which depict Dathan and Abiram, or even Miriam and Aaron, disputing the right of Moses to special privileges (Num. xii. and xvi.).

Concerning the relation between this priestly fraternity of the Levites and the ancient warrior tribe of Levi we have no certain information. There are reasons for thinking that *lewi* was formerly a common noun meaning priest : it is

---

[1] 1 Kings xii. 31 ; *cf.* pp. 415–6.
[2] Judges xvii. 7–13 ; xviii. 30 (read " Moses " instead of " Manasseh ").
[3] 1 Sam. i. 3 ; ii. 34, etc. *Cf.* Exod. vi. 25 ; Num. xxv. 7, 11 ; etc.

used in this sense in Exodus iv. 14, and the words *lw'* and *lw't* occur several times in the Minæan inscriptions of el-Ela, probably with the meaning " priest " and " priestess." [1] It is a possible view that the ancient warrior tribe of Levi received this name because, being in possession of the holy places of Kadesh, it provided, from these revered sanctuaries, a continuous supply of priests, of whom Moses was the most famous.[2] When, as a result of its disastrous attack on Shechem, the tribe was scattered,[3] the survivors retained as a relic of their former greatness the sacred prestige which accrued to them by reason of the association of their fathers with the cradle of the religion of Jahweh.

2. *The Prophets.* Side by side with the priests, who were attached to a particular sanctuary, the Israelites settled in Palestine also possessed, as did their nomad ancestors,[4] individuals who were endowed with a special power of influencing or foreseeing the future : magicians, diviners, ecstatics. Among these various types of " divine men," there was one which, at least from the time of the early kings, assumed pre-eminence over all the rest : this was the *nabi'* or prophet. An undoubtedly reliable archæological note which occurs in the book of Samuel tells us : " He who is now called a prophet was formerly called *roeh* (seer) " (1 Sam. ix. 9). Hence, in the time of the writer, the name *nabi* had replaced that of *roeh*. It is true that certain Hebrew writers ascribe the title of prophet to individuals of remote antiquity, such as Abraham, Moses or Deborah, or to a " seer " like Samuel ; but this is, no doubt, an anachronism.

The change of name represented a very definite change in methods. According to Hoelscher, the difference between the seer and the prophet lay in the fact that the latter was an ecstatic, a visionary, while the *roeh* " obtains his supernatural knowledge without ecstasy by the observation of external phenomena, especially of the phantasies born of the darkness of the night, of dream, and of the state between sleep and waking " [5] : he interprets signs and omens like

---

[1] D. H. Müller, *Epigraphische Denkmäler aus Arabien* (*Denkschr. der Wien. Akad., phil. Kl.,* 37, 1889) ; **XXX**, p. 103.

[2] *Cf.* the Koreish at Mecca, **CLXXXIX**, p. 171.

[3] *Cf.* pp. 154, 188, 331.

[4] See pp. 299–300. [5] **XXX**, pp. 125–6.

the Babylonian *baru*, whose name also means " seer," and like the οἰωνοσκόπος of the Greeks or the *auspex* of the Romans. Moreover, the " seer " was not originally in touch with the great gods of the clan or tribe : like the Arab *kahin*, he obtained his supernatural knowledge from a spirit or a demon.

The hypothesis is attractive, and it is very possible that the word " seer " may have originally denoted, not a man who was specially subject to *visions*, but, broadly, anyone who possessed the power of " seeing " things hidden from men in general. However, Hoelscher seems to exaggerate somewhat artificially the differences between the seer and the prophet when he makes ecstasy the special characteristic of the latter. It is not likely that the nomad Hebrews and the ancient Arabs should have been entirely unaware of ecstatic phenomena.[1] Hoelscher grants that " seers " had *auditory* hallucinations in the night and that they believed themselves to be inspired : hence it seems somewhat rash to maintain that they never had *visual* hallucinations. Furthermore, the Hebrew words *mar'eh*, *hazon*, which correspond to the names given to the seer (*roeh*, *hozeh*), were generally and almost exclusively applied to the ecstatic vision. On the other hand, we find cases among the Arabs of seers inspired by the great gods, such as the *kahina* Zarifat al-Shair, inspired by " the lord of all the peoples " [2]; the Hebrew seers are all represented as instructed by Jahweh (1 Sam. ix. 15).

What then was the difference between the seer and the prophet ? [3] According to the account in which the two terms are used side by side,[4] it appears that the former denoted a solitary inspired person, living in his own city, who for a small fee gave information to those who consulted him concerning the trivial problems of daily life ; such being the description of Samuel ; while the inspiration of the *nebi'im* was collective, violent and contagious : when Saul left the " seer," he met a band of these " prophets," coming down from the high place, preceded by the sound of harps, timbrels, flutes and lyres. Under the influence of this

---

[1] P. 300.   [2] Kitâb al-agâni, **XIII**, 110, 4ff (**XXX**, p. 95).
[3] Cf. Herbert Junker, *Prophet und Seher in Israel*, Trèves, 1927.
[4] 1 Sam. ix. 1–10, 16.

tumultuous music, and moved by the sight of the dancing and wild gestures of the *nebi'im*, Saul too was seized by the spirit and began to " prophesy " with them (1 Sam. x. 10–11), that is, he was overpowered by the same sacred ecstasy.

Another account, late and legendary, but none the less valuable as a picture of the customs of the time, represents the messengers of the King's anger, and then the King himself, as seized by the spirit on reaching the prophets, with the result that they stripped themselves and remained prostrate on the ground for a whole night (1 Sam. xix. 18–24).

We evidently have here phenomena similar to those observable among the whirling or howling dervishes of the East, and, in a measure, to those which took place in France among the persecuted Protestants of the Cevennes. The occurrence was particularly noticeable among the peasants of the Cevennes, of the same phenomenon of an almost physical contagion ; in the meetings in the desert, where these cases of inspiration occurred, it was not uncommon to see people who were uninterested and even Catholics who had come for the purpose of spying, suddenly seized by the same mental disturbance as the " prophets," and uttering the same words. Even in modern times, among the Malgaches, when the " tromba," *i.e.* the spirit of an ancestor, becomes active in an assembly, women who have determined not to succumb to the contagion are compelled in spite of themselves to join their companions.[1]

We have seen [2] that a collective inspiration expressing itself in dances and shouts, although not wholly unknown to the nomad Semites,[3] was nevertheless uncommon among them, while this type of religious experience was fostered by the cults of Phenicia,[4] Syria [5] and Asia Minor, whence the phenomena of orgiastic prophecy may have spread to Syria and Palestine.[6] Hence there is every reason to suppose that the earliest bands of *nebi'im* may have arisen among

[1] Rusillon, *Un culte dynastique avec évocation des morts chez les Sakalaves de Madagascar. Le " Tromba,"* Paris, Alph. Picard, 1912, p. 94, *cf.* p. 122.

[2] **XXX**, pp. 129–30.   [3] See p. 300.

[4] 1 Kings xviii. 19 ; Heliodorus, *Æthiopica*, iv, 16. A Phenician god was called Baal marqod, " the Lord of the dance." *Cf.* Golenischeff Pap., **RT**, xxi, pp. 22–3 ; Celsus (in Origen, *Contra Celsum*, vii, 9).

[5] *De dea Syria*, 43, 50 ; Apuleius, *Metamorph*, viii, 24–9 ; Florus, iii, 29 ; *cf.* **XXX**, pp. 132–9 ; **XLV**, p. 244.   [6] **XXX**, pp. 140–2.

the Israelites as the result of contact with and imitation of the Canaanites. The sacred madness of these ecstatics impressed the newcomers as a higher manifestation of the divine power, hence Jahweh must show himself the equal of the Baals.

The very word *nabi* does not seem to be of Hebrew origin. Nor is it necessary to suppose, as some have maintained, that the " hairy mantle " of the prophet [1] was a proof of his Hebrew origin : nomads did not often wear skins. The mantle in question might be the skin of a sacrificed animal, with which the individual who desired inspiration clothed himself in order thereby to enter into communion with the god [2] ; the ecstasy often seized the *nabi* in the high place and at the moment of the mysterious act of sacrifice : we have examples in the case of the young ecstatic of Byblos,[3] of the Tyrian sailors mentioned by Heliodorus, and of the *nebi'im* whom Saul met as they came down from the high place (1 Sam. x. 5).

The object of these practices, wherever they are found, is to imbue the participant with a sense of immediate contact with the deity. Dazed by the crashing music, the shouts, the motion of the dance, the violent shaking of the head, often by drinking some intoxicating beverage,[4] he experiences the sensation of having become another man (1 Sam. x. 6, 9), sundered from his everyday life, insensible to pain (the *nabi*, in Phenicia and in Syria, doubtless also in Israel,[5] used to wound himself with a sword or spear), he becomes a sharer in the life of the god.

As a consequence of this experience, he becomes a source of oracles and a wonder-worker : since the inarticulate sounds which he utters, his incoherent words, his gestures, are regarded as the activities of the god himself by whose spirit he is possessed.

In the time of Elisha (second half of the ninth century), the companies of Israelite *nebi'im* were organized into permanent communities. They settled in small colonies near certain cities (usually sacred cities), like Gilgal, Bethel and Jericho. The general name for the members of these com-

---

[1] **LXXXV**, p. 67. [2] **XXX**, pp. 145–6. [3] Golenischeff Pap.
[4] Mic. ii. 11 ; Isa. xxviii. 7, 8 ; xxix. 9 (?) ; 4 Esdras xiv. 40.
[5] Zech. xiii. 6 ; Hos. vii. 14 (emended) ; 1 Kings xx. 35–7, 41.

munities was *bene han-nebi'im*, " sons of the prophets," a
phrase whose meaning was not that they were sons or disciples
of the prophets, but that they belonged to a brotherhood
of *nebi'im*, just as a member of a guild of craftsmen was
called " a son of the perfumers " (Neh. iii. 8), or " a son of
the jewellers " (Neh. iii. 8, 31), or as the singers were called
" the sons of the singers " (Neh. xii. 28), or the exiled Israelites " the sons of the dispersion " (Ezra iv. 1).

The members of these communities of prophets ate at
a common table (2 Kings iv. 38–44) ; they were subject
to the orders of chiefs whom they called " lords " (1 Kings
ii. 3 ; vi. 5), before whom they prostrated themselves (2 Kings
ii. 15) and to whom they rendered the most menial services
(2 Kings iii. 11). They were allowed to marry and there
is no reason to suppose that they practised any kind of
asceticism (2 Kings iv. 1).

Their members were drawn chiefly from the poorer classes,
and it was unusual to find among them a substantial farmer
like Elisha (1 Kings xix. 19) ; people were surprised to see
a man of good family like Saul among them : " What has
happened to the son of Kish ? Is Saul also among the
prophets ? . . . And who is their father ? " [1] Their strange
dress and eccentric behaviour occasionally caused ridicule,
even among the children (2 Kings ii. 23). Sceptics treated
them with contempt as madmen, but were none the less
ready to give credence to " the word of the Lord " in the
mouth of one of these " men of the spirit." [2] The common
people loaded them with tokens of honour ; both kings and
private individuals consulted them on all kinds of problems
of private or public life. They were credited with the power
of giving or withholding rain, of healing springs, of multiplying food, of healing the sick, and even of raising the dead.
They had inherited the prestige, the powers and even the
methods of their predecessors, the seers and magicians :
when they were asked for signs, they performed genuine
feats of magic,[3] with the single reservation that all their
acts of power were done in the name of Jahweh.[4]

[1] 1 Sam. x. 11, 12.
[2] 2 Kings ix. 11–13 ; *cf.* Jer. xxix. 26 ; Hos. ix. 7.
[3] See particularly 2 Kings iv. 29, 40–1 ; vi. 6 ; xiii. 18–19.
[4] 2 Kings ii. 19–22.

In payment for these consultations they received presents in kind or in money.[1] Whoever entertained them was thought to bring good luck to his house (2 Kings iv. 8–11). The 400 prophets whom Ahab was in the habit of consulting must have been more or less in his pay : perhaps they ate at his table like the prophets of Baal who were maintained by Jezebel (1 Kings xviii. 19). Apparently, like the seers of earlier times,[2] there were prophets who were attached to various sanctuaries, and whose function in the cult it was to ensure the response of Jahweh to the prayers of the worshippers [3] : for this they must have received some remuneration. Hence prophesying had become a regular means of livelihood. The writers of the eighth and sixth centuries complain bitterly that many of the prophets allowed the oracles which they gave as the word of Jahweh, to be determined by their material interests :

" That bite with their teeth,
    and cry, Peace ;
and whoso putteth not into their mouths,
    they even prepare war against him." [4]

If we may judge by the stories, often of the most childish nature, related concerning Elisha, and clearly emanating from the communities of the " sons of the prophets," the spiritual level of the religious conceptions characteristic of these circles was not a very lofty one.

Situations, however, arose in which the religious excitement which prevailed in these fraternities of prophets found an outlet in the service of a higher cause : whenever a national war broke out they played a part which was, no doubt, similar to that of the Moslem fraternities in the holy wars of Islam, and became centres of patriotic zeal for Jahweh and Israel. The prophets accompanied the armies, placing their supernatural powers at the disposal of the leaders, and usually insisting on the most rigorous treatment of the enemies.[5] It was a proverbial saying about Elisha that he was the chariots and horsemen of Israel (2 Kings xiii. 14).

[1] 1 Kings xiii. 7 ; 2 Kings iv. 42 ; v. 5, 15, 20–7 ; viii. 8–9 ; cf. Mic. iii. 5, 11 ; Ezek. xiii. 19.
[2] Moses, Samuel.   [3] Cf. LXX, iii.
[4] Mic. iii. 5, cf. 11 ; Ezek. xiii. 19.
[5] 1 Kings xxii. 6, 10–12 ; cf. xx. 13, 22, 28, 35–42 ; 2 Kings iii. 11–20 ; vi. 8–23 ; xiii. 14–19 ; xiv. 25.

The prophetic ecstasy of the *nebi'im* acted in Israel as a powerful ferment in the direction of religious individualism. Indeed, the humblest layman, if he were possessed by the spirit, might become the recipient and the interpreter of the divine communications, the counsellor or the reprover of kings, and the guide of the nation. However, this potentiality of a more personal religious development was offset by the gregarious tendency which prevailed in these circles, and by their dependence on the power of the king and on the mass of the people to whom they looked for their livelihood. In the time of Ahab, on the occasion of the great struggle between Jahweh and the Tyrian Baal, 400 prophets of Jahweh were on the side of the King ; Micaiah, the son of Imlah, was the only prophet in Samaria who dared to oppose the King (1 Kings xxii. 8–28). It was only later, under the influence of Elisha, that the " sons of the prophets " took sides with the opponents of the foreign god (2 Kings ix. 1).

Hence it cannot truly be said that the decisive part played by prophecy in the religious development of Israel was due to the members of these fraternities, for, as far as we know, Elisha was the only strong personality who arose among them. The importance of prophecy in Israel was due rather to a few outstanding individuals who, although apparently belonging to the *nebi'im* in virtue of their activity as prophets, were always eager to disclaim any connexion with the organized body of these ecstatics. Amos affirmed to Amaziah : " I am neither a prophet nor the son of a prophet," that is to say, neither a prophet by profession nor a member of a prophetic fraternity (Amos vii. 14). During the whole of his career Jeremiah was opposed to those whom he calls " the prophets." [1]

3. *Consecrated Persons.* The high places and, no doubt, the great royal sanctuaries in particular, tended to attract a considerable following of men, and even of women, who in various ways had acquired the title of " holy to Jahweh."

(*a*) A woman who had no children might make a vow that if Jahweh would grant her offspring she would " lend " to Jahweh the firstborn of her sons ; the child would then

[1] Jer. xxvi. 7–16 ; xxiii. 9–40 ; *cf.* Mic. iii. 5, 11 ; Ezek. xiii.

become a servant of the priests and a keeper of the sanctuary.[1] Some of the children so " lent " may have become priests ; they might also be redeemed by the payment of a sum of money to the sanctuary (Lev. xxvii. 1–8). Similar customs are still practised in Syria ; when it is a girl who has been thus vowed to a *wely*, one of the priests of the saint has the right to marry her, or else the girl's *mohar* (the marriage price paid by her future husband) is brought into the sanctuary.[2]

According to Exod. xxxviii. 8 and 1 Sam. ii. 22, there were also women who " served at the entrance of the Tent of Meeting." But these two passages are late interpolations. Moreover, it is not clear whether they relate to servants of the sanctuary,[3] pious persons living within the precincts of the temple (*cf.* Luke ii. 37), or merely to female worshippers taking part in the festivals.[4]

(*b*) Slaves, in the strict sense of the word, were also attached to the temple, usually foreigners and heathen, who fulfilled the menial tasks of the sanctuary (Ezek. xliv. 7–14). Most of them will have been prisoners of war given to the temple by the kings. Even a century after the return from exile, when most of their functions had, in theory, been transferred to the " Levites," they still figured in the staff of the temple under the title of *nethinim* (given) and " Solomon's servants." [5]

(*c*) There was also a class that might be designated as " sacred serfs " : the Canaanite population of certain cities, such as Gibeon, Kephirah, Beeroth and Kirjath Jearim, were obliged to supply hewers of wood and drawers of water for the altar of the house of God (Joshua ix. 23), that is, for the temple at Jerusalem, according to the Deuteronomic editor (Joshua ix. 27), originally, perhaps, for the high place of Jahweh at Gibeon.

(*d*) Lastly, there were those who were called " sacred men " and " sacred women " (*qedeshim* and *qedeshoth*) : these were men and women who devoted themselves to sacred prostitution. The men who belonged to this class were also

---

[1] 1 Sam. i.–iii. ; *cf.* Exod. xxxiii. 11.
[2] **XV**, pp. 189–93.
[3] **III**, p. 356.
[4] *Cf.* Judges xxi. 21 ; Ps. lxviii. 26.
[5] Ezra ii. 43–58, 70 ; viii. 20 ; Neh. vii. 46–60, 72 ; xi. 21 ; etc.

known by the more derogatory title of "dogs." We have
seen that this practice was probably borrowed from the
Canaanites, among whom it was widely prevalent.[1]

Although it does not seem to have been extirpated, or
nearly so, until the time of Josiah's reform,[2] it was attacked
by Asa and Jehoshaphat in the beginning of the ninth
century,[3] then by the prophets Amos (Amos ii. 7 probably)
and Hosea (Hos. iv. 14). Hence Jahwism early undertook
the task of sweeping away these doubtful customs in spite
of the religious prestige which surrounded them. There
can be no doubt that this was one of the effects of the severity
and the high moral standards which, from the first, seem to
have characterized the national religion of Israel.

To sum up, it may be said that the ritual practices and
religious institutions of the Israelites after their settlement
in Palestine were in the main the legacy of primitive Semitism
or borrowed from the Canaanites. Although they were
accommodated to the requirements of Jahwism, they only
give us a very imperfect view of the true nature of this
religion. In order to get to the heart of the religious life
of the Israelites of this period, we must study their beliefs,
their religious outlook, their morality and their attempts
at religious speculation.

[1] Pp. 103, 408–9.
[2] 2 Kings xxiii. 7 ; Deut. xxiii. 18–19 ; but see also Lev. xix. 29.
[3] 1 Kings xv. 22 ; xxii. 47 ; cf. xiv. 24.

CHAPTER III

RELIGIOUS BELIEFS OF THE ISRAELITES SETTLED IN PALESTINE

BEFORE the preaching of the eighth-century prophets introduced new points of view, the religious life of the Israelites settled in Palestine was wholly dominated by two cardinal beliefs, which constituted, so to speak, the compass which guided its religious development : Jahweh is the God of Israel, and Jahweh is a holy God.

I

JAHWEH, THE GOD OF ISRAEL

1. *Jahweh's Dwelling-place.* In the early days of the settlement, the old idea persisted that Jahweh dwelt *in the deserts of the south* (Judges v. 4) ; but this soon disappeared, and only survived in the imaginative descriptions of the poets, by nature conservers of tradition.[1]

Israel had far too intense a feeling of the divine intervention in daily life to remain long content with a belief that placed their God so far away from them.

When the people had become firmly rooted in Palestine, a new conception grew up, namely, that Jahweh was *the God of the land of Canaan*. So close a bond was formed between Jahweh and this land that Palestine was often represented as being the only abode of Jahweh. The peoples who live on the frontiers of the chosen land are " nigh unto Jahweh " (Jer. xii. 14). To be banished is to be " driven out from the face of Jahweh."[2] He cannot be worshipped in any other country : a foreign soil, belonging to other gods, permeated

[1] Deut. xxxii. 2 ; Hab. iii. 3 ; Ps. lxviii. 8–9 ; *cf.* 1 Kings xix.
[2] 2 Kings xiii. 23 ; xvii. 20 ; xxiv. 20 ; Jer. vii. 15 ; Jonah i. 3, 10 ; *cf.* Gen. iv. 14 ; Exod. xx. 3.

451

with their effluvia, is unclean in the eyes of the God of Israel.[1]
Hence, in order to obtain the help of Jahweh in a foreign
country, it is necessary either to make a vow to him, that is,
to promise him a sacrifice, a vow which can only be paid on
returning to Palestine, as Absalom did,[2] or to have recourse
to the more original method of Naaman, the Aramean general
whom Elisha healed of his leprosy : he carried off into his
own country two mules' loads of earth from the land of
Canaan, and set up an altar which was thus on the land of
Jahweh (2 Kings v. 17).

According to a third conception, no doubt closely connected with the previous one, but which on examination
proves to be quite distinct, Jahweh dwells *in the sanctuaries
of the land of Canaan*. When the Israelite went on a pilgrimage to one of these holy places, he spoke, thought, felt
and acted as if his God were really permanently and completely present within the limits of this one sacred enclosure.
To go to a sanctuary was " to seek " or " to visit Jahweh,"
or " to behold the face of Jahweh." A temple was " the
house of God." These beliefs persisted in spite of the most
spiritual teaching of the great prophets, even among the
prophets themselves. According to Ezekiel the destruction
of the temple in 586 was only possible because Jahweh had
previously abandoned his sanctuary (cc. viii.–xi.). The whole
priestly legislation is unintelligible unless it is recognized that
the post-exilic Jews believed in a real though mysterious
presence of the God of the heavens within the Holy of Holies
of the second temple.

The source of this conception is evident : the Israelites,
after their settlement in Palestine, had transferred to their
own God the beliefs which were prevalent among the ancient
inhabitants of the land concerning the baal, the special
divinity of each of these high places. The assimilation was
facilitated by the fact that the Hebrews had entirely analogous ideas about the holy springs or mountains of their
deserts.[3]

In addition to these three conceptions concerning the
dwelling-place of Jahweh, we can see a fourth beginning to

[1] Hos. ix. 3–6 ; Amos vii. 17 ; Exod. v. 1–2 ; vii. 16, 26 ; viii. 16 ;
etc.
[2] 2 Sam. xv. 7–8.　　　　[3] See pp. 264–7 ; 269–76.

appear : namely, that *Jahweh dwells in heaven*. The point has been disputed, but seems to be established by the texts.[1] The story ran that the tower of Babel was to reach to heaven —clearly the abode of the gods—and Jahweh " came down " —again, from heaven, no doubt—in order to see the building (Gen. ii. 1–9). According to the Jahwist, he " came down " on Sinai when the people were collected at the foot of the mountain (Exod. xix. 11, 20). Manoah's mysterious visitor ascended in the flame, when it " went up on the altar towards heaven " (Judges xiii. 20).

According to the Elohist, when the angel of Jahweh wishes to communicate with a mortal he calls to him from heaven (Gen. xxi. 17 ; xxii. 11). The same cycle contains a curious attempt to reconcile this belief with the previous one. When Jacob, on the site of the future sanctuary of Bethel, had received the famous dream of the ladder, he cried : " This is the gate of heaven ! " (Gen. xxviii. 17). Thus the divine dwelling is in heaven ; but the earthly sanctuary of Bethel received the distinction of being the starting-point of the invisible ladder which leads to the gate of the divine palace, and hence was the place where the divine messengers were most likely to be met with.

The belief in a ladder or stairway between earth and heaven is found among many peoples ; [2] it is often associated with the rainbow, or with the daily ascent of the heavenly bodies from the horizon to the zenith and their descent again from the zenith to the horizon.[3] If the Palestinian belief reflected in our story (Gen. xxviii.) is also of astral, and possibly of Babylonian, origin,[4] it must be confessed that the original bearing of the story had been forgotten ; for it was certainly never claimed that the stars rose and set at Bethel. We have here an original and probably spontaneous application of the popular theme of the heavenly ladder to the glorification of a local sanctuary.

This thought of Jahweh as dwelling in heaven did not necessarily involve the abandonment of the terrestrial limits which popular belief imposed upon him. It is possible that the God of Israel was thought of as reigning only in that part of the heavens corresponding to the land of Canaan, in " the heaven of Jacob," as a poet of that period expresses it (Deut. xxxiii. 28). However, such a representation would suggest

---

[1] **LXXXV**, p. 104.
[2] Egyptians, **XXI**, p. 98 ; Persians, Oceanians, Scandinavians, folk-stories of Germany, **XXVI**, *ad loc.*
[3] **XXVI**, *ibid.*   [4] **XXXVII**, p. 234.

a more superhuman, less material conception of the nature of Jahweh and one which would harmonize better with the increasing recognition of the wider extent of his kingdom.

2. *Jahweh and Foreign Gods.* Up to the eighth century, the Israelites believed firmly in the existence of many other deities beside their national God. This fact, which we have already given evidence for, is confirmed by the limitation of Jahweh's authority to Palestine. Jephthah, in the course of diplomatic negotiations with the King of Moab,[1] says to him : " Wilt thou not possess that which Chemosh thy god giveth thee to possess ? So whomsoever the Lord our God hath dispossessed from before us, them will we possess " (Judges ii. 24). It is such a well-recognized fact that Chemosh is master in his own domain that an Israelite historian assigns the anger of that god as the cause of a defeat inflicted upon the kings of Israel and Judah in Moabite territory (2 Kings iii. 27).

The worship of " strange gods," as they were called, was regarded as perfectly legitimate within the limits of their respective territories.[2] The view which placed the true God in sharp opposition to the false gods, God over against the " no-gods," and the true religion in contrast with the worship of lies, was still unknown.

Hence, during this period, the relations between Israelites and foreigners were in the main unrestricted. Elijah, the fiery champion of Jahweh, lives in Phenician territory, in the house of a worshipper of Baal, and shares her food (1 King xvii. 8–24). Israelites have no hesitation in taking wives from among Arameans, Egyptians and Moabites, and are astonished at the refusal of the Egyptians to eat with Hebrews (Gen. xliii. 32).

In the ancient East it was a common practice to consult foreign oracles and wonder-workers. The Pharaoh, Ameno-phis III, sent for the statue of Ishtar of Nineveh, perhaps in order to obtain healing from her.[3] It was said that the daughter of the Hittite king was delivered from a demon through the intervention of the Egyptian god Khonsu, whose

---

[1] And not of Ammon, as the present text, which is composite, suggests.
[2] 1 Sam. xxvi. 19 ; *cf.* Jer. xvi. 13 ; Ruth i. 15 ; ii. 12.
[3] TA(W), 20 (K, 23).

image had been sent to her.[1] Moabites and Arameans believed in the word of Israelite men of God.[2] Similarly the people of Jahweh were very proud of having been blessed by Balaam, the famous foreign diviner,[3] whose blessings and curses were always effectual (Num. xxii. 6). An old Israelite tradition tells of the fulfilment of an oracle given by Philistine priests and diviners (1 Sam. vi. 2–9). Ahaziah, the King of Israel, sends to consult Baal Zebub, the Philistine god of Ekron ; it is true that Elijah blames him severely for the step ; but his censure is not directed so much against his superstition in consulting an idol which could not answer him, as against his lack of respect for the God of his own country. " Is there not a God in Israel, that thou sendest to consult Baal Zebub, the god of Ekron ?·" (2 Kings i. 1–4).

Ancient Israel shared the universal belief of that time in a world peopled by supernatural powers, gods, spirits, invisible beings, who could endow man with something of their own power or superhuman knowledge. In the minds of the Israelites of this period, that which distinguished genuine Israelite prophecy from the rest was not that the latter were false and the former alone true ; it was rather that Israelite prophecy was inspired by Jahweh, the sole God whom it was legitimate for Israel to consult, while other prophets depended upon the revelations of all kinds of *elohim*. From this belief arose the prohibition against consulting the dead—in spite of the superhuman foreknowledge which these *elohim* possessed (1 Sam. xxviii. 4–25)—as well as the *yiddeoni*, who were, perhaps, familiar spirits, similar to the companions (*sahib*, *tabi*) who were the usual sources of inspiration for the Arab diviners.[4]

However, even if the Israelite did not yet believe that there was a fundamental difference in nature between Jahweh and the foreign gods, he was convinced that his God was much more powerful than the gods of his neighbours. He took pride in the story of the humiliations which the ark, after it had been captured by the Philistines, inflicted upon Dagon in his own temple (1 Sam. iv.–v.).

Hence, many an Israelite, even in a foreign land, readily recognized in all good or evil fortune that befell him the

---

[1] Cf. **LXVIII**, p. 384. [2] Judges iii. 20 ; 2 Kings v. ; viii. 7–15. [3] See pp. 219–20. [4] **XXX**, p. 82.

evidence of Jahweh's protection or displeasure.[1] Jahweh was conceived of somewhat after the fashion of a powerful king who is able to protect his subjects even beyond the boundaries of his own domains, and will if necessary spread death and destruction in the lands of those who oppress his people. Although these conceptions were still capable of being contained within the pattern of the polytheism which prevailed among the ancient Israelites, they, nevertheless, prepared the way for a loftier view of the power of the national God. The pious Israelite had an increasing sense of his continual dependence upon Jahweh, wherever he happened to be. While still polytheistic in his ideas, in feeling and practice he was almost a monotheist.[2]

As we have already been reminded, the religious man inevitably tends, as he contemplates the god who is the object of his worship, to ascribe to him titles of the widest implication, and to recognize his supremacy over the celestial realm as well as over the terrestrial. Among peoples possessing many gods these attributions, being applied to each of them, tend to limit each other. But among the Israelites, who had only one national God, " cathenotheism," that instinctive monotheism of the religious mind, could develop along its logical lines without counteracting influences.

3. *Conceptions of Jahweh. Attendants and Agents of the National God.* Some of the features of the conception of Jahweh are derived from ancient times, prior to the age of Moses, when the God of Sinai was associated with certain natural phenomena such as lightning, storm, earthquake and fire, possibly because the sacred mountain was a volcano.[3] The story was told that, like the volcano, Jahweh had appeared to the Israelites in the wilderness under the form of

---

[1] The adventure of Abraham in Egypt (Gen. xii. 17) and with Abimelech (xx. 3–7), the journey of Abraham's servant into Aram (xxiv. 7, 12–27, 40), the sojourn of Isaac at Gerar (xxvi. 12–13), of Jacob with Laban (xxviii. 15 ; xxix. 31 ; xxx. 22–4, 27, 30 ; xxxi. 3, 5–7) and in Egypt (xlvi. 4), of Joseph and his brothers in the same country (xli. 16, 51 ; xlii. 21 ; xliv. 16 ; xlv. 7–9), and above all the triumphant intervention of Jahweh in Egypt at the time of the deliverance of his oppressed people (Exod. iii. 7–8 ; etc.). Jahweh answers prayer even in a foreign land (1 Kings xvii. 20–2 ; 2 Kings v. 17).

[2] See particularly 1 Kings xviii. 39 ; 2 Kings v. 15.

[3] See p. 179.

a pillar of fire by night and a pillar of cloud by day. He had revealed himself to Abraham as a blazing torch and a smoking furnace (Gen. xv. 17). The temple was filled with smoke when the ark was brought into it in the time of Solomon (1 Kings viii. 10–11) and when Isaiah received the vision there which called him to the prophetic office (Isa. vi. 4). Thunder was the voice of Jahweh.[1] Poets described the march of Jahweh shrouded in dark clouds, discharging hailstones and coals of fire.[2] The God of Sinai appeared to Moses " in a flame in the midst of a bush." " The glory of Jahweh " was a divine fire of dazzling brightness flashing at intervals from the storm-cloud which concealed it;[3] sometimes this fire seems to be thought of as surrounding,[4] sometimes as constituting the body of the deity. The chariots and horses of the heavenly host are of fire.[5]

But the traces of what we might call the *naturistic* conception of Jahweh are replaced, in the period with which we are dealing, by an *animistic* conception which usually results in an anthropomorphic representation of God. For the animist all that lives contains a principle by which it lives, breathes, thinks and wills, and which many peoples denote by a word which literally means " breath " (soul, spirit). In the mind of the Israelite, Jahweh had thoughts, passions, feelings, entirely similar to those of man : he could be provoked and appeased, be grieved and repent. Hence Jahweh also is essentially a spirit. The Israelite went still further in this assimilation of God to man : he ascribed to Jahweh the bodily organs which in man are the seat or organs of expression of feelings or thoughts : Jahweh had eyes, ears, a mouth, nostrils, hands, a heart, bowels, his breath was long or short (quiet or disturbed).

These were not mere metaphors. Doubtless the Israelite might affirm that, following the distinction between man and the animal, the *elohim* were spirit and not flesh.[6] But by " spirit " he did not understand an immaterial principle, incapable of apprehension by the senses : for him, as for most

---

[1] Amos i. 2 ; Ps. xxix. 3–9 ; etc.
[2] Judges v. 4–5 ; Ps. lxviii. 8–10 ; Isa. xix. 1 ; Ps. xviii. 8–15 ; Ezek. i. ; etc.
[3] 1 Kings viii. 11 ; Isa. vi. 3–4 ; *cf.* Exod. xvi. 10 ; xxiv. 15–17.
[4] For example, Exod. xxxiv. 29–35.
[5] 2 Kings ii. 11 ; vi. 17.   [6] Isa. xxxi. 3 ; Gen. vi. 3.

animistic peoples, spirit was an extremely subtle substance, nebulous and ethereal, but nevertheless material : it could be poured out like a fluid (Isa. xxix. 10). Jahweh takes a portion of the spirit which was on Moses and puts it upon the seventy elders, who thereupon begin to prophesy (Num. ii. 17, 25). Elisha asks for a double portion, the eldest son's share, of the spirit of Elijah, implying that the latter can allot his *ruach* as if it were an inheritance (2 Kings ii. 9). The soul of man, spiritual though it is, may be snared, smitten, killed. Similarly, the Israelite did not think that his God was invisible *by nature* ; he did not say : " no man can see God," but : " no man can see an *elohim* and live," a state-ment with an entirely different implication, namely, that the mortal who chanced to see a divine being would certainly

FIG. 38. SEAL OF SHEBANJAU

die, no doubt because, for the primitive mind, seeing was the same as physical contact.[1]

Hence the Israelite probably thought of Jahweh as possessing a kind of ethereal body, " a spiritual body," to use Paul's expression, capable of appearing under various forms. Jahweh could assume the appearance of fire or of an animal, especially of a bull : hence the representation of the God of Israel in the form of a " calf," that is, of a bull-image, of gold, in the sanctuaries of Dan and Bethel ; hence also the title of " the bull of Jacob,"[2] or " the bull of Israel,"[3] which seems to be ascribed to him by some of the poets. Possibly two texts ascribe to him the horns of a buffalo (Num. xxiii. 22 ; xxiv. 8). The personal name *Egelyahu*, occurring on an ostrakon found at Samaria (ninth century), may be inter-preted : " Jahweh is a young bull." Elsewhere the bull is

[1] Gen. xix. 26 ; Num. xxii. 41 ; xxiii. 9 ; xxiv. 2 ; *cf.* **LXXVIII**, p. 187 ; Lods, **LXXVI**, p. 68.
[2] Gen. xlix. 24 ; Isa. xlix. 26 ; lx. 16 ; Ps. cxxxii. 2, 5.
[3] Isa. i. 24.

not a representation of Jahweh, but the sacred animal of the God of Israel : hence its place in the temple decoration [1] and its appearance on the seal of Shema'yahu.[2] Horns were, as we know, the attribute of divine beings among the Babylonians. The bull was specially sacred to Adad and Marduk.[3] It was, no doubt, from the cult of Adad, a storm-god like Jahweh, that the Israelites borrowed this symbol.

But usually Jahweh was supposed to appear in the form of a man. Early traditions represent him as walking in the garden of Eden in the cool of the day, closing the roof of the ark over Noah, coming down to see the city of Babel or to stop the building of the tower, accepting the hospitality of Abraham or of Gideon, allowing his back parts to be seen by Moses or Elijah, etc.

It is Jahweh, apparently, who is represented on the seal of Elishama, the son of Gedalyahu, seated on a throne enclosed by palm-trees, in a boat decorated with birds' heads.[4]

The anthropopathic and anthropomorphic conception of Jahweh was an advance on the naturistic and theriomorphic representations : this explains why the great prophets, far from opposing this mode of conceiving of Jahweh, commonly made use of the metaphors which served to express it.

Only rarely is Jahweh represented by the winged disk,[5] or described in the terms of solar theology.[6]

The conception of the God of Israel was too vital and exclusive to allow much room for subsidiary deities. Here and there, however, we catch sight of beings who attend him or express his will. They are of very diverse origins ; some of them even appear to be composite beings.

The kerub (from its plural kerubim we have formed the word cherubim) was originally, no doubt, the storm cloud upon which Jahweh rode, and was represented as a winged being ;[7] its connexion with the storm is still to be discerned in the highly

---

[1] 1 Kings vii. 25, 29, 44. [2] **III**, p. 228 (fig. 265).

[3] See, for example, in Palestine the bull of Rihab and that of er-Rummân ; **XXII**[2], ii, figs. 352 and 353 ; cf. **CLIX**, pp. 164 (fig. 107), 168 (fig. 114), 170 (fig. 116) and above, pp. 110–1, fig. 35 and pl. viii.

[4] **XXIII**[2], ii, fig. 598.

[5] Seal of Shebanyau (fig. 38) a contract from Gezer (**III**, p. 229, fig. 273).

[6] Deut. xxxiii. 2 ; cf. Ps. l. 2 ; Num. vi. 25 ; Mal. iii. 20 ; Ps. xvii. 8 ; xxxvi. 8 ; lvii. 2 ; lxi. 5 ; lxiii 8 ; xci. 4 ; Ruth ii. 12.

[7] Ps. xviii. 10–12 ; cf civ. 3 ; Isa. xix. 1.

elaborate conception of Ezekiel.[1] This naturistic figure may be
of early Hebrew origin. But the *kerub* was also the guardian of
sacred things, of the tree of life (Gen. iii. 24), and of the ark in the
temple at Jerusalem.[2] Hence it had been assimilated to the
winged genii, half-animal in form, which are found in the myths
of Babylon, Egypt and the Syro-Hittite region. The animals
with human heads, moulded on the sides of the object found at
Taanach and supposed to be an Israelite censer of the eighth
century,[3] may represent *kerubim*, although they are not winged
(pl. xv, 2).

The *seraphim*, a plural form from which we have derived our
seraphim, were originally winged serpents, in which, according to
Arab folklore, were embodied the jinns and ghouls which inhabited
the desert.[4] The *seraphim* were, no doubt, identified with the
gods and spirits in serpent form whom the Canaanites worshipped
at Jerusalem,[5] as also at Debir and Bethshan.[6] In this way,
apparently, they became the attendants of Jahweh, hymning the
glory of the God of Israel in his temple. According to another
theory, *seraph* was in the Canaanite period a name of Nergal. It
may be recalled that this god, according to V R 46, 23 c.d., was
called *sharrapu* in Amurru, and that the god of Byblos was sometimes represented with four [7] or with six wings.[8] But this parallel
is doubtful : *sharrapu* or *sharrabu* may correspond with the
Hebrew *sharab*, a mirage.[9]

The vague entities known as " *the face of Jahweh*,"[10] " *the name
of Jahweh*," [11] " *the angel of Jahweh*," and which were sometimes
distinguished from the God of Israel,[12] and sometimes treated as
identical with him,[13] seem, like the *genius* of the Roman gods or
the *fravashi* of the gods of Persia, to come under the same category
as those doubles which, according to animistic belief, can be sent
out either by gods or men, to journey wherever they will.[14] The
Egyptians of Thebes distinguished " Khonsu who sits still," who
could not leave his temple, and " Khonsu who carries out his
plans," who could even journey to a foreign country.[15]

Angels (in the plural) only appear later (in the Elohist narrative). We also hear of *the host of Jahweh*, commanded by a chief,
with chariots and horses of fire,[16] of a *destroyer* who sometimes,
though not often, takes the place of Jahweh in the execution of

---

[1] i. 4, 13, 24, 28 ; x. 5, 13.
[3] 1 Kings vi. 23–8 ; *cf.* Exod. xxv. 18–22.
[4] See p. 435.   [2] See pp. 238–9.
[5] 2 Kings xviii. 4 ; *cf.* 1 Kings i. 9 ; Neh. ii. 13.
[6] See pp. 108–9 and pls. iv, 2 ; ix, 1 and 3.
[7] Philo of Byblos, Fr. ii, 26.
[8] Coins of the city published by Rouvier ; **XLIX**, p. 430.
[9] **XCIII**, p. 415.   [10] Exod. xxxiii. 12–15.
[11] Exod. xxiii. 21 ; 2 Kings xxiii. 27 ; 2 Chron. xxxiii. 4 ; Isa. xxx.
27 (M.T.).
[12] With the Phenicians " the face of Baal " was the goddess Tanit.
Ra is called the face of Amon (*cf.* **XXXVI**, ii, p. 354).
[13] So Isa. lxiii. 9 ; Ps. xx. 2 ; Gen. xlviii. 15–16 ; etc.
[14] **CCLXXI**.   [15] *Cf.* **CCLXXX**, pp. 19–21.
[16] Joshua v. 13–15 ; 2 Kings vi. 17.

his punishments.[1] The presence of these subordinate beings in Jahwism was doubtless due to the desire to give a place in the religion to the ancient deities of the local sanctuaries and to the spirits of popular belief.

Lastly, there is *the spirit*. This was originally, according to animistic conceptions, an alien soul or force that gained an entrance into the human body and there became the cause of disease, madness, irresistible passions, vertigo, supernatural sleep. It was also the source of the ecstasy and the foreknowledge of inspired persons, the skill of specially gifted craftsmen, and the courage of warriors. In Israel the spirit which possessed certain individuals was sometimes called " the spirit of Jahweh," sometimes " a spirit sent by Jahweh " (1 Sam. xvi. 14) ; sometimes, indeed, the view was entertained that an impersonal portion of that ethereal fluid which constitutes the divine substance, distinct from God who sent it, had entered into the inspired person ; sometimes the spirit was regarded as a personal being, also distinct from God who sent it : Micaiah, the son of Imlah, in his vision of the heavenly council, sees the spirit which inspired the prophets come forth and speak in the presence of Jahweh and his train (1 Kings xxii. 19–23).

4. *Jahweh's activities on behalf of Israel.* Abstract ideas about what God is *in himself* have never possessed more than a secondary importance in religions. The real centre of interest for worshippers is *what God is for them.* However much the ancient Israelites may have been impressed with the inscrutability of the divine will, they were, at all events, thoroughly convinced that the will of Jahweh was always directed towards to the good of his people.

They did not occupy themselves much with speculations concerning the nature of the tie that bound Jahweh to Israel. Traditions relating to the Mosaic age assigned the origin of this tie to a covenant made at the time of the exodus from Egypt, while a Jahwist historian found its source in an immemorial relation going back to the third human generation (Gen. iv. 26). The one certain fact was that Jahweh was bound to Israel.

In general, his attitude toward his people was regarded as resembling that feeling of community which unites a sheikh to his tribe, or a king to the nation which he rules, an attitude which is expressed in the Hebrew word *hesed*,[2] very closely corresponding to the Latin *pietas*.

This care of Jahweh for his people appears in all the cir-

---

[1] Exod. xii. 23 ; 2 Sam. xxiv. 16–17 ; *cf.* 2 Kings xix. 35, but Exod. xi. 4, 5 ; xii. 23ª ; Gen. xix. 14 ; Exod. iv. 24–6 ; Amos v. 17 ; etc.

[2] Gen. xxiv. 27 ; xxxii. 11 ; 2 Sam. ii. 6.

cumstances in which Israel is involved as a nation, and always takes the form of a personal intervention, thought of in the most vivid and anthropomorphic fashion.

(1) The foremost of such situations was war. The national struggles of Israel were called " the wars of Jahweh." The enemies of the nation were the enemies of its God. Israelite warriors were merely his allies (Judges v. 23). Jahweh in person was present in the midst of the host (Deut. xxiii. 15), either invisibly, or in the form of a material object such as the ark or the ephod.

The ancient taboos intended to protect the combatants were regarded as practices of " sanctification " or purification necessary because of the presence of Jahweh ; [1] the *herem* was intended to appease his anger against his foes. [2]

In time of war, Jahweh aided his people in counsel as well as in action : he aided them in counsel by revealing through oracles, dreams, or omens, the fortunate or fatal result of the intended campaign, and by pointing out the necessary strategy ; the prophet Elisha hears at a distance and reports to the King of Israel all that passes in the inner room where the King of Aram takes counsel with his generals (2 Kings vi. 8–12) ; in action he aided them by spreading panic among the enemy, by pouring down hail upon them, by causing the sun and moon to stand still in order to allow his people to dispatch the fugitives, [3] by producing a storm or an earthquake. David waits to give battle until he hears the sound of marching on the tops of the trees ; it is the sound of Jahweh going forth to lead the host of Israel (2 Sam. v. 22–5). In Hebrew poetry Jahweh is " a man of war " ; he overwhelms his enemies with his arrows and smites them with his sword. [4]

(2) When we come down to the period of the monarchy, Israel has become less warlike, and values more highly than victory that blessing which is the fruit of victory, the peaceful possession of the land. In their gratitude to Jahweh, the Israelites were never weary of celebrating the praises of the land " flowing with milk and honey," whose fertility they

[1] See pp. 294–6.   [2] See pp. 287–9.
[3] Joshua x. 12ᵃ, 14.
[4] Exod. xv. 3 ; Ps. xxiv. 8 ; Deut. xxxii, 41–2 ; Isa. xxxi. 8 ; Ps. xviii. 15 ; etc.

proudly compared with the barren steppes of Edom,[1] Moab and Ammon.[2] In the tradition the settlement in Palestine began to assume the miraculous aspect of an incredibly swift conquest. After the victories of David, and later on, after those of Jeroboam II over the Arameans, the people, " delivered from their enemies," felt that they had reached the height of prosperity. They thought that the peaceful enjoyment of the land of Canaan was the ultimate blessing which Jahweh had predestined for his people from the beginning.[3]

(3) In the next place, the value of the possession of the land depended on the fruitfulness of the soil; to this end it was necessary that the harvests should be preserved from blight, swarms of locusts, and other scourges, and above all, that the heaven should yield rain and dew in their season. All these things, from the time of the settlement in Palestine, were regarded as depending on Jahweh, the true baal of the land. Thus rain, like victory over their enemies, was the chief blessing promised by Jahweh to his people.[4]

(4) Furthermore, it was Jahweh who watched over the increase of the population. He had promised the patriarchs to multiply their seed as the dust of the earth (Gen. xiii. 16 ; xxviii. 14), the stars of heaven (Gen. xv. 5 ; xxii. 17) or the sand which is by the seashore (Gen. xxxii. 13). According to a widely prevalent popular belief, it was sacrilegious; or at any rate highly dangerous, to number a people or a tribe, or to take stock of one's possessions.[5] " The merchants of the Levant believe that if man knows the exact value of his property he will soon lose a portion of it."[6] Even at the end of the nineteenth century, Russian peasants preferred to be put to death rather than submit to a census, regarding such a measure as a sacrilege.[7] The Israelites shared this feeling. When David numbered the people in spite of Joab's warnings, Jahweh decimated them with a terrible plague (2 Sam. xxiv.). The priestly legislation also provides that each of those who are numbered shall give to Jahweh half a shekel " as a ransom

---

[1] Gen. xxvii. 27–8, 39, 40.
[2] Gen. xiii. ; xix.   [3] See p. 419.
[4] Gen. xxvii. 27–9 ; xlix. 24–5 ; Deut. xxxiii. 13–16, 27–9.
[5] CLXXXVII, ii, pp. 555–63 ; XXV, ii, 1, p. 150.
[6] CLXX, iii, p. 7.
[7] *Journal des Débats*, Sept. 2, 1897.

for his life," in order that the numbering may not bring a disaster upon them.[1] These statistics were probably regarded as an impious attempt to pierce the mystery surrounding Jahweh's methods of multiplying population or property.

(5) Israel was also in the habit of ascribing to Jahweh the origin of its social organization, its law and its morality. At his command Moses had instituted the elders,[2] and the first king had been appointed by Samuel,[3] at least, according to certain versions of the tradition. The short codes known as the second Decalogue (Exod. xxxiv.) and the Book of the Covenant (Exod. xx. 23 ; xxiii. 19), are represented as having been communicated to Moses by Jahweh. However, in the earlier texts, blessings of this character are not mentioned among the signal marks of the care of the national God, although, in a later age, the gift of the Book of the Law was to be hailed as the supreme favour granted by Jahweh to his people. The reason for this was, no doubt, that the people still remembered that the customary law and organization of the tribes belonged, in the main, to the period prior to Jahwism (the blood-feud, the levirate, the organization of the family and the clan, etc.). It was also due to the fact that Israel did not yet think that its superiority over other nations consisted in its institutions or its morality so much as in its military and numerical preponderance. But most of all it was due to the fact that the ancient Israelites had no conception of a fixed code, given once for all from the creation of the world. They believed that they possessed what was infinitely better, the continual guidance of a divine Counsellor, ever ready to enlighten his people in all their difficulties, internal or external.

(6) Jahweh was Israel's Guide. This was, perhaps, the most important of his blessings, the source of all the rest. He guided his people, not only, as we have said, by his providence, controlling the course of events for the good of his own ; for Israel's national history was to them the great occasion of thanksgiving to Jahweh and the book in which they might read his revelations ; but he guided them, too, by imparting his instructions to, or acting through, certain

---

[1] Exod. xxx. 12–13.   [2] Num. xi. 16–17, 24–5.
[3] According to 1 Sam. ix. 15–17 ; x. 1, and even according to viii. 9 ; x. 20–4.

individuals, chiefs, priests, prophets, Nazirites.[1] Advice
given by the elders, the oracle (*torah*) of the priests, and the
word of the prophets, were the three recognized means by
which, under normal circumstances, Israel could learn the
will and guidance of its God.[2]

Thus the national religion, naïve, sometimes crude, but
always full of vitality and spontaneity, permeated all the
activities of public life.

II

JAHWEH IS A HOLY GOD

1. *The Conception of the Holiness of God.* It was natural
that confidence in a God who was so watchful over the good
of his people should be a dominant feature in the national
religion. But with this feeling there became mingled an
entirely opposite one, which served as a corrective to the
first, providing both its necessary contrast and complement ;
this was the profound feeling of awe and helplessness in the
presence of the divine majesty.

This feeling was not peculiar to the Israelites. It was
common to all the Semites and was expressed in the very
ancient idea of holiness.[3]

For the Semites the word " holiness " was not, as it is for
us, equivalent to moral perfection. This is a later association
of ideas of which we can discern only the first faint traces in
the great prophets of Israel. In ancient documents, in
Hebrew literature in general and in other Semitic languages,
the term " holy " is applied to everything that is divine or
connected with the gods to indicate that such things or beings
are hedged about with sanctity, inviolable, that contact with
them is dangerous for the man who has not observed the
most meticulous precautions in his approach to them. Contact with a holy being or sacred object is certainly desirable,
since the establishment of communication with the divine
may procure for a man supernatural force or life ; but such a
contact is as much a source of fear as of desire. For example,
an ancient tradition relates that when the ark was brought

---

[1] See pp. 296–307 ; 440–8.
[2] Jer. xviii. 18 ; Ezek. vii. 26 ; Lam. ii. 9.
[3] See pp. 248–9 ; 265–6. *Cf.* **CCLXIX**, ch. iv.

back from the country of the Philistines, seventy Israelites died because they looked into the sacred object, or, according to a more probable variant, because they had not displayed sufficient joy at its return, and that the people of the place, terror-stricken, cried out : " Who shall stand before Jahweh, this ·holy God ? *And to whom shall he go up from us ?* " That is to say : " We may no longer entertain so terrible a guest : whither shall we send him ? " (1 Sam vi. 20). The synonyms for " holy " are " terrible " (Isaiah viii. 13), " jealous " (Joshua xxiv. 19), " divine " (Hos. ii. 9) ; the equivalents for " holiness " are " glory " (Isa. vi. 3), " majesty," " splendour " (Ps. lxxvii. 14).

Holiness was thought of by the ancient Semite as a kind of formidable fluid which could be imparted by mere contact and might be fatal to the profane person.[1] This very primitive conception of holiness was still in the main that of the Israelites immediately after their settlement in Palestine, save that the discharge of divine energy was conceived of somewhat less after the fashion of a blind physical force, and rather more after the pattern of human anger.[2]

2. *The Anger of Jahweh. Its Effects and its Causes.* The Israelites were the more inclined to ascribe to Jahweh this easy irascibility in that it seemed to harmonize with the character of a storm-god and perhaps with the volcanic nature which he had brought from Sinai.

Hence, as a rule, there was no hesitation in attributing to the anger of Jahweh the misfortunes which overtook the nation, especially sudden calamities : drought and swarms of locusts—with the resultant famine—pestilence, defeat, the rulers' lack of understanding, the silence of the priestly oracle, the lying visions of the prophets.

It then became necessary to discover, if possible, the cause of Jahweh's wrath, in order to appease it.

The answers which the ancient Israelite gave to the question why Jahweh was angry are significant ; they enlighten us as to the conception then held concerning the relation between religion and morality.

According to the great prophets and especially according to their disciples of post-exilic times, the sole cause of the

---

[1] Isa. lxv. 5 ; Ezek. xliv. 19 ; Exod. xix. 12, 13, 23 ; etc.
[2] So 2 Sam. vi. 6–10.

anger of God was the injustice of man : the people, the generation or the individual who committed the crime fell inevitably under the divine wrath. The anger of Jahweh was identified with the execution of justice. In ancient Israel the idea of the relation between God and man was not too lofty and abstract to be understood by the ordinary man. It was conceived of in vivid and human fashion. True, the ancient Israelite believed, like all the early peoples who had made some progress in moral ideas, that his God avenged the crimes which were committed among the people, or in the land, under his rule; that he punished perjurers, decided by means of his oracles the cases which were submitted to his arbitration, protected widows, orphans and foreign sojourners, exacted the due penalty of breaches of national custom. But many other reasons might exist why the divine anger should be kindled or slumber, be appeased or provoked, reasons beyond the rules of a strict justice which all could understand.

In the first place, Jahweh might forget or pass over sins which had been committed : he might only punish them when he happened to observe them or when they were pointed out to him (1 Kings xvii. 18). A custom which bears the stamp of extreme antiquity prescribed the offering, for this purpose, of a special sacrifice called " an oblation of memorial, bringing iniquity to remembrance " (Num. v. 15). When, many years after their crime, Joseph's brothers are falsely accused of theft, Judah says to the governor : " God hath *found out* the iniquity of thy servants " (Gen. xliv. 16).

On the other hand, the wrath of Jahweh would burn most fiercely when it was a question of an offence against his own person ; no atonement was possible in such a case. This conception is expressed in Eli's naïve explanation to his sons : " If one man sin against another, God shall judge between them : but if a man sin against the Lord, who shall intreat for him ? " (1 Sam. ii. 25). The crime of the sons of Eli consisted in having taken their portion of the sacrifices, due to them as priests, before Jahweh had received his portion (1 Sam. ii. 15–16), or, according to another version, in merely having helped themselves before the other guests at the sacred meal (1 Sam. ii. 13–14). For this offence, Jahweh destroyed them and took away the priesthood from their house for ever.[1]

Jahweh also appears as the aggrieved party to exact vengeance, and not as an impartial arbiter, when his people are concerned. It is not related in the early texts that Jahweh ever took sides against Israel in their quarrels with other nations : he might deliver them occasionally into the hands of their enemies, not because the latter's cause was just, but because he had a personal reason for anger with his people—the Moabites in the same way explain their own defeats as due to the anger of Chemosh, their god.[2] Hence the partiality shown by Jahweh, according to the tradition, to the patriarchs, even when they are in the wrong : for instance, to Abraham and Isaac, when they deceive the Pharaoh or Abimelech, and to Jacob after he has deceived his blind father, or when he had robbed Laban. It is because the patriarchs represent Israel in its relations with other nations. Jahweh himself commands the Israelites, at the time of the exodus, to spoil their Egyptian neighbours (Exod. iii. 21–2).

Similar instances occur in the execution of law in ancient Israel,[3] Jahweh punishes the children with the guilty father, or in his stead.[4] He chastises the whole people for the sin of an individual, especially of its king (2 Sam. xxiv.). Such a proceeding was even one of the regular means employed by Jahweh to compel the reparation of a crime : he would smite the community in order to force it to discover and punish the guilty person.[5] Hence the purpose of the penalties inflicted by the judges was not so much to right the wrongs of the victim as to take away from the midst of the nation the evil which might draw down upon it the wrath of God.

The Israelites had not wholly emerged from the point of view of primitive peoples who only recognize crimes of fact. They knew that the justice or injustice of an act consisted in its motive ; nevertheless, numerous traces remained of the older and cruder conception, both in the grounds of

---

[1] 1 Sam. iii. 14. See also the accounts in 2 Sam. xxiv. ; Joshua vii.–viii. ; 1 Sam. xv. ; 1 Kings xx. 42.
[2] The Mesha Stone, ll. 5–6.
[3] See pp. 480–1.
[4] Num. xvi. 32 ; 2 Sam. xii. 13–14 ; etc.
[5] Joshua vii.–viii. ; 1 Sam. xiv. 37–45 ; 2 Sam. xxi. 1–14.

action which they attributed to their God, and in their own customary law. It was the duty of the avenger of blood to slay the manslayer, even if the latter's act had been unpremeditated (Exod. xxi. 13). When Abimelech took Sarah into his harem without knowing that she was married, he committed a crime for which he was obliged to obtain Abraham's intercession; if he had lain with her, he would have committed a crime for which God would have slain him, although by God's own admission *he was perfectly innocent* (Gen. xx. 3–7).

It was believed that ritual could change the feelings of Jahweh. God might be appeased by the smell of a sacrifice, as the story of the deluge frankly acknowledges.[1]

On the other hand, Jahweh has his likes and dislikes. He shows mercy to whom he will show mercy, and is gracious to whom he will be gracious (Exod. xxxiii. 19). The J tradition does not state that he had any reason for rejecting Cain's offering and accepting Abel's : which proves that no need of an explanation was felt to exist. The sight of these apparently arbitrary displays of favour or displeasure did not, however, induce the early Israelites to accuse their God of partiality, but rather to bow in awe before the mystery of his ways. Possibly they felt that the laws of divine justice were not the same as those of human justice.

Hence, if the Israelite found no difficulty in the arbitrary character of the divine activity, it was because, at heart, he believed that everything, especially everything of an unusual nature, was the work of his God, and did not distinguish what God willed from what he permitted in view of a higher end. These inequalities exist, hence they must be the immediate result of the loves and hates of Jahweh.

This state of mind produced an attitude still more disconcerting to our modern point of view. The ancient Israelite did not shrink from regarding Jahweh as the instigator of acts that were morally bad.

Quos perdere vult Jupiter dementat, is a famous dictum, dating from the sixteenth century, but expressing a very ancient idea. The Israelites shared this belief.[2] But they went further and admitted that sometimes, when Jahweh

---

[1] Gen. viii. 21 ; *cf.* 1 Sam. xxvi. 19 ; Judges ix. 13 ; etc.
[2] 2 Sam. xv. 31 ; 1 Kings xxii. 20–3 ; 2 Kings iii. 10–13 ; etc.

wished to destroy an individual, *he caused him to sin.* He
sends an evil spirit to stir up the men of Shechem to rebel
against Abimelech (Judges ix. 23). He hardens Pharaoh's
heart.[1] The sons of Eli did not listen to their father's reproofs
" because Jahweh would slay them " (1 Sam. ii. 25). Rehoboam arrogantly refused to grant the just demands of his
subjects because Jahweh intended to fulfil his oracle concerning the breach of national unity (1 Kings xii. 15). Zedekiah
did evil because Jahweh sought an occasion to cast off Judah
(2 Kings xxiv. 19–20). It was because Jahweh was angry
with Israel that he stirred up David to take a census, a step
which he proceeded to punish by decimating the people with
a pestilence (2 Sam. xxiv. 1).

It is significant that the later editor of Chronicles, in
reproducing this passage, says that it was Satan who stirred
up David to give the orders for the fatal census (1 Chron.
xxi. 1). The ancient Israelite, on the other hand, had hardly
any place in his beliefs for supernatural beings whose function
was wholly evil, for evil demons like the Satan of the apoc-
alyptic writings and the Gospels. He had no need of them.
The ancient Semite, impressed above all by the inscrutable
nature of the divine will, found no difficulty in believing
that the intervention of the same God might express itself,
now by marks of favour, and now by sinister activities.
Even today there are Arabs who speak of " sins coming from
Allah."[2]

Finally, as the result of all these reservations, the ancient
Israelite, persuaded though he might be that in a general
sense Jahweh desired the welfare of his people and intended
that righteousness should reign in their midst, was never
absolutely certain of the immediate will of his God. There
was always the possibility that someone had sinned—that is,
had displeased Jahweh—unwittingly, with a perfectly clear
conscience. Hence the high importance attached to oracles,
which made it possible to obtain a knowledge of the divine
will, and to ritual as the means of securing, in some measure,
the favour of Jahweh.

[1] Exod. x. 20 ; etc.
[2] *Cf.* **XV**, pp. 288–9 ; **CCV**, p. 51, n. 1.

CHAPTER IV

THE EFFECT OF RELIGION ON LIFE IN ANCIENT ISRAEL

I

THE RELIGIOUS LIFE OF THE NATION

THE great feasts were the occasions when Jahwism, an essentially national religion, lived most consciously and intensely, when the Israelite, mingling with the crowd of pilgrims gathered from all parts of the country to the principal sanctuaries, *felt* the existence of the people of Jahweh and its relation with its God.

Other times of intense religious consciousness were the periods of warfare, and those times of national misfortune when Israel believed that she had incurred the anger of her God. At such times the sense of distress was the more acute by reason of the fact that the Israelites had lost the old conviction that they possessed infallible methods of appeasing the wrath of Jahweh. They might have recourse to sacrifices [1] or make propitiatory offerings to the sanctuary. But such methods were only felt to be efficacious in unimportant matters (1 Sam. iii. 14).

Sometimes they sought to arouse God's compassion by appearing before him in the piteous garb of captives or mourners : they put on sackcloth, cast ashes on their heads and fasted. [2] Or else they appealed to the intercession of a man of God, who was, presumably, a *persona grata* with

---

[1] 2 Sam. xxiv. 17–25 ; *cf.* 1 Sam. xxvi. 19.
[2] Joshua vii. 6 ; Judges xx. 26 ; 1 Sam. vii. 6 ; 1 Kings xxi. 9, 27 ; 2 Kings xix. 1 ; *cf.* Joel i, 14 ; ii. 15 ; Jonah iii. 5 ; Ps. lxix. 11 ; Jer. xxxvi. 9, 24 ; Esther iv. 1–3 ; Ezra x. 6 ; Neh. ix. 1 ; Lev. xvi. 29 ; xxiii. 27 ; Num. xxix. 7 ; 1 Macc. iii. 47 ; and in case of private misfortune, 2 Sam. xii. 16–23 ; Ps. xxxv. 13.

Jahweh.[1] When they succeeded in discovering by means of the oracle the cause of the divine wrath, they lost no time in removing from the midst of Israel the individuals who were the source of the national misfortune.[2] But it might also happen that Jahweh refused to answer,[3] or that, in spite of their efforts, he would not turn away his anger from them. It was the way of wisdom, when the storm of divine wrath raged strongly, to bow before it, letting it take its course without attempting to avert it, without even uttering the name of Jahweh for fear of attracting his attention (Amos. vi. 10), nor venturing to offer a sacrifice until his anger showed signs of abating.[4]

In any case, the first duty of the people or the individual, when Jahweh's anger fell upon them, that is, when some misfortune overtook them, was to make their confession and to humble themselves before their God,[5] even if they were unaware of the reason for his anger.

Moreover, just as the Israelite easily succumbed to despair in the face of adversity, so did his spirits rise swiftly in the sunshine of returning prosperity. Nothing was left in the mind of Israel nor, as they thought, in the heart of God, of the misunderstanding which had disturbed the relations of Jahweh with his people. When his child was sick, David recognized in this misfortune the punishment of his adultery and displayed the deepest grief and humiliation in his attempt to avert the fatal stroke; but as soon as he knew that the child was dead, he ate and drank and went into the sanctuary of Jahweh as if nothing had happened (2 Sam. xii. 15–23): God's anger was assuaged, all was forgotten. Generally speaking, it was the prick of suffering that awakened the sense of guilt, and this disappeared with the suffering that had aroused it.

Hence, one of the characteristic features of the religious life of the nation was hope. During the depressing period which followed the glorious age of David and Solomon, the

---

[1] Exod. xxxii. 30–4 ; 1 Sam. vii. 7–9 ; xii. 18–25 ; cf. Exod. xx. 19 ; xxxii. 11–14 ; Jer. iv. 10, 14, 15, 1 ; etc.
[2] Joshua vii. ; 1 Sam. xiv. 36–45 ; 2 Sam. xxi. 1–9. Cf. Jonah 4–15 ; Deut. xix. 19 ; xxii. 22, 24 ; Judges xx. 13.
[3] 1 Sam. xiv. 37 ; xxviii. 6.
[4] Gen. viii. 20–1 ; 2 Sam. xxiv. 17–25 ; Jonah i. 15–16.
[5] 2 Sam. xv. 23–9.

people confidently awaited " the day of Jahweh " (Amos v. 18–20), that is to say, a golden age when Jahweh would restore to his people their pristine glory. The question has been much discussed recently whether Israel's glowing hopes were not, to some extent, derived from foreign beliefs. Hugo Gressmann has maintained that, from remote antiquity, predictions were widely current throughout the ancient East announcing a cosmic rebirth, preceded by terrible and world-wide catastrophes and followed by the return of the Golden Age of the world's dawn, a return which was as certain as the return of spring after winter. Hence there must have existed long before the eighth century, an elaborate system of Oriental eschatology, similar to that of Judaism or Mazdeism.[1]

But the Egyptian texts appealed [2] to in support of this view are of very doubtful interpretation and the Babylonian evidence is also quite vague ; for instance, the prayer which occurs in a hymn to the fire-god : " Let thy terrible day overtake them." [3] The most definite evidence, so far, con-sists of allusions to the myth of the Golden Age and to the return of the peaceful paradisal state, contained in certain predictions belonging to the Jewish epoch. But we are hardly justified in drawing from texts of so late a date conclusions concerning the beliefs of the Israelites prior to the eighth century.[4]

According to Mowinckel's very plausible hypothesis, on the other hand, Israel's messianic hope is a purely national product : it is the projection into the more remote future of the glorious accession of Jahweh, the renewal of which, from the earliest times of the monarchy, was eagerly awaited at the beginning of each new year, and which was celebrated by the feast of Jahweh's enthronement,[5] with the cry : " Jahweh reigns ! " either in person, or as embodied in his anointed, the human king.

Whatever we may think of these questions of origin, the hope of the restoration of Israel, the germ of the messianic hope, was certainly not the creation of the great prophets of the eighth century, but a living product of the old national

[1] **XXIV.**
[2] **XXIII²**, i, pp. 46–55 ; A. von Gall, βασιλεία τοῦ θεοῦ , 1926, p. 43.
[3] **XXXIV**, i, pp. 305–07.
[4] *Cf.* Th. H. Robinson, **ZATW**, 1927, pp. 3–9.
[5] **LXX**, ii. *Cf.* pp. 506–7.

religion, and which, in so far as it was admitted into the prophetic religion, long remained an alien element there.[1]

II

The Religious Life of the Individual

While the nation might believe that, come what may, Jahweh would never forsake her, the same did not hold good of the individual. The national God was not directly concerned with his protection or his desires. It was the part of the individual, even more than of the people, to cultivate an almost fatalistic resignation [2]; for he could claim no right to escape destruction.

When a mere individual wished to obtain a favour from Jahweh, his wisest course was to avail himself of sacrifices and vows,[3] this being the accepted method of establishing a relation between himself and the God of the community, or else to secure the friendship of one of those men for whom everything seems to succeed, and who are therefore the favourites, the " blessed " of Jahweh.[4]

The comparative indifference of the national God helps to explain why, side by side with Jahwism, all kinds of petty cults and lower forms of worship persisted so long ; for instance, the worship of household idols,[5] seeking after the dead,[6] the use of amulets and talismans. Such practices were especially prevalent among the women,[7] whose relations with the God of Israel were of a very precarious nature.

If the links between Jahweh and the individual were somewhat uncertain during his lifetime, after death they ceased altogether. Although in the pre-exilic period the belief persisted that the dead had a real existence, either in the grave or in Sheol,[8] the ancient Israelite was convinced that Jahweh was no longer interested in them, nor they in Jahweh, even those who in their lifetime had been

---

[1] Already seen by P. Volz (**CCLXXVIII**).
[2] 1 Sam. iii. 18 ; 2 Sam. xv. 23-9.
[3] Gen. xxviii. 20-2 ; 1 Sam. i. 11 ; 2 Sam. xv. 7.
[4] Gen. xxvi. 26-33 ; xxxix. 3-5.
[5] 1 Sam. xix. 13-16 ; Exod. xxi. 6 ; Isa. lvii. 8.
[6] *Cf.* **LVIII**, i, pp. 242-62.
[7] Gen. xxxi. 19, 30, 32, 34, 35 ; 1 Sam. xxviii, 7-25 ; Exod. xxii. 17 ; Isa. iii. 16-23 ; Jer. vii. 18 ; xliv. 15-19 ; Ezek. viii. 15.
[8] See pp. 219-23.

his most faithful servants. In his sickness, Hezekiah made use of this accepted principle as an argument why Jahweh should grant him an extension of life :

> " For the grave cannot praise thee,
>   death cannot celebrate thee :
> they that go down into the pit
>   cannot hope for thy truth.
> The living, the living, he shall praise thee,
>   as I do this day.
> The father to the children
>   shall make known thy truth." [1]

Hence when he thought about his future life after death, or about his relations who were already dead, the ancient Israelite ceased to think and act as a believer in the religion of Jahweh and fell back under the sway of the old cult of the dead [2] : he brought offerings and sacrifices to his dead ancestors, their grave conferred a sacred character upon his land, handed on to him by his fathers, and the dead became for him *elohim*. [3]

However, in the course of the period preceding the eighth century, we can see a growing tendency to extend the range of Jahweh's intervention in the life of the individual. Personal names compounded with Jahweh, which are rare in early times, [4] become common from the time of Elijah and Jonadab. [5] There is a tendency to ascribe to Jahweh all the events, even the most trivial, in daily life, which, according to the mind of the ancient world, signalize the activity of a supernatural power. An unusually deep sleep, especially when it proves fatal, is called " a sleep of Jahweh." [6] When a sudden or violent death overtakes a man, it is Jahweh who has smitten him. [7]

The nature of the speeches which the storytellers put into the mouths of obscure individuals who are all unaware that they are destined to play a part in the history of the

---

[1] Isa. xxxviii. 18–19 ; *cf.* Ps. vi. 6 ; xxx. 10 ; lxxxviii. 6, 11–13 ; cxv. 17.

[2] See pp. 223–30.

[3] 1 Sam. xxviii. 13 ; Isa. viii. 19.

[4] Joshua, Jonathan, Joash, Joab, Joiada.

[5] See, for example, the names of the kings or of those which appear on the ostraca from Samaria (p. 421).

[6] 1 Sam. xxvi. 12 ; *cf.* Gen. ii. 21 ; xv. 12 ; Isa. xxix. 10.

[7] 1 Sam. xxv. 38 ; xxvi. 10 ; *cf.* Exod. xxi. 13 ; code of Hammurabi, § 249 ; Hittite code, § 75.

nation, suggests that simple shepherds, hunters in quest of
game, women longing to become mothers, believed that in
their daily lives Jahweh could protect them, guide them,
and answer their prayers.[1] Occasionally, though rarely,
we meet with generalizations such as the following:

" Who hath made man's mouth ? or who maketh a man dumb or
deaf, or lame,[2] or blind ? is it not I the Lord ? " (Exod. iv. 11).

Jahwism even begins to show some interest in the dead,
in that it opposes the cult of the dead as an offence against
Jahweh who has the sole right to Israel's worship : there is
no reason for doubting that Saul had forbidden the practice
of seeking to the dead,[3] although unsuccessfully.[4] In the
ensuing periods the champions of Jahwism condemned other
practices connected with this cult, and, apparently in order
to facilitate its extermination, declared that the dead were
without strength or knowledge, and that their state was
an almost complete negation of existence.[5] It was not till
very much later, about the second century B.C., that Jahwism,
having destroyed the old animistic belief in survival as a
false and dangerous superstition, actually replaced the con-
solations, gloomy at best, which it offered, by a new hope,
namely, that of a resurrection or immortality accompanied
by judgment after death. Hence Jahwism presents the
phenomenon, somewhat disconcerting to our modern ideas,
of a religion in which the belief in a future life for the individual was long an alien and unwelcome element.

III

THE MORAL LIFE [6]

During the first centuries of the settlement in Palestine,
morality remained much what it had been in nomad times :
an ethic based on the unquestioned solidarity which desert
life imposes on the members of the same clan. However,

[1] 1 Sam. xvii. 37 ; Gen. xxvii. 20 ; 1 Sam. i. 13–27 ; Gen. xxv. 22 ;
etc.
[2] Massoretic Text : " seeing."
[3] 1 Sam. xxviii. 3, 9–13.
[4] Isa. viii. 19 ; 2 Kings xxi. 6 ; Deut. xviii. 11 ; 2 Kings xxiii. 24 ;
Lev. xix. 31 ; xx. 6, 27 ; Isa. lvii. 9 ; lxv. 4 ; cf. LVIII, i, pp. 242–3.
[5] So in Job iii. 13–19 ; xiv. 7–12, 18–22 ; Eccl. ix. 4, 5.
[6] CCLXX, pp. 65–76.

we can trace a characteristic development in the sphere of
morals : as the old tribal organization lost its hold, the rules
of conduct were brought into an increasingly conscious
relation with the national religion ; on the other hand they
lost something of their severity and bore less heavily upon
the individual.

It is always custom which furnishes the *norm* of conduct :
it is necessary to refrain from that which " is not done "
among a people or in a country.[1] On the other hand, the
origin of many Israelite customs and institutions was already
being ascribed to Jahweh. In fact, there is no doubt that
by this time the main purpose of his intervention by means
of his oracles was to interpret or elucidate the custom on
certain points. Occasionally, however, the priests' *torah*
was applied in restraint of certain customs which were foreign
to the spirit of Jahwism, such as the blood-feud (Exod. xxi. 13)
and the levirate,[2] institutions connected with ancestor-
worship.

Among the motives which induced the Israelite to order
his daily life in conformity with the rule of law must be
mentioned the ingrained respect for custom which carried
its own sanction, to say nothing of the fear of the vengeance
or the curse of the injured party.[3] The simple statement :
" it is not so done in Israel," or " it would be an infamy
in Israel," [4] contained a motive of sufficient strength to prevent
the commission of such an act.

This very respect for custom sprang from the feeling of
the close tie which united the members of a clan, a feeling
which was another extremely potent support of morality
in ancient Israel. This, too, was a heritage from nomad
times ; Jahwism had merely extended this sense of unity
to all the members of the nation. The patriotism of the
Israelite was hardly less spontaneous than his love for his
family. The biblical writers do not often speak of it, simply
because it seemed perfectly natural, but there are several

---

[1] Gen. xx. 9 ; xxix. 26.

[2] One can follow the progress of the limitation of this right :
Gen. xxxviii. ; Deut. xxv. 5–10 ; Ruth ; Lev. xviii. 16 ; xx. 21 ;
Num. xxvii. 1–11 ; xxxvi. *Cf.* LVIII, ii, pp. 75–6.

[3] Gen. xxvii. 12 ; xxxi. 21 ; xxxiv. 30 ; Judges xvii. 2.

[4] Gen. xxxiv. 7 ; 2 Sam. xiii. 12 ; *cf.* Deut. xxii. 21 ; Judges xx. 6,
10 ; Jer. xxix. 23.

examples of the delicacy of moral feeling and occasionally
of the heroism to which this sense of national solidarity gave
birth. Uriah declines to enjoy the comforts of civilian life
while Israel and Judah were enduring the hardships of a
campaign (2 Sam. ii. 8–11); Moses asks that he may be
blotted out of Jahweh's book rather than suffer his fate to
be severed from that of his guilty people.[1]

To these motives which were not purely religious, must
be added the fear of God. In the mind of the Israelite,
this was the chief source of morality : where there was no
fear of God any kind of crime might be expected (Gen. xx. 11).
Joseph declares that he will not slay his brothers on a mere
suspicion, and adds : " for I fear God " (Gen. xlii. 18).
In general, fear of God implied fear of the divine judgment.
Strenuously as the relation between religion and morality
might be affirmed, it was still mainly an external relation,
similar to that which existed in all the religions which had
attained some stage of development, and which certainly
obtained among the Hebrew tribes before the rise of Jahwism :
for instance, in the case of the punishment of murder, it is
evident that Jahweh has been associated with, and then
has replaced, the spirit of the murdered man which originally
itself undertook to punish the living if they neglected their
duty of exacting vengeance.[2] The main purpose of divine
intervention was to provide protection and sanction for
national custom.

Sometimes, however, though seldom, the duties of individuals towards one another were brought into a more
vital relation with the religion of Jahweh, as when the sons
of Jacob say to their brother Joseph : " Forgive the sin of
the servants of the God of thy father " (Gen. l. 17), or when the
author of the ancient poem of Deborah curses some of the
Israelite warriors for not having " *come to the help of Jarweh*
among the mighty " (Judges v. 23).

It was especially in the realm of *sanctions* that the link
between religion and morality found a place. Nor is this
difficult to understand : Jahweh, the God of Israel, compels
individuals to observe the law because the maintenance of

---

[1] Exod. xxxii. 10, 32.
[2] 2 Sam. xxi. 1–14 ; Gen. iv. 10 ; xxxvii. 26 ; Job xvi. 18 ;
xxiv. 12 ; Ezek. xxiv. 7–8 ; Isa. xxvi 21 ; Deut. xxi. 1–9 ; etc.

order is one of the basic necessities of national life. Hence he rewards those who love justice and foster national unity.[1] Above all, he punishes, with temporal penalties, of course, those who violate the national custom. " He rewards the wicked according to his wickedness," " he rendereth to every man according to his works." [2] An injured wife can appeal against her husband to the judgment of Jahweh : " Let Jahweh judge between me and thee." [3] He protects a slave like Hagar ; he will smite his people if they deal harshly with the sojourner, the widow or the orphan [4] ; he brings back the banished.[5]

However, as we have shown in speaking of the anger of Jahweh, this avenging function of the national God was regarded as subject to various failures, changes and restrictions. Hence the individual, in order to ensure that the wrongs suffered or apprehended by him should be punished, still frequently resorted to very ancient practices which were magical in essence. When the person who had committed a theft could not be discovered, the injured party uttered against the thief and those who were sheltering him a curse whose effects were greatly dreaded.[6] Or else the suspected person was compelled to pronounce against himself a curse which was fatal to the perjurer.[7] The formula took effect by virtue of its own inherent power, whether Jahweh were appealed to or not to guarantee its efficaciousness (Judges ix. 57[b]).

In other cases the Israelite might depend for the punishment of a crime, upon other supernatural agencies than the national God : on the Earth, for instance, as in the case of Cain.[8] The sin itself is sometimes thought of as a baleful power which " lays hold of " the guilty person.[9] Such ideas and practices were survivals from pre-Mosaic times.

Within the sphere of operation of sanctions it is easy to discern the degree to which the interests of the individual

[1] So Gen. xviii. ; xix. ; Exod. i. 21.
[2] 1 Sam. xxvi. 23 ; 2 Sam. iii. 39.
[3] Gen. xvi. 5 ; cf. 1 Sam. ii. 25.
[4] Exod. xxii. 20–3.   [5] 2 Sam. xiv. 14.
[6] Judges xvii. 2 ; cf. Prov. xxix. 24 ; Lev. v. 1 ; Zech. v. 3–4.
[7] So 1 Kings viii. 31, 32 ; Num. v. 11–31.
[8] Gen. iv. 11–12.
[9] Ps. xl. 13. Cf. Johs. Pedersen, *Israel, its Life and Culture*, London, Milford, 1926, pp. 432–3, 441 ff.

were still subordinated to those of the community. It was generally agreed that, in the execution of vengeance or of justice,[1] especially of divine justice, the children of a guilty person, the other members of his family, his fellow-citizens or his subjects, should be punished with, or instead of him.[2]

It may, however, be pointed out that the civil legislation of the so-called " Book of the Covenant " (probably belonging to the ninth century) never prescribes collective or substitutionary penalties, a fact which is the more significant in that the Code of Hammurabi allows such penalties in exceptional cases (§ 210), and the Deuteronomist himself prescribes the collective punishment of those guilty of the crime of religious apostasy (Deut. xiii. 13–19). The book of Kings is careful to point out that when Joash was assassinated (about 797), the sons of the regicides were not put to death with their fathers, which suggests, moreover, that this mitigation of ancient custom must have been an innovation at that time.[3] Hence the mind of the Israelite was beginning to admit, at least in the realm of human justice, the principle of individual responsibility, while Ezekiel, in the sixth century, reached the point of announcing that this principle was also the sole standard of divine justice.[4]

Moral ideals were also advancing. The type held up for admiration is no longer the warrior eager for the prey,[5] jealous of his honour,[6] avenging himself seventy and seven fold.[7] The later writers praise the generosity of Abraham towards his nephew Lot, the magnanimity of Joseph to his brethren, David's chivalrous treatment of Saul (1 Sam. xxiv. 26). Whereas the ancient poet exalts Jael, the slayer of a conquered foe who had sought shelter in her tent, above all women, the Israelite rulers of the ninth century pride themselves on being " merciful kings," generous toward a defeated enemy.[8] It was admitted in the ninth century, that it was contrary to the principles of justice to slay prisoners of war,[9]

[1] For example, 2 Sam. iii. 29 ; xxi. 1–9.
[2] See pp. 468–9.　　　　　[3] 2 Kings xiv. 5–6.
[4] Ezek. xviii., xxxiii.
[5] Gen. xlix. 17, 27 ; Judges xvii.–xviii.
[6] Judges viii. 21 ; ix. 54.
[7] Gen. iv. 24 ; Judges viii. 18–21.
[8] 1 Kings xx. 31 ; *cf.* v. 32–43.
[9] 2 Kings vi. 21–23.

whereas in earlier times they might be mutilated, massacred, and even offered up as sacrifices, without scruple.[1]

Hence we can see that in every department of human activity, although some dark places remained, there was a remarkable advance in moral conceptions. In a marked degree the national religion became increasingly permeated with morality, and morality was more and more identified with the national religion.

IV

THE FIRST ATTEMPTS AT RELIGIOUS SPECULATION

In the course of human history man's earliest attempts to explain the origin of the most striking facts of life have always taken the form of myth. Where we endeavour to explain phenomena by the method of scientific hypothesis or abstract thought, primitive peoples explain them by the dramatic method of a concrete episode which took place at the beginning and in which the actors are usually gods, ancestors, divine animals and magical plants, that is to say, beings and things which are the product of an age of animism and the belief in magic. These stories are then handed on to more enlightened ages, which regard them as literal history, preserve them with reverence, and attempt to interpret them by means of such expansions or abbreviations as will enable them to fit into their new conceptions of the world and of the gods.

It was in such myths that the wisdom of the Babylonians and the Egyptians, the chief exponents of the science of the ancient East, found expression. Nor did the Israelites escape this tendency. Their first attempts at a philosophy of religion, if we may use so modern a term to describe the naïve traditions which the J portions of the first eleven chapters of Genesis have preserved for us, are expressed in the form of ancient myths, transformed and adapted to the religion of Jahweh. This section of Genesis consists of a series of stories originally independent of one another, each of which constitutes a unity, and is intended to explain a group of facts.

The series begins with a story of the beginnings of the

[1] Judges i. 6 ; 2 Sam. viii. 2 ; xii. 31 ; 1 Sam. xv 32–3.

world (Gen. ii. 4^b–24) which differs widely from the better
known account which now constitutes the first chapter of
Genesis, and in which a priestly editor of the exilic period
relates the orderly creation of the world in six days.   In
the Jahwist version, the creative acts are connected by a
thread of much more primitive logic.   In the beginning
there were no plants because there was no rain to water the
earth nor men to till it.   Hence Jahweh began by causing
a spring (or a mist) to come up ; then he made man, and not
till then did he create trees.   After man and plants, Jahweh
brought animals into existence with the definite purpose of
providing man with " a help meet for him."   When Jahweh
perceives by the names which Adam gives to the animals
that none of them fulfils the intended purpose, he finally
fashions woman out of a rib taken from the man.

This ancient story with its significant simplicity cannot
have originated among the nomad Hebrews, since it represents man as having been destined from the beginning to be
a tiller of the soil.   The problem of the origin of things can
only have forced itself upon the attention of the Israelites
after they came into contact with the more advanced civilization of Canaan ; we can see in the story to which we have
referred, that they were still unable to grasp the real extent
of the problem : the narrator is only concerned with the
origin of the things or beings which people the petty world
of the peasant : the cultivator himself and his fields, plants
suitable for cultivation, rain, domestic animals.   The story
has affinities with several of the very various cosmogonies
which were current among the Babylonians and the Egyptians.   Many of them, for instance, begin with an enumera-
tion of the things which did not yet exist in the beginning.
It was also a widely distributed idea that man was made
from the mixture of a little earth with some divine element,
the breath, blood,[1] or tears [2] of a god.   However, up to the
present, there has not been found among the records of the
ancient East, a narrative exactly parallel to the Hebrew
story.   It would appear that the Jahwist narrative, if it
is of foreign origin, must, nevertheless, have received a
strong Palestinian colouring, either among the Israelites,

---

[1] The Babylonian poem *enuma eliš*, vi, 5 *ff*.
[2] " The Book of Apophis," 27, 2–3 (**XXIII**[2], i, pp. 1–3).

or among the Canaanites before them. On the one hand, the Babylonians, followed by the priestly editor of the first chapter of Genesis, represent the primæval chaos as a vast expanse of water, after the pattern of lower Mesopotamia at the time when the rivers are in flood; the Jahwist historian, on the contrary, conceives of it as an arid desert: in Palestine and Syria, the scorching summer is the bad season, and the rain is the beneficent element, causing life to spring up everywhere.

Although it may have been originally distinct, the story of Paradise lost is closely connected with the Jahwist version of the Creation.[1] In order to understand the original point of view of those who first told or listened to the story, it is necessary to clear away the gloomy and grandiose theories which Jewish and Christian theologians have erected around it, making it the corner stone of their soteriological systems. What the ancient Israelites looked for in stories such as this was the explanation of the facts which emerge at the conclusion of the story; in this case the conclusion consists of the sentences pronounced by God upon each of the guilty parties. They asked why man should be compelled to wrest his daily bread from a reluctant earth until he died; or why the woman must suffer the pangs of childbirth and be subject to the man. These disabilities were the more irksome in that they contrasted so strongly with the divine power which man possessed of distinguishing good from evil, that is, with the faculty of discrimination.[2] It is not a question here, as is often thought, and as Budde, for example, maintains, of the faculty of distinguishing good and evil *in the moral sense*; for it is clear that, in the mind of the narrator, the man and the woman already knew *before they ate the fruit of the tree*, that in disobeying they were doing evil. What they gained was intelligence, reason. Hence the problem

---

[1] The interpretation of this story has recently given rise to many fresh controversies among the commentators: see, *e.g.* that of Brunner with Köhler (**KRS**, 1926, Nos. 27, 29, 31, 32, 36) and Gressman (**CW**, 1926, No. 21) and the criticism of K. Budde (**CW**, 1927, No. 1), or the theory of Obbink (**LXXVI**, pp. 25–8; **ZATW**, 1928, pp. 105–12), approved by Ungnad (**ZATW**, 1929, p. 62) and Stärk (**RHP**, 1928, pp. 66–9) and criticized by K. Budde (**ZATW**, 1929, pp. 54–62). See also the daring hypothesis of R. Eisler (*Monde Oriental*, 1929, pp. 48–112).

[2] *Cf.* 2 Sam. xix. 36; Isā. vii. 16; Deut. i. 39.

was to explain this mingled greatness and wretchedness of which man's life consists.

The answer was, that man acquired intelligence by disobedience, against the will of God, who did not intend that a creature made of clay should be equal to the *elohim*. Formerly, man lived a life of happiness in the garden of God, but only possessed the intelligence of a child ; now, however, that he had become " as an *elohim* " in intelligence, it was necessary that he should be deprived of happiness, according to the earliest form of the tradition ; that he should be shut off from the tree of life : since, if he had acquired immortality in addition to intelligence, he would have become wholly an *elohim*.[1] But this might not be : to the Israelite it was fitting that Jahweh should resist all the attempts of human pride to encroach on the divine prerogatives.[2]

This story is probably not of purely Hebraic origin, any more than that of the Creation ; nomads would not have depicted man as condemned to till the ground. Neither is the gloomy conception of life which underlies this tradition in keeping with the general outlook of ancient Israel which was essentially optimistic. On the other hand, the central idea of the story was familiar to the Babylonians : it resembles several of their myths : that of Adapa, for instance, the wise man who, deceived by a god, refuses the food and drink of immortality offered to him by another god ; then there is the myth of Etana who ascends to heaven on an eagle in

[1] Gen. iii. 22. We cannot believe, with Budde, that this verse is a later addition—the idea which it expresses is much more archaic and more logical than the point of view of the main body of the narrative,—nor, with Obbink, that it is perfectly in keeping with the whole story of Paradise : according to this commentator, the only tree forbidden to the first man was the tree of knowledge ; he was free to eat of the tree of life, and partook of it until the Fall ; after man's disobedience, Jahweh wished to deprive him of this food, which ensured an endless life with the gods. As Budde has shown, this interpretation is excluded by the whole tenor of the verse : " Behold the man is become as one of us, to know good and evil. And now, lest he put forth his hand and take also of the tree of life, and eat and live for ever." What Jahweh was concerned to prevent was a fresh attempt on man's part, an act which would at once secure for him eternal life, just as the eating of the fruit of the other tree had given him knowledge, once and for ever.

[2] See the account of the Tower of Babel (Gen. xi. 1–9) or Isa. ii. 9–22.

order to procure from Ishtar the plant that causes child-bearing, but falls as he is on the point of succeeding; or again, the myth of Gilgamish, who, after having endured unimaginable hardships to win the herb of immortality, was robbed of it by a serpent. It has even been supposed that a Babylonian seal depicts the scene of the temptation of Adam and Eve by the serpent; but this interpretation is improbable; the two individuals represented are clothed, and one of them wears the horned cap characteristic of the gods.[1] It is also doubtful whether, in the Sumerian poem published by Professor Langdon, we are dealing with the story of an ancestor of mankind who draws down all kinds of ills upon his descendants by eating of a forbidden plant, in a garden which he was set to cultivate.[2] It is none the less true that the garden of the gods, the tree of life, the guardian *kerubim* are frequently met with in Babylonian mythology.

On the other hand, the distinctive contribution of the Israelite narrators seems to be the significant and delicate conciseness, of the description of the gradual stages of the disobedience from the moment of the woman's succumbing to the tempter up to the excuses with which the guilty pair endeavour to throw the blame upon each other. The stress laid upon the moral aspect of the story foreshadows and, one might almost say, justifies the dogmatic interpretation which sees nothing in the story but the original sin of our primordial ancestors, the most disastrous event in human history : namely, the Fall, by which death came into the world. Whereas, for the ancient historian, the sin is introduced merely as an explanation, not as a thing to be explained, and death, that is, the return to the earth, is the natural end of a being who sprang from the earth.

The rest of the Jahwist story of the origins of the race need only be touched on lightly.

The story of the slaying of Abel was originally a short ethnographic tale explaining why the Kenites led the detested life of nomads.[3] The story assumed a symbolic value because Cain was identified with the son of the first man, and the

---

[1] *Cf.* for example, **XXXVII**, pp. 104–06 and fig. 36.

[2] See the criticisms of Prince and M. Jastrow in America, Fossey and P. Dhorme in France : bibliography in **CCLXXIII**, pp. 40–1 ; P. Dhorme, **RB**, 1921, pp. 309–11.

[3] See pp. 324–5.

historian, with the psychological insight characteristic of the
Israelite story-tellers, drew the unforgettable picture of the
erstwhile callous slayer fleeing in terror before the voice
of God.

Then follow two genealogies of the descendants of Adam,
one through Cain and the other through Seth, belonging to
two parallel Jahwist recensions, and consisting mainly of the
same names. Attached to these lists, which are certainly
related to the Babylonian list of the ten antediluvian kings,
we find a number of fragments of legends and myths, especially
the remains of a story of human inventions, similar to those
which are found among the Phenicians and the Greeks.

The strange episode of the " sons of the *elohim*," that is,
divine beings, who took to themselves wives of the daughters
of men and begot giants, affords clear proof that mythology
had taken root among the Israelites.

The deluge tradition is evidently of Babylonian origin :
in the epic of Gilgamish we possess the prototype of the two
Hebrew versions which have been fused in the narrative of
Genesis, and we can observe the transformations which the
Babylonian story has undergone in the hands of the Israelite
narrators with the purpose of purging it from its crude polytheism and emphasizing its moral lessons. It is probable
that this tradition was not taken over by the Israelites until
a fairly late date, possibly in the eighth or seventh century,
during the principal period of contact with the Assyrians, for
it seems to have been absent from the two earliest versions of
the Jahwist recension. One of these regards the three sons
of Lamech as the ancestors of the present divisions of mankind (Gen. iv. 20–2), while the other seems to regard the
invention of wine as the outstanding incident in the life of
Noah (Gen. v. 29).

The episode of the curse pronounced by Noah on Canaan,
his undutiful son, is at the same time an explanatory patriarchal narrative giving the reasons for the subjection of the
Canaanites to the Hebrews and probably to the Philistines,
and also a link in the chain of the history of civilization :
Noah discovers the art of planting vines and making wine.

The table of races (Gen. x.) represents a quasi-scientific
attempt on the part of the Israelite historian to enumerate
and classify the nations who at that time constituted the

Israelite's universe : it is the first attempt to define and extend the idea of the " world."

The story of the city of Babel built by mankind " to make themselves a name," or of the tower which they erected in order that they might not be scattered (there are two variant forms of the story fused into the narrative as we have it), is an etiological story whose principal purpose is to explain the diversity of tongues and the distribution of mankind in the earth.   The underlying motive is the same as that which we have already observed in the story of paradise : if mankind had remained united they would have scaled heaven and overpowered Jahweh himself.   It is clear that the story is not, as has been maintained, of Babylonian origin : a Babylonian would never have explained the glorious name of his city, which means " the gate of God " or " of the gods," by a contemptuous pun on the Hebrew word *balal*, which means " to confound."   This tradition reflects the impression made upon the minds of the Ishmaelite or Midianite camel-drivers by the great cities of the lower Euphrates, with their cosmopolitan markets, and the colossal stepped towers, generally in ruins, of their brick temples.

To sum up, from the pages in which the Jahwistic writers have collected the beliefs of ancient Israel concerning the beginnings of the world and of human history, we learn that Israel received its problems and the myths in which they sought their solution mainly from outside, and especially from Babylon, but that Israel completely transformed these myths and traditions and adapted them to the spirit of the national religion.   This assimilation of elements borrowed from the wisdom of alien nations is the strongest possible proof of the lofty conception of the power of their God which the Israelites already possessed : they did not hesitate to claim for him the creation of the world and the shaping of man's destiny from the beginning.

On the other hand, there is evidence that these speculations remained for many centuries without any real influence upon the religious life of the nation.   For instance, the idea of creation only began to assume an important place in the thought of Israel with 2 Isaiah (sixth century).   The far-reaching effect of the story of the lost paradise was not felt until later still, in the Wisdom of Solomon, the writings of the Apostle Paul, and 4 Esdras. In the national period of Jahwism these realms of thought were too recent an acquisition to have been properly assimilated by the national religion.

Hence, the great advances in religion were not due to these attempts at speculation, interesting as they are, but to the deep-seated protest against the narrowness and poverty of a purely national religion—a protest which led the prophets of the eighth century to discover the one God and, more important still, the God of absolute righteousness, and thus to lay the foundation, for the first time in the world's history, of a universal religion.

BIBLIOGRAPHY

PERIODICALS, DICTIONARIES, AND COLLECTIONS

Abhandlungen der koen pr. Akad. der Wiss. (Phil-hist. Klasse) . . . . **AAW**

Académie des Inscriptions et Belles-Lettres, comptes rendus des séances . . . . **AI**

The American Journal of Semitic Languages and Literatures . . . . **AJSL**

Anneé sociologique . . . . **AS**

Anthropologie . . . . **An**

Archœologischer Anzeiger . . . . . . **AA**

Archiv fur Religionswissenschaft . . . . **AR**

Bulletin de correspondance hellénique . . . **BCH**

Bulletin de l'Inst. fr. arch. du Caire. . . . **BIA**

Christliche Welt . . . . **CW**

Corpus inscriptionum latinarum . . . . **CIL**

Corpus inscriptionum semiticarum . . . . **CIS**

Encyclopœdia of Religion and Ethics . . . **ERE**

The Expositor . . . . **EX**

Expository Times . . . . **ET**

The Harvard Theological Review . . . . **HTR**

Jahrbuch des kaiserlich deutschen Archœol. Instituts . **JAI**

Journal of the American Oriental Society . . . **JAOS**

Journàl Asiatique . . . . **JA**

The Journal of Egyptian Archœology, Londres . . **JEA**

Journal of the Palestine Oriental Society . . . **JPOS**

The Journal of Philology . . . . . . **JPh**

Journal de Psychologie, Paris, Alcan . . . **JP**

Journal of theologic. Studies . . . . . **JTS**

Kirchenblatt f. d. ref. Schweiz. . . . . . **KRS**

Klio . . . . **Kl**

Kurzer Hand-Commentar zum Alten Testament (Marti) **KHC**

Mélanges de la Faculté orientale de Beyrouth . . **MOB**

Mémoires de la Société des Antiquaires de France . **MAF**

Mitteilungen der Deutschen Orient-Gesellschaft 1898 ff. . . **MDOG**

Mittheilungen und Nachrichten des deutschen Palœstina-Vereins . . . . **MN**

490 BIBLIOGRAPHY

Museum Journal, Philadelphia . . . . **MJ**
Nachrichten der K. Ges. der Wiss. zu Goettingen (Phil-hist. Klasse) . . . . **NGG**
Neue Kirchliche Zeitschrift, Erlangen-Leipzig, Deichert **NKZ**
Nieuw Theologisch Tijdschrift . . . . . **NTT**
Oesterreichische Monatschrift für den Orient . . **OMO**
Orientalistische Literaturzeitung . . . . **OLZ**
Palestine Exploration Fund . . . . . **PEF**
Palestine Exploration Fund, Quarterly Statement . **PEF, QS**
Migne's Greek Patrology . . . . . . **PG**
Proceedings of the Society of Biblical Archæology . **PSBA**
Real-Encyklopædie für prot. Theologie und Kirche (Herzog-Plitt) . . . . **HRE**
Die Religion in Geschichte und Gegenwart, Tübingen, Mohr . . . . **RGG**
Revue d'Assyriologie . . . . . . **RA**
Revue Biblique, Paris, Gabalda . . . . **RB**
Revue de l'Égypte ancienne . . . . . **REA**
Revue des Études juives . . . . . . **REJ**
Revue d'Histoire et de Philosophie religieuses, Strasbourg-Paris, Alcan . . . . **RHP**
Revue de l'Histoire des Religions . . . . **RHR**
Revue historique . . . . **RH**
Revue de théologie, Montauban . . . . **RT**
Revue de théologie et de philosophie, Lausanne . . **RTP**
Sitzungsberichte der Berliner Akademie . . . **SBA**
Syria, revue d'art oriental et d'archéologie, Paris, Geuthner **SY**
Tell el-Amarna, ed. J.A. KNUDTZON (See **CXXXIII**). **TA(K)**
Tell el-Amarna (die Thontafeln von), ed. HUGO WINCKLER (**XLII, V**), 1896 . . . . **TA(W)**
Theologische Literaturzeitung . . . . . **TL**
Theologische Studien und Kritiken . . . . **TSK**
Zeitschrift für ægyptische Sprache und Altertumskunde, Leipzig . . . . **ZAS**
Zeitschrift für die alttestamentliche Wissenschaft, Giessen, Toepelmann. . . . . **ZATW**
Zeitschrift der Deutschen Morgenlaendischen Gesellschaft, Leipzig, Brockhaus . . . . . . **ZDMG**
Zeitschrift des Deutschen Palaestina-Vereins, Leipzig, Bædeker . . . . **ZDPV**
Zeitschrift für Ethnologie . . . . . **ZE**
Zeitschrift für Assyriologie . . . . . **ZA**

GENERAL WORKS

KARL BAEDEKER, *Palestine et Syrie*, Leipzig, 2 edit., 1893, ; 4 edit., 1912 . . . . . . **I**

BIBLIOGRAPHY 491

Bruno Baentsch, *Numeri* (Handkom. z. A.T.), Goettingen, Vandenhoeck and Ruprecht, 1903 . . II

I. Benzinger, *Hebræische Archæologie*, 3 edit., Leipzig, Pfeiffer, 1927 III

Alfred Bertholet, *Histoire de la civilisation d'Israel*, french translation by Jacques Marty, Paris, Payot, 1929 IV

Alfred Bertholet, *Kulturgeschichte Israëls*, Goettingen, Vandenhoeck and Ruprecht, 1920 . . V

La sainte Bible, traduction nouvelle d'apres les meilleurs textes, avec introduction et notes (Bible du Centenaire), Paris, Société biblique de Paris, 1916 et suiv VI

J. H. Breasted, *Ancient Records of Egypt*, Chicago, Univ. Press, 5 vols., 1906–1907 VII

J. H. Breasted, *Geschichte Ægyptens*, transl. Ranke, 2 edit., 1911 VIII

Karl Budde, *Das Buch der Richter* (Kurzer Hand-Comm. z. A.T.), Fribourg, Mohr, 1897 . . . IX

Karl Budde, *Die altisraelitische Religion*, 3 edit., Giessen, Toepelmann, 1912 X

Karl Budde, *Geschichte der althebraeischen Litteratur*, Leipzig, Amelang, 1906 XI

C. F. Burney, *The Book of Judges*, 2 edit., London, Rivingtons, 1920 XII

Stanley Arthur Cook, *The Cambridge Ancient History*, Cambridge Univ. Press, vol. ii, 1924 . . . XIII

Samuel Ives Curtiss, *Primitive Semitic Religion To-day*, London, 1902 XIV

S. I. Curtiss, id., translated into German by Stocks, *Ursemitische Religion im Volksleben des heutigen Orients*, Leipzig, Hinrichs, 1903 XV

L. Desnoyers, *Histoire du peuple hebreu des Juges a la Captivité*, i, Paris, Desclée et Picard, 1922 ; ii et iii, Picard, 1930 XVI

René Dussaud, *Introduction à l'histoire des religions*, Paris, Leroux, 1914 XVII

R. Dussaud, *Le sacrifice en Israël et chez les Phéniciens*, Paris, Leroux, 1914 XVIII

R. Dussaud, id., 2 edit., *Les origines cananéennes du sacrifice israélite*, Paris, Leroux, 1921 . . . XIX

R. Dussaud, *Topographie historique de la Syrie antique et médiévale*, Paris, Geuthner, 1927 . . . XX

Adolf Erman, *Die aegyptische Religion*, Berlin, Reimer, 1905 XXI

Heinrich Ewald, *Geschichte des Volkes Israel*, i, 3 edit., Goettingen, Dieterick, 186 XXII

Gressmann, Ungnad, Ranke, Ebeling et Rhodokanakis, *Altorientalische Texte und Bilder zum Alten Testament*, 2 vols., Tübingen, Mohr, 1 edit., 1909 ; 2 edit., 1926–7 XXIII

HUGO GRESSMANN, *Der Ursprung der israelitisch-jüdischen Eschatologie*, 1905 XXIV

H. GRESSMAN, HERMAN GUNKEL, MAX HALLER, HANS SCHMIDT, WILLY STAERK, PAUL VOLZ, *Die Schriften des Alten Testaments in Auswahl uebersetzt*, Goettingen, Vandenhoeck and Ruprecht, 1 edit., 1910 . XXV

HERMANN GUNKEL, *Genesis, Handkommentar zum Alten Testament*, 3 edit., Goettingen, Vandenhoeck and Ruprecht, 1910 XXVI

HERMANN GUTHE, *Geshichte des Volkes Israel*, 3 edit., Tübingen, Mohr, 1914 XXVII

JOSEPH HALÉVY, *Mélanges de critique et d'histoire*, Paris, Maisonneuve, 1883 XXVIII

J. HALÉVY, *Mélanges d'épigraphie et d'archéologie sémitiques*, Imp. Nat., 1874 XXIX

GUSTAV HOELSCHER, *Die Profeten, Untersuchung zur Religions-geschichte Israels*, Leipzig, Hinrichs, 1914. XXX

FRITZ HOMMEL, *Altisraelitische Ueberlieferung*, Munich, Franz, 1897. XXXI

FRITZ HOMMEL, *Grundriss der Geographie und Geschichte des alten Orients*, ii, Munich, Beck, 1926 . XXXII

FRÉDÉRIC HROZNY, *Code hittite provenant de l'Asie Mineure* (vers 1350 av. J.C.) Paris, Geuthner, 1922 XXXIII

MORRIS JASTROW, jr., *Die Religion Babyloniens und Assyriens*, Giessen, Toepelmann, 1912 . . . XXXIV

CHARLES F. JEAN, *La littérature des Babyloniens et des Assyriens*, Paris, Geuthner, 1924 XXXV

C. F. JEAN, *Le milieu biblique avant Jésus-Christ*, Paris, Geuthner, 1 vol., 1922 ; 2, 1923 . . . XXXVI

ALFRED JEREMIAS, *Das Alte Testament im Lichte des alten Orients*, Leipzig, Hinrichs, 1904 . . . XXXVII

ANTON JIRKU, *Altorientalischer Kommentar zum Alten Testament* XXXVIII

EMIL KAUTZSCH, *Biblische Theologie des Alten Testaments*, Tübingen, Mohr, 1911 XXXIX

E. KAUTZSCH, *Die Heilige Schrift des Alten Testaments*, Tübingen, Mohr, 4 edit., 1922 XL

KEIL et DELITZSCH, *Bibl. Comment. über das A.T.*, Leipzig, Doerffling-Franke, 1861 ss. XLI

Keilinschriftliche Bibliotek, Berlin, Reuther and Reichard XLII

RUDOLF KITTEL, *Die alttestamentliche Wissenschaft in ihren wichtigsten Ergebnissen*, 2 edit., Leipzig, Quelle and Meyer, 1912 XLIII

R. KITTEL, *Geschichte der Hebraer*, 1888, 1892 . . XLIV

R. KITTEL, *Geschichte des Volkes Israel*, Gotha, Perthes, 6 edit., vol. ii, 1925 XLV

R. KITTEL, *Studien zur hebraeischen Archœologie und Religions-geschichte*, Leipzig, Hinrichs, 1908 . . XLVI

RICHARD KREGLINGER, *La religion d'Israël*, Bruxelles, Lamertin, 1 edit., 1922 ; 2 edit., 1926 . . . XLVII

BIBLIOGRAPHY 493

P. Marie-Joseph Lagrange, *Le livre des Juges*, Paris, Gabalda, 1903 . . . . **XLVIII**

M.-J. Lagrange, *Études sur les religions sémitiques*, 2 edit., Paris, Lecoffre, 1905 . . . . **XLIX**

C. F. Lehmann Haupt, *Israel, seine Entwicklung im Rahmen der Weltgeschichte*, Tübingen, Mohr, 1911 . **L**

Louis-Germain Lévy, *La famille dans l'antiquité israélite*, Paris, Alcan, 1905 . . . . . . **LI**

Lucien Lévy-Bruhl, *La mentalité primitive*, Paris, Alcan, 1922 . . . . **LII**

Lexa, *La magie dans l'Égypte antique*, 3 vols., Paris, Geuthner, 1925 . . . . **LIII**

Mark Lidzbarski, *Ephemeris für semitische Epigraphik*, Giessen, Ricker, i, 1902 . . . . . **LIV**

M. Lidzbarski, *Handbuch der nordsemitischen Epigraphik*, Weimar, Felber, 1898 . . . . **LV**

Adolphe Lods, *Les idées des Israélites sur la maladie, ses causes et ses remédes* (*vom A.T., Karl Marti . . . gewidmet*), Giessen, Toepelmann, 1925, pp. 181-93 . **LVI**

Ad. Lods, *Quelques remarques sur l'histoire de Samson* (Actes du congrès internat. d'hist. des religions tenu à Paris en Oct. 1923), Paris, Champion, i, pp. 504-16 . . . . **LVII**

Ad. Lods, *La croyance à la vie future et le culte des morts dans l'antiquité israélite*, 2 vols., Paris, Fischbacher, 1906 . . . . **LVIII**

Alfred Loisy, *Essai historique sur le sacrifice*, Paris, Nourry, 1920. . . . . **LIX**

A. Loisy, *La religion d'Israél*, 2 edit., Ceffonds, 1908 **LX**

Alexis Mallon, *Les Hébreux en Égypte* (*Orientalia*, num. 3) Rome, Inst. bibl. pontif., 1921 . . **LXI**

Karl Marti, *Geschichte der israelitischen Religion*, 5 edit., Strasbourg, Bull, 1907. . . . . **LXII**

Gaston Maspero, *Histoire ancienne des peuples de l'Orient classique*, Paris, Hachette, 1897 . . **LXIII**

G. Maspero, *Les contes populaires de l'Égypte ancienne*, Paris, Maisonneuve . . . . . **LXIV**

Eduard Meyer, *Geschichte des Altertums*, 3 edit., Stuttgart, Cotta, 1913 ss. . . . . . . **LXV**

Edouard Montet, *Histoire du peuple d'Israel*, Paris, Payot, 1926 . . . . . . **LXVI**

George F. Moore, *A Critical and Exegetical Commentary on Judges*, 2 edit., Edinburgh, Clark, 1898 . **LXVII**

A. Moret et G. Davy, *Des Clans aux Empires* (*L'Evolution de l'humanité*, no. 6), Paris, Renaissance du Livre, 1923 . . . . **LXVIII**

A. Moret, *Le Nil et la civilisation égyptienne* (*L'Evolution de l'humanité*, no. 7), Paris, Renaissance du Livre, 1926 . . . . **LXIX**

494   BIBLIOGRAPHY

SIGMUND MOWINCKEL, *Psalmenstudien*, 6 vols., Kristiania, Dybwad, 1921–4 LXX

W. MAX MULLER, *Asien und Europa nach altaegyptischen Denkmaelern*, 1893 LXXI

ALOYS MUSIL, *Arabia Petraea*, Vienna, Hoelder, 1908   LXXII

TH. NOELDEKE, *Die alttestamentliche Litteratur*, Leipzig, Quandt, 1868 LXXIII

WILHELM NOWACK, *Lehrbuch der hebraeischen Archæologie*, 2 vols., Fribourg, Mohr, 1894 . . LXXIV

W. NOWACK, *Richter, Ruth* (Handk. z. A.T.), Goettingen, Vandenhoeck and Ruprecht, 1900 . . . LXXV

Old Testament Essays, London, Griffin, 1927 . . LXXVI

VON ORELLI, *Allgemeine Religionsgeschichte*, 2 edit., 1911   LXXVII

OTTO PROCKSCH, *Die Genesis* (Komm. zum A.T. Sellin), Leipzig, Deichert, 1913 LXXVIII

THÉODORE REINACH, *Textes d'auteurs grecs et romains relatifs au judaïsme*, Paris, Leroux, 1895 . . LXXIX

GEORG-ANDREW REISNER, CLARENCE-STANLEY FISHER, DAVID-GORDON LYON, *Harvard Excavations at Samaria*, Cambridge (Mass.), Harvard University Press, 1924 LXXX

ERNEST RENAN, *Histoire du peuple d'Israël*, Paris, Lévy, 1887 ss. LXXXI

R. W. ROGERS, *A History of Babylonia and Assyria*, 6 edit., 1915 LXXXII

R. W. ROGERS, *Cuneiform Parallels to the Old Testament*, Oxford University Press, 1912 LXXXIII

W. ROBERTSON SMITH, *Lectures on the Religion of the Semites*, London, Black, 2 edit., 1894; 3 edit., 1927, with intro. and notes by Stanley A. COOK . . LXXXIV

BERNHARD STADE, *Biblische Theologie des Alten Testaments*, Tübingen, Mohr, 1905 LXXXV

B. STADE, *Geschichte des Volkes Israel*, 2 vols., Berlin, Grote, 2 edit., 1889 LXXXVI

HERMANN STAHN, *Die Simsonage*, Goettingen, Vandenhoeck and Ruprecht, 1908 LXXXVII

JULIUS WELLHAUSEN, *Israelitische und jüdische Geschichte*, Berlin, Reimer, 2 edit., 1895 . . LXXXVIII

J. WELLHAUSEN, *Prolegomena*, 4 edit., Berlin, Reimer, 1895 LXXXIX

J. WELLHAUSEN, *Skizzen und Vorarbeiten*, iii, 1 edit., Berlin, Reimer, 1887 ; 2 edit. under the title of *Reste arabischen Heidentums gesammelt und erlaeutert*, 1897   XC

HUGO WINCKLER, *Altorientalische Forschungen*, Leipzig, Pfeiffer, 1893–1906 XCI

H. WINCKLER, *Geschichte Israels*, Leipzig, Pfeiffer, 1895   XCII

HEINRICH ZIMMERN et HUGO WINCKLER, *Die Keilinschriften und das Alte Testament*, 3 edit., Berlin, Reuther and Reichard, 1902 XCIII

BIBLIOGRAPHY

SPECIAL WORKS

1.—CANAAN

BRUNO BAENTSCH, *Altorientalischer und israelitischer Monotheismus*, Tübingen, Mohr, 1906 . . . **XCIV**

F. BAETHGEN, *Beiträge zur semitischen Religionsgeschichte*, 1888 . . . . **XCV**

WOLF-WILHELM GRAF BAUDISSIN, *Adonis und Esmun*, Leipzig, Hinrichs, 1911 . . . . . **XCVI**

HANS BAUER, *Zur Entzifferung der neuentdeckten Sinaischrift und zur Entstehung des semitischen Alphabets*, 1918 . . . . **XCVII**

PHILIPPE BERGER, *Histoire de l'écriture dans l'antiquité*, Paris, Imp. Nat., 1891. . . . . . **XCVIII**

M. BLANCKENHORN, *Die Strukturlinien Syriens und des Roten Meeres*, 1903 . . . . . . **XCIX**

F. J. BLISS, *Excavations at Jerusalem*, 1894–7, London, PEF, 1898 . . . . **C**

F. J. BLISS, *A Mound of many Cities*, London, Watt, 1894 . . . . **CI**

BLISS et MACALISTER, *Excavations in Palestine during the years 1898–1900*, London, PEF, 1902 . . **CII**

BOEHL, *Kananaeer und Hebraer*, Leipzig, Hinrichs, 1911 **CIII**

BOEHL, *Die Sprache der Amarnabriefe* . . . **CIV**

MAX BURGHARDT, *Die altkananaeischen Fremdworte und Eigennamen im Aegyptischen*, Leipzig, Hinrichs, 1909–10 . . . . **CV**

ALBERT T. CLAY, *A Hebrew Deluge Story in Cuneiform and other Epic Fragments in the Pierpont Morgan Library* (Yale Univ. Series, Researches, vol. v-3), New Haven, Yale Univ. Press, 1922 . . . **CVI**

CH. CLERMONT GANNEAU, *L'imagerie phénicienne*, Paris, Leroux, 1880 . . . . **CVII**

CH. CLERMONT GANNEAU, *Recueil d'archéologie orientale*, Paris, Leroux . . . . **CVIII**

CH. CLERMONT GANNEAU, FR. CUMONT, R. DUSSAUD, R. NAVILLE, E. POTTIER et CH. VIROLLEAUD, *Les travaux archéologiques en Syrie de 1920–1922*, Paris, Geuthner, 1923 . . . . **CIX**

G. CONTENAU, *La glyptique syro-hittite*, Paris, Geuthner, 1922 . . . . **CX**

G. CONTENAU, *La civilisation phénicienne*, Paris, Payot, 1926 . . . . **CXI**

G. CONTENAU, *Éléments de bibliographie hittite*, Paris, Geuthner, 1922 . . . . **CXII**

G. CONTENAU, *Manuel d'archéologie orientale*, i, Paris, Picard, 1927 . . . . **CXIII**

STANLEY A. COOK, *The Religion of Ancient Palestine in the Second Millenium B.C. in the Light of Archæology and the Inscriptions*, London, Constable, 1908 . . **CXIV**

G. A. Cooke, *A Text Book of North-Semitic Inscriptions*, Oxford, Clarendon Press, 1903 . . . . **CXV**

Une Croisière autour de la mer Morte, Paris, Gabalda, 1911 . . . . **CXVI**

G. Dalman, *Palaestina als Heerstrasse im Altertum und in der Gegenwart* (Palaestinajahrbuch, 12, 1916), pp. 15 *ff.* . . . . **CXVII**

Paul Dhorme, *Choix de textes religieux assyro-babyloniens*, Paris, Lecoffre, 1907 . . . . **CXVIII**

Bernhard Duhm, *Die Gottgeweihten in der altestamentlichen Religion*, Tübingen, Mohr, 1905 . . . **CXIX**

René Dussaud, *Les civilisations préhelléniques dans le bassin de la mer Egée*, Paris, Geuthner, 2 edit., 1914 **CXX**

R. Eisler, *Die kenitischen Weihinschriften der Hyksoszeit im Bergbaugebiet der Sinaihalbinsel*, Friburg in B. Herder, 1919 . . . . **CXXI**

Adolf Erman, *Aegypten und aegyptisches Leben im Altertum*, Tübingen, Laupp, 1885 . . . . **CXXII**

A. J. Evans, *Scripta Minoa*, Oxford, Clarendon Press, 1909 *ss.* . . . . **CXXIII**

Ch. Fossey, *La magie assyrienne*, Paris, Leroux, 1902 **CXXIV**

Sir James Frazer, *The magic Art* . . . . **CXXV**

Arnold van Gennep, *Les rites de passage*, Paris, Nourry, 1909 . . . . **CXXVI**

G. Glotz, *La civilisation égéenne* (*Évolution de l'humanité*, no. 9) Paris, Renaissance du Livre, 1923 . . **CXXVII**

Hugo Gressmann, *Die Ausgrabungen in Palaestina und das Alte Testament*, Tübingen, Mohr, 1908 . . **CXXVIII**

H. Gressmann, *Palaestinas Erdgeruch in der israelitischen Religion*, Berlin, Curtius, 1909 . . . **CXXIX**

H. Gressman, *Hadad und Baal nach den Amarnabriefen und nach Aegyptischen Texten* (Baudissin- Festschrift), 1918 . . . . **CXXX**

Hubert Grimme, *Althebraeische Inschriften vom Sinai*, Hanover, Heinz Lafaire, 1923 . . . . **CXXXI**

H. V. Hilprecht, *Die Ausgrabungen im Bel-Tempel zu Nippur*, Leipzig, Hinrichs, 1903 . . . . **CXXXII**

J. A. Knudtzon, Beiträge zur Assyriologie . . **CXXXIII**

J. A. Knudtzon, *Die El-Amarna Tafeln mit Einleitung und Erlaeuterungen*, 2 vols., Leipzig, Hinrichs, 1915 **CXXXIV**

Ad. Lods, *La chute des anges, origine et portée de cette spéculation* (Congrès d'histoire du christianisme, Paris, Rieder, 1928, pp. 29–54) . . . . . **CXXXV**

Ad. Lods et Paul Alphandéry, *Jean Astruc et la critique biblique au XVIII siècle*, Strasbourg-Paris, Istra, 1924 **CXXXVI**

R. A. S. Macalister, *The Philistines, their History and Civilisation* (The Schweich Lectures, 1911) . . **CXXXVII**

R. A. S. Macalister, *The Excavation of Gezer*, 1902–1905 and 1907–1909, 3 vols., London, 1912 . . **CXXXVIII**

F. H. Marshall, *The Collection of Ancient Greek Inscriptions in the British Museum*, p. iv, sect. ii, Oxford, 1916   **CXXXIX**

Joh. Meinhold in *Beiträge*, Karl Budde, Giessen, Toepelmann, 1920, pp. 122–31 . . . .   **CXL**

Eduard Meyer, *Reich und Kultur der Chetiter*, Berlin, Curtius, 1914 . . . .   **CXLI**

A. Moret, *Le rituel du culte divin journalier en Egypte*, Paris, Leroux, 1902 (Annales du Musée Guimet, t. xiv et xv) . . . .   **CXLII**

E. H. Palmer, *The Desert of the Exodus*, 2 vols., Cambridge, Deighton, 1871 . . . . .   **CXLIII**

W. M. Flinders Petrie, *Researches in Sinai*, London, Murray, 1906 . . . .   **CXLIV**

Flinders Petrie, *Tools and Weapons*, London, British School of Arch. in Egypt, 1917 . . . .   **CXLV**

Flinders Petrie, *Tell el Hesy (Lachish)*, London, Watt, 1891 . . . .   **CXLVI**

De Rougé, *Mémoires Acad. Inscriptions*, xxv, 1866   **CXLVII**

De Rougé, *Mémoire sur l'origine égyptienne de l'alphabet phénicien*, Paris, 1874 . . . . . .   **CXLVIII**

A. H. Sayce, *The Archæology of the Cuneiform Inscriptions*, London, Soc. for Prom. Christ. Knowl., 1907   **CXLIX**

Hermann Schneider, *Der kretische Ursprung des phoenikischen Alphabets*, Leipzig, Hinrichs, 1913 .   **CL**

Schumacher, *Tell el Mutesellim*, i, Halle, 1908 .   **CLI**

Ernst Sellin, *Eine Nachlese auf dem Tell Ta'annek*, Vienna, Hoelder, 1905 . . . . . .   **CLII**

E. Sellin, *Tell Ta'annek, Bericht über eine . . . Ausgrabung in Palaestina*, Vienna, Gerold, 1904 . .   **CLIII**

E. Sellin et C. Watzinger, *Jericho, Die Ergebnisse der Ausgrabungen*, Leipzig, Hinrichs, 1913 . . .   **CLIV**

Kurt Sethe, *Die Aechtung feindlicher Fuersten, Voelker und Dinge auf altaegyptischen Tongefaessscherben des mittleren Reiches* (Abhandl. der preuss. Akad. der Wiss., Jahrg. 1926, phil.-hist. Klasse, no. 5) Berlin, 1926 . . . .   **CLV**

K. Sethe, *Ursprung des Alphabets, Die neuendeckte Sinaischrift*, Berlin, 1926 . . . . .   **CLVI**

F. Staehelin, *Die Philister*, 1918 . . . .   **CLVII**

Usener, *Milch und Honig*, Rhein. Mus. für Philologie, N.F., lvii, 177 . . . .   **CLVIII**

Hugues Vincent, *Canaan d'apres l'exploration récente*, 2 mille, Paris, Gabalda, 1914 . . .   **CLIX**

H. Vincent, *Jérusalem, recherches de topographie, d'archéologie et d'histoire*, Paris, Gabalda (in course of publication) . . . . . .   **CLX**

H. Vincent, *Jérusalem sous terre, les récentes fouilles d'Ophel*, London, Cox, 1911 . . . .   **CLXI**

I.

DANIEL VOELTER, *Die althebraeischen Inschriften vom Sinai und ihre historische Bedeutung*, Leipzig, Hinrichs, 1924 . . . .   **CLXII**

RAYMOND WEILL, *La cité de David*, Paris, Geuthner, 1920 . . . .   **CLXIII**

2.—THE HEBREW NOMADS

GEORGE AARON BARTON, *A Sketch of Semitic Origins*, New York, Macmillan, 1902 . . . .   **CLXIV**

GEORG BEER, *Pesachim* (*Die Mischna*, ii, 3), Giessen, Toepelmann, 1912 . . . . . .   **CLXV**

G. BEER, *Der biblische Hades* (Holtzmann-Festschrift, pp. 3–29), Tübingen-Leipzig, Mohr, 1902 . .   **CLXVI**

BERNARD et N. LACROIX, *Étude sur le nomadisme* (Annales de Géographie, 1906, pp. 152–65) . .   **CLXVII**

ALFRED BERTHOLET, *Die israelitischen Vorstellungen vom Zustande nach dem Tode*, Friburg, Mohr, 1889, 2 edit., 1914 . . . .   **CLXVIII**

A. BERTHOLET, *Die Stellung der Israeliten und der Juden zu den Fremden*, Friburg, Mohr, 1896. .   **CLXIX**

J. L. BURCKHARDT, *Voyages en Arabie*, Traduits de l'anglais par J. B. B. EYRIES, 3 vols., Paris, Bertrand, 1835 . . . .   **CLXX**

C. F. BURNEY, *Israel's Settlement in Canaan* (published for the British Academy), London, 1918 . .   **CLXXI**

MAURICE A. CANNEY, Givers of Life, 1923 . .   **CLXXII**

CASALIS, *Les Basutos*, Paris, Meyrueis, 1860 . .   **CLXXIII**

ANTONIN CAUSSE, *Les plus vieux chants de la Bible*, Paris, Alcan, 1926 . . . . . .   **CLXXIV**

PH. CHAMPAULT, *Les patriarches bibliques*, dans *La science sociale*, Paris, Firmin Didot, xxiii, 6 (1897); xxiv, 1 (1897); xxv, 2 (1898) . . . .   **CLXXV**

ALBERT T. CLAY, *The Empire of the Amorites*, New Haven, Yale Univ. Press, 1919 . . . .   **CLXXVI**

GUSTAF DALMAN, *Petra und seine Felsheiligtümer*, Leipzig, Hinrichs, 1908 . . . . . .   **CLXXVII**

CH. H. DOUGHTY, *Travels in Arabia Deserta*, Cambridge Univ. Press, 1888 . . . .   **CLXXVIII**

RENÉ DUSSAUD, *Le Cantique des Cantiques*, Paris, Leroux, 1919 . . . .   **CLXXIX**

R. DUSSAUD, *Les Arabes en Syrie avant l'Islam*, Paris, Leroux, 1907 . . . .   **CLXXX**

R. DUSSAUD et F. MACLER, *Voyage archéologique au Safa et dans le Djebel ed-Druz*, Paris, Leroux, 1901 .   **CLXXXI**

EERDMANS, *Alttestamentliche Studien*, Giessen, 1908, 1910 . . . .   **CLXXXII**

H. J. ELLHORST, *Die israelitischen Trauerriten* (Wellhausen-Festschrift), Giessen, Toepelmann, 1914, pp. 114–28 . . . .   **CLXXXIII**

WILHELM ENGELKEMPER, *Heiligtum und Opferstaetten in den Gesetzen des Pentateuch*, Paderborn, Schoeningh, 1908 . . . . **CLXXXIV**

Sir JAMES FRAZER, *Le Rameau d'or, étude sur la magie et la religion* (trnsl. by R. STIEBEL et J. TOUTAIN), Paris, Schleicher, 1903 . . . . . **CLXXXV**

Sir J. FRAZER, *Scapegoat*. . . . . . **CLXXXVI**

Sir J. FRAZER, *Folk Lore in the Old Testament*, 3 vols., London, Macmillan, 1919 . . . . . **CLXXXVII**

Sir J. FRAZER, *Anthropological Essays Presented to Edw. Burnett Tylor*, Oxford, 1907 . . . . . **CLXXXVIII**

GAUDEFROY DEMOMBYNES, *Contribution a l'étude du pélerinage de la Mekke*, Paris, Geuthner, 1923 . **CLXXXIX**

ARNOLD VAN GENNEP, *L'état actuel du problème totémique*, Paris, Leroux, 1920 . . . . **CXC**

H. GRESSMANN, *Mose und seine Zeit*, Goettingen, Vandenhoeck and Ruprecht, 1913 . . . . **CXCI**

H. GRESSMANN, *Musik und Musikinstrumente im Alten Testament*, Giessen, Ricker, 1903 . . . **CXCII**

J. S. GRIFFITHS, *The Exodus in the Light of Archæology*, London, Scott, 1923 . . . . . **CXCIII**

CARL GRUENEISEN, *Der Ahnenkultus und die Urreligion Israels*, Halle, Niemeyer, 1900 . . . . **CXCIV**

IGNAZIO GUIDI, *Della sede primitiva dei popoli semitici*, 1879 (*Atti. d. R. Acad. dei Lincei, iii, Memorie*, vol. 3, p. 566) . . . . **CXCV**

H. R. HALL, *The Ancient History of the Near East*, 1913 **CXCVI**

EDWIN SIDNEY HARTLAND, *The Legend of Perseus*, London, Nutt, 1896 . . . . . . **CXCVII**

PAUL HAUPT, *Babylon, Elements in the Levitical Ritual* (*Journal of Bibl. Lit.*, pp. 58–81) . . . . **CXCVIII**

SVEN HERNER, *Athlaja* (Marti-Festschrift, pp. 137–41), Giessen, Toepelmann, 1925 . . . . **CXCIX**

HENRI HUBERT et MARCEL MAUSS, *Essai sur la nature et la fonction du sacrifice*, Paris, Alcan, 1899 . . **CC**

G. JACOB, *Das Leben der vorislamischen Beduinen*, 1895 **CCI**

JACOB, *Altarabisches Beduinenleben*, 2 edit., 1897 . **CCII**

MORRIS JASTROW, jr., *Aspects of Religious Belief and Practice in Babylonia and Assyria*, New York-London, Putnam, 1911 . . . . . **CCIII**

J. A. JAUSSEN, *Coutumes des Arabes au pays de Moab*, Paris, Gabalda, 1908 . . . . . . **CCIV**

RR. PP. JAUSSEN et SAVIGNAC, *Coutumes des Fuqara*, Paris, Geuthner, 1914 . . . . . . **CCV**

ANTON JIRKU, *Die Daemonen und ihre Abwehr im Alten Testament*, Leipzig, Deichert, 1912 . . . **CCVI**

A. JIRKU, *Materialen zur Volksreligion Israels*, 1914 . **CCVII**

ANDREW LANG, *Myth, Ritual and Religion*, London, Longmans, 1887 . . . . **CCVIII**

Lucien Lévy-Bruhl, *L'âme primitive*, Paris, Alcan, 1927   CCIX

L. Lévy-Bruhl, *Les fonctions mentales dans les sociétés inférieures*, Paris, Alcan, 1922   CCX

Julius Lippert, *Der Seelencult in seinen Beziehungen zur althebraeischen Religion*, Berlin, Hofmann, 1881 .   CCXI

Ad. Lods, *Rites et sacrifices* (dans *Dieux et Religions*, pp. 90–121), Paris, Rieder, 1926   CCXII

Max Loehr, *Einfuehrung in das A.T.*, Leipzig, Quelle et Meyer, 1912   CCXIII

M. Loehr, *Das Deuteronomium* (Schriften der koenigsberger Gelehrten Ges., 1, 6), Berlin, 1925 . .   CCXIV

Frédéric Macler, *Correspondance épistolaire avec le ciel*, Paris, Leroux, 1905   CCXV

Karl Marti, *Jahwe und seine Auffassung in der aeltesten Zeit*, Gotha, Perthes, 1908   CCXVI

Eduard Meyer, *Die Israeliten und ihre Nachbarstaemme*, Halle, Niemeyer, 1906   CCXVII

G.-F. Moore, *Old Testament and Semitic Studies*, 1908   CCXVIII

De Morgan, *Délégation en Perse*, Paris, Leroux, 1908 *ss.*   CCXIX

Sigmund Mowinckel, *Le décalogue*, Paris, Alcan, 1927   CCXX

N.-M. Nicolsky, *Spüren magischer Formeln in den Psalmen*, ZATW Beih. 45, Giessen, Toepelmann, 1927   CCXXI

Dietlef Nielsen, *The Site of the Biblical Mount Sinai, a Claim for Petra*, Paris, Geuthner ; Copenhagen, Busck ; Leipzig, Harassowitz, 1928   CCXXII

Orr, *The Problem of the Old Testament*, fr. trnsl. by E. Thouvenot, *Le problème de l'A.T.*, Geneva, 1908   CCXXIII

R. Pettazzoni, *Dio ; formazione e sviluppo del monoteismo nella storia delle religioni*, i, Rome, 1922 .   CCXXIV

R. Pettazzoni, *Le problème du monothéisme* (Actes du Congrès international d'hist. des rel. tenu à Paris en Oct. 1923), Paris, Champion, i, 70–82 . . .   CCXXV

W. M. Flinders Petrie, *Hyksos and Israelite Cities*, London, Quaritch, 1906   CCXXVI

Flinders Petrie, *A Hist. of Egypt*, London, Methuen, 1898 *ss.*   CCXXVII

Theophilus G. Pinches, *The Religion of Babylonia and Assyria*, London, Constable, 1906   CCXXVIII

Otto Procksch, *Die Voelker Altpalaestinas*, Leipzig, Hinrichs, 1914   CCXXIX

P. Saintyves, *Le miracle de Josué* (Actes du Congrès international d'hist. des rel. tenu à Paris en Oct. 1923), Paris, Champion, 1925, i, 219–41 . .   CCXXX

V. Scheil, *Le prisme d'Assarhaddon, roi d'Assyrie* (Bibl. de l'École des Hautes Études, fasc. 208, pp. 36 *ff.*), Paris, Champion, 1914   CCXXXI

V. Scheil, *Recueil de lois assyriennes*, Paris, Geuthner, 1921   CCXXXII

HANS SCHMIDT, *Ob* (Marti-Festschrift, 253–61), Giessen,
Toepelmann, 1925 CCXXXIII

P.-W. SCHMIDT, *Der Ursprung der Gottesidee*, Muenster,
Aschendorff, 2 edit., 1926 CCXXXIV

FRIEDRICH SCHWALLY, *Das Leben nach dem Tode*, Giessen, Ricker, 1892. CCXXXV

F. SCHWALLY, *Semitische Kriegsaltertuemer*, i, Leipzig,
Deichert, 1903 CCXXXVI

ERNST SELLIN, *Mose und seine Bedeutung fur die isr.-jud.
Rel. gesch.*, Leipzig, Deichert, 1922 . . . CCXXXVII

E. SELLIN, *Gilgal, ein Beitrag zur Geschichte der Einwanderung Israels in Palaestina*, Leipzig, Deichert, 1917 CCXXXVIII

NAHUM SLOUSCHZ, *Judéo-Hellènes et Judéo-Berbères*,
Paris, Leroux, 1909 CCXXXIX

W. ROBERTSON SMITH, *Kinship and Marriage in Early
Arabia*, Cambridge Univ. Press, 1885 . . . CCXL

SNOUCK HURGRONJE, *Mekka* CCXLI

HERBERT SPENCER, fr. trnsl. *Principes de sociologie*,
Paris, Germer-Baillière, 1880. CCXLII

JOHN SPENCER, *De legibus Hebraeorum ritualibus*, Hagæ,
1686 CCXLIII

W. M. THOMSON, *The Land and the Book, Central Palestine*, 1861 CCXLIV

PAUL TORGE, *Seelenglaube und Unsterblichkeitshoffnung
im A.T.*, Leipzig, Hinrichs, 1909 . . . CCXLV

TRUMBULL, *The Threshold Covenant*, New York, 1896. CCXLVI

H. CLAY TRUMBULL, *Kadesh-Barnea*, New York, 1884 CCXLVII

EDWARD B. TYLOR, fr. trnsl. by BRUNET et BARBIER, *La
civilisation primitive*, Paris, Reinwald, 2 vols., 1876 et
1878 CCXLVIII

ARTHUR UNGNAD, Beiträge zur Assyriologie . . CCXLIX

MAURICE VERNES, *Sinaï contre Kades* (École prat. des
Hautes Études, sciences religieuses), Paris, Imp. nat.
1915 CCL

DANIEL VOELTER, *Aegypten und die Bibel. Die
Urgeschichte Israels in Lichte der aegyptischen Mytho-
logie*, 3 edit., Leyde, Brill, 1907 CCLI

PAUL VOLZ, *Der Geist Gottes*, Tübingen, Mohr, 1910. CCLII

JULIUS WELLHAUSEN, *Die Ehe bei den Arabern*, NGWG,
1883, pp. 431–81. CCLIII

HAROLD M. WIENER, *Essays in Pentateuchal Criticism*,
London, Stock, 1910 CCLIV

H. M. WIENER, *The Date of Exodus*, Bibliotheca sacra,
1916 CCLV

HUGO WINCKLER, *Abraham als Babylonier, Joseph als
Aegypter*, Leipzig, Hinrichs, 1903 CCLVI

H. WINCKLER, *Alttestamentliche Studien* . . . CCLVII

HEINRICH ZIMMERN, *Beiträge zur Kenntniss der babyl.
Religion*, Leipzig, Hinrichs, 1901 . . . CCLVIII

3.—ISRAEL IN PALESTINE

WILLIAM FREDERICK BADE, *The Old Testament in the Light of To-day*, Boston-New York, Houghton Mifflin, 1915   CCLIX

Beiträge zur Wissenschaft des Alten Testaments, herausgeg. von R. Kittel   CCLX

ALFRED BERTHOLET, *Das Buch Hesekiel* (**KHC**), 1897.   CCLXI

FRANTS BUHL, *Die sozialen Verhältnisse der Israeliten*, Berlin, Reuther, 1899   CCLXII

ANTONIN CAUSSE, *Les " Pauvres " d'Israël (prophètes, psalmistes, messianistes)*, Strasbourg-Paris, Istra, 1922   CCLXIII

G. DALMAN, *Orte und Wege*, Gütersloh, Bertelsmann, 1 edit., 2 edit., 1919   CCLXIV

BERNHARD DUHM, *Theologie der Propheten*, Bonn, Marcus, 1875   CCLXV

HERMANN GUNKEL, *Schoepfung und Chaos in Urzeit und Endzeit*, Goettingen, Vandenhoeck and Ruprecht, 1895   CCLXVI

RUDOLF KITTEL, *Die Buecher der Koenige* (H.K. z. A.T.), 1900   CCLXVII

STEPHEN LANGDON, *Sumerian Epic of Paradise, the Flood and the Fall of Man* (Univ. of Pennsylv., Babyl. Section, vol. x, no. 1), 1915 ; fr. trnsl. by CH. VIROLLEAUD, Paris, Leroux, 1919   CCLXVIII

FRANZ-J. LEENHARDT, *La notion de sainteté dans l'Ancien Testament, Étude de la racine Q Dh Sh*, Paris, Fischbacher, 1929   CCLXIX

AD. LODS, *La morale des prophètes* (Morales et religions, pp. 61–96), Paris, Alcan, 1909   CCLXX

AD. LODS, *L'ange de Yahwé et l' " âme extérieure "* (Wellhausen-Festschrift, pp. 263–78), Giessen, Toepelmann, 1914   CCLXXI

AD. LODS, *Les sources des récits du premier livre de Samuel sur l'institution de la royauté* (Études de théologie et d'histoire . . . pp. 257–84), Paris, Fischbacher, 1901   CCLXXII

JOHN A. MAYNARD, *A Survey of Assyriology during the Years 1915–1917*   CCLXXIII

E. MEYER, *Der Papyrusfund von Elephantine*, Leipzig, Hinrichs, 1912   CCLXXIV

OTTO PROCKSCH, *Elohimquelle*   CCLXXV

G. A. REISNER, *Israelite Ostraka from Samaria* . .   CCLXXVI

STEUERNAGEL, *Einwanderung*   CCLXXVII

PAUL VOLZ, *Die vorexilische Jahweprophetie und der Messias, in ihrem Verhaeltniss dargestellt*, Goettingen, Vandenhoeck and Ruprecht, 1897. . . .   CCLXXVIII

ALEXANDRE WESTPHAL, *Les dieux et l'alcool*, Montauban, Granié, 1903   CCLXXIX

ALFRED WIEDEMANN, *Magie und Zauberei im alten Aegypten* (der Alte Orient, vi, 4), Leipzig, Hinrichs, 1905 CCLXXX

H. M. WIENER, *The Altars of the Old Testament*, Leipzig, Hinrichs, 1927. CCLXXXI

H. WINCKLER, *Die Gesetze Hammurabis*, Leipzig, Hinrichs, 2 edit., 1903 CCLXXXII

H. WINCKLER, *Alttestamentl. Untersuchungen*, Leipzig, Pfeiffer, 1892 CCLXXXIII

INDEX